THE INTERNATIONAL MONETARY FUND 1945-1965

Twenty Years of International Monetary Cooperation

VOLUME II: ANALYSIS

By

Margaret G. de Vries *and* J. Keith Horsefield

with the collaboration of

Joseph Gold, Mary H. Gumbart, Gertrud Lovasy,
and Emil G. Spitzer

Edited by
J. Keith Horsefield

INTERNATIONAL MONETARY FUND
WASHINGTON, D. C.
1969

CONTENTS

PART III: EXCHANGE RESTRICTIONS

PART IV: THE FUND'S RESOURCES AND THEIR USE

PART V: CONSTITUTIONAL DEVELOPMENT
AND CHANGE

INDEXES

TABLES

Page

PREFACE TO VOLUME II

The first four parts of this volume deal successively with the process of policy formation and the objectives of the Fund, and with its policies in three main aspects of its work. These chapters are concerned wholly with the period covered by this history, viz., the twenty years 1945–65. Part V differs from the rest of the volume in two respects: in this, the General Counsel of the Fund deals with the constitutional development of the Fund rather than with its economic activities; and he includes a brief description of the amendments to the Articles which entered into force in July 1969, in order to relate past constitutional developments to special drawing rights and the reform of certain features of the Fund.

As indicated in the title, *Analysis,* given to this volume, the intention is to examine here, more intensively than was possible in Volume I, the Fund's activities in the various fields chosen for study. The additional dimension here provided has several facets. By bringing together the Fund's decisions on a given subject, instead of discussing them seriatim as they were taken, it has been possible to bring into sharper focus the reasoning which led to the Fund's actions. Similarly, where its decisions have been diffused among discussions with a number of different countries, the underlying policy has here been brought out. Further, an attempt has been made to take into account the economic background against which the Fund's decisions were taken. Finally, some reference has been made to comments on and criticisms of the Fund's actions by officials and economists not connected with it.

❖ ❖ ❖

The foundation for this volume was laid by the late Oscar L. Altman, then Historian of the Fund, with the assistance of Mrs. Margaret G. de Vries, Mr. Allan G. B. Fisher, and Miss Mary H. Gumbart. Half of the final text has been written by Mrs. de Vries. Other contributors are Mr. Joseph Gold, the General Counsel of the Fund, who wrote Chapters 22 through 27; Miss Gumbart, who wrote Chapter 8 and contributed preparatory work for parts of Chapters 11, 15, and 17; Mr. Emil G. Spitzer, who wrote Chapters 20 and 21 and prepared early drafts of parts of Chapters 18 and 19; and Mr. J. Keith Horsefield, Mr. Altman's successor as Historian of the Fund, who wrote Chapters 9, 17, 18, and 19 and has also edited the volume. A part of Chapter 18 was written by Miss Gertrud Lovasy, and Mr. Evan B. Hannay prepared early drafts for some other sections. All those mentioned are or have been members of the staff of the Fund.

At all stages the authors have been greatly assisted by advice and comments from present and former members of the Executive Board and of the staff of the Fund. In particular, Mr. Fisher has made most helpful comments on the draft of each chapter in Parts II, III, and IV. Mrs. de Vries expresses appreciation to Professor Gerard Curzon, of the Graduate Institute of International Studies, University of Geneva, and to Professor Gardner Patterson, of Princeton University, for sharing with her some of their experiences as authors of volumes in related fields and for making suggestions for the contents of this volume. She is grateful also to Professor Robert A. Mundell, of the University of Chicago, for his encouraging interest in the project.

The staffs of the Archivist of the Fund and of the Joint Bank-Fund Library have much facilitated the task of identifying and consulting the relevant documents and volumes.

Mrs. Jane B. Evensen, Assistant Editor of the Fund, has greatly assisted in clarifying the final text.

Mrs. Margaret P. Estes has helped with some of the statistical material and has patiently typed several versions of the manuscript.

Responsibility for the contents of this volume is, however, that of the authors and editor alone.

M. G. de V.

J. G.

M. H. G.

J. K. H.

G. L.

E. G. S.

ABBREVIATIONS AND DEFINITIONS

Annual Meetings, 19—

Annual Meetings of the Boards of Governors of the Fund and the Bank, in the year specified. The Meetings of the two institutions are held at the same time and in the same place, and some of the sessions are held jointly. Other sessions, however, are held separately by the Fund and the Bank. When the term Annual Meeting (in the singular) is used, the reference is to a Meeting of the Fund Governors.

Annual Report, 19—

Annual Report of the Executive Directors for the Fiscal Year Ended April 30, 19—

Articles of Agreement; Articles; Fund Agreement

Articles of Agreement of the International Monetary Fund

Bank; World Bank

International Bank for Reconstruction and Development

BIS

Bank for International Settlements

Bretton Woods

[Site of] United Nations Monetary and Financial Conference, July 1944

Consultations

Annual consultations with members by the Executive Board under Article XIV, and parallel consultations with members that have accepted the obligations of Article VIII

Drawing

Purchase from the Fund by a member of another member's currency (or other members' currencies). Amounts are always expressed in U.S. dollars.

E.B. Decision

Decision of the Executive Board. Until Meeting 630 (at the beginning of 1951), the formal decisions and policy actions of the Executive Board were numbered x-y, where x was the number of the meeting and y that of the decision taken at that meeting (e.g., 2-1 was the first decision taken at Executive Board Meeting 2). Beginning with Meeting 630, the decisions were numbered consecutively; thereafter

xv

the number was z-(x), where z was the consecutive number of the decision and x that of the meeting (e.g., 7-(648) was the seventh policy decision taken since Meeting 630, and was taken at Meeting 648). From January 1, 1952, the number of the decision has been followed by the last two figures of the year and the number of the meeting in that year in parentheses (e.g., Decision No. 102-(52/11) was the 102nd decision since Meeting 630, and was taken at the eleventh meeting in 1952).

ECA — Economic Cooperation Administration (U.S.)

ECOSOC — Economic and Social Council (UN)

EEC — European Economic Community

EMA — European Monetary Agreement

EPU — European Payments Union

ERP — European Recovery Program (U.S.)

FAO — Food and Agriculture Organization (UN)

FIFO — First in, first out (pertaining to Fund transactions)

GAB — General Arrangements to Borrow

GATT — General Agreement on Tariffs and Trade. The term CONTRACTING PARTIES in capital letters denotes the adherents to the General Agreement acting in concert. The terms contracting parties and contracting party in lower case letters refer to the individual adherents to the General Agreement.

Group of Ten — The countries associated in the General Arrangements to Borrow, viz., Belgium, Canada, France, Germany, Italy, Japan, the Netherlands, Sweden, the United Kingdom, the United States

IDB — Inter-American Development Bank

IFNS — *International Financial News Survey*

IFS — *International Financial Statistics*

ITO — International Trade Organization

Joint Statement	*Joint Statement by Experts on the Establishment of an International Monetary Fund*
Keynes Plan	Proposals for an International Clearing Union
LIFO	Last in, first out (pertaining to Fund transactions)
OAS	Organization of American States
OECD	Organization for Economic Cooperation and Development
OEEC	Organization for European Economic Cooperation
Proceedings	*Proceedings and Documents of the United Nations Monetary and Financial Conference, Bretton Woods, New Hampshire, July 1–22, 1944*, 2 vols. (Washington, 1948)
Repurchase	Purchase of its own currency from the Fund by a member country, in reduction of the Fund's holdings of that currency. Amounts are always expressed in U.S. dollars.
Resolution	Resolution of the Board of Governors of the Fund. Resolutions at the Annual Meetings of Governors are referred to by the number of the Annual Meeting followed by a dash and the number of the resolution. Resolutions passed at the Inaugural Meeting (Savannah, March 1946) are listed as IM-1, etc., those at the First Annual Meeting (Washington, September 1946) as 1-1, and so on. Resolutions passed by Governors between Annual Meetings are given the number of the next succeeding Annual Meeting.
Selected Decisions	*Selected Decisions of the Executive Directors and Selected Documents*, 3rd issue, January 1965
Selected Documents	*Selected Documents, Board of Governors Inaugural Meeting, Savannah, Ga., March 8 to 18, 1946* (compare *Summary Proceedings* below)
Summary Proceedings, 19—	*Summary Proceedings of the . . . Annual Meeting of the Board of Governors* (issued after each Annual Meeting). In early years *Summary Proceedings* were really summaries, but latterly most speeches made at the Annual Meetings have been printed in full. In these printed

reports Governors are named, but in the records maintained in the Fund's files they are not, being referred to as "Governor" whether they were in fact Governors, Alternate Governors, or Temporary Alternate Governors. Unless, therefore, the speaker can be identified in other ways, it has been necessary, in those parts of this volume that are drawn from unpublished reports, to cite only "Governor for . . . ".

UN	United Nations
UNCTAD	United Nations Conference on Trade and Development
White Plan	Proposals for an International Stabilization Fund
World Bank; Bank	International Bank for Reconstruction and Development

PART I

The Formation and Objectives of Fund Policy

CHAPTER

1

The Process of Policymaking

Margaret G. de Vries

O NE OF THE DISTINGUISHING CHARACTERISTICS of the international economic scene since World War II is the existence of multi-member economic institutions, such as the International Monetary Fund. The Fund was established to substitute cooperation and consultation in monetary and financial affairs for the unilateral and independent decision-making concerning these matters in which countries had previously engaged. Subsequently, in accordance with its Articles of Agreement, the Fund has been evolving policies in the fields for which it has responsibility that are of considerable significance to its members.

IMPORTANCE OF THE FUND'S POLICIES

The Fund's attitudes and policies are an important factor circumscribing the monetary and financial policies of each member country. For several of its policies, a member is accountable to the Fund. Regular consultations between the Fund and the member provide the Fund with an opportunity to review and to criticize the monetary and financial policies being pursued by the member. Some actions contemplated by the monetary authorities of a member—such as a change in the exchange rate or the imposition of exchange restrictions—must receive the concurrence of the Fund even before these steps can be taken.

A member has a vested interest in securing the Fund's approval: not only may the member then be regarded as one in good standing in the international economic community, but it is enabled should the need arise to draw upon the pool of resources which the Fund has at its disposal. Through the medium of the Fund, a member has opportunities to comment upon the policies of other members and, should it feel that its interests are adversely affected by the policies of another, it has the right to object.

Just as the Fund's policies are of concern to a member individually, so are they important to its members collectively. These policies aim at making harmonious the conduct of trade and payments among all members. And, through the Fund, members as a group have worked out additional forms and techniques of international monetary cooperation as new problems in international trade and payments have arisen.

The upcoming chapters in this volume are devoted to explaining many of the specific policies of the Fund. This chapter provides background by describing the process by which these policies are formed. As an example of the machinery of international organizations, the process of policymaking in the Fund is, in fact, a subject of interest in itself. Because this process has changed significantly over the years, note is also taken of some of the important ways in which the process differs from that in the early years.

INSTRUMENTS OF POLICYMAKING

The process of policymaking in the Fund consists of a complex of relations between member governments, the Board of Governors, the Board of Executive Directors, the Managing Director, and the international staff, and the line of formal authority moreover proceeds in that order.

Members

The Fund is, of course, an entity composed of its members. It is the members who determine the Fund's policies. Thus the Fund can go only as far in fulfilling its objectives and deciding what policies will be pursued as its members will allow.

At the end of 1965 there were 103 members, compared with 40 at the end of 1946. Until 1960 the growth of membership was relatively slow; on average, there were about two new members each year. Thereafter membership increased sharply, as former colonial territories which had achieved their independence joined. These countries were especially eager to be admitted to the Fund, not only because of the benefits of such membership itself, but also because Fund membership is a condition for membership in the International Bank for Reconstruction and Development (the World Bank). Of the Fund's 103 members at the end of 1965, 48 had not existed as sovereign states when the Fund was formed. Apart from the U.S.S.R., mainland China, and some countries closely associated with one or the other of these, the only considerable countries that were independent at the end of 1965 and had not joined the Fund were Cambodia, Switzerland, and Yemen.[1]

The composition of the Fund's membership at the end of 1965, although roughly the same as that of the United Nations, differed in some important

---

[1] Switzerland does, however, have an agreement with the Fund parallel to the Fund's General Arrangements to Borrow.

respects. Among the member countries of the Fund were some, such as Germany, Korea, and Viet-Nam, that were not members of the United Nations. On the other hand, the U.S.S.R. and states associated with it that were members of the United Nations were not members of the Fund. The U.S.S.R. sent a delegation to the Bretton Woods Conference and took an active part in the deliberations there; indeed, some of the Articles of Agreement were reworded in an effort to meet the points of view of the U.S.S.R. A member of the staff of the U.S.S.R. Purchasing Commission in Washington also attended as an observer the Inaugural Meetings of the Boards of Governors of the Fund and the Bank in March 1946. By that time, however, relations between the Soviet bloc and its wartime allies had sharply deteriorated, and the U.S.S.R. never joined the Fund. Poland, Cuba, and Czechoslovakia were original members, but the first two withdrew in 1950 and 1964, respectively, and Czechoslovakia's membership terminated at the end of 1954.[2]

This composition of membership meant, inter alia, that the tensions of the cold war did not cause the same conflict among the Fund's members as had occurred in the United Nations. On the contrary, rather quickly after the Fund's establishment, members developed harmonious working relationships and a sharing of confidences concerning their economic situations and policies that, in all probability, would not have been possible if there had been acute political differences among the membership.

At the time that it joins the Fund, each member country agrees to a *quota*. These quotas play a unique role in the organization and operation of the Fund: they determine the contribution that a member makes to the Fund (and hence the size and composition of the Fund's resources), the drawings permitted to members and the charges and repayments on these drawings, and members' voting power.

No formal principles have been laid down for the determination of quotas. The quotas agreed at Bretton Woods for the original members were based on a complicated formula which employed various percentages of the member's national income, its holdings of gold and U.S. dollars, and its average annual exports and imports. The idea was that quotas would be in accordance with the relative economic circumstances of members.

Although quotas of subsequent members have continued to be based primarily on their economic circumstances, a good deal of consideration is also given to fitting the quota into the existing structure of quotas. In accordance with its Articles, the Fund conducts a comprehensive review of quotas every five years. In 1958–59 and 1965–66, general increases for all members were proposed and

---

[2] The membership at the end of 1965 and the date that each member joined are listed in Table 2 of Chapter 4 (below, pp. 87–89).

accepted. There have also been many special increases in the quotas of individual countries. By early in 1966, the total of the Fund's quotas had reached nearly $21 billion.

Unlike the United Nations and some other international organizations, members do not have to make periodic contributions for the administrative expenses of the Fund: these are met from the charges the Fund receives from its members for drawings from its resources. Although in its first ten years the Fund ran an annual deficit, subsequently there was a sharp rise in transactions, which increased the Fund's income.

BOARD OF GOVERNORS

As its highest-ranking representatives in the Fund, every member appoints a Governor (usually the Minister of Finance or the Governor of the central bank) and an Alternate Governor. In late September or early October of each year there is a meeting attended by all the Governors and Alternate Governors, held jointly with that of the World Bank. Because of the high-level representation of member countries at the Joint Bank-Fund Meetings, these meetings have become the occasion not only for conducting the immediate business of the Fund but also for holding informal discussions among members on a variety of financial matters of mutual concern. Such informal discussions have become part of the process by which international monetary cooperation has gradually been extended.

Although the Articles of the Fund provide also for special meetings of the Board of Governors, such meetings have never been called. Convening Governors—and by 1965 there were more than one hundred—from all over the world would be a cumbersome way to make decisions. When a vote of the Governors is needed, they are polled by mail or cable.

EXECUTIVE DIRECTORS

The Articles also provide for Executive Directors who are to exercise whatever powers are delegated to them by the Board of Governors. At its Inaugural Meeting in 1946, the Board of Governors delegated to the Executive Directors all its powers except for a few reserved subjects, notably the admission of members and changes in quotas. The Board of Governors, however, retains authority to issue policy decisions for the guidance of the Executive Directors, and all decisions and actions of the Executive Directors may, upon the proposal of any member, be reviewed by the Board of Governors.

On December 31, 1965, the Executive Board consisted of twenty Executive Directors.[3] The five members with the largest quotas—the United States, the

---

[3] For a list of the Executive Directors and their Alternates from the Fund's inception to the end of 1968, see above, Vol. I, Appendix A.

United Kingdom, France, Germany, and India—are each entitled to appoint one Director. The two countries whose currencies are drawn on the most in the preceding two years are also entitled to appoint a Director each, on the occasion of the biennial elections of Executive Directors. Usually these countries are among the five with the largest quotas, but Canada appointed a Director under this provision for the two years beginning November 1958.

The remaining Directors are elected for two-year terms by the other members. Three seats are specifically reserved for the Latin American Republics. The other members arrange themselves informally into groups. For example, the five Nordic countries customarily form a single group. Some members are, however, represented by an Executive Director from a country which is not geographically close. For example, at the end of 1965 eight Middle Eastern countries were represented by Mr. Saad (from the United Arab Republic), but Mr. Saad also represented Afghanistan, Ethiopia, Pakistan, Somalia, and the Philippines; Mr. Lieftinck (a Dutch national) cast the votes of Cyprus, Israel, the Netherlands, and Yugoslavia; and Mr. van Campenhout (from Belgium) those of Austria, Belgium, Korea, Luxembourg, and Turkey. The groupings of countries that combine to elect Directors have changed little since 1954.

Voting in the Fund is not conducted, as in most other international organizations, on the basis of one country, one vote. The system in the Fund is one of weighted voting, that is, the voting strength wielded by each member's representative is based on the quotas of the members (or quota of the member) which he represents. The intent is to give the greatest "say" to those countries which have contributed the most to the Fund's assets.

On April 30, 1966, the U.S. Director had 23.82 per cent of the total voting power in the Fund, the British Director 11.33 per cent, the Directors from France and Germany 3.73 per cent each, and the Indian Director 3.56 per cent. With the steady increase in the number of members and the disproportionate increases in many quotas in 1959–60, these percentages were somewhat smaller than when the Fund was first established. The voting power of the elected Directors in April 1966 ranged from 5.53 per cent of the total (Mr. Saad) to 1.89 per cent.

Some of the Directors have served for long periods of time. Among appointed Directors, for example, Mr. de Largentaye was the French Director from June 1946 until June 1964 and Mr. Southard represented the United States from March 1949 to October 1962 (the United States has had only four Directors since 1946). Among elected Directors, Mr. Saad has been a Director since the establishment of the Fund; Mr. Rasminsky (Canada) served from 1946 to 1962; Mr. Lieftinck has been on the Board since 1955, Mr. Tann (China) since 1950, and Mr. van Campenhout since 1954. Other groups, for example, the Nordic countries and sometimes the countries of Central America, vary the countries from which their Directors are elected.

Usually the Directors are experts in international monetary affairs. Most of them have been officials of treasuries, ministries of economics, or central banks; a number have been former Ministers of Finance or Governors of central banks. Many are highly qualified economists; some have already been on the senior staff of the Fund and some have been appointed later to senior staff posts.

The Executive Board functions in continuous session, meeting as often as Fund business requires. Through the Executive Directors, members exercise a closer control over the day-to-day activities of the Fund than is generally the case with international organizations, with one or two exceptions such as the Organization for Economic Cooperation and Development (OECD).

A few countries formerly made it a practice to appoint as Executive Director a high official whose main work was at home, and who visited Washington on Fund business only at irregular intervals. But nowadays the Directors usually devote full time to their Fund duties. Some also represent their countries on the Executive Board of the World Bank, or combine with their work as a Director of the Fund other duties in Washington on behalf of their governments. Mondays, Wednesdays, and Fridays are reserved for meetings of the Fund Board; this permits Executive Directors who also serve on the Board of the Bank to attend its meetings on Tuesdays and Thursdays. When business demands it, meetings are also held on holidays and on week-ends.

Each Executive Director appoints an Alternate from the country or countries which appointed or elected him. Some of the elected Directors appoint Alternates from member states other than those from which they themselves come. The presence of Alternates in Washington makes it possible to maintain the principle of continuous session for the Board, even though some Executive Directors may not themselves be continuously available. A member not entitled to appoint an Executive Director may send a special representative to an Executive Board meeting when a matter particularly affecting the member is under consideration. The representative may speak at meetings but may not vote.

With a few exceptions, such as a change in quota, a simple majority of votes cast is all that is necessary to carry a decision. But some actions—for instance, changes in quotas or in par values—must have the concurrence of the member concerned as well.

In practice, nearly all decisions of the Executive Board are taken without a vote. Down to the end of 1965, only 45 recorded votes were taken; of these, many were purely a matter of form, relating to changes in the Fund's schedule of charges, for which a three-fourths majority of the Directors is required by the Articles. Several more of the 45 recorded votes dealt with administrative and personnel matters. Since 1953 votes on substantive issues have occurred only infrequently. Apart from the approval of changes in the schedule of Fund charges, there was, between 1953 and the end of 1965, only one issue on which a vote was taken. Instead, the Chairman of the Board customarily obtains what is agreed to be *the sense of the meeting*. These words were explicitly defined by the Directors in 1947 to be a position supported by those Directors having sufficient votes to carry the question if a vote were to be taken.

One other special attribute of the Executive Board should be noted—the responsibility for interpreting the Articles of Agreement. Indeed, the Articles give the Executive Directors the power to interpret questions relating to the range and limits of their own authority.[4]

Managing Director

The Managing Director is Chairman of the Executive Board as well as chief of the international staff. He is appointed by the Board for a five-year term. He presides over meetings of the Board but has no vote. He is also in charge of the organization, appointment, and dismissal of the staff, and is responsible for the work of the staff and for the formulation of staff positions on policy matters.

The Managing Director is the principal representative of the Fund; for example, he addresses the Board of Governors at Annual Meetings, and gives formal statements on behalf of the Fund to other high-level international gatherings. When the Fund is invited to meetings at the ministerial level, it is the Managing Director who attends.

The Fund has been under the leadership of four Managing Directors: Camille Gutt, from Belgium (May 1946–May 1951); Ivar Rooth, from Sweden (August 1951–October 1956); Per Jacobsson, also from Sweden (November 1956–May 1963); and Pierre-Paul Schweitzer, from France (September 1963 to the present). Each has been well known in the fields of money, banking, and finance. Mr. Gutt had been Minister of Finance in Belgium; Mr. Rooth, Governor of the Sveriges Riksbank; Mr. Jacobsson, Economic Adviser and Head of the Monetary and Economic Department of the Bank for International Settlements; and Mr. Schweitzer, Deputy Governor of the Bank of France.

Since 1949 there has also been a Deputy Managing Director. So far three persons, all from the United States, have served in this capacity: Andrew N. Overby (February 1949–January 1952); H. Merle Cochran (March 1953–October 1962); and Frank A. Southard, Jr. (November 1962 to the present). The Deputy Managing Director assists the Managing Director and, in his absence, chairs the meetings of the Executive Board and directs the staff.

---

[4] On the significance of this feature, see Chapter 25 below and Joseph Gold, *Interpretation by the Fund*, IMF Pamphlet Series, No. 11. For an earlier study, see Ervin P. Hexner, "Interpretation by Public International Organizations of their Basic Instruments," *American Journal of International Law*, Vol. 53 (1959), pp. 341–70.

STAFF

The Fund is relatively small as organizations go these days: on April 30, 1966, the staff consisted of 750 persons in total. About half were professional staff—economists, lawyers, statisticians, and fiscal experts—drawn from 69 member countries. The staff is selected with a view to securing the highest standards of efficiency and technical competence, with due regard to the importance of having as wide a geographical basis as possible. Because it has often been difficult to recruit from the less developed countries staff members who have the necessary qualifications and who can be spared from duties in their home countries for several years, a high proportion of the staff—especially of the senior staff—has come from the United States, the United Kingdom, other European countries, Canada, and Australia. However, many of the less developed countries have also been represented on the senior staff; in 1965, for example, senior staff officers included persons from Burma, Chile, Ghana, India, Pakistan, and Paraguay. Senior staff appointments are subject to the approval of the Executive Directors, who also pass on the annual administrative budget.

Members of the staff owe their duty entirely to the Fund; each staff member is, on appointment, required to sign a statement that he will accept no instruction from any country. The majority of staff members stay with the Fund for long periods; most of the senior staff, in April 1966, had been with the Fund for close to fifteen years, and many for twenty years. Hence, over time, the Fund's staff has become part of an international civil servant group, similar to staff serving in other international organizations, such as the United Nations, the World Bank, the GATT, and the FAO.

The staff at the end of 1965 was organized into fourteen departments–five functional departments (Exchange and Trade Relations, Fiscal Affairs, Legal, Research and Statistics, and Treasurer's) and five area departments (African, Asian, European, Middle Eastern, and Western Hemisphere). Two departments (the Central Banking Service and the IMF Institute) were devoted to technical assistance and training, and in addition there was an Administration Department, for internal administration, and a Secretary's Department, to provide services to the Executive Directors and to Governors. In addition to the headquarters in Washington, there were small offices in Paris and Geneva.

EVOLUTION OF THE PROCESS OF POLICYMAKING

As early as the Inaugural Meeting in Savannah in 1946, a distinction was made between the roles of the Executive Directors on the one hand and of the Managing Director and the staff on the other: the Executive Directors are responsible to the countries that appointed or elected them; the Managing

Director and the staff to the Fund as a whole. This division of responsibility has persisted, although, over time, the implementation has changed substantially.

In the Fund's first two years, Executive Directors headed field missions to member countries, frequently accompanied by senior staff. In 1948, after the Board took a decision clarifying the division of responsibility, Directors ceased as a rule to head such missions, and these were now headed by members of the staff. Mr. Saad (Egypt) continued until 1955 to act as head of the Fund's missions to the meetings of the GATT, but since then the Fund has been represented at international meetings by members of the staff, or, on occasion, by the Managing Director or Deputy Managing Director.

From 1948 until well into the 1950's, the composition of each staff mission was subject to Board approval, and the Board outlined detailed instructions for them. Sometimes the Board would pass a general decision outlining the Fund's official position; at other times Board meetings were held so that, prior to the staff's departure, Directors could indicate their points of view on a particular topic. Several instances of this process can be noted in the forthcoming chapters.

There was also a tendency for member governments, before submitting a formal proposal or request to the Fund, to ask their Executive Directors to discuss it with other Directors first. Quite frequently the Executive Director for the member concerned went to the Director of the United States—the country with the largest quota. If the U.S. Director concurred with the proposal or request, the member would then continue with the formal procedures of the Fund. It was in this sense that some observers commented that the United States "dominated" the Fund. By 1952 this practice had begun to wane and by 1956 it had virtually ended.

What emerged by the late 1950's and early 1960's, and has continued, is a process in which the five instruments of policymaking are closely interwoven, but in which the management and the staff have a large measure of responsibility. There were several reasons for the change. Increasing contacts between individual members of the staff and individual Directors, frequently on a first-name basis, both enabled the staff to convey informally to the Directors suggestions for the improved operation of the Fund and gave Directors greater confidence in the staff. As the staff conducted missions and technical assistance to member countries, it had to make on-the-spot decisions, subject only later to Board review and confirmation. As missions became more frequent, and a regular part of the Fund's procedures, members themselves were inclined to place more confidence in the staff. In addition, members became less concerned that the presence of a staff mission would be interpreted by the press or outsiders as a sign of pending exchange devaluation: the extreme secrecy which had attended missions could be dispensed with. Henceforth, representatives of member governments and the Fund staff could have more open contacts and exploratory discussions that did not commit the Board.

The public speeches commenting on countries' domestic policies made by Mr. Jacobsson during his tenure gave separate and important identity to the Managing Director. Furthermore, as the membership grew, the Board grew, and the new Directors did not have the accumulated experience of their predecessors. Meanwhile, the staff was gaining experience, especially as senior staff stayed on in the service of the Fund. As the same staff representatives returned time and again to member countries, the staff developed insight into the problems of members and an intimate acquaintance with their officials; indeed, several members of the staff, in the course of providing technical assistance to the member, have resided for long periods in a country.

Now as the Fund's policies are gradually worked out, an almost continuous interchange of ideas, both formally and informally, takes place between the members, the Governors, the Executive Directors, the Managing Director, and the staff. The nature of this interchange is somewhat different for policies pertaining to individual member countries and for general policies.

POLICIES FOR INDIVIDUAL MEMBERS

DAY-TO-DAY WORK

In the day-to-day operations of the Fund, the procedure is almost the inverse of the formal line of authority described above. Preparatory work is done by the staff, whose appraisal and recommendations are approved by the Managing Director; and the agreed staff position is then reviewed and decided upon by the Executive Directors. Only after decision by the Board do proposals become official Fund policy. Later action is taken by the Governors, if required, and then, if need be, by the members. As noted above, the Governors must approve quota changes and applications for membership. They have also passed several resolutions requesting the staff and the Executive Board to look into broad general policy questions facing the Fund. Action at the member level is also necessary for certain procedural changes, as, for example, the ratification of amendments to the Articles by the legislatures of member governments.

The primary responsibilities of the staff are to keep abreast of developments in member countries, especially of those financial and monetary developments directly pertinent to the Fund's interests; to carry out the Fund's policies vis-à-vis members; and to handle negotiations with members. The staff examines a regular inflow of documentary and statistical material from member countries. But in addition, both junior and senior staff make frequent visits to the member countries to gather data, to confer with technicians, to evaluate economic trends, and to conduct discussions with the authorities concerning the member's monetary and financial policies, as part of the policy of annual consultation with members. (The evolution of these consultations and the way in which they are conducted forms the subject of Chapter 11.)

As a result, the staff is often engaged not only in becoming familiar with members' economies, but in assisting them to work out monetary and financial policies. For example, if a member is trying to stabilize its economy, the staff may help the government team to formulate monetary and credit measures, or budget and tax policies, or both. If the country wishes to relax restrictions on international payments or to move to an alternative exchange rate, the staff may help to analyze the impact of these actions and to judge the need and nature of supporting measures. Not infrequently, high-ranking officials of member countries, at an early stage in their deliberations on new monetary and financial policies, explore informally the likely reactions of the Fund management and staff.

Most of the work with the countries is carried on by the area departments. But functional departments also perform specialized day-to-day work that helps to shape the Fund's policies vis-à-vis individual countries. The Exchange and Trade Relations Department, for example, analyzes developments in members' restrictive systems. The Fiscal Affairs Department concerns itself with tax and budgetary problems. The Research and Statistics Department has, among its other duties, the making of calculations and projections for the operation of the compensatory financing facility, and the important job of collecting from members the basic financial, monetary, and balance of payments statistics essential for assessing the nature and magnitude of a member's problems. The Treasurer's Department undertakes the Fund's financial operations, including drawings, repurchases, and charges, and is responsible also for quotas and calculations of monetary reserves. The Legal Department ensures that the Fund and its members are fulfilling their obligations under the Articles of Agreement. The Central Banking Service provides advice and technical assistance on the setting up and operating of central banks, especially in less developed countries. The Joint Library, to provide the basic source materials needed by both the Fund and the Bank, is continuously adding to its collection of documents, reports, books, and periodicals in more than thirty languages. Indeed, there is virtually no staff member whose work is not in some way or another pertinent to the Fund's dealings with its member countries.

Generally, an attempt is made to avoid having a staff member negotiate with his own country. The availability of staff from the functional departments makes this task easier, while at the same time giving the member countries the benefit of the specialized experience of the staff of functional departments and keeping this staff informed on the current problems of members.

In carrying on these functions, the staff has close discussions, which take place before field missions as well as immediately thereafter, with the Managing Director and his Deputy. Senior staff officials from various departments are also frequently involved in these discussions, as part of many informal interdepartmental meetings between staff and management.

Staff recommendations

Upon return from a mission, the staff team reports directly, within forty-eight hours, to the Managing Director and the Deputy Managing Director. Should any issues need to be resolved, meetings of the staff team and senior staff officers are called by the Managing Director. The staff team then prepares a detailed report of its activities and discussions with the member, and drafts recommendations for action by the Fund. This report is considered by an informal interdepartmental committee, which includes at least some of the members of the mission. In any case, the reviewing committee includes members of the relevant area department, the Exchange and Trade Relations Department, and the Legal Department.

In formulating an agreed position, the staff is guided by previous decisions taken by the Executive Directors. As time has gone on, and general guidelines have emerged delimiting what the Board will or will not approve, the staff has been able to work informally with member countries in drafting programs and requests that are likely to be acceptable to the Board. As a result, for example, no request for a drawing which reached the Board for several years before 1965 was rejected, although a considerable number of requests which members would have liked to make were not made because the staff advised them that the attendant circumstances were not in line with the Fund's policy.

The Managing Director, in his continuous contacts with the Executive Directors, may well have explored informally with the Director of the country concerned his reactions to the staff's appraisal and recommendations. In some instances, the Executive Director may even have attended, as an observer, the discussions in the member country between the staff and the member's representatives.

Board decisions

Once a staff report has been written and approved and an agreed staff and management position has been formulated, the subject is ready for the agenda of the Board of Executive Directors. Although any Director may propose items for the agenda, usually it is determined by the Managing Director after informal consultation with individual Directors.

The meetings on the topics on the agenda are formal ones, of which detailed minutes are kept. In discussions concerning a particular country, the Director appointed or elected by that country customarily speaks first, presenting his (or the government's) views of the staff's evaluation and recommendations and any additional explanations and comments he wishes. Comments by virtually all of the Directors on most topics are common. The positions taken by an appointed Director naturally reflect closely those of his government. He keeps his government more or less continuously informed about the Fund's deliberations and receives appropriate instructions, although he may also have participated within his government in the formulation of those instructions. An elected Director, too, does his best to accommodate the views and suggestions of all his constituents, including the one which nominated him. In fact, placing an important item on the agenda may be delayed for a while if a Director does not receive instructions from his home country. Usually, too, the Managing Director attempts to iron out important controversies between Directors prior to placing an item on the agenda.[5]

Although in the first few years of the Board's deliberations, many Directors were concerned primarily with safeguarding the legal rights of their members against the Fund's overstepping its bounds, or with preventing the Fund from jeopardizing the vested financial interests of members, an international viewpoint quite rapidly evolved. Directors soon began to express points of view that took into account the interests of all members or of the Fund as a whole. The changes in the process of policymaking just described were also part of the process by which the Fund became more truly international, with members gradually submerging many of their conflicting national interests.[6] Frequently Directors speak as technical experts on a particular problem on which they have expertise.

Staff members concerned with a particular country or a general topic are present at Board meetings. Senior staff members explain and defend the staff position, and answer specific questions raised by the Directors. Even if a Director disagrees with a staff appraisal or recommendation, he usually values an independent staff position. Directors often make minor changes in the wording of draft stand-by arrangements or draft conclusions to consultations. Discussion of items in which there is little interest or controversy may last for only a few minutes; discussions of other items may go on for two or three hours—the usual length of a meeting—or even be extended to two or three sessions.

---

[5] Further details on the functioning of the Executive Board can be found in articles by two former members of the Fund staff: Allan G. B. Fisher, "The Political Framework of an International Institution," *The Manchester School*, Vol. XXX (May 1962), pp. 121–51; and Ervin P. Hexner, "The Executive Board of the International Monetary Fund: A Decision-Making Instrument," *International Organization*, Vol. XVIII (1964), pp. 74–96.

[6] See below, pp. 31–33.

Final decisions of the Board are drafted with great care. Terms which might adversely affect the prestige or domestic affairs of a member are avoided. Recommendations for action are couched in phrases which carefully reflect the limits of the Fund's authority. Efforts are made to incorporate the points of view of as many Directors as possible, consistent with a meaningful decision. Once a decision is taken by the Board, it becomes the decision of the Board as a whole. No publicity is given to the dissenting view of individual Directors.

Decisions on individual countries are communicated to the members by the Managing Director. Some, such as recommendations concerning changes in quotas or membership resolutions, require action by the Board of Governors. The precise language submitted to the Governors for consideration is drafted by the staff and approved by the Board of Executive Directors before being taken to the Governors. The relations between the Governors and Executive Directors make it unlikely that the Governors will vote differently from the Directors; only rarely, and not since 1951, have Governors even made statements critical of Directors.

To complete the policymaking circle, after decisions have been taken by the Executive Board or resolutions have been adopted by the Board of Governors, the staff has the responsibility for carrying out these instructions in its day-to-day work with the member countries.

There are several advantages to these procedures. First, efficient use is made of the staff. A field mission is competent to deal with a wide range of topics and is treated by the member country as a negotiating team. Also, a minimum amount of time is involved in eliciting and reconciling the views of the staff, so that an agreed staff position can be formulated. Thus, the Fund's operations with over a hundred member countries have been handled by a relatively small staff. Second, Fund actions, such as drawings or exchange rate changes, can be taken quickly. Close acquaintance with the problems of members means that staff position papers can be prepared at short notice. The fact that the Executive Board is in continuous session, meeting as the occasion requires; the periodic review by the Board of member countries' economic situations; and the rapid preparation by the staff of papers to be considered, together make possible the taking of decisions by the Fund very promptly.

GENERAL POLICIES

In the formation of the general policies of the Fund on such subjects as restrictions, exchange rates, changes in quotas, and use of resources, the procedures differ somewhat from those followed in respect of individual countries. An issue may arise in the course of Executive Board discussions, which is then pursued by an ad hoc committee of officials from the departments immediately concerned. Or an issue may arise during the course of a discussion by senior staff of some other problem. The small group of senior officials which first explores a general problem usually consists of the Managing Director, the Deputy Managing Director, the General Counsel (the head of the Legal Department), the Economic Counsellor (the head of the Research Department), and, depending on the issue at hand, possibly the Directors of the Exchange and Trade Relations Department, the Fiscal Affairs Department, the Treasurer's Department, and some of the area departments. Then if, after discussion, the group decides that further study is desirable, the topic is assigned to one of the departments, usually a functional department, or an interdepartmental working group. There is then intensive study by the staff, and general analytical papers are circulated to the Board, for information only. The possibilities of compensatory financing through the Fund were, for example, exhaustively investigated by the staff for two years prior to the Board's decision.

The Executive Directors frequently hold preliminary meetings to explore a general issue and possible alternative policies. The technique of informal sessions of the Board was introduced in January 1950, when the Board adopted a proposal by Mr. Southard (United States) that it meet from time to time to discuss multiple currency policy. The purpose of informal sessions is to allow Directors to express their views without necessarily committing the countries which they represent. Minutes are not circulated, though an unofficial record is kept in the Secretary's Office for reference. The discussions are purely between the management, the Directors, and the senior staff. The Managing Director, meanwhile, may be exploring with various Governors their reactions and views, including discussions in meetings of the Group of Ten (see below). Only after a considerable sorting out of ideas and views has taken place, and virtual agreement by the Governors has been assured, are proposals considered formally by the Board of Executive Directors.

Here, again, the process of formulating general policy differs significantly from the process in the Fund's early days. In 1947, for example, examination of the major policy problem facing the Fund—what action to take concerning multiple exchange rates—had been undertaken by an Ad Hoc Committee of Executive Directors, and it had been that committee which made policy proposals to the Board.

THE GROUP OF TEN

What has come to be known as the Group of Ten is not part of the structure of the Fund; however, because of the close relations involved, a few words about the nature of this group are appropriate. In October 1962 the General Arrangements to Borrow came into effect. Under these Arrangements, ten major industrial countries—Belgium, Canada, France, Germany, Italy, Japan, the Netherlands, Sweden, the United Kingdom, and the United States—agreed to stand ready to lend their currencies to the Fund up to specified amounts when the Fund and these countries considered that supplementary resources were needed by the Fund to forestall or cope with an impairment of the international monetary system. The total of the supplementary resources made available was equivalent to $6 billion. On October 15, 1965, the Executive Directors approved a four-year renewal of these Arrangements for the period October 1966–October 1970.

The Ministers of Finance and Governors of central banks of the ten countries concerned have met on several occasions to discuss major international monetary and financial problems of mutual interest. The Managing Director has been invited to attend these meetings. Deputies of the Group of Ten meet at the official level; senior staff members of the Fund participate in these meetings. In addition, shortly after the end of the period covered by this volume, in 1966–67, four joint meetings were held between the Executive Directors and the Deputies of the Group of Ten.

2

Objectives

Margaret G. de Vries

W HEN THE FUND was established, the founders had six purposes in mind. These were, as stated in Article I of the Fund Agreement:

(i) To promote international monetary cooperation through a permanent institution which provides the machinery for consultation and collaboration on international monetary problems.

(ii) To facilitate the expansion and balanced growth of international trade, and to contribute thereby to the promotion and maintenance of high levels of employment and real income and to the development of the productive resources of all members as primary objectives of economic policy.

(iii) To promote exchange stability, to maintain orderly exchange arrangements among members, and to avoid competitive exchange depreciation.

(iv) To assist in the establishment of a multilateral system of payments in respect of current transactions between members and in the elimination of foreign exchange restrictions which hamper the growth of world trade.

(v) To give confidence to members by making the Fund's resources available to them under adequate safeguards, thus providing them with the opportunity to correct maladjustments in their balance of payments without resorting to measures destructive of national or international prosperity.

(vi) In accordance with the above, to shorten the duration and lessen the degree of disequilibrium in the international balances of payments of members.

INTERDEPENDENT OBJECTIVES

The intention was that countries which joined the Fund would conform to certain standards of behavior in international financial matters. An elaborate and detailed code of what was considered good conduct was drawn up; it called for exchange stability, orderly exchange arrangements, the avoidance of competitive exchange depreciation, and a liberal regime of international payments— that is, convertibility of currencies and freedom from exchange restrictions.

Adherence to this code of conduct was not an end in itself. The specific goals of exchange rate stability, freedom from exchange restrictions, and convertibility of currencies were rather viewed as essential for the achievement of full employment and the maximum development of productive resources—objectives which were regarded by practically all countries at the close of World War II as primary.

The logic was that good conduct in international financial relations would foster a high level of international trade and investment. More specifically, the Fund's purposes implied that fixed exchange rates, freedom from exchange restrictions, and multilateral trade and payments were the best basis for international financial cooperation and for promoting world trade and investment. Expanding world trade and investment were, in turn, regarded as essential for the attainment of the even broader objectives of full employment and economic development in all member countries.

In the past, national economic policies had frequently led to restrictive measures in the international field, and thereupon to international economic conflict. The purpose of the new cooperation to be achieved through the Fund was to reconcile domestic and international objectives.

It was recognized that such reconciliation could not be assumed. In the forefront of economists' attention at the time were the questions whether full employment and balance of payments equilibrium could be attained simultaneously and, if so, what policies in the international field were compatible with the maintenance of full employment at home.[1] There were those who argued that, under certain assumptions, multilateral trade and payments might not maximize world trade.[2] The issue of the consistency of economic development—especially in what were only later to be called "the less developed countries"—with the international objectives of exchange stability and free trade and payments was still in the wings, rather than on stage, in economists' thinking.[3] While these questions were being debated, those who were proceeding with setting up and operating the International Monetary Fund took the view that these goals were not only compatible but even mutually reinforcing.

However, the architects of the Fund were fully aware that a permanent institution would be needed if the specified aims were to be accomplished. International

---

[1] These questions were discussed, for example, at the 59th annual meeting of the American Economic Association in January 1947; see "Papers and Proceedings," *American Economic Review*, Vol. XXXVII, No. 2 (May 1947), pp. 560–94. And they formed the subject of James Meade's *The Theory of International Economic Policy*; Vol. I, *The Balance of Payments*.

[2] Ragnar Frisch, "On the Need for Forecasting a Multilateral Balance of Payments," *American Economic Review*, Vol. XXXVII, No. 4 (September 1947), pp. 535–51.

[3] The second volume of James Meade's *The Theory of International Economic Policy*, entitled *Trade and Welfare*, was, however, devoted to the related question of how direct trade and payments controls can increase welfare.

cooperation was now to replace the exclusive authority of governments in fields in which decisions had previously been taken solely in the national interest. Resolving the conflicts that would arise and making the necessary day-to-day decisions would inevitably require continuous consultation and collaboration among the member countries. The Fund was thus intended as part of the permanent machinery of international monetary cooperation to be set up after World War II, rather than as an emergency agency to meet the temporary needs associated with the aftermath of war.

But it was also realized that the Fund would need to do more than enforce a code of conduct. The harmful financial practices which had characterized international relations prior to the Fund's establishment had been adopted because countries were short of foreign exchange. The Fund was, therefore, provided with large resources which it could make available to its members. Consequently, while countries joining the Fund agree to strict rules for the conduct of their international financial relations, they become members of an institution that possesses a large reserve of gold and foreign currencies with which it can assist any member that gets into payments difficulties.

The Fund can thus be thought of as having two types of function. What are sometimes called its regulatory functions consist of determining and enforcing the code of behavior in international financial and monetary matters. Its financial functions consist of making available to its members the resources to which it has access.

Other agencies of international cooperation were to supplement the Fund's functions. The International Bank for Reconstruction and Development was established to assist countries in obtaining funds for long-term investment. The International Trade Organization was planned—but never came into being —to reduce barriers to international trade, such as tariffs and trade quotas, and to set standards of behavior in the international trade field analogous to those established by the Fund in international financial matters.

We now turn to a brief description of the code of conduct administered by the Fund and of its financial assistance, as envisaged in the Articles.

EXCHANGE RATE STABILITY

The first part of the code of conduct consists of rules about exchange rates. Article IV provides for fixed exchange rates. Members agree to decide through the Fund on a system of exchange rates—that is, par values—for their currencies, and not to change these rates without consulting the Fund. Related obligations concern the price of gold.

Exchange rate stability is not, however, tantamount to rigidity. On the contrary, the exchange rate is to be adjusted when necessary to correct a fundamental disequilibrium in the member's balance of payments. But it is implicit in the Articles that exchange rates should be adjusted at only infrequent intervals: fundamental disequilibrium (although it has never been formally defined) is distinguished from merely ephemeral balance of payments disequilibria, such as those associated with seasonal, speculative, or possibly even short cyclical, disturbances.

The initiative for changing an exchange rate is reserved to the member concerned: the Fund cannot propose it. With minor exceptions, however, the member must seek the Fund's approval for the proposed change, and the Fund concurs if it is satisfied that the change is necessary and sufficient to correct a fundamental disequilibrium. If a member changes the par value of its currency despite the Fund's objection, the Fund may declare the member ineligible to use its resources and, subsequently, may even require the member to withdraw from membership.

The principal intention is to empower the Fund to prevent undue fluctuation or undue depreciation of exchange rates, or both. It is one of the explicit purposes of the Fund to outlaw competitive exchange depreciation—that is, depreciation in excess of that required to remove a fundamental disequilibrium.

CURRENCY CONVERTIBILITY AND FREEDOM FROM EXCHANGE RESTRICTIONS

The second part of the code of conduct consists of rules about exchange restrictions and similar practices, and requires members to establish and maintain a multilateral system of payments. It is envisaged that each member, after a transitional period of varying duration, will accept certain obligations set out in Article VIII. This Article provides that no member may, without the approval of the Fund, impose restrictions on the making of payments or transfers for current international transactions, or engage in discriminatory currency arrangements or multiple currency practices. Article VIII further provides for the convertibility of currencies—namely, for arrangements by which any trader exporting from one member country to another can secure effective payment in his own currency, and by which a member is free to use a payments surplus with any other member to pay for its deficit with a third country.

The aim of the Articles is that exchange restrictions shall be minimized— indeed eliminated—in the conviction that they are harmful to the growth of world trade and result in distortions in the domestic economies of members which discourage maximum economic growth and rising standards of living.

However, it was recognized at Bretton Woods that conditions after World War II would probably be such as to make it impossible, for some time to come, for many countries to accept in full the obligations pertaining to abolition of restrictions and establishment of convertibility. A transitional period, during which members might maintain and adapt their exchange restrictions, was therefore provided by Article XIV. But even members taking advantage of this

Article were to do their best to remove restrictions as soon as possible. After five years they were to consult with the Fund annually regarding any remaining restrictions, and the Fund was given authority to apply pressure on them to withdraw such restrictions.

FINANCIAL ASSISTANCE

The Fund's financial assistance to a member takes the form of an exchange of currencies. When a member wishes to draw on the Fund's resources, it purchases from the Fund some foreign currency that it can use and pays in a corresponding amount of its own currency, which the Fund then holds. Conversely, when a member pays back the drawing, it repurchases its own currency from the Fund with gold or some currency acceptable to the Fund. Such transactions are analogous to borrowing and repaying.

These transactions affect the Fund's holdings not only of the currency of the drawing or repurchasing member, but of the currencies of other members as well. While a drawing, for instance, increases the Fund's holdings of the currency of the member making the drawing, it reduces the holdings of the currency drawn. The Articles provide that the Fund shall be a revolving fund; that is, whatever the Fund pays out to its member countries is sooner or later to be returned to it. The drafters at Bretton Woods planned that in ideal conditions the Fund would hold 75 per cent of each member's quota in that member's currency.

The purpose for which the Fund's resources are to be made available is stated in Article I (v) to be that of providing members "with the opportunity to correct maladjustments in their balance of payments without resorting to measures destructive of national or international prosperity." This purpose implies *temporary* use of the Fund's resources.

The provisions for repurchase and for charges on drawings also indicate the temporary nature of the Fund's assistance. The idea on which the repurchase provisions in the Agreement are based is that an increase in a member's monetary reserves indicates an improvement in its balance of payments position. Any member that has drawn from the Fund an amount equal to more than half of its balance of payments deficit in any one year has to pay back the excess; thereafter, half of any payments surplus, or rise in reserves, has to be paid to the Fund in the form of a repurchase of the member's currency, although such repurchases are not required of a member whose reserves have fallen sharply or are less than its quota. Charges on drawings increase not only with the amount of the drawing outstanding relative to quota, but also with the time for which the drawing has been outstanding.

The concept of the Fund's assistance is that the Fund's resources form a secondary source of reserves for a member with a temporary balance of payments deficit; the member's own reserves constitute its first line of defense. Use of the Fund's resources makes it unnecessary for a member, in the absence of adequate reserves of its own, to resort to other means for coping with a temporary payments deficit. The solutions especially to be avoided for short-term deficits are exchange rate devaluation—reserved by the Fund's Articles for balance of payments deficits of a *fundamental* character—and exchange restrictions which curb the flow of trade and payments.

WORKING TOWARD THE OBJECTIVES

So much for the Fund's objectives as intended by its Articles. In working toward these goals the Fund has encountered many problems and a series of ever-changing circumstances in the world economy. Questions have continually arisen as to how the Fund should go about implementing its code of conduct. Examples during the years 1945 to 1965 were: What should the Fund do about members that did not believe that they could establish par values? What initiative could, and should, the Fund take if members did not of their own accord adjust their par values? What attitude should the Fund take toward countries that maintained multiple exchange rates rather than a single one? Since the convertibility of European currencies did not appear feasible for many years, what other exchange restrictions could be removed? The Fund also had to decide whether to permit the use of its resources in the absence of ready compliance with its code of conduct. Should drawings from the Fund, for example, be automatic, on the strength of a member's representation that the currency was needed for payments consistent with the Fund's Articles? Or could the Fund reject a request or impose conditions on drawings? If so, what should the conditions be?

The policies formulated to answer the foregoing and many similar questions form the subjects of the subsequent chapters of this volume. The evolution from 1945 to 1965 of the Fund's policies on exchange rates is traced in Chapters 3–7; Chapters 8 and 9 describe the related policies for transactions in gold. The policies adopted as regards exchange restrictions are surveyed in Chapters 10–14. Separate accounts of the Fund's relations with the European Payments Union (EPU) and with the CONTRACTING PARTIES to the General Agreement on Tariffs and Trade (GATT) are given in Chapters 15 and 16 respectively. Chapters 17–19 explain how the size and composition of the Fund's resources have changed over the years, and how access to the Fund's resources has gradually been implemented by the enunciation of various drawing policies and by the introduction of stand-by arrangements. Chapters 20 and 21 discuss the relation between stand-by arrangements and stabilization programs; these programs emerged as part of the Fund's objective of internal financial stability for its member countries, immediately discussed below. Finally, Chapters 22–27 study the constitutional development of the Fund from 1945 to 1968.

THE OBJECTIVE OF INTERNAL FINANCIAL STABILITY

As the Fund began to evolve precise principles and detailed procedures, it soon became apparent that one facet of economic policy which had not been an explicit feature of the Articles was a prerequisite for the implementation of the Fund's objectives, namely, the maintenance of internal financial stability. Domestic financial policy had not been made a matter of international obligation. On the contrary, care had been taken to ensure that the obligations laid upon countries with respect to international transactions should not impede the use of internal monetary and financial policies to achieve national goals.

Shortly after the Fund commenced operations, it was evident that the problem of inflation was creating serious economic difficulties. Though the fundamental forces of inflation had had their origins in World War II, their effects became more apparent after the war. The public, long deprived of the goods to which it had been accustomed, had expectations far beyond the capacity of the war-depleted economies; and large-scale investments to restore and increase productive capacity further limited the supply of consumer goods. Government expenditure was expanded on an unprecedented scale, and in many countries the extension of credit to finance investment was excessive.

It soon became clear, and the Fund began to emphasize, that achievement of the international goals of free exchange and exchange stability would be frustrated unless government and monetary authorities took appropriate measures to prevent inflation.[4] The next step was that the Fund, while recognizing that there was no single program of fiscal, credit, and monetary measures which could be applied to every country, began to enunciate general principles for the attainment of internal monetary stability.[5] These principles related to a wide range of fiscal and financial policies, involving inter alia the level of government expenditure, the rate of domestic taxation, the measures to promote domestic savings, and the rate and nature of bank credit expansion.

Because the Fund had no authority or jurisdiction over these matters, it had to proceed with caution. The Fund cannot impose any particular domestic policies upon its members. It can, of course, refuse to provide financial assistance to a member whose policies are conducive to acute and persistent balance of payments difficulties. But the Fund has preferred a more positive role.

In the circumstances, much of the work of the Fund in its formative years consisted of securing a wider recognition of the close relationship between the domestic financial policies of a member and that member's balance of payments. In later years, as inflation continued to prevail in many countries, the Fund devoted a great deal of attention to studying the internal financial problems of

---

[4] *Annual Report, 1948*, pp. 19–20.

[5] *Ibid.*, p. 20.

its members, to advocating particular policies to cope with these problems, and to providing technical assistance in the application of such policies.

From time to time fears have been expressed that the Fund was overstepping its jurisdictional bounds. These fears have lessened in recent years, however, and attacks have more frequently been made on the Fund's emphasis on sound monetary management, the term often used for anti-inflationary measures, sometimes derogatorily. Indeed, not a few economists and government officials have continued to contend that moderate amounts of inflation are necessary to achieve full employment or rapid economic development, although this is a view which the Fund's experience makes it difficult to support.

Despite periodic debates among economists, both within and outside the Fund, about the degree of inflation that is compatible with broader economic objectives, and even about the nature and causes of inflation,[6] the working out with members of programs of internal financial stabilization has gradually become one of the main activities of the Fund. These stabilization programs go fairly deeply into internal policies; they include, for example, rather precise undertakings by members with respect to public finance, quantitative limitations on expansion of central bank credit, and minimum reserve requirements for commercial banks.

LINKING ACTIVITIES TO OBJECTIVES

Another theme which has emerged as the Fund has developed its policies is that all of the Fund's activities should be aimed toward a common set of objectives. In other words, the Fund's regulatory functions should be unified, and the operation of its financial functions—that is, the use of its resources—should be made conditional on a member's progress toward the Fund's objectives or toward compliance with the Fund's code of conduct.

Article I provides that the resources of the Fund be made available to members "under adequate safeguards." In effect, Fund assistance is to be made available to countries that make efforts to eliminate those aspects of their exchange and monetary policies that are detrimental to their own interests or those of other members. The degree and nature of the conditions that could and should be attached to drawings must, however, be determined. And much of the Fund's history pertaining to its resources is concerned with the determination of the type and degree of conditionality that should govern access to its resources.

The formal linking of the use of its resources with practical programs of action was an important step in the Fund's policy, taken in 1951. But the search for a means of reducing the uncertainty about the conditions of access to its resources continued. Eventually, conditions for some drawings were to become

---

[6] See, for example, Martin Bronfenbrenner and Franklin D. Holzman, "A Survey of Inflation Theory," in *Surveys of Economic Theory; Vol. I, Money, Interest, and Welfare*, pp. 46–107.

very specific indeed. They have included, for example, reduction or removal of exchange restrictions, simplification of a multiple rate system, and adoption of a detailed program of internal financial stabilization.

By the mid-1960's, support of stabilization programs designed to eliminate inflation and reduce reliance on restrictions had become the most common purpose of Fund assistance. Members using the Fund's resources were thus encouraged to adopt measures consistent with the Fund's basic objectives.

DEVELOPING THE NECESSARY PROCEDURES

As the Fund worked toward its objectives, various procedures which had not been envisaged in the Articles also had to be developed. One procedure that has evolved over the years has been the annual consultations with all members, including those with no exchange restrictions requiring the Fund's approval. Another is the stand-by arrangement.

The Articles provide for annual consultations, after the Fund has been in operation for five years, covering exchange restrictions still maintained by members under Article XIV. Accordingly, consultations under Article XIV commenced with most member countries in 1952. Intense debates took place at that time about the conduct of these consultations and the subjects to which the discussions should be confined. Within a few years, however, these consultations had become the principal vehicle by which the Fund and its members explored a whole range of topics of mutual interest, including exchange rates and par values, multiple currency practices, exchange restrictions, internal financial policies, use of the Fund's resources, and quotas. In 1961 it was agreed that annual consultations would take place with members that had discarded the transitional regime of Article XIV as well as with those which still availed themselves of that regime.

These periodic exchanges of views have become of key importance to the Fund and its members and have proved to be a valuable instrument of international monetary cooperation. Indeed, they have become essential instruments for promoting the purposes of the Fund, paving the way to the use of its resources where appropriate and facilitating adjustments in payments imbalances where these have existed. The consultations have made members' policies more responsive to the aims of the international community, and have equipped the Fund to be more fully appreciative of the problems of its individual members.

The other innovation is the stand-by arrangement. These arrangements are not expressly provided for in the Fund's Articles. They were introduced because of the need for some procedure by which members could be sure of being able to purchase exchange during an agreed period, if they needed to do so. Under a stand-by arrangement a country is assured that, following a review of its policies and position, and subject to such conditions as are included in the arrangement, it can, without further consideration of its position by the Fund, purchase from the Fund the currencies of other members up to an agreed amount during a stated period. Such an arrangement is usually granted for twelve months (or six months if the member's request is purely seasonal), but is renewable. In considering a request for a stand-by arrangement, the Fund applies the same policies as it applies to requests for immediate drawings. The arrangement is usually accompanied by a precise agreement between the Fund and the member specifying the policies the member will pursue and how the drawings conferred by the stand-by arrangement are to be phased over time.

ATTAINMENTS BY 1965

Although at the end of 1965 important problems persisted in the international monetary system, and others were already on the horizon, it was nonetheless evident that considerable progress toward the Fund's initial objectives had been made since 1945. Exchange rates, exchange arrangements, exchange restrictions, and currency convertibility, all afforded many favorable contrasts with those prevailing at the end of World War II.

THE STARTING POINT

When the Fund opened its doors in May 1946, international economic relations were very much restricted. One of the legacies of World War II had been the imposition of additional problems on the already burdened flow of international commerce. For countries in Europe and for Japan, the war had left difficulties arising from destruction and disruption, the loss of overseas resources, and the rupture of long-established trade connections. Not only did most of these countries have sizable trade and payments deficits, but the whole pattern of world trade was seriously unbalanced. This imbalance reflected the sharp contrast between the capacity of the Western Hemisphere to produce for export and that of other areas, where postwar productive facilities were inadequate to meet the greatly increased demands of their populations for goods and services.

In these circumstances, many countries in Europe, the Middle East, and Asia were compelled to ration available supplies of domestically produced goods and to continue and even to extend their stringent wartime restrictions on imports. Only a handful of members—all in the Western Hemisphere—assumed the obligations of Article VIII of the Fund Agreement.

Moreover, by 1947 the payments problem, which was shortly to become generally known as the "chronic world dollar shortage," had forced many countries to change the character of their restrictions. Where before restrictions had been placed on imports of certain goods, such as nonessential and luxury items, rather than on imports from specific currency areas, during 1947 the restrictions of most countries were altered so as to reduce their deficits in U.S. dollars and save their gold and dollar reserves. In short, restrictions commonly became discriminatory against the dollar area—that is, against imports from the United States, Canada, and parts of Latin America. In addition, the attempt to render convertible all sterling accruing from current transactions, under the terms of the Anglo-American Financial Agreement of 1945, had failed by the summer of 1947. All European currencies were still inconvertible.

Restrictions also prevailed elsewhere. In many Latin American countries the demand for imports—swollen partly because of deferred demand and partly because of postwar inflation—had made necessary an intensification of restrictions, even though foreign exchange receipts were large. In several Eastern European countries exchange restrictions, although severe, were themselves subordinated to even more direct and comprehensive state intervention through state trading and barter arrangements.

As regards exchange rates, although most original members agreed par values with the Fund at the end of 1946, some did not, and others had multiple exchange rate systems which made their par values more or less nominal. Of the 40 countries that were Fund members at the end of 1946, some 13 were using multiple rates. And within a few years several members gave up conducting transactions at exchange rates based on their par values and adopted fluctuating rates of exchange.

PROGRESS BY 1965

By the end of 1965, the great majority of the Fund's 103 members were adhering to a regime of parity exchange rates: if they did not have institutionally agreed par values, they at least maintained exchange rates which were fixed or had been stable for several years. The extent and complexity of multiple exchange rate systems had also vastly diminished, and restrictions on current payments in the world as a whole were far fewer in the early 1960's than they had been for some decades.

Convertibility of the currencies of the European countries had been fully maintained since 1961, when 10 European members had given up the transitional arrangements of Article XIV. By the end of 1965, 27 of the Fund's members, from all geographic regions, had assumed the obligations of Article VIII. The introduction and successful maintenance of widespread currency convertibility had also brought about a virtual end to discriminatory exchange restrictions.

Many countries had gone even farther in reducing restrictions on payments than they were obliged to do; although the Articles permitted controls on capital movements, liberalization of restrictions was gradually extended even to these. Moreover, the industrial countries had begun to concentrate on the liberalization of trade as well as of payments. In particular, in 1962–63 efforts were initiated to reduce tariffs which eventually culminated in the "Kennedy Round" of tariff cuts effected through the GATT in 1967.

At the same time as countries had progressed toward following the Fund's code of conduct, there had been a signal expansion of the world economy and of international trade, and although only modest progress had been made in raising the incomes of the developing countries, relatively high levels of employment had been maintained in most countries.

Since the intra-European trade liberalization program of the OEEC and several consultations of the GATT were going forward simultaneously with the activities of the Fund in the field of restrictions, it is difficult, if not impossible, to disentangle the precise role of the Fund in the substantial liberalization of restrictions that occurred. Three contributions of the Fund may, nonetheless, be noted: it repeatedly stressed the dangers of permanent regional blocs; it emphasized the need for freeing trade and payments on a world-wide nondiscriminatory basis; and, by highlighting the importance of countries' domestic financial policies and by making its resources available, it helped to create the conditions essential for the restoration of currency convertibility and the relaxation of restrictions.

THE OTHER SIDE OF THE PICTURE

Admittedly the picture was not entirely unmixed, and the Fund was not without its problems or its critics. Not all countries had been able to abolish their exchange restrictions. By and large the less developed countries, hampered by structural problems, notably the unsatisfactory expansion of their export earnings, had found it difficult to achieve simultaneously the goals of rapid economic growth and internal and external stability. Hence, although by the 1960's the industrial countries were generally able to maintain their external economic relations with few limitations on the acquisition or use of foreign exchange, many less developed countries continued to rely on exchange restrictions, and some still had multiple or fluctuating exchange rates. Many that had reduced their exchange restrictions had turned to other devices, frequently in the trade field, to stem imports, and had introduced export bonuses and subsidies to encourage exports. Possibly worst of all, in some less developed countries restrictions seemed to have lost their temporary character.

The mid-1960's also saw the reintroduction of exchange controls on capital movements by some of the leading industrial countries. After restrictions on capital movements had been lifted in the early years of the decade, transfers of short-term capital had become sizable and frequent. Because such capital movements were often speculative and disequilibrating rather than equilibrating, they presented the financial authorities, especially in industrial countries, with new problems. Sterling, for example, was subjected from time to time to severe strains in the world's exchange markets, at least partly because of rather sharp movements of short-term capital. The unexpected magnitudes of capital flows from the United States were also responsible in part for the emergence and persistence of a sizable deficit in the balance of payments of that country.

These disturbances often necessitated official intervention—sometimes on a large scale—to enable countries to maintain their exchange rates within the margins specified by the Fund. In order to avoid impairing the freedom already allowed to foreign payments, large amounts of reserves were utilized, and there was heavy resort to the Fund.

Devaluations and rumors of devaluation of important European currencies were recurrent. Consequently, the principal industrial countries took special measures to curb capital flows. In 1964, the United States imposed a tax on purchases of foreign stocks and bonds. This tax was extended in February 1965, at which time the United States also introduced a voluntary program to discourage capital exports by banks and other financial institutions. As one of several steps to correct its balance of payments in 1964–65, the United Kingdom made changes in its exchange control regulations affecting capital movements.

As one international monetary crisis after another occurred, and were solved by ad hoc decisions, the Fund's mechanisms began to be criticized as unequipped to deal with the problems at hand. Major reforms, especially in the field of exchange rates, were suggested. Some critics were disappointed that the Fund had not itself come forward with proposals for exchange reform. Others cited as evidence of the deficiencies of the Fund the fact that since 1962 the Ministers of the Group of Ten had considered several key questions of international finance prior to their discussion by the Executive Board of the Fund.[7]

THE GROWTH OF INTERNATIONALISM

Over a considerable part of its field, therefore, the Fund's achievements by 1965 were partial rather than complete. But in one important direction the aim of its founders, as expressed in Article I, had been fulfilled with conspicuous success. By the mid-1960's the Fund had developed a system of international cooperation and consultation in the monetary and financial field which was in sharp contrast to the situation of the interwar period, particularly the 1930's, when countries had pursued their financial policies with little regard for, and little understanding of, the effects of these policies on other countries. Indeed, the way in which countries were working together in the Fund by 1965 was in sharp contrast to that prevailing during the Fund's first decade.

---

[7] See, for example, Fritz Machlup, *Plans for Reform of the International Monetary System*; Fritz Machlup and Burton G. Malkiel, eds., *International Monetary Arrangements: The Problem of Choice*; and Harry G. Johnson, *The World Economy at the Crossroads*, Chap. 3.

At the outset of the discussions on the organization of the Fund, it was evident that countries had profoundly conflicting views as to how vital and effective a force in international monetary affairs the Fund should be. Sharply conflicting views surfaced as early as the Inaugural Meeting of the Board of Governors at Savannah in March 1946: White argued for a strong, currently informed Board of Executive Directors, which would take the initiative and make decisions, while Keynes envisaged the Board more as an arbiter of disputes, meeting as the occasion required.[8] Conflicts of national interests were, in the next several years, to occasion many debates among Directors. Especially contended were questions about the Fund's jurisdiction and how it should be implemented. The United States, eager to restore normal international relations as quickly as possible, sought to enhance the authority and activities of the Fund, while European countries, faced with reconstruction and major readjustments of their economies and of their trading relations, had much narrower ideas as to what the Fund should or could do.

There was also a sharp division in the Board between those who believed that members had automatic rights to draw on the Fund's resources and others, notably the U.S. Directors. The European countries, with urgent needs for U.S. dollars, clung strongly to conceptions of "automaticity" about the Fund's resources, while the United States, deluged with requests for aid, and with a Congress anxious to keep close watch over disbursements, took the line that access to the Fund's holdings of dollars should be made subject to fairly strict conditions.

This atmosphere resulted in many decisions by the Board which in effect tied the Fund's hands in its initial years: there were to be few transactions, no participation in European payments arrangements, and little action against restrictions. The Fund's attention was given mainly to broken cross rates and multiple currency practices. Moreover, as effective power lay with the Board, there was little that management and staff could do to alter the situation. The morale of the staff, already low, was further depressed by curbs on administrative expenditures necessitated by the Fund's persistent budgetary deficits. Following the suggestion of the Governor for the United Kingdom in 1951 that ways be found for cooperation with the World Bank so as to reduce the Fund's expenditures, there were even fears that some of the Fund's functions might be eliminated or absorbed by the World Bank, which was operating very profitably.

This story, in detail, is clearly traceable in the chronicle related in Volume I, as is the subsequent turnaround after 1952–53 and the growth of the Fund into an effective organization. By the 1960's the Fund was operating with relatively little controversy in all its fields of responsibility: practically all members, including the largest ones, the United States and the United Kingdom, had concluded

[8] See above, Vol. I, pp. 130–34.

stand-by arrangements or had made drawings; the Fund's resources had been enlarged; all the major European countries had undertaken the obligations of Article VIII; and all members, including those under Article VIII, were regularly consulting with the Fund concerning a wide range of economic policies. A by-product of the extensive use of the Fund's resources has been that, despite a severalfold increase in the size of the staff, there have been budgetary surpluses in each year since 1955–56.

A number of factors, political as well as economic, contributed to the dramatic change. Many of these are described in Volume I, some of them have been mentioned in the previous chapter, and still more are considered in Part V of this volume. But two elements making for improved relations between the Fund and its members may here be mentioned; they are (1) the development from 1952 onward of policies opening up use of the Fund's resources, and (2) the successful conduct of the annual consultations which commenced in March 1952. Both of these factors gave new and meaningful form and substance to collaboration among members, Executive Directors, the management, and the staff.

PROGRESS AND CHANGE

In the last resort, any attempt to assess the over-all achievements of the Fund necessitates the weighing of intangibles. One would need to discover what the postwar world would have been like without the Fund, or with a Fund that had acted in a different way. Moreover, one must keep in mind that the complex of political considerations that determine relations between governments inevitably affects the operations and policies of specialized international agencies. In addition, there is a reverse flow of effects from international agencies to governments. Finally, the operations and policies of the international agencies are themselves influenced by contacts and discussions between these agencies and between their staffs.

In attempting to strike a balance it is also necessary to take into account that the Fund has shown a capacity to adapt to new situations which may not have been anticipated by its founding fathers. For example, in the 1960's new and wider solutions were being sought for the trade and payments problems of the less developed countries. In 1963 a decision on compensatory financing introduced a new drawing policy, chiefly for the benefit of these countries. Under this decision, members can draw on the Fund's resources to meet payments difficulties arising out of temporary export shortfalls, provided that the shortfall is largely attributable to circumstances beyond the control of the member, and provided that the member is willing to cooperate with the Fund in seeking appropriate solutions for its balance of payments difficulties where such solutions are called for. This second provision is much less strict than the conditions generally stipulated for drawings of a substantial amount—that is, in the technical terminology of the Fund, for drawings beyond the first credit tranche (see Chapter 18). In other words, there was recognition that even countries which had difficulty in meeting the Fund's standards should be able to obtain assistance to meet difficulties arising out of genuinely short-term export fluctuations.

Technical assistance to the less developed countries has also been expanded in many areas within the Fund's competence—the improvement of statistics, taxation, budgeting, central banking operations, banking legislation, exchange reforms, and programs of monetary stabilization—and the Fund has established a special institute for the training of technicians from the less developed countries.

Even more significantly, the Fund has increasingly recognized that, while monetary stability is a prerequisite for sustained economic development, resolute efforts by developing countries to increase productivity and capital formation, and to reallocate productive resources, are equally essential. Moreover, the Fund has taken an active interest in such matters as the level of external indebtedness of primary producing countries and the impact on them of the hard-core trade barriers of the industrial countries, especially on imports of agricultural commodities from the less developed countries. These activities have expanded further since 1965. To help to alleviate the continuing difficulties of the less developed countries, the compensatory financing scheme has been expanded and the Fund has put forward proposals to deal with the instability of prices of primary commodities in world markets.

In the same vein, when, after convertibility had become widespread, it became obvious that capital transfers would be an important feature of the payments scene, the Fund took steps to deal with the problems then presented. First, in 1962 it augmented its resources through the General Arrangements to Borrow (GAB), under which ten main industrial countries agreed to stand ready to lend their currencies to the Fund up to specified amounts when the Fund and the countries considered that supplementary resources were needed to forestall or cope with an impairment of the international monetary system, especially because of sizable short-term capital movements.

Second, during the early 1960's the Fund re-examined the legal and policy aspects of the provisions of its Articles respecting the use of its resources to finance capital movements.[9] The Articles preclude use of the Fund's resources "to meet a large or sustained outflow of capital" (Article VI, Section 1 (a)). Immediately after World War II, there had been great apprehension lest the

---

[9] E.B. Decision No. 1238-(61/43), July 28, 1961; below, Vol. III, p. 245.

resources of the Fund be wasted in financing capital flight from countries whose currencies were overvalued. But as the years passed and circumstances changed, it came to be appreciated that disturbances to the normal flow of capital, provided they are temporary, are eminently suitable for Fund financing. Hence, in 1962 the Fund announced that it should not, on account of its Articles, be precluded from assisting a member because the latter's difficulties are caused or accentuated by an outflow of short-term capital that could not be deemed large or sustained. The Fund let it be known that, if a country facing an outflow of capital turned to the Fund for assistance, the test to be applied by the Fund would be in accordance with its accepted principles, i.e., that appropriate measures were being taken to restore equilibrium in the balance of payments, and that assistance provided by the Fund would be repaid within a maximum period of three to five years.[10]

The possible need for greater Fund resources which evoked the GAB stemmed from a more general concern for international liquidity—that is, the stock of the world's gold and foreign exchange reserves and other assets with which countries can finance payments deficits, such as facilities to draw on the Fund or to borrow from other international institutions, or various arrangements to borrow from foreign central banks or governments. For several years the Fund debated whether these resources were adequate. Searching questions were raised, e.g.: Was international liquidity increasing fast enough to keep pace with the rising levels of world trade, investment, and capital movements? How great was the danger that additional liquidity in the international monetary system would cause countries to pursue excessively inflationary policies? Was the stock of international liquidity so low that countries encountering payments deficits would again have to resort to exchange restrictions?

The gradual recognition of a possible inadequacy of reserves had led to a long process of international discussion and negotiation, both in the Fund and among the ten countries that had signed the GAB. In 1964–65 there had been a wide-ranging exploration of a variety of possible techniques of reserve creation, and, as 1965 came to a close, discussions were proceeding which aimed at finding a basis for agreement among governments on contingency plans for deliberate reserve creation.

The outcome of these discussions was to produce perhaps the greatest evidence that the Fund contained capacity for growth and change—that is, agreement among its members at the Annual Meeting in 1967 on an Outline of a Facility Based on Special Drawing Rights. This system of special drawing rights—which was agreed to by the Board of Governors shortly after the close of the period here reviewed—was sufficiently new and different as to require significant modifications in the Articles of Agreement of the Fund.

---

[10] *Annual Report, 1962*, p. 33.

PART II

Exchange Rates and Gold Markets

The Par Value System: An Overview

Margaret G. de Vries

SINCE THE PAR VALUE SYSTEM was initiated in 1945, there have been several ups and downs—or, more literally, downs and ups—in the extent to which it has been adhered to. In the first decade of the Fund's life—that is until about 1955—several countries found it necessary to deviate from parity exchange rates. Some suspended their parities; others resorted to one or more of the myriad types of multiple exchange rate systems which made meaningless the par values to which they had originally agreed.

In the second decade of the Fund's operations, however, a pronounced trend toward adherence to agreed par values appeared. Par values were agreed by most countries which had not previously had them; fluctuating exchange rates were abolished in favor of agreed parities; and many multiple rates were eliminated. In many countries where par values had not been established, exchange rates of a fixed nature were introduced.

This trend toward par values, or at least toward fixed exchange rates, became especially marked after 1960. By the end of 1965, some 57 of the Fund's 103 members were using their par values for all transactions; another 4 had only minor deviations from the par value system; and 28, although without par values, were using fixed or stable single rates of exchange. In this sense, by the mid-1960's the par value system was for the first time operating in the great majority of countries.

These broad trends are traced in this chapter, following a brief description of the genesis of the par value system and how it was meant to work. Focus on these general trends, however, is merely introductory to the main story of exchange rates in the twenty years reviewed here. Much occurred quietly and behind the scenes, as it were. As the Fund administered the par value system, a variety of policies on different aspects of exchange rates had to be formulated and implemented. Answers had to be provided, for example, to such questions as the circumstances in which par values should be instituted or when they might be delayed; and policies had to be worked out governing the adjustment of par values in instances of fundamental disequilibrium. In the same way, it was essential that policies on multiple rates and on fluctuating rates be developed.

These matters are covered in detail in the next four chapters. Chapter 4 elaborates the policies that the Fund evolved from 1945 to 1965 on the establishment and maintenance of the par value system. Chapter 5 is concerned with policies on exchange rate adjustment—that is, with the alteration of par values or, where no par values exist, with the changing of existing exchange rates— and also contains a statistical picture of the extent to which exchange rates were actually altered between the time the Fund was established and the end of 1965. Chapter 6 traces the policies of the Fund as regards multiple rates, and Chapter 7 as regards fluctuating rates.

GENESIS OF THE PAR VALUE SYSTEM

From very early in World War II, there had been extensive discussion about the nature of the exchange rate system which would be appropriate after the war. What was believed to be needed was some sort of international mechanism by which an individual country's exchange rate could be set and altered under mutually agreed conditions. The interwar years seemed to have demonstrated two primary needs as regards exchange rates. First, exchange rates should be established and changed in the context of an international review, rather than by countries acting alone. Since countries had a vital interest in each other's exchange rates, international cooperation was essential. It was unilateral action that had led to the economic chaos of the 1930's. Second, stable exchange rates were regarded as more likely than fluctuating or frequently changing rates to produce good financial relations between countries and an orderly working of the international monetary system. Following the "beggar-my-neighbor" experiences of the 1930's, exchange rates that were frequently changed were thought to run the risk of creating opportunities for competitive exchange depreciation and of exporting unemployment.

Some influential economists, then as now, believed in the merits of fluctuating exchange rates, at least in certain circumstances. In the forthcoming years much ingenuity was to be devoted to producing schemes for almost automatic fluctuations in exchange rates which, it was hoped, would not involve competitive exchange depreciation. Nonetheless, the par value system was generally accepted as a central core of the new international cooperation.

Procedures are set out in the Articles, first for establishing and then for maintaining an international par value system. The principal Article in this regard is Article IV, of which the contents, partly quoted and partly summarized (in brackets) follow:

SECTION 1. *Expression of par values.*—(*a*) The par value of the currency of each member shall be expressed in terms of gold as a common denominator or in terms of the United States dollar of the weight and fineness in effect on July 1, 1944.

(*b*) [All computations relating to members' currencies necessary for carrying on Fund activities are to be based on par values.]

SEC. 2. [Gold purchases and sales are to be based on par values.]

SEC. 3. *Foreign exchange dealings based on parity.*—The maximum and the minimum rates for exchange transactions between the currencies of members taking place within their territories shall not differ from parity

(i) in the case of spot exchange transactions, by more than one percent; and

(ii) in the case of other exchange transactions, by a margin which exceeds the margin for spot exchange transactions by more than the Fund considers reasonable.

SEC. 4. *Obligations regarding exchange stability.*—(*a*) Each member undertakes to collaborate with the Fund to promote exchange stability, to maintain orderly exchange arrangements with other members, and to avoid competitive exchange alterations.

(*b*) [Provisions for exchange of currencies based on par values.]

SEC. 5. *Changes in par values.*—(*a*) A member shall not propose a change in the par value of its currency except to correct a fundamental disequilibrium.

(*b*) A change in the par value of a member's currency may be made only on the proposal of the member and only after consultation with the Fund.

(*c*) When a change is proposed, the Fund shall first take into account the changes, if any, which have already taken place in the initial par value of the member's currency as determined under Article XX, Section 4. If the proposed change, together with all previous changes, whether increases or decreases,

(i) does not exceed ten percent of the initial par value, the Fund shall raise no objection;

(ii) does not exceed ten percent of the initial par value, the Fund may either concur or object, but shall declare its attitude within seventy-two hours if the member so requests;

(iii) is not within (i) or (ii) above, the Fund may either concur or object, but shall be entitled to a longer period in which to declare its attitude.

(*d*) . . .

(*e*) A member may change the par value of its currency without the concurrence of the Fund if the change does not affect the international transactions of members of the Fund.

(*f*) The Fund shall concur in a proposed change which is within the terms of (*c*) (ii) or (*c*) (iii) above if it is satisfied that the change is necessary to correct a fundamental disequilibrium. In particular, provided it is so satisfied, it shall not object to a proposed change because of the domestic social or political policies of the member proposing the change.

SEC. 6. *Effect of unauthorized changes.*—If a member changes the par value of its currency despite the objection of the Fund, in cases where the Fund is entitled to object, the member shall be ineligible to use the resources of the Fund unless the Fund otherwise determines; and if, after the expiration of a reasonable period, the difference between the member and the Fund continues, the matter shall be subject to the provisions of Article XV, Section 2 (*b*) [that is, the member may be expelled from Fund membership].

In addition, Article XX, Section 4, specifies the procedures for the determination of initial par values. This Article states in part (summarized portions in brackets):

SEC. 4. *Initial determination of par values.*—(*a*) When the Fund is of the opinion that it will shortly be in a position to begin exchange transactions, it shall so notify the members and shall request each member to communicate within thirty days the par value of its currency based on the rates of exchange prevailing on the sixtieth day before the entry into force of this Agreement. [Enemy-occupied members still in the midst of hostilities were to be given extra time.]

(*b*) [The par value so communicated, except for enemy-occupied countries, is to become the par value unless, within ninety days after the Fund's request for communication of a par value, the member notifies the Fund that it regards that par value as unsatisfactory or the Fund notifies the member that the par value is likely to cause undue use of the Fund's resources. If such notification is given either way, the Fund and the member are to agree on a par value within a period determined by the Fund.]

(*c*) When the par value of a member's currency has been established under (*b*) above, either by the expiration of ninety days without notification, or by agreement after notification, the member shall be eligible to buy from the Fund the currencies of other members to the full extent permitted in this Agreement, provided that the Fund has begun exchange transactions.

(*d*) In the case of a member whose metropolitan territory has been occupied by the enemy, the provisions of (*b*) above shall apply [but, (i) the period of ninety days shall be extended to a date fixed by agreement between the Fund and the member; meanwhile, (ii) the member may have recourse to Fund resources, under conditions and in amounts prescribed by the Fund and, (iii) may, by agreement with the Fund, change its par value].

(*e*) [Provision for an enemy-occupied country to adopt a new monetary unit.]

(*f*) Changes in par values agreed with the Fund under this Section shall not be taken into account in determining whether a proposed change falls within (i), (ii), or (iii) of Article IV, Section 5 (*c*).

(*g*) [Provision for par values for separate currencies of nonmetropolitan territories.]

(*h*) The Fund shall begin exchange transactions at such date as it may determine after members having sixty-five percent of the total of the quotas set forth in Schedule A have become eligible . . . to purchase the currencies of other members [that is, after they have agreed initial par values with the Fund]. . . .

The par value technique can be characterized as one of managed flexibility of exchange rates; it stands between permanently fixed exchange rates, such as would exist under the gold standard, and freely fluctuating rates. In recent years, economists have come to refer to it as the "adjustable peg" system, par values being thought of as pegs that can be changed under specified conditions.

Late in 1946, for reasons made clear in the next chapter, the Fund decided to go ahead with the establishment of initial par values for its 39 members. All but seven of these members set such par values in December 1946. However, several problems already existed in connection with the system established. Most of the exchange rates prevailing were those that had been operative during World War II; some had been in use even earlier. It was, of course, known— and the Fund's studies of individual countries at the time also revealed—that on the basis of price, wage, and cost of living comparisons, the rates for many currencies were out of line with the U.S. dollar and a few other currencies. In addition, it was explicitly recognized that the initial par values for some countries might later be found to be incompatible with the maintenance of full employment in those countries. The possibility was also envisaged that the initial par values agreed might have an unduly contractionist effect, reducing the exports of several countries and adversely affecting the flow of world trade. In this regard the Fund noted that the continuation of price inflation in a number of countries threatened to impair their ability to compete in world trade. Inflationary fiscal and credit policies, warned the Fund, would undermine the parities just established.[1]

Nevertheless, the Fund believed it preferable to make a start with these exchange rates rather than to wait until a better set of initial par values could be agreed. Many parities were thus accepted which the Fund was fully cognizant could not long be held. Some of them were already used in conjunction with other effective rates. For example, among the countries for which par values were accepted, eleven had various forms of multiple exchange rate systems. Ten of these—Bolivia, Chile, Colombia, Costa Rica, Cuba, Ecuador, Honduras, Nicaragua, Paraguay, and Peru—were in Latin America; the eleventh was Iran. Venezuela joined the Fund in December 1946 but did not establish a par value until 1947; it too had multiple rates.

EARLY BREAKS WITH THE SYSTEM

Establishing and maintaining the par value regime just after World War II was not an easy task. The Fund was immediately confronted with three kinds of deviations from the system of agreed par values. First, because of concern with the uncertainties in their economies, a few countries delayed setting initial par values at all. This postponement involved large countries, such as Italy, as well as small ones. Second, because of the inconvertibility of European currencies, broken cross rates—an exchange rate between two currencies in a third

---

[1] *Annual Report, 1947*, p. 27.

market which differs from that derived from their par values—were to emerge in several markets throughout the world. The third deviation from the par value system occurred almost at once. France, Mexico, Peru, and Canada took measures between 1948 and 1950 which suspended all transactions at their par values. The last three introduced fluctuating rates; France set up a limited free market.

The French proposal, in January 1948, to change its par value was a significant one: France was the first nation under the new international regime to propose a change in its exchange rate. Instead of making the change unilaterally, as it would have done before the days of the Fund, it came to an international organization to ask its opinion and concurrence. Subsequent developments, however, led to disagreement between France and the Fund. In addition to the change in the par value, France proposed a concurrent free market. In the free market were to be sold half the export proceeds and all receipts from investments in U.S. dollars and Portuguese escudos, and these currencies were to be bought in this free market for certain transactions. While the Executive Directors were prepared to concur in a devaluation of the franc to a realistic rate which would be applicable to transactions in all currencies, they objected to the proposed free market for a few currencies.

In July 1948 the Mexican Government informed the Fund that, unless Mexico could obtain substantial financial support, its par value could not be held. When this assistance was not forthcoming, Mexico suspended its par value in favor of a fluctuating rate; this rate lasted until June 1949, when a new par value was established. In November 1949 Peru proposed to abandon its official parity for the sol and to permit the exchange rate to fluctuate freely until it found its natural and stable level. In September 1950 Canada introduced a fluctuating rate.

ATTITUDES TOWARD DEVALUATION IN THE LATE 1940's

Another stumbling block for the Fund and the par value system in these early years was the discovery, shortly after the Fund commenced operations, that members were reluctant to devalue their currencies. At the time of Bretton Woods it had been the fear in some circles that countries would resort to frequent exchange rate changes in the postwar period. Indeed, one of the objectives of the Fund was to be the curbing of excessive devaluation. By 1948, however, it had become apparent that these fears were misplaced. Countries had in fact tended to lean in the opposite direction, maintaining exchange rates which should have been changed. Apart from a devaluation by Italy in 1947, and the devaluations of France, Mexico, and Peru just noted, only Colombia and French Somaliland had altered their par values by mid-1949.[2]

---

[2] For statements on the devaluations of Italy, Colombia, and French Somaliland, see *Annual Report, 1948*, pp. 63–64, and *1949*, pp. 57, 58.

Many reasons explain the lack of shifts in exchange rates in these initial years. Prior to 1949 there was still considerable concern that supply and production facilities had not yet been sufficiently restored in Western Europe to make relative prices a key factor in world trade. Inability to produce enough exportable goods remained the principal limitation on exports, and devaluation would not reduce imports, which were already held in check by restrictions. Moreover, inflation in European countries, as well as in much of the rest of the world, had not yet been brought under control. Until these countries achieved a reasonable amount of internal stability, any improvement in their balances of payments brought about by devaluation would be quickly dissipated by price rises.

By the latter part of 1948 and early in 1949, production in Western Europe had recovered and a reasonable degree of internal financial stability had been attained. Debate among economists then arose as to the need for an adjustment of European currencies. In a world which seemed to be increasingly characterized by controlled economies and imperfect markets, some economists questioned the relevance of the price mechanism for restoring balance of payments equilibrium. Others believed that the world dollar shortage was due to deep-seated differences in productivity between the United States and Western Europe. These economists argued that, until these differences in productivity were reduced, the devaluation required to achieve equilibrium would cut real incomes and consumption to intolerable levels. There was also a widely held belief that the U.S. demand for imports was inelastic with respect to relative price changes for imports and domestic commodities. Hence it was argued that devaluation by European countries would not increase their dollar earnings sufficiently to make the devaluation successful.[3] Many economists, including some on the Fund staff, focused attention on and debated all these arguments.

Eventually the pound sterling was devalued, on September 17, 1949, from £1 = $4.03 to £1 = $2.80, or by 30.5 per cent, and this set off a series of devaluations literally around the world. Some countries had been waiting for sterling devaluation in order to adjust their own exchange rates. Others recognized that they had no alternative but to follow sterling.

INSTITUTION OF PROCEDURES

One of the consequences of the week of devaluations in September 1949 was an important institutional one for the Fund, for it brought to light the need for quick-acting procedures for handling changes in par values. Many such changes would have to be effected over week-ends, while exchange markets were closed.

---

[3] The various economic and political arguments against devaluation at this time can be found in Raymond F. Mikesell, *Foreign Exchange in the Postwar World*, pp. 136–44.

Speedy consideration and decision by the Fund was crucial. The Fund therefore instituted rush procedures for dealing with cables coming in late on Friday afternoons, for the preparation on Friday night and Saturday morning of reports by the staff, and for their immediate distribution to the Executive Directors. It was established that the Board would meet to consider the request on Sunday or at the latest Monday morning, depending on the circumstances.

The effects of the 1949 exchange devaluations on trade, payments, and prices became the object of special study by the Fund staff.[4] The data were intensively examined as well for the lessons that might be learned for economic analysis,[5] and for the estimation of trade elasticities.[6] Appraisal of the immediate impact of the devaluations on international trade and the world dollar shortage was, however, made difficult by the host of other factors which came into play in 1950. These included recovery of the U.S. economy, a rapid acceleration of imports by the United States, and large increases in world demand and prices for raw materials after the middle of 1950, in connection with the outbreak of hostilities in Korea.

By the mid-1950's many of the debates among economists and government officials concerning the benefits of the 1949 exchange rate devaluations had subsided. It was generally agreed that these devaluations and the subsequent expansion in dollar earnings by the countries of Western Europe had helped to lay the basis for the restoration of convertibility of European currencies which was achieved in 1958. Indeed, the expansion of European exports was so successful that by the mid-1960's the view had emerged in some circles that the 1949 devaluations had been too great.

FURTHER FRACTURES IN THE PAR VALUE REGIME

During the early 1950's more departures from the par value system took place. True enough, the Fund had gained several new members, most of which agreed initial par values: Burma, Ceylon, Germany, Haiti, Japan, Jordan, Pakistan, and Sweden. However, by this time there were several countries—

---

[4] See, for example, J. J. Polak, "Contribution of the September 1949 Devaluations to the Solution of Europe's Dollar Problem," *Staff Papers*, Vol. II (1951–52), pp. 1–32; and Barend A. de Vries, "Immediate Effects of Devaluation on Prices of Raw Materials," *ibid.*, Vol. I (1950–51), pp. 238–53.

[5] See Sidney S. Alexander, "Devaluation versus Import Restriction as an Instrument for Improving Foreign Trade Balance," *Staff Papers*, Vol. I (1950–51), pp. 379–96.

[6] Barend A. de Vries, "Price Elasticities of Demand for Individual Commodities Imported into the United States," *Staff Papers*, Vol. I (1950–51), pp. 397–419; Sidney S. Alexander, "Effects of Devaluation on a Trade Balance," *ibid.*, Vol. II (1951–52), pp. 263–78; and Ta-Chung Liu, "The Elasticity of U.S. Import Demand," *ibid.*, Vol. III (1953–54), pp. 416–41. For a listing of other statistical studies dealing with trade elasticities, see Hang Sheng Cheng, "Statistical Estimates of Elasticities and Propensities in International Trade," *ibid.*, Vol. VII (1959–60), pp. 107–58.

Canada, Lebanon, Peru, Syria, and Thailand—which, instead of adhering to par values or even to fixed exchange rates, had turned to fluctuating rates. Moreover, there was considerable speculation that other countries—including the United Kingdom—were seriously contemplating the use of fluctuating rates. The advantages and disadvantages of fixed versus fluctuating exchange rates were intensively discussed, not only in academic circles but by highly placed government officials. In part because a few countries already had fluctuating rates, and in part because from time to time there emerged exchange difficulties with other currencies, there was some advocacy not only of fluctuating exchange rates for a particular country, but even of a large number of fluctuating rates.[7]

The Fund continued to defend the par value system, and contended that in the circumstances of the early 1950's it was essential that the cooperative endeavor represented by the Fund be extended and improved, rather than undermined; but it was evident that a universal system of fixed par values was far from being achieved. Problems arising from the world dollar shortage—bilateralism and currency inconvertibility—had led to the temporary use of a variety of practices in Western Europe which deviated from the concept that all transactions should take place at rates based on par values. These practices included separate free markets for tourist receipts or other invisibles or capital transactions, and arrangements to increase dollar export earnings, such as retention quotas, import entitlement schemes, or "transit dollar" arrangements. In addition, multiple exchange rates, which had been introduced in the 1930's in a few Latin American countries to cope with depression-oriented situations, were increasingly being used to cope with the postwar problems of currency inconvertibility, severe inflation, and economic development. As a result, there had been a continued spread of multiple rates.

By the end of 1956—a decade after the initial par values had been established in 1946—the Fund had 60 members. Eleven of these (Afghanistan, Argentina, China, Greece, Indonesia, Israel, Italy, Korea, Thailand, Uruguay, and Viet-Nam) had not yet established initial par values. France, having given up its initial par value in January 1948, had not yet set a new one. Canada continued to rely on a fluctuating rate. Twelve countries (Brazil, Colombia, Costa Rica, Ecuador, Finland, Iceland, Iran, Jordan, Nicaragua, Syria, Venezuela, and Yugoslavia) had multiple rate systems of some significance. Five (Bolivia, Chile, Lebanon, Paraguay, and Peru) that had abolished their multiple rates did so in favor of fluctuating rather than fixed rates. Six others (Cuba, Denmark, Egypt, the Netherlands, Sweden, and Turkey) had various minor multiple currency practices for some current transactions (many more had such practices for capital transactions). This left only 24 members out of 60 conducting all their

---

[7] A summary of the arguments for and against fluctuating exchange rates, as presented at that time, can be found in Bank for International Settlements, *Twenty-Second Annual Report* (Basle, 1952), pp. 142–49.

current transactions at exchange rates within 1 per cent of their par values. In other words, only these had what can be defined as "fully effective par values," that is, par values agreed with the Fund and all transactions (except certain minor practices affecting only capital transactions) conducted at parity rates.[8] The first decade of the Fund's existence had proved to be a most difficult environment for the attainment of its exchange rate objectives.

ACCELERATED TRENDS TOWARD PAR VALUES, 1957–65

In the next decade the setback to the par value system was to be overcome. In the second half of the 1950's countries began to return to fixed exchange rates and to agree with the Fund on par values for their currencies. Once par values were set, they were effectively maintained for long periods of time. These trends, apparent by 1960, became even stronger thereafter.

A series of events brought about the gradual re-establishment of effective parity exchange rates. First was a progressive elimination of the minor multiple currency practices and retention quotas that had been maintained earlier by Western European countries. By 1958 the Fund was able to report that, for the most part, Western European currencies were traded in official exchange markets at rates fluctuating within official limits, and that in view of the closeness of the free market rates to the official market quotations, the problem of broken cross rates in these currencies was no longer important. Thus the Annual Report for 1958 was able to state that

> most Fund members maintain exchange systems in which for the most part transactions take place within the prescribed margins of their respective par values agreed with the Fund. The currencies of these members include all that are most used as means of payment in international trading and financial transactions.[9]

Second, the major countries which had not previously established par values did so. On March 31, 1960, Italy agreed a par value of 625 lire = $1. In March 1961 Greece declared a par value (30 drachmas = $1). In May 1962 Canada, after nearly twelve years with a fluctuating rate, established a new par value of 1 Canadian dollar = 92.5 U.S. cents.

Third, beginning in 1955–56 a series of exchange reforms led to the elimination of many multiple rate systems in the less developed countries. For some of these countries the setting of new par values took place immediately. For others, experimentation with different rates of exchange was to occur before a new parity was finally selected and established.

Fourth, during 1958–65 initial par values were set for many of the countries then joining the Fund—twenty in all.

---

[8] This definition is used here for statistical purposes only; it does not represent the official definition of the Fund.

[9] *Annual Report, 1958*, p. 20.

By 1965 there had been attained a regime in which the majority of Fund members had par values. By December 31 of that year, 57 of the Fund's 103 members (55 per cent) were carrying out all their transactions at "fully effective par values," [10] viz., the United States and Canada; all 19 European members; Australia, New Zealand, Jamaica, and Trinidad and Tobago; 6 out of 12 members in the Far East; 12 out of 34 in Africa; 6 out of 13 in the Middle East; and 8 out of 19 in Latin America.[11] Nine years earlier, as previously noted, only 24 members out of 60 (40 per cent) had been in such a position, and the proportion had been even lower (36 and 38 per cent) in 1954 and 1955.

Because of the addition over time of many new members, the trend from 1954 to 1965 toward par values may be more clearly seen by use of a constant sample. At the end of 1954, out of a total of 56 member countries, 36 were without "fully effective par values," although 10 of these had only minor deviations from the Fund's standard. Among these 36 members, 21 had, by December 31, 1965, attained "fully effective par values." This included many countries which had previously had systems of multiple rates, fluctuating rates, or long-standing absence of par values: Canada, Costa Rica, Finland, Greece, Iceland, Iran, Israel, Italy, Jordan, Nicaragua, the Philippines, and Yugoslavia.

The trend toward adherence to fixed exchange rates was even more marked than that toward legally instituted par values. By December 1965, more than 86 per cent of Fund members (89 out of 103) had fixed exchange rates or rates which, while nominally fluctuating, had been stable for several years; the comparable figure for the end of 1954 was 59 per cent (33 out of 56 members).

Furthermore, members with "fully effective par values" accounted for by far the bulk of world exports. Even in 1954, the approximately one third of Fund members that continued to adhere fully and formally to the par value regime had accounted for 76 per cent of world (noncommunist) exports; by 1965, the share in world exports of countries with par values had risen to 91 per cent.

CRITICISM AND DEFENSE OF THE SYSTEM IN THE 1960's

By one of the ironies of international economic life, the effective attainment of a par value system and of stable unitary exchange rates coincided with renewed attacks by several economists on the par value regime. Their complaint was that par values were too infrequently altered; "adjustable pegs" were rarely adjusted. As a result, exchange rate changes were no longer an important instrument of balance of payments policy.

---

[10] As defined above, p. 48.

[11] Details concerning the gradual attainment of the par value system can be found in Margaret G. de Vries, "Fund Members' Adherence to the Par Value Regime," *Staff Papers*, Vol. XIII (1966), pp. 504–32.

In the mid-1960's, a number of economists, especially in academic circles but also in some official and semiofficial groups, were once again recommending fluctuating exchange rates for the major currencies of the world. But other specific suggestions for enhancing the flexibility of exchange rates were also forthcoming. A proposal was advanced for widening the range of fluctuations permitted under the par value regime to something like 5–7 per cent either side of the par value rather than the 1 per cent required by the Fund's Articles. The necessary width of the band under this "band proposal" was said to depend on whether the effects of exchange rate changes on trade or capital were stressed; doubling the range of fluctuation from the present 2 per cent to 4 per cent was thought to be possibly sufficient for capital. Several economists favored a "shiftable-parity" or "crawling peg" arrangement: automatic adjustments in par values could be made at intervals which might be annual or, conceivably, even quarterly.[12]

The system of par values was, of course, not without academic defenders. In addition, the official views of the Fund and also of practically all central banks continued to favor—strongly—fixed exchange rates. Accordingly, when the Group of Ten agreed in August 1964 to study proposals for the reform of the international monetary system, changes in the exchange rate system were explicitly ruled out.[13]

Reluctance to tamper with the par value system reflected at least in part the experience of the Fund and its members during the previous twenty years. The greater use by Fund members of fully effective par values, described in this chapter, could be attributed to a variety of factors. Decisive among these, as is made clear in the next chapters, were the unsatisfactory results encountered with alternative exchange rate systems.

But there were other arguments in favor of fixed exchange rates—that they put national monetary authorities under pressure to integrate their policies; that they have to be defended by anti-inflationary measures; that they eliminate the danger of competitive depreciation. In addition to these arguments in favor of fixed exchange rates, the Fund had yet another reason for preferring the par value system: in the Fund's view an alternative exchange rate system would make the process of international collaboration far more difficult.

As the year 1965 drew to a close, the debates over exchange rates were continuing and becoming even more heated.

[12] The literature on these proposals is extensive. Summaries of the arguments of academic economists may be found in *International Monetary Arrangements: The Problem of Choice*, Fritz Machlup and Burton G. Malkiel, eds., pp. 94–100; and in William Fellner, "On Limited Exchange-rate Flexibility," in Fellner, Machlup, Triffin, and others, *Maintaining and Restoring Balance in International Payments*, pp. 111-22. An illustration of official argumentation may be found in Federal Republic of Germany, Sachverständigenrat zur Begutachtung der gesamt-wirtschaftlichen Entwinklung, *Jahresgutachten*, 1964, par. 240.

[13] *Ministerial Statement of the Group of Ten and Annex Prepared by the Deputies* (Paris, August 1964), Ministerial Statement, par. 2.

CHAPTER

4

Setting Par Values

Margaret G. de Vries

A S THE PAR VALUE SYSTEM has evolved, many questions have confronted the Fund. Since par values are central to the Fund Agreement, one set of questions has concerned their establishment. How quickly should initial par values be agreed? What should be the attitude of the Fund toward delays by members in proposing parities? How much pressure should the Fund put on countries to set parities? What exceptions might be made to the requirement of the Articles that an initial par value must be set before a country may draw on the Fund's resources? What considerations ought to govern appraisal of a proposed parity? Once initial par values are no longer used for any transactions, when should a new effective par value be instituted? Can a country be regarded as having a fully convertible currency—that is, subject to the requirements of Article VIII—if it does not have a par value?

Still other questions have arisen in connection with the adjustment of par values and exchange rates. By what criteria should the need for a change in an exchange rate be determined? Inasmuch as the Articles provide that devaluations shall be proposed only by members, what informal role might the Fund play in suggesting to members the advisability of changes in exchange rates? What constitutes *fundamental disequilibrium* and what *competitive exchange depreciation*, the two concepts of the Articles relating to changes in exchange rates?

The ways in which the Fund has attempted to find answers to these questions make up, in part, the policy of the Fund on exchange rates. A few of the issues involved have been covered by decisions of general applicability taken by the Executive Board. But for most of these issues, no broadly stated policy lines have been formulated. Rather, as is customary in most fields, policy is mainly an accretion of the attitudes and actions taken in particular situations over the years.

This chapter and the next three provide some generalizations of the Fund's policies on par values and exchange rates. These generalizations are based on an examination of the decisions taken by the Board and the views expressed by several Directors in a variety of individual country situations; in a number of instances the reasoning of the staff, reflected in the papers prepared for the discussions in the Board, has also been included. The present chapter covers those policies which have applied to the setting of par values. It describes considerations which have guided the Fund in timing the introduction of par values, the criteria used for approving the parities proposed, and the views of the Fund as to whether a par value must first be agreed if a member is to draw on the Fund's resources.

Several countries, after they had established initial par values, took measures which meant that these par values were no longer applied to any transactions. The Fund, therefore, has also had to consider the extent to which it should urge countries to institute effective par values, and whether countries without effective par values may assume the convertibility status of Article VIII. Moreover, once par values have been established, certain requirements follow for cross rates with third currencies, for the margins within which exchange rates may move around parities, and for rates in forward exchange markets. These matters are also discussed in this chapter. Policies relating to the adjustment of par values and of exchange rates are deferred until Chapter 5.

Tracing the growth of the Fund's exchange rate policies over the years reveals the flexibility and adaptability with which the Fund has administered the par value system. Yet adaptability and flexibility have not meant the absence of basic policies. Some general guidelines can be discerned, demonstrating that the policies have not been merely a series of ad hoc reactions to particular situations. Nonetheless, since generally formulated policies cannot always be applied to the particulars of individual situations, some anomalies and inconsistencies in the application of policy have inevitably occurred.

ESTABLISHING INITIAL PAR VALUES

Immediate parities in early years

In the first years the Board was anxious that members should establish par values as soon as possible. This was manifested when the initial par values for original members were agreed at the end of 1946. Although both the Board and member countries recognized the many uncertainties then attending exchange rate determination, initial par values were quickly set for most original members.

Weighty arguments could have been marshaled against setting initial par values in 1946. Many members had been devastated by the war and had to undergo extensive reconstruction. These countries, and others, were in the grip of serious inflation. Shortages of goods and services were widespread and international trade was badly distorted.

However, the Board wished to go ahead. In the first place, Article XX, Section 4, provided that initial par values for members having at least 65 per cent of the total of quotas must be established before exchange transactions could begin, and that (except for countries that had been occupied by the enemy) a par value must be agreed with the Fund before a member could use the Fund's resources. Moreover, the Board recognized the desire of the drafters of the Articles to put the par value regime into operation at an early stage. It had been foreseen at Bretton Woods that the Fund would have to begin in a period of disorder, but the conferees were convinced that a start toward an improved world exchange rate structure could be made.

On September 12, 1946, therefore, the Fund called upon its 39 members to communicate par values, and on December 18, 1946 the initial par values of 32 countries were announced, viz., Belgium, Bolivia, Canada, Chile, Colombia, Costa Rica, Cuba, Czechoslovakia, Denmark, Ecuador, Egypt, El Salvador, Ethiopia, France, Guatemala, Honduras, Iceland, India, Iran, Iraq, Luxembourg, Mexico, the Netherlands, Nicaragua, Norway, Panama, Paraguay, Peru, the Philippines, the Union of South Africa, the United Kingdom, and the United States.

Initial par values were also agreed with Belgium for the Belgian Congo; with France for Algeria, Cameroun, French Antilles, French Equatorial Africa, French Guiana, French possessions in India, French possessions in Oceania, French Somaliland, French West Africa, Madagascar and dependencies, Morocco, New Caledonia, New Hebrides, Réunion, St. Pierre and Miquelon, Togoland, and Tunisia; with the Netherlands for Curaçao and Surinam; and with the United Kingdom for Bahamas, Barbados, Bermuda, British Guiana, British Honduras, Burma, Ceylon, Cyprus, Falkland Islands, Fiji, Gambia, Gibraltar, Gold Coast, Hong Kong, Jamaica, Kenya, Malaya (Singapore and Malayan Union), Malta, Mauritius, Nigeria, Northern Rhodesia, Nyasaland, Palestine, Sarawak (British North Borneo), Seychelles, Sierra Leone, Southern Rhodesia, Tanganyika, Tonga, Trinidad, Uganda, and Zanzibar.

The determination of par values for six members (Brazil, China, the Dominican Republic, Greece, Poland, and Yugoslavia) was deferred at their request because their domestic monetary situation was not sufficiently stable to warrant the adoption of par values. The Uruguayan submission of a par value was not definite enough to permit its formal acceptance. The determination of initial par values for the French dependent territories in Indo-China and for the Netherlands Indies was also deferred.

Since imports were subject to controls by nearly all countries, the main criterion for judging the rates proposed was their effect on exports. So long as exports continued to flow, it could fairly be assumed that the prevailing exchange rate would help to attain by the end of the transitional period a "tolerable balance of payments."[1] Existing exchange rates did not seem to be impairing the ability of any country to export. Supply shortages were so acute that, despite the current exchange rates and despite the import controls, there was no difficulty in disposing of any exports that a country was in a position to offer. Difficulties of production and transport and other prevalent obstacles to a smooth supply of goods were by far the most serious impediments to an expansion of exports. The Executive Directors were also aware that to encourage a general revision of exchange rates would have been quite unacceptable to member countries. Such a revision "would have gravely dislocated exchange relationships which were already working in practice and enabling trade to be carried on."[2]

For members subsequently joining the Fund, a procedure for the establishment of an initial par value is prescribed which gives the Fund the right to initiate the process. The standard membership resolution provides (paragraph 5) that the Fund is to request the member to communicate, within thirty days of receipt of the Fund's request, a proposed par value for its currency. Within sixty days of receipt of the proposed par value by the Fund, the Fund and the member must agree on an initial par value. In practice, the period of thirty days is not introduced until the member is known to be ready to establish a par value, and the sixty-day period is extended if this is found to be necessary. Should no agreement be reached at the end of the extended period, the member will be deemed to have withdrawn from the Fund.

In the late 1940's and early 1950's, the Fund made persistent efforts to get original members to agree initial par values if they had not already done so. Brazil and the Dominican Republic, having postponed theirs in 1946, set them in 1948; Yugoslavia's par value was agreed in May 1949. Most countries that joined the Fund in these years very quickly agreed initial par values. These included Australia, Lebanon, Syria, Turkey, and Venezuela in 1947, Sweden and Pakistan in 1951, Ceylon in 1952, Burma, Germany, Japan, and Jordan in 1953, and Haiti in 1954. Table 1 at the end of this chapter lists the initial par values agreed with the Fund for each year from 1946 through 1965.

DELAYED PARITIES

There were, of course, some instances of initial parities being delayed. Two illustrations of relatively short delays are provided by Finland and Austria. Both joined the Fund in 1948 but Finland did not set its first parity until 1951 and Austria not until 1953. Finland agreed as an initial par value the exchange rate which had been in effect since the devaluations of September 1949. The establishment of Austria's parity, however, was dependent on further drastic devaluation. The rate adopted for the schilling after the war was S 10 = $1. In Novem-

---

[1] Camille Gutt, *The Practical Problem of Exchange Rates*, p. 4.
[2] *Annual Report, 1947*, p. 27.

ber 1949 Austria introduced multiple rates; these were replaced by a single rate in May 1953, at which time an initial par value of S 26 = $1 was established.

As to long delays in establishing initial parities, Italy is a case in point, and also serves to illustrate the caution exercised both by members in communicating par values and by the Fund in not applying strong pressure to do so. Italy joined the Fund in March 1947. The Membership Resolution, drafted soon after the Fund came into being, contained terms similar to those in the Articles of Agreement. In effect, Italy was declared a country whose metropolitan territory had been occupied by the enemy.[3] It was specifically granted the privileges of Article XX, Section 4 (d) (ii), which provided that an enemy-occupied country could, with the permission of the Executive Board, draw on the Fund's resources prior to establishing an initial par value.

On April 24, 1947, in accordance with its usual procedure, the Board requested the Government of Italy to communicate within thirty days a par value for the lira based on the exchange rate prevailing on March 27, 1947, the date on which Italy joined the Fund. The Italian economy was then encountering several difficulties. Prices were rising rapidly, owing to inflation, and the balance of payments was in marked disequilibrium. Production was stagnating and the rate of unemployment was high. Multiple currency practices existed: there was an official rate of Lit 225 = $1 and a free rate of Lit 585–600 = $1. A rate of Lit 410 = $1 seemed to the Italian Government at the time as the only rate which could reasonably be proposed as a par value. But this rate could not be considered definitive. Moreover, the Fund's request was for a rate based on the rate on March 27, 1947, which was presumably already outdated.

Therefore, on May 23, 1947 the Government requested an extension of the usual period of ninety days for agreeing on a par value with the Fund, and on May 28 the Board informed the Government that it had extended the period indefinitely and was prepared to discuss with a representative of the Government a new date for communication of a par value.

During the following three years Italy made great progress in the achievement of economic stability, as a result of the adoption in November 1947 of a comprehensive anti-inflationary program and of financial assistance from the United States. By mid-1950 a reasonable degree of monetary stability had been attained, production had expanded beyond the prewar peak, and the increase in exports had helped to reduce substantially the balance of payments deficit. In 1949 the exchange rate for the lira, only theoretically a fluctuating rate, had been devalued from Lit 575 = $1 to about Lit 625 = $1. This rate applied to all transactions in the official market, there was no currency discrimination, and the rates of various other currencies were pegged to the lira-dollar rate.

---

[3] Resolution No. 1-6; *Summary Proceedings, 1946*, pp. 49–50.

During the 1950's, consequently, there were frequent contacts between the Italian Government and the Fund to explore the possibility of agreement on a par value. The Board's belief was that the setting, and defense, of a par value would help to consolidate the strength of the lira both internally and externally. On all these occasions the Government showed extreme caution and suggested that continuing uncertainties, such as the process of trade liberalization under the OEEC and the establishment of a new tariff system, counseled delay. Between September 1949 and the establishment of external convertibility for the lira on December 29, 1958, Italy maintained a unitary exchange rate of between Lit 624.60 and Lit 625.10 = $1. The Italian authorities, nonetheless, argued for the need to maintain a rate for the lira which was, at least potentially, a fluctuating one.

In September 1959 the Government asked the Fund to agree to a rate of Lit 625 = $1 for determination of the amount of Italy's currency subscription in connection with the increase in its quota. The Board took the occasion to suggest again that a par value be instituted. A few months later, on March 15, 1960, Italy proposed an initial par value of Lit 625 = $1. Foreign trade had been liberalized. Reserves had increased fivefold since 1950. The national product was growing at an average annual rate of more than 5 per cent. It was difficult, if not impossible, to justify any further delay in setting a par value. The Board agreed with the communicated par value, expressing satisfaction that the rate prevailing for many years had at last become the par value.

The instance of Italy is by no means unique. Greece, Thailand, and Uruguay, among others, joined the Fund early on but set their par values only many years thereafter. Table 2 at the end of this chapter gives the date of membership and the date that the initial par value became effective for all countries that were Fund members in the years 1945–65.

A variety of circumstances help to explain delays in establishing par values: chronic inflation, a multiplicity of rates, the need to experiment with devaluation. The continuous ebb and flow of opinion about fluctuating rates no doubt also contributed, at least in part. Countries that already had fluctuating rates, albeit nominally, were reluctant to give them up. Their hesitation did not stem from the fact that they gained any advantages from their fluctuating rates; in most instances rate fluctuations were smoothed out by official intervention in the exchange market. Rather, the authorities concerned believed that it would be easier to change a rate if it had not been instituted as a par value. This consideration became less important as the Fund established its authority over changes in all exchange rates.

What motivated Fund concurrence in these delays was not any weakened faith in the system of par values. In part the Board concurred because of the realization as time went on that it was preferable to have parities set at realistic and maintainable levels rather than to have them established prematurely. By the late 1940's it had become apparent that par values would not be adjusted frequently; the appropriateness, therefore, of a particular parity was of greater significance than its timing. In part, too, the Fund did not wish to jeopardize the improving Fund-member relations in the exchange rate field. As Chapter 5 indicates, the Fund had managed to bring under its jurisdiction virtually all changes in exchange rates, whether par values or not, and the Fund's views were frequently being sought. In this environment, to attach excessive significance to the formal status of a par value at the expense of workable, even affable, member relations might be foolhardy.

SHORT-LIVED PARITIES

Despite the pragmatism of the Fund's policy on the establishment of initial parities, a few par values were set which quickly proved untenable. Because countries changed the multiple rates that coexisted with their par values, their par values were within a short time not meaningful. The examples of Argentina and Uruguay best illustrate this phenomenon.

The Fund agreed in January 1957 to an initial par value for Argentina. An exchange rate of M$N 18 = US$1 had been introduced in October 1955 in connection with a devaluation and as part of a major effort to liberalize and stabilize the economy. The Argentine authorities now proposed this rate as a par value. At the time, this exchange rate applied to the bulk of exports and imports (approximately 85 to 90 per cent of total trade transactions), although retention taxes applied to most exports and a free market also existed.

The staff found it difficult to make any analysis of the appropriateness of the proposed par value based on a comparison of prices, and believed that the rate of M$N 18 = US$1 had not been in effect long enough to judge whether it was an equilibrium rate. Nonetheless, the staff recommended to the Board that it should agree to the proposed par value. This recommendation was based on the expectation of the Argentine authorities that the rate would prove to be appropriate in the light of their domestic financial policies and the anticipated improvement of exports. Relying on this expectation, the Board accepted the rate, but with some misgivings.

It soon became doubtful whether the par value could be maintained. Already by May 1957, changes in the effective exchange rates for imports were being made by transfers of certain commodities to the free market, and throughout 1958 the exchange rates for exports were frequently adjusted. On January 12, 1959, the Argentine authorities introduced a single, free, exchange market for all transactions; at the outset the rate in this free market was M$N 66.60 = US$1. The par value of M$N 18 = US$1 thereafter applied only to the proceeds of exports effected before December 30, 1958, and to payments for imports contracted for before that date.[4] No new par value had been suggested by Argentina down to the end of 1965, and no transactions were then taking place at the par value agreed in 1957.

The Uruguayan par value agreed in 1960 provides another example of a short-lived initial parity. In connection with a stabilization plan supported by a stand-by arrangement, the Fund in October 1960 agreed to an initial par value for the peso of Ur$7.40 = US$1. This rate was the effective one for exports of greasy wool; it resulted from the application of a retention tax of approximately 25 per cent to the sale of exchange receipts for this product at the free market rate (at that time approximately Ur$11.42 = US$1). The Uruguayan authorities believed that this rate was adequate and viable for the wool exports to which it was applicable (wool accounted for somewhat more than half of the country's total exports). Hence, although the staff had been pressing for the adoption of the free market rate as the basis for an initial par value, it recommended that the Fund should concur in the rate proposed by Uruguay. The Board agreed. However, by January 1, 1961—only a few months later—all exchange transactions were moved to a free market with a fluctuating rate, where the prevailing rate was about Ur$11.00 = US$1.[5]

CRITERIA FOR ACCEPTING PROPOSED PAR VALUES

According to the Articles of Agreement (Article XX, Section 4 (b)), the criterion for Fund concurrence in a proposal for an initial parity is a negative one: the par value must not in the Fund's opinion cause "recourse to the Fund on the part of that member or others on a scale prejudicial to the Fund and to members." In practice, the prospects for a country's exports have been a crucial factor in the consideration of a proposed parity. As noted above, in the selection of initial parities for original members in 1946, considerable emphasis was given to the effect on exports;[6] and for the next several years this consideration continued to be given the most weight. "So long as an exchange rate does not hamper a country's exports, there is little to be said in present world conditions for altering it."[7] The Fund has continued to rely heavily on the effect-on-exports test. However, once world markets again became competitive, in the 1950's, the Fund was more inclined to accept a par value that differed from the existing exchange rate.

Since the middle of the 1950's, members have generally not proposed par values unless they were fairly certain that the rate suggested would be

---

[4] *Ninth Annual Report on Exchange Restrictions* (1958), pp. 23–31; *Tenth Annual Report on Exchange Restrictions* (1959), pp. 29–33.

[5] *Twelfth Annual Report on Exchange Restrictions* (1961), pp. 360–63.

[6] "Statement Concerning Initial Par Values," December 18, 1946, *Annual Report, 1947*, pp. 70–71.

[7] *Annual Report, 1948*, p. 23.

acceptable to the Fund and that they could maintain that rate. The nature of the circumstances prevailing when countries have proposed parities suggests some of the criteria the Fund has developed for accepting them. One such circumstance is that exchange rates proposed as par values have commonly been in effect for a number of years. From 1957 to the end of 1965, twenty-seven countries proposed initial par values shortly after they accepted membership. Most of these countries, especially those in the sterling area, selected as initial parities the exchange rates that had been in effect since the devaluations of September 1949. Both more and less developed countries were among those that proposed as par values exchange rates that had already been in effect for some eight to fifteen years: Cyprus, Ghana, Ireland, Jamaica, Kuwait, Liberia, Libya, New Zealand, Nigeria, Portugal, Sierra Leone, Somalia, and the Sudan.

Because it was known that the Fund wished to approve as par values only exchange rates which were clearly stable, only countries which had such rates offered them as par values. Indeed, assuming that the rate proposed is appropriate for a member's exports, stability has often been the principal factor noted in the Board's discussions of proposed par values. This is, of course, in accordance with the Fund's emphasis on the achievement of general economic stability. In addition, a stable exchange rate usually has had a close link with other currencies. Thus, for example, when the Fund considered an initial par value for New Zealand, the long-standing relation of the New Zealand pound to the pound sterling was recognized. Another reason why the Fund has used the test of stability for judging a proposed par value is that a stable rate provides good evidence that the authorities can maintain the par value proposed. Still a further reason for adopting the criterion of stability has been that where an exchange rate has not been stable, the correct level for a par value has been extremely hard to gauge. The difficulties of finding an appropriate rate, in the absence of an already stable rate, was evident, for example, in the Canadian experience of the early 1960's. After the authorities had decided to give up the fluctuating rate they still delayed the institution of an effective par value, partly because of the difficulty of choosing an exchange rate satisfactory for both current and capital account. (The details of Canada's fluctuating rate are discussed in Chapter 7.)

In addition to stability, the Fund has, since the mid-1950's, considered the uniformity and general applicability of the exchange rate suggested as a par value. When a member proposes a parity, exchange reform has usually already been completed. Few, if any, transactions continue to be carried out at exchange rates other than the proposed one. In this sense the par value must be an effective one. Austria, Saudi Arabia, and Spain, for example, all introduced par values only after exchange reform had been made fully effective. This policy, emerging after 1955, was in contrast to that followed earlier when the Board had been eager that members should establish par values even if multiple rates coexisted with these par values.

A final criterion of the suitability of a proposed par value is that the country concerned should have a strong balance of payments and reserve position, and few restrictions. Malaysia and Nigeria, for example, had few restrictions and the former had been contemplating coming under Article VIII. Preferably, the country should be able to relax any prevailing restrictions. Thus, simultaneously with their new parities, Jamaica and Kuwait accepted the obligations of Article VIII.

SOME TROUBLESOME EPISODES

Although generally the initial par values of member countries have been agreed with little controversy, some problems have attended the establishment of a few initial parities. One such instance involved a dispute in which one country believed itself to be adversely affected not by the devaluation of another country's currency but by that other country's abstaining from devaluation. Such a situation is, in effect, the opposite of competitive devaluation. Difficulties have also arisen in connection with the establishment of, or alteration of, par values for totally planned economies. One such instance was the establishment of a par value by Yugoslavia in 1949; another involved a change in par value by Czechoslovakia in 1953.

A CONTROVERSIAL PARITY—PAKISTAN

A dispute about an exchange rate arose when the Fund deliberated on an initial par value for the Pakistan rupee, after Pakistan had become a member early in 1950. In September 1949 Pakistan had elected not to follow the United Kingdom and the rest of the sterling area in devaluation, and maintained the rate for the Pakistan rupee at PRs 1 = $0.30225. This was the same as the rate for the Indian rupee before the 1949 devaluation, and Pakistan proposed this rate to the Fund in 1950 as an initial par value. India's new rate was Rs 1 = $0.21.

India refused to trade with Pakistan at its current rate of exchange and Pakistan was adamant that it would not devalue. Consequently, trade between the two countries—which had previously been extensive and essential to both— had come to a virtual halt. The balance of payments of both countries was being seriously harmed. Pakistan's exports at the time consisted almost entirely of raw jute, most of which went to India for the manufacture of burlap. Inasmuch as India produced most of the world's burlap, Pakistan had no other outlet for its jute. And India had no other source of supply.

Pakistan's position was that, on the basis of price comparisons, exchange devaluation would not help to expand raw material exports; nor would it aid in diversifying exports, whether in composition or trading pattern, as industrialization progressed. Devaluation would also turn the terms of trade against imports—which were mainly consumer goods—and especially textiles from India. India's position was that Pakistan's exchange rate made it impossible for India's burlap producers to operate profitably.

A special staff working party was set up in the Fund to examine the economic merits of Pakistan's proposed par value. In September 1950 the Executive Board, at a special meeting in Paris during the Fifth Annual Meeting, discussed the problem. Not wishing to add to the contention between the two members, the Board agreed to postpone indefinitely the establishment of a par value for Pakistan, and reserved the right to fix the date when the matter would be further considered.

The issue was settled in March 1951, when the Board agreed with Pakistan on an initial par value of PRs 1 = $0.30225. The upward movement of world prices following the outbreak of hostilities in Korea, together with an increasing demand for Pakistan's exports, had strengthened the case for maintaining the original exchange rate of the rupee. But intrinsic to the Fund's action was that in February 1951 the Governments of India and Pakistan had concluded a new trade and payments agreement, providing for the purchase and sale of each other's currencies and for conversion of balances at the par value of the Pakistan rupee as declared to the Fund. Therefore, the Indian Government no longer pressed its objection to acceptance by the Fund of the par value proposed by Pakistan.

This rate for the Pakistan rupee was maintained until July 1955, when the Board concurred in a devaluation of 30.5 per cent, bringing the Pakistani rate into line with other sterling area currencies. This move followed a period in which the prices of Pakistan's exports had been declining under the impact of increased competition in agricultural markets, while at the same time the prices of home-consumed goods had risen because of the monetary expansion induced by the financing of large capital expenditures.

An exchange rate for a planned economy—Yugoslavia

One of the questions about exchange rates which was receiving heightened attention toward the end of 1965, especially in discussions about Eastern European economies, was one with which the Fund had grappled in its early days: what is the role of the exchange rate in a centrally planned economy? This question had arisen at Bretton Woods. The delegation of the U.S.S.R. had proposed the provision which became Article IV, Section 5 (e), that a member may change the par value of its currency without the concurrence of the Fund *if the change does not affect the international transactions of members of the Fund.* The question of the significance of the exchange rate in a socialist economy became a practical one for the Fund in August 1947 when Yugoslavia, an original member, requested the Fund to consider a par value for the dinar. The establishment of a par value had been postponed in December 1946 because Yugoslavia had found it difficult to supply adequate basic data to the staff.

The Yugoslav authorities communicated a rate of Din 50 = $1. A report by the staff on the Yugoslav proposal commented that comparisons with the cost of living in other countries and with wholesale prices in the United States showed the dinar only slightly overvalued at this rate, but pointed out that these comparisons were of doubtful validity since supply, demand, prices, and wages in Yugoslavia were all governmentally controlled. But the staff also noted that devaluation of the dinar would not help to increase that country's exports in the short run. The Executive Board considered the staff's findings, but believed that more information was required before a par value could be agreed.

It was not until May 1949 that the Board again considered this matter. Meanwhile, in the course of 1948 the staff examined the significance for the Fund of an exchange rate in a state-controlled economy. Two main conclusions were reached. One was that a state-controlled economy could have a fundamental disequilibrium in the Fund sense of that term. The second was that a member could alter its par value in order to correct a fundamental disequilibrium only after consultation with the Fund; this obligation applied to all members.

When the par value for the dinar was discussed by the Board in May 1949, the Fund agreed to the communicated rate of Din 50 = $1. Mr. Kolovic (Yugoslavia), Alternate to Mr. Sucharda, argued that, although the function of the par value in a planned economy was somewhat different from its function in a free economy, it was of equal importance for either type of economy. He contended that, although in Yugoslavia imports were limited by an economic plan, in drawing up that plan the calculations of trade items were based on the purchase prices of these items expressed in terms of foreign currencies at existing parities plus distribution costs. Hence, the exchange rate played the same role for trade items in a planned economy as in a free one.

Mr. Southard (United States) questioned this line of reasoning. In his view, the real function of a par value in a centrally controlled economy was difficult to understand. The exchange rate was probably a subordinate policy instrument, the main adjustments being made through internal controls. Because of the unusual nature of the economy and the absence of the usual criteria, Mr. Southard could not regard the acceptance by the Board of the Yugoslav par value as implying that the economy was in complete equilibrium.

Mr. Sucharda (Czechoslovakia) insisted that any reservations about the par value for Yugoslavia were unnecessary. He asked that the staff make comprehensive studies so as to dispel any doubts about the Yugoslav parity.

These antipodal views were in practice fused on January 1, 1952, when the par value for the dinar was altered from Din 50 = $1 to Din 300 = $1. This change in the exchange rate not only represented a drastic devaluation but also signified a far-reaching reform of the Yugoslav economic system, a reform which gave a much greater role to the exchange rate. It had been the Fund's view that, under the previous system, the exchange rate had not been one of the determinants of foreign trade transactions.[8] Such transactions were carried out by the state foreign trade monopoly according to a plan, without much regard to the relations between prices in Yugoslavia and abroad. Now, as a result of a process of reorganizing and liberalizing the Yugoslav economic system and equilibrating Yugoslav prices, begun in 1950, a new rate came into being.

The Fund concurred in the devaluation. Explaining its action, the Board stated that the new exchange rate would help to forge a link between domestic and foreign prices, and put the exchange rate in line with the intended level at which prices were to be unified and stabilized.[9]

Later on, Yugoslavia was to encounter serious difficulties in synchronizing domestic and foreign prices while at the same time attempting to use relative domestic prices both as incentives to producers and as taxation of consumers. This use of the price system was made inordinately difficult because of the absence of customs tariffs in Yugoslavia. Utilization of the exchange system for too many objectives led to the emergence of a complex maze of multiple rates: by 1955 the Yugoslav exchange rate system had become one of the most complicated of any maintained by a Fund member. By 1961, however, following a series of steps closely worked out between Yugoslavia and the Fund, this rate system had gradually been unified.

A DISPUTE WITH CZECHOSLOVAKIA

The issue of the role of the exchange rate in a totally controlled economy came up again in 1953. But this time the circumstances were entirely different. On a minor level, the Czechoslovak proposal in 1953 was not for the establishment of an initial par value but for a change in its par value. On a major level, the Fund's relations with the member were in great contrast. Whereas cordial and friendly relations between Yugoslavia and the Fund had developed very early, the Fund's relations with Czechoslovakia had by 1953 become extremely stiff.

On June 2, 1953, the State Bank of Czechoslovakia sent a cable informing the Fund of a change in the par value of the koruna that had become effective the day before. On July 1, the Managing Director, Mr. Rooth, notified the member that since it had not consulted the Fund on this matter, the item would be placed on the agenda of the Board for July 20, 1953, that the member

[8] *Annual Report, 1952,* pp. 64–65.
[9] *Ibid.*

was entitled to send a representative, and that the Fund would wish information on the reasons for the lack of consultation. Czechoslovakia replied that it would be represented by its Ambassador in Washington.

At the meeting on July 20, the representative of Czechoslovakia took the position that his Government's action was covered by Article IV, Section 5 (*e*), of the Fund Agreement. Since Czechoslovakia conducted the overwhelming majority of its international transactions in foreign currencies, the change in the par value of the koruna did not and could not in any way affect international transactions.

Mr. Southard emphasized that consultation with the Fund was to take place *before* changes in the par values were made, and that such consultation was more than a matter of form. In his view, there was no basis for arguing that changes in par values which members claimed did not affect international transactions were not subject to the obligation of advance consultation. No such exception was stated in the Fund Agreement; on the contrary, advance consultation was required even where the Fund had no right to object (Article IV, Section 5 (*c*) (i)).

A salient question was whether the change in the exchange rate did in actuality affect international transactions. Unless the rate had some international effect, why was it being changed? The Executive Directors took the view that, before the Fund could judge the impact of the alteration in the par value on international transactions, it would have to have information on how the country's foreign trading system operated. Were any of the outstanding debts which were altered by the monetary reform owed to foreign countries or their residents? At what exchange rates were the koruna clearing balances of foreign countries converted from old to new korunas? At what rates were other koruna debts to foreign countries converted? What were the total balances, both in korunas and in foreign currencies, between Czechoslovakia and other countries before the exchange rate was changed, how were they distributed between countries, and how were they affected by the revaluation of the rate?

The representative of Czechoslovakia forwarded these questions to his Government. Temporary postponements of the date set for further consideration by the Board were granted, and it was the middle of September 1953 before Czechoslovakia was ready to reply. The representative of Czechoslovakia then read a prepared statement in which he argued that the economy of his country was very different from that of other Fund members and that the change in par value did not affect international transactions. The gist of his contention was that the Czechoslovak balance of payments was the result of a national economic plan. The balance of payments expressed the country's foreign trade plan; equilibrium in the balance of payments was always maintained. The principal motives for the change in par value were internal. The change in no way affected either the current or the capital transactions of other members of the Fund. The Czechoslovak representative thought it was significant that some Fund members—in their payments agreements with Czechoslovakia—had already recognized the new par value. He further supplied brief information on the questions asked by the Fund but did not provide basic background material.

Meanwhile Mr. Southard had suggested that action be taken under Article XV, Section 2 (a), to make Czechoslovakia ineligible to use the Fund's resources. He noted the several occasions on which the member had failed to supply adequate information to the Fund, and pointed out that in its financial relations with the Fund Czechoslovakia was using an unauthorized exchange rate which reduced the number of korunas due to the Fund. However, by October 1953 the issue of the par value was just one of several controversies between Czechoslovakia and the Fund. From September until mid-December 1953, the Directors repeatedly deliberated the par value issue per se. Representatives of Czechoslovakia were present at a series of meetings. Their contention continued to be that, as the change in the par value was not intended to correct a fundamental disequilibrium, and did not affect international transactions, it had not been necessary for Czechoslovakia to consult the Fund. The representatives discussed detailed items of the balance of payments accounts in an effort to prove that the change in parity had not affected these accounts. They explained how foreign trade was conducted in Czechoslovakia. However, such important information as data on the levels and composition of exports and imports, or quantitative estimates for the balance of payments and for national income, could not, they insisted, be revealed for security reasons.

The Executive Directors were unable to accept the arguments put forward by Czechoslovakia. The staff had shown that diplomats and tourists were affected by the new rate. That being the case, Czechoslovakia was not justified in claiming the right to alter its exchange rate without Fund approval. The contrast with the position taken by Yugoslavia, also a socialist economy, on the relevance of its exchange rate was especially noted.

On December 16, 1953, the Board took the following decision:

> The Government of Czechoslovakia on June 1, 1953, changed the par value of its currency, the koruna, and subsequently informed the Fund that concurrence of the Fund with this change was not required because Czechoslovakia had taken the action in accordance with the provisions of Article IV, Section 5 (e). Having considered the arguments offered by Czechoslovakia, and such information as was made available, the Fund concludes that the change of par value by Czechoslovakia does not come under Article IV, Section 5 (e).

PAR VALUES AND FUND RESOURCES

The establishment of an initial par value is, by Article XX, Section 4 (c), a prerequisite to the use of the Fund's resources. Hence, countries without initial par values are, in the absence of any further Fund decision or action, ineligible to draw upon the Fund. Prima facie, this deprives members of financial support from the Fund even when they are, for example, contemplating extensive exchange reforms or coping with a temporary balance of payments problem.

THAILAND QUERIES ITS POSITION

Exceptions to the above provisions were possible to members whose metropolitan territory had been occupied by the enemy. Such a member was granted certain privileges under Article XX, Section 4 (d). According to subsection (i) of this Section, the ninety-day period prescribed by Article XX, Section 4 (b), could be extended. Subsection (ii) further provided that:

> Within the extended period the member may, if the Fund has begun exchange transactions, buy from the Fund with its currency the currencies of other members, but only under such conditions and in such amounts as may be prescribed by the Fund.

The privileges of Article XX, Section 4 (d), had been automatically accorded to original members whose metropolitan territories had been occupied by the enemy. When Italy became a member in 1947, the Membership Resolution incorporated references to Article XX, Section 4 (d), thus making explicit the possibility that Italy could draw on the Fund prior to agreeing a par value. The question of drawings for countries without parities was queried rather forcefully at the Annual Meeting, 1952, by the Governor for Thailand, Prince Viwat. The Membership Resolution for Thailand, which became a member in 1949, had contained no provision to the effect that the privileges of Article XX, Section 4 (d) (ii), be accorded to that country. Therefore, the Executive Directors were not authorized to permit exchange transactions with Thailand under that provision. Furthermore, paragraph 5 of the Resolution stated categorically that the member "may not engage in exchange transactions with the Fund before the thirtieth day after the par value of its currency has been agreed."

This particular clause relating to exchange transactions with the Fund had appeared for the first time in 1948 in the Membership Resolution for Finland and had subsequently been repeated for Austria and Burma, as well as for Thailand; the same paragraph also occurred in the Membership Resolution for Indonesia, which was, in 1952, in the process of joining the Fund. The staff explained to the Board that the wording for those countries joining the Fund after Italy had been changed because it had been cumbersome to draft membership resolutions in such detail as that for Italy. Now, in 1952, Thailand was asking whether there were any circumstances which would prevent Thailand from enjoying the privileges of Article XX, Section 4 (d) (ii), and, if so, whether these obstacles could be removed by any action of the Fund.

Prince Viwat, in September 1952, pointed to the nature of the balance of payments difficulties of Thailand. His country's deficits, when they occurred, seemed to exemplify the classic textbook case for use of the Fund's resources. Thailand was a large exporter of rice and normally had little balance of payments problem. But since the successful production of rice depended upon the quantity of rainfall, he expressed Thailand's potential predicament in 1952 in four words—"no rain, no rice." [10] Any balance of payments difficulty would be temporary and likely to be self-correcting, since a two-year failure of the monsoon was a rarity. Therefore, he asked, should a country which is creditworthy and has a good record as a debtor, if faced with a temporary and self-correcting balance of payments difficulty, be barred from using the Fund's resources simply because it has not been able to declare a par value? The Managing Director replied that he hoped that countries in positions similar to that of Thailand would soon be able to agree with the Fund on par values for their currencies. Should an emergency develop, however, the Fund and the member would endeavor to find a practical solution for the problem.[11]

The question of the need for par values prior to Fund drawings was carefully considered by the Board beginning in mid-1953. Mr. Rajapatirana (Ceylon), Alternate to Mr. Yumoto (who had been elected by Thailand) called attention to Prince Viwat's statement of several months before and urged the Directors to reconsider whether the relevant paragraph of the Membership Resolution for Thailand was the correct condition to be imposed. In his opinion, an injustice had been done to Thailand and should not be perpetuated because that country, owing to circumstances beyond its control, could not comply with the technicality of declaring a par value. (These circumstances concerned cross rates, which are discussed later in this chapter.)

Action considered for a few countries

The staff's first recommendations on this subject were considered by the Board in June 1953. The conclusion of the staff was that, under the Articles of Agreement and paragraph 5 of the Membership Resolution for Thailand, the Executive Directors could not permit Thailand to buy exchange from the Fund before a par value for its currency was agreed. However, the Board of Governors could authorize the Executive Directors to permit exchange transactions with Thailand, or any other member in similar circumstances, on terms substantially similar to those prescribed in Article XX, Section 4 (d) (ii), notwithstanding any provision of the original membership resolutions for such countries.

A draft text of a resolution for adoption by the Governors was therefore submitted by the staff to the Executive Board for consideration. This draft resolution covered Thailand and Burma, and would cover Indonesia if it accepted membership under the terms of its Membership Resolution. For addi-

---

[10] *Summary Proceedings, 1952,* p. 65.

[11] *Ibid.,* p. 124.

tional new members the staff proposed that the problem be handled in the drafting of the membership resolutions.

When this draft resolution came before the Board, a few Directors insisted that the communication of a par value should be retained as a requirement for drawings. But several Directors believed that new members without par values should have at least the same privileges for drawings as those members which, while having agreed par values with the Fund, were not necessarily maintaining them.

Mr. Southard went further and wondered whether the staff suggestions were too limited. He questioned the wisdom of the distinction, implicit in the staff approach, between enemy-occupied countries and those not so occupied; the draft resolution would, moreover, provide a solution only for Thailand, Burma, and possibly Indonesia. There still remained the problem of Uruguay, an original Fund member without an initial par value, which could not be accorded the privileges of Article XX, Section 4 (d) (ii), since its territory had not been occupied by the enemy in World War II. The Board thereupon agreed to post-pone discussion of the draft resolution pending a further review by the staff.

General action considered

The next discussions by the Executive Board weighed the pros and cons of action on this issue for a great number of countries. Directors recognized that the Board of Governors had the legal authority to provide in a membership resolution for exchange transactions between the Fund and a new member prior to agreement on a par value, even in those instances where the member had not been occupied by the enemy within the meaning of the Articles. But several Directors were concerned that any general action might grant new members which had not been occupied by the enemy a privilege which some original members did not have. Several Directors recognized that with the passing of time there was a diminution of the original significance of occupation by the enemy. However, they doubted the wisdom of proposing at this time any action by the Governors which would be generally applied to all new members; such action would amount to discrimination against original members that had not yet set par values.

On the other hand, some Directors noted that there was only one original member, namely Uruguay, that did not have the right to purchase exchange from the Fund because it had not agreed a par value with the Fund.[12] Perhaps some solution might be found for that case. These Directors stressed that the Fund already seemed to have a new category of members not mentioned in the Articles, namely those which did not make their par values effective. They

---

[12] China was also an original member without a par value, but had not paid its subscription (also a prerequisite to the use of the Fund's resources).

suggested that there seemed to be no point in requiring new members to declare a par value as a prerequisite to using the Fund's resources if original members did not live up to their obligations under Article IV, Section 3, and yet remained eligible to engage in transactions with the Fund.

In line with this reasoning, the staff then proposed a broad approach, viz., that the Board of Governors should be asked to give the Executive Directors discretion to engage in transactions on an ad hoc basis before a par value was agreed, when the circumstances of a particular country justified assistance from the Fund. If this approach was too comprehensive, the staff recommended as a minimum that a proposal be made to the Board of Governors covering new members whose territories had been occupied by the enemy.

Although two Directors favored the general approach suggested by the staff, most had difficulties with any broadly applying resolution. Universal action would grant the privileges of Article XX, Section 4 (d) (ii), to countries never occupied by the enemy, thereby granting greater privileges to some new members than were given to original members. A clear-cut distinction between old and new members raised many delicate points which would provoke lengthy debate in the Governors' Meeting.

AGREEMENT FOR THAILAND AND INDONESIA

Accordingly, the Board went back to considering a limited action which would apply only to Thailand and Indonesia. (Burma, in the meantime, had agreed an initial par value.) No new category of members would thus be set up. The Board, aware of the economic situations in Thailand and Indonesia, acknowledged that the establishment of par values might not be possible for some time. It was clear that special action for Thailand and Indonesia could not be regarded as discriminatory against Uruguay, and that such special action for two countries would not set a precedent.

In August 1953, the Executive Directors approved a report to the Board of Governors and two draft resolutions amending the Membership Resolutions for Thailand and Indonesia.[13] The draft resolution for Thailand read as follows (that for Indonesia was similar):

RESOLVED:

That paragraph (5) of Resolution No. 3-4 of the Board of Governors on Membership for Siam [Thailand] be amended to read as follows:

(5) That Siam may not engage in exchange transactions with the Fund before the thirtieth day after the par value of its currency has been agreed in accordance with (4) above and its subscription shall be paid in full before such thirtieth day; provided, however, that at any time before such thirtieth day the Executive Directors are authorized to permit exchange transactions with Siam on the same terms

---

[13] *Summary Proceedings, 1953*, Appendix VI, Annex A, pp. 120–22.

and conditions as those prescribed by Article XX, Section 4 (*d*) (ii), of the Articles of Agreement.

These two resolutions were passed by the Board of Governors in September 1953.[14] The amended paragraph 5 has served as an archetype for later membership resolutions.

AGREEMENT FOR ALL NEW MEMBERS

The Governors' resolutions on Thailand and Indonesia were precursors to much broader action ten years later. The question of the need for initial par values prior to drawings again came up in 1962–63 following the admission to Fund membership of 24 new African countries. The circumstances of these countries suggested that many of them might not be able to establish initial par values for some years. Would they, on that account, not be eligible to draw on the Fund? When, in 1964, the Executive Directors considered this question for a second time, they were no longer disturbed at the idea that countries might use the Fund's resources prior to the establishment of par values, and thus were able to accept a general change in the Fund's policy that they had rejected eleven years earlier.

The first step taken to make new members eligible to use the Fund's resources without waiting for the establishment of initial par values was to reduce the waiting period between the time when a member country had agreed to a par value with the Fund and had paid its subscription and the time when it was eligible to use the Fund's resources. The standard provision in membership resolutions had been a waiting period of at least thirty days.

Mr. Saad (United Arab Republic), who had been elected by Afghanistan, in a discussion of a proposed par value for Afghanistan in January 1963, made the suggestion that there be an "acceleration of eligibility" by reducing this period to one day. In March 1963 the Board agreed to eliminate the delay altogether and recommended to the Board of Governors that the change should apply both to future membership resolutions and to all past ones. This was agreed by the Governors in April 1963.[15] The countries for whom membership resolutions were retroactively amended in this way were Cameroon, Central African Republic, Chad, Congo (Brazzaville), Dahomey, Gabon, Guinea, Ivory Coast, Jamaica, Korea, Kuwait, Laos, Liberia, Nepal, Niger, Nigeria, Sierra Leone, Somalia, Tanganyika, Togo, Tunisia, Upper Volta, and Viet-Nam.

On April 22, 1964, in a series of three decisions, a much more sweeping policy was formulated. First, the Executive Directors recommended to the Board of Governors an amendment of the membership resolutions for all those members

[14] Resolutions 8-4 and 8-5, *Summary Proceedings, 1953*, pp. 96–97.
[15] Resolution No. 18-2, *Summary Proceedings, 1963*, p. 227.

that had paid their subscriptions but had not yet agreed initial par values with the Fund, viz., Algeria, Burundi, Cameroon, Central African Republic, Chad, Congo (Brazzaville), Congo (Leopoldville), Dahomey, Gabon, Guinea, Ivory Coast, Kenya, Korea, Laos, Malagasy Republic, Mali, Mauritania, Nepal, Niger, Rwanda, Senegal, Sierra Leone, Tanganyika, Togo, Trinidad and Tobago, Tunisia, Uganda, Upper Volta, and Viet-Nam. This amendment authorized the Executive Directors to permit exchange transactions with any of these members prior to establishment of an initial par value, under such conditions and in such amounts as might be prescribed by the Executive Directors. The Board of Governors approved the amendment on June 1, 1964.[16]

The second decision was to the effect that the provision permitting transactions with new members prior to the setting of par values should be incorporated in all future membership resolutions, and the Directors agreed on guidelines for implementing this provision.

In the third decision, the Board emphasized that the two foregoing decisions should not be interpreted as a sign of weakened emphasis on the par value system. It was agreed that, when considering requests to draw by members that had not established par values, the Fund would be guided by the purposes of the Articles. Moreover, the Fund would encourage members to follow policies leading to the establishment of realistic exchange rates and to the adoption at the earliest feasible date of effective par values, and would take into account the efforts being made to achieve these objectives.

However, the Fund would give the overwhelming benefit of the doubt to requests for exchange transactions within the gold tranche. Further, members might expect that requests for drawings would be met where they were made in accordance with the decision on compensatory financing of shortfalls in export receipts.[17] A further condition for transactions with a member without an initial par value was that the member should complete the payment of its subscription on the basis of a provisional rate of exchange agreed with the Fund.[18]

Why had such comprehensive action finally been taken? First, the terms on which Fund resources would be made available were becoming more liberal. At about this time the Fund was increasing the availability of the gold tranche to members in general. Also, in 1963 the Fund had introduced facilities for compensatory financing of export fluctuations and wished to permit the use of these facilities by members who, although otherwise eligible, had not declared par values.

Second, the staff presented several arguments in favor of permitting exchange transactions before par values were agreed. The use of the Fund's resources by

---

[16] Resolution No. 19-8, *Summary Proceedings, 1964*, p. 260.
[17] See below, pp. 403, 421.
[18] E.B. Decision No. 1687-(64/22), April 22, 1964; below, Vol. III, p. 243.

members suffering temporary payments difficulties could encourage them to follow policies leading to the establishment of adequate exchange rates and, ultimately, to realistic par values. Moreover, allowing members to draw on the Fund before they had established par values would make it unnecessary for them to propose possibly unrealistic par values in order to become eligible to draw. The staff argued that unrealistic par values should be avoided because, once set, they were often adjusted only after severe damage had been done to the economy of the country concerned. Also, the acceptance by the Fund of unrealistic par values for some members might discourage other members from adopting appropriate ones, or make it difficult for them to do so.

Third, to preclude transactions with new members which had not established initial par values, while permitting transactions with other members which did not use their par values or whose par values were not realistic, might also be regarded as unfair.

Finally, the staff found little logic in the practice of withholding the right to use the Fund's resources from countries that had joined the Fund after Indonesia and Thailand and which had also been occupied by the enemy, for example, Korea and Viet-Nam.

On the other side of the argument, the staff recognized the need to bear in mind the risk of weakening the authority of the Fund in the field of par values. Any concession might be interpreted as a departure from the Fund's general policy of encouraging members to establish realistic and effective par values. It might also lead to the relaxation by some members of their efforts to establish such par values at an early date.

At the Board meeting at which these staff recommendations were discussed, the Directors focused on the question: If general action was taken permitting drawings by countries without parities, would the principle of fixed par values, so important to the Fund, be threatened? The Directors indicated a strong awareness of the likelihood that the establishment of par values in many developing countries might take a long time. They agreed that where a developing country could establish an initial par value at an early stage in its membership, it should do so, their reasoning being that where countries had reached an appropriate stage of development par values were desirable. At the same time, some Directors voiced the thought that the establishment of a par value could not be regarded as a precondition of economic progress, and in certain circumstances might even be detrimental.

Both the Managing Director and Mr. Saad reminded the Board that the proposed third decision was really a reaffirmation of the Articles. Stress was placed on the statement in the draft that the Fund would "encourage members to follow policies leading to the establishment of realistic exchange rates." The purpose of the decision would be to avoid any impression that the Fund was no longer giving the same pre-eminence as in the past to the par value principle.

Directors also agreed that the impact of the proposed decisions was that exchange transactions should not *generally* be permitted prior to the establishment of an initial par value, but only in appropriate cases. The Board recorded its obligation to make a careful and individual approach to requests for drawings, considering the particular aspects of each application and not losing sight of the purposes of the Articles of Agreement, in which the establishment of an initial par value was a basic principle.

Mr. Kiingi (Uganda), Alternate to Mr. Kandé, emphasized that while the adoption of these decisions would make it possible for the 29 member countries which had not yet established par values, and any countries which later joined the Fund, to participate fully in the major benefits to be derived from Fund membership, this possibility did not mean that the African countries would not try to establish realistic par values whenever possible.

Another problem which concerned the Directors as they reached the decisions mentioned was that the Board might be more lax in granting requests to use the Fund's resources from the new members affected by the decisions than requests from old members, some of which also did not have par values, or did not have effective par values. For these reasons, some Directors suggested that it might be desirable later to review this departure from past Fund policy. The Managing Director emphasized that no discrimination between old and new members was intended.

Par values and stand-by arrangements

The Directors have agreed to stand-by arrangements with several member countries which had not established par values or did not have effective par values. The first such member was Peru, in February 1954.[19] This arrangement was approved by the Directors even though, in the view of the staff, Peru's economic circumstances seemed favorable for setting a par value and its current exchange rate appeared stable.

REINSTITUTING PARITIES

The Fund's policies toward the setting of new par values by members that had suspended parities agreed earlier, or had made them nominal by subsequent changes in their exchange systems, have been as pragmatic as its policies toward initial par values.

---

[19] See below, p. 471.

PAR VALUES AND MULTIPLE RATES

In the Fund's early years, it was not prepared to see initial par values remain unaltered while members made changes in their *de facto* exchange rates. Consequently, many countries with multiple rates not only established initial par values despite the multiplicity of their exchange rates; they also altered those par values when they changed their exchange systems. In effect, countries made an effort to keep their par values in line with their current exchange rate structures. For example, until 1956 Bolivia from time to time introduced new parities as it made alterations in its multiple rate system. Similarly, Ecuador adjusted its par value in 1950 when making changes in the rate structure. An extreme example is offered by Paraguay, which changed its par value once in 1951, twice within eight months in 1953–54, and again early in 1956—all of these par values being accompanied by a continued multiplicity of exchange rates. The logic of changing par values in these instances was that changes in the exchange system represented genuine steps toward more realistic rate patterns; hence par values should be moved in line with the improved exchange rate structures.

After the mid-1950's, however, as the difficulties of final elimination of multiple exchange rates became more apparent, there was less resetting of par values in line with frequent adaptations of multiple rates. Most changes in multiple exchange rate systems, and even unifications of multiple rates, took place without the establishment of new par values, either immediately or even for some years thereafter. Only after the new system had proved itself to be enduring did new par values tend to be proposed.

Paraguay again provides an interesting example. In 1957, it replaced its multiple rate system with a fluctuating rate of exchange. Subsequently, although the guaraní has depreciated by some 50 per cent, Paraguay has not declared a new par value. Similarly, several other countries which had eliminated their multiple rate systems and had had stable, unitary rates for many years, still had not instituted new par values by the end of 1965. These included Bolivia, Lebanon, and Peru. Still others—for example, Venezuela—had considerably simplified their exchange systems but had not yet set a new parity.

URGING PAR VALUES

Where conditions have been considered eventually to have become appropriate, the Fund has urged countries to set par values—either initial parities or realigned parities in accordance with their *de facto* exchange rates. Thailand provides an example of such action by the Fund. After Thailand had eliminated multiple rates in favor of a fluctuating rate, and after the fluctuating rate had been stabilized, the Fund urged the Thai authorities to set a par value: from early in 1960 until late in 1963, when a par value was agreed, several statements were made in Board decisions on Article XIV consultations to the effect that the Fund would welcome the establishment of a par value.

PAR VALUES AND CONVERTIBILITY STATUS

The facts that some countries did not establish an initial par value, and that others did not establish a new parity after their earlier ones had become outdated, raised a further question: Should such countries be permitted to undertake the obligations of Article VIII? Canada, which had suspended transactions at its par value in 1950, had come under Article VIII in 1952. At that time, however, the question of the need for a member to have an effective par value prior to assuming Article VIII status had not been pointedly discussed. In 1960 this question was one of several considered by the Board at length.

The preparatory paper by the staff had suggested that countries assuming Article VIII status should conduct their international transactions through a uniform rate system based on a par value agreed with the Fund. This paper outlined various categories of countries which should probably not assume Article VIII status. One such category was of countries which had few or virtually no restrictions but where considerable uncertainty prevailed concerning balance of payments prospects. Doubt was cast on the ability of such countries to cope with a deterioration of the balance of payments without resort to restrictions. Countries which had been unable to establish effective par values were included in this category, on the ground that avoiding restrictions was not a sufficient test of the strength of a country's external position; what was needed as well was a demonstration that the country's exchange rate could remain stable.

As the Board considered the possible requirements of Article VIII status, some European Directors expressed the conviction that the establishment of an effective par value was an essential qualification for a country moving to Article VIII. Mr. Southard, however, although wholeheartedly supporting the par value system, argued that the Fund should not put undue emphasis on this point. He agreed that where a country seemed to have no justifiable reason for not having a par value, the Fund should try to convince the member that it should establish one. But he also believed that the Board should recognize that there were instances where it was to a member's advantage to have a fluctuating rate.

Other Directors also believed that it was desirable for the Fund to keep open the possibility that a country could come under Article VIII even if that country had no par value. They recognized that many countries which did not have par values were, nonetheless, relatively free of restrictions. These countries maintained dual exchange rates on the premise that they could keep capital movements unrestricted provided that a free exchange rate was applied to those transactions. Although in the 1950's many countries that had dual exchange rates also had par values, countries that established par values in the 1960's usually had first unified their exchange systems.

The question of whether a country coming under Article VIII should have a par value came to the fore in a specific instance in February 1961. Ten European countries and Peru had indicated to the Fund that they intended to accept the obligations of Article VIII; but Peru's situation was somewhat different from that of the others in that it did not have a par value and, in fact, had a fluctuating rate. Some Directors believed that the significance of Peru's move to Article VIII was reduced by the fact that its exchange rate situation was irregular. They stressed that fulfillment of the Fund's purposes required the removal of two obstacles, variations in exchange rates and restrictions on current transfers. The attainment of Article VIII status, in their view, should be indicative of economic stability, which should be reflected in a fixed rate of exchange. Several Directors, however, were especially gratified that Peru could join the list of Article VIII countries together with the European countries. Mr. Klein (Argentina), who had been elected by Peru, argued that a country could not always fix a parity without at the same time adopting a number of restrictive regulations. Some of the other countries then moving to Article VIII had at least some restrictions, while Peru did not.

The Board decided to note Peru's intention of accepting the obligations of Article VIII from February 15, 1961, the same action as was taken for the other ten countries then assuming Article VIII status.

CROSS RATES

Once an economic issue has been closed, the passions that it once engendered are difficult to recapture or even to imagine. Such is the situation with regard to the Fund's actions in connection with cross rates. The existence of "broken" or "disorderly" cross rates was the source of repeated discussions between the Fund and its members and among Board members from 1946 until about 1952–53, after which the prevalence of broken cross rates diminished. By 1958, most of such problems had disappeared, largely because the general economic environment which had occasioned them had changed.

CAUSES AND THE FUND'S EARLY POSITION

Broken cross rates are rates of exchange between two currencies which differ from the parity relationships between these currencies. If, for example, in 1948 in a free market in a third country, the U.S. dollar sold for 10 pesos and the pound sterling for 35 pesos, the cross rate between dollars and sterling would have been $3.50 rather than the official $4.03. In the late 1940's and in the early 1950's, even after the devaluation of sterling, broken cross rates occurred almost everywhere that limited free market rates or fluctuating rates prevailed.

These broken cross rates resulted from the inconvertibility of currencies. In normal circumstances, where currencies are freely interchangeable, their values in terms of each other are as a rule the same in exchange markets throughout the world. Any temporary divergence which may appear is quickly eliminated by arbitrage operations. However, when currencies are inconvertible, exchange dealers are prevented from carrying out the necessary arbitrage transactions. If the exchange control authorities do not cooperate to maintain agreed exchange rates, the rate for each currency is affected by the special circumstances of local supply and demand or by unilateral controls, and the resulting cross rates may have little relation to the parities agreed with the Fund.

Deviations from an orderly pattern of cross rates in the late 1940's and early 1950's were part of the abnormal circumstances of the times. Not only were currencies inconvertible, but transactions in exchange markets were very limited. Most central banks fixed exchange rates unilaterally and based their official quotations on parities, maintaining a small and usually uniform spread between their buying and selling prices for each currency. There was little scope for even minor movements of exchange rates. Exchange markets for transactions in the same currency in different countries were not interrelated.

Countries that had free markets in which broken cross rates existed usually had an excess supply of inconvertible currencies—some of which had accumulated during the war years—and a shortage of convertible currencies (mainly U.S. dollars). Broken cross rates helped these countries to encourage imports requiring inconvertible currencies and to make it more profitable to export to the dollar area than to countries with inconvertible currencies.

On the other hand, given the world shortages of goods and the buyers' markets then prevailing, the trade effects produced by broken cross rates were adverse for the countries whose currencies were sold at implicit discounts. The discounted rate, while making it easier for the country with an inconvertible currency to sell goods to countries in which cross rates were broken, made it more expensive to buy from them. In the circumstances of the late 1940's, the latter consideration was the more important one: shortages of supplies so limited exports that an exchange rate inducement was considered of no value. Instead, countries were eager to obtain an abundant flow of imports as cheaply as possible.

The United Kingdom was particularly concerned about broken cross rates for sterling. When, for example, the Italian authorities indicated to the Fund in 1947 that Italy would have a broken cross rate between sterling and the U.S. dollar because of its fluctuating rate, the British Government made a formal protest to Italy.

Partly, the United Kingdom was troubled by the adverse effects of broken cross rates, wherever they existed, on confidence in the sterling rate. But the unfavorable implications for British imports were also of consequence. In addition, broken cross rates induced traders to buy British goods for resale in the United States and thus diverted part of the dollar receipts which would otherwise have accrued to the United Kingdom and other countries in the sterling area. And broken cross rates diminished the incentive of countries in whose markets broken cross rates prevailed to seek to earn dollars directly.

The Fund Agreement contains no express provisions regarding cross rates. But as a matter of interpretation and policy, the Fund's approaches at the outset were based on an insistence on orderly cross rates. The Fund recognized the adverse consequences for some members of broken cross rates, and also had various legal arguments against these rates. The General Counsel's view was that to comply with the Fund Agreement a country with a single rate should not have cross rates differing from parity. Where such cross rates resulted from multiple rates, they were discriminatory. And, clearly, the general philosophy of the Fund Agreement made discriminatory practices undesirable.

In addition, in formulating policy on cross rates, the Fund used a broader test: What would be the implications of broken cross rates for the quick restoration of the convertibility of currencies? It was the Fund's view at the time that disorderly cross rates distorted trade relations and made future convertibility even more difficult to attain. Changes in the direction of trade in response to the movements of disorderly cross rates were likely to be determined by short-run considerations and local peculiarities which had little to do with the fundamental influences by which a new pattern of world trade should be determined. Hence, the Fund attached great importance to the maintenance of orderly cross rates based on parities (1) because of its Articles, (2) as a means of protecting its members, and (3) as a way to encourage the appropriate reorientation of trade on a multilateral basis.[20]

Debates over policy

By March 1949 a few Directors, while recognizing the importance in the long run of orderly cross rates, had begun to question the extent to which the Fund should continue to insist on orderly cross rates in the circumstances then prevailing. Mr. Tasca (United States), Alternate to Mr. Southard, pointed out that in many cases the only alternative to breaking the cross rates was overt discrimination through quantitative restrictions against imports from the United States. In his view, therefore, the Fund could press for parity cross rates only as part of a larger program looking toward the elimination of all currency discrimination and inconvertibility. When after the devaluations of September 1949 a few countries continued to have problems in maintaining orderly cross rates, some Directors again queried whether the Fund should press the matter.

---

[20] See, e.g., *Annual Report, 1948*, pp. 26–27.

These Directors were beginning to believe that some revision of Fund policy might be desirable. The issues raised are exemplified by the cross-rate problem of Thailand.

In March 1950 Thailand, which had a multiple exchange rate system, proposed a new exchange market in which broken cross rates would prevail. The argument was that broken cross rates in markets in other Far Eastern countries made it impossible for Thailand to maintain parity cross rates. The cross rates in these other markets fluctuated a great deal; however, by buying and selling dollars in the free market, the Thai authorities could compensate for these fluctuations, hold the free market rate stable, avoid large changes in the cost of living, and maintain a fairly satisfactory payments position. The staff thought that within eighteen months, or earlier if the sterling-dollar cross rate improved, Thailand might establish a par value.

The majority of Directors acknowledged that any attempt by Thailand to maintain orderly cross rates would result in Thailand's reserves ending up in Hong Kong or other Far Eastern free markets. Certainly the system proposed would put little pressure on sterling. In the future, should the position of sterling in the Far East improve sufficiently, Thailand would, after unification of its rates, be in a good position to establish a par value and maintain regular cross rates. If, on the other hand, the sterling cross-rate problem was not solved for a considerable time, the arrangement proposed should still make it possible for Thailand to look forward to establishing a par value, even though a disparate cross rate would remain. These Directors reasoned that no member should be expected to undertake a stabilization of cross rates which was beyond its ability to achieve, nor should the objective of orderly cross rates be allowed to prejudice a member's efforts to achieve and maintain an appropriate parity.

On the opposite side were Directors who had grave misgivings about any change in the Fund's policy on cross rates. They contended, for example, that a broken cross rate in Thailand might afford the country an unfair competitive advantage over other areas, such as Latin America, exporting similar products. Mr. Crick (United Kingdom), Alternate to Sir George Bolton, was especially concerned about the prospect that the volume of transactions taking place at broken cross rates would increase considerably. To support his concern, Mr. Crick cited the major discounts for sterling which continued to prevail in markets other than the one in Thailand—those in Peru, Lebanon, and Hong Kong.

Because of these conflicting views, the Board, in 1950, 1951, and 1952, undertook a general reassessment of the Fund's cross-rate policy. The staff paper prepared for these discussions suggested that the Fund should not sanction any exceptions to the obligations of orderly cross rates except in situations where it was clearly evident that a particular problem faced by members had no acceptable solution other than a break in cross rates. In general, Fund policy would continue to be not to approve of broken cross rates, but for the first time the Fund would recognize some exceptional cases.

After consideration, the Board concluded that a general decision on cross rates would not be desirable; rather, each case should be determined on its merits. The Board's public statement ran as follows:

> The area within which broken cross rates threaten to distort the normal flow of trade is now much narrower than it was two or three years ago. The cross rates of greatest significance are the sterling-dollar rates, and the increased relative strength of sterling has been the basic reason for the improvement. There are, however, still a number of countries, including Hong Kong, Peru, Syria, Lebanon, and Thailand, where cross rates have not been brought under control, and countries confronted with special exchange problems are still sometimes disposed to look for an easy solution to practices that involve broken cross rates.[21]

Thereafter it was increasingly recognized, by both the Board and the staff, that broken cross rates for inconvertible currencies could not be avoided in free exchange markets. The only way to eliminate them was to abolish the free markets; yet most free markets were regarded as desirable both by the country concerned and by the Fund.

The extent of broken cross rates subsequently decreased further. In 1953, under the EPU agreement, eight European countries—Belgium, Denmark, France, Germany, the Netherlands, Sweden, Switzerland, and the United Kingdom—set up a multilateral arbitrage system. These countries allowed their banks (when authorized) to buy from and sell to authorized banks in the other cooperating countries any of their currencies in exchange for the currency of any of the other cooperating countries. The central banks concerned undertook to intervene at stated margins, usually ¾ of 1 per cent either side of parity. Cross rates between the eight currencies involved henceforth became approximately the same in all eight markets. After the establishment of external convertibility for sterling and other major European currencies in 1958, the U.S. dollar also came into the circuit of multilateral arbitrage facilities. Hence, there were no longer any broken cross rates involving European currencies and the U.S. dollar. Earlier that year the Fund had specifically noted the marked decline in broken cross rates for sterling and other key currencies.[22] Thus, although some broken cross rates have continued to prevail in free markets, they no longer constitute a serious issue for the Fund.

MARGINS AROUND PARITY

Once countries have set par values, they are obliged under the Articles to keep their spot exchange rates within a margin of 1 per cent on either side of

---

[21] *Annual Report, 1951*, p. 48.
[22] *Annual Report, 1958*, p. 127.

parity. If two countries fix margins for their currencies in terms of the U.S. dollar, the cross rate between their two currencies can, under the Articles, vary up to 2 per cent from that calculated on the basis of their parities. After European countries introduced external convertibility (in 1958), although they did not in fact allow their currencies to move all the way to the 1 per cent margin—stopping at ¾ per cent—the possibility of an illegal cross rate still arose. This was because the margins from par for the exchange rates between EPU currencies in the market were the sum of the margins prevailing for each currency against the U.S. dollar. In the extreme case, if one currency moved to the maximum permitted premium against the U.S. dollar while another currency moved to the maximum discount, the rate of exchange between the two currencies would move to a point approximately 1.5 per cent from parity. Because of this potential margin of 1.5 per cent, the central bank whose currency was involved in the differential would find it useful to buy and sell interchangeable currencies at exchange rates related to their quotations in foreign exchange markets. Central banks would thereby be engaging in transactions at exchange rates of more than 1 per cent from parity.

In recognition of such situations, and to avoid the possibility of excessive rate movements, the staff recommended to the Board that countries should fix the margin vis-à-vis the currency which they selected within 1 per cent and then ensure that the cumulative margins on either side of parity in relation to other convertible currencies would not exceed 2 per cent. This approach, the staff believed, would in general meet member countries' needs; any exceptional problems could be dealt with by the Fund on an individual basis.

When the Executive Board considered this recommendation, most Directors agreed with the staff's analysis. The question arose, however, as to the legal basis for the Fund to allow larger margins than those prescribed by Article IV, Section 3 (a). Was the Fund departing from its Articles either by amendment or by interpretation? The view of the General Counsel was that the proposed margins were technically multiple currency practices and could be approved by the Board under Article VIII, Section 3, which states that "no member shall engage in . . . any discriminatory currency arrangements or multiple currency practices except as authorized under this Agreement or approved by the Fund." Moreover, and even more important, the exchange systems in which these rates might develop already met or went far to meet the standards laid down in Article IV, Section 4 (a). Therefore, the General Counsel contended that the Fund could declare rates within a 2 per cent margin to be consistent with the Fund Agreement.

A few Directors noted that if rates outside the 1 per cent margin were legally approved under the authority of the Fund to deal with multiple currency practices, there might be some question that, like multiple currency practices, these rates were approved "on a temporary basis." But the decisive element, in the Board's view, was that the decision on margins about to be taken could not be interpreted as a violation of Article IV, Section 3. In any event, this decision could always be reversed later.

With these considerations in mind, the Board took the following decision on July 24, 1959:

> The Fund does not object to exchange rates which are within 2 per cent of parity for spot exchange transactions between a member's currency and the currencies of other members taking place within the member's territories, whenever such rates result from the maintenance of margins of no more than 1 per cent from parity for a convertible, including externally convertible, currency.[23]

FORWARD EXCHANGE RATES

Quite early in the Fund's existence, the question of the relation of forward to spot exchange rates arose. That the Fund was obliged to see that forward exchange rates bore a proper relation to spot rates was immediately recognized by both the staff and the Board. Provision had been made in Article IV, Section 3 (ii), for the Fund to determine what constituted a "reasonable" spread between spot and forward rates.

In 1946 the Board discussed a proposed section for the Rules and Regulations to the effect that agreed parities should not be circumvented by rates for forward exchange transactions. However, it was decided that it was not necessary for the Board to adopt a special regulation concerning forward transactions.

During the early 1950's concern about the relation of forward to spot rates was somewhat intensified. Spreads in forward rates from spot rates began to emerge after free markets in forward exchange had been re-established in a number of countries. When the Exchange Restrictions Report was discussed in the Board in 1953, attention focused on exchange arrangements which had recently gone into effect in some countries. These arrangements limited the purchase and sale of certain currencies at spot rates. As a result, transactions in forward markets had increased at the same time that there was little, if any, official intervention to support forward exchange rates.

While the Directors agreed that the Fund should not at the time attempt to take a position with respect to forward exchange arrangements, they recognized that an increase in forward transactions might constitute a rather significant development. Traders would naturally deal in the forward market if they could obtain more favorable exchange rates for certain currencies than the rate within 1 per cent of parity available in the spot market. Possibly forward market arrangements could even put in jeopardy the principle of orderly cross rates.

---

[23] E.B. Decision No. 904-(59/32), July 24, 1959; below, Vol. III, p. 226.

It was noted that discounts for certain currencies already existed in the forward exchange markets of some countries.

This problem was examined further during the course of 1953. The specific question of how the Fund was to determine a "reasonable" spread between a forward and a spot rate had arisen during the 1953 consultations under Article XIV with Belgium, in connection with the forward rate for Egyptian pounds. In first analyzing the factors responsible for a spread between spot and forward rates, the staff related premiums (or discounts) of forward rates over spot rates to interest rates. According to this analysis, at any given time the forward rate of exchange between two currencies is determined by the conditions of supply and demand in the forward market. But if, for example, the premium of the forward rate over the spot rate exceeds a certain margin, it becomes profitable for a bank to undertake interest arbitrage—that is, to sell the foreign currency forward and cover the exchange risk by buying the currency involved at the spot rate and investing that currency abroad. Therefore, under conditions of free competition, interest arbitrage will narrow down the forward premium (or discount) until it equals the difference in short-term (open market) interest rates in different countries.[24]

Wider spreads between forward and spot exchange rates resulted from limitations on access to spot markets, expectation of devaluation, or intervention in the forward market by monetary authorities. The Fund would, so the staff thought, have to judge instances of wider spreads in relation to the particular factor responsible for such a spread. For example, if an excessive spread between a forward rate and a spot rate resulted from controls on spot transactions, the Fund might treat the forward rate as a multiple currency practice.

The problem of spreads between forward and spot exchange rates diminished in the late 1950's as external convertibility was established. Subsequently, the staff undertook studies of the implications of government intervention in forward markets.[25] Later, as the world became more concerned about the role of interest rates in stimulating short-term capital movements and hence in facilitating balance of payments adjustment, the staff also examined the scope for movements of short-term funds in response to changes in forward rates.[26] But in the absence of the need for policy decisions, these analyses, while of interest to the Board, were not generally discussed.

[24] For a detailed exposition of forward exchange theory, see Paul Einzig, *A Dynamic Theory of Forward Exchange.*

[25] S.C. Tsiang, "The Theory of Forward Exchange and Effects of Government Intervention on the Forward Exchange Market," *Staff Papers,* Vol. VII (1959–60), pp. 75–106; J. Marcus Fleming and Robert A. Mundell, "Official Intervention on the Forward Exchange Market," *ibid.,* Vol. XI (1964), pp. 1–19.

[26] William H. White, "Interest Rate Differences, Forward Exchange Mechanism, and Scope for Short-Term Capital Movements," *Staff Papers,* Vol. X (1963), pp. 485–503.

Table 1. Initial Par Values Established, 1946–65

Date [1]	Member [2] and Rate
1946	
Dec. 18	Belgium — 2.28167 U.S. cents per franc
Dec. 18	Bolivia — 2.38095 U.S. cents per boliviano
Dec. 18	Canada — 100.000 U.S. cents per dollar
Dec. 18	Chile — 3.22581 U.S. cents per peso
Dec. 18	Colombia — 57.1433 U.S. cents per peso
Dec. 18	Costa Rica — 17.8094 U.S. cents per colón
Dec. 18	Cuba — 100.000 U.S. cents per peso
Dec. 18	Czechoslovakia — 2.00000 U.S. cents per koruna
Dec. 18	Denmark — 20.8376 U.S. cents per krone
Dec. 18	Ecuador — 7.40741 U.S. cents per sucre
Dec. 18	Egypt — 413.300 U.S. cents per pound
Dec. 18	El Salvador — 40.0000 U.S. cents per colón
Dec. 18	Ethiopia — 40.2500 U.S. cents per dollar
Dec. 18	France — 0.839583 U.S. cent per franc
Dec. 18	Guatemala — 100.000 U.S. cents per quetzal
Dec. 18	Honduras — 50.0000 U.S. cents per lempira
Dec. 18	Iceland — 15.4111 U.S. cents per króna
Dec. 18	India — 30.2250 U.S. cents per rupee
Dec. 18	Iran — 3.10078 U.S. cents per rial
Dec. 18	Iraq — 403.000 U.S. cents per dinar
Dec. 18	Luxembourg — 2.28167 U.S. cents per franc
Dec. 18	Mexico — 20.5973 U.S. cents per peso
Dec. 18	Netherlands — 37.6953 U.S. cents per guilder
Dec. 18	Nicaragua — 20.0000 U.S. cents per córdoba
Dec. 18	Norway — 20.1500 U.S. cents per krone
Dec. 18	Panama — 100.000 U.S. cents per balboa
Dec. 18	Paraguay — 32.3625 U.S. cents per guaraní
Dec. 18	Peru — 15.3846 U.S. cents per sol
Dec. 18	Philippines — 50.0000 U.S. cents per peso
Dec. 18	South Africa — 403.000 U.S. cents per pound
Dec. 18	United Kingdom — 403.000 U.S. cents per pound
Dec. 18	United States — 100.000 U.S. cents per dollar
1947	
Apr. 18	Venezuela — 29.8507 U.S. cents per bolívar
June 19	Turkey — 35.7143 U.S. cents per lira
July 29	Lebanon — 45.6313 U.S. cents per pound
July 29	Syrian Arab Republic — 45.6313 U.S. cents per pound
Nov. 17	Australia — 322.400 U.S. cents per pound
1948	
Apr. 23	Dominican Republic — 100.000 U.S. cents per peso
July 14	Brazil — 5.40541 U.S. cents per cruzeiro

Footnotes on page 86.

Table 1 *(continued).* Initial Par Values Established, 1946–65

Date [1]	Member [2] and Rate
1949	
May 24	Yugoslavia — 2.00000 U.S. cents per dinar
1951	
Mar. 19	Pakistan — 30.2250 U.S. cents per rupee
July 1	Finland — 0.434783 U.S. cent per markka
Nov. 5	Sweden — 19.3304 U.S. cents per krona
1952	
Jan. 16	Ceylon — 21.0000 U.S. cents per rupee
1953	
Jan. 30	Germany — 23.8095 U.S. cents per deutsche mark
May 4	Austria — 3.84615 U.S. cents per schilling
May 11	Japan — 0.277778 U.S. cent per yen
Aug. 7	Burma — 21.0000 U.S. cents per kyat
Oct. 2	Jordan — 280.000 U.S. cents per dinar
1954	
Apr. 9	Haiti — 20.0000 U.S. cents per gourde
1957	
Jan. 9	Argentina — 5.55556 U.S. cents per peso
Mar. 13	Israel — 55.5556 U.S. cents per pound
1958	
May 14	Ireland — 280.000 U.S. cents per pound
July 23	Sudan — 287.156 U.S. cents per pound
Nov. 5	Ghana — 280.000 U.S. cents per pound
1959	
July 17	Spain — 1.66667 U.S. cents per peseta
Aug. 12	Libya — 280.000 U.S. cents per pound
Oct. 16	Morocco — 19.7609 U.S. cents per dirham
1960	
Jan. 8	Saudi Arabia — 22.2222 U.S. cents per riyal
Mar. 30	Italy — 0.160000 U.S. cent per lira
Oct. 7	Uruguay — 13.5135 U.S. cents per peso
1961	
Mar. 29	Greece — 3.33333 U.S. cents per drachma
Oct. 27	New Zealand — 278.090 U.S. cents per pound
1962	
June 1	Portugal — 3.47826 U.S. cents per escudo
July 20	Malaya — 32.6667 U.S. cents per dollar
July 25	Cyprus — 280.000 U.S. cents per pound

Table 1 *(concluded).* Initial Par Values Established, 1946–65

Date [1]	Member [2] and Rate
1963	
Mar. 8	Jamaica — 280.000 U.S. cents per pound
Mar. 13	Liberia — 100.000 U.S. cents per dollar
Mar. 22	Afghanistan — 2.22222 U.S. cents per afghani
Apr. 17	Nigeria — 280.000 U.S. cents per pound
Apr. 26	Kuwait — 280.000 U.S. cents per dinar
June 14	Somalia — 14.0000 U.S. cents per shilling
Oct. 20	Thailand — 4.80769 U.S. cents per baht
1964	
Sept. 28	Tunisia — 190.476 U.S. cents per dinar
1965	
Jan. 26	Burundi — 1.14286 U.S. cents per franc
Feb. 10	Trinidad and Tobago — 58.3333 U.S. cents per dollar
Aug. 6	Sierra Leone — 140.000 U.S. cents per leone

[1] The date given is that on which the initial par value became effective, usually a few days later than that on which the par value was agreed with the Fund.

[2] Excludes nonmetropolitan territories.

Table 2. Dates of Membership and of Initial Par Values,
December 27, 1945–December 31, 1965 [1]

Member [2]	Date of Membership	Effective Date of Initial Par Value [3]
1. Afghanistan	July 14, 1955	Mar. 22, 1963
2. Algeria	Sept. 26, 1963	Not established
3. Argentina	Sept. 20, 1956	Jan. 9, 1957
4. Australia	Aug. 5, 1947	Nov. 17, 1947
5. Austria	Aug. 27, 1948	May 4, 1953
6. Belgium	Dec. 27, 1945	Dec. 18, 1946
7. Bolivia	Dec. 27, 1945	Dec. 18, 1946
8. Brazil	Jan. 14, 1946	July 14, 1948
9. Burma	Jan. 3, 1952	Aug. 7, 1953
10. Burundi	Sept. 28, 1963	Jan. 26, 1965
11. Cameroon	July 10, 1963	Not established
12. Canada	Dec. 27, 1945	Dec. 18, 1946
13. Central African Republic	July 10, 1963	Not established
14. Ceylon	Aug. 29, 1950	Jan. 16, 1952
15. Chad	July 10, 1963	Not established
16. Chile	Dec. 31, 1945	Dec. 18, 1946
17. China	Dec. 27, 1945	Not established
18. Colombia	Dec. 27, 1945	Dec. 18, 1946
19. Congo (Brazzaville)	July 10, 1963	Not established
20. Congo, Democratic Republic	Sept. 28, 1963	Not established
21. Costa Rica	Jan. 8, 1946	Dec. 18, 1946
22. Cuba	Mar. 14, 1946	Dec. 18, 1946
23. Cyprus	Dec. 21, 1961	July 25, 1962
24. Czechoslovakia	Dec. 27, 1945	Dec. 18, 1946
25. Dahomey	July 10, 1963	Not established
26. Denmark	Mar. 30, 1946	Dec. 18, 1946
27. Dominican Republic	Dec. 28, 1945	Apr. 23, 1948
28. Ecuador	Dec. 27, 1945	Dec. 18, 1946
29. El Salvador	Mar. 14, 1946	Dec. 18, 1946
30. Ethiopia	Dec. 27, 1945	Dec. 18, 1946
31. Finland	Jan. 14, 1948	July 1, 1951
32. France	Dec. 27, 1945	Dec. 18, 1946
33. Gabon	Sept. 10, 1963	Not established
34. Germany	Aug. 14, 1952	Jan. 30, 1953
35. Ghana	Sept. 20, 1957	Nov. 5, 1958
36. Greece	Dec. 27, 1945	Mar. 29, 1961
37. Guatemala	Dec. 27, 1945	Dec. 18, 1946
38. Guinea	Sept. 28, 1963	Not established
39. Haiti	Sept. 8, 1953	Apr. 9, 1954
40. Honduras	Dec. 27, 1945	Dec. 18, 1946
41. Iceland	Dec. 27, 1945	Dec. 18, 1946
42. India	Dec. 27, 1945	Dec. 18, 1946
43. Indonesia	Apr. 15, 1954	Not established
44. Iran	Dec. 29, 1945	Dec. 18, 1946
45. Iraq	Dec. 27, 1945	Dec. 18, 1946

Footnotes on page 89.

Table 2 *(continued).* Dates of Membership and of Initial Par Values,
December 27, 1945–December 31, 1965 [1]

Member [2]	Date of Membership	Effective Date of Initial Par Value [3]
46. Ireland	Aug. 8, 1957	May 14, 1958
47. Israel	July 12, 1954	Mar. 13, 1957
48. Italy	Mar. 27, 1947	Mar. 30, 1960
49. Ivory Coast	Mar. 11, 1963	Not established
50. Jamaica	Feb. 21, 1963	Mar. 8, 1963
51. Japan	Aug. 13, 1952	May 11, 1953
52. Jordan	Aug. 29, 1952	Oct. 2, 1953
53. Kenya	Feb. 3, 1964	Not established
54. Korea	Aug. 26, 1955	Not established
55. Kuwait	Sept. 13, 1962	Apr. 26, 1963
56. Laos	July 5, 1961	Not established
57. Lebanon	Apr. 14, 1947	July 29, 1947
58. Liberia	Mar. 28, 1962	Mar. 13, 1963
59. Libya	Sept. 17, 1958	Aug. 12, 1959
60. Luxembourg	Dec. 27, 1945	Dec. 18, 1946
61. Malagasy Republic	Sept. 25, 1963	Not established
62. Malawi	July 19, 1965	Not established
63. Malaysia	Mar. 7, 1958	July 20, 1962
64. Mali	Sept. 27, 1963	Not established
65. Mauritania	Sept. 10, 1963	Not established
66. Mexico	Dec. 31, 1945	Dec. 18, 1946
67. Morocco	Apr. 25, 1958	Oct. 16, 1959
68. Nepal	Sept. 6, 1961	Not established
69. Netherlands	Dec. 27, 1945	Dec. 18, 1946
70. New Zealand	Aug. 31, 1961	Oct. 27, 1961
71. Nicaragua	Mar. 14, 1946	Dec. 18, 1946
72. Niger	Apr. 24, 1963	Not established
73. Nigeria	Mar. 30, 1961	Apr. 17, 1963
74. Norway	Dec. 27, 1945	Dec. 18, 1946
75. Pakistan	July 11, 1950	Mar. 19, 1951
76. Panama	Mar. 14, 1946	Dec. 18, 1946
77. Paraguay	Dec. 27, 1945	Dec. 18, 1946
78. Peru	Dec. 31, 1945	Dec. 18, 1946
79. Philippines	Dec. 27, 1945	Dec. 18, 1946
80. Poland	Dec. 27, 1945	Not established
81. Portugal	Mar. 29, 1961	June 1, 1962
82. Rwanda	Sept. 30, 1963	Not established
83. Saudi Arabia	Aug. 26, 1957	Jan. 8, 1960
84. Senegal	Aug. 31, 1962	Not established
85. Sierra Leone	Sept. 10, 1962	Aug. 6, 1965
86. Somalia	Aug. 31, 1962	June 14, 1963
87. South Africa	Dec. 27, 1945	Dec. 18, 1946
88. Spain	Sept. 15, 1958	July 17, 1959
89. Sudan	Sept. 5, 1957	July 23, 1958
90. Sweden	Aug. 31, 1951	Nov. 5, 1951

Table 2 *(concluded).* Dates of Membership and of Initial Par Values,
December 27, 1945–December 31, 1965 [1]

Member [2]	Date of Membership	Effective Date of Initial Par Value [3]
91. Syrian Arab Republic	Apr. 10, 1947	July 29, 1947
92. Tanzania	Sept. 10, 1962	Not established
93. Thailand	May 3, 1949	Oct. 20, 1963
94. Togo	Aug. 1, 1962	Not established
95. Trinidad and Tobago	Sept. 16, 1963	Feb. 10, 1965
96. Tunisia	Apr. 14, 1958	Sept. 28, 1964
97. Turkey	Mar. 11, 1947	June 19, 1947
98. Uganda	Sept. 27, 1963	Not established
99. United Arab Republic	Dec. 27, 1945	Dec. 18, 1946
100. United Kingdom	Dec. 27, 1945	Dec. 18, 1946
101. United States	Dec. 27, 1945	Dec. 18, 1946
102. Upper Volta	May 2, 1963	Not established
103. Uruguay	Dec. 27, 1945	Oct. 7, 1960
104. Venezuela	Dec. 30, 1946	Apr. 18, 1947
105. Viet-Nam	Sept. 21, 1956	Not established
106. Yugoslavia	Dec. 27, 1945	May 24, 1949
107. Zambia	Sept. 23, 1965	Not established

[1] As 4 of the 107 countries listed in this table withdrew from membership (Cuba, Czechoslovakia, Indonesia, and Poland), the actual membership on December 31, 1965 was 103.

[2] Excludes nonmetropolitan territories.

[3] The date given is that on which the par value became effective, usually a few days later than that on which the par value was agreed with the Fund.

CHAPTER

5

Exchange Rate Adjustment

Margaret G. de Vries

JUST AS THE FUND has had to develop policies pertaining to the establishment and maintenance of par values, so it has had to evolve policies relating to changes in those par values and in other exchange rates. The issues which have come to the fore include the reasons for devaluation, the magnitudes of the changes, and the possibility of adverse consequences for other members. The role of the Fund in a matter explicitly stated by the Articles to be reserved to the initiative of members has also had to be clarified. Furthermore, the Fund has had to decide what to do when members change exchange rates that have not been agreed as par values: adjustment of exchange rates is not always effected by the simple mechanism set up in the Articles—that is, from one unitary par value to another.

The major examples of rate adjustment between 1946 and 1965 through what, in the parlance of economists, is called "altering the pegs" were the devaluations of the major currencies in September 1949, devaluations by Mexico (1954) and Pakistan (1955), and the German and Dutch revaluations of 1961. These rate adjustments form the subject of this chapter. Exchange rates have also been altered in three other ways. The first comprises partial and selective devaluations through the alteration of multiple rates; these were very frequent until the late 1950's. The reasons for devaluation in this manner, and the Fund's views, are discussed in Chapter 6. Second, in a few countries devaluation has been effected by the temporary institution of a fluctuating exchange rate; only later was a new par value established. Canada, the Philippines, and Thailand afford noteworthy examples of this type of devaluation. Third, devaluation has occurred through the use of steadily depreciating fluctuating rates. Some countries which had introduced fluctuating rates subsequently undertook to support these rates. Later, they were obliged to devalue again. These last two types of devaluation are discussed in Chapter 7.

TWO BASIC CONCEPTS

The Fund's Articles contain two basic concepts applicable to changes in par values. The first provides a criterion by which to judge the *need* for a change in par value: par values are to be altered only to correct a fundamental disequilibrium. The second relates not only to the need for devaluation but also to its *size:* competitive depreciation is to be avoided.

In the twenty-odd years since these concepts were formulated, the Fund has never attempted to define precisely either "fundamental disequilibrium" or "competitive depreciation." In its first years, in response to members' requests, the Fund did make two interpretations of its Articles involving the first term. And in the early 1950's some sizable devaluations excited in at least one Executive Director the fear of excessive, if not competitive, depreciation.

Subsequently, the need for exact definitions of these terms has not been a pressing one; therefore such definitions, which could limit the leverage of future Fund actions, have been avoided. In fact, even when the Fund has taken decisions denoting its concurrence with the proposed rate changes of individual countries, it has rarely used these terms. But the absence of definitions has not meant that the conditions described could not be recognized when they were thought to occur. Over the years member countries have proposed a number of changes in par values and, where par values did not exist, in their prevailing exchange rates, and the Fund has generally concurred. In these instances, several different reasons for devaluation can be discerned, all tending to suggest the nature of fundamental disequilibrium.

In a postwar world in which economic conditions have been in direct contrast to those of the interwar period, there has been little temptation to indulge in competitive depreciation of exchange rates. Whereas unemployment had been widespread in the 1930's, high levels of employment have prevailed in most countries since the end of World War II. The economic dangers have stemmed from inflation rather than from deflation. Consequently, countries have been less, rather than more, inclined since the war than in the interwar period to use devaluation as an instrument of balance of payments policy. In this environment it is understandable that the Fund has not found it necessary to disapprove, certainly not formally, any proposed change in exchange rates as constituting competitive depreciation.

EARLY INTERPRETATION OF
FUNDAMENTAL DISEQUILIBRIUM

While the plans for a postwar international monetary organization were being drawn up, considerable interest centered on how to limit the frequency of exchange rate adjustments. To this end many economists distinguished fundamental disequilibrium—for which rate adjustments were appropriate—from cyclical or seasonal disequilibrium—for which rate adjustments were not suitable. Furthermore, a prime concern, both for Fund member countries and for economists, was how to reconcile domestic objectives, especially the attainment of full employment, with the requirements of external balance. Therefore, the question raised by the United Kingdom at the outset of the Fund's activity in 1946 could be expected. The British Government stated its intention to maintain full employment and asked whether steps necessary to protect a member from unemployment of a chronic or persistent character, arising from pressures on its balance of payments, would be considered measures necessary to correct a fundamental disequilibrium.[1] In other words, would countries threatened by unemployment due to loss of exports, now (with the advent of the Fund) have the option of devaluing their currency with the approval of an international body? Their choice had previously been restricted to deflation, as required by the gold standard, or to devaluation in circumstances likely to induce retaliatory depreciation, as during the 1930's.

In answer to the British request for an interpretation of fundamental disequilibrium, the Executive Directors took what proved to be one of two unique decisions pertaining to that expression—that steps necessary to protect a member from unemployment of a chronic or persistent character, arising from pressure on its balance of payments, were indeed among the measures necessary to correct a fundamental disequilibrium. The Board further decided that, in each instance in which a member proposed a change in the par value of its currency to correct a fundamental disequilibrium, the Fund would be required to determine, in the light of all relevant circumstances, whether in its opinion the proposed change was necessary to correct the fundamental disequilibrium.[2]

THE FUND'S AUTHORITY

Another early issue in connection with the interpretation of fundamental disequilibrium focused on the question of the exact powers of the Fund. Although the Fund Agreement specified that exchange rate changes could be proposed only by members—not by the Fund—and only where there was fundamental disequilibrium, this still left scope for wide differences in view as to how much of a role the Fund might play, and in what way. How much informal initiative could the Fund take in suggesting exchange rate changes? Who in the Fund—the Executive Board, the Managing Director, or, informally, the staff—might take such initiative, and in what ways and to what degree?

---

[1] Resolution IM-5, *Selected Documents*, p. 19.
[2] E.B. Decision No. 71-2, September 26, 1946; below, Vol. III, p. 227.

In fact, as the Fund and its members learned to work closely together, a *modus operandi* was evolved without any formalized arrangements having been agreed. However, at the outset of the Fund's deliberations in the late 1940's, countries were understandably jealous of their sovereignty in this important field. This was the first time that such a previously unilateral matter had been turned over to an international body. Moreover, there was much mistrust of the Fund, especially among Western European countries. They feared especially that changes in exchange rates or relaxation of restrictions might be forced upon them. They doubted that the Fund was adequately aware of the difficulties of postwar reconstruction. And in their fears and concerns they were mindful of the strong voting position in the Fund of the United States and of the eagerness of the U.S. authorities to have international trade and payments relations restored to normal. In these circumstances the power of the Fund even to object to a proposed par value had to be agreed upon explicitly by the Board.

AN INSUFFICIENT DEVALUATION

In the course of the Executive Board's discussion concerning the first devaluation referred to the Fund—that of the French franc early in 1948 [3]—Mr. de Largentaye (France) brought up an ancillary, but crucial, question. Although under its Articles the Fund could object to a change in par value if no fundamental disequilibrium existed, could the Fund also object if it considered the proposed degree of change in par value not sufficient to correct that disequilibrium? Did the Fund not have to concur in a proposed change of parity if (a) there was a fundamental disequilibrium, and (b) a change in the par value was necessary to correct the fundamental disequilibrium?

Mr. de Largentaye believed that the Fund had no power to object to an insufficient change in parity. His reasoning was that if the Fund had the right to object to a proposed change in a par value because it found the change insufficient, the Fund would, in the long run, force the member to accept an additional depreciation of its currency. The Fund, rather than the member, thereby would initiate a change in the par value. The purpose of the Fund was to oppose competitive alterations of par values. In order to prevent competitive depreciation, it was not necessary for the Fund to be able to object to an insufficient alteration; it was enough to empower it to object to an excessive alteration.

The question at stake was vital. The Board, in addition to discussing France's devaluation, held extra sessions to consider this matter of the Fund's authority. In the preparatory staff paper for these discussions, the General Counsel expressed the opinion that the Fund could object if the degree of proposed devaluation was insufficient. In effect, the Fund must be satisfied that not just two but three conditions existed before it was required to concur in a change in

---

[3] See below, pp. 129–30.

par value: first, a fundamental disequilibrium must exist; second, the fundamental disequilibrium could not be corrected without a change in par value; and third, *the change would, in fact, correct the disequilibrium.*

The Directors, however, did not consider the question resolved so simply. Mr. de Selliers (Belgium) concurred with Mr. de Largentaye in his belief that the Fund had no power to object to an insufficient devaluation. Article IV, he contended, was intended to avoid competitive devaluations. Its whole emphasis was on keeping changes in par values as small as possible. There was no indication that members could be made to devalue further than they wished because the Fund thought that only a greater change would correct a fundamental disequilibrium.

Mr. Martínez-Ostos (Mexico), Alternate to Mr. Gómez, agreed with Mr. de Largentaye and Mr. de Selliers on purely legal grounds. He recalled that the Fund was debarred from objecting to a change in par value amounting to less than 10 per cent of the original parity. If a member could make a change of up to 10 per cent with freedom, he doubted that the Fund could object to an even greater change on the ground that it was insufficient.

Other Directors had a broader view of the Fund's powers. Mr. Overby (United States) thought that the Fund would be in a ridiculous position if it was forced to concur in a change in par value which it was convinced was not adequate. The acceptance of an inadequate change would jeopardize exchange stability for the member and endanger orderly exchange arrangements for all members. He emphasized that, with the establishment of the Fund, a new regime had come into being. Par values were no longer matters of unilateral decision. They were now subject to agreement with the Fund. And the term *agreement* necessarily meant that the parties must have the power to concur or reject. Consultation and collaboration in the true sense involved more than mere form.

Although he did not ordinarily intervene in discussions such as this, the Chairman, Mr. Gutt, believed the issue to be so significant that he wished to express his opinion. From the practical point of view, he believed that the Fund would be placed in an absurd position before the public if it was forced by interpretation to concur in inadequate changes. To protect its integrity, the Fund would have to declare that the concurrence was purely formal, and that it really opposed the new par value; such a declaration would be confusing to the public and would bring discredit on the Fund.

THE CONCEPT OF "REASONABLE DOUBT"

Mr. Saad (Egypt), who was away from headquarters at the time, cabled a statement of his position and successfully resolved the debate with a concept of "reasonable doubt." He believed that the Fund, which could not legally require a member to change its par value in order to correct a fundamental disequilibrium, could not justifiably express disagreement with a proposed depreciation merely because it questioned whether the depreciation was sufficient to correct the fundamental disequilibrium. However, he thought that a different situation prevailed if it was *proved beyond doubt* that the proposed depreciation would not correct even partially the fundamental disequilibrium, or that the damage done to a member's interest by such a depreciation would absorb any possible advantage that the depreciation would give to the member. In such circumstances, the Fund could rightly consider that a proposed depreciation could not be justified as correcting a fundamental disequilibrium.

In effect, Mr. Saad's concept acknowledged the Fund's power to object to a proposed devaluation if the inadequacy of that devaluation could be proved beyond doubt; if it could not, the Fund could not object. Moreover, in its deliberations, the Fund must give the member the benefit of any reasonable doubt.

On this basis the Board was able to take the second of two decisions on fundamental disequilibrium. On March 1, 1948, it decided that the Fund had authority under Article IV, Section 5, to object to a change in par value proposed by a member when the extent of the proposed change, in the judgment of the Fund, was insufficient to correct a fundamental disequilibrium. The Fund recognized, however, that the extent of the necessary change could not be determined with precision, and that, in reaching a decision on a member's proposal to change its par value, whether during the transitional period or thereafter, the member should be given the benefit of any reasonable doubt. In addition, due consideration should be given to the views of the member regarding the political and social consequences of a change in par value greater than the one proposed.[4]

CHANGES IN RATES OTHER THAN PAR VALUES

Since members did not always devalue their currencies by altering an agreed par value, the Fund found it necessary to establish its authority to agree to other kinds of exchange rate changes. From 1947 to 1951, the Executive Board took a series of decisions to the effect that all alterations of exchange rates, regardless of whether par values were involved or not, were subject to review by the Fund. In December 1947 procedures and policies were outlined for reviewing changes in multiple rates, to apply to all members including those for whose currencies par values had not been established.[5] In April 1951, the Board took a further decision requiring new members that had not yet agreed initial par values to consult with the Fund and obtain its agreement before changing the exchange rates which had prevailed when they accepted membership. Thus, as countries

---

[4] E.B. Decision No. 278-3, March 1, 1948; below, Vol. III, p. 227.

[5] Footnote to E.B. Decision No. 237-2, December 18, 1947; below, Vol. III, p. 264.

joined the Fund, they were required to consult with the Fund before changing their exchange rates, even though they might not yet have set par values.

THE DEVALUATIONS OF 1949

A TEST FOR THE FUND

Both the staff and the Executive Directors were well aware of the arguments against devaluation being advanced by many economists in the late 1940's. Differences of opinion as regards the need for exchange rate adjustment in Western Europe also occurred among the staff, who had been studying the need for devaluation, and among the Directors. Nevertheless, in their Annual Report for 1948 the Executive Directors distinguished between exchange stability and exchange rigidity:

> The Fund Agreement makes it clear that the provisions for the regulation of exchange rates are not intended to impose upon the Fund the duty of perpetuating in the name of stability exchange rates which have lost touch with economic realities.[6]

By that time there were indications that in some countries the exchange rate was restraining exports and adding to the difficulty of earning convertible currencies. The Fund stressed that in the timing of an exchange rate adjustment, the function of the rate in promoting exports, which had been a major element in the determination of the initial par values, was still of great importance.[7]

Significantly, the Directors also said that

> although the Fund is not entitled to propose a change in the par value of a currency it has an obligation to keep the exchange rate situation constantly under review, and its views may properly find expression in its informal consultations with members. When an exchange rate is no longer appropriate the Fund will, of course, give prompt and realistic consideration to a member's request for adjustment in the par value of its currency.[8]

But this statement was as far as the Directors, as a whole, were prepared to go. The European Directors especially were unready, even by mid-1949, for any decision by the Fund to review countries' exchange rates. Some did not want the Board even to discuss the problem. Jealous of members' sovereignty in this field, they believed that a decision by the Board to study exchange rates was unnecessary and likely to be detrimental to the interests of both the Fund and members. They were especially fearful that the Fund might *propose* a devaluation and thereby usurp a prerogative of members.

---

[6] *Annual Report, 1948,* p. 21.

[7] *Ibid.,* p. 23.

[8] *Ibid.,* p. 24.

The position of the U.S. Executive Director was exactly the opposite. In the U.S. Government the conviction had gradually grown that the establishment of a stronger economic structure in Europe required a substantial depreciation of sterling and other Western European currencies. Early in 1949 this attitude found public expression. The U.S. National Advisory Council proposed that "the exchange rate question should be reviewed with a number of European countries in the course of the next year." [9] In discussions in the Executive Board of the position of individual members during the first eight months of 1949, Mr. Overby and Mr. Southard (who succeeded him in March 1949) found frequent opportunities to raise the question of exchange rate adjustment.

At the suggestion of Mr. Southard, an Ad Hoc Committee of the Board was established in August 1949 to consider the problems arising out of the international payments situation and the relation of exchange rates to these problems. Some Directors objected to the establishment of such a committee and took a very unfavorable view of its discussions. The last meeting of this committee was held on September 8, about a week before the devaluation of sterling. The committee's report advocated that member countries in Western Europe review their rate structures and determine, in consultation with the Fund, to what extent adjustment should be made in each individual case where it was appropriate. Several Directors, among them Mr. Beyen (Netherlands), Mr. Bolton (United Kingdom), Mr. de Largentaye, Mr. Madan (India), Alternate to Mr. Joshi, Mr. McFarlane (Australia), and Mr. Rasminsky (Canada), opposed adoption of any formal report in which members were "invited" to change their exchange rates. Their opposition continued even after the devaluations of September. In their view the Fund should refrain from coming to formal decisions in advance on the exchange rates of its members. Eventually, the committee's report was adopted by formal vote of the Directors.

THE DEVALUATION OF STERLING

What finally precipitated the devaluation of sterling was a large outflow of sterling reserves during the summer of 1949, such as had occurred in the attempt at convertibility in 1947. In the three months April–June 1949, gold and dollar reserves of the sterling area fell by 14 per cent, to $1,650 million. This level of reserves was less than half the amount of gold alone held at the beginning of 1938, and less than a quarter of that amount in terms of purchasing power, after making allowance for the increase in U.S. prices in the intervening decade. As anticipations of devaluation grew, speculative action increased. In the eleven weeks from June 30 to September 18 reserves declined by nearly 20 per cent, to $1,340 million, and the British authorities came to look

---

[9] U.S. Congress, Senate, Committee on Foreign Relations, *Extension of European Recovery,* Hearings . . . on S. 833, a Bill to Amend the Economic Cooperation Act of 1948, 81st Cong., 1st sess., 1949, p. 388.

upon devaluation as an unavoidable step in order to end a situation which was being made more difficult by the expectation of devaluation.

The choice of an appropriate new rate presented a most difficult problem. Obviously, the lower the new rate, the more expensive in sterling terms American imports would be, and the greater, therefore, the difficulty of controlling increases in manufacturing and living costs; in addition, the lower the rate, the greater the difficulty of servicing the dollar debts of the United Kingdom. On the other hand, the disparity in export price levels was such as to call for a drastic change. Perhaps even more important was the need to establish a rate low enough to create expectations that the British Government would be able to maintain it.

The Managing Director of the Fund was informed by the Chancellor of the Exchequer on September 15, 1949, the penultimate day of the Fund's Fourth Annual Meeting, that the U.K. Government intended to devalue sterling by approximately 30.5 per cent. The exchange rate of £1 = $4.03 which had been accepted by the Fund as the initial par value for sterling would be replaced by a new rate of £1 = $2.80. Formal notification of the proposal to establish a new par value was submitted to the Fund on Saturday, September 17, and on the afternoon of that day the Executive Board concurred in the proposal.

The Directors considered that the causes of the devaluation of sterling were to be found both in the United Kingdom itself and in other countries of the sterling area. Among the long-term factors that had shaped the problem of the United Kingdom in 1949, the most important were the severe deterioration of its external position on capital account compared with ten years earlier, the deterioration in its terms of trade, the difficulties it had experienced in recapturing an adequate share of the dollar markets, its abnormal dependence on dollar imports, the persistence of inflationary pressures in its economy, and the existence of large sterling balances.

Subsequently the role of the Fund in the devaluation of sterling was, variously, questioned, criticized, and defended. Had not the Fund been merely a "rubber stamp"? Had not the Fund been too passive—some said "by-passed"— in this devaluation?

Clearly the magnitude of the devaluation as well as the timing had been determined by the British authorities before the Fund was notified. However, the test had been met that plans to change the rate were presented to an international body prior to action. The Fund, recognizing the need for devaluation, and that the extent ought to be large, agreed to the proposed change. The Fund could therefore be regarded as putting into operation the guidelines of the general decision taken a year and a half earlier. At that time, as noted above, it had stated that the extent of a necessary change in par value could not be determined with precision and that, as the Fund reached a decision on a member's proposal to change its par value, the member should be given the benefit of any reasonable doubt. Also the Fund might, and did, stress the need for monetary and fiscal policies to back up the new exchange rate.

DEVALUATIONS OF OTHER CURRENCIES

The devaluation of sterling was immediately followed by devaluations of several other currencies—those of the sterling area and of all the Western European countries. This was indeed a week in which the Fund's machinery— Board and staff—went into operation. A detailed staff study evaluating the new exchange rate was prepared for each of the several countries and was discussed by the Executive Board. Much relevant preparatory work had laid the basis for expediting the staff's papers and the Board's consideration of them. Nonetheless, much preparation and discussion still had to be done quickly— within the course of four days and mostly over a week-end. Furthermore, complete secrecy was mandatory. Those who were closely involved at the time recall several measures to maintain secrecy and to keep up the pace of staff preparation and Board consideration of the exchange rate changes being proposed. The staff, for example, was not permitted to leave the building for any purpose on Saturday, September 17, meals being brought in. And senior officials did not go home for three days, sleeping at a nearby hotel.

Most of the currencies involved, including not only those of other countries in the sterling area (Australia, Iceland, India, Iraq, and the Union of South Africa), but those of Egypt, Denmark, and Norway, were also devalued by 30.5 per cent. The Netherlands guilder was devalued from f. 2.65285 to f. 3.80 = $1, i.e., by 30.2 per cent.

The devaluation of the currencies of Belgium and Luxembourg from 43.8275 francs to 50.000 francs = $1 involved a depreciation of only 12.3 per cent. For a few days the Belgian Government had considered the possibility of introducing a fluctuating rate. After discussion with the Fund, however, the Government concluded that the disadvantages of a floating rate were too grave to be worth-while, and proposed a new par value. The rate chosen was designed to adjust the export and import prices of the Belgian-Luxembourg Economic Union (BLEU) to the trend of world prices which was expected to follow the devaluations, and to improve the payments position of the BLEU vis-à-vis the dollar area. Since the end of World War II the international financial position of the BLEU had been strong; its current account deficit with the dollar area had been declining and its surplus with other countries had increased. The position of the Belgian steel industry was also relatively strong. However, the Belgian authorities believed it necessary to adjust the parity of the Belgian franc somewhat in the face of the general devaluation. These considerations led the Belgian Government to adopt a middle course between maintenance of the former parity and devaluation to the same extent as sterling.

The problem of the appropriate rate for Canada was dominated by two considerations. Had the rate been left unchanged, Canada would have been subjected to the strains arising from the improved competitive position of the devaluing countries, although still needing to alleviate the imbalance in its trade with the United States. On the other hand, a devaluation equal to that of sterling would not have helped to expand imports from the devaluing countries, which was required if such countries were to correct the serious disequilibrium in their payments position vis-à-vis Canada. In light of these considerations, the Canadian dollar was devalued by 9.1 per cent.

The Fund also agreed to changes in the exchange rates of Finland and Greece, for which no par values had been agreed, and to a change in the exchange rate for France, for which the agreed par value had been suspended. In July 1949, Finland had devalued the markka by 15 per cent, from Fmk 135 = $1 to Fmk 160 = $1. The devaluation in September 1949 was to Fmk 230 = $1. The Government of Greece, on September 22, changed the effective exchange rate for the drachma to Dr 15,000 = $1 and Dr 42,000 = £1, a depreciation of 33.3 per cent in respect of the dollar.

The French Government proposed to unify its system as well as adjust the exchange rate. Since October 1948 the free rate for the franc had applied only to nontrade transactions in certain currencies. For commercial transactions the daily average of the free rate and the previous fixed official rate of 214.392 francs per U.S. dollar had been used. Financial as well as commercial transactions in all other currencies except the Italian lira were conducted at exchange rates based on this average dollar rate. The rates for financial transactions were approximately 20 per cent more depreciated than the rates for commercial transactions. After unification in September 1949, the exchange rate applicable to transactions in U.S. dollars was allowed to rise from F 330.80 to F 350.00 = $1. This represented a depreciation vis-à-vis the dollar of 5.7 per cent for financial transactions and 21.8 per cent for commercial transactions, but it represented an appreciation vis-à-vis sterling of about 12.5 per cent.

COMPETITIVE DEPRECIATION

THE ISSUE ARISES

The onset of the first devaluations—those of September 1949—demonstrated that differences in points of view about the need for and magnitudes of devaluation were inevitable. The Latin American Directors, exercised lest the devaluations of the outer sterling area in line with that of the pound sterling should harm the export prospects of their countries, thought that there was a need for a "definitional examination" of competitive depreciation. Both Mr. Paranaguá (Brazil) and Mr. D'Ascoli (Venezuela) doubted whether a clear case of fundamental disequilibrium could be made in support of the devaluations of the dependent territories, and felt certain that no such case could be made for a devaluation by 30 per cent.

This objection raised a related legal question. When a member proposed to the Fund a change in the par value of its metropolitan currency and corresponding changes in the par values of the separate currencies of its nonmetropolitan areas, could the Fund consider the various pieces of the proposal separately or did the Fund have to deal with the proposal as a whole? The Legal Department's opinion in the preparatory staff paper was that the Fund was required to consider and decide on such proposals as a unit. It could object to the entire proposal if it was not satisfied that the changes proposed in the par value of the metropolitan currency or in the par value of one or more of the separate currencies were necessary to correct a fundamental disequilibrium. But it was not required to decide on the proposal as a unit if the intended changes in the par values of the separate currencies did not correspond to that in the metropolitan currency.

Several Directors did not concur. Mr. D'Ascoli thought that the conclusion that the Fund had to accept or reject the entire proposal of a country was wholly impractical. It put the Board in the situation of either (a) accepting an unjustified change in the par value of a separate currency (i.e., a colonial currency) purely for the sake of not having to reject at the same time a justified and even very necessary change in the par value of a metropolitan currency, or (b) rejecting both proposals, even if the member making the proposal was taking the very action that the Board thought it should have taken long before with respect to the metropolitan currency.

There seemed, Mr. D'Ascoli stated, to be an assumption that colonial empires possessed economic uniformity. In actuality, the differences between metropolitan and dependent territories were so great that separate currencies had been created for many dependent territories. The Fund should be entitled to decide upon the changes in those separate currencies without being influenced by considerations independent of the payments position of the territory concerned. Mr. Hooker (United States), Alternate to Mr. Southard, supported Mr. D'Ascoli's position. But he commented that, as a practical matter, if the Fund had any doubts on a joint proposal, these doubts could be expressed to the member during the course of the Fund's preliminary discussions with that member.

Most of the European Directors, on the other hand, agreed with the interpretation put forward by the staff. Mr. Tansley (United Kingdom) and Mr. McFarlane (Australia) argued that a member which proposed a change in the par values of its metropolitan currency and its separate currencies made a single proposal which the Fund had to accept or reject as a whole, although the

Fund had the right to look at each separate currency. Mr. de Largentaye's opinion was that the drafters of the Articles of Agreement could not have intended to give the Fund the right to object or concur in only part of a proposal. The Fund's rejection of a part of the proposal would amount to a change in the par value of the separate currency in terms of the metropolitan currency which the member had not proposed.

Mr. Southard's reasoning was that on economic grounds there was no necessity for a separate currency to follow the metropolitan currency. The Fund should consider each currency independently after economic analysis of each proposal. He did not believe that the Articles of Agreement denied the Fund the right to concur in part of a proposal if it had arrived at the conclusion that only a portion of a proposal was justified and other portions were not. Mr. Southard's argument was also that the Fund was not necessarily serving the best interests of members that administered dependent territories by treating a joint proposal as a unit. It was of more help to the metropolitan members for the Fund to examine carefully the exchange rates of dependent territories. Accordingly, Mr. Southard suggested and the Board agreed that further discussion should be postponed until the Directors for these members had had an opportunity to consider the problem further.

There has not, however, been any further discussion in the Board of the question whether devaluation of nonmetropolitan currencies should be considered separately from that of the member. Another instance of devaluation of nonmetropolitan currencies occurred in December 1958. After France had devalued and proposed a new par value for the franc, it also proposed parities for the separate currencies of its nonmetropolitan territories, but the rates proposed were not uniform. The new par value established for the franc for Algeria, the French Antilles, and French Guiana was the same as that for the French franc, 0.202550 U.S. cents per franc. The par value of the CFA franc, for Cameroun, French Equatorial Africa, French West Africa, Madagascar and dependencies, Réunion, St. Pierre and Miquelon, and Togoland, was 0.405099 U.S. cent per CFA franc; the CFA franc was thus equal to 2.00 French francs. The par value agreed for the CFP franc, applying to the French possessions of Oceania, New Caledonia, and New Hebrides, was 1.11402 U.S. cents per CFP franc, equal to 5.50 French francs. But, in any event, no question was raised in the Board about these devaluations, and the decision was taken without discussion.

WHAT IS COMPETITIVE DEPRECIATION?

The possibility that competitive depreciation might be involved in a member's proposal to devalue has come up on only a few occasions. One such occasion was when Iceland, which had already devalued by 30.5 per cent in September

1949, proposed to devalue by another 42.5 per cent in February 1950. The problem posed for the Fund was made the more difficult by the fact that the second devaluation, according to the member, was not needed to sustain exports; in fact, in order to prevent excessive export price cutting, sizable export taxes were being introduced. The extra depreciation was necessary rather to curb imports: import demand was swollen and the country could not introduce import duties. Inasmuch as European markets for fish, the chief Icelandic export, had become much more competitive, concern by several European Directors over this devaluation was more pronounced than it might otherwise have been.

Several questions confronted the Fund: Should a country be permitted, because of import considerations, to cut its par value below a point adequate to move exports? Could devaluing a currency so as to balance imports with exports be regarded as competitive depreciation? If export taxes were to be applied after devaluation because otherwise the profits to exporters would be too great, could such a devaluation be considered necessary to correct a fundamental disequilibrium?

In effect, the Icelandic devaluation had raised the question of the nature of competitive depreciation. How could it be defined or identified? The staff undertook a careful examination of the subject.

Meanwhile, a decision on Iceland's exchange rate could not wait. When the Board considered the proposal, several Directors agreed that a devaluation was necessary and saw no reason to object to the degree proposed. In their view, because of its payments deficits, Iceland needed some protection for its exports. And they were pleased at the well thought out program of fiscal measures that would accompany devaluation. However, Mr. de Largentaye believed that the devaluation should be held to the lowest possible level so as to keep down the inflationary and other undesirable effects that would follow. He also questioned whether the country was taking all possible steps to deflate the economy, which, in his view, was a better alternative than devaluation where it was possible.

Mr. van der Valk (Netherlands), Alternate to Mr. Beyen, and Mr. Santaella (Venezuela), Alternate to Mr. D'Ascoli, had similar doubts about the degree of devaluation proposed. So large a devaluation as was proposed might mean that other countries would be subjected to unjustified competition from Icelandic exports only because of Iceland's need to curb imports.

After an assurance by Iceland that it was not intending to engage in competitive depreciation, the Fund concurred in the proposed change in the par value, noting with approval the intention to impose export taxes which would help to prevent undue pressure on highly competitive markets for particular exports. A year later, to cope with a similar set of circumstances, Iceland introduced a multiple rate system which lasted for several years.

After studying the question of a definition of competitive depreciation, the consensus of the staff was that a devaluation which merely corrected the payments position of a country could not be considered competitive, even if that devaluation had adverse effects on other countries.   Admittedly, devaluation might be disturbing to other countries exporting the same goods, and even to countries importing such goods if they competed with home output, but this did not make the devaluation competitive.   Only an excessive devaluation—that is, one that overcorrected for a fundamental disequilibrium—could be regarded as competitive depreciation in the sense of the Fund Agreement.   The question was how to determine an excessive devaluation.

The staff approach to this question was to measure an excessive devaluation in terms of its departure from a "correct" exchange rate.   The "correct" level of an exchange rate was defined to be one that over a period of years tended to restore external balance *and* to yield a moderate increase in reserves if these were previously deficient.   In this light, devaluation was competitive only when it resulted in so marked a surplus in the devaluing country that reserves grew at an excessive rate.[10]   This definition was, of course, influenced heavily by the circumstances of the time, when all countries except the United States were suffering from low foreign exchange reserves.   But this definition also made clear that, in order to judge whether a proposed exchange adjustment is correct, the Fund must have a broad concept of (1) the appropriate distribution of reserves in the world, (2) the effects on the world pattern of exchange rates and the need for continuing direct controls that the proposed adjustment would involve, and (3) the extent to which the new exchange rate would enable the devaluing country, over a period of years, to acquire reserves.

From time to time other devaluations aroused some concern, at least for one or two Directors; these are discussed immediately below.   On these occasions, although some members of the staff suggested a general discussion by the Board of competitive depreciation, one was never held.   The need for a definition of competitive depreciation had waned.

OTHER DEVALUATIONS OF CONCERN

In the next few years the magnitudes of some other proposed devaluations, although acceptable to nearly all the Executive Directors and defensible as far as staff analysis was concerned, were to elicit expressions of disapproval from at least one Director when the proposals were discussed by the Board.

---

[10] See Walter R. Gardner and S.C. Tsiang, "Competitive Depreciation," *Staff Papers*, Vol. II (1951–52), pp. 399–406.

GREECE AND AUSTRIA

In 1953 two countries—Greece and Austria—both of which had devalued in late 1949, again proposed sizable devaluations in moves to unify their multiple rates. When Greece proposed to unify its exchange structure at a new rate of Dr 30,000 = $1, Mr. de Largentaye (France) queried the rate. The free rate in New York was only 16,000 to 17,000 drachmas per U.S. dollar. According to staff calculations, the average effective rate for all exports under the multiple rate system was approximately 20,000 drachmas per U.S. dollar. The average effective rate for imports subject to tax was also estimated at about 20,000 drachmas per U.S. dollar. Mr. de Largentaye was of the opinion, therefore, that a devaluation to Dr 30,000 = $1 was extreme, especially for a country which was in near equilibrium. Such a sizable devaluation would, he believed, be apt to bring a considerable reflux of capital, which might well destroy the newly won internal economic stability and might ruin the deflationary efforts of the Government.

The consensus of the Board did not coincide with this view. As had the staff, the Directors reasoned that the inflation which continued in Greece after the devaluation of September 1949 had made the drachma by 1953 again considerably overvalued. Moreover, Greece had had great difficulty in moving its principal exports, even at exchange rates of 20,000 drachmas per U.S. dollar and more. Additionally, Greece was proposing to remove virtually all quantitative restrictions on imports, except for those on some luxury goods. Therefore, the new rate had to be high enough to keep in check the hitherto suppressed import demand which might otherwise emerge. But because of the point made by Mr. de Largentaye, the Board, in its decision, impressed upon the Greek authorities the importance of firm anti-inflationary measures.

In May 1953 Austria similarly proposed a unification of its multiple rates and a devaluation to S 26 = $1. Austria also proposed this rate as an initial par value. Once again Mr. de Largentaye commented that the proposed devaluation was rather severe. He was not convinced that a smaller devaluation would not have been possible: Austria's reserves had doubled in one year, its credit in the EPU had increased, and its exports had been expanding.

The majority of Directors, however, were in favor of sizable devaluation. A new price-wage spiral which had developed after the outbreak of the Korean War had weakened the competitive position of Austria's exports, and the country was liberalizing restrictions.[11]

BOLIVIA AND MEXICO

About the same time Bolivia also proposed a large devaluation of its currency. This was the second change in its par value in three years. Mr. de Largentaye

---

[11] *Annual Report, 1953*, pp. 63–64.

again questioned the size of the devaluation. In his view, the fundamental disequilibrium involved could be corrected by a much smaller devaluation, provided wages and salaries were held at their then-current levels rather than being permitted to rise. However, the Board concurred in the Bolivian proposal on several grounds. The country's exchange earnings had declined, both because of a drop in the price of its main export (tin) from the level reached during the Korean War, and from adjustments in connection with the nationalization of various industries. Meanwhile, import demand had remained high. Bolivia's system of multiple rates had become most complex, and the new devaluation would enable a simplification of the exchange rate structure.

In answer to Mr. de Largentaye, some Directors commented that the devaluation could scarcely be considered excessive when quantitative restrictions were still required. Interestingly enough, at this time some Directors thought that the Fund was not required to pass judgment on the entire stabilization program, but only on the devaluation; it was later that the Fund adopted the policy of assessing the over-all stabilization programs of its members.

Another example of a unitary rate change which seemed to some Directors to be possibly unnecessary or excessive was that of Mexico in 1954. That country proposed a devaluation of 30.8 per cent from its par value, although it had devalued substantially just five years earlier. As in the Icelandic case in 1950, the evidence of a fundamental disequilibrium was not to be found in a falling off of exports. Although the demand for the country's exports had slackened, this was attributable to a decline in world demand and prices.

As the staff pointed out, the more difficult part of Mexico's problem was twofold. First, because of the decline in exports, business conditions had become depressed. The Government wished to neutralize the export decline through compensatory fiscal policies, but without a devaluation such fiscal policies would have tended to place additional pressure on the monetary system and the balance of payments. Second, there had been massive speculative capital outflows—the largest in Mexico's history. The gradual reduction over three years of the country's reserves had impaired Mexico's ability to cope with balance of payments deficits or with recurrent sizable outflows of capital. A foreign exchange crisis had in fact emerged.

To cope with these developments, the country was proposing a devaluation which it expected would restrain imports, give a stimulus to foreign tourist receipts, and encourage an inflow of private investment. Simultaneously, the Government planned to impose a special 25 per cent ad valorem tax on all exports to absorb the windfall profits on exports and to increase government revenues.

Mr. Martínez-Ostos, a former Executive Director, attended the Board meeting as the representative of Mexico. He stressed that his Government was not resorting to this exchange rate depreciation as a competitive device to increase Mexican exports at the expense of other countries. Not only had Mexico always deprecated such practices as unfair, but it considered that competitive depreciation would be self-defeating: competitive depreciation would impair the country's terms of trade without bringing any significant gains in the volume of exports.

The Directors reviewed the reasons why devaluation seemed the only alternative. Since Mexico had relatively small reserves, the peso was susceptible to speculative pressures. Again the point was made that the Mexican authorities wished to avoid exchange controls; they were not certain that such controls could be enforced. These characteristics of Mexico's situation had been impressed upon the Directors in 1948–49, when Mexico had previously devalued the peso. Thus what Mr. Southard referred to as a "premature devaluation" seemed the only solution.

Mr. Southard also commented that he was prepared to accept the judgment of the Mexican authorities about the degree of devaluation required. It had to be large enough to provoke a backflow of capital and to meet the country's needs for some years hence. However, the danger of competitive depreciation in the years ahead was increased, and he reserved the right of the United States to take appropriate action if unfair competition resulted from Mexico's action. After expressing similar concerns, but with a recognition that no alternative was open to Mexico, the Directors took a decision noting the Fund's concurrence with the devaluation.

FEARS OF COMPETITIVE DEPRECIATION THROUGH MULTIPLE RATES

Multiple rates have also given rise to fears of competitive depreciation, especially insofar as they have suggested that certain exports were being subsidized. There was grave concern about this prospect in the middle 1950's, when several countries intensified their use of multiple rates for exports. The intention of these countries was to promote exports at a time when their particular products were encountering stiffer competition in world markets. Early in 1955, Brazil introduced a series of export bonuses and gradually added to the number of its effective exchange rates, eventually ending up with a complex system. Indonesia considerably revised its exchange system in order to assist its exports. Uruguay announced a special premium for exports of wool, including wool tops. Israel devised a system in which export premiums were applied to various commodities on the basis of net domestic value added.

THE STORMS OF THE 1950's

As world export markets in the mid-1950's were becoming increasingly competitive for all countries, the alarm of the Executive Directors from nearly all the major countries at any exchange rates which favored exports became more vocal. Were multiple rates subsidizing the exports of certain countries? How could a subsidy within a multiple rate system, which also included penalty rates, be identified? At one time Mr. Southard, for example, announced that he reserved the right of his Government to impose countervailing duties if export subsidies were found to be involved in new export rates introduced in Brazil. Mr. Warren (Canada), Alternate to Mr. Rasminsky, drew attention to the interest of the GATT, as well as of the Fund, in export measures, because of their commercial aspects.

Requests for the Fund's approval to shift individual commodities from one exchange rate category to another within a complex rate structure were regarded by both the Board and the staff as especially difficult to appraise. The mere fact that the rate for a given export was being devalued did not suggest competitive depreciation. Indeed the Fund, in its informal contacts with members, had been encouraging—or at least not discouraging—countries to alter their exchange rates toward more depreciated rates where exports were not moving satisfactorily and where it appeared likely that a unification of multiple rates would involve further depreciation.

The criterion by which the staff judged a change in an export rate was whether the change was in the direction of an exchange rate at which future unification might take place. If so, no subsidy was considered to be involved; shifting an export to such a rate was really equivalent to reducing an export duty. If, however, a subsidy was involved, the staff was guided by the Board's view that the exchange system was not an appropriate instrument for providing subsidies. Straight budgetary subsidies were usually preferable, as they made clear the costs of the subsidy and avoided misuse of the exchange system.

This anxiety over multiple export rates brought about renewed attempts by the Fund to assist countries to eliminate multiple rates more quickly, and by the late 1950's the number of multiple rates was greatly reduced and the problem of export subsidies—and of possible competitive depreciation via multiple rates—much diminished.[12]

NEW VIEWS IN THE 1960's

A changed climate had emerged by the 1960's. The gravity of the problem faced by the less developed countries in exporting primary products had become more apparent. Empirical evidence had revealed that the exports of the less developed countries had been expanding much less rapidly than those of the industrial countries. During the 1950's, the former had increased at an annual rate of 3.6 per cent; this was only about one-half the rate at which the exports of the industrial countries had advanced. Moreover, since there had been a

[12] See Chapter 6 above, especially pp. 143–44.

deterioration in the terms of trade of the less developed countries, the purchasing power of their exports had risen at an annual rate only slightly above
2 per cent.[13] Trade in primary products had fallen even farther behind that of
manufactured goods. In the three decades between 1928 and 1955–57, the
increase in total world trade of primary commodities had been less than one-third
that in manufactured goods; excluding petroleum, a special case since it is
exported by only a few countries, the growth of world trade in primary products
had amounted to only about one-seventh that in manufactures.[14]

But another factor contributed even more to a new attitude toward the exports
of the less developed countries. This was the growing realization that exports
were the key to successful economic development. Several studies by the
United Nations, the Economic Commission for Latin America, the Economic
Commission for Asia and the Far East, and the World Bank, as well as various
private studies, pointed up a striking correlation between the expansion of
exports of developing countries and the rates of growth of their economies. The
trade and exchange policies of the less developed countries shifted markedly away
from policies which emphasized restriction of imports to those which stressed
stimulation of exports.[15]

There was a parallel change in emphasis away from the policies of individual
countries to the policies of international bodies or of groups of countries acting
in unison. A new general awareness emerged that, except for possible temporary
and unusual circumstances, the problems of expanding the exports of the less
developed countries could be tackled only as a cooperative venture. Various
new exceptions to its rules for the less developed countries were worked out by
the GATT. A United Nations Conference on Trade and Development (UNCTAD)
was held in March 1964 to consider proposals for dealing with their special trade
problems. Shortly thereafter, UNCTAD was set up on a permanent basis to
give continuing attention to the trade problems of these countries. The Fund
itself, in 1963, introduced a new facility known as "compensatory financing," to
provide short-term financial assistance to countries suffering from fluctuations in
exchange receipts from exports of primary products (see Chapter 18).

The widespread search for new ways to promote the exports of the less
developed countries caused some changes in the Fund's policies on exchange
rates, stress being placed on the close relation between realistic rates of
exchange and exports. Where exchange rate flexibility was thought useful and
feasible, countries were encouraged to adjust their exchange rates periodically,
or even, temporarily, to institute fluctuating exchange rates. The widespread
prevalence of inflation had caused Executive Directors to fear that, in the

[13] United Nations, *World Economic Survey, 1961*, p. 7, and *1962*, p. 1.
[14] United Nations, *World Economic Survey, 1958*, pp. 17–18.
[15] For details on these trends see Margaret G. de Vries, "Trade and Exchange Policy and
Economic Development," *Oxford Economic Papers*, Vol. 18 (1966), pp. 19–44.

absence of exchange rate adjustments, domestic price increases would affect exports adversely and shift demand to imports. Increasingly, the Fund placed emphasis on the benefits to exports likely to accrue from exchange depreciation, and by 1965 had come to the view that possibly the most important gain from devaluation was the effect on exports of the realignment of external prices with domestic prices.[16]

Export promotion programs were introduced by a number of countries. In part because of the general world emphasis on the need for developing countries to increase their exports, but probably even more because many developing countries were eliminating multiple rates and devaluing to unitary rates, these export promotional devices no longer occasioned the adverse reactions among Executive Directors that similar schemes in the 1950's had done. And some Directors recognized the usefulness of many of these arrangements: they frequently did give a pronounced fillip to exports.

Nonetheless, the Board continued to be very cognizant of the undesirable consequences of promoting exports through special export schemes or multiple currency practices favoring exports. Indeed, when such arrangements became complex and yielded exchange rates widely different from the par value, the Board urged their elimination. Moreover, export promotion schemes were still regarded as temporary palliatives. The Fund called the attention of its developing members specifically to two more enduring solutions: improving the supply and the quality of their exports by altering resource allocation patterns, and maintaining the competitiveness of their exports.[17] But by the mid-1960's all methods of enlarging the export earnings of the less developed countries were certain to receive serious discussion and consideration by both the Fund staff and the Board.

REVALUATION BY GERMANY AND THE NETHERLANDS

In the early 1960's the exchange rates of two of the major currencies that had been devalued in 1949 were adjusted upward—that is, they were appreciated. On March 4, 1961, Germany proposed to the Board a change in the par value of the deutsche mark from DM 4.20 to DM 4.00 = $1, effective on March 6. Germany argued that it wished to make a useful contribution to the common task of reaching a better equilibrium in international payments. Some steps had already been taken in the monetary field. Moreover, considerable speculative capital had come to Germany. The appreciation of the deutsche mark by 5 per cent—chosen to allow some leeway for internal adjustment—was

---

[16] *Annual Report, 1966,* p. 25.
[17] *Annual Report, 1963,* pp. 71–72.

believed to be sufficient to bring down the current balance of payments surplus, and to cheapen imports so as to offset excessive inflationary tendencies.

Because the change in the value of the currency was less than 10 per cent of the initial par value, and because no previous change had been made in the initial par value, the proposal did not require a decision by the Fund. The Board, however, recorded its view that the move was a useful one because it reflected the improvement in Germany's competitive position.

On March 6, 1961—two days later—the Netherlands Government took a similar decision, to be effective on March 7. As the guilder had already been devalued in 1949 by more than 10 per cent of its initial par value, this change required the approval of the Fund. Mr. Lieftinck (Netherlands) laid stress on the surplus in the Dutch balance of payments on current account and the increased liquidity in the domestic economy. He contended, moreover, that the labor market in particular had become excessively strained by the continuing boom. Before the revaluation of the deutsche mark there had already existed a large and growing discrepancy between the wage levels in the Netherlands and in Germany, resulting in a significant outflow of Dutch workers across the eastern frontier. The Fund accepted the Netherlands' proposal and a new par value of f. 3.62 = $1 was set.

Table 4, at the end of this chapter, presents a chronological list of all changes in par values from 1948 through 1965.

MAGNITUDES OF DEPRECIATION

As shown in the foregoing sections, the years 1948 through 1965 witnessed a number of changes in par values. Briefly, the industrial countries undertook relatively little devaluation of their exchange rates. Of the fourteen members of the Fund classed as industrial countries in 1965, only five altered their exchange rates between September 1949 and the end of 1965.[18] The adjustments of two of these countries—Germany and the Netherlands in March 1961—were appreciations. Austria devalued by stages until 1953. France devalued twice. Canada devalued once, by a small amount, in the course of its return to parity from a fluctuating rate in 1962. (The Canadian dollar had appreciated by some 5 per cent while it was fluctuating.)

However, many less developed countries experienced a greater frequency and degree of exchange depreciation than often is realized. Countries in Africa, Asia, Latin America, and the Middle East undertook several exchange rate adjustments. Among a third group of countries, classed as primary producing but

---

[18] The member countries specified here as industrial are those listed in the *Annual Report, 1967*, p. 55: Austria, Belgium, Canada, Denmark, France, Germany, Italy, Japan, Luxembourg, the Netherlands, Norway, Sweden, the United Kingdom, and the United States.

more developed,[19] exchange devaluation was not uncommon. Finland and Iceland each devalued twice again between 1949 and 1965, and Turkey and Yugoslavia once.

This section presents some measurements of the extent of these devaluations. The focus is on the accumulated magnitudes over a long period of years.

MEASURING THE MAGNITUDES

Percentage changes in the exchange rates for 105 countries for the seventeen years from the end of 1948 to the end of December 1965 are summarized in Table 3. The 105 countries comprise the membership of the Fund at the end

Table 3. Magnitudes of Exchange Depreciation, End 1948 to End 1965:
Distribution of 105 Countries by Degree of Depreciation

(Magnitudes in per cent)

Category [1]	Magnitude of Depreciation	Number of Countries
A	Appreciation	1
B	Zero	10
C	Less than 30.5	14
D	30.5	29
E	31–65	13
F	66–90	28
G	More than 90	10
Total		105

[1] The countries are distributed among the categories as follows (for each category they are listed in order of increasing depreciation, or in alphabetical order where the depreciation was the same for all countries in the group):

A. Lebanon

B. Cuba, Dominican Republic, El Salvador, Guatemala, Haiti, Honduras, Japan, Liberia, Panama, United States

C. Ethiopia, Canada, Italy, Belgium, Luxembourg, Ecuador, Costa Rica, Germany, Syrian Arab Republic, Saudi Arabia, Portugal, Venezuela, Netherlands, Nicaragua

D. Australia, Burma, Ceylon, Cyprus, Denmark, Ghana, Iraq, Ireland, Jamaica, Jordan, Kenya, Kuwait, Libya, Malawi, Malaysia, New Zealand, Nigeria, Norway, Pakistan, Sierra Leone, Somalia, South Africa, Sudan, Sweden, Tanzania, Trinidad and Tobago, Uganda, United Kingdom, Zambia

E. Burundi, United Arab Republic, Nepal, Afghanistan, Philippines, Rwanda, Thailand, India, Iran, France, Austria, Finland, Mexico

F. Turkey, China, Cameroon, Central African Republic, Chad, Dahomey, Gabon, Guinea, Ivory Coast, Malagasy Republic, Mali, Mauritania, Niger, Senegal, Togo, Upper Volta, Viet-Nam, Peru, Algeria, Tunisia, Democratic Republic of Congo, Morocco, Spain, Congo (Brazzaville), Colombia, Greece, Iceland, Laos

G. Israel, Yugoslavia, Uruguay, Paraguay, Argentina, Chile, Brazil, Bolivia, Indonesia, Korea

[19] Australia, Finland, Greece, Iceland, Ireland, New Zealand, Portugal, South Africa, Spain, Turkey, and Yugoslavia.

of 1965 plus Cuba and Indonesia, which were Fund members during part of the period. As a starting date, the end of 1948 has been preferred to an earlier postwar date (that is, the end of 1945, or of 1946, when the Fund set initial parities for its original members) because the exchange rates of several countries were more settled by that year (or by early in 1949) than they were immediately after World War II. Moreover, data for 1948 are readily available.[20]

Because the results depend on the particular exchange rate used, and because in some instances (e.g., for countries with multiple exchange rates) there was a choice of rates, an endeavor has been made to select exchange rates that were currently used for most transactions. For most countries par values, or at least fixed official rates, could be used for both initial and end years. For other countries, a free market rate or one of the multiple rates was used for either the initial or end year, and in some instances midpoints among multiple rates were used. Table 5, at the end of this chapter, specifies which rates were used for each country.

Exchange rate changes were measured relative to gold; that is, with the initial period as the base, the percentage was calculated of the change in the exchange rate expressed in terms of grams of fine gold per local currency unit. This is the customary Fund way of measuring exchange rate changes: it produces, for example, the familiar 30.5 per cent devaluation of the pound sterling in September 1949. Measured in this way, 100 per cent is the maximum that a currency can depreciate. Inasmuch as the gold content of the U.S. dollar has remained unchanged, measurements relative to gold are, of course, identical with measurements relative to the U.S. dollar.

How much depreciation?

In Table 3 the countries covered are distributed over seven categories according to the degree of their exchange depreciation from the end of 1948 to the end of 1965. In Lebanon a slight appreciation occurred. Group B comprises 10 countries which did not devalue at all: the United States, 7 Central American countries, Liberia, and Japan.[21] Group C comprises 14 countries that devalued less than 30.5 per cent—that is, less than the amount by which sterling was devalued in September 1949; in this group are several industrial nations (Belgium, Canada, Germany, Italy, Luxembourg, and the Netherlands), 4 Latin American countries (Costa Rica, Ecuador, Nicaragua, and Venezuela), and Ethiopia, Portugal, Saudi Arabia, and the Syrian Arab Republic. Germany and the Netherlands, after depreciating by approximately 30 per cent in September 1949, both appreciated their currencies by 5 per cent in 1961.

[20] The annual supplement to *International Financial Statistics* regularly presents series beginning with 1948.

[21] Japan's official rate was set in April 1949, and has since remained unaltered.

Group D comprises 29 countries which devalued by 30.5 per cent in September 1949, or (Pakistan) some years later. These countries are mainly those of the sterling area, plus Denmark, Norway, and Sweden.

What is often not fully realized is that for 50 countries (groups E, F, and G), the magnitude of exchange depreciation in these years exceeded 30 per cent. Thirteen countries devalued by between 31 and 65 per cent; these included Austria, Finland, France, India, Mexico, and the Philippines. For another 28 countries devaluation ranged from 66 to 90 per cent. Among European countries in this group were Greece, Iceland, Spain, and Turkey. Other countries devaluing by these large amounts were two Latin American countries (Colombia and Peru), much of the French franc area of Africa, and Viet-Nam. Finally, there were 10 countries—6 Latin American countries plus Indonesia, Israel, Korea, and Yugoslavia—for which depreciation exceeded 90 per cent.

Developed countries, even in Europe, are distributed among all the five groups C through G. Among less developed countries two patterns of depreciation are apparent. One follows that of the major currencies. Countries in Central America conformed generally to the U.S. dollar and devalued either not at all or very little. Many others in Asia and Africa followed the lead of either sterling or the French franc. The second pattern was related to the price and balance of payments experiences of the individual country. Quite a number of countries, in all geographic regions, devalued independently of the major currencies, by from 40 to nearly 100 per cent.[22]

THE FUND AS A PARTICIPATOR

The role of the Fund in exchange rate adjustments has grown appreciably over the years. By 1965 the Board could, as it discussed a member's economic situation, consider the exchange rate without setting off the same touchy debates among Directors about the Fund's jurisdiction as had characterized 1948 and 1949. Individual Directors had become less desirous of defining the precise limits of the Fund's authority in this field.

This change in attitude had come about mainly because Fund-member relations in general had grown easier. One of the primary benefits of the annual consultations, begun in 1952, was that the Fund and its members learned how to talk to each other informally and quietly about a range of topics of mutual concern (see Chapter 11). In addition, precedents had gradually been set for the inclusion in Board decisions of sentences relating to exchange rates. When the atmosphere first tended to become more relaxed—about the mid-1950's—decisions merely reminded countries to keep their exchange policies under

---

[22] Further details can be found in Margaret G. de Vries, "Exchange Depreciation in Developing Countries," *Staff Papers*, Vol. XV (1968), pp. 560–78.

review. But individual Directors went so far as to note freely at Board meetings that they considered certain currencies overvalued, or at least questionable. Later, increasingly stronger sentences were incorporated into decisions. It became commonplace for decisions to contain phrases urging countries to adopt more realistic exchange rates or policies which would permit unification of multiple rates at realistic levels. In one instance in 1964 the Board went so far as to comment explicitly, in its decision, on the overvaluation of the currency of a member and its unrealistic exchange rate.

Some Directors have continued to be fearful that the Fund might overstep its bounds. A few, for instance, have questioned the propriety of inserting in a decision any exhortations to a country to correct a growing disparity between external and internal prices, or have wanted to know precisely the precedents for inclusion of the term overvaluation in decisions. As time has gone on, however, anxieties over the Fund's jurisdiction in exchange rate matters have tended to diminish. This lessening of the sensitivities of the Executive Directors, and in effect of the members they represented, concerning the Fund's role in deliberations of exchange rate policy, also had implications for the work of the staff. Staff discussions with authorities in member countries could increasingly include consideration of exchange rate policies. Over time the staff has undertaken informally to explore with members the need for exchange rate adjustment or the likely consequences of devaluation, and, at times, even to suggest specific exchange reforms. Nonetheless, both the staff and the Board have proceeded cautiously in these matters, mindful both of the paramount need for secrecy concerning possible exchange rate changes and of members' prerogatives in this field.

By the 1960's, a more serious problem for the Fund than that of immediate jurisdiction was the onset of new debates about exchange rates in general. To many economists, countries seemed to be eschewing devaluation. The experience of the Fund had revealed a variety of reasons why, since World War II, countries often avoided or at least postponed devaluation. Domestic political resistance to reductions in the external values of currencies, especially if elections were to be held in the near future, was a factor. In a world of general inflation, the danger of further price advances following devaluation was another. Authorities were often preoccupied with the effects of devaluation on the prices of imported goods, and hence on the cost of living. There was also a strong apprehension that, where the country was an important supplier to world markets, and where the demand for its exports was inelastic, devaluation would lower world market prices and yet not enhance the country's export earnings.

The environment in which the Fund operated in the 1960's was made even more complex by the re-examination of questions central to the operation of the international monetary system. What was the mechanism by which balance of payments adjustment took place? Could fundamental disequilibrium be corrected by a change in the exchange rate? Had it not been demonstrated that policies of several kinds—exchange rate, monetary, fiscal, and, more recently, incomes policies—worked together to alter a given balance of payments situation? What was the appropriate "policy mix" for attaining external equilibrium? What was the function of international capital flows in balance of payments adjustment? Were capital movements equilibrating, as had once been thought, or disequilibrating? Finally, new proposals were being advanced for enhancing the liquidity of the international monetary system.

In this climate, steering between the Scylla of taking upon itself the initiative that rightfully belongs to its members, and the Charybdis of ignoring exchange rate adjustment as a vital policy tool, was not easy for the Fund. Indeed, the passive role in exchange rate changes assigned to the Fund, and the continued sensitivities of several members, had the result that, in the midst of the crucial concerns of the middle 1960's—the balance of payments deficits of major nations and the problem of international liquidity—the Board had not, by the end of 1965, discussed the general role of exchange rates in balance of payments adjustment.

Table 4. Changes in Par Values, 1948–65 [1]

Date [2]	Country	Change in Par Value
1948		
Jan. 26	France	Initial par value suspended
July 22	Mexico	Initial par value suspended
Dec. 17	Colombia	Par value changed to 51.2825 U.S. cents per peso
1949		
June 17	Mexico	New par value set at 11.5607 U.S. cents per peso
Sept. 18	Australia	Par value changed to 224.000 U.S. cents per pound
Sept. 18	Denmark	Par value changed to 14.4778 U.S. cents per krone
Sept. 18	Norway	Par value changed to 14.0000 U.S. cents per krone
Sept. 18	South Africa	Par value changed to 280.000 U.S. cents per pound
Sept. 18	Egypt	Par value changed to 287.156 U.S. cents per pound
Sept. 18	United Kingdom	Par value changed to 280.000 U.S. cents per pound
Sept. 19	Canada	Par value changed to 90.9091 U.S. cents per dollar
Sept. 20	Iraq	Par value changed to 280.000 U.S. cents per dinar

Footnotes on page 118.

Table 4 *(continued).* Changes in Par Values, 1948–65 [1]

Date [2]	Country	Change in Par Value
Sept. 21	Iceland	Par value changed to 10.7054 U.S. cents per króna
Sept. 21	Netherlands	Par value changed to 26.3158 U.S. cents per guilder
Sept. 22	Belgium	Par value changed to 2.00000 U.S. cents per franc
Sept. 22	Luxembourg	Par value changed to 2.00000 U.S. cents per franc
Sept. 22	India	Par value changed to 21.0000 U.S. cents per rupee
Nov. 15	Peru	Par value suspended
1950		
Mar. 20	Iceland	Par value changed to 6.14036 U.S. cents per króna
Apr. 8	Bolivia	Par value changed to 1.66667 U.S. cents per boliviano
Sept. 30	Canada	Par value suspended
Dec. 1	Ecuador	Par value changed to 6.66667 U.S. cents per sucre
1951		
Mar. 5	Paraguay	Par value changed to 16.6667 U.S. cents per guaraní
1952		
Jan. 1	Yugoslavia	Par value changed to 0.33333 U.S. cent per dinar
1953		
May 14	Bolivia	Par value changed to 0.52632 U.S. cent per boliviano
Oct. 5	Chile	Par value changed to 0.90909 U.S. cent per peso
1954		
Jan. 1	Paraguay	Par value changed to 6.66667 U.S. cents per guaraní
Apr. 19	Mexico	Par value changed to 8.00000 U.S. cents per peso
Aug. 18	Paraguay	Par value changed to 4.76190 U.S. cents per guaraní
1955		
July 1	Nicaragua	Par value changed to 14.2857 U.S. cents per córdoba
July 30	Pakistan	Par value changed to 21.0000 U.S. cents per rupee
1956		
Mar. 1	Paraguay	Par value changed to 1.66667 U.S. cents per guaraní

Table 4 *(concluded).* Changes in Par Values, 1948–65 [1]

Date [2]	Country	Change in Par Value
1957		
May 22	Iran	Par value changed to 1.32013 U.S. cents per rial
Sept. 15	Finland	Par value changed to 0.31250 U.S. cent per markka
1958		
Dec. 29	France	New par value set at 0.20255 U.S. cent per franc
1960		
Jan. 1	France	Par value changed to 20.2550 U.S. cents per (new) franc
Feb. 22	Iceland	Par value changed to 2.63158 U.S. cents per króna
Aug. 20	Turkey	Par value changed to 11.1111 U.S. cents per lira
1961		
Feb. 14	South Africa	Par value changed to 140.000 U.S. cents per rand
Mar. 6	Germany	Par value changed to 25.0000 U.S. cents per deutsche mark
Mar. 7	Netherlands	Par value changed to 27.6243 U.S. cents per guilder
July 14	Ecuador	Par value changed to 5.55556 U.S. cents per sucre
Aug. 4	Iceland	Par value changed to 2.32558 U.S. cents per króna
Sept. 3	Costa Rica	Par value changed to 15.0943 U.S. cents per colón
1962		
Feb. 9	Israel	Par value changed to 33.3333 U.S. cents per pound
May 2	Canada	New par value set at 92.5000 U.S. cents per dollar
1963		
Jan. 1	Finland	Par value changed to 31.2500 U.S. cents per (new) markka
Dec. 31	Ethiopia	Par value changed to 40.0000 U.S. cents per dollar
1965		
July 26	Yugoslavia	Par value changed to 0.080000 U.S. cent per dinar
Nov. 8	Philippines	Par value changed to 25.6410 U.S. cents per peso

[1] Excludes nonmetropolitan territories.

[2] Dates specified are those on which the change took effect, which is not necessarily the same date on which the change was agreed with the Fund.

Table 5. Exchange Rates Used in Table 3

Country	1948 [1]	1965
1. Afghanistan	Free	Free
2. Algeria	Official	Official
3. Argentina	Free	Free
4. Australia	Par value	Par value
5. Austria	Official	Par value
6. Belgium	Par value	Par value
7. Bolivia	Par value	Free
8. Brazil	Free	Free
9. Burma	Par value	Par value
10. Burundi	Official	Par value
11. Cameroon	Official	Official
12. Canada	Par value	Par value
13. Central African Republic	Official	Official
14. Ceylon	Official	Par value
15. Chad	Official	Official
16. Chile	Free	Free
17. China	Official	Official
18. Colombia	Free	Free
19. Congo (Brazzaville)	Official	Official
20. Congo, Democratic Republic	Par value	Official
21. Costa Rica	Par value	Par value
22. Cuba	Par value	Official
23. Cyprus	Par value	Par value
24. Dahomey	Official	Official
25. Denmark	Par value	Par value
26. Dominican Republic	Par value	Par value
27. Ecuador	Official [2]	Official [2]
28. El Salvador	Par value	Par value
29. Ethiopia	Par value	Par value
30. Finland	Official	Par value
31. France	Official	Par value
32. Gabon	Official	Official
33. Germany	Official	Par value
34. Ghana	Par value	Par value
35. Greece	Official	Par value
36. Guatemala	Par value	Par value
37. Guinea	Official	Official
38. Haiti	Official	Par value
39. Honduras	Par value	Par value
40. Iceland	Par value	Par value
41. India	Par value	Par value
42. Indonesia	Free	Free
43. Iran	Par value	Par value
44. Iraq	Par value	Par value
45. Ireland	Official	Par value

Footnotes on page 121.

Table 5 *(continued).* Exchange Rates Used in Table 3

Country	1948 [1]	1965
46. Israel	Official	Par value
47. Italy	Official	Par value
48. Ivory Coast	Official	Official
49. Jamaica	Par value	Par value
50. Japan	Official [3]	Par value
51. Jordan	Official	Par value
52. Kenya	Par value	Par value
53. Korea	Official	Official
54. Kuwait	Official	Par value
55. Laos	Official	Free
56. Lebanon	Free	Free
57. Liberia	Official	Par value
58. Libya	Official	Par value
59. Luxembourg	Par value	Par value
60. Malagasy Republic	Official	Official
61. Malawi	Par value	Par value
62. Malaysia	Par value	Par value
63. Mali	Official	Official
64. Mauritania	Official	Official
65. Mexico	Par value	Par value
66. Morocco	Official	Par value
67. Nepal	Official	Par value
68. Netherlands	Par value	Par value
69. New Zealand	Official	Par value
70. Nicaragua	Par value	Par value
71. Niger	Official	Official
72. Nigeria	Par value	Par value
73. Norway	Par value	Par value
74. Pakistan	Official	Par value
75. Panama	Par value	Par value
76. Paraguay	Free	Free
77. Peru	Principal	Free
78. Philippines	Par value	Par value
79. Portugal	Official	Par value
80. Rwanda	Official	Par value
81. Saudi Arabia	Official	Par value
82. Senegal	Official	Official
83. Sierra Leone	Par value	Par value
84. Somalia	Official	Par value
85. South Africa	Par value	Par value
86. Spain	Official	Par value
87. Sudan	Official	Par value
88. Sweden	Official	Par value
89. Syrian Arab Republic	Free	Free
90. Tanzania	Par value	Par value

Table 5 *(concluded).* Exchange Rates Used in Table 3

Country	1948 [1]	1965
91. Thailand	Official	Par value
92. Togo	Official	Official
93. Trinidad and Tobago	Par value	Par value
94. Tunisia	Official	Par value
95. Turkey	Par value	Par value
96. Uganda	Par value	Par value
97. United Arab Republic	Par value	Official
98. United Kingdom	Par value	Par value
99. United States	Par value	Par value
100. Upper Volta	Official	Official
101. Uruguay	Free	Free
102. Venezuela	Non-oil exports	Non-oil exports
103. Viet-Nam	Principal	Free
104. Yugoslavia	Official	Par value
105. Zambia	Par value	Par value

Sources: *International Financial Statistics,* monthly issues and Supplement to 1966–67 issues; and *Annual Report on Exchange Restrictions,* various years.

[1] For some members the par values used here were those that had been established for them while they were nonmetropolitan areas.

[2] Selling rate.

[3] 1949.

CHAPTER

6

Multiple Exchange Rates

Margaret G. de Vries

 ULTIPLE EXCHANGE RATES were one of the first problems that faced the Fund in 1946, and have probably been its most common problem in the field of exchange rates. An impressive number and diversity of countries in the last twenty years have experimented with one form or another of what the Fund has called *multiple currency practices*, at least for a few, if not for most, of their transactions.[1] And, although the use of such practices has been much reduced in recent years, a succession of countries that had not previously tried multiple rates has been experimenting with them. In the mid-1960's, some new suggestions for multiple exchange rates were put forward. Economists, especially those outside official circles, have continued to propose exchange rate schemes as a means of assisting primary producing countries. Moreover, a few have suggested that subsidies-cum-tariffs—in a sense a form of multiple rates—or two exchange rates, one a floating rate for capital, might be possible compromises between fixed and fluctuating rates for the industrialized nations. The problem of multiple rates, then, never seems entirely at an end.

THE BACKGROUND

THE INTERWAR PERIOD

Multiple rates originated in the exchange control mechanisms of the 1930's. First used by Germany in 1934 in dealings with its bilateral agreement partners, multiple rates allowed considerably more exchange rate manipulation than did

---

[1] The established technical term of the Fund for any multiple rate is *multiple currency practice*. In what follows, the terms *multiple exchange rate* and *multiple currency practice* are used interchangeably.

ordinary clearing agreements with a fixed exchange rate.[2] German exports to a particular country could enjoy the benefits of sudden exchange depreciation. Through such devices, Germany succeeded in expanding its trade with certain countries in southeastern Europe and with a number of Latin American countries, especially those which had their own exchange controls, for example, Brazil, Chile, and Peru. Brazil's imports from Germany rose from 13 per cent of its total imports in 1929 to 25 per cent in 1938, and its exports to Germany rose from 9 per cent to 19 per cent. In the same period, Peru's imports from Germany rose from 10 per cent to 20 per cent of the total.[3] Although Germany's methods met with increasing resistance, Latin American countries tended to encourage bilateral transactions with Germany, even at unfavorable exchange rates, when raw material prices were low and exports to free exchange countries were depressed.

Multiple rates also began to be employed by other countries during the Great Depression. After 1932, the majority of European countries with exchange controls resorted eventually to some form of currency devaluation. Although some countries, like Czechoslovakia and Italy, devalued in one step, other countries passed through a period of gradual depreciation, usually through the use of multiple rates. Black markets developed, and later became legal free markets: Austria, Hungary, Yugoslavia, and Rumania were among the countries in Europe which, after a time, gave official recognition to black markets and thus to the multiple exchange rates prevailing in them.

Several Latin American countries similarly embarked on programs of multiple rates, essentially as exchange control devices. The purposes in Latin America, however, differed from those in Europe in two respects. Although the initial purpose of exchange controls in Europe was to control capital movements, this was taken less seriously in Latin America: several countries there permitted capital transactions through free markets. Secondly, in Latin America one of the main objectives of differentiated rates of exchange was to secure, at preferential rates, foreign exchange to service the government debt. Exchange depreciation had increased the cost of this service in terms of domestic currency, and the compulsory surrender of part of export proceeds at official rates operated in effect as a special tax to meet that cost. The obligation of exporters to surrender exchange receipts was sometimes confined to one or a few of the chief export products, to make it easier to enforce. In European countries, on the other

[2] Further details of the interwar experiences with multiple rates can be found in Margaret S. Gordon, *Barriers to World Trade*, Chapters V and VII; and in League of Nations, *International Currency Experience*. A detailed description of European exchange controls in the interwar period is in Howard S. Ellis, *Exchange Control in Central Europe*. League of Nations, *Report on Exchange Control*, briefly examines the economic effects of exchange controls, especially on the domestic economies of the countries concerned.

[3] League of Nations, *World Economic Survey, 1938/39*, p. 202.

hand, generally because of their creditor status, debt service was not an important stimulus to exchange control.

What precipitated international concern about these practices was that the trend in most countries with multiple rates was toward discrimination. The discrimination was seldom explicit. More often the allocation of foreign exchange among different countries became subject to administrative discretion, and in these circumstances some form of discrimination, or "preferential allotment," became virtually inevitable. The objective of discrimination was usually to evade the most-favored-nation clause of trade agreements and to force trade into bilateral channels.

Free exchange countries, therefore, when concluding trade agreements with exchange control countries, frequently insisted on the insertion of various formulas to ensure a "fair and equitable share" in any allotment of foreign exchange. However, because such formulas were difficult to prescribe in such a way as to give real equality of treatment, most of them had in practice little real meaning.

MULTIPLE RATES AT BRETTON WOODS

Against this background the delegations at Bretton Woods treated multiple currency practices in the same way as they treated quantitative exchange restrictions. In the Keynes Plan no specific mention had been made of multiple currency practices. But in the White Plan, one of the stated purposes of the Fund was

> 5. To reduce the use of such foreign exchange restrictions, bilateral clearing arrangements, multiple currency devices, and discriminatory foreign exchange practices as hamper world trade and the international flow of productive capital.[4]

Clause IX of the *Joint Statement by Experts on the Establishment of an International Monetary Fund*, paragraphs 2 and 3, under the heading The Obligations of Member Countries, contained statements to the effect that each member country is

> 2. Not to allow exchange transactions in its market in currencies of other members at rates outside a prescribed range based on the agreed parities.
>
> 3. Not to impose restrictions on payments for current international transactions with other member countries (other than those involving capital transfers or in accordance with VI, above) or to engage in any discriminatory currency arrangements or multiple currency practices without the approval of the Fund.[5]

"VI, above" referred to the provisions for allocating a scarce currency.

In June 1944, the scope of these provisions was interpreted by the U.S. Treasury in *Questions and Answers on the International Monetary Fund.* Ques-

---

[4] Vol. III below, p. 86.
[5] Vol. III below, p. 135.

tion 20 was: Would differential rates of exchange for different classes of imports and exports (visible and invisible) be permitted by the Fund? The answer suggested that what was considered most objectionable in multiple currency practices was the uses to which such devices might be put, rather than the multiplicity of rates itself. Multiple rates should be avoided because they might so easily become the means for discrimination in trade relationships, and because they usually involved control of the exchanges so complete as to offer a strong temptation to restrict transactions on current account. Nonetheless, it was made clear that, conceivably, the Fund might decide that a member's multiple currency practices did not conflict with the principles of the Fund. Moreover, where conflict did occur, the Fund would allow adequate time for the abolition of multiple currency practices.[6]

As finally drafted, Article VIII of the Articles of Agreement obliges members (Section 2 (a)) not to "impose restrictions on the making of payments and transfers for current international transactions," nor (Section 3) to

> engage in, or permit any of its fiscal agencies . . . to engage in, any discriminatory currency arrangements or multiple currency practices except as authorized under this Agreement or approved by the Fund. If such arrangements and practices are engaged in at the date when this Agreement enters into force the member concerned shall consult with the Fund as to their progressive removal unless they are maintained or imposed under Article XIV, Section 2, in which case the provisions of Section 4 of that Article, shall apply.

Article XIV makes no explicit reference to multiple currency practices.

PREVALENCE OF MULTIPLE RATES IN 1946

By the time the Fund was organized, multiple rates were in use not only in the six countries of Latin America that had used them during the 1930's (Argentina, Brazil, Chile, Ecuador, Peru, and Venezuela), but also in Bolivia, Colombia, Costa Rica, Nicaragua, and Uruguay; and Cuba and Honduras had introduced small exchange taxes that had somewhat the same effect as multiple rates.[7] The use of multiple rates in Iran suggested that the problem might not remain confined to Latin America.

The countries adopting multiple currency practices had problems which did not seem to be solvable in any other way. Mr. (now Professor) Robert Triffin, then with the Board of Governors of the Federal Reserve System, had in fact, when helping a number of Latin American countries to overhaul their monetary, exchange control, and banking systems, suggested policies which, in his own

---

[6] Vol. III below, pp. 160–61.

[7] Argentina was not an original Fund member; the other Latin American countries mentioned were.

words, were "highly unorthodox . . . for the newly born International Monetary Fund." [8]

The problem to which Mr. Triffin was seeking a solution was that of a primary producing country facing balance of payments disequilibrium due to a cyclically depressed world market for raw materials or for its own particular exports. This situation, in which over-all exchange depreciation was regarded as ineffective, was distinguished from that of fundamental disequilibrium, where an over-all exchange rate adjustment was required. For the cyclical problem, Mr. Triffin advocated two markets—a normal market and an "auction" market. Exchange proceeds from exports or other easily controllable sources would be channeled into the normal market, and be available for essential imports and current invisibles. Exchange proceeds from less controllable transactions, such as capital movements, would be sold in a free or "auction" market; purchasers could use these proceeds to make payments for nonessential imports or for outgoing capital. Such a dual exchange system would, Mr. Triffin argued, prevent the emergence of a black market and the need for administrative allocations, and would provide an escape valve: capital movements could take place without upsetting the markets or rates for normal transactions. [9]

These arguments were not merely theoretical; they expressed the objectives of countries' actual policies. They explained, for example, the initial establishment of multiple rates in Argentina and of dual markets in several other countries, e.g., Chile, Costa Rica, Ecuador, and Paraguay.

THE FUND'S POLICIES INAUGURATED (1946–51)

INITIAL QUESTIONS FOR THE FUND

When the Fund opened its doors, 13 of its 39 members were using multiple exchange rates. Specific questions began to arise almost immediately. Even before concluding membership formalities, Venezuela (in September 1946) asked for assurance from the Fund that adherence to the Articles would not prevent it from taking a suitable period to eliminate its multiple currency practices. When the establishment of initial par values was considered at the end of 1946, the question arose as to what rates could be used as par values where multiple rates existed. When, in the early months of 1947, the Fund asked countries to state whether or not they were going to take advantage of the transitional arrangements, the significance of multiple rates again came to the fore. Cuba indicated that it would avail itself of the transitional arrangements primarily because of its small exchange tax.

---

[8] Robert Triffin, *The World Money Maze*, p. 141.

[9] *Ibid.*, pp. 142–77.

Questions of definition hampered consideration of these practices. What precisely constituted a multiple currency practice under the Fund Agreement? Could the small exchange taxes of Cuba and Honduras be so defined? Did an unusually large difference between the effective buying and selling rates for a currency constitute a multiple currency practice? Were multiple currency practices to be regarded as a restriction and therefore subject to the Fund's transitional arrangements, or were these practices to be considered solely as exchange rates?

More basic were questions pertaining to the Fund's authority in this field. Could a member maintaining a multiple currency practice under the transitional arrangements introduce a new multiple rate without Fund approval? Could a member with a multiple currency practice change the classifications of commodities subject to different multiple rates without prior consultation with the Fund? Could a member which did not have any multiple currency practices, but which took advantage of the transitional arrangements, introduce a multiple currency practice without the Fund's approval?

Important questions of policy also had to be answered: What was the economic significance of these practices? What should be the Fund's attitude toward the multiple rates already in existence? Under what conditions might these rates be temporarily retained? What should be the view of the Fund toward new practices?

THE DECEMBER 1947 LETTER

During its first year, the Fund studied these questions at great length. It was evident from a review of individual country situations in 1947 that the extent of multiple currency practices warranted early discussion between members and the Fund as well; the Board agreed that most of these discussions should be held in the territory of the members concerned.

In order that a detailed examination could be made of the economic, legal, and procedural issues raised by all the questions on multiple rates, the Board set up an Ad Hoc Committee on Spreads and Multiple Currency Practices in the middle of 1947. The members of the committee were Mr. Mládek (Czechoslovakia), Chairman; Mr. Bruins (Netherlands); Mr. Joshi (India); Mr. Luthringer (United States), Alternate to Mr. Overby; and Mr. Martínez-Ostos (Mexico), Alternate to Mr. Gómez. This committee held many meetings and undertook a careful assessment of the extent of the multiple rate problem, of the Fund's powers in this field, and of possible policies. In its report to the Board the committee urged moderation in the Fund's approach to multiple rates. It emphasized that the Fund was especially interested in multiple rates because they were not simply restrictive practices but rates of exchange as well, and hence could be a primary source of exchange instability. Exchange rate stability, the report stressed, was one of the Fund's main objectives. In order to make a start toward this objective the Fund had already, late in 1946, decided to set initial par values. While the mere existence of multiple exchange rates might not endanger exchange stability, frequent changes and extensions of such rates could well undermine the whole par value system. Moreover, multiple rates might also endanger the Fund's objective of the avoidance of competitive depreciation.

A multiple currency practice was defined as any practice which, as a result of official action, gives rise to an effective buying or selling rate differing from the par value by more than 1 per cent. Such a practice was explicitly recognized to include any of a series of fixed exchange rates, exchange taxes, exchange surcharges, free markets, and auction systems. Although on several future occasions debates were to occur between a member and the Fund, and even within the Fund, as to whether particular exchange systems did in fact constitute multiple currency practices, this definition proved to be sufficiently comprehensive to cover the vast majority of cases for the next twenty years.

After deliberation, the Board adopted the committee's recommendations unanimously. It agreed with the committee that the Fund had broad powers over the introduction of new practices and the adaptation of old ones, even during the transitional period; and decided that member countries should, as a minimum, consult the Fund before introducing a multiple currency practice, before making any change in a multiple exchange rate, before reclassifying transactions subject to different rates, and before making any other significant change in their exchange systems.

The Board also spelled out the policies to be followed. It recommended that early steps should be taken toward the removal of multiple currency practices that were not necessary for balance of payments reasons, although ample time should be provided for members to take these steps and to install appropriate substitutes where necessary. The Fund would encourage members engaging in multiple currency practices for balance of payments reasons to establish, as soon as possible, conditions which would permit the removal of these practices, with the general objective of seeking this removal not later than the end of the transitional period. Where complete removal by the end of the transitional period proved impossible, the Fund would assist the members concerned to eliminate the most dangerous aspects of their multiple currency practices and to exercise reasonable control over those retained.

As a consequence, there was circulated to the members in December 1947 a letter and memorandum outlining the Fund's powers and policies in the matter of multiple rates. This letter and memorandum, which together came to be known as "the December 1947 letter on multiple currency practices," [10] laid

---

[10] Reproduced below, Vol. III, pp. 262–65.

the basis for relations with members in this field, although there have subsequently been modifications in the policies and procedures which it set forth.

A few Directors had had some difficulty with the terms of the letter.
Mr. de Largentaye (France), among other points of disagreement, was of the
opinion that members which had been occupied by the enemy and which were
availing themselves of Article XIV could independently (i.e., without authorization from the Fund) introduce and modify multiple currency practices. In his
view, such a member's only obligation was to consult the Fund. And this
obligation did not mean that the Fund could object. Some weeks later (in
January 1948) this difference of opinion led to the vexing difficulties between
France and the Fund described below.

Mr. Martínez-Ostos, while not disagreeing with the committee's conclusions,
pointed out two factors not mentioned in its analysis which he thought would
have to be taken into consideration when specific courses of action were considered: the importance of the monetary management (nontrade) functions of
multiple rates, and the negligible amount of world trade conducted by a few
Latin American countries which maintained multiple rates.

It is noteworthy, in retrospect, that despite the importance that other Executive
Directors attached to exchange rate stability *during* as well as *after* the transitional period, Mr. Martínez-Ostos stressed at this time that fixed multiple rates
were not to be preferred over multiple rate systems with a floating rate (that is,
a fluctuating or free market rate). He believed the opposite: since floating rates
did not freeze particular rates into the economy, members would have less
difficulty in moving to a single rate later on. Thus, floating rate mechanisms
tended to be self-liquidating. This point is the more memorable because some
ten years later, as noted below, this was to be the road by which many members
were to move to unitary rates and a gradual change in Fund policy became
necessary.

DISAGREEMENT WITH FRANCE

Immediately after the December 1947 letter—that is, in January 1948—the
first example of a multiple currency practice was brought to the Board and led
to disagreement with a major member. France proposed a devaluation of the
franc from 119.107 francs to 214.392 francs per U.S. dollar. In addition, France
proposed a free market for certain convertible currencies—namely, U.S. dollars
and Portuguese escudos; Swiss francs were added subsequently.

The French authorities were willing to maintain orderly cross rates between
all inconvertible currencies and between all convertible currencies. Thus, there
would be only one case of disorderly cross rates—between the official rates of
all currencies and the free rates of the convertible currencies. Mr. de Largentaye
adduced two arguments in support of the French proposal. Legally, Article XIV,

Section 2, permitted France, as an enemy-occupied country, to introduce a multiple currency practice. Economically, the free market in certain currencies would help to meet the deficit in the French balance of payments. A premium on exports to the dollar area would encourage such exports, while the penalty on dollar imports would encourage the substitution of European imports for dollar imports. In addition, the repatriation of French assets held abroad would be encouraged, and tourist receipts and other invisibles would be diverted from black markets into a legal free market.

The Executive Directors objected to the free market. In the first place, they thought that it was an introduction of a multiple currency practice which was not necessary to achieve the trade objectives sought by France. In the second place, many Directors thought that the free market would be liable to have adverse effects on other members. There would be scope for competitive depreciation. Trade could be distorted by French traders purchasing goods in soft currency areas and selling them for hard currencies. France would be able to buy raw materials for soft currencies and sell finished goods for dollars, thereby giving French manufactures a substantial price advantage. This would hamper the eventual achievement of multilateral trade.

As an alternative to its proposal, France was prepared to institute a free market for all currencies, but this was also objected to by the Fund, as in effect destroying the whole system of fixed and stable par values. The Directors proposed that the free market should be limited to nontrade transactions, but this was not acceptable to the French authorities. A considerable effort was made by the Executive Directors to work out some alternative acceptable to all countries, but without success. France proceeded with its measures, and the Fund declared France ineligible to use its resources.

These difficulties between the Fund and France were, however, short-lived. In October 1948 France made changes in its exchange system which restored orderly cross rates for trade transactions. In September 1949, following the devaluation of sterling, the French Government consulted the Fund on a proposal to unify its exchange system at the exchange rate for the U.S. dollar prevailing in the free market—350 francs per U.S. dollar—which involved a further depreciation of the franc against the dollar. The Fund welcomed the modifications proposed by the French Government. Between September 20, 1949 and May 1950, the range of fluctuation in the franc-dollar rate was less than 0.3 per cent. Thus France had introduced a stable unitary exchange rate, although not a new par value.

IMPLEMENTING THE DECEMBER 1947 LETTER

In the next few years, a flood of multiple exchange rates was proposed for consideration and action by the Executive Board. There were, for example, some twenty occasions in 1948 and some twenty-five in 1949 on which broad changes in their exchange systems were proposed by members, and several smaller changes of rates or shifts of commodities from one rate to another.

Ways of implementing the general policies laid down in the December 1947 letter had to be worked out to deal with individual cases. Formulas had to be found for approving or disapproving specific practices. In addition, some procedure had to be developed for dealing with countries—although these were a minority—which did not consult the Fund at all.

The member's action in one or two instances seemed almost like deliberate flouting of the Fund. But in most cases the lack of consultation was due to misunderstanding. Changes were sometimes made after informal discussion with the staff, or after a visit to the member country of a staff mission, which the member had regarded as "consulting" the Fund. Other changes represented progress toward a unitary rate structure, and some members believed that steps of this sort should not be subject to prior consultation and approval. In instances of nonconsultation, the Directors either communicated with the member in an informal way, calling the member's attention to its obligations and requesting an explanation, or took a decision drawing the member's attention to the need for prior consultation.

A question related to nonconsultation arose where the member did not allow adequate time for the Fund to consider a measure before it went into effect: What constitutes effective consultation? In December 1949, the Board sent a letter to all members carefully explaining the need for time for the staff to prepare economic and legal analyses, as well as time for consideration by the Executive Directors, and specifically requesting members to notify the Fund at least seven days before multiple rate changes were to go into effect.

From time to time the details of a particular practice had to be examined by both the economic and the legal staff in order to determine whether or not a multiple currency practice as defined by the Fund existed. Many different practices, in addition to straightforward fixed or free market rates, were soon uncovered, some of which gave rise not to explicit but to implicit rates. Among these practices were "mixing" rates, import surcharges, compensation arrangements, *aforo* techniques, negotiable and nonnegotiable exchange certificates, a variety of export bonus and import entitlement schemes, and "cheap currency" schemes. Of these, "mixing" rates were by far the most common. A "mixing" rate occurs when a specified proportion of exchange proceeds is sold at the official rate and the remainder is sold in a free market, resulting in an effective rate of exchange which is a weighted average of the two rates at which the exchange has been sold.[11]

---

[11] Detailed descriptions of all these various arrangements can be found in the individual country surveys of the *Annual Report on Exchange Restrictions*, especially for the years 1950–55, and in the monthly issues of *International Financial Statistics*.

Because of the number of multiple exchange rate changes it had to consider, the Executive Board, early in 1949, requested the staff to study and recommend a procedure by which at least some changes in multiple currency practices— for example, "minor" ones—might be acted upon simply. Several Directors, however, were uneasy lest a procedure might be adopted which would result in changes in multiple rates being made without Directors having adequate time to consult their governments, or without their even being informed of the changes. How, they asked, would it be decided what was a "minor" change? What appeared to be a minor change on the surface might be of material significance to a particular country exporting a given commodity. And certainly it must not appear to members that the Board was relinquishing any authority in this field.

Nevertheless, a procedure for dealing with minor changes in multiple rates had finally been worked out by May 1951. When a member country proposed to the Fund a change in its multiple currency practices which the Managing Director (with the assistance of the staff) regarded as minor, the Managing Director was to inform the Executive Directors, stating that he did not intend to place the matter on the agenda unless a Director so requested by a specified date. In the absence of any such request, the minutes of the next Board meeting would record the proposal as being approved. This gradually became known internally in the Fund as the "minor change procedure" or the "lapse of time procedure."

This procedure was similar to one that had been worked out earlier for China's multiple rates. While still on the mainland, the Chinese authorities began to maintain a series of multiple exchange rates which were, in the midst of civil war and severe inflation, almost continuously being altered. In view of the unusual difficulties that confronted the exchange authorities in China, a special procedure for dealing with them was evolved in 1948 by which China would inform the Fund of changes in advance where possible, or in any case at the earliest possible time, and the Managing Director would reply to China promptly on behalf of the Fund, without a Board meeting, unless the Managing Director preferred to raise the matter with the Board.

In addition to problems of procedure, issues of substance, even more intractable, concerned the Board. Member countries, and also economists who were closely concerned with the subject, came to realize that cogent arguments might be advanced for multiple rates. Some of these were economic, others administrative. It was contended, for example, that multiple currency practices represented an attempt to use the exchange rate mechanism to adjust the balance of payments when it was not politically possible to change the par value.

There were even times when selective exchange rate devaluation was preferable to general devaluation—when general devaluation would be inflationary, or would raise the cost of living of essential items, or would bring excessive windfall profits to exporters but would not help significantly to solve the balance of payments deficit. In regard to the last mentioned, much was made of the price inelasticity of both the demand for and the supply of primary products. It was argued that these inelasticities made multiple rates necessary so that import demand might be restrained without the export rate being depreciated. In these circumstances, use of an exchange spread—that is, maintenance of the exchange rate for exports but depreciation of the effective rate for imports— might be preferred to the depreciation of a single rate.[12]

Multiple rates were also defended as merely another form of exchange control, like quantitative restrictions. Here it was important that they were easier to administer than quantitative controls. A multiple rate system could be handled by a small group of trained bankers who bought and sold foreign exchange, whereas quantitative controls required a comprehensive system of licensing, exchange budgeting, and exchange allocation. It was argued, in addition, that if a choice had to be made, multiple rates were preferable to quantitative restrictions because they distributed foreign exchange on a basis of price rather than of ability to obtain a license. They constituted a mechanism by which the arbitrary decisions of exchange control authorities, inherent in quantitative restrictions, were thought to be avoided. They imposed less interference on consumer choice

Another rationale of multiple rates was that they might have monetary effects which would alleviate inflation. Multiple rate systems usually yield profits in local currency to the exchange authorities: exchange is sold to importers at higher rates (that is, more units of local currency per unit of foreign exchange) than the authorities pay out to the exporters surrendering foreign exchange. If these profits are spent by the authorities, no money is withdrawn from circulation. But to the extent that the authorities refrain from spending these profits—that is, if they freeze them—a decline in money occurs. This anti-inflationary effect of a multiple rate system has repercussions on the balance of payments of the country concerned additional to the effects of devaluation. Both help to restrain import demand.

In these early years the objections of the Fund to multiple rates were of several types. Most frequent were the fear of harmful effects on other countries, especially through broken cross rates, and, although to a lesser extent, the fear of competitive depreciation. Another was that multiple exchange rates tended to perpetuate themselves, as vested interests in their continuation developed: complicated exchange systems had not, in practice, led eventually to a unitary rate; multiple rates had, in fact, proliferated.

---

[12] These economic objectives of multiple exchange rates are explained by E. M. Bernstein in "Some Economic Aspects of Multiple Exchange Rates," *Staff Papers*, Vol. I (1950–51), pp. 224–37.

Another objection to multiple currency practices was that, by making official rates nominal, multiple rates tended to undermine par values. Because most of the countries using multiple rates were subject to strong inflationary pressures, their exchange rates had to be adjusted frequently. Experience had demonstrated that, shortly after a country instituted multiple rates, its official exchange rates or its agreed par value no longer applied to many transactions.

Many Directors objected to multiple currency practices on yet another ground: they did not help to overcome the underlying economic problems of the countries employing them. Devaluation via multiple rates was usually inadequate and partial. Resort to multiple rates in many instances had not avoided the need for quantitative controls to curb import demand. When used for their anti-inflationary effects, multiple rates were insufficient to restrain inflationary pressures; primary reliance still had to be placed on the usual monetary and fiscal policies.

The Fund was, in the next few years, to learn even more about the adverse consequences of multiple rates, as well as the circumstances in which they might be useful; these are discussed below.

ADAPTATION OF POLICIES

As the arguments about the relative merits of multiple rates continued, it became evident that multiple rates usually resulted from balance of payments deficits, which in turn were most often caused by inflation. Until inflation was brought under control, the removal of multiple rates would necessitate, in their place, the introduction or tightening of quantitative restrictions on imports and payments. Since quantitative restrictions were themselves a form of control, and gave rise to many difficulties, the replacement of multiple rates by such restrictions would achieve little. (The Fund's first Exchange Restrictions Report, dated March 1, 1950, used the term *cost restrictions* for multiple currency practices and referred to quantitative restrictions as *supply-type* restrictions. These expressions did not subsequently become common Fund usage, although they occur in unofficial discussions of multiple rates.)

There was also increasing evidence of the widespread use of multiple rates for purposes not concerned with the balance of payments, such as taxation and protection. Therefore, the Fund realized that insistence on the immediate discontinuation of multiple rates might compel members to put into effect hastily devised tax substitutes, different in form but no better in practice than the existing systems of multiple rates. Preferable substitutes would require comprehensive reforms of fiscal systems and customs tariff schedules, and these had first to be carefully designed and then had to go through prolonged legislative procedures.

In these circumstances the general principles outlined in the 1947 letter had to be adapted to deal with specific problems. This adaptation took several forms.

One, rather than insisting on the immediate elimination of multiple rates, the Fund came to put stress on the achievement of general economic conditions which would facilitate this elimination as soon as practicable. Most important among these conditions was domestic financial stability. Thus, as part of its early consideration of multiple currency practices, the Fund came to concentrate heavily on the domestic inflation of its members.[13]

Two, there was gradually evolved what was in effect a case-by-case approach: each member's request for approval of multiple rates was decided on its own merits. In certain inflationary conditions, for example, members' exchange difficulties were considered to be related to the inadequacy of their import rates for restraining excessive import demand. Among the recommendations which the Fund made to members, along with anti-inflationary measures, were higher penalty selling rates for nonessential imports. At times the further restriction of import demand—including, occasionally, tightened quantitative restrictions—was advised.

Members were also encouraged to avoid the use of many particular practices—such as auction systems, compensation arrangements, and "mixing" rates, especially for exports—which might unduly complicate their exchange rates or harm other countries. "Mixing" systems were considered to be unduly susceptible to pressure from exporters for further rate multiplicity, as well as to administrative juggling. Compensation arrangements also gave rise to extensive multiplication of rates. In order to keep exchange rates as stable as possible, the Fund urged that free market rates be limited to balance of payments items other than trade, such as capital or invisibles. This sort of "code of fair practices," it was thought, would keep continuing systems within tolerable limits.

Despite these difficulties, the Fund still hoped for progress in the elimination of multiple rates. Not wishing to disapprove multiple rates or to approve them outright, the Board gave approval to those proposed by individual countries as "temporary measures," and remained in consultation with the members concerned.

During these early years, the Fund worked intensely with its members on multiple rate problems. Innumerable informal contacts were made, many staff missions were sent out, sundry reports were written, and frequent discussions took place in the Board. All this activity was almost entirely concerned with the Fund's Latin American members, especially Chile, Colombia, Costa Rica, Ecuador, Honduras, Nicaragua, and Paraguay.

In many respects, these years were frustrating ones. The Fund was criticized at times for too much and at times for too little attention to multiple rates.

---

[13] *Annual Report, 1948*, p. 28.

Some of the Latin American countries began to ask whether the Fund, in a world of extensive exchange controls and the continued inconvertibility of key currencies, was not devoting excessive attention to the multiple rates of a few countries that contributed little to total world trade. On the other hand, some economists, both in academic and in some official circles, anxious for evidences of successful international monetary cooperation within the new organization, frequently lamented the lack of progress, even in the field of multiple rates, which was thought to be easier than that of other controls.

REASSESSMENT OF POLICIES

In January–February 1950 these problems were brought to a head in the Executive Board, which undertook a series of informal sessions on multiple currency practices. In these sessions it was stressed that the Fund had been willing to approve multiple rates *only* for balance of payments reasons. Much discussion centered, therefore, on the other reasons for multiple rates, including the use of such rates for taxation and subsidization and for protection.

To assist in formulating a new policy, Directors considered a model system of multiple rates. This model was designed to take account of balance of payments deficits without making concessions to the other purposes of multiple rates. The model had one import and one export rate with a fixed spread in excess of 1 per cent, and a free market as a safety valve for excessive import demand. The various advantages and disadvantages of the model were debated. But the basic question remained, and was left unanswered: Would such a model imply the *permanent* use of multiple rates? No firm consolidation of views among Directors took place even after these informal sessions.

THE MIDDLE YEARS (1952–55)

SECOND PHASE IN THE FUND'S APPROACH

The beginning of consultations under Article XIV in 1952 led to what may be seen as a second phase in the Fund's policies on multiple exchange rates. This phase continued until about the end of 1955. Although the legal obligation of members to consult the Fund in advance of multiple rate changes, set forth in the December 1947 letter, continued to apply, the Board's operating procedures were altered in important respects. The Directors no longer reviewed changes in multiple exchange rates when such changes were made. Instead, they gave temporary approval to a proposed change in a multiple rate system without immediate review of a particular practice, pending the forthcoming annual Article XIV consultation. In the course of that consultation a review of the total exchange rate system was undertaken and a final decision reached on the particular rate changes made.

This change in procedure had two important advantages. First, it enabled the Fund and the member country to consider the reasons for, and possible alternatives to, multiple rates in a broad, regular (annual) context, and eventually to work together toward the elimination of multiple rates. Second, as such consultations came to be held with practically all members, including the major European ones, the dualism in the Fund's policy between multiple exchange rates and other types of exchange restrictions seemed more or less at an end. After 1952, the consultations became the main activity of the Fund, in contrast to the previous situation, when multiple currency practices had been the great generator of the work of the Fund.

This switch in procedure—from considering multiple currency practices as they were introduced to considering them more fully in the course of the Article XIV consultations—culminated in a decision of the Executive Board, taken in February 1956, to use much more extensively the so-called lapse of time procedure for changes in multiple rates. The changes approved by the Managing Director under this procedure were, of course, more fully examined at the time of the Article XIV consultations. However, it was understood that this procedure would not be used for multiple rate changes involving shifts of payments from an official market to a new or narrow free market or to a free market in which the prevailing exchange rates were far out of line with the official rate at which most exports were handled. The Directors were particularly sensitive to multiple rate changes that jeopardized fixed exchange rates or that might in effect subsidize exports.

During this second phase, it was still evident that multiple currency practices could not be eradicated easily or quickly, and that the case-by-case approach would have to be continued for some time. A search was therefore begun for some new policy that could be implemented on a case-by-case basis.

Spread of multiple rates

The question of what policy to apply had been made even more difficult by an increasing divergence in practice between the Fund's ultimate goal of unification of exchange systems and the existing situation. Despite the Fund's efforts, multiple currency practices continued to spread.[14] Several countries that were already employing multiple exchange rates joined the Fund: Afghanistan, Indonesia, Israel, and Korea. Many countries that were already members introduced multiple currency practices: China, Egypt, Finland, Greece, Iceland, the Philippines, Turkey, and Yugoslavia. Even a number of Western European countries, although retaining unitary fixed rates for the bulk of their transactions, felt compelled to open free markets for the sale of certain bilateral or EPU currencies, or for certain capital flows. Belgium, for example, established a free

[14] *Fourth Annual Report on Exchange Restrictions* (1953), pp. 40–50.

market for EPU currencies; Germany introduced a free market for "Brazilian accounting dollars." Multiple rates were thus no longer confined to Latin America; they had spread to Asia, the Middle East, and Western Europe. Table 6 at the end of this chapter, which provides a detailed chronological summary of the principal developments in multiple rates, shows this extension.

REASONS FOR EXTENSION OF MULTIPLE RATES

The increased use of multiple currency practices during these years reflected two distinct kinds of problem, each of which gave rise to different practices. One problem was what was commonly known at the time as the world dollar shortage. The currencies of the world had become divided into "hard" currencies, mainly the U.S. and Canadian dollars, which were convertible, and "soft" currencies, including the pound sterling, the French and Belgian francs, the deutsche mark, and the guilder, which were inconvertible. Although a country might have achieved equilibrium in its aggregate balance of payments, a surplus in an inconvertible currency could not be used to settle deficits where convertible currencies were needed.

This situation had led, in Western Europe as elsewhere, to some multiple currency practices—such as limited free markets and broken cross rates in broader free markets—and to retention quotas, which aimed at increasing a country's supply of "hard" currencies and decreasing its holdings of "soft" ones.

The trend to such practices began to be reversed in 1954–55 as a result of the marked general improvement in the international payments situation which had started to take place. On January 23, 1954, the Report of the Randall Commission of the U.S. Government noted, for example, that the conditions prerequisite to currency convertibility were more nearly in prospect at that time than at any previous time since the war.[15]

By the spring of 1954 the Fund was able to discern a general tendency toward the removal of barriers to trade and payments; restrictive practices had been considerably reduced or modified.[16] The Exchange Restrictions Report for 1955 called attention to continued—although more gradual—progress in relaxing restrictions and, in particular, to increased facilities for nonresidents to convert inconvertible currencies into dollars.[17]

The second reason for the spread of multiple rates, applying to the less developed countries, was a more difficult one to counter. Multiple exchange rates, originally introduced to alleviate the depression-based payments problems of the 1930's, now seemed useful instruments to support economic development

[15] U.S. Commission on Foreign Economic Policy, *Report to the President and the Congress*, p. 470.

[16] *Annual Report, 1954*, p. 74.

[17] *Sixth Annual Report on Exchange Restrictions* (1955), pp. 2–6.

efforts, particularly in the economic and institutional environment of developing countries.

The problems of establishing or maintaining internal monetary stability were often intensified by the pressing claims of development programs. Multiple rates could, as described above, have an anti-inflationary effect if exchange profits were frozen. Dual exchange markets could isolate speculative capital from trade transactions. Alternatively, dual markets could separate exports of primary products, which might not benefit from devaluation, from exports of manufactured goods, where an exchange rate incentive might induce new export industries, so essential to development. On the import side, multiple rates might offer protection to some domestic industries; or they might provide subsidies to essential consumer goods, thereby keeping down the cost of living. Additional arguments for multiple rates as an aid to development were also advanced by member countries.

Multiple rates thus persisted in developing countries. Several countries, dissatisfied with the results of quantitative controls, switched to multiple rates. The Annual Report of the Executive Directors for 1955, after noting that world trade and payments were less subject to restriction than they had been a year earlier, commented that much less progress had been made in the elimination of multiple currency practices.[18]

At the same time, the problem of multiple export rates had become of added concern to countries not employing them. The less developed countries had begun to increase their use of multiple rates for exports, and keener competition in international markets made countries with unitary rates increasingly fearful that competitors using multiple rates might derive unfair advantages in export markets. It seemed certain that tension between the Fund's members concerning multiple rates might again increase, as it had in the Fund's first days.

In these circumstances both the staff and the Board began to consider even more intensively the economic functions and effects of multiple rates, especially the relation between multiple rates and economic development. The conclusion was that the use of exchange restrictions and multiple rates to foster economic development would be unnecessary if substitute measures were introduced. Since multiple rates were, for example, often used in place of customs duties or taxes, they could be eliminated if equivalent revenue was raised in another way. Similarly, multiple rates that provided protection to domestic producers could be abolished if protective tariffs were appropriately raised. Increasingly the devising of acceptable alternative measures for multiple rates became a main problem for the Fund. Meanwhile, the questions facing the Fund were these: Should it condone, or at least not object to, these uses of multiple

---

[18] *Annual Report, 1955*, p. 76.

rates for reasons other than the balance of payments? Should it recommend specific alternatives?

As background for the Board's consideration of these problems, the staff also prepared studies of the revenue-raising functions of multiple currency practices [19] and of the desirability of substituting increases in tariffs for exchange surcharges. In the latter study, a series of propositions was advanced as to the economic circumstances for which tariffs and surcharges, respectively, were most appropriate. Essentially, surcharges were considered best suited to meet temporary balance of payments deficits. Consequently, when surcharges were used to help cope with temporary payments deficits, they should not be incorporated in the customs tariff schedule. When, however, surcharges were serving a longer-run balance of payments purpose, the study deemed it advisable for the country concerned to introduce anti-inflationary measures or to adjust its exchange rate rather than to revise its customs tariff rates. On the other hand, the study concluded that tariffs were preferable to surcharges as a long-run source of revenue and for protection.

Consideration of these staff suggestions showed that Directors held widely differing views. After much discussion the Board came to the conclusion that generalizations on alternative measures for multiple rates were difficult and dangerous, and that it was preferable to consider the individual circumstances of each country.

By the end of 1955, membership of the Fund had grown to 58. But, despite some lessening of multiple rates, there were still 36 members that had some kind of practice which the Fund considered a multiple currency practice. Many of these practices, especially in Europe, were minor, and most transactions were still conducted at exchange rates based on par values. But there remained very complex systems with many different rates in many countries throughout the world.

EVENTUAL BREAKTHROUGH (1956–62)

Toward the end of 1955, a third phase in the history of the Fund's dealings with multiple rates began. In the Exchange Restrictions Report for 1956, the Fund was able to report considerable progress toward the lessened use of multiple rates:

> In the past year, many countries maintaining multiple exchange rates and similar practices made some changes in these practices, which varied considerably in character and significance. The countries that did not change their multiple currency practices are, for the most part, those in which the practice is only a

[19] W. John R. Woodley, "The Use of Special Exchange Rates for Transactions with Foreign Companies," *Staff Papers*, Vol. III (1953–54), pp. 254–69; Joyce Sherwood, "Revenue Features of Multiple Exchange Rate Systems," *ibid.*, Vol. V (1956–57), pp. 74–107.

minor element in the exchange rate structure. The number of countries in which multiple currency practices were simplified appreciably exceeded those in which there was an increase in multiple rates.[20]

The intensive postwar investment programs, especially in Western Europe, had borne fruit, and production was rising rapidly. Increased supplies of goods, together with the improved domestic financial and monetary positions of Western European countries following the realignment of exchange rates in 1949, brought the world dollar shortage to an end. Hence, from 1956 onward, the main industrial countries relaxed many of the barriers to trade and payments and made their currencies convertible. Multiple currency practices, as well as discriminatory quantitative restrictions, which distinguished between "hard" and "soft" currencies could be, and were, quickly removed. By 1958 the free markets in which some but not all transactions took place, broken cross rates, retention quotas, and other special devices of a number of Western European countries had all been discontinued.

Toward the end of 1955 and in 1956 events occurred which were, in some ways, even more unexpected. Three less developed countries—Bolivia, Chile, and Paraguay—which had maintained multiple rates since the 1930's and had believed them imperative for primary producing economies, undertook comprehensive exchange reforms, eliminating multiple rates at a single stroke and introducing unitary fluctuating rates. Thailand also achieved a unitary fluctuating rate, but gradually. In addition, several other multiple rates, such as an exchange tax in the Philippines and the application of an official rate to oil company transactions in Syria, were eliminated.

New Fund approaches

The time was ripe for an intensification of the Fund's efforts to eliminate multiple rates. The countries employing them now were less convinced of their usefulness than they had been several years before. Greater emphasis was being placed on the practical difficulties of eliminating multiple rates than on a preference for them over unitary rates.

The experiences of the Fund in the previous ten years had demonstrated that, for most countries with complex systems, unification of the exchange system required the mapping out of a special course of action. The elimination of multiple rates could not be expected to come about automatically as internal monetary conditions were brought satisfactorily under control, or even as balance of payments positions were strengthened. Moreover, in many countries, unification at a realistic par value was not likely to be attained in one step: what was required was either a process of simplification to a few fixed rates or to one fixed and one free rate, or, alternatively, unification at a fluctuating rate.

---

[20] *Seventh Annual Report on Exchange Restrictions* (1956), p. 5.

The Fund had also learned that it was much easier for a country to simplify its exchange rate structure than to unify it. The necessary degree of stringency in internal monetary policies was significantly smaller for simplification than for unification, and fewer reserves were required if a simplified system included a fluctuating rate. Over the years it had become evident that floating rate mechanisms were often more self-liquidating than a group of fixed rates. Another advantage of simplification as against unification was that an exchange spread, such as often characterized simple multiple rate systems, might absorb part of any internal monetary expansion; such absorption was not possible with a unitary rate.

Moreover, it had been learned that it was the *complexity* of multiple rates that was especially at fault. Complex exchange systems brought into economic decisions many more elements of arbitrariness and uncertainty. Extensive differentiation of rates among export and import commodities was particularly likely to distort domestic prices and output and made it more difficult for the authorities to resist pressures for special treatment of a given commodity. Further, an excessive number of rates increased the possibilities of hidden subsidization and encouraged the continuation of overvalued rates. But perhaps the most important condemnation of complex rate systems was that they tended to perpetuate themselves until the countries using them experienced crises which might well have been avoided.

For several months in 1957 the Board carefully considered the possibility of making new and intensified efforts to reduce multiple rates. All the Directors were anxious to reach a decision that would be widely supported, especially by the developing countries that maintained multiple rates. In June 1957 this consensus was reached, and the Board decided to send to the members a new communication on multiple currency practices.[21] This memorandum urged countries using such techniques to simplify considerably their existing rate structures. Such a simplification meant more than a mere reduction in the number of existing rates: emphasis was placed on limiting the system to two or three rates which would be sufficiently realistic to maintain a satisfactory balance of payments with a minimum of restrictions. A simpler system could include, where necessary, the temporary use of a widened free market or of a fluctuating rate as a step toward a stable unitary rate.

The Fund undertook to help countries to plan specific exchange systems. Technical assistance could also be made available to cover the formulation, where appropriate, of substitute fiscal arrangements. Most important of all, where the exchange reform was sufficiently broad and was accompanied by a domestic stabilization program, the Fund was willing to consider permitting

---

[21] Reproduced below, Vol. III, pp. 265–66.

members to use its resources in support of exchange reforms. Meanwhile, the Board would be reluctant to approve changes in multiple rate systems which would make them more complex.

While not insisting on the immediate unification of exchange rates, this communication sounded a warning that the Board would no longer approve complex systems except in certain circumstances.

ACCELERATED ELIMINATION OF MULTIPLE RATES

For several years after the issue of the June 1957 memorandum, there was a strong trend toward elimination of multiple exchange rates by the developing countries. Significantly, the countries abandoning multiple rates included Argentina (1958), which in the 1930's had been one of the first Latin American countries to use them, and Yugoslavia (1961), which had had in the mid-1950's an exchange system often regarded as the most complex of all. Table 6 at the end of this chapter gives additional details of the decline in the use of multiple rates.

Some countries devalued, eliminated multiple rates, and set a new fixed rate, all at the same time. Generally these were the European countries, but they included Israel. This was the pattern in Finland, Spain, and Turkey. Many of these countries also set new par values. Others—especially the less developed countries—reached a par value by stages, first eliminating multiple rates and introducing a unitary fluctuating rate, then gradually stabilizing the fluctuating rate, and eventually converting it into a par value. Costa Rica, Iran, Jordan, Korea, Nicaragua, the Philippines, Saudi Arabia, and Thailand attained fixed rates (or even par values) via fluctuating rates, at least for some transactions.[22]

A few countries eliminated multiple rates when they were enjoying a favorable balance of payments; usually the strong payments situation was the result of peak production or high world prices for exports, or both. More frequently, however, countries reshaped their exchange rate structures as part of a broad program to meet balance of payments crises. These general reforms of the exchange system were usually accompanied by exchange devaluation and by internal policies designed to remove price distortions and to restrain inflation.

Frequently also tariff adjustments, usually upward, were undertaken simultaneously with exchange reform. In some countries, comprehensive fiscal reforms were carried out. Other countries, introducing a single fluctuating rate, temporarily applied taxes or surcharges to some imports. Apart from whether or not these taxes and surcharges were different from multiple rates insofar as the Fund's Articles were concerned, their economic function was different. Because

---

[22] These alternative approaches have been described in Margaret G. de Vries, "Fund Members' Adherence to the Par Value Regime," *Staff Papers*, Vol. XIII (1966), at pp. 516–20.

they were now superimposed on unitary exchange rates that were unrestricted and hence presumably realistic, these taxes and surcharges were regarded purely as fiscal devices; previously, because they comprised part of the exchange system, they had been considered at least in part as balance of payments measures. The main reason why countries used taxes and surcharges, after exchange reform, was that alternative revenue sources could not be quickly developed. Some countries proposed explicitly to undertake tariff revision at a later date, at which time these taxes and surcharges were to be incorporated into the tariff structure.[23]

In sum, between 1955 and 1962, not only did several Western European countries eliminate their minor exchange practices, but major systems of multiple rates were unified in many other countries as well, in every geographic region. By the end of 1962, only 15 Fund members out of a total of 82 had multiple rates of any type, in contrast to 36 out of 58 members seven years earlier.

EXPLANATIONS OF DECLINE IN MULTIPLE RATES

One of the principal reasons for the decline in multiple rates was the adverse experiences with these practices that many countries had had. Although some countries had been able to use them to advantage, the experiences of most had been disappointing and frustrating. In order to achieve any of the professed purposes of multiple exchange rates—that is, to tax a major export, to restrain imports of luxury commodities, to raise revenue, to alleviate inflation, to stimulate minor exports, or to isolate capital movements from trade transactions—countries had found that certain conditions had to prevail.

First, it was essential that the exchange system be simple; that is, there should be only a few exchange rates rather than many. Complex systems worked out much less well; they rarely achieved several objectives concurrently. Finding a rate structure suitable for such diverse purposes as holding down external deficits, redistributing internal income, and checking inflation seemed to be virtually impossible, even where several rates existed. Seeking to make multiple rates perform both balance of payments and taxation functions, especially under conditions of chronic inflation, led to complex systems and the dissipation of the initial objectives.

Second, periodic adjustments had to be made in the exchange system or else fluctuating rates had to be used in order to keep at realistic levels the exchange rates applicable to most exports and imports; otherwise, there was a danger that the exchange rates prevailing would become overvalued.

---

[23] A discussion of the techniques of unification of multiple rates is to be found in F. d'A. Collings, "Recent Progress in Latin America Toward Eliminating Exchange Restrictions," *Staff Papers*, Vol. VIII (1960–61), pp. 274–86.

Third, a reasonable amount of domestic monetary stability had to be maintained.[24] Under conditions of inflation, traditional export industries were harmed by being subjected to penalty rates of exchange at overvalued levels. New and potential export industries were neglected, even where special exchange rates for so-called minor exports existed. Multiple import rates had adverse effects on the structure of domestic production and investment.

These conditions for successful use of multiple rates had not always, or even frequently, been fulfilled in the countries that had employed multiple rates, and multiple rates had then proved worse than practicable alternatives.

Following the memorandum of June 1957, the Fund vigorously encouraged countries to eliminate multiple rates. On many occasions the Fund urged countries not to be unduly cautious in moving toward simplified exchange systems. It drew attention to specific circumstances where, in the Fund's view, greater simplification was feasible and even essential. Frequently it singled out for comment to a member exchange rates that were considered especially troublesome. The Fund provided technical assistance to work out specific exchange reforms and internal stabilization programs. Finally, there were stand-by arrangements to bolster countries' reserves.

Once some countries had eliminated complex systems of multiple rates, the Fund could point to the favorable aftermath. In their Annual Report for 1961 the Directors had this to say:

> In arguing the advantages of [the removal of multiple rates], the Fund has been able to point to the generally favorable experience of several members that have eliminated complex multiple exchange rate systems in the recent past. In general, these countries have found that their economies are better able than previously to deal with both domestic and balance of payments problems. In some countries, this improvement occurred despite lower prices for major export products upon which they largely depend for foreign exchange. In several of the countries which adopted freely fluctuating exchange rates when they abolished their multiple exchange [rate] systems, these rates remained virtually unchanged for long periods. For some, moreover, the initial, sometimes difficult, period of adjustment to the new conditions that inevitably follows a major economic reform has been succeeded by a period of renewed progress, accompanied at the same time by monetary and exchange rate stability and an increasingly satisfactory reserve position.[25]

SOME CONTINUING PROBLEMS (1963–65)

Developments in multiple exchange rates in the eighteenth to twentieth years of the Fund's history were of three types.

---

[24] A fuller account of the economic experiences of countries with multiple rates can be found in Margaret G. de Vries, "Multiple Exchange Rates," *Staff Papers*, Vol. XII (1965), pp. 282–313.

[25] *Annual Report, 1961*, p. 117.

(1) Countries which had long made use of multiple rates continued to join others which had considerably simplified or unified their exchange rates. In 1964–65 Venezuela and Brazil simplified their exchange systems in a series of steps. The Philippines, which had introduced multiple rates with a fluctuating rate in 1962, eliminated them and set a new par value in November 1965. Also in 1965, Korea replaced its multiple rates with a unitary fluctuating rate.

(2) A few countries, including Afghanistan, Colombia, Indonesia, and Viet-Nam, continued to maintain significant multiple rate systems, although some of these became somewhat less complex.

(3) On the other hand, certain countries where multiple rates had been eliminated or very much simplified reintroduced them or reverted to complex systems. And in some countries which previously did not have them, multiple rates appeared. Chile, for example, following a virtual unification of its exchange rate in 1956, introduced in 1962 a dual market system which still continued at the end of 1965. Multiple rates were adopted in several countries where they had not been used previously. Pakistan, to assist exports of all except its major primary products, had in 1959 introduced an export bonus scheme patterned along the lines of the retention quota employed by Germany in the mid-1950's. This system was still in use at the end of 1965, and its scope and complexity had been increased. A few new African countries had begun to use devices reminiscent of those used in Latin America in the 1940's.

Some other devices, such as import surcharges and advance deposit requirements, which are in many respects similar to multiple currency practices, were instituted by several countries to deal with recurrent payments or fiscal deficits. Among these countries were Argentina, Brazil, Ceylon, Colombia, Ecuador, India, Iran, Ireland, Japan, Pakistan, and Uruguay. Moreover, among the measures introduced by a number of industrial countries to reduce the outflow of capital were special taxes or markets with premiums for investment currencies, as in the United Kingdom.[26]

The problem of multiple exchange rates may never be entirely solved. The nature of and reasons for the practices used differ, their locale shifts, and there is a constant need for vigilance by the Fund. Despite some continued and some newly emerging problems, however, the extent and complexity of multiple rates were clearly less at the end of 1965 than they had been twenty years earlier.

---

[26] See *Seventeenth Annual Report on Exchange Restrictions* (1966), p. 6.

Table 6. Principal Developments in Multiple Exchange Rates, 1946–65

1946

Sept.   *Venezuela* asked Fund assurance that membership would not prevent it from taking suitable time to eliminate multiple currency practices.

Nov.   The question arose whether an initial par value could be agreed if multiple rates prevailed.

1947

Jan.–Feb.   The Board discussed several matters pertaining to multiple rates. Do differences exceeding 2 per cent between buying and selling rates constitute a multiple currency practice? Are multiple rates subject to Article XIV? How prevalent are they?

May   The Board set up an Ad Hoc Committee on Spreads and Multiple Currency Practices to study the application of the Articles to multiple rates.

June–Aug.   The Board considered the recommendations of the Ad Hoc Committee.

Dec.   A letter setting forth the decisions on policy and procedures for multiple currency practices was sent to all members.

1948

Jan.   *France* devalued the franc and instituted a multiple currency practice, to which the Fund objected.

June   The Fund agreed to a special simple procedure for changes in *China's* exchange system because of special problems in the case: the Managing Director approved in writing changes proposed by the Chinese authorities, and circulated the correspondence to the Board for information, Board consideration of the change not being first required.

Oct.–Nov.   The Fund reviewed Latin American exchange problems and policies. No Board decision was taken but it was stressed that continuing inflation had been found to be a major cause of exchange difficulties and that, in view of the diversity of conditions in Latin America, proposals by each country would have to be considered separately.

1949

Feb.   During a review of the exchange position of one country, the question first arose whether a member could properly maintain multiple rates if they were not necessary for balance of payments reasons.

Apr.   Instructions given to a Fund mission to one country required it to investigate the possibility of substituting nonexchange measures for the existing exchange surcharges in order to restrain imports.

1950

Jan.–Feb.   The Board held a series of informal sessions on multiple currency practices.

Mar.   A separate Multiple Currency Practices Division was created in a staff reorganization.

Table 6 *(continued).* Principal Developments in Multiple Exchange Rates, 1946–65

1951

Mar.   *The Philippines* imposed a 17 per cent tax on sales of foreign exchange.

Mar.–Apr.   *Paraguay* devalued the guaraní, removed taxes on sales of exchange, and transferred various transactions to the free market in an attempt to meet objections of the Fund to its exchange system.

May   An internal Fund procedure for minor changes in multiple rates was established to lessen the need for consideration by the Board of all changes in multiple rate systems.

Sept.   *Costa Rica* abolished surcharges, reducing the complexity of its multiple rate structure; the abolition was facilitated by upward revisions in its tariffs. It was agreed by the Board that the staff should look into the general problem of surcharges versus tariffs.

1952

Jan.   After consideration of a staff paper on tariffs versus surcharges, the Board decided that no general line either favoring or disapproving elimination of multiple rates through upward tariff revisions could be taken and that each case must be considered on its merits.

Jan.–June   *Yugoslavia,* in a series of steps, introduced a complex system of multiple rates.

Feb.   *Ecuador* simplified its exchange system by abolishing its compensation system.

Sept.   *Germany* introduced a free market for "Brazilian accounting dollars" (used in payments transactions under the payments agreements between Germany and Brazil).

1953

Feb.   *Brazil* inaugurated a free market for invisibles and most capital transactions and for certain trade items.

Apr.   *Greece* unified its exchange structure and devalued the drachma.

May   *Austria* unified its exchange structure and set an initial par value.

Aug.   *Brazil* reduced the list of export products subject to a "mixing" arrangement, but a complex system remained.

1954

Jan.   *Israel* (not yet a member) substituted a single official rate for three fixed official rates, but for certain transactions either one of two premiums or a surcharge applied.

July   *The Netherlands, Belgium,* and *Luxembourg,* in connection with arrangements to facilitate capital movements between them and other EPU countries, extended the free market for capital to residents of other EPU countries; previously the free market had been confined to transactions between their own residents.

Aug.   *Paraguay* depreciated to a new par value and made other substantial alterations in its exchange system, but a complex system remained.

                Israel (now a Fund member) extended its surcharge to all imports.

Table 6 *(continued).* Principal Developments in Multiple Exchange Rates, 1946–65

1955

Jan.–Feb.	*Brazil* established export bonuses.
Feb.–May	*Colombia* abolished a differential rate for coffee exports and introduced a broad free market; imports were made subject to stamp taxes.
Mar.	*China* introduced a system of negotiable exchange certificates.
May	*Chile* eliminated the special exchange rate for copper companies.
July	*Nicaragua* removed surcharges and depreciated its par value but retained an exchange spread.
	Belgium's free market was opened to capital transfers to all destinations.
July–Oct.	*Indonesia* considerably revised its system in an attempt at simplification, but a wide range of rates, especially on imports, continued.
Sept.–Dec.	*Uruguay* announced a special premium for exports of wool, including wool tops.

1956

Jan.	*Thailand* completed unification of its exchange system; all transactions were to be effected at a fluctuating free market rate.
Mar.	*Paraguay* depreciated its par value and greatly simplified its complex multiple rate system. A broad internal monetary stabilization program was introduced.
	The Board agreed to more extensive use of the lapse of time procedure for multiple rates: it could now be used for all changes that did not, in the opinion of the Managing Director, seem to require immediate discussion by the Board.
Apr.	*Chile* considerably simplified its multiple rate system, abolished the import licensing system, and instituted a fluctuating free market for all commodity transactions.
Dec.	*Bolivia* undertook an exchange reform and comprehensive economic stabilization measures, replacing the complex multiple rate system with a single fluctuating rate.

1957

Mar.	The Board began consideration of a staff paper on a change in policies for multiple currency practices which would put an end to Fund approval of complex systems and would encourage genuine and substantial simplification.
May	*Iran,* as a final step in unifying its multiple rates, changed its par value to what was the *de facto* unitary exchange rate.
June	The Board reached a second general decision on multiple currency practices. The Fund notified countries that it would no longer approve complex systems unless the countries maintaining them were making reasonable progress toward simplification.
Aug.	*Paraguay* gave up all transactions at the par value, eliminated all multiple rates and quantitative restrictions, and adopted a freely fluctuating rate.
	France introduced a 20 per cent surcharge and premium on most transactions, which was extended to all transactions shortly thereafter.
Sept.	*Finland* depreciated its par value and abolished its multiple currency practices.
Nov.	*Nicaragua* applied the official rate to exports of cotton and minor exports, thus moving toward unification.

Table 6 *(continued).* Principal Developments in Multiple Exchange Rates, 1946–65

1958

Jan.–Dec. *Uruguay* made various changes in its rate structure, making it more complex.

Apr. *China* simplified its exchange system, abolishing its 20 per cent defense tax and other rates. There were now two effective rates.

May *Iceland* introduced three exchange premiums on export proceeds, replacing the assistance previously granted to exports through different forms of subsidization. Discrimination as to country destination was terminated.

July *Yugoslavia* continued to simplify its complex rate structure by reducing the number of export and import coefficients.

Aug. *Turkey* replaced its complex system with a simpler one.

Oct. *Nicaragua* extended the par value rate to coffee exports; thus by the end of the crop year all trade transactions were unified at a rate based on the par value.

Dec. *Argentina,* as part of an economic stabilization program, abolished multiple rates and introduced a single fluctuating rate.

1959

Jan. *Chile* combined its two fluctuating exchange markets.

Pakistan introduced an export bonus scheme.

July *Spain* set a par value and abolished all multiple rates.

Aug. *China* established a single fluctuating rate for all transactions except government payments.

Indonesia abolished its exchange certificate system and introduced other multiple rates.

Turkey modified its export premiums so that a single rate applied to all transactions except exports of two commodities.

1960

Feb. *Iceland* eliminated its multiple rate system, and depreciated its par value.

Apr. *The Philippines* introduced a fluctuating free market for most transactions, with a "mixing" rate for exports.

May *Peru* unified its two exchange markets.

Dec. The special procedure for changes in *China's* exchange system arranged in June 1948 was discontinued.

1961

Jan. *Yugoslavia* abolished its multiple rate system and introduced a unified fixed rate for all transactions except receipts from tourism.

May–July *Brazil* introduced new exchange arrangements for coffee export proceeds and transferred to the free market all imports previously at preferential rates.

June *China* introduced a fixed rate for all transactions.

July *Ecuador* replaced a complex multiple rate system with a new par value applying to most transactions; only a minor free market with a fluctuating rate was retained for some transactions in invisibles and unregistered capital.

Sept. *Costa Rica* set a new par value and except for temporary arrangements abolished all multiple rates.

Table 6 *(concluded).* Principal Developments in Multiple Exchange Rates, 1946–65

1962

Jan.	*Chile* again instituted two exchange markets.
	The Philippines introduced a fluctuating rate for all transactions except merchandise exports, to which a "mixing" rate would apply.
Feb.	*Israel* set a new par value and eliminated multiple rates.
May	*The United Arab Republic* replaced its multiple rates with a single rate.
Aug.	*Costa Rica* removed its last multiple rate.
Oct.	*Indonesia* reclassified imports in its complex rate structure.

1963

Mar.	*Nicaragua* transferred the remaining items from the free to the official market, so that a single rate of exchange applied to all transactions.
	Afghanistan devalued its official rate, set an initial par value, and greatly simplified its complex rate structure.

1964

Jan.	*Laos* devalued its official rate and established a legal free market for imports other than aid goods, and for tourism, capital transfers, and other payments.
	Venezuela considerably simplified its exchange system through a series of steps worked out with the Fund.
Mar.–July	*Brazil* undertook several simplifications of its exchange system.
May	*Korea* established a unitary rate which was only nominally fluctuating, and abolished multiple rates.

1965

Jan.–Dec.	*Brazil* changed the effective rates applicable to coffee exports on several occasions throughout the year.
Mar.	*Korea* established an exchange market in which the rate was allowed to fluctuate, and substantially liberalized its restrictive system.
Nov.	*The Philippines* unified its exchange system, and set a new par value of ₱ 3.90 = US$1.
Dec.	*Somalia* introduced a temporary 3 per cent exchange tax for revenue purposes.

CHAPTER

7

Fluctuating Exchange Rates

Margaret G. de Vries

IN NO FIELD of the Fund's endeavor have principle and expediency been more thoroughly interwoven than in that of fluctuating rates. Fixed exchange rates have remained the Fund's main principle; but temporarily, and in certain circumstances, fluctuating rates have been recognized as useful expedients.

Reconciliation between the aim of exchange rate stability and awareness of the need for flexibility of exchange rates has come by degrees: over the years it is possible to discern almost step-by-step movements in the Fund's policy in this regard. In its very early days the Fund put primary stress on the fact that fluctuating rates were inconsistent with the Articles. Quite soon, however, pragmatic considerations began to overshadow the more technical ones, and a less rigid approach was adopted. Hoping that a few exceptions would not cause a general return to the unstable rates of the pre-Fund era, the staff and the Board recognized the possibility that unusual circumstances might justify temporary departures from the standard prescribed by the Articles.

This toleration was not entirely a mere giving in to circumstances. Already the useful possibilities of less exacting policies toward exchange rates could be envisaged. Consequently, as successful experiences mounted, the Fund's policy gradually extended to outright advocacy of fluctuating rates for those situations where they seemed especially fitting.

Nevertheless, these shifts in the Fund's attitude toward flexible rates from 1948 to 1965 were not at the expense of the Fund's belief in exchange rate stability. There were two reasons why the Board could accept fluctuating rates on a number of occasions without surrendering the prime objective of rate stability. First, fluctuating rates have, for several countries, turned out to be part of the journey to a fixed exchange rate. Second, the circumstances in which fluctuating rates could meet with Fund approval have been carefully delineated. Although liberalizing its policies on flexible rates, the Fund opposed all suggestions that a general scheme of fluctuating rates be instituted.

CONCERN WITH THE ARTICLES

MEXICO IN 1948

That members of the staff and nearly all the Directors were anxious about the status under the Articles of a country that had suspended its par value, is clear from the action taken when the first such example came up for the Fund's consideration. In July 1948 Mexico suspended all transactions at the par value, and proposed to allow exchange transactions to take place at whatever exchange rates the market set. Although imports were to some extent excessive, the country's payments difficulty was due not so much to the balance of trade as to capital flight.

When the Mexican proposal was considered, the legal staff made much of the point that the Fund had no authority, under the terms of the Agreement, to *approve* a fluctuating rate. Not wishing to disapprove the Mexican action, the Board therefore did not take any decision, on the understanding that Mexico would establish a new parity "within three weeks." It soon became evident that a new parity would not be so quickly set, and the situation then posed for the Fund, as a new international agency, was a most difficult one. The two questions regarded as basic were: Could the Fund *agree* to a continued violation of the Articles? Could access to the Fund's resources be permitted during the period in which the par value was ineffective?

Mr. Gómez (Mexico), when explaining to the Board Mexico's request for an extension of time, argued the necessity for Mexico to ascertain the level at which a new rate could be maintained before agreeing a new parity. The Mexican Government had adopted all the strict internal stabilization measures the Fund had recommended, but more time was still required. Although it was possible that a stable exchange rate might be maintained if exchange controls were introduced, Mr. Gómez made it clear that the Mexican authorities were especially reluctant to resort to exchange controls. It was not even certain that the authorities could enforce exchange controls.

Nonetheless, Mexico did not wish to place itself in the position of violating the Articles of Agreement. Mr. Gómez suggested, therefore, that Mexico's situation might be considered as falling within the provisions of Article IV, Section 5 (c) (iii), which entitles the Fund to "a longer period in which to declare its attitude" concerning a proposed change in par value. Recognizing that this Section might not have been intended to cover the exact circumstances of the Mexican case, he urged that the Fund and Mexico should be guided by the principles rather than by the strict letter of the Articles.

Most Executive Directors feared dangerous implications in an interpretation of the Fund's Agreement which would permit a member to change its par value by introducing a free rate. Although the staff and the Directors considered at some length the economic feasibility of fixing a new parity, they were even more concerned about Mexico's formal status under the Articles. Mexico was not meeting the basic obligations of Article IV, Section 3, which required members to maintain exchange transactions within 1 per cent of parity. The request for an extension of time under Article IV, Section 5 (c) (iii), amounted to a request that the Fund condone a technical violation of its Agreement during the extended period of time.

ARGUMENTS FOR A NEW PARITY FOR MEXICO

In the next several months a number of staff missions went to Mexico and the situation was discussed by the Board several times. The reasons why Mexico hesitated to set a new par value were considered, and each time the Fund stressed the economic advantages to Mexico of quickly doing so—the promotion of exports, the encouragement of foreign capital inflow, the return of domestic funds held abroad, and support for the determination of the Government to take the strong fiscal and credit measures necessary to redress Mexico's economic difficulties.

In the early part of 1949 the United States was in the midst of a recession. Hence, one issue to which special attention was given was whether a country closely affected by business conditions in the United States could determine a new par value so long as the recession there continued. Following the experiences of the 1930's, the fear continued to prevail in the late 1940's that fluctuations in U.S. business conditions would seriously harm the United States' trading partners.

The Fund took the view that the fixed rate system of its Agreement had already taken into account the possibility of changing business conditions in its largest member countries. Swings in business conditions should, therefore, not be the occasion for members to break away from the par value regime. Depressions and recessions were, instead, to be relieved by use of the Fund's resources.

What disturbed the legal staff and several Directors most was the continuation of Mexico's anomalous formal position in the Fund. Mexico's exchange system remained unapproved by the Fund. Accordingly, in January 1949 a proposal was made in the Board, which received general support, to write to Mexico urging the establishment of a new par value by the end of March.

Another staff mission to Mexico followed the dispatch of this communication and intensive consideration by the Board was renewed. In July 1949—one year after suspension of the initial par value—a new par value was agreed and Mexico was declared again eligible to use the Fund's resources.

EROSION OF FORMAL APPROACHES

THE BELGIAN PROPOSAL

Preoccupation with the formal status under the Articles of members with fluctuating rates was short-lived. In September 1949, at the time of the general European devaluations, the Belgian Government requested the Fund to agree to its abandoning its existing par value and delaying establishment of a new one until an appropriate rate could be determined. The Executive Directors raised no objection to the plan, there being a general feeling that the Fund had to recognize the difficulties facing Belgium. Nonetheless, deliberation took place over the precise wording of a decision. The Fund could not *agree* to the Belgian proposal because it had no authority to *approve* the adoption of fluctuating rates. There was the further question as to how far the Fund should go in condoning Belgium's action. The problem seemed simple: if Belgium found that circumstances made a fluctuating exchange rate imperative, the Fund should not try to prevent the introduction of that rate. However, it was quite another matter for the Fund to lend moral support to a fluctuating rate by formally expressing "approval" or "no objection." Mr. Rasminsky (Canada), for example, was disturbed at the change in the attitude of the Directors toward fluctuating exchange rates. Previously, the Fund had held strictly that fluctuating rates were illegal under the Articles; now the Board was considering a decision in which the Fund would agree to the need for a fluctuating rate, or at least would not object. In his view, the Fund should only note the Belgian proposal, treat it as a situation of *force majeure*, and refrain from imposing any sanctions against the member.

Mr. Tansley (United Kingdom) agreed with Mr. Rasminsky. He was especially uneasy lest the decision be taken as an invitation to other members to have recourse to fluctuating rates for indefinite periods. Moreover, he thought that any intimation of approval would be unfair to those members who had taken the risks of deciding on a new par value.

Because of these considerations, the Board discussed imposing a one-month time limit, but decided that such a limit would be unwise. A draft decision in which the Fund agreed to Belgium's plan was withdrawn. Two other alternatives—one in which the Fund *raised no objection* to Belgium's proposal, and a second in which the Fund merely *noted the Belgian measures*—were formally voted upon. The first of these two won, by a vote of 53,600 to 38,490. The final decision was, therefore:

1. Belgium has informed the Fund that it proposes to abandon the existing par value of the Belgian franc, beginning September 20, 1949, and, until the situation in the monetary field can be properly assessed so as to make possible a decision on the appropriate level for a new par value, no new fixed par value would be estab-

lished; instead a free market for the U.S. dollar would be established in Brussels for the time being. Cross rates between the dollar and other currencies would be maintained and the normal operation of payments agreements would not be affected. The firm resolve of the Belgian Government would be to propose a new fixed par value for the Belgian franc as soon as circumstances warrant it. In the meantime the member would keep in close contact with the Fund concerning developments in the free market. The Fund has been requested to concur in the plan as an appropriate step in the light of existing circumstances. . . .

2. The Fund recognizes that the plan proposed by the Government of Belgium is an appropriate step in view of the exigencies of the situation. The Fund therefore raises no objection to the plan and takes note of the intention expressed by the Belgian Government to consult with the Fund and to propose a new parity as soon as circumstances warrant.

Two days later, on September 21, 1949, Belgium, fearful of the dangers of a fluctuating rate, proposed a new par value and the Fund agreed. The decision quoted above was revoked.

PERU TURNS TO FLUCTUATING RATES

That the Fund's views on fluctuating rates had been considerably modified was further evidenced in November 1949, when Peru suspended all transactions at the par value. The country had had an exchange system consisting of three separate markets, the rates in one of which were fixed on the basis of the par value. It now proposed that the market with fixed rates should be abolished and all transactions should be conducted in two markets, one for trade and the other for nontrade transactions. Although the rates in both markets would fluctuate, they were expected to remain close to each other.

The Peruvian authorities explained that the weakening of demand abroad had created problems for Peru's metal exports. In addition, the accumulation of more sterling than could be used under Peru's import restrictions had caused difficulties for exports to the sterling area. The authorities contended that the parity rate had thus become unrealistic but that it was impossible for the time being to determine the level at which a new rate should be fixed. A prestabilization period was needed.

In a preparatory paper, the staff, guided by the less rigid view toward fluctuating rates that the Board had taken in the Belgian instance, suggested that the Fund should merely note the Peruvian proposal and take no further action. The staff reasoned that, since a system of unitary, fixed rates was fundamental to the Fund Agreement, the Fund should do no more than recognize the circumstances in which a fluctuating rate was introduced and refrain from applying sanctions. It was to be understood that Peru could not use the Fund's resources. The staff suggested that a time limit should be set within which a new par value should be proposed; otherwise, the Peruvian authorities might not have sufficient incentive to take the difficult steps necessary to stabilize the internal economy.

Several Directors, including Mr. Southard (United States), wished to go further in support of Peru's action, and suggested that the Board should commend Peru's new rate system as an effective step toward realizing the Fund's objectives. Observing that the exchange system was essentially unified and that the new rates seemed realistic, they viewed Peru's action as a substantial improvement on the complex multiple rate systems of many other countries.

As described in the preceding chapter, the Fund was becoming increasingly aware at this time that multiple rates would be difficult to abolish. Many countries had complex exchange systems based on par values which were clearly overvalued. By contrast, Peru's simple dual market system with two fluctuating rates seemed much closer to a unitary, realistic exchange rate.

EMERGENCE OF A CASE-BY-CASE APPROACH

Not all Executive Directors shared this favorable view of Peru's fluctuating rates. Recalling that a fluctuating rate had been under discussion only two months earlier when proposed by Belgium, some Directors insisted that the Fund's action on Peru should not be taken as introducing a new general policy on fluctuating rates; as in the field of multiple rates, so with fluctuating rates, a preferable solution lay in a policy which considered each country's situation on its merits.

The Board accepted this view and, on the understanding that the purpose of Peru's fluctuating rates was the establishment of a unitary exchange system on a more appropriate level, decided not to object to the use of fluctuating rates as a temporary measure. It asked the Peruvian Government to remain in close consultation with the Fund in order to fix a new par value when circumstances permitted. Meanwhile, the Board considered it urgent that Peru should adopt appropriate fiscal and credit policies in order to restrain inflationary forces and assure internal financial stability, and instructed the staff to submit a complete review of Peru's problems within six months.

THE REQUIREMENTS OF THE ARTICLES ONCE AGAIN

During the foregoing discussion of the Peruvian proposal, the status under the Articles of a country with a fluctuating rate was again reviewed. This time some Directors considered it possible for the Fund to *approve* a fluctuating rate. They argued that Sections 6 and 8 of Article IV envisaged the eventuality that some members would have to abandon existing par values without immediately fixing new ones. Section 6 provided for sanctions against members who fixed par values over the Fund's objection, but not against members who abandoned par values without moving to new ones. Section 8 provided for interim payments to maintain the value of the Fund's assets by countries without par values.

The General Counsel did not agree. His view was that, although Article IV, Section 6, did give evidence that the Fund Agreement envisaged situations in which a member might operate temporarily without a par value, these situations would remain unauthorized and thus inconsistent with the Agreement. The member would be required to agree with the Fund on a par value within a reasonable period or the sanctions provided in Article XV, Section 2, might have to be invoked.

Also in November 1949, the Board considered the procedure for dealing with the exchange system of Thailand, which had a fluctuating rate as part of a multiple rate system. A staff mission was then in Thailand; and the Thai authorities, presumably prompted by its presence, had cabled the Fund requesting authorization for its then prevailing policies, and for a change in one of its rates. Mr. de Largentaye (France) questioned whether a member that had no par value but had a fluctuating rate needed to secure the Fund's approval for changes in that rate. He did not accept that the Fund was to be the judge of whether circumstances required a change in the fluctuating rate. If it had been intended by the drafters of the Articles that the Fund's approval was required, Article XIV would have so specified. Accordingly, he abstained from any decision on the change in the Thai rate. The decision taken was in fact quite limited. In view of the lack of information at the time on Thailand's exchange system, the Fund did not object to the continuance of Thailand's existing policies, pending the return of the staff mission and consideration of its report.

Continued deferment of a par value for Peru

At the end of 1950, the Board took up a first request from Peru to defer establishing a new par value. The country's two fluctuating rates had been close together and had remained stable, but in the Government's view a new parity could not yet be fixed. The Board discussed setting a time limit within which Peru must take action on a par value. Mr. Southard questioned the desirability of this. He thought that the Fund should not take an inflexible attitude toward such cases, particularly since most members seemed convinced of the advantages of stable exchange rates and the use of fluctuating rates did not seem especially contagious. The most important consideration was to find amicable ways of genuine consultation with members having such arrangements, so that the Fund could periodically review with them the feasibility of establishing a formal parity. Mr. Crick (United Kingdom) similarly questioned a proposed six-month deadline. Hence, the decision was merely to the effect that the Fund would from time to time review with Peru its exchange situation, with a view to determining whether action respecting a new parity would be feasible.

In 1960, by combining its two markets, Peru introduced a unitary fluctuating rate. This rate was still in existence on December 31, 1965, having remained, or been held, stable at 26.8 soles per U.S. dollar. In the intervening years, the Fund had permitted Peru to draw on the Fund's resources and to assume the obligations of Article VIII—that is, to be regarded as a country which has a convertible currency.[1]

FLUCTUATION OF A MAJOR CURRENCY

Why Canada turned to a fluctuating rate

A further example of the Fund's acceptance or toleration of a fluctuating rate in exceptional circumstances is afforded by Canada. At the end of September 1950, Mr. Rasminsky informed the Fund that Canada had decided for the time being to suspend the par value of the Canadian dollar and to allow its foreign exchange value to fluctuate in response to market forces. The main purpose was to restrain a heavy inflow of capital, especially of speculative capital and mainly from the United States. This inflow, which had become especially great in 1950, was adding to the money supply and tending to depress interest rates, thus augmenting inflation. The object of the Canadian proposal was thus in contrast to most other exchange rate adjustments, which are intended to rectify an unfavorable balance of trade and to check an outflow of capital. In the view of the Canadian Government, it was impossible to determine in advance with any reasonable assurance what new rate level would be appropriate.

When the Canadian proposal was received, the staff recommended that one or both of two alternatives to the contemplated fluctuating rate should be considered: (1) the absorption of additional reserves by open market operations; (2) the introduction of additional controls to restrain the inflow of capital. In the staff view, a basic principle of the Fund was that exchange rates should not be used as an instrument of domestic monetary policy. The rationale of the Canadian proposal was the hope that a small appreciation of the exchange rate would have a minor effect on the current payments position but would have an important restraining effect on the capital inflow; the absorption of the residual dollar inflow could be handled by open market operations.

The staff, however, believed that it was unlikely that small changes in the exchange rate would have important effects on capital flows. Continued fluctuation of the rate would encourage and even justify the expectations of speculators. The Canadian problem was a fundamental one: capital movements had recurrently led to pressures on the exchange rate. The Canadians should act on the

---

[1] See p. 76 above.

assumption that the world-wide instability leading to pressures on its exchange rate would continue and might even grow worse.

Mr. Rasminsky explained to the Directors that the suggestions made by the staff had already been submitted to the Finance Minister for consideration and had been referred to the Canadian Cabinet. The Canadian authorities, however, had rejected these alternatives as inadequate. As for open market operations, the Government could not take on additional debt of an unpredictable amount. And there were technical and political difficulties in controlling capital movements: direct controls would impose a tremendous, if not impossible, administrative burden; they might create hostility toward American capital; and, in addition, the Canadian Government was opposed to exchange controls of any kind.

The Fund's immediate response

The decision which the Executive Directors took at the time was that the Fund, unable under its Articles of Agreement to approve a fluctuating rate, recognized the exigencies of the situation and took note of the intention of the Canadian Government to remain in consultation with the Fund and to re-establish an effective par value as soon as circumstances warranted. This decision reflected the position of the majority of Directors that Canada should, in the light of its special circumstances, be permitted to try a fluctuating exchange rate for a short period. If, at the end of that period, the Canadian Government had to conclude that the alternatives were either to declare a new par value at parity with the U.S. dollar or to restore the old par value and impose effective capital controls, at least there was a better prospect of reaching general agreement that no other alternatives existed. At the same time, the language of the decision was not as forthright as in the Belgian case in 1949; it made no reference to "an appropriate step."

A few Directors again commented that possibly the Articles had been somewhat deficient: they made no provision for the case of a country which could not immediately propose a new par value. It was the view of Mr. Beyen (Netherlands), for example, that where a country could not propose a new parity, the Board could not ask the government to take the responsibility of doing so; the Fund had to give the member the benefit of the doubt in instances of this kind, since the responsibility for the action was the government's.

The Chairman, however, stressed that the position taken by Mr. Beyen called for very definite qualification because, if too widely interpreted, it might amount to a negation of one of the main principles of the Fund. He could not agree that the Fund was obliged to accept any proposal submitted by a member, on the theory that the responsibility for the proposed action and its effect were the government's alone. The Fund also had a responsibility to all its members, and each member in turn had a responsibility to other members.

Debates over the Canadian rate

For the next decade, until Canada returned to the par value system, there were intensive discussions among the staff and in the Board about the Canadian rate. The discussions in the Board began only a few months after the introduction of the fluctuating rate. In April 1951, in the course of a review by the Board of the Canadian economy, Mr. Rasminsky defended the fluctuating rate. He stressed that the excessive capital inflow had been reduced and import and exchange restrictions had been liberalized. Mr. de Largentaye insisted, however, that the Canadian Government could have used alternative arrangements to deal with the capital inflow. Mr. Melville (Australia) believed that the Canadian example, and the fact that the Fund had not objected, had made it difficult for the Fund to refuse other requests for fluctuating rates.

In another review in February 1952, several Directors inquired what economic factors, if any, prevented Canada from establishing a par value and whether the fluctuating rate had not had greater disadvantages than a fixed rate even for a member in Canada's circumstances. Mr. Rasminsky replied that the Canadian experience had been that a fixed rate of exchange produced wide swings in capital movements: foreign capital came in when the fixed rate looked too low and tended to leave when the rate looked high. The Canadian Government believed that, where foreign capital movements were large, a fluctuating rate controlled them better than a fixed rate. A fluctuating rate discouraged oscillations in capital flows because of its own fluctuations. Moreover, the size of the capital flows was not enhanced by further speculative capital movements in anticipation of a change in a pegged exchange rate.

Several Directors were concerned that the Canadian problem was not a temporary one, and that the fluctuating rate, also, was not temporary. Therefore, Mr. Stamp (United Kingdom) argued that the Fund should review the general policy at issue, with emphasis on the possible result if the practice of exchange rate fluctuation spread more widely.

Mr. Rasminsky argued, in rebuttal, that Canada's current circumstances were abnormal. Moreover, Canada's adaptation to these circumstances had contributed to its attainment of two of the three main Fund objectives—the elimination of exchange restrictions and the establishment of a convertible currency with no discrimination. Some Directors supported his position. They believed that the world's exchange situation had been abnormal for some time and in such circumstances fluctuating exchange rates were of great help to countries, particularly in permitting the removal of restrictions.

By 1956 the Fund had come to regard Canada's relative success with a fluctuating rate as reflecting the uniqueness of that country's circumstances. Canada had a trade deficit with a large capital inflow. There was confidence in the Canadian dollar because of the fiscal and credit policies being followed; Canada was relatively free of restrictions and had a convertible currency. Moreover, the institutional background led many to regard as natural a parity for the Canadian dollar somewhere near that of the U.S. dollar. Close interdependence between short-term capital movements and movements of the exchange rate had caused capital flows on the whole to be equilibrating rather than disturbing. Finally, the exchange rate fluctuated by only about 3–5 per cent, despite the absence of intervention by the authorities except to maintain an orderly exchange market.

For all these reasons, Canadian trade and normal capital transactions had not lost the important benefits commonly associated with exchange rate stability. The Canadian example was not a precedent, for the circumstances of other countries were quite different.

AT THE CROSSROADS

Thus, from 1950 until about 1956, Canada's fluctuating rate had achieved the primary objectives for which it had been established. Massive inflows of long-term capital had continued and had provided net additional savings with which Canada had been able to finance a high rate of investment and growth. Yet the potentially disequilibrating effects of these long-term capital inflows on the balance of payments had been sufficiently offset by current account balances and compensating short-term capital movements. Exchange stability had been preserved. Short-term capital movements appeared to have responded much more to changes in the exchange rate than to relative interest rates in Canada and the United States.

After 1957, however, Canada began to encounter several difficulties. A very large current account deficit emerged and persisted; at 3–4 per cent of the gross national product, it was among the largest in the world. The rate of growth of the economy had slowed down measurably, and unemployment was high— 7½ per cent by mid-1961. By then disenchantment with the way the Canadian rate had been operating since the late 1950's was discernible both among Canadian authorities and in the Fund.

The Canadian authorities attributed the country's economic reverses in large part to the now unduly appreciated level of the exchange rate; the inflow of capital had caused the rate to reach a point at which it acted as a stimulus to imports and as some deterrent to exports. In presenting his budget to Parliament on June 20, 1961, the Minister of Finance announced several new policies, including a switch in exchange rate policy. Whereas the Government previously had had a neutral attitude toward the level of the exchange rate, there was now to be some direct official intervention in the exchange market. Canada was thus to have a *managed* flexible rate.

Describing the Canadian policy to the Board in the middle of 1961, Mr. Rasminsky recognized that the shift in the exchange rate policy of the Canadian

Government might create some special problems for the Fund. Other Fund members might well have anxiety about the degree to which the Canadian Government would devalue the Canadian dollar, but would not have an opportunity to sanction, or object to, the rate that emerged. Mr. Rasminsky sought to reassure the other Fund members by stating that Canada did not intend to operate its rate policies so as to cause competitive depreciation. The intention of the Canadian Government was not to determine the level of the exchange rate in the market but rather to reduce the inflow of capital and the size of the current account deficit.

The assessment of the Canadian exchange rate situation which the Fund staff made differed from that of the Canadian authorities. The staff agreed with the authorities that the period prior to 1956–57 had shown the usefulness of the fluctuating rate, and that the post-1956 experiences had been more disturbing than equilibrating. But the explanation offered by the staff for what had gone wrong since 1956–57 differed from that of the authorities.

In the staff view, the primary cause of the unsatisfactory results of the fluctuating exchange rate after the first few years was not any change in the mechanism of the Canadian balance of payments, but the effect of governmental policy on that mechanism. Governmental policy had resulted in the emergence of a wide differential between Canadian interest rates and those of the United States. A spread in which interest rates in Canada were higher than those in the United States had attracted liquid funds into Canada. The inflow of these funds kept the exchange rate appreciated during a period when basic trade and long-term capital flows that were normally motivated would have tended to push it downward.

The staff pointed out that after 1956–57 the size and composition of the long-term capital inflow into Canada had changed markedly. While direct investment inflows had continued on a more or less steady and generally upward course, they had been supplemented by huge and erratic movements of portfolio capital. Various types of capital flowed in unevenly at different times. Many of these flows seemed to have been highly sensitive to divergences between monetary and credit conditions in Canada and the United States. By the late 1950's capital movements which were induced primarily, or solely, by interest differentials were much larger than they had been in the early 1950's. Another factor which had made the fluctuating rate increasingly difficult to handle by 1960 had been the mounting uncertainties as to the prospects for the Canadian economy and as to the Government's economic policies. The staff concluded, therefore, that "Canada should re-establish an effective par value as soon as circumstances permit."

The foregoing report by the staff was before the Board when, in February 1962, it undertook the first consultation with Canada under Article VIII. At this consultation, the uneasiness of most of the Executive Directors concerning the continuance of the fluctuating rate was readily manifest. The Board did not press for an immediate re-establishment of a par value. But many Directors questioned whether Canada still had a plausible case for continued noncompliance with the Fund Agreement. What economic situation would enable a par value to be restored? Were not Canada's special circumstances, in effect, permanent? Did not Canada's large reserves seem sufficiently ample to enable the authorities to defend a fixed rate? How should the Fund assess the declared intention of the Canadian authorities to bring the rate down to a lower level? How far would the rate actually be depreciated? How could depreciation be achieved without endangering exchange rate stability, if large fiscal deficits and low interest rates were permitted?

The Directors observed that Canada presented a rare example of an exchange depreciation being undertaken largely to stimulate the growth of national income rather than to influence the current balance of payments. They also expressed considerable concern over the possibility that Canada's internal policies were too expansionary.

From Canada's experiences the Directors drew conclusions regarding fluctuating rates in general. Had not Canada's experience demonstrated that it was difficult and potentially harmful for a country to conduct a monetary policy isolated from that of other countries? Even a flexible exchange rate had not given Canada freedom in its internal monetary policy. Had not another danger of flexible rates also been revealed—that feeling safe under the shelter of a flexible rate and deprived of the symptoms of movements in reserves, the authorities tended to disregard the external repercussions of their domestic policies? It was significantly noted that Mexico, like Canada a neighbor of the United States and a recipient of heavy inflows of U.S. capital, had also found a fluctuating rate unworkable.

Several Directors, therefore, supported the conclusions of the staff that Canada should re-establish an effective par value as soon as circumstances permitted. Some of the Directors were fairly specific that the new par value should be introduced as soon as the Canadian Government's policies were clearly established and the authorities had reached a conclusion as to the appropriate level for the new parity.

On May 2, 1962, in the midst of exchange difficulties, Canada gave up its fluctuating rate and proposed a new par value to the Fund. The authorities stated that the new par value was necessary to correct a fundamental disequilibrium. Moreover, they expressed their awareness, deriving from the discussions at the meetings of the Board in July 1961 and February 1962, of the widespread international concern at Canada's deviation from the established exchange system.

Having decided to re-establish a par value, the Canadian authorities faced the question of selecting a rate. Mr. Rasminsky explained that a par value at the current rate of 95 U.S. cents per Canadian dollar was thought to be too high to eliminate uncertainty in the market; the Government had already lost substantial reserves in defending that rate. Alternatively, a rate of 90 U.S. cents per Canadian dollar was rejected as being lower than the Canadian economy required. Furthermore, Canada could not count on international acceptance of such a depreciated rate. Consequently, the authorities proposed a new rate of 92.5 U.S. cents per Canadian dollar.

The Directors, agreeing with the new par value, welcomed the return of Canada to the par value system.

A REMAINING HURDLE

With the acceptance by the Board during the 1950's of Canada's fluctuating rate, the formal objections of the Fund to fluctuating rates had quietly come to an end. But yet another hurdle had had, in the meantime, to be surmounted. This concerned the valuation of the Fund's holdings of currencies of countries where fluctuating rates prevailed. Article IV, Section 8, of the Agreement requires countries to maintain the gold value of the Fund's assets. Hence, in the event of a depreciation in its par value, a member has to pay additional local currency to the Fund. Was there not a need for such payments to be made by countries without par values and with fluctuating rates? If payments were required, what rate of exchange should be applied? The staff pointed out that a similar difficulty covering the exchange rate to use for computations would arise if another member wished to draw from the Fund the currency of the country with the fluctuating rate.

These questions became a matter for consideration and decision by the Board in 1954. At that time members with fluctuating rates included not only Canada but also Lebanon, Peru, Syria, and Thailand. Even if only for the purposes of the auditors, some rules were essential. In addition, it was imperative to preserve the gold value of the Fund's assets. And it was desirable to ensure that the Fund was not used in lieu of the outside market for short-term arbitrage gains.

With little debate the Board decided that for currencies with a single fluctuating rate, computations were to be based on the mid-point between the highest and lowest exchange rates for the U.S. dollar for cable transfers for spot delivery in the main financial center of the country of the fluctuating currency on specified days. If a mid-point could not be determined in the main financial center of the country of the fluctuating currency, rates quoted in New York could be substituted.[2]

---

[2] E.B. Decision No. 321-(54/32), June 15, 1954; below, Vol. III, p. 222.

The Directors had, however, some difficulty in deciding upon the scope of application of these rules. How should they be applied to currencies with multiple exchange rates, some of which might fluctuate? The Directors from Latin America stressed that it was vital that the Fund should not embarrass a country which was struggling to maintain a par value. Such embarrassment might result from the Fund's computing an effective rate other than the par value for use in Fund transactions in the currency of that country. Hence, a preamble to the decision on computed exchange rates explicitly specified that multiple rate systems were not to be covered by these special rules, and that the Fund would not determine computed rates except where there was a practical interest for the Fund or its members to do so.

These rules have the practical purpose of facilitating the operations of the Fund. They make it possible for the Fund to engage in transactions in the currencies of members with fluctuating exchange rates on an equitable basis and to make the computations required by the Fund Agreement—that is, to facilitate the periodic revaluations of the Fund's holdings of fluctuating currencies, as well as their valuation for the purpose of actual transactions. Other members of the Fund are thus not precluded by the fluctuations in the rate for a member's currency from purchasing it from the Fund, nor is a member whose currency fluctuates necessarily deprived of its right to purchase the currencies of other members. These rules become operative in any given case only after the Fund has decided to apply Article IV, Section 8, to its holdings of a fluctuating currency.

In July 1954, this general decision on computed rates for fluctuating currencies was made applicable to Canada and Peru. Canada, of course, had had a single fluctuating rate since September 20, 1950, and this rate was used as the basis for the rate computed for Fund transactions.

Peru had had two exchange markets since November 1949; the par value of 6.50 soles per U.S. dollar no longer applied to any transactions. The exchange rates in the two markets fluctuated freely and there was only a small spread between the rates. The Fund's holdings of Peruvian soles had been adjusted under Article IV, Section 8 (b) (ii), in April 1951. This adjustment had been made on the basis of a rate of 15 soles per U.S. dollar, a rate which had been proposed by Peru and accepted by the Board "subject to further adjustment in the event of a significant change in the foreign exchange value of the currency or when a new par value for the sol is established in agreement with the Fund." The rate in the certificate market—more important than the free market as measured by the volume of transactions—had been adopted as the rate for purposes of a stand-by arrangement with the Fund approved in February 1954. Paragraph 2 of the stand-by arrangement had specified that "currencies drawn from the Fund shall be used only for the support of the certificate market rate."

Paragraph 19 of the arrangement had specified that the rate of exchange to be used for drawings and repurchases would be the rate determined from time to time under Article IV, Section 8. In computing this rate for the currency of Peru, the mid-point stated in the general rules was to be that of the rate in the certificate market.

Computations under the general decision have been made only for countries where no transactions any longer take place at the par values. At the end of 1965, for example, computed effective rates applied only to Argentina, Bolivia, Brazil, Chile, Colombia, Paraguay, and Peru.[3]

The question of a country's formal status in the Fund if it had no par value, while quiescent, was not entirely dead in 1954. Discussing the application to Canada of the decision on computed rates, Mr. Saad (Egypt) said that he had serious difficulty with the Fund's adopting rules which in a sense helped to perpetuate a member's technical violation of the Articles. However, the decision passed without objection by other Directors.

Subsequently, two technical amendments were made to the decision on the determination of rates for transactions in currencies of countries with fluctuating rates.[4] The first was introduced in August 1961 when the Fund decided that it should sell gold to replenish its holdings of certain currencies. Because the currencies of some countries with fluctuating rates were involved—for example, the Canadian dollar—the earlier decision on transactions and computations involving fluctuating currencies was amended to cover such sales of gold by the Fund. The second amendment was made in December 1961 when the Board took a decision on the General Arrangements to Borrow. At that time, the decision on computed rates for fluctuating currencies was amended to cover such borrowing and the repayment of borrowing in fluctuating currencies.

FLUCTUATING RATES AND EXCHANGE REFORM

The gradually evolving policies in connection with the fluctuating rates of Mexico, Peru, and Canada illustrate one major direction in which the Fund's attitude toward fixed rates was not immutable. In these instances, the Fund, in effect, tolerated fluctuating rates; later, it went somewhat further.

Beginning in 1956, the Fund has supported programs which, in conjunction with exchange reforms and stabilization plans, have included a fluctuating rate. To some extent Peru's fluctuating rate, described above, had been introduced as part of an exchange reform. But even before reform, Peru's exchange system had been fairly simple, inflation had not been massive, and the devaluation involved was modest. In the late 1950's, however, the technique of using a

---

[3] *Schedule of Par Values,* February 15, 1966.

[4] E.B. Decision No. 1245-(61/45), August 4, 1961, and E.B. Decision No. 1283-(61/56), December 20, 1961; below, Vol. III, p. 224.

fluctuating exchange rate to effect reform of a complex exchange system became widely used.

The circumstances

Many of the less developed countries in which there has been prolonged inflation have found it necessary to change their exchange rates frequently. Several of these countries, for various reasons, have instituted fluctuating rates. Countries undertaking stabilization of their economies are frequently uncertain about the effects of the internal measures being adopted. Future movements in prices and wages have been difficult to estimate. In these circumstances, countries have been unable to determine in advance an appropriate level for the exchange rate. Where a combination of restrictions and multiple rates exist, it is difficult to ascertain even the average effective exchange rate being applied. Determination of an equilibrium rate is virtually impossible. In still other instances, a new par value cannot be determined until after a new tariff system has been established. For these reasons, as exchange reforms have been undertaken, several countries have instituted single fluctuating rates.

The changing Fund policy

Bolivia was among the first, in 1956, to effect exchange reform via a fluctuating rate. Its example was soon followed by Chile, Paraguay, and Argentina. At first, the Fund merely agreed to these fluctuating rates. But as more instances occurred, it was clear that the Fund had, in effect, adopted a general policy of permitting fluctuating exchange rates as a temporary instrument of exchange depreciation and liberalization of restrictions.

This policy was made manifest in the Board's reaction to a proposal put forward by the Philippines in 1962. At this time the Philippines, which had had a fixed exchange rate, introduced a fluctuating one. When presenting to the Board the Philippine proposal for exchange reform and request for a drawing from the Fund, Mr. Saad (who had been elected by the Philippines) emphasized that the proposed fluctuating rate was clearly in line with the Fund's policy. The Government of the Philippines was resorting to a fluctuating rate just as had other countries as a means of eliminating restrictions on payments and of finding a realistic level for the exchange rate. The proposed change in the exchange rate represented the culmination of a program, which the Philippines had been following for the previous two years, of steadily simplifying its exchange system and of reducing reliance on quantitative restrictions. The Philippine authorities regarded the fluctuating rate as temporary and looked forward to the establishment of an appropriate new par value.

The Directors agreed that the proposed exchange reform, except for a few transitional features, followed a plan with which they were already familiar.

They would have preferred that the Philippine authorities move to a single fixed rate system, but they recognized the circumstances which necessitated delay in introducing a new par value. These circumstances included the persistence of a great deal of inflationary pressure, a change in government administration, and a need to revise the tariff. The Managing Director, Mr. Jacobsson, while reasserting that a floating rate was not, in general, desirable, emphasized the difficulty which a country with slender reserves experienced in adopting a fixed rate without imposing exchange restrictions. Were restrictions to be instituted, a black market would inevitably emerge.

Some Directors questioned how capital movements, both in and out of the Philippines, would react to a fluctuating exchange rate. The effect of the new rate on capital was important, especially because capital outflows had been partly responsible for the deterioration in the balance of payments. These Directors hoped that the proposed exchange reform would help to curb capital flight and even to stimulate capital repatriation. They favored a fixed rate, which in their view was more likely to make capital movements normal. Therefore, they placed a great deal of emphasis on the intention of the Philippine authorities to use the fluctuating rate only temporarily.

Experiences with temporary fluctuating rates have, in general, proved quite successful. Several such rates were eventually stabilized and furnished the basis for new par values. Indeed, by 1962–63 the Fund had even begun to initiate suggestions for fluctuating rates as temporary ways of altering exchange rates and of achieving exchange reforms. Several countries were advised—even urged—to take this road to depreciation and exchange reform. Where countries introduced greater rate flexibility, the Fund welcomed the action.

APPROPRIATE CONDITIONS FOR A FLUCTUATING RATE

The questions that have come up as the Fund has considered individual fluctuating rates reveal the difficulties of deciding the circumstances in which fluctuating rates are appropriate. Many of these questions have concerned reserves and reserve policy. What is the level of reserves required before an exchange rate can be maintained? When should the central bank enter the market in order to accumulate reserves? Do not central bank purchases in the market to repay short-term liabilities differ from purchases for reserves? (The former may be treated as a genuine market force, while the demand for foreign exchange for reserve accumulation represents a policy decision of the authorities rather than a market force.) May it not be best to accumulate reserves by taking advantage of special occurrences in the exchange market rather than by exerting a continuous downward pressure on the rate?

Another group of questions has concerned the reactions of capital movements to a fluctuating exchange rate. For example, is a fluctuating rate appropriate where underinvoicing and smuggling as well as an excessive outflow of capital have been a problem? The use of fluctuating rates in circumstances of continuous inflation has given rise to still other questions. For, if internal prices are not stabilized, flexible rates are necessary to prevent overvaluation. Yet under conditions of unstable internal prices, the rate depreciates regularly; this depreciation in turn contributes to continued instability of internal prices, and also possibly induces speculative capital movements.

One situation in which a unitary fluctuating exchange rate has been found unworkable is that in which a particular exchange rate is required for a given commodity. When Colombia, for example, attempted to introduce a fluctuating rate in 1957–58, it was found to be inappropriate because of the need for a special exchange rate for coffee exports.

Pegging of fluctuating rates

The Fund's view has been that, once a fluctuating rate is introduced, the authorities should let the rate change freely in response to market forces, intervening only to maintain orderly market conditions. The Board has, therefore, often warned against pegging of fluctuating rates. Similarly, the Board has suggested that, where two markets exist, sales of exchange by the central bank in the free market should not result in a spread of fixed size between the official rate of exchange and that in the free market. The fear of the Board has been that intervention by the central bank could lead to an undue loss of foreign exchange reserves as well as establish an inappropriate exchange rate. Where the member has drawn on the Fund, the Board has been concerned lest the Fund's resources be used to peg a potentially unrealistic exchange rate.

In some countries where a flexible exchange rate policy is considered essential, certain "balance of payments tests" have been developed and have become part of stabilization programs.[5] The object of these tests is to ensure that an exchange rate will be maintained which conforms to the basic trends in the economy. A level at which the country's foreign exchange reserves are to be maintained during a stated period is prescribed. The country undertakes that if there is a danger that reserves will fall below this level, it will take appropriate action, for example, by allowing the exchange rate to fall. Even so, since most countries have been reluctant to see their exchange rates depreciate excessively, the Fund has frequently had to call upon countries with flexible rates not to stabilize prematurely.

FIXED RATES AS AN OBJECTIVE

Nonetheless, the Fund's ultimate objective in cases of exchange reform has been to create the conditions for the restoration of a stable and unified exchange

---

[5] See below, pp. 506–10.

rate. The fluctuating rate has been regarded as a temporary means to an end. The Fund has also continued to regard a general system of fixed rates and institutionally agreed par values as decidedly superior to a system of fluctuating rates.

As early as 1951 the Fund gave several reasons for its belief that a system of fluctuating rates would not be a satisfactory alternative to the par value system. To those who advocated allowing rates to find their "natural" level it replied that there was no such thing as a natural level for the rate of exchange of a currency. The "natural" rate differed in each case, as it was dependent upon the economic, financial, and monetary policies followed by the country concerned, and by other countries with whom it had important economic relationships. In addition, whether a given exchange rate was at the correct level could be determined only after there had been time to observe the course of the balance of payments in response to that rate.

Furthermore, implicit in the arguments for fluctuating rates was the assumption that some major currency would remain stable as a point of reference. The limited number of countries that had used flexible rates had done so within the framework of fixed parities for the currencies of well-nigh all the industrial countries. Chaos would result if a substantial number of rates were allowed to fluctuate.[6]

By 1958 the Fund's views were based on its widening experiences. As in the 1930's, so in the 1950's, fluctuating rates had been found to be inappropriate where outflows of capital were excessive or underinvoicing and smuggling were troublesome. Fluctuating rates often induced additional capital inflows which were prompted by speculation on exchange rate movements. It had also become clear that countries preferred to make adjustments in their exchange rates in some manner other than through fluctuating rates, so as to minimize speculation. Most countries seemed to recognize, in practice, the importance of orderly exchange arrangements and exchange stability. Even in countries where the authorities were not prepared formally to stabilize the exchange rate on the basis of a realistic parity, *de facto* stable rates, the Board observed, were often maintained for long periods of time.[7]

In its Annual Report for 1962 further examples were cited of the Fund's postwar experience with fluctuating exchange rates.[8] The conclusion was that a short period of fluctuation might be a means of reaching a rate which could subsequently be maintained. But in other circumstances fluctuating rates gave rise to difficulties. In exceptional circumstances, such as the large capital inflows into Canada in the early 1950's and into Peru for brief periods, a fluctuating rate might have an upward tendency. The more general experience, however, was

---

[6] *Annual Report, 1951,* pp. 36–41.

[7] *Annual Report, 1958,* p. 20.

[8] *Annual Report, 1962,* pp. 62–67.

that if a country did not clearly and quickly adopt a monetary policy aimed at stability, the movements of its fluctuating rate were likely to be oscillations not around a stable value but around a declining trend.

If an exchange rate fluctuated widely, it might be expected to depreciate over time. Any circumstance leading to a temporary depreciation of the rate raised the domestic currency cost of imports and directly and indirectly led to price increases. These increases encouraged demands for higher money wages, at least some of which were met. Hence, depreciations were likely to induce increases in domestic costs. On the other hand, institutional rigidities limited reductions in money wages, so that exchange appreciations were unlikely to lead to any significant lowering of domestic costs. Therefore, a fluctuating rate might be expected to encourage a rising trend in domestic costs, which in turn put downward pressure on the rate.

Pegging of a fluctuating rate had still other disadvantages. A fixed rate subject to frequent changes, or a temporarily pegged fluctuating rate, was likely to encourage destabilizing speculation which would create even more serious problems than those which arose under a system of freely fluctuating rates.

It was concluded therefore that it was an illusion to expect a fluctuating rate to ease the problems facing monetary authorities. On the contrary, by eliminating the rallying point of the defense of a fixed par value, a fluctuating rate made it necessary for the authorities to exercise greater caution in determining monetary policy.

In 1964 the Deputy Managing Director summarized the Fund's position as follows:

> Some economists argue the case for freely fluctuating rates of exchange as an instrument for balance of payments adjustment. But financial officials in most countries today—even in those developing countries which temporarily have fluctuating rates—have been convinced by experience that greater flexibility than that sanctioned by the Fund's Articles of Agreement would be undesirable and impractical. Fluctuating rates create great uncertainty for traders and investors and set up stresses in the financial and economic relationships within a country and in its international position. Moreover, far from being simple, the problems of managing a flexible rate are no less complex than those which arise in maintaining an effective par value, and in addition present their own mixture of financial, economic, and political difficulties. Indeed, countries which have endeavored to conduct their affairs on the basis of a fluctuating rate have found it extremely hard to let the exchange rate perform its intended functions. It also is generally true that exchange rate policy under a system of flexible rates tends to become much more a matter of unilateral action, which would make the whole process of international collaboration in financial matters far more difficult.[9]

[9] Speech by Frank A. Southard, Jr., Dallas, Texas, March 27, 1964, in *International Financial News Survey*, April 3, 1964, pp. 115–16.

Thus, while the Fund's policy as regards fluctuating rates became more flexible, the Fund continued, strongly, to favor a system of fixed exchange rates. Nonetheless, events on the horizon forewarned that the debates concerning the merits of fluctuating rates would, shortly, be intensified. Among the suggestions being made in the mid-1960's for ways to improve the system of par values was that fluctuating rates, at least for major currencies, should be substituted for par values. When, in 1964 and 1965, one large industrial country after another began to be plagued by balance of payments stresses for which there seemed no adequate solutions, the advocates of fluctuating rates were able to muster additional adherents.

Changes in fixed rates seemed ruled out because the authorities of the major countries concerned found it difficult politically to alter the exchange values of their currencies. Further, in the absence of adequate world gold stocks, most countries had come to hold sizable amounts of the currencies of the major countries as foreign exchange reserves. Therefore, among other effects of exchange rate alteration, the authorities in charge of the currencies used as reserves were concerned with the implications of changes in exchange rates for the reserve holdings of all trading nations. Tighter monetary and fiscal policies had already been introduced in most of the large industrial nations; the imposition of still more stringent internal measures to alleviate or reverse external deficits was considered contrary to the domestic objectives to which these countries were committed. Stricter credit or tax measures might jeopardize employment; reduced public expenditure might mean that urgent domestic programs would have to be postponed or foregone. Some countries had reintroduced, or enacted for the first time, controls on capital movements, but they shunned controls on current transactions.

All these difficulties with alternative solutions strengthened the arguments for enhanced flexibility of exchange rates. Nevertheless, the monetary authorities of all the large industrial nations, and especially the central bankers, as well as the officials of the Fund, continued to view as untenable any general system of fluctuating rates.

CHAPTER

8

Gold Transactions at Premium Prices

Mary H. Gumbart

THE OBLIGATIONS OF FUND MEMBERS in connection with the price of gold are set out in Article IV, Section 2, of the Fund Agreement, which reads as follows:

> *Gold purchases based on par values.*—The Fund shall prescribe a margin above and below par value for transactions in gold by members, and no member shall buy gold at a price above par value plus the prescribed margin, or sell gold at a price below par value minus the prescribed margin.

Because of this link between par values and the price of gold, the Fund's policy on gold transactions at premium prices has sought to prevent international transactions in gold being effected at prices substantially above par values. (Transactions below par values have never been at issue.) The purposes of the policy were twofold: first to prevent such sales from undermining the stability of members' exchange rates, and second to minimize the loss to monetary reserves resulting from private hoarding, which was the main source of demand in the premium market. The achievement of both aims required the prevention of premium gold sales.

The dilemma facing the Fund was as follows: If the premium market was kept supplied in order to lower or eliminate the premium, this would result in a larger portion of newly mined gold going into private hoards and, possibly, in the diversion of official gold holdings to hoards. As long as newly mined gold was sold at a premium above the margin set by the Fund, the monetary authorities of Fund members would be precluded, under Article IV, Section 2, from purchasing the new gold. This would reduce the amount of international liquidity (i.e., gold) available to monetary authorities. If, on the other hand, the supply to the premium gold market was not maintained, the premium would continue and might increase, thus possibly leading to instability of exchange rates. The reason that exchange rates might be undermined was that they are denominated in terms of gold, so that international transactions in gold at other than official rates must affect the established rates; premium transactions at least establish another rate for the currency in which the transactions take place.

174

FIRST STATEMENT ON GOLD TRANSACTIONS AT PREMIUM PRICES

History of first statement

The first time that the issue of premium gold sales was raised in the Board was in August 1946, when Peru inquired whether its Central Reserve Bank might, after the par value for the sol had been fixed, sell gold coins at a premium price in any market for the account of private concerns. The divergences of opinion on the economic, legal, and political aspects of the problem that characterized all considerations of it by Executive Directors emerged during a discussion of a draft reply to Peru. The minutes of the Board meeting include the following:

> It was generally agreed that [Peru's] project . . . was not specifically prohibited by any provision of the Fund Agreement. One view was that the Fund's reply should not appear to condone the practices, which resulted in smuggling of gold against the laws of various governments. . . . such a position would give the impression that the Fund approved dual prices for gold, whereas such dual prices were harmful to exchange stability.

> The other view was that in its infancy, the Fund should avoid any impression of rendering opinions on matters beyond its actual authority, and for the sake of its relations with members should not attempt to enforce a broad interpretation, where such might properly be disputed.

> It was agreed that the Ad Hoc Drafting Committee should prepare a final draft letter indicating that while the proposed project could not be said to contravene the Fund Agreement, the Fund did not wish this opinion to be construed as encouragement of the proposed action.

Such a letter was produced and sent to Peru on September 11, 1946.

Six months later Colombia asked (a) whether the Fund Agreement would permit mine owners to sell their output at a premium price (i) on the free international market, or (ii) on the local market for industrial purposes, and (b) in either event, whether the Colombian central bank could intervene in the prospective markets for purposes of control and management.

At the first discussion of this request, Mr. Gómez (Mexico), who had been elected by Colombia, urged that the Fund should reply to Colombia, as it had to Peru, that, with appropriate qualifications, the proposed actions would not in themselves "be inconsistent with any particular provision of the Fund Agreement." There was considerable opposition to Mr. Gómez' proposal, mainly on the ground that the Fund Agreement enabled the Fund to intervene against a member's permitting external gold sales at premium prices, if official rates of exchange were likely to be undermined. Any action that siphoned newly mined gold into private hoards and away from monetary systems where it could support exchange rates and finance world trade should be opposed. On the other hand, it was argued that the effects of premium gold sales might not, in fact, be as bad as assumed.

The discussion also touched on the problem of nonmember countries, which the Fund could not control, and on the question whether responsibility for stopping the trade should not rest with the buying nations rather than the selling. The discussion ended when, at the Managing Director's suggestion, the Directors agreed to set up a Committee on External Sales of Gold to study the question. The committee members were Messrs. Luthringer (United States), Chairman, Bolton (United Kingdom), Bruins (Netherlands), de Selliers (Belgium), Gómez, and Rasminsky (Canada).

The committee's first report to the Board, on May 19, 1947, was agreed by all members of the committee except Mr. Gómez, whose views were presented to the Board in writing by his Alternate, Mr. Martínez-Ostos (Mexico). The report made the following main points:

1. *General policy.* In the interest of world monetary stabilization and in view of the purposes of the Fund, the Fund should take a strong position deprecating external sales of gold at premium prices. It was recognized, as pointed out by Mr. Gómez, that the immediate value of the Fund's taking such a position might be limited owing to the action of nonmember countries. But the moral and psychological effect of the Fund's action would be internationally favorable. The committee felt that exchange stability would be undermined by continued external sales of gold at premium prices and there would be increased pressure by producers on governments of large gold producing countries to permit their production to be sold at premium prices.

2. *Authority of the Fund.* The Fund has authority under Article I and Article IV, Sections 2 and 4 (*a*), of the Fund Agreement to take action to prevent members from engaging in gold sale practices which would undermine exchange stability.

3. *Recommended action.* The committee was of the opinion that a general statement of policy should be prepared and circulated to the members recommending the adoption of effective measures by member countries to prevent exports and imports of gold at premium prices. It was felt that a legalistic statement of interpretation of the Articles of Agreement would not be desirable.

On the questions raised by Colombia, the report suggested that no reply should be sent until the general policy had been settled, and that Colombia should then be told that further consideration would be given to the question of intervention by the central bank if Colombian producers were allowed to sell their gold at a premium in the domestic market.

The committee's report was twice discussed in the Board. At the first of these meetings, some Directors urged that the question of whether the Fund had the legal authority to prevent members and/or their nationals from engaging in external gold transactions at premium prices be referred to the Committee on Interpretation, and the discussion was confined to questions of substance. These questions included the following: whether continued sales of gold at premium prices would in fact undermine exchange rate stability; the status under the Fund Agreement, and the effects of, official versus private transactions in gold; the volume and character of the premium gold trade; and whether continued premium gold sales by some members would lead to irresistible pressures on other members to permit such sales.

The only two points on which Directors were generally agreed were, first, that official agencies of members would not be permitted, under the Fund Agreement, to engage in international gold transactions outside official rates; and, second, that (as the committee proposed) the Fund should not object to internal sales of gold above parity, provided that such sales did not in effect establish new rates of exchange or undermine existing rates of other members. Opposing views were expressed in the Board on the question whether members' obligations under the Fund Agreement extended to private transactions in gold, as well as on the other points discussed.

However, at the next meeting of the Board it was decided to waive the problem of a formal interpretation of the Articles and instead to approve point 2 (Authority of the Fund) in the committee's report.

Mr. Martínez-Ostos opposed the committee's recommendations. He said that while he did not deny the obligation of members regarding exchange stability, this obligation rested on buyers of gold as much as on sellers, and premium sales were permitted under Article IV, Section 2. Perhaps as a result of these representations, the decision of the Board departed from the committee's proposals by making no reference to Article IV, Section 2, and by altering the phrase "gold sale practices" to "gold transactions."

The Board also approved points 1 and 3 of the committee's report, and agreed that a statement expressing the policy of the Fund and recommending action to members should be prepared by the staff and transmitted to members after approval by the Board. It was also decided that, before the statement was transmitted, the Board should prescribe the margins for members' gold transactions as required in Article IV, Section 2.

The decision setting the margin for members' gold transactions at $\frac{1}{4}$ of 1 per cent, plus certain handling charges, was adopted on June 10, 1947. Colombia then requested that its inquiry be withdrawn, and the letter in which the inquiry had been made be returned. The Board noted the request for withdrawal, agreed to return the original letter to Colombia, and decided that the other records of the Fund on the matter would not be altered.

The Board then approved the drafts of the proposed general statement on premium gold transactions and the letter of transmittal to members. The discussion of the latter document was chiefly concerned with the question whether the Fund itself would make the statement public. The committee had previously suggested that the Fund should not do so, although the letter of transmittal would make it clear that members could make such use of the statement as they considered desirable. This position was the one finally adopted, being apparently influenced by Mr. Martínez-Ostos' statement that Colombia's withdrawal of its inquiry might have depended to a certain degree on his personal assurance that no public statement would be made by the Fund, and that if a Fund statement were to be made, he would want to make a general reservation on the whole problem.

TEXT OF FIRST STATEMENT

The text of the statement, which was communicated by the Fund to all members in a letter of June 18, 1947 from the Managing Director, is set out in Volume III of this history.[1] The operative paragraphs were the following:

> A primary purpose of the Fund is world exchange stability and it is the considered opinion of the Fund that exchange stability may be undermined by continued and increasing external purchases and sales of gold at prices which directly or indirectly produce exchange transactions at depreciated rates. From information at its disposal, the Fund believes that unless discouraged this practice is likely to become extensive, which would fundamentally disturb the exchange relationships among the members of the Fund. Moreover, these transactions involve a loss to monetary reserves, since much of the gold goes into private hoards rather than into central holdings. For these reasons, the Fund strongly deprecates international transactions in gold at premium prices and recommends that all of its members take effective action to prevent such transactions in gold with other countries or with the nationals of other countries. . . .
>
> The Fund has not overlooked the problems arising in connection with domestic transactions in gold at prices above parity. The conclusion was reached that the Fund would not object at this time to such transactions unless they have the effect of establishing new rates of exchange or undermining existing rates of other members, or unless they result in a significant weakening of the international financial position of a member which might affect its utilization of the Fund's resources.
>
> The Fund has requested its members to take action as promptly as possible to put into effect the recommendations contained in this statement.

That the statement is in the form of an expression of the Fund's views and recommendations rather than a formal interpretation of the Articles of Agreement, reflects the fact that there were conflicting points of view among Directors as to the legal basis for the Fund's authority. It should be noted also that, while

---

[1] Below, Vol. III, p. 310.

external and internal transactions are distinguished, the statement makes no distinction between monetary gold and nonmonetary (processed) gold. This point was to be of importance later in connection with South Africa's proposals for sales of semiprocessed gold at premium prices. However, Mr. Martínez-Ostos later commented that although he and Mr. Gómez had pointed out the problems that would arise from the exclusion of processed gold from the Fund's statement of June 1947, the Fund had exempted such transactions in August of the same year. Other Executive Directors then recalled that processed gold had been excluded from the Fund's statement because the Fund did not wish to curtail normal commercial enterprises. However, where it appeared that an increase in commercial activity was in reality a negation of the Fund's policy statement, the Fund would have to be concerned.

THE MEXICAN INQUIRY

Shortly after the statement was issued, Mexico asked (a) for the legal grounds of the Fund's statement, and (b) whether members were required to suspend gold sales to nonmember countries.

When this inquiry was considered on July 28, 1947, the Executive Board approved a reply to (a) in the following terms:

> The legal basis of the statement in connection with Transactions in Gold at Premium Prices is to be found in Article I (iii), and Article IV, Section 4 (a). Article I makes it the duty of the Fund to promote exchange stability, maintain orderly exchange arrangements, and avoid competitive exchange depreciation. Where the Fund finds a threat to exchange stability or orderly exchange arrangements, Article IV, Section 4 (a), gives the Fund the right to call for collaboration by members to eliminate the threat.

As regards (b), the Legal Department suggested that the reply might explain that "the reference to 'other countries' in [the Fund's statement of June 18, 1947] was intended and should be interpreted to embrace both members and nonmembers."

However, on this second issue the Board disagreed. In the discussion, Executive Directors raised two further problems. The first was whether the Fund's statement covered transactions with nonmembers clearly and satisfactorily: nonmembers necessarily had no par value, which created a possible ambiguity as to the meaning of premium prices. The special case of a nonmember with multiple rates of exchange was also considered. The second problem was whether the June 18 statement applied or should apply to sales of gold for manufacture into jewelry, or sales of gold in the form of jewelry. It was agreed to defer an answer to Mexico until these matters had been further studied.

At a further Board meeting on August 26, Mr. Gómez observed that there was no indication that the gold which Mexico sold returned to international channels where it might affect par values. For that reason he could not support the proposed draft reply on this point.

Other Directors, however, pointed out that stable exchange rates could be weakened by premium sales even if the gold did not move out of the buying country. If Mexico sold gold at a premium for a particular currency, it would be getting that currency at a more favorable rate than other Fund members. Cross rates for member currencies might result which would be significantly different from the pattern of rates established by the Fund. Thus there might be a tendency to undermine the stability of members' currencies. The Fund's concern would certainly extend to such cases. Mr. Gómez accepted that the argument about disorderly cross rates was valid; it was therefore embodied in a reply sent to Mexico covering both points in the member's second letter.

RESULTS OF FIRST STATEMENT

Parallel with the consideration of the letters from Mexico just discussed, the Board had under consideration a further inquiry from Peru. This described the adverse effect that the Fund's statement would have on the prospects of gold mines in Peru, and asked advice on ways of protecting the industry. The Board decided to request the Committee on External Sales of Gold to study the question of what measures, acceptable to the Fund, could be taken to encourage domestic gold production. In preparation for the work of the committee, the staff was asked for "studies of the developments and results which had occurred since the Fund's policy on premium transactions had been announced, the movements of gold in recent years, and the nature of the 'underground' gold traffic." A further general statement about the price of gold which emerged from the committee's work dealt primarily with subsidies to gold producers, and is therefore reported in the next chapter. However, it is appropriate here to set out the result of the staff's studies, as summarized in a memorandum circulated in January 1948.

The staff found that the Fund's requests had been anticipated in India, China, and Hong Kong, and had been followed by immediate action in Mexico and the Philippines toward ending gold exports at a premium. In the United Kingdom, the United States, and Canada, supplementary measures had been taken to tighten controls having the same purpose. Following these measures there had in general been an upward movement in the price of gold in Eastern free markets, and there might also have been a shrinkage in the volume of transactions in those markets.

During the discussion of this memorandum, Mr. Overby (United States) told the Board that U.S. mining and smelting interests had complained that they were at a disadvantage because the Fund's policy was enforced in the United States, whereas it did not seem to be in certain other countries. Another Director pointed out that cooperation by the large producing countries was essential to any reduction of premium transactions in gold, as the number of receiving countries and their tendency toward lax administration made effective control unlikely at the receiving end.

Mr. Martínez-Ostos doubted that the Fund's policy was having any beneficial effect. He believed that unless there was a noticeable drop in the volume of premium transactions, the Fund's policy could be regarded as having increased the premiums and hence the incentives for trade in the black markets. The premiums had in fact continued to rise since the date of the Fund's statement, and apparently the amounts involved in the transactions were not less than when the Fund made the statement.

The Director of Research replied that the volume of transactions had probably decreased somewhat. Measurement of the drop was difficult. However, the very fact that the prices for gold were going up in black markets was evidence that the Fund's policy and members' actions were having a noticeable effect.

Mr. de Largentaye (France) believed that the Fund would have done better to urge that gold be made available in plentiful supply at the official price. He felt that this would soon have eliminated the premium in terms of dollars on the free markets. The Director of Research said that sales above $35 an ounce probably could be eliminated in this way without excessive offerings. However, he doubted that the same would be true of the premium prices in inconvertible currencies.

At the conclusion of the meeting, the Board decided that the Fund should ask its members, through a letter from the Managing Director, for information on their laws, decrees, administrative practices, etc., concerning monetary, processed, and nonprocessed gold; those measures that were taken subsequent to the Fund's first statement; recent data on trade in such gold; and other pertinent details relating to the implementation of the first statement. The letter together with a questionnaire was sent out on April 6, 1948.

SUBSEQUENT DEVELOPMENTS—BELGIUM AND CHILE

The evolution of the Board's policy on gold during the years 1948–51 was closely connected with developments in South Africa. In order not to interrupt the discussion of these developments, we may here mention briefly the Board's attention to practices bearing on the price of gold introduced in Belgium and Chile during 1948 and 1949.

The Belgian Government informed the Fund in October 1948 that it was considering an arrangement for an internal free gold market. It gave two reasons: (1) it believed that the black market in gold which already existed and was tolerated should be legalized, and (2) certain gold producers in the Belgian Congo needed relief because of increased costs of production. After some discussion, the Board decided on a reply to Belgium which stated that sales in a member's metropolitan territory of gold produced in a nonmetropolitan territory in respect of which the member had accepted the Fund Agreement were not international transactions, and that the proposed arrangement would not be in conflict with the Fund's first statement on premium gold transactions because the Belgian Government intended to prevent international transactions. However, the reply also drew attention to a number of unfavorable comments by Executive Directors. Some doubted that international transactions could be entirely prevented. Furthermore, the establishment of a free market would divert gold from central reserves and put pressure on other countries to take the same step. The reply concluded by asking Belgium to consider these unfavorable views carefully before coming to a decision on the proposal.

As a result of this reply, the Belgian Government revised its proposal so as to limit sellers in the free market to Belgian Congo gold producers, and buyers to bona fide dentists, industrialists, and goldsmiths residing in Belgium or the Congo; the price in Belgian francs was to be fixed by the seller. Buyers would not be allowed to resell the gold except in processed form. No imports of semi-processed or fabricated gold would be allowed. When the Board discussed the revised proposal, Mr. Southard (United States) said that he believed the proposal represented an effort to bring a gold subsidy arrangement within a range to which the Fund would not object, and he appreciated the effort made to eliminate the monetary implications. His Government, however, believed that all premium sales arrangements would necessarily have monetary aspects, and it continued to oppose them. It was also concerned at the apparent intention to increase Congolese gold production by this means. Mr. de Selliers defended the plan, saying that it was not intended to expand output but to protect a major Congolese industry. The Board's decision on the matter did not specifically approve the plan; after describing the revised arrangements it stated as follows:

> 2. Considering its previous decision . . . the Fund notes the proposal and the revisions from the previous plan. It will expect to review developments under the arrangement from time to time and to receive current statistics on the operation of the market.

In November 1949 access to the market was extended to buyers of the specified occupations who were resident in the Belgian Trust Territory of Ruanda Urundi.

Another relevant decision taken at this time arose from a consideration of the multiple currency system of Chile, which included an import rate fluctuating around 125 pesos = $1 (compared with a par value of 31 pesos = $1) resulting from the method of marketing newly mined gold; this applied to authorized nonessential imports. The Board's decision included the following:

5. While it regrets that the gold practice authorized by the Chilean law of December 2, 1948, results in creation of a new effective rate of exchange for nonessential imports, the Fund approves this aspect of the gold practice. However, because of the inconsistency with the Fund's established policy on external transactions in gold at premium prices, the Fund disapproves the practice of permitting exportation of gold from Chile at premium prices.

SOUTH AFRICAN SALES

During 1948 and 1949 the Fund had a prolonged discussion with South Africa on a proposal to sell semiprocessed gold at premium prices. South Africa was in balance of payments difficulties at the time because of excessive import demand, and in fact drew on the Fund's resources.

SEPTEMBER-OCTOBER 1948

In September 1948, South Africa requested an opportunity for Mr. M. H. de Kock, the Alternate Governor for South Africa, to discuss, at the time of the forthcoming Annual Meeting, a proposal made to the South African Mint that it sell for export, at a premium price, a considerable quantity of semiprocessed gold. The gold would be in the shape and form normally used by manufacturing goldsmiths and jewelers and would be alloyed to required standards and hall-marked to show the actual fineness. All the gold would be exported, and all payments would be made in dollars. The proposal had been made to the South African Mint by a London firm. It was the intention of the Government to share any financial benefit from the transaction with the producers of gold.

The Legal Department advised the Board as follows:

(i) External transactions in semiprocessed gold at premium prices are within the scope of the Fund's Statement on Transactions in Gold at Premium Prices if such gold will be held, used, or disposed of for monetary purposes and not for industrial, professional or artistic purposes.

(ii) The contemplated profit-sharing with producers might involve a price paid for gold by the Government in violation of Article IV, Section 2, or, depending on the form of profit-sharing arrangements, constitute a subsidy which, under the Fund's Statement on Gold Subsidies [see p. 205 below], would be regarded as an increase in the purchase price beyond that permitted by Article IV, Section 2. Even though the additional payments might not have these effects, they might be subsidies which, as pointed out in the Statement on Gold Subsidies, would, directly or indirectly, undermine or threaten to undermine exchange or monetary stability and thus be of concern to the Fund.

These two conclusions were incorporated in a letter that the Managing Director sent to the South African Government on October 5, 1948 following the Board's discussion of the proposal with Mr. de Kock. In addition, the letter made further points that indicated, but did not state explicitly, the Fund's general disapproval of the proposal. First, the letter stated that members of the Executive Board were "disturbed by the fear that the proposed transactions would involve considerable sales of gold for purposes other than legitimate industrial, professional, or artistic uses," a consequence that would almost certainly occur if the scale of the proposed transactions was large enough to ensure an appreciable profit to South African gold producers. Accordingly, the letter went on to say that

> in these circumstances, the Fund believes that South Africa should not engage in the proposed plan unless it is satisfied that it can take effective measures to ensure that gold sold under the plan will in fact be used for bona fide and customary industrial, professional or artistic purposes

Second, the letter noted the Fund's pleasure at Mr. de Kock's statement that South Africa had no specific plan in mind for sharing any profit with producers and would consult with the Fund before putting any plan into effect.

During the discussions that preceded the dispatch of this letter, the principal opposition to the South African proposal came from Mr. Overby and Mr. Tansley (United Kingdom). Mr. Overby believed that any substantial sales of semi-processed gold by South Africa would be destined for private hoards, because the United States and the United Kingdom were prepared to supply, at prices based on $35 an ounce, all the gold needed for legitimate industrial, professional, and artistic purposes. In reply Mr. de Kock said that his Government had been told that the sales by the United States and the United Kingdom were so restricted that the real demand for processed and semiprocessed gold was by no means met. He believed that "legitimate" demands were hard if not impossible to define. However, Mr. de Kock added that "the demand for gold in artistic forms had always included a large element of desire for gold as a store of value."

Mr. Martínez-Ostos again stated his belief that the Fund had never given adequate consideration to the theoretical and factual background of its whole policy on premium gold transactions, and that a full study was necessary before action could be taken in the South African case. Some other Directors supported Mr. Martínez-Ostos by urging that a full review of the Fund's gold policies be undertaken, and Mr. Martínez-Ostos said he would abstain from taking a position on South Africa's question until such a general discussion could be held.

February-March 1949

On Saturday, February 5, 1949, the South African Legation in Washington handed to the Managing Director a cable from its Government in which the Fund was informed of the outline of a plan to sell for dollars 100,000 ounces of semi-processed gold at a price of $38.20 an ounce, over a period of eight weeks beginning on that day. The cable indicated that the gold would be sold to a firm of London bullion brokers, on the understanding that the gold would be used for specific and customary industrial, professional, and artistic purposes. The method of transferring the premium benefit to the gold producers would be settled later in a way that would not conflict with the Fund's purposes. The arrangement was regarded as an experiment, and any subsequent sales would be subject to new negotiation.

The staff advised the Board that as South Africa appeared to be already fully committed to the initial transaction, no useful purpose would be served by asking the Government to consult further with the Fund before entering into the contract. Instead, South Africa might be requested to enter into discussions with the Fund before further negotiations for the sale of semiprocessed gold were undertaken. However, on February 9 the Managing Director circulated to the Board a memorandum that he had received from Mr. Tansley. This stated that the South African gold was to be sold for delivery in Switzerland (the London brokers acting as agents for a Swiss-French syndicate) and that such a transaction could not be carried out in the United Kingdom. Mr. Tansley added that unless the Fund took a strong position regarding premium sales, his Government would be compelled to open the London bullion market to unlimited transactions in industrial gold. He said that the British Government asked to be informed by the evening of the next day, i.e., Thursday, February 10, of the action the Fund proposed to take.

Accordingly, a Board meeting was held on Thursday morning. It revealed that the South African proposal aroused strong feelings, both pro and con. Two questions were raised: first, whether South Africa should have consulted the Fund before entering into the contract, and second, whether there was adequate assurance that the gold would in fact be used only for legitimate industrial purposes.

On the first question, Mr. McFarlane (Australia), who had been elected by South Africa, pointed out that the Fund had not asked the member to consult again before engaging in any premium gold sales, but had only asked that it satisfy itself on the proposed uses of the gold. Mr. Tasca (United States), on the other hand, thought that the spirit if not the letter of the Fund's recommendation had been violated. He repeated Mr. Overby's doubts that any gold sold would be used for legitimate industrial purposes, as the buyers would be paying a premium price whereas the United States and the United Kingdom would meet any such legitimate demand at a price of $35 an ounce. Mr. Parkinson (Canada) supported the U.S. view, but Mr. de Largentaye dissented, saying he was not satisfied that all bona fide demands were being met by the United States and the United Kingdom, especially as part of the demand for industrial gold had been supplied through the free market.

At the end of the meeting, the Board took a decision which expressed doubts similar to those which had been brought forward during the meeting, and asked

South Africa to take all practicable steps to ensure that the gold sold was in fact used for bona fide industrial, professional, or artistic purposes.

At a further meeting that afternoon the Board approved a reply to South Africa and a press release. The reply, sent on the same day, incorporated the substance of the Board's decision and also requested South Africa to provide the Fund with a copy of the contract or the text of the relevant terms. The press release referred to news reports about a gold sale at premium prices made by South Africa, and emphasized that the Fund had never approved any specific gold sale at a premium price. It then recited the Fund's view of the undesirability of such sales as those which South Africa was making, and explained that the Government was being asked for further information to enable the Fund to judge whether the safeguards in the contract were adequate.

An answer from South Africa to the Fund's inquiries, dispatched by airmail on February 16, failed to arrive. Meanwhile the South African Legation stated that Mr. Havenga would make a public statement on the premium gold sale in the South African Parliament before it recessed in the following week. On February 22 a copy of the letter of February 16 was received by cable and at the same time Mr. Havenga undertook to postpone his speech until February 24, the last day before the recess. On February 23 the Board met to consider a draft reply to South Africa. The Managing Director commented that consideration of the matter was urgent, since receipt of the member's explanation had been delayed, and since the Fund had been informed that South Africa's Finance Minister would make a statement in Parliament on the matter in less than twenty-four hours.

South Africa's reply was summarized by Mr. McFarlane as follows:

(1) The text of the agreement South Africa had made with the London brokers was being sent to the Fund as requested.

(2) This agreement put into effect safeguards which were considered as meeting the requirements of the Fund's letter of October 5, 1948. If any breach of the undertakings came to the member's attention, the defaulting house would be debarred from further participation.

(3) In fact the legitimate and bona fide market for semiprocessed gold had expanded very considerably in recent years, so that an increased supply was appropriate.

(4) The contract could not be broken or postponed without exposing South Africa to action for breach of contract.

(5) South Africa would give serious consideration to any further practicable precautions that the Fund might suggest during the period of the present contract.

(6) The South African authorities would consult with the Fund regarding the plan for distributing the premium among gold producers.

The discussion that followed was concerned principally with the point that South Africa's safeguards relied mainly on the argument that the use of the gold would be controlled until it was fabricated. Directors felt that effective safeguards against hoarding would control the volume of sales, not the form of the gold. Accordingly, the reply to South Africa approved by the Board stated that the Fund was still not satisfied with South Africa's safeguards and recommended more effective procedures, citing regulations enforced by the United States.

Two days later, the Board met twice to consider a draft press release explaining the Fund's position in reply to the Finance Minister's statement to Parliament. The speech had included criticism of the Fund's gold policies and the maintenance of the dollar price of gold, and stigmatized as a "fiction" that gold was worth only $35 an ounce. The press release, a long one, added further details to what had been said in the previous release, and defended the Fund's position on premium sales and on the price of gold. Several Directors questioned the wisdom of the Fund's issuing a press release, and Messrs. McFarlane, de Largentaye, and D'Ascoli (Venezuela) recorded their objections to its terms.

The Managing Director had become increasingly unhappy about the situation and accordingly, with Board approval, sent personal and private letters on March 9 to Mr. Havenga and Mr. Holloway (Secretary for Finance in the South African Treasury), proposing direct, face-to-face talks either in South Africa or in Washington. Mr. Havenga accepted the proposal and expressed his preference for a meeting in South Africa and his hope that the Managing Director himself would come.

April-May 1949

Before the Managing Director went to South Africa, the Board in April 1949 had two discussions on the $35 an ounce price of gold, on premium transactions in gold, and on the Fund's gold policy, based on a number of staff memoranda. At the first discussion Mr. de Largentaye made a long statement in favor of increasing the price of gold, a proposal with which Mr. Southard disagreed, saying that his Government opposed a change in the price of gold. At the end of the second discussion the Managing Director summed up the views expressed, particularly as they bore on his coming talks with the South African authorities. He discerned no desire to stiffen the Fund's policy on international gold transactions at premium prices. At the same time only one Executive Director had proposed a reversal of that policy. Thus the matter appeared to come down to presenting the Fund's view that it was in the interest of all members, including South Africa, to carry out the spirit and purpose of the policy which had been established; also that there should be discussion on the arrangements that should govern any sales of semiprocessed and fabricated gold. Mr. Gutt believed that the aim of the talks should be to arrive at a full understanding on principles, so that both the Fund and the member could be assured of each other's continuing cooperation.

During his ensuing visit to South Africa in May the Managing Director cabled to the Fund the terms of some further proposals for the sales of semiprocessed gold which had been communicated to him by the Government. These included additional precautions to ensure that the gold was confined to legitimate industrial uses. When the Managing Director's cable was discussed at the Board, however, some Directors still had misgivings about the adequacy of these precautions, and the Board asked the Managing Director to convey these misgivings to the Government.

Mr. Gutt issued a public statement during his stay in South Africa, and Mr. Havenga made a statement in Parliament on their discussions. Mr. Gutt stressed the cordial atmosphere and desire of South Africa to reach agreement with the Fund, the safeguards that had been adopted, the undertaking of South Africa to keep a watch on developments, and the intention of the Fund to keep premium gold sales under review with all its members. Mr. Havenga referred not only to the discussions on premium gold sales (and subsidies), but also to the discussions held at the same time on South Africa's economic and foreign exchange position, both of which he noted had been cordial. However, he also implied that the question of the price of gold would have to be taken up again in view of the world exchange position. These statements ended the matter until the Annual Meeting in September 1949, except for a short factual report made to the Board, in the absence of the Managing Director, by the Director of Operations, who had also been in South Africa.

SOUTH AFRICAN RESOLUTION

At the Fourth Annual Meeting, in September 1949, Mr. Havenga, Governor for South Africa, introduced a resolution [2] that mentioned a number of factors, among them the long period during which the price of gold had remained fixed while prices of other commodities had risen, and proposed that the Governors resolve

> that nothing in the Articles of Agreement of the Fund shall be interpreted to prevent the sale, by the Government of any member, of newly-mined gold in any market at such premium prices as may be ruling in that market *provided* the said member sells to the Fund or to one or more members of the Fund, or transfers to its own monetary reserves at least fifty percent of its newly-mined gold at the price from time to time current in terms of the Articles of Agreement of the Fund.

---

[2] *Summary Proceedings, 1949,* p. 34.

The Board of Governors referred this proposal to a Committee on Gold, which reported back to the Governors a resolution, which was adopted, that the

> resolution of the Governor for the Union of South Africa be referred to the Executive Directors of the Fund for study of all relevant considerations and report to the Board of Governors.[3]

It will, of course, be realized that the devaluations which immediately followed the Annual Meeting, 1949, and included that of the South African pound, materially improved the position of the gold producers.

The Executive Board took up the Governors' resolution at two meetings in October 1949, and at the second meeting directed the staff to prepare a study for Executive Directors' consideration. The decision provided that a determination as to the scope of the phrase "all relevant considerations" should be reserved until the staff study was considered by the Board.

FIRST STAFF REPORT

A lengthy report by the staff and a draft of a public statement on the report's recommendations were circulated to the Board on February 2, 1950. The report was in two parts: the first, an examination of the Fund's policy on external transactions in gold at premium prices and related matters, and the second, a country-by-country analysis of premium gold markets and regulations on gold transactions. In a brief consideration of the appropriateness of the $35 price of gold, the report touched on the extent to which the purchasing power of gold and the profitability of gold mining had fallen out of line with that of other industries and other commodities, and reviewed the extent to which these were suitable criteria for determining the price of gold.

While in form the report was one by the staff to the Executive Board, it had been so written that it could be converted into a report from the Executive Board to the Governors. The principal alternatives confronting the Fund at the time were stated to be (1) continue the present policy; (2) strengthen the policy by calling on members to tighten their regulations covering international gold trade in a number of fields (i.e., exports of processed gold, gold transit trade and agency deals, re-exports of gold imported for refining, and gold imports); (3) adopt the South African proposal; (4) permit all newly mined gold to be sold in premium markets but continue the policy with respect to all other gold; and (5) modify the present policy.

The report concluded that the preferable alternative was to modify the present policy. The following summary of the principal arguments for this course is taken from a paper prepared by the staff working party at a later stage in the discussions:

---

[3] See *ibid.*, pp. 34–36, for the text of the committee's report.

(1) While the Fund's policy helped to limit the flow of gold into hoards, it was not the only or the most important limitation, other limitations being the import restrictions and the exchange control machinery of importing countries, the demand in the gold markets in these countries, and the national policies of exporting countries to the extent that these would be maintained independently of the Fund's premium gold policy.

(2) A relaxation of the Fund's policy might be expected to lower the dollar price of gold in premium markets and thus to strengthen confidence in the basic parity between the dollar and gold.

(3) The limited extent to which the policy was implemented (or such degree of implementation as might reasonably be hoped to be achieved on the most optimistic assumption) left serious inequities, and the persistence of such inequities would be a source of international irritation and would be likely to set up increasing pressures within countries that might lead to the ultimate collapse of the policy.

The staff report proposed that the Fund's policy should be modified so as to leave the countries exporting gold substantial freedom of action, subject to the provisions of Article IV, Section 2, of the Fund Agreement, and subject (1) to the undertaking of members to cooperate with the Fund to maintain orderly exchange arrangements with other members; (2) to the unenforceability in members' courts, pursuant to Article VIII, Section 2 (b), of contracts involving the currency of any member which are contrary to the exchange control regulations of that member maintained or imposed consistently with the Articles of Agreement; and (3) to any accord between members under Article VIII, Section 2 (b), to cooperate in any further measures for the purpose of making each other's exchange control regulations more effective.

CONSIDERATION OF STAFF REPORT

The Board first discussed the staff report, shortly after it was issued, at two informal sessions. The recommendations were given a generally cool reception, suggesting that Directors representing a majority would oppose changing the Fund's policy.

The Board's first formal session on the staff's report was held on April 11, 1950, when the only speaker was Mr. Holloway, who made a statement as the representative of South Africa. Describing and defending South Africa's position, Mr. Holloway made, inter alia, the following points: South Africa had understood at Bretton Woods that Article IV, Section 2, of the Fund Agreement gave members a legal right to sell gold at premium prices and had accepted this Article with that understanding. However, while South Africa still took the position that members had this legal right, it was prepared to reserve the legal question for the purposes of the discussion and deal instead with the policy. On this he stated that South Africa challenged not only the Fund's policy on premium gold sales but also the official price of gold. The Fund had evaded this latter challenge, and if it could not prove that the present official price for gold was the right one, it would have failed to meet the challenge.

At the next discussion of the staff report, a number of Directors supported the continuation, or even the strengthening, of the Fund's policy rather than its modification. Mr. Southard said that while there were admissible arguments for modifying the policy, the U.S. Government had decided that on balance there was no conclusive reason for changing the policy as it now stood. As to South Africa's proposal for a uniform change in par values, he said that he believed that discussion by the Executive Directors was appropriate, but he made it clear that the policy of the U.S. Government was still the same as it had been a year earlier. Although the United States was mindful of the gains that a uniform change in par values would bring to gold producers and gold holding countries, it had decided against a change in the present period of struggle against disequilibrium and inflation. He added that the U.S. Government was aware of the imperfect enforcement of the policy and the loopholes in its own and other members' regulations, which were the main reason for the recommendation of the staff report, but it believed that the present policy was still serviceable.

Mr. Crick (United Kingdom) indicated that his Government could not contemplate an abandonment of the Fund's policy; he supported maintaining and, if possible, strengthening it. Messrs. Falaki (Egypt), Joshi (India), and Rasminsky also supported the policy.

On the other hand, Mr. de Largentaye favored modification of the policy because he thought it was legally untenable, and because he did not agree that premium gold transactions undermined exchange stability and tended to reduce official reserves. Mr. de Selliers supported Mr. de Largentaye's position.

The Board's decision

At a further meeting, on April 13, 1950, the Board decided to recommend to the Governors that they should *not* adopt the South African resolution. The votes were 51,740 for so recommending, and 7,280 against, seven Directors abstaining. Mr. de Largentaye was the only one to state his reason for abstaining, which was that he could not see any legal basis on which different rules could be applied to various parts of gold production.

Following the vote, Mr. Holloway made a number of criticisms of the Fund's treatment of South Africa, and stated that he assumed that the Executive Board, in view of the trend of previous discussions, would reaffirm the 1947 policy. This, he said, would pose a question of high policy for his Government. The Government would have to decide whether, in the spirit of altruistic, international cooperation, it would still adhere to the Fund's policy and its agreement of 1949, or whether it would act solely on the basis of self-interest. His Government had instructed him to inform the Executive Board that this question would be decided only after his report had been submitted; meanwhile South Africa reserved all its rights under Article IV, Section 2, of the Articles of Agreement.

At its next meeting, on April 14, the Executive Board, without further discussion of the staff report, voted against the recommendations in that report and decided by 55,290 votes to 16,530 that the policy expressed in the first statement (June 1947) should be continued. While no Director changed his position from the preceding vote, three who had previously abstained voted this time, one to continue the policy and two against the decision.

DISCUSSION OF UNIFORM CHANGE IN PAR VALUES

Following the vote, the Board took up the question of a uniform change in par values. Mr. Holloway stated that discussion of this matter was called for if the Executive Directors were to meet the requirements of the Governors' resolution. While South Africa accepted the provisions of Article IV, Section 7, which gave any member having 10 per cent or more of the total of the quotas the power to veto a uniform change in par values, it thought that the exercise of the power in the face of an approval of such a change by a majority of the Board of Governors would be undemocratic. Mr. Southard took exception to the word "undemocratic," and said that the question could not be considered a substantive one in the light of the U.S. Government's position.

In reply to a question, the staff representative said that Article IV, Section 7, had not been intended to grant undemocratic veto powers to any members but had merely recognized that exchange rates would move with those of the countries having the largest quotas, not because of votes but because of economics.

The staff then commented on the principal economic arguments used by the proponents of a uniform change in par values, as follows:

A premium price in gold markets did not prove that gold was worth more than $35 an ounce. The recent sharp fall in the dollar premium price of gold reflected much more the better pattern of exchange rates after devaluation. If the dollar premium price of gold should rise again, the fundamental reason for it would be further inflation in gold hoarding countries and a worsening of the balance of payments situation.

The argument that a change in the price of gold was needed to give the world more liquidity was generally advanced because the public ordinarily thought of liquidity in terms of gold. But national liquidity in terms of gold had not been a factor in any major country. As for other countries, the ratio of money supply and national income to gold would be inconsequential even if gold stocks were doubled.

International liquidity, however, was a more important element. With a uniform change in par values, the ratio of gold to total world liquidity would increase somewhat, but the countries with the greatest shortage of reserves would benefit least. In fact, it would be quite impossible to increase international liquidity substantially unless the balance of payments of countries outside the United States were improved simultaneously.

Those favoring a uniform change in par values argued that an increase in the price of gold would correct the present balance of payments disequilibrium of the world. However, the payments difficulties of the world did not arise from the $35 price of gold and a change in the price would merely postpone solution of the real problem, which could be satisfactorily met only by an increase in production for export at competitive prices.

Moreover, a change in the price of gold was not needed to do justice to the gold producers of the world. Profitability for gold producers, while lower than in 1934, was considerably higher than in the years prior to 1934. There was no special obligation to keep the return to gold producers constant.

Mr. de Largentaye, and Messrs. Holloway and Busschau, who represented South Africa, indicated at the next meeting that they did not accept the staff's arguments. The Managing Director asked the Directors whether they wished to report to the Governors on the question of a uniform change in par values, and it was agreed that the Board would decide later the nature of its report to the Governors and what, if anything, should be included on the par value question.

THE BOARD'S REPORT

The Research Department then produced for the Board a revised draft of a report to the Governors. The Board's discussions of this draft, from April 21 to 25, 1950, revolved principally around two questions: the extent to which dissenting or minority views should be given, and whether a reference to uniform changes in par values should be included. On the former point the Board decided that its report would contain the decisions on the South African resolution and on the continuance of the policy on premium gold transactions taken on April 13 and 14. It would also set out the various considerations which led to those decisions, but would not give a minority view or indicate that the decisions were not unanimous.

On the question of a reference to the Board's consideration of a uniform change in par values, Mr. Parkinson proposed the omission of this paragraph in the report. When it was agreed to include the paragraph, in view of South Africa's desire to have it and the fact that the South African resolution contained a reference to it, he expressed formal dissent. Further difficulties arose over the inclusion of the word *present* in the draft sentence giving the Executive Directors' view of the par value question: "In their view there is no present economic justification for recommending such a change to the Board of Governors." The word was deleted from the report as approved by the Executive Directors, but Mr. McFarlane asked at the following meeting that it be reinstated, saying that the deletion made the sentence unsatisfactory to the South African representative, who had not been in attendance when the report was adopted. However, the sense of the meeting opposed changing the previous decision.

The Executive Board's report, as approved, quoted part of the Fund's first statement on premium gold transactions, the resolution of the Board of Governors, and the resolution proposed by the South African Governor, recorded that after full consideration the Directors were not in favor of changing the policy, and then developed in full the arguments for that policy which have been indicated above.

The Executive Board decided that its report should be sent to the Governors without delay and released to the public on May 3, 1950. The report was reproduced as an Appendix to the Annual Report of the Executive Directors for 1950, and was discussed in a chapter on Gold Policy in that Report.[4] At the ensuing Annual Meeting, in September 1950, Mr. Havenga, as Governor for South Africa, criticized the Executive Directors' treatment of the matter in a speech on September 7.[5] Four days later the Governors' Committee on Gold discussed the report and the related chapter in the Annual Report. Some Governors agreed with the Executive Board and others did not.[6] This divergence of views was reported by the committee to the Governors, who accepted the committee's report without comment. The South African resolution, as such, was not formally considered by the Governors.

TWO MINOR ISSUES

During 1949 and 1950 two minor questions concerning South Africa's gold sales were dealt with by the Executive Board. Both involved, in somewhat different ways, problems created by the Fund's policy.

---

[4] *Annual Report, 1950,* Appendix II, pp. 90–95, and Chap. IV, pp. 70–74.

[5] *Summary Proceedings, 1950,* pp. 93–98.

[6] *Ibid.,* pp. 42–43.

Among the measures of control adopted by the United States, and recommended to South Africa, was a rule that not more than 80 per cent of the value of fabricated gold sold abroad might represent the value of the gold itself. Adapting this rule to local conditions, the South African Government prescribed that the elements of the cost of any fabricated gold article which represented labor and overhead must represent at least 25 per cent of the value of the gold (at $35 an ounce) included in it. This meant a minimum of £2 3s. 1½d. for labor and overhead added for each ounce of gold used. Announcing this to the Fund in August 1949, however, the South African authorities said that they regarded it as an unsatisfactory requirement because it put a premium on inefficient manufacturing processes, and because mark-ups arising from inter-company sales afforded an easy way of escaping it. They preferred to rely upon inspection of all consignments of gold articles by the police. Three months later, Mr. Holloway wrote to the Fund to say that the revision of the price of gold due to the devaluation of the South African pound had raised the value of 25 per cent of an ounce of gold to £3 2s. 0d. To require manufacturers to incur minimum costs of this order would, however, run counter to South Africa's anti-inflationary policy. The Government had accordingly decided to change the requirement to a minimum of £1 10s. 0d. for labor and overhead per ounce of gold.

In May 1950, however, Mr. Holloway sent a further letter, announcing that his Government had decided to abandon the imposition of a minimum mark-up for labor and overhead, partly because it was so easily evaded and partly because of the inducement to inefficiency. South Africa intended for the future to rely solely upon police inspection. This letter was considered by the Board in July, and a reply was sent explaining that the purpose of the "80 per cent test" applied in the United States was to distinguish between fabricated gold and semi-processed gold, which was subject to export licensing. The reply expressed the hope that, in the absence of a similar test, South Africa would take special precautions to avoid semiprocessed gold being exported as fabricated gold.

The second question raised by South Africa's gold transactions concerned a proposed sale of gold sovereigns equivalent to 1,800,000 ounces of gold to the Arabian American Oil Company for use in payment of oil royalties to the King of Saudi Arabia. Mr. Holloway consulted the Fund in December 1949 about the transaction, which involved payment by the company of handling, conversion, transport, and minting charges equivalent to $1.3175 per fine ounce. Following discussion of the matter in the Board, Mr. Overby (Acting Chairman) replied, drawing attention to Rule F-4 of the Fund's Rules and Regulations. Inquiries made by the staff had shown that normal charges for the operations proposed by South Africa would be approximately $0.90 an ounce less than the figure quoted by Mr. Holloway. The Fund would therefore have to regard the proposed sale of sovereigns as a premium transaction.

SECOND FUND STATEMENT

Establishment of staff Working Party

The flow of gold to private hoards, after declining in 1949 and the first half of 1950, increased sharply in the second half of 1950, following the outbreak of the Korean War, to an annual rate of 60 per cent of world gold production. The staff became concerned about the possibility that gold from official reserves was reaching private hoards through the premium markets. The Managing Director therefore wrote to all members on February 9, 1951, requesting information on any sales made recently from their reserves to nonmonetary authorities.

Shortly after the inquiry had been sent, the staff circulated to the Board two memoranda on gold transactions. The first, dated February 14, 1951, drew the Board's attention to the large increase in the volume of gold exports at premium prices authorized by South Africa since the outbreak of the Korean War. The second, dated February 26, described the large increase in hoarding, expressed the fear that continued hoarding on such a scale would in time lead to a complete breakdown of attempts to conserve gold for central reserves, and gave as the staff's judgment that the amount of gold exported by South Africa at a premium far exceeded what was required for arts and industries. It therefore recommended that the Board should review the arrangement with South Africa reached in May 1949, and also that the Managing Director should be authorized to consult appropriate gold producing and gold importing countries to ascertain whether further steps could be taken to make the Fund's policy more effective.

The staff memoranda and recommendations were discussed at a number of Board meetings in February and early in March 1951, at which the main points at issue were (1) the legal authority for the Fund's gold policy, (2) whether there was, in fact, any agreed arrangement between the Fund and South Africa, and (3) whether any Board decision on the staff's recommendations should single out South Africa.

The legal question was raised again by Mr. Martínez-Ostos, but he agreed to defer it for the time being to enable the Board to consider questions of substance. Mr. Melville (Australia), who had been elected by South Africa, on the other hand, asked that the legal authority should be clearly established, e.g., by Board interpretation, before any decision was taken that involved a question of a member's compliance with the Fund Agreement. Mr. Melville sharply attacked not only the Fund staff for concentrating on South Africa in its memorandum of February 14, but also the Fund's premium gold policy, stating that it was impracticable. He advocated flooding the premium markets to destroy them as the only possible policy, if the price of gold was not to be increased. Referring to the two countries that had elected him, he said, "As a South African I am, of course, in favour of premium sales of gold. As an Australian I must add that my instructions are to oppose them."

After some discussion, in which differences of opinion were expressed as to the terms in which the decision should refer to South Africa, the Board decided on March 7, 1951 as follows, agreeing at the same time that the text should be made public:

> Since the amount of sales and purchases in the world markets of gold for jewelry, artistic and industrial purposes has recently been increasing at a rate indicating that at least a part of it finds its way to private hoards, contrary to the gold policy of the Fund established in June 1947, the Executive Board considers the existing arrangements and practices of several countries, including South Africa, are no longer a satisfactory basis to implement the Fund's gold policy and directs the staff of the Fund urgently to elaborate, after consultation with the countries concerned, more effective methods than the existing ones.

The Managing Director appointed a committee of four staff members to plan action to carry out the Board's decision. However, the committee was unable to agree on a report, one plan being advocated by the Treasurer and a member of his Department, and another by the other two members of the committee, who were drawn from the Legal and Research Departments. The Acting Chairman (Mr. Overby) then appointed a staff Working Party on Gold with terms of reference which included the stipulation that the Fund's gold policy was to be taken for granted. The Working Party was to have unlimited scope to investigate what measures might be taken to make the policy more effective. To this end, major gold producers and importers were to be consulted on existing practices and arrangements. Following such consultation, the Working Party might make recommendations to the Executive Board in accordance with its decision of March 7. The Working Party was also to consider the question of sales of gold from monetary reserves and, in this connection, was to study the replies received from members to the general letter of February 9.

REPORT OF STAFF WORKING PARTY

The Working Party held discussions in Washington during April and May 1951 with technical representatives from Canada, France, Mexico, the Netherlands, South Africa, the United Kingdom, and the United States.[7] The discussions, which included both separate conversations with the representatives from each member and joint meetings, were concerned with the members' regulations and practices for dealing with gold transactions, and their experience in carrying

---

[7] Italy and Egypt had also been invited to send representatives. However, Italy did not nominate a representative until after the discussions had been held, and the information supplied by him was received too late to be included in the Working Party's report. Although Egypt stated that it would supply written information, this had not been received by the time the report was issued.

them out. In addition to the discussions, the Working Party obtained statistical and other information from the representatives and supplemented its discussions with further studies and inquiries on the subject.

The Working Party's report, which was prepared on the basis of all the information received, was issued on July 18, 1951. The report was circulated to the Board with a covering note by the Acting Managing Director, which emphasized that the Board's decision required that the Fund's gold policy as it stood should be the basis of the report and that the report therefore dealt with more effective measures for implementing the existing policy, which deprecated external premium gold sales. Accordingly, the main recommendations of the report were as follows:

> Countries should permit exports and imports of gold only in accordance with the following principles:
>
> (1) Except for movements of gold between monetary authorities, gold in whatever form, such as gold-bearing materials, raw gold, semiprocessed gold, bullion, coin, fully fabricated gold, or scrap gold, should not be imported into any country from any source except
>
> > (a) for the purpose of satisfying the demand for gold required for local industrial, professional, or artistic consumption, and not for re-export; or
> >
> > (b) for the purpose of refining, processing, or fabrication of the gold for export in accordance with paragraph 2 below:
>
> (2) Except for movements of gold between monetary authorities, no gold in whatever form should be exported from a country to any other country, whether a member or nonmember of the Fund, unless the importing country has agreed to subscribe to the principles outlined in paragraph 1 above.

The Board considered the Working Party's recommendations on September 18, 1951. During the course of the discussions, it became clear that for a variety of reasons the Board was unwilling to recommend the adoption of the much more stringent measures that the Working Party's report had shown would be necessary, if the Fund's existing gold policy was to be better implemented. Among the reasons were that enforcement of the policy required the cooperation of all members and a general will to support the policy, whereas certain members were opposed to the policy and to the imposition of further controls. Also, more stringent measures would probably fail, especially in times of uncertainty; gold premiums were only a symptom of financial ills, and the Fund would do better to attack the disease rather than trying to control the symptoms.

Other Directors argued that the Fund's policy was mistaken because a curtailment of premium markets raised the premium in them, and this reduced public confidence in currencies. Another view expressed again was that the proper course was for importing countries to stiffen their controls against gold imports, and not for exporting countries to be required to limit their exports. Finally, Mr. Melville made it clear that South Africa was still wholly opposed to the Fund's policy, and was in any event unwilling to go beyond the arrangement reached in May 1949. However, Mr. Southard said that he did not believe that the Fund could solve the problem by throwing the gold policy overboard on the ground that it was unenforceable.

Accordingly, the Board decided that "the recommendations [of the Working Party report] are not adopted and the staff is asked to prepare further recommendations."

Staff recommendation

In accordance with this decision, the Working Party prepared another memorandum which included a brief review of the premium gold policy and a new recommendation. The staff had considered whether it should explore alternative techniques of enforcing the policy that would be more acceptable to members, but had concluded that this would not be fruitful in the present circumstances. The fact was that the Fund's policy was bound to be ineffective so long as there remained a strong demand for gold at prices above parity, with payment to be made in dollars. Accordingly, the staff's new recommendation was that "the Fund, while reaffirming its belief in the economic principles underlying its premium gold statement, should withdraw its request to members to prevent external transactions in gold at premium prices" because it had become clear that the flow of gold into hoards could not effectively be checked except by much more extensive and hence much more onerous controls, which members did not feel able to accept. The memorandum also discussed briefly the likely consequences of the proposed change in policy, finding them not wholly adverse to the Fund's objectives.

Second Board statement

The staff also prepared a draft statement incorporating its new recommendation. This proposal was not acceptable to Mr. Southard and was considered too drastic by other Directors. Mr. Joshi stated that his Government was completely opposed to scuttling the Fund gold policy. Accordingly, the Board's discussions were mainly based on alternative drafts put forward by Mr. Southard and Mr. Saad (Egypt).

Mr. Southard's draft was specific about the controls members should maintain to distinguish between transactions in monetary and nonmonetary gold, whereas Mr. Saad's did not mention any, nor did the final statement. Both drafts contained the essential paragraph of the statement finally adopted on September 28, 1951, which read as follows:

> . . . the Fund's continuous study of the situation in gold-producing and -consuming countries shows that their positions vary so widely as to make it impracticable to expect all members to take uniform measures in order to achieve the objectives of the premium gold statement. Accordingly, while the Fund reaffirms its belief in the economic principles involved and urges the members to support them, the Fund leaves to its members the practical operating decisions involved in their implementation, subject to the provisions of Article IV, Section 2 and other relevant Articles of the Articles of Agreement of the International Monetary Fund.[8]

Mr. de Largentaye said he would have to object to the proposed statement and could take no responsibility for it, having never agreed with the Fund's gold policy. He offered a different statement that he thought would be a better way out of the difficulty; this put the primary burden for preventing premium transactions in gold on importing countries and also stressed the need for tight monetary policies.

Mr. Rasminsky, in a statement highly critical of the proposed decision, said that it was misleading to suggest that members had obligations other than those imposed by Article IV, Section 2. The Canadian Government would not feel obliged to pretend otherwise, and would take the decision to mean that it would cover such actions as the Government thought necessary to pursue.

Mr. de Selliers disliked the fact that the paragraph did not clearly indicate what the Fund expected of its members, and said that he would have to reserve the position of Belgium because of the vague wording.

In reply to Sir George Bolton (United Kingdom), Mr. Southard said that he believed the intent of the new statement to be that members would make effective as far as possible an operating distinction between hoarding and non-hoarding sales. Other Directors indicated their views that the new statement meant that the judgment as to whether it was desirable to sell gold bars and coins was left to the discretion of each member.

The Managing Director stated his understanding of what the new statement involved so that those who would be working with it would know exactly what its implications were. His statement, on which no Director commented, read in part as follows:

> I take it that we are not withdrawing the Fund's gold statement of June 1947. What we are doing instead is to modify that statement in certain important respects. For example, where the original statement requested members to take effective measures to prevent external transactions in gold at premium prices, the new statement will urge members to support the basic principles underlying the policy under which, to the maximum extent practicable, gold should be held in

---

[8] For the full text of the statement, see E.B. Decision No. 75-(705), September 28, 1951; below, Vol. III, p. 225.

official reserves rather than go into private hoards, so that it should contribute to monetary and exchange stability.

I understand that it is left to members to decide what measures they consider practicable. Some members may take strong measures, others weaker measures, and yet others, perhaps, no measures at all. Each member will be the judge of just how and to what extent it will implement this statement. So far as premium sales are concerned they do not come within the purview of the statement as long as they are not designed to direct gold into private hoards.

Finally, it should be clear that although the Fund will continue to study all aspects of gold transactions, and will remain the instrument of collaboration available at all times to its members to discuss any question relating, for instance, to gold, the Fund will not be expected to represent to any member which sells significant amounts of gold for any nonmonetary purpose that for this reason it is failing to support the statement. Of course, if at any time the failure of gold to enter or remain in official reserves threatens to become dangerous to its members or to some of them, the Fund will review the whole situation, and this statement will not prevent it from performing this normal function or from taking the initiative in consulting with members on any problems which may arise.

This was the last occasion during the period covered by this history on which the Board discussed the problem of the sale of gold at premium prices.

REVIEW OF POLICY

During the years 1947–51, the Fund was faced with the alternatives of attempting to maximize the accretion of gold to reserves, or attempting to drive down the price of gold in premium markets. Had the latter course been followed, it seems likely that most of the flow of newly mined gold ($800 million a year), apart from that needed for legitimate industrial or artistic demands, would have been absorbed by hoarders. In the event, the Board decided to disregard the possibility of reducing the premium, and concentrate on securing as much gold as possible for reserves. There is little doubt that this was the right choice. At least, some $1.5 billion of gold was added to world reserves in the four years 1948 through 1951, whereas if the Fund had been inactive it seems likely that little of this would have been secured.

It is arguable, also, that the contribution made by this increase in reserves to the stability of exchange rates itself helped, in the longer run, to lessen the premium in gold markets. Nor did this influence cease with the Board's decision to leave the implementation of its policy to individual member countries. Its known views assisted members to continue to encourage the accretion of gold to reserves, and to discourage premium markets, so that as the demand for gold for hoarding diminished, reserves were able to benefit increasingly from the steadily growing output from the mines.

SUBSEQUENT ACTION

In their Annual Reports since 1951 the Executive Directors have continued to pay attention to the price of gold. The Reports for 1953 and 1954 recorded the gradual removal of restrictions on the sale and movement of gold, and a fall in the premium.[9] The reasons for this fall were given in the 1953 Report as being the relaxation of controls and the creation of new marketing facilities; the continuance of the legal restrictions imposed in certain countries on the purchase and holding of gold; and the general tightening of monetary policy and the decline of inflationary pressures.[10] The Report for 1954 recorded the reopening of the London gold market on March 22, 1954.[11]

In September 1954, at the instance of Lord Harcourt (United Kingdom), the Board agreed to amend Rule F-4, which set the margins above and below $35 an ounce outside which members may not buy and sell gold, because the existing margins made it impossible for the Bank of England to intervene to regulate the London market when the price moved outside $35 plus/minus ¼ per cent.[12] The new rule, which was established for a month on a temporary basis and then made permanent, sets an alternative margin of 1 per cent including all charges.

The Annual Report for 1956 stated that there had been virtually no premium obtainable by several members that had previously obtained relief for their mining industries by selling part of their output at a premium, and the 1957 Report recorded that there had actually been some dishoarding during the year.[13]

After 1954 the price of gold on the London market remained within limits close to the gold points based on the buying and selling prices of the U.S. Treasury ($35.0875 and $34.9125) until the winter of 1960–61, when the price rose briefly to a maximum of $40. Recording this in its Annual Report for 1961, the Board also referred to the measures taken in several countries to reduce the abnormal demand for gold that had caused the increase.[14] No other major disturbance occurred during the period covered by this chapter.

Prices in other markets, which continued to show substantial premiums above $35 an ounce, were recorded annually with some indication of the probable cause of fluctuations, but with no general comment.[15]

---

[9] *Annual Report, 1953,* pp. 58–60, and *1954,* pp. 114–19.

[10] *Annual Report, 1953,* p. 60.

[11] *Annual Report, 1954,* p. 116.

[12] *Annual Report, 1955,* pp. 97–98.

[13] *Annual Report, 1956,* p. 112, and *1957,* p. 109.

[14] *Annual Report, 1961,* pp. 128–29.

[15] See, e.g., *Annual Report, 1966,* p. 118.

CHAPTER

9

Subsidies to Gold Producers

J. Keith Horsefield

THE FUND'S POLICY of discouraging sales of gold at premium prices, described in the last chapter, has had a parallel in connection with the payment of subsidies to gold producers. This practice too has been held by the Board to run the risk of infringing Article IV, Section 2, which reads as follows:

> *Gold purchases based on par values.*—The Fund shall prescribe a margin above and below par value for transactions in gold by members, and no member shall buy gold at a price above par value plus the prescribed margin, or sell gold at a price below par value minus the prescribed margin.

The margin referred to was fixed by the Board in June 1947 at ¼ of 1 per cent plus certain handling and transportation charges. In October 1954 this was altered to either ¼ of 1 per cent plus handling and transportation charges, or 1 per cent, at the option of the member.

FORMULATION OF POLICY

The problem of subsidies to gold producers first came to the notice of the Board in August 1947, when Peru, having been discouraged from assisting its gold miners to profit from the premium on gold available in free markets, asked the Fund to suggest what alternative methods of aiding its producers were open to it. This problem was remitted to the Committee on External Sales of Gold, which had been set up in May 1947 to consider a request from Colombia for the Board's views on a plan similar to that originally proposed by Peru.[1] (It may be noted that at Bretton Woods Colombia had offered an amendment— which was not accepted—authorizing member countries to pay bonuses in order to promote gold production within their territories.)[2]

---

[1] See above, p. 175.
[2] Alternative C, *Proceedings*, p. 432.

Before the committee was able to consider the matter, the need for a decision was precipitated by an announcement by the Canadian Minister of Finance that his Government proposed to offer to each Canadian gold mine a subsidy of Can$7 for each ounce of gold produced in excess of the output for the year ended June 30, 1947. When communicating this to the Board in November 1947, Mr. Rasminsky (Canada) explained that he was in effect informing the Fund what his Government intended to do, leaving it up to the Fund to take what action it thought necessary.

Meanwhile the committee, having made a preliminary examination of the question posed by Peru, had some doubts whether it was competent to give an answer; the view was expressed that it could not give useful advice to members without having consulted, for example, gold mining experts. It therefore came back to the Board and asked for clarification of its terms of reference. This was given in the form of an instruction to examine whether the Canadian scheme or a variant of it was consonant with the provisions of the Fund Agreement, and what general methods of encouraging gold production in Peru would meet the same test. In its considerations, the committee was enjoined to pay due attention to the implications of these questions for general monetary policy, and to their effect upon the policies and actions of other members.

The discussion of the Canadian plan in the committee showed that there was a difference of opinion between Mr. Overby (United States) and Mr. Martínez-Ostos (Mexico) on the one hand, and Mr. Bolton (United Kingdom) and Mr. Bruins (Netherlands) on the other. Messrs. Overby and Martínez-Ostos believed that the proposed subsidy amounted to an increase in the price of gold, and therefore contravened Article IV, Section 2. Mr. Overby also contended that the economic effects could be serious, and in particular that the subsidy would cause irresistible pressure on the governments of other gold producing countries to assist their gold miners in similar ways. Mr. Bolton and Mr. Bruins, on the other hand, regarded the Canadian proposal as a domestic matter, and not tantamount to an increase in the official price of gold. Mr. Bruins, however, deplored the probable effect, mentioned by Mr. Overby, on other gold producing countries.

Shortly afterwards the Canadian Government, responding to the criticisms in the committee, put forward a new proposal. This provided for a subsidy comprising some percentage (e.g., 30 per cent, 40 per cent, 50 per cent) of the amount by which a mine's actual production costs per fine ounce of gold exceeded a stated basic cost (e.g., $18, $20, $25) per fine ounce. This would be paid on the amount by which the production in any year exceeded a certain percentage (e.g., 66⅔ per cent, 75 per cent) of gold production in the base year. For new mines the subsidy would be paid on the entire production for the first year, and on the amount by which output exceeded a certain percentage (e.g., 66⅔ per cent, 75 per cent) of the first year's production in subsequent years.

The staff advised the committee that this revised plan need not be objected to, particularly in the light of the comment by the reporting delegate of Committee 1 of Commission I at Bretton Woods, to the effect that members were free to encourage their local gold mining industries by means other than paying a higher price for gold.[3] At the instance of Mr. Overby, however, the committee decided that it would be preferable first to draft a general statement on the Fund's attitude toward subsidies, and after three meetings of the committee and three of the Board, at which drafts were discussed, a detailed statement was adopted on December 11, 1947.[4] The following are the operative paragraphs:

> The International Monetary Fund has a responsibility to see that the gold policies of its members do not undermine or threaten to undermine exchange stability. Consequently every member which proposes to introduce new measures to subsidize the production of gold is under obligation to consult with the Fund on the specific measures to be introduced.
>
> Under Article IV, Section 2, of the Articles of Agreement of the Fund members are prohibited from buying gold at a price above parity plus the prescribed margin. In the view of the Fund, a subsidy in the form of a uniform payment per ounce for all or part of the gold produced would constitute an increase in price which would not be permissible if the total price paid by the member for gold were thereby to become in excess of parity plus the prescribed margin. Subsidies involving payments in another form may also, depending upon their nature, constitute an increase in price.

Some reservations to this statement were expressed by Executive Directors. Mr. Tansley (United Kingdom), who had objected to a provision in an earlier draft requiring members to consult the Fund about proposed changes in regulations and practices relating to external transactions in gold, expressed similar concern at the terms of the statement as issued, because there was in it no definition of subsidies. Mr. de Largentaye (France) would have preferred the Board to state that the Fund disapproved of subsidies on gold production, but contended that the Fund Agreement did not empower it to object, since Article IV, Section 2, referred only to price. Mr. Martínez-Ostos sought, and obtained, an assurance that the issuance of the statement would not prevent members from asking the Fund to reconsider any of the related questions involved, or from requesting a formal interpretation by the Executive Directors.

In the light of the general policy just expressed, the Board considered the Canadian plan as acceptable, and took the following decision:

> The Canadian Government has consulted with the Fund regarding its proposed gold production subsidy and has today made an announcement on this subject. The Fund has examined the present Canadian proposal in the light of its own

---

[3] *Proceedings*, p. 575.

[4] E.B. Decision No. 233-2, December 11, 1947; below, Vol. III, p. 225.

general statement of policy published today. The Fund has determined that in the present circumstances the proposed Canadian action is not inconsistent with the policy stated by the Fund.

The crucial element in the policy formulated in the statement quoted above was that it brought within the prohibition in Article IV, Section 2, all subsidy schemes providing for uniform payments per ounce. It is arguable that the consequential recourse by gold producing countries to subsidies adapted to the circumstances of individual producing units stimulated gold production more than uniform subsidies would have done.

APPLICATION OF POLICY

The next opportunity to apply the newly framed policy came in March 1948, when Mr. McFarlane (Australia) sought the approval of the Board for a plan prepared by the Australian Government. This was designed to enable certain marginal gold mines in Western Australia to remain in production despite rising costs—a socially necessary measure since the local population was economically dependent on their continuance. The Government proposed to determine the amount of assistance to be given to each mine individually, on the basis of its costs, ore reserves, value, and dependent population. Mr. McFarlane said that the measures would not affect the price of gold, nor increase output; the Government was opposed to any subsidies for the latter purpose.

Mr. Overby called attention to a statement issued by the U.S. National Advisory Council on the day after the enunciation of the Board's general policy. This expressed the view, inter alia, that there were no grounds which would justify instituting a subsidy to encourage the production of gold in the United States. Mr. Overby said that, in the light of this, he would have to object to any proposal by another member country to subsidize gold production in order to increase it. However, as this feature was absent from the Australian proposal, he would not oppose its approval. The Board then decided that the plan as put forward was consistent with the principles enunciated in its statement of December 11, 1947; therefore the Fund would not object to it.

Six months later the Board considered a staff report on subsidy arrangements in Southern Rhodesia. These had come to light as a result of an article in the London *Economist* in May 1948.[5] Mr. Tansley, having made inquiries, explained to the Board in June that the Government of Southern Rhodesia, which was a self-governing territory, had included the proposal in good faith in its budget for the year. The plan provided for a minimum payment of £1 7s. 6d. an ounce for all gold produced, with additional benefits up to £1 0s. 0d. an ounce for mines of economic benefit to Southern Rhodesia which otherwise would have to close.

[5] "Rhodesia's Gold Subsidy," *The Economist*, Vol. CLIV (January-June 1948), p. 855.

It was regarded as a cost of living payment to the industry to compensate for sharply increased costs. The Government had considered that a system of subsidies to individual mines, such as the Canadian Government had instituted, would be impracticable because of the large number of small mines whose costs would be difficult to determine. Mr. Tansley concluded by saying that the British Government felt that it had gone as far as it could in drawing the attention of Southern Rhodesia to the difficulties inherent in the proposal.

Mr. Overby suggested that Mr. Tansley's last statement raised serious questions about responsibilities to the Fund, since the United Kingdom had included Southern Rhodesia in the nonmetropolitan territories for which it had accepted the Articles of Agreement. He asked that the question should be further studied, and discussions between the staff, the U.K. delegation, and representatives of Southern Rhodesia were held during the Annual Meeting in Washington. As a result, Mr. Tansley reported to the Board on October 5 that the British Government accepted responsibility vis-à-vis the Fund.

Mr. Tansley went on to say that the British Government realized that Southern Rhodesia had unwittingly adopted measures which were not consistent with Article IV, Section 2, and with the Fund's statement of December 11, 1947. Southern Rhodesia was unable to modify the arrangements during the current budget year, but had undertaken to introduce legislation to remove the inconsistency at the next session of the Southern Rhodesian Parliament. Mr. Overby pointed out that the measures criticized had been introduced in Southern Rhodesia without consultation with the Fund, and suggested that the Fund's disapproval be made clear. This was done in the ensuing Annual Report.[6]

In April 1949 the promised legislation was introduced. It replaced the flat rate subsidy by assistance on a graduated scale related to the gold content of the ore processed. The new scale rose from 1s. 0d. a ton for ore yielding 0.75 dwt. per ton to 5s. 0d. a ton for ore yielding 4.0 dwts., and then fell off to zero for ore yielding 10 dwts. This was considered by the Board on May 4. The discussion raised for the first time the significance of the phrase in the statement of December 11, 1947, "a uniform payment per ounce for . . . part of the gold produced. . . ." The Legal Department advised the Board that the broad intention of the statement had been to prohibit a flat rate subsidy for all gold produced or for such a substantial part of it as to violate the spirit. The Southern Rhodesian plan could not, the Department thought, be said to set up a uniform payment for all or for a substantial part of the gold produced.

Mr. Southard (United States) again referred to the U.S. Government's disapproval of gold subsidies instituted for the purpose of expanding gold production to enhance a country's balance of payments position. Commenting on this, Mr. Parkinson (Canada) said that Canada's subsidy continued to be for the

---

[6] *Annual Report, 1949*, p. 36.

purpose of maintaining production in an industry whose output was substantially below normal. In 1948 the value of gold produced was some $10–15 million higher than in 1947, but this was only a negligible part of the improvement in the Canadian balance of payments during the year. Mr. McFarlane said that the purpose of the Australian subsidy plan was similar, and that output in 1948 had not increased at all. Mr. Tansley said that in Southern Rhodesia the previous subsidy scheme, which the Fund did not approve, had done no more than slow down the rate of decline of gold production, and as the new system would cost little, if anything, more than the previous one, it was clear that the Government's objective remained a modest one. The Board then decided that the proposed subsidy did not contravene the requirements of Article IV, Sections 2 and 4, or of the Board's statement of December 11, 1947.

Following the devaluations in September 1949, Australia and Southern Rhodesia canceled their subsidies and Canada reduced the amount of its subsidy, while still avoiding payment of a uniform amount per ounce.[7] When in September 1950 Canada adopted a fluctuating exchange rate, its subsidy was increased by 10 per cent, but in the rush of events the Government overlooked obtaining the Fund's consent, for which Mr. Parkinson subsequently expressed the Government's regret.

Shortly thereafter Canada sought the Fund's approval for a change in the cost limits used for the calculation of the subsidy for individual mines, raising the minimum limit and lowering the maximum one. It also proposed to change the base year to 1949. The cost to the Government was expected to fall from $9.4 million in 1950 to $7 million in 1951. Asked under what conditions Canada could visualize that the subsidy could be eliminated, Mr. Parkinson said that this would probably have to depend primarily upon increased efficiency and declining costs in the industry. He agreed that the latter development did not seem likely, at least for some time to come. The Board accepted the proposed change in the subsidy arrangements as being within the terms of its statement of December 11, 1947. A minor change in the plan, introduced early in 1951, was similarly accepted, the Board referring in its decision to the continuing rise in operating costs. A further minor change was approved in June 1951.

Up to this time the Canadian subsidy had been renewed from year to year; but in December 1951 the Government sought the Board's concurrence in its extension for two years. Mr. Wolfson (Canada) explained that Canadian producers had been given the option of continuing to receive the subsidy or of selling their output in the free market; this had followed from the Board's statement of September 28, 1951.[8] (When that statement was prepared, Mr. Rasminsky had said that his Government would not "feel obligated . . . to resort

---

[7] *Annual Report, 1950*, p. 74.

[8] See above, p. 200.

to any form of pretence with regard to gold transactions at premium prices.")
Some Executive Directors questioned whether, in view of the option available to
gold producers, there was any justification in continuing the subsidy; insofar
as this kept gold off the free market, it would lessen the desirable tendency for
the free market price to fall. Pressing this argument, Mr. Martínez-Ostos said
that he still believed that any subsidy contravened the requirements of Article IV,
Section 2. However, as the Board had so frequently approved the Canadian plan,
he would not vote against it.

Mr. Southard denied that the intention of the Board's statement of September 1951 was to channel more gold into free markets; on the contrary, it was
the Fund's wish that as much as possible should find its way into monetary
reserves. He therefore saw no contradiction between that statement and the
Canadian subsidy. While he himself thought that subsidies for gold production
were unwise, the Canadian plan had previously been approved, and the Board's
decision of September 28 made no difference. He therefore supported the
Canadian request. The Board then agreed to it.

In November 1952 the Canadian Government decided that it would be necessary to increase the scale of its subsidy. Rising costs and declining yields had
led to the closing of ten mines during the previous eighteen months, and more
were threatened with closure. Executive Directors commented in terms similar
to those used on previous occasions, but the Board decided again that the plan
was compatible with the Fund's policy.

Later developments in connection with the Canadian subsidy may be briefly
noted. It was prolonged without alteration in December 1953, the Government
at that time still regarding it as a temporary measure. In January 1955 the rate
of subsidy was reduced to two thirds of the excess of costs of production over
Can$26.50 an ounce, up to a maximum of Can$12.33 an ounce.[9] It was payable
on two thirds of the amount produced. This new plan was initially to be limited
to two years, but in 1956 it was extended for a further two years.[10] In 1958
the rate of subsidy was increased by 25 per cent (to offset the decline in the gold
price corresponding to the appreciation of the Canadian dollar), and the arrangement was extended for a further two years.[11] In June 1960 it was further
extended through 1963.[12] Finally, in April 1964 it was extended to the end of
1967, with a modification excluding new lode mines commencing production after
June 1965 unless they provided direct support to an existing gold mining community.[13] These successive adjustments were all considered by the Board, and
the schemes as revised were deemed consistent with Fund policy.

[9] *Annual Report, 1955*, p. 95.
[10] *Annual Report, 1957*, p. 105.
[11] *Annual Report, 1959*, pp. 149–50.
[12] *Annual Report, 1961*, p. 125.
[13] *Annual Report, 1964*, p. 109.

MODIFICATION OF POLICY

In 1954 three other countries joined Canada in offering subsidies for gold production—Australia, Colombia, and the Philippines. The first of these to submit a proposal was the Philippines, which consulted the Fund in June 1954 about a proposal to provide subsidies at three levels, to corresponding categories of mines, classified on the basis of profits and production costs.

Commenting on this proposal, the staff suggested that it was scarcely consistent with the policy enunciated on December 11, 1947, since uniform payments per ounce would be made to the mines in each group. Nevertheless the staff recommended that the proposal should be approved, being influenced by the belief that in the past the application of the 1947 policy had led to the drawing of fine distinctions which were difficult to defend. Since the number of mines in the Philippines to be assisted was in any case quite small, there would be no large groups receiving identical assistance. While it could not be denied that the contemplated subsidy would amount to "a uniform payment per ounce for . . . part of the gold produced," the structure of the subsidy was so similar to others which had been approved that the staff believed the Board could consent.

Discussing the proposal, Executive Directors recognized that gold mines in the Philippines were gravely disadvantaged by high production costs. Mr. Saad (Egypt), who had been elected by the Philippines, supported the recommendation of the staff, while recognizing that the phrase quoted from the 1947 decision created a problem. He agreed with a suggestion by the staff that the policy should be re-examined. Mr. Eriksen (Norway) agreed with the proposal but suggested that meanwhile the Philippine plan should be approved for one year only. Other Directors, however, observed that the Philippines had proposed to apply the subsidy for two years, and it seemed inappropriate to refuse this request merely in order that the policy might be re-examined. One Director indeed suggested that experience with the Canadian subsidy suggested that there was no good purpose to be served by approving such a plan for a fixed term; he thought it would be better to approve the Philippine proposal without a time limit, on the understanding that any changes would be brought before the Board.

Mr. Southard believed that the plan met the test of a subsidy and not an increase in the monetary price of gold. Mr. de Lattre (France) recalled that Mr. de Largentaye had frequently indicated his dislike of subsidies, but considering the small number of mines involved in the Philippines he would not object to the proposal. Mr. Bury (Australia) saw no advantage in re-examining the Fund's policy; he thought it was clear that it would be unreasonable to deny the Philippine request to meet their serious problems. He and Mr. Warren

(Canada) both welcomed the implicit change in the application of the Fund's policy. On this footing the Board decided that the Philippine proposal was deemed to be consistent with the objectives of the Fund's statement of December 11, 1947. The plan was subsequently modified on two occasions and approved by the Board for continuance until July 1957, when it was allowed to expire.[14] For some years thereafter producers were assisted through the Philippines' exchange system. The resulting multiple currency practice was considered by the Board in January 1958 and not objected to.

In June 1961, however, the Philippines reintroduced subsidies. This time, producers were divided into two categories only—marginal and over-marginal—depending on whether or not their profits fell short of "base profits" calculated separately for each mine.[15] The Board agreed that these arrangements were consistent with the Fund's policy. This plan was modified in the following year as a result of the inauguration of a floating exchange rate on January 22, 1962. While the rates of subsidy remained unchanged, it was proposed that the total of the official price plus the subsidy should not exceed ₱ 200 an ounce nor fall below ₱ 160 an ounce for both classes of producers. (At the free rate, these figures were approximately equivalent to $55 and $44.) As there appeared to be a danger that these arrangements might lead to the payment of a uniform premium price for gold should the exchange rate appreciate or depreciate sufficiently far, the Board asked for assurances that, if this seemed likely to happen, corrective measures would be taken in consultation with the Fund. These assurances were forthcoming, and the Board then accepted the plan, which has since been maintained in operation.[16] A new par value for the Philippine peso was agreed with the Fund on November 8, 1965.

In June 1954 Colombia also introduced a subsidy for gold producers. The Government then set aside the sum of Col$80,000 a month to assist certain small mines and gold-pan miners whose production had not exceeded 180 ounces of gold during the first six months of 1953.[17] Provided that these mines and miners agreed to sell their gold to the central bank, they would be eligible to receive not more than Col$20 per fine ounce (equivalent at the official rate to US$8) on not more than 30 ounces a month. This plan was brought to the notice of the Board in January 1955, during the 1954 consultation with Colombia, and was deemed to be consistent with Fund policy. The subsidy was discontinued in 1962, but since then Colombian gold producers have been assisted through the exchange market and fiscal incentives.

Australia reintroduced subsidy arrangements in October 1954.[18] Its gold

[14] *Annual Report, 1958*, p. 144.

[15] *Annual Report, 1962*, p. 164.

[16] *Annual Report, 1963*, p. 181, *1964*, p. 109, *1965*, pp. 102–103, and *1966*, p. 119.

[17] *Annual Report, 1955*, pp. 94–95.

[18] *Ibid.*, p. 94.

producers were divided into two groups. Those with an output exceeding 500 ounces a year and satisfying certain conditions were to be eligible during the two financial years 1954/55 and 1955/56 for a subsidy equal to three fourths of the excess cost of production over £A 13 10s. 0d. (US$30) an ounce, subject to a maximum subsidy of £A 2 0s. 0d. an ounce. Producers whose output was less than 500 ounces a year were to be eligible for a flat rate subsidy of £A 1 10s. 0d. an ounce. This flat rate was adopted for administrative convenience because of the great number of small mines affected and the possible imperfection of their records. The output of the small mines represented only 4 per cent of Australia's total production. Mr. Southard commented that a good case had been made out for the flat rate subsidy to small producers, and he believed that it would not result in any measurable breaking down of the Fund's policy; he therefore supported the Australian request for approval of the plan. The Board accepted it as being consistent with the objectives of Fund policy.

In September 1957 and May 1959 the rates of subsidy paid to both classes of producer were increased.[19] With these alterations the scheme remained in operation until October 1961, when it was modified to remove the sharp distinction between large and small producers. Under the revised plan producers with an annual output of between 500 and 1,075 ounces could opt to be paid a flat rate subsidy at a rate diminishing from £A 2 8s. 0d. an ounce at 500 ounces to zero at 1,076 ounces a year.[20]

In August 1962 Australia granted a subsidy for developmental purposes to mines not previously eligible; the allowance was not to exceed the amount by which their expenditure on development in any year exceeded their annual rate of expenditure on development in a selected base period.[21] The latter provision was removed in 1965, when the rates of subsidy were again increased.[22] All these changes were submitted to the Board and were accepted as consistent with the Fund's policy.

It may be added that the possibility of revising the statement of policy enunciated in December 1947, suggested during the discussion of the original Philippine proposal mentioned above, was reviewed by the staff in December 1954 and January 1955. In view of the legislative history of Article IV, Section 2, however, the Legal Department formed the view that any payments made in addition to the official price of gold must be construed as additions to its price. No reformulation of the 1947 decision which would be consistent with the Articles could therefore be found, and the matter was not again submitted to the Executive Board.

[19] *Annual Report, 1958*, p. 145, and *1960*, p. 144.
[20] *Annual Report, 1962*, pp. 163–64.
[21] *Annual Report, 1963*, p. 181.
[22] *Annual Report, 1965*, p. 103.

LATER DEVELOPMENTS

For nearly ten years after 1954 the only new plan to subsidize gold production brought to the notice of the Board was one introduced by Fiji for the three fiscal years 1958/59, 1959/60, and 1960/61. In these years the Fiji Government undertook to pay an annual subsidy not exceeding £150,000 a year to the one mining company in the colony, on condition that the company would expend an equal or greater amount on development. The maximum subsidy was to be reduced by £2 for each ounce that output fell below 75,000 ounces in any one of the three years. This plan was accepted by the Board at the instance of the United Kingdom, of which Fiji was a nonmetropolitan territory, in February 1959.[23]

In August 1963 South Africa obtained the Board's approval for a plan to assist twelve marginal gold mines to meet the cost of pumping out underground water in order that they might remain in production. The total cost for the year 1963–64 was not to exceed R 1 million. In April 1964 this assistance to the marginal mines was supplemented by the grant of unsecured loans by the state to cover working losses up to 10 per cent of revenue, plus certain capital expenditures approved by the Government Mining Engineer.[24] These arrangements have since been continued from year to year.[25]

The only other subsidy plan introduced during the period covered by this history was a new arrangement by Southern Rhodesia in December 1963. This was designed to subsidize potentially economic mines that otherwise would for the time being operate at a loss and possibly have to close down. The amount of assistance to be given was left to the discretion of the Minister of the Treasury.[26] The plan was accepted by the Fund as being consistent with its objectives, and has since remained in force.[27]

RESULTS OF SUBSIDIES

The size of the output of gold is determined by a number of factors, including the availability and yield of ores, the ability of the mines to compete for necessary resources of labor and capital, and the attractiveness of the price of gold in relation to its cost of production. Compared with these three factors, the effects of a subsidy can only be marginal, so that one can hardly expect to detect it from the figures of output.

---

[23] *Annual Report, 1959*, pp. 150–51.

[24] *Annual Report, 1964*, p. 109.

[25] *Annual Report, 1965*, pp. 102–103, and *1966*, p. 119.

[26] *Annual Report, 1964*, p. 109.

[27] *Annual Report, 1965*, p. 103, and *1966*, p. 119.

In general, however, it appears that subsidy arrangements have at best succeeded in maintaining output at the level at which it stood when they were introduced. The exceptions have been Canada, from 1948 to about 1955, and South Africa. Canadian output rose from $124 million in 1948 to $159 million in 1955, fluctuated around the latter figure until 1961, but then fell off, to $126 million in 1965. South Africa's production rose from 58 per cent of world output (excluding communist countries) in 1945 to 75 per cent in 1965, but its subsidies affected only about 4 per cent of its output. Colombia's output was a little larger than usual in 1956 and 1960, but if the former year is averaged with 1957 the improvement disappears, and the higher figure achieved in 1960 has not been repeated. Figures for the most recent years show a decline also in Australia, despite the continuance of the subsidy. It seems clear, therefore, that subsidies have not led to any material increase in the output of gold.

On the other hand, the spread of subsidy payments has certainly slowed the pace of mine closures and thereby averted a significant fall in output from a growing number of marginal and submarginal mines. The proportion of gold produced from mines with reported production costs above the equivalent of $35 an ounce was perhaps 30 per cent in Canada in 1965 and some 45 per cent in Australia in the year ended June 30, 1966. On less complete information it may be inferred that the proportion of gold produced from such mines in Ghana was about one fourth, in the Philippines a large proportion, and in Rhodesia a substantial part. In all, among gold producers other than South Africa, somewhere between 22 per cent and 27 per cent of output may have been made economic by subsidy payments. This would represent between 5½ and 7 per cent of world production outside the communist countries; without subsidy payments, most if not all of this output might have been expected to cease.

PART III

Exchange Restrictions

10

Exchange Restrictions: The Setting

Margaret G. de Vries

THE SECOND PART of the code of conduct implicit in the Articles of Agreement (as described in Chapter 2) concerns exchange restrictions and convertibility of currencies. When the Articles were signed at the end of 1945, the flow of international commerce and payments was very much restricted. The preceding fifteen years had seen the introduction and extension of fairly rigid controls over international trade and payments by all except a few countries, mainly in the Western Hemisphere. The depression of the 1930's had forced most countries to abandon the gold standard. Faced with drastically reduced supplies of foreign exchange, countries had had to take measures to curb the demand for exchange. Many adopted exchange controls.[1]

THE BREADTH AND DEPTH OF RESTRICTIONS IN 1945

By 1945, European countries could be classified in three groups. (1) A first group of countries had formed a "sterling bloc." In September 1931 Denmark, Finland, Norway, Portugal, and Sweden devalued along with the United Kingdom, and thereafter their currencies were pegged to the pound sterling, the rate for which fluctuated. They retained their free markets and, with minor exceptions, did not impose exchange controls. (2) Another group of countries—Belgium, France, the Netherlands, and Switzerland—had constituted a "gold bloc."[2] These countries in general maintained both the pre-1931 parities for their exchange rates and the convertibility of their currencies into gold until 1936, after which they departed from the gold standard but avoided introducing

---

[1] The term *exchange controls* in this volume is used to designate a broad course of action and an entire apparatus of control, which usually includes *exchange restrictions*.

[2] Italy was part of the gold bloc until 1934, and Poland until 1936.

exchange controls.[3] (3) A third group of countries in Central and Eastern Europe had taken the exchange control route. Germany adopted controls in August 1931, and shortly thereafter Austria, Bulgaria, Czechoslovakia, Greece, Hungary, Rumania, and Yugoslavia did likewise. Italy held out until 1934, and Poland until 1936, when exchange controls were adopted by those two countries also.[4]

Exchange controls had also been adopted by countries outside Europe. Japan resorted to controls in July 1932; and in 1931–32 several Latin American countries, notably Argentina, Bolivia, Brazil, Chile, Colombia, Paraguay, and Uruguay, found it necessary to restrict transactions in foreign exchange. The exchange depreciation already undertaken by most of these Latin American countries had failed to alleviate sufficiently the acute shortages of foreign exchange brought about after 1929 by severe declines in the demand for their exports and a marked deterioration in their terms of trade.

With the outbreak of World War II, practically all countries had been compelled to bring their international payments and reserves under strict regulation. In September 1939 the United Kingdom had set up a comprehensive system of controls over foreign exchange transactions. Moreover, what had been the informal and voluntary arrangements of the "sterling bloc" had become the formal and legal arrangements of the "sterling area." Regulations similar to those of the United Kingdom had been put into effect in the British Dominions (except for Canada and Newfoundland) and throughout the British colonies, protectorates, and mandated territories. Thus exchange controls had been put in force in what were then—or were to become after the war—Australia, Burma, Ceylon, Egypt, India, Iraq, Ireland, Israel, Jamaica, Jordan, Kenya, Kuwait, Malaysia, New Zealand, Nigeria, Pakistan, Sierra Leone, South Africa, the Sudan, and Uganda. Furthermore, as Germany had occupied the continent of Europe, the system of German controls and clearing arrangements had been extended. By early 1942, some seventeen countries, including Belgium, Denmark, France, the Netherlands, and Norway, had been linked to the German arrangements.[5]

Exchange controls and quantitative restrictions on trade had become major instruments of national policy, and their manipulation had become a plausible new alternative to exchange rate adjustment when a country's balance of payments fell into disorder. Moreover, exchange controls had become not only a method of adjusting the external financial position of a country, but also a way

[3] Belgium introduced controls in March 1935 but rescinded them soon afterward.

[4] Details of the introduction, extent, and nature of controls in Europe during the 1930's can be found in League of Nations, *Report on Exchange Control.*

[5] Details of the extension of exchange controls as a result of World War II can be found in Raymond F. Mikesell, *Foreign Exchange in the Postwar World,* pp. 3–21.

in which countries could pursue internal monetary policies in their own interests independent of external considerations. Behind a protective wall of controls, countries could, for example, employ expansionary monetary policies aimed at stimulating full employment.[6]

It was hoped by many economists and government officials that, once the war was over, most of these controls would be removed. They favored a return to some mechanism which would again permit freedom of international transactions on a multilateral rather than a bilateral basis. To this end, the convertibility of sterling was looked upon as a key element. The Anglo-American Financial Agreement of 1945 had, therefore, envisaged an early restoration of sterling convertibility: under the terms of this Agreement, sterling was to be made convertible by July 16, 1947.

The problem of eliminating exchange restrictions—and of subsequently maintaining freedom of international payments—was, however, inextricably bound up with the question of how reconcilable was the pursuit of domestic full employment with the maintenance of free and multilateral international trade and payments—a question discussed in Chapter 2. Countries agreed to the code of conduct of the Fund in the realization that much harm had been wrought both to the system of international payments and to their own domestic economies by the wide use of exchange controls. But they were by no means confident that they could live without such controls. It was evident that the Fund's task in this field would not be an easy one. Controls would not wither away merely because World War II had come to an end, or because the Fund's Articles had come into effect.

THE FUND'S ASSIGNMENT

This was the environment in which the Fund came into being. One of its major purposes, as noted in Chapter 2, is "to assist in the establishment of a multilateral system of payments in respect of current transactions between members and in the elimination of foreign exchange restrictions which hamper the growth of world trade" (Article I (iv)). Beyond that, its Articles spell out several obligations that members must assume. Article VIII defines the general obligations of members; Sections 2, 3, and 4 specify those regarding exchange restrictions and convertibility of currencies. These are, in part:

> SEC. 2. *Avoidance of restrictions on current payments.*—(a) Subject to the provisions of Article VII, Section 3 (b), and Article XIV, Section 2, no member

---

[6] The details of how countries had learned to use controls and of their harmful consequences are given in League of Nations, *International Currency Experience*; in Margaret S. Gordon, *Barriers to World Trade*; and in Howard S. Ellis, *Exchange Control in Central Europe.*

shall, without the approval of the Fund, impose restrictions on the making of payments and transfers for current international transactions.[7]

(b) Exchange contracts which involve the currency of any member and which are contrary to the exchange control regulations of that member maintained or imposed consistently with this Agreement shall be unenforceable in the territories of any member. . . .[8]

SEC. 3. *Avoidance of discriminatory currency practices.*—No member shall engage in, or permit any of its fiscal agencies . . . to engage in, any discriminatory currency arrangements or multiple currency practices except as authorized under this Agreement or approved by the Fund. . . .

SEC. 4. *Convertibility of foreign held balances.*—(a) Each member shall buy balances of its currency held by another member if the latter, in requesting the purchase, represents

(i) that the balances to be bought have been recently acquired as a result of current transactions; or

(ii) that their conversion is needed for making payments for current transactions.

However, these obligations did not have to be fulfilled immediately. Article XIV, Sections 2, 3, 4, and 5, provided for a transitional period:

SEC. 2. *Exchange restrictions.*—In the post-war transitional period members may, notwithstanding the provisions of any other articles of this Agreement, maintain and adapt to changing circumstances (and, in the case of members whose territories have been occupied by the enemy, introduce where necessary) restrictions on payments and transfers for current international transactions. . . . members shall withdraw restrictions maintained or imposed under this Section as soon as they are satisfied that they will be able, in the absence of such restrictions, to settle their balance of payments in a manner which will not unduly encumber their access to the resources of the Fund.

SEC. 3. *Notification to the Fund.*—Each member shall notify the Fund before it becomes eligible under Article XX, Section 4 (c) or (d), to buy currency from the Fund, whether it intends to avail itself of the transitional arrangements in Section 2 of this Article, or whether it is prepared to accept the obligations of Article VIII, Sections 2, 3, and 4. . . .

SEC. 4. *Action of the Fund relating to restrictions.*—Not later than three years after the date on which the Fund begins operations and in each year thereafter, the Fund shall report on the restrictions still in force under Section 2 of this Article. Five years after the date on which the Fund begins operations, and in each year thereafter, any member still retaining any restrictions inconsistent with Article VIII, Sections 2, 3, or 4, shall consult the Fund as to their further retention.

---

[7] Article VII, Section 3 (b), refers to the special situation when the Fund has formally declared its holdings of a given currency to be scarce; see Vol. I, p. 193. Article XIV, Section 2, provides for a postwar transitional period. For the full text of the Articles, see below, Vol. III, pp. 185–214.

[8] For a discussion of the interpretation of this provision and of the legal proceedings involved in the courts of member countries in enforcing this provision, see Joseph Gold, *The Fund Agreement in the Courts.*

The Fund may, if it deems such action necessary in exceptional circumstances, make representations to any member that conditions are favorable for the withdrawal of any particular restriction, or for the general abandonment of restrictions, inconsistent with the provisions of any other article of this Agreement. The member shall be given a suitable time to reply to such representations. If the Fund finds that the member persists in maintaining restrictions which are inconsistent with the purposes of the Fund, the member shall be subject to Article XV, Section 2 (a).

SEC. 5. *Nature of transitional period.*—In its relations with members, the Fund shall recognize that the post-war transitional period will be one of change and adjustment and in making decisions on requests occasioned thereby which are presented by any member it shall give the member the benefit of any reasonable doubt.

Not only did these Articles specify the obligations of members, but they made clear that despite the considerable powers of the Fund, there were certain limitations on its objectives and on its jurisdiction in the field of exchange restrictions.

LIMITATIONS ON THE FUND

RESTRICTIONS ON PAYMENTS

The first point to be noted about the obligations of Article VIII is the phrase in Section 2 (a), *restrictions on the making of payments and transfers* (referred to in this volume as exchange restrictions). This phrase has the effect of demarcating the Fund's authority.

At the time of the Bretton Woods Conference in 1944, it was expected that two agencies would be established in the international economic field: one, a trade organization, to deal inter alia with restraints on international *trade,* such as tariffs, quotas, import controls, and the like; the other, the International Monetary Fund, to deal with restrictions on international *payments and transfers.* Later, in its first Annual Report, the Fund stressed that it "was conceived as one element in a many-sided approach to the task of re-establishing a functioning world economic system," and pointed reference was made to the plans for a parallel International Trade Organization.[9]

For a variety of reasons, the trade organization was not in fact ever set up. But most of the matters that were to have been under its jurisdiction eventually came to be handled through the CONTRACTING PARTIES to the General Agreement on Tariffs and Trade (GATT). The GATT, accordingly, has jurisdiction over *trade* and *import* restrictions. Many economists have argued that distinctions between the various types of obstacles to international transactions—and in particular between restraints labeled "import restrictions" and others called "exchange

---

[9] *Annual Report, 1946,* p. 15.

restrictions"—have little economic significance. Nonetheless, the Fund's competence was delimited by the specific words of Article VIII, Section 2 (*a*).

In the Fund's early years there were repeated discussions among both the staff and the Executive Directors as to the extent of the Fund's jurisdiction. Frequently, such internal discussions focused on the questions of just how an *exchange* restriction should be defined and how it should be differentiated from a *trade* restriction. Clearly, something called restrictions on trade—including import licensing—were to be the concern of the GATT, while restrictions on payments —including payments for imports through an exchange licensing procedure— were the proper province of the Fund. It was to prove difficult in practice, however, to distinguish trade restrictions from payments restrictions. Differences between the exchange control systems of one country and another often seemed to result more from variations among countries' legal requirements and administrative procedures than from the economic intent of the controls. In some countries—including those of the sterling area—goods could not be imported without import licenses; and such licenses were not freely issued. However, once an import license had been obtained, foreign exchange could be automatically obtained for the permitted import. On the surface of things, this type of regulation seemed to constitute a restriction on trade but not a restriction on foreign exchange payments. The converse, a restriction on foreign exchange payments but not on trade, seemed to exist in other countries, where it was the foreign exchange which was subject to license and where such exchange licenses were limited in issue but, once obtained, conferred an automatic right to import or to obtain an import license.

Hence, important questions had to be answered: Was there an essential difference between a situation where an importer was unable to import a commodity because he could not obtain an import license, and one where he was denied the foreign exchange with which to purchase it? Was the point at which a restriction was applied—i.e., on imports or on exchange—an adequate basis for deciding which countries would have to consult the Fund or obtain the Fund's approval for their restrictions? If so, were many of the Fund's principal members that applied controls to imports, such as those in the sterling area, to be left free of the Fund's code of conduct as regards restrictions?

If the *form* alone of a restriction did not constitute a sufficient basis for differentiating an exchange restriction from a trade restriction, it quickly became evident that neither did the *purpose* for which a given restriction might be applied. Licensing of imports could easily be used as a means of restricting payments in foreign exchange—that is, import restrictions could be introduced to restrain deficits in the balance of payments. In fact, the GATT charter explicitly recognized the possibility of "quantitative restrictions for balance of payments purposes." Similarly, restrictions on payments originally applied in order to conserve foreign exchange could be retained, after the need to conserve foreign exchange no longer existed, for the benefit of domestic industry that had grown up under its protection. Thus, a division of the jurisdiction between the Fund and the GATT using the purpose of the restrictions as a guide was not feasible.

Debates within the Fund over how to define and characterize an exchange restriction became especially intense early in 1952, just before the first consultations under Article XIV were to take place. For it was then that it had to be decided what types of restrictive and other policies of members would be made subject to consultation. Although an explicit definition of an exchange restriction was not agreed until 1960,[10] the Directors, the member countries, and the staff worked out arrangements by which, in the meantime, the Fund could discuss, even if it did not comment formally on, a wide range of members' restrictions.

Although on other occasions the problem of a clear differentiation between the jurisdiction of the Fund and of the GATT has been a subject of discussion by the Executive Directors, the Fund and the GATT have not had any actual disputes over jurisdiction; on the contrary, cooperation has been close and substantive.

THE EUROPEAN PAYMENTS UNION

Shortly after its establishment, the Fund found itself operating in a world that contained not only the GATT but also various regional groupings which, like the Fund, concerned themselves with payments arrangements across national boundaries. The most important of these was the European Payments Union (EPU), which was founded in Paris in September 1950 under the auspices of the Organization for European Economic Cooperation (OEEC), also relatively new. The EPU led to the creation of a new monetary area known as the "EPU monetary area," the main features of which were that currencies of EPU members (as well as currencies of the countries in the members' own monetary areas) held by residents of other EPU members became, in practice, transferable, i.e., convertible within the EPU area. Intra-EPU payments hence became "multilateralized." Furthermore, members of the EPU were committed to liberalize their restrictions on intra-European trade and payments. Trade liberalization ratios were established which applied to each member's total trade with the whole area rather than to trade with each member separately.

The Fund's task of achieving liberalization of exchange restrictions and convertibility of currencies was thus made both more complex and easier. It was more complex because there was now another formal organization in the same field, and the loyalties of countries that were members of both organizations

---

[10] E.B. Decision No. 1034-(60/27), June 1, 1960; below, Vol. III, pp. 260–61.

might be divided. Initially, the establishment of the EPU monetary area gave rise to anxiety among the staff, the management, and some of the Executive Directors, who feared that the EPU might become a permanent monetary area and that discrimination against outside countries, especially those in the dollar area, might be prolonged. At the same time, however, the achievement of the Fund's objectives was facilitated by the corresponding efforts of the OEEC in liberalizing the restrictions of the members of the EPU and in restoring the convertibility of their currencies.

CURRENT TRANSACTIONS

In addition to the limitations described above, the Fund's regulatory functions apply only to certain kinds of international transactions, some kinds being deliberately left out. The Articles recognize that members might find it necessary to control capital movements. The obligation of members under Article VIII, Section 2, with respect to freedom of exchange transactions is explicitly limited to the avoidance of restrictions on payments and transfers on *current* international transactions. To underscore the point, Article VI, Section 3, explicitly provides that "members may exercise such controls as are necessary to regulate international capital movements," although it goes on to provide that, with certain exceptions, "no member may exercise these controls in a manner which will restrict payments for current transactions or which will unduly delay transfers of funds in settlement of commitments. . . ."

As the Fund's Articles were drafted against the background of the disturbing capital movements that had taken place during the 1930's, there was an understandable desire to prevent movements of "hot" money and to minimize the risk that inadequate foreign exchange reserves would be depleted by more or less panic-inspired capital transfers. Hence, it was thought that controls over capital movements might be necessary and beneficial.

The freedom of the members of the Fund to exercise such controls as are necessary to regulate capital movements for any reason, without prior Fund approval, was restated in a decision by the Executive Board interpreting Article VI, Section 3.[11]

TRANSITIONAL ARRANGEMENTS

Finally, the Articles provided that the Fund was not to pursue to the full its objectives in the field of restrictions during a "transitional period." This limitation affected the Fund's activities in a very important way in the early years, and has continued to be relevant until the present time for the majority of the Fund's members. As quoted above, Article XIV provides for the retention

---

[11] E.B. Decision No. 541-(56/39), July 25, 1956; below, Vol. III, p. 246.

of restrictions during this transitional period. After World War II, when supplies of foreign exchange nearly everywhere were running far short of probable demands for imports, it was obviously impossible to expect any country to abandon at once the elaborate control machinery which had been built up; and it was certain that, at least during an interim period whose length no one could predict, countries where the whole economic structure had to be painfully reconstructed after enemy occupation would feel obliged to impose strict controls upon their international trade and payments.

No period of time was set by the Articles for this transitional period. No definitional criteria of any kind were given. The Fund was merely admonished to recognize that the "post-war transitional period" would be a period "of change and adjustment" and in making any decisions to "give the member the benefit of any reasonable doubt." Two periods were mentioned in Article XIV—three years between the time the Fund started operations (i.e., March 1947) and the time when it was required to make a report to its members on any exchange restrictions still in force, and five years between the time the Fund began operations and the start of consultations on restrictions maintained under Article XIV. But neither of these periods was intended to define the transitional period.

The provision for a transitional period has had several implications for the formation of the Fund's policies on restrictions. First, for several years, the Fund hesitated to take much, if any, action concerning the exchange restrictions maintained by its members. Indeed, prior to the publication of the first Exchange Restrictions Report, in 1950, the only time that the Executive Directors undertook to make any general pronouncements on exchange restrictions was in the course of agreeing on their Annual Reports to the Board of Governors. Second, inasmuch as the Fund had already subjected multiple currency practices to its review (as early as 1947), it seemed to many members, especially those in Latin America, that there was an unfair dichotomy in the Fund's policies. With other forms of control so prevalent and the Fund doing little about them, harping on the elimination of multiple rates which seemed to many relatively minor was a source of irritation to a lot of members. Third, most members were to continue to take advantage of the transitional arrangements for a number of years. Before 1961, only Canada, Cuba, the Dominican Republic, El Salvador, Guatemala, Haiti, Honduras, Mexico, Panama, and the United States had accepted the obligations of Article VIII.

Therefore, from time to time the question arose whether the Fund should not declare the transitional period ended. The Legal Department, in 1959, advised that the Board had no power to terminate the transitional period. By 1965 the issue was no longer much debated, although all but 27 of the Fund's members still took advantage of these arrangements.

THE GENERAL VERSUS THE PARTICULAR

In addition to the limitations imposed by the Articles, Article VIII defines a general and ultimate objective. It does not catalog the particular types of restrictions that usually make up an exchange control system. No differentiation is made, for example, between *payments made* by a member's residents, and *payments received* by residents, e.g., payments made by nonresidents.

Of course, when the Fund began to take action concerning restrictions on payments and transfers, it had to seek to apply these general principles to individual restrictions. Moreover, it became necessary to formulate separate lines of action in respect of certain *particular* forms of restrictions or payments arrangements. Additionally, as the Fund specified its goals from time to time, it had to formulate a lesser objective than the total elimination of restrictions. Only gradually could its ultimate objectives be attained.

Three particular aspects of exchange restrictions were to become the focus of the Fund's attention during the years 1945 to 1965: partial (or external) convertibility, discrimination, and bilateralism.

PARTIAL CONVERTIBILITY

In the exchange control regulations with which the Fund was faced when it undertook consultations on restrictions in 1952, various monetary or currency areas were usually differentiated. Payments by residents of one monetary area to those of another were subject to restrictions of varying degrees. For instance, countries in the sterling area applied much stricter rules to payments to countries in the dollar area than to payments to other sterling area countries.

After the Fund had been in operation for some eight or nine years, the concepts of *external* and *internal* convertibility became regularly used to distinguish different degrees of convertibility. Such concepts had not been part of the Articles. When convertibility of sterling was attempted in 1947, total convertibility, not partial, was the aim. Yet as time went on, it became evident that currencies would be made convertible by degrees, and not all at once. Hence the distinction between external and internal convertibility became a useful one.

The payments system of a country whose currency is *externally* convertible has two important characteristics. First, all holdings of that currency by nonresidents are freely exchangeable into any foreign (nonresident) currency at exchange rates within the official margins. Second, all payments that residents of the country are authorized to make to nonresidents may be made in any externally convertible currency that residents can buy in foreign exchange markets. On the other hand, if there are no restrictions on the ability of a country's residents to use their holdings of domestic currency to acquire any foreign currency and hold it, or transfer it to any nonresident for any purpose, the country's currency is said to be *internally* convertible. Thus *external* convertibility alone is tantamount to *partial* convertibility whereas *total* convertibility involves both *external* and *internal* convertibility.

The Fund members that initially opted for Article XIV and that subsequently moved to Article VIII (mainly countries in Western Europe), in general established external convertibility first and internal convertibility later. Only a few countries—Germany, for example—established the two simultaneously. Both types of convertibility were achieved gradually by most of the European countries, and not without setbacks. Formal recognition was usually eventually given to the *de facto* convertibility established by a series of administrative acts which had in successive stages liberalized the country's system of restrictions. In this process, a number of stages of less than total convertibility were reached.

Discrimination

The second distinction of which the Fund has had to take account is that between *discriminatory* and *nondiscriminatory* restrictions. Prior to the establishment of external convertibility, there was considerable discrimination in the restrictions applied to different monetary or currency areas. Again, as an illustration, the tighter restrictions imposed on transactions in dollars than on transactions in sterling constituted discrimination against the dollar area. In general, discrimination refers to a situation where a country treats its international transactions differently depending on which foreign countries, or which currencies, or both, are involved.

The issue of discrimination in international trade and finance has been a long-standing one, extending far beyond the payments restrictions falling under the jurisdiction of the Fund. Discrimination may be involved, for example, in trade restrictions, in regional arrangements, in customs unions, and in customs tariffs.[12] Discrimination in payments was for many of the years reviewed here especially pronounced and prolonged against countries in the dollar area; transactions with the dollar area were, as a rule, the last to be freed from restrictions.

Thus, the field of discrimination was a *particular* aspect of exchange controls that the Fund also had to tackle. Indeed, discrimination was one of the first problems pertaining to exchange restrictions considered by the Fund; the question of discrimination arose as early as 1949 in connection with South Africa's restrictions. The problem of discrimination against the dollar area persisted to some extent even after the establishment of the external convertibility of European currencies at the end of 1958. Hence, in 1959 the Executive Board took a special decision pertaining to discrimination in exchange restrictions.

---

[12] For a study of discrimination in these broader aspects covering the same years as this volume, see Gardner Patterson, *Discrimination in International Trade.*

BILATERALISM

Another feature of restrictive systems consists of bilateral payments agreements, i.e., agreements between two countries on how payments between them will be settled. Under a typical bilateral agreement, payments between the partner countries have to be made through the bilateral accounts held by the countries' central banks with each other. The outstanding balances on these accounts are generally subject to limits which represent the amount of credit each country is willing to extend to the other; when one of the limits is reached, further amounts accruing to the creditor are to be settled in gold or convertible currencies. The Fund has often used the term *bilateralism* to mean the use of such agreements.

Although the Articles of Agreement do not refer specifically to bilateral payments agreements, they do specify as one of the aims of the Fund the attainment of a multilateral system of payments. Consequently, the Executive Directors have had no difficulty in accepting the view that bilateral payments agreements fall within the Fund's jurisdiction. In 1955 the Board took a special decision stating the Fund's policy on bilateralism.

OUTLINE OF THE DETAILED CHAPTERS

Against this background, the next several chapters have been organized. Chapter 11 explains in detail how the Fund carries on its consultations with individual members. In addition, there are described the reasons why the present procedures were agreed, and the way in which the Fund resolved the question of which restrictions should be the subject of consultation. The chapter also explains how the consultations, which started as consultations on exchange restrictions under Article XIV, evolved into full-blown discussions on many other topics, even with countries not under Article XIV.

Chapter 12 traces developments in the Fund's policies on restrictions from 1945 to the end of 1958 when European countries established external convertibility for their currencies. This chapter interweaves the related developments in world economic conditions during these years and the process by which restrictions were gradually liberalized. Chapter 13 explains these same developments from 1959 to 1965, as well as some special problems of the 1960's, such as those of the less developed countries and some newly emerging difficulties with regard to capital movements among industrial nations. Chapter 14 relates the separate story of bilateral payments agreements. The Fund's relations with the EPU are briefly described in Chapter 15. The discussion of exchange restrictions is then concluded with a résumé of the Fund's relations with the GATT in Chapter 16.

11

The Consultations Process

Margaret G. de Vries

THE FIVE YEARS specified by Article XIV as the period after which the Fund was to consult annually with members on exchange restrictions came to an end on March 1, 1952. The staff and the Executive Board spent some months prior to that date working out how to conduct the consultations. At that time, the climate for the initiation and acceptance of effective consultations was anything but propitious. Hence, although consultations commenced on schedule, many issues concerning their pattern and content remained to be resolved, and the initial procedures were viewed as experimental. In the course of the next few years discussions in the Board, especially during the annual reviews of the procedures for the consultations, focused on these issues. The basic procedures were, with some adaptations, retained. By 1955 the process was working smoothly.

In subsequent years few changes have been made in the procedures, but over time the scope of the consultations has been very much broadened and they have come to serve a growing number of purposes and to involve the effective international scrutiny of members' policies. Significantly, both the Fund and its members decided in 1960 to institute similar annual consultations for members accepting the obligations of Article VIII, although such consultations are not required by the Articles.

Toward the end of 1965 the Fund re-examined its consultations procedures. A few minor alterations were made, but essentially the process was retained unchanged.

A CAUTIOUS BEGINNING

AN UNEASY ENVIRONMENT

In 1952 the Fund's reputation and its relations with many of its members were at a low ebb. The Fund had not yet developed close and frequent contacts with the senior officials of the member governments. While some contacts had been made with the less developed countries, these were not on a regular basis, and some of them had been characterized by friction. In particular, a few less developed countries resented the greater attention being paid to their restrictions than to those of the major powers. Furthermore, the use of the Fund's resources had been minimized by, among other things, the decision of the Fund in April 1948 to limit the use of its resources by European recipients of Marshall Plan Aid (see Chapter 18).

Other elements contributing to disquietude among Fund members with the onset of consultations were uncertainty about the policies on restrictions that the Fund might evolve, and disagreement over the Fund's authority in this field. Little if any progress had been made since 1945 toward the achievement of the objectives of currency convertibility and the elimination of exchange restrictions, and a number of members feared a push by the Fund for a more rapid relaxation of restrictions.

Disagreements in the Board in 1950 on the occasion of the Fund's participation in the Torquay Session of the GATT had already foreshadowed the kind of struggle that could arise. Anticipating that the Fund's own consultations were to commence in 1952 and were likely to take place with practically all of the Fund's members, several Executive Directors sought to create precedents that would circumscribe the Fund's activities vis-à-vis restrictions. It was argued that the Fund's advice to the GATT could not be based on current economic conditions; rather, it should be limited to an appraisal of the circumstances at the time that the member imposed the restrictions. In other words, the Fund was merely to determine whether the initial restrictions had been justified and not to appraise whether such restrictions were currently necessary. Some Directors also contended that the Fund's reports to the GATT should be limited to the facts of the situation, and that the Fund should not draw from these facts any conclusions about the need for restrictions. The very participation of the Fund in these GATT consultations was challenged by Australia, which went so far as to refuse to allow the GATT secretariat to send to the Fund certain documents necessary to the Fund's preparations for the consultations.

The reports that the staff had prepared added to the difficulties among the Executive Directors. The staff had found that while further relaxation of dollar imports by Chile, India, and Pakistan did not then seem practicable, it would be feasible for Australia, Ceylon, New Zealand, Southern Rhodesia, and the United Kingdom to begin a progressive relaxation of their restrictions on imports from "hard" currency areas, although it was recommended that this should be undertaken with due caution.[1] It became necessary to vote formally on the decisions

---

[1] Fund Press Release of December 13, 1950, reprinted in the *Second Annual Report on Exchange Restrictions* (1951), p. 159.

before the Board, and in two series of votes the Directors decided that the Fund should both analyze current conditions and put forward conclusions.

INSTITUTING PROCEDURES

Against this background, the Fund's consultations were started in an experimental way. Certain procedures were proposed by the staff and accepted by the Board in January 1952 as a way to get going. Later these same procedures continued to be the crux of the Fund's consultations process, but only after several troublesome issues had been ironed out. The decisions taken in January 1952 were as follows:

First, the consultations should begin on time, that is, on March 1, 1952, and not, for any reason, be delayed.

Second, the staff should hold discussions with representatives of the members concerned and then prepare recommendations for consideration by the Board.

Third, consultations should be far-reaching. They should cover not only the detailed characteristics of the restrictive system, but the factors necessitating the retention of restrictions as well. And "for appropriate situations" the consultations were to go further. They could include consideration of the ways and means of eliminating or adapting restrictions, the feasibility of substituting alternative measures, and possible technical and financial assistance from the Fund.

That these proposals, with their broad terms of reference, were accepted by the Board was most auspicious for the future development of consultations. But agreement was not reached without anxieties being expressed.

One Executive Director suggested postponing the consultations altogether, on the ground that the requirement for consultations might have been the result of a miscalculation at Bretton Woods of the postwar conditions of the world, which were far different from what had been envisaged at that time. This point was not, however, seriously debated, as the Board as a whole agreed that the consultations were clearly required under Article XIV. Another suggestion was that the procedure should explicitly recognize that the initiative for a consultation had to come from the member rather than from the Fund: some Directors were eager that the Fund should not give the impression that it was exercising the initiative. Had this approach been accepted, members might have avoided consulting the Fund. However, as discussed below, the question of initiative was among those resolved most readily.

Several Directors also expressed a caveat about the Fund's power to communicate its views after a consultation had taken place. They pointed to the terms of Article XIV, Section 4: before the Fund could make formal "representations" to a member about removing restrictions, there would have to be a finding by the Board that "exceptional circumstances" existed. These remarks on "representations" disclosed the fears of a number of countries that the Fund might make representations to many members, in order to end the transitional period. Without coming to any agreement as to their form or content, the Executive Directors tentatively agreed that some conclusions could probably be reached that would be "appropriately notified to the members."

RESOLVING THE ISSUES

Desirous as some Directors had been that vexing issues should be settled in advance, this did not prove possible. Various troublesome questions kept coming up during the next three to four years as the Fund consulted with individual countries, and to a greater extent as annual reviews of consultation procedures took place in the Board. How and by whom—the member or the Fund—should the consultation be initiated? Are annual consultations necessary and worthwhile, or should they be held less frequently? What should be the form and content of the Fund's conclusions for each country's consultation? If the Fund does not make representations, is the Fund in effect giving "approval" to the retention of restrictions? What particular restrictions can the Fund ask members to consult about? Precisely which restrictions does the Fund have authority to "approve"? To what extent can the Fund, in the process of consulting about exchange restrictions, probe into—and comment on—the domestic policies of its members?

Recurrent discussion, widening experience, and improving Fund-member relations were gradually to settle these questions, or at least to make them quiescent.

WHO SHOULD INITIATE THE CONSULTATION?

A formula was quickly found to answer the question whether the Fund or the member should take the initiative in setting up the consultation each year. It was readily recognized that consultations had to be a two-way action, involving cooperation between the Fund and the member, and that practical procedures were of greater importance than the formal rights of initiative.

Nowadays the Fund starts the process by sending letters each year to members announcing the beginning of another round of consultations. But in these letters the Fund recognizes the members' right to initiate them. Simultaneously, the Fund proposes to individual members through their Executive Directors, or after conferring with them, a specific date for the consultations. Over the years, a convenient time of the year has come to be settled upon for most members, governed by such considerations as when the budget is prepared, when legislative sessions are held, and the season of the year. But the date has often been put forward or postponed because of special factors, such as changes in members' governments (due, e.g., to elections), variations in members' attitudes toward the Fund and its usefulness, and sudden crises in a member's balance of payments situation giving rise to a need for the member to use the Fund's resources. Proposals for an alteration in the consultation date have usually been made by the member. Sometimes changes in a member's situation have prevented a consultation being held at all for that year.

How frequently should consultations be held?

Closely related to the foregoing was the question of how frequently consultations should be held. Were annual consultations useful? In the early years, some Executive Directors expressed the view that the consultations could not be expected to achieve any results until there was a change in basic economic conditions, that is, until the problems created by World War II had been overcome. They reiterated that so long as key currencies, especially sterling, remained inconvertible, there was little hope for the elimination of restrictions. Why then was it necessary to have elaborate machinery for annual consultations with the Fund, especially if no changes had taken place in a member's restrictive system since the previous year's consultation? Had not experience shown that the Fund could hardly expect to have a profound consultation with every member more than once every two years? Implicit in these queries was the assumption that the Fund could not help to overcome the fundamental difficulties restricting international commerce.

On the other hand, even in those early years, some Executive Directors—especially the U.S. Director—took exception to the idea that annual consultations were not profitable. These Directors did not wish to limit the frequency of consultations. In their view, if the Fund did not take a rather intensive look at the situation in each member country about once a year through the consultations, some other way would have to be devised to keep up with the developments in each country.

Because of the expressed skepticism about the usefulness of the consultations, and even more because of the considerable work and expense involved for both Fund and members, the staff and management made several suggestions in 1953 and 1954 for simplifying the procedures. Consultations would be advanced, wherever possible, by a preliminary exchange of correspondence—or, in some instances, conducted entirely by correspondence—and the number of formal discussions would be reduced. However, 1954 was also the year when several Directors, during consideration of the Fund's annual budget, suggested that, while expenditures should be limited, more travel by senior staff to member countries should be allowed for. These conflicting views could not easily be reconciled.

Shortly thereafter, however, annual consultations began to be more generally accepted, with due regard to timing problems. It was evident that the regularity of the consultations was not only helping to keep the Board informed of developments, but was also enabling the Fund to avoid any air of crisis in arranging staff contacts with the authorities of its members. The Fund had become much more able than before to act quickly on exchange reforms, drawings, and stand-by arrangements; the consultations had, in fact, frequently led directly to action by the Fund on these matters.

SHOULD THE FUND "APPROVE" RESTRICTIONS?

Despite the initial concern of some members that the Board might make formal representations under Article XIV, Section 4, the Directors did not in fact do so. The closest they came to making representations was in the decision taken on the first consultation, with Belgium-Luxembourg in August 1952. In this decision, the Board expressed the opinion that the strong balance of payments and reserve position of Belgium-Luxembourg made relaxation of restrictions feasible. Accordingly, it requested Belgium-Luxembourg to reconsider the necessity for the level of restrictions maintained on dollar imports.

This decision had been reached by vote after extensive discussion, during which some Directors urged that the decision was tantamount to a representation and, more important, a dangerous precedent. This was the only time in the period covered by this history that a formal vote was taken on a decision after a consultation, although there have been a number of abstentions from decisions. After 1952 the question of making representations did not come up again.

Nonetheless, once it was clear that no representations were to be made, the related questions emerged: Would the Fund then "approve" a member's restrictions, in whole or in part? If so, what language should be used? This problem of approval first came up during the Board's discussion of the draft decision on the first consultation with Denmark, the seventh to be considered by the Board in 1952. The staff had recommended that the Fund "agree" to the temporary retention of Denmark's transitional arrangements and that, if Denmark introduced new restrictions on payments or substantially adapted existing ones, the changes should be made in consultation with the Fund. A number of Directors, especially the Europeans, had difficulties over the implication of this recommendation. Did "agree" mean that the Board was authorizing the continuance of restrictions? Had the Fund any such authority? The Director appointed by the United States had difficulties of an opposite nature with the staff recommendation: How could the Fund question certain restrictions and yet "agree" to their retention?

The issue that had to be resolved can be simply stated: Should the conclusions following a consultation make explicit that the Fund had, in essence, decided *not* to make representations? If there were to be no representations, should the words "agree to" be used, with their implications of Fund approbation of continuing restrictions? The first question—that of representation—was laid to rest by a decision on August 15, 1952, on the basis of a proposal by Mr. Southard (United States). It was agreed that, except under special circumstances, two sentences would be used to open and close, respectively, all decisions taken in the 1952 Article XIV consultations:

> 1. The Government of [*name of country*] has consulted the Fund under Article XIV, Section 4, of the Fund Agreement concerning the further retention of its transitional arrangements.
>
> 2. In concluding the 1952 consultations, the Fund has no further comments to make on the transitional arrangements maintained by [*name of country*].

These innocuous sentences were a way of saying that, after considering the country's restrictions, the Fund did not wish to make any representation.

The second question—of "agreeing" to a country's restrictions—was not dealt with but was left in abeyance. Any conclusions embodied in an Article XIV decision had the status of advice and recommendation rather than of approval by the Fund. Thus, the question of whether the Fund was legally approving a country's restrictions had been skirted. The decisions on Article XIV consultations for several countries taken before August 15, 1952 were correspondingly revised. And the two sentences continued to be used for all Article XIV consultation decisions until early in 1966.

WHAT RESTRICTIONS SHOULD BE REVIEWED

It had been generally understood—by the staff, the management, and the Executive Directors—that the "approval" jurisdiction of the Fund did not go beyond restrictions on current payments and transfers, multiple currency practices, and discriminatory currency arrangements. Nevertheless, difficult definitional and jurisdictional questions still remained. When the consultations began in 1952, a *restriction on payments* (i.e., an exchange restriction) had not yet been defined. Just what restrictions the Fund could discuss with its members remained uncertain. Similarly, whether the Board could comment to its members on what were mutually regarded as trade policies and practices, as distinct from exchange policies and practices, was undetermined.

Debates and definitions

Not only did various Directors hold opposing views on these questions, but so did members of the staff. For this reason, and because of the GATT's jurisdiction over trade restrictions, it was only to be expected that the question of what types of restrictions should be covered by the consultations, and by the Executive Board's decisions on them, would frequently plague the Board in the early years of consultations. Even before the Article XIV consultations had begun, such debates had occurred. The Australian Director had held the extreme view that since the Fund had no jurisdiction over quantitative restrictions on imports, a case could be made for limiting consultations to restrictions on current payments for transactions in invisibles only. On the occasion of considering one of the early Exchange Restrictions Reports, Mr. Melville (Australia) had objected to the proposed description of Australia's restrictive system. Distinguishing between import licenses and exchange licenses, he wished the description to make it abundantly clear that Australia's restrictions on imports were exercised only through import licenses and not through exchange licenses. Mr. Saad (Egypt), who had represented the Fund at the General Sessions of the GATT, argued in rebuttal that import licenses in the Australian system implemented *both* trade and exchange restrictions. He pointed out that many countries had mixed systems of trade and exchange restrictions, and any form of licensing technique might be used to enforce the two kinds of restrictions simultaneously.

With the support of Mr. Stamp (United Kingdom) and Mr. Savkar (India), whose countries had similar control systems, Mr. Melville requested an opinion from the General Counsel on what constitutes an exchange restriction. Mr. Saad, in his capacity as Governor of the Fund for Egypt, then requested a decision by the Executive Board giving a formal interpretation of the meaning in Article VIII, Section 2, of the phrase *restrictions on the making of payments and transfers for current international transactions.* The Board, in a sense-of-the-meeting decision, approved for inclusion in the Exchange Restrictions Report the staff's description of Australia's restrictive system, and referred Mr. Saad's request to the Committee on Interpretation. However, neither the committee nor the Board was able to reach agreement on the question, and after the Board had discussed the question in executive session, general consideration of the matter was, at least temporarily, dropped.

The issue of jurisdiction, therefore, had not really been decided. And it recurred persistently in the Board's consultations during the next several years. On various occasions the Directors for Australia and the United Kingdom pointed out that Fund decisions must be limited to restrictions on payments. Or that while the Fund, as a party to a GATT consultation, could *comment* on any restrictive measures affecting a country's balance of payments, any *recommendations* in Article XIV consultations should be confined to restrictions on current payments and transfers. Mr. Bury (Australia) opposed "any attempt to bring trade matters into a Fund decision," because it would "raise the fears of certain governments that the Fund was going beyond its proper sphere." In the view of Sir Edmund Hall-Patch (United Kingdom), for the Fund to give advice in areas where its jurisdiction was not clear would tend to weaken its influence in areas where it was intended to have authority. The sensitivity of these Directors on such points was evidenced, for example, when Mr. Southard proposed, for the conclusions to the first consultation with Colombia, a reference to the adjustment of import prohibitions. And it was apparent again in 1954 and 1955, when during the first two consultations with Germany comments were made on import restrictions to protect agriculture. Subsequently, the issue has recurred from time to time but has not been so intensely debated as in those early years.

A closely related question was how far the Fund could go in suggesting specific ways of reducing restrictions. This problem had arisen during the first consultation with Burma. The staff's draft decision contained the suggestion that "wherever possible, Burma should increase the proportion of imports under open general license." Mr. Crick (United Kingdom) and Mr. Melville argued for the deletion of this reference, on the ground that the Fund should not comment on one particular type of licensing technique. In contrast, Mr. Southard and Mr. Perry (Canada) urged that on grounds of principle the Fund had not only the right but the duty to transmit technical advice, especially in the area of exchange controls.

EMERGENCE OF BROAD DISCUSSIONS

In the course of time jurisdictional disputes and fears of the Fund's overstepping the mark subsided, allowing the economic realities to guide the Fund's activities. These realities were that various forms of restrictions were interrelated both in their operation and in their effects on the domestic situation and on other Fund members, and that it was impossible to make sensible judgments regarding a particular restriction on payments without taking account of the totality of restrictive practices of a member. Practice began to demonstrate that jurisdiction was not being usurped. Without further debate, the staff's discussions with members came gradually to cover all quantitative and other trade restrictions operated for the purpose of restricting exchange payments. Eventually, restrictions maintained for protective as well as for balance of payments reasons were also included in these discussions.

At the same time, however, the decisions on restrictions taken by the Board at the end of each consultation were made more precise. For a time, the working principle used for Board decisions was that only restrictions for balance of payments purposes could be maintained under Article XIV, whereas restrictions for other reasons would have to be approved under Article VIII. This principle had been enunciated as an ad hoc guide during the first consultation with Italy. It was made explicit in the decision on the 1952 consultation with Cuba: Cuba's 2 per cent exchange tax on remittances abroad was not maintained for balance of payments purposes and consequently was maintained in accordance with the provisions of Article VIII.

Later, for the same reasons that staff discussions with the member encompassed the broad range of restrictions, Executive Board decisions also came to include statements of views regarding the general level of restrictions and the possibility of removing them, but did not "approve" or "disapprove" them. The language used over the years ranged from urging action to suggesting re-examination of the practices, depending upon the severity of the restrictions and their harmfulness to the international community.

COMMENTING ON TRADE POLICY

THE AUTHORITY OF THE FUND

The legal authority of the Fund to consider and comment on trade policies and practices—as distinct from the jurisdictional character of its authority with respect to exchange practices—was finally formulated in 1960. At that time the Legal Department, distinguishing between the Fund's official authority to consider and comment on the trade policies and practices of its members and its power to approve exchange practices, worked out a legal position which met with little opposition. While members are not required to submit their trade policies and practices as such to the Fund for its approval, and the Fund cannot disapprove these policies and practices in the sense that if members persist in them they can be regarded as violating international obligations under the Fund's Articles, these trade policies and practices can be evaluated in the light of the Fund's purposes.

In defense of its reasoning, the legal staff cited various provisions of the Articles. Since Article I (ii) specified as a purpose of the Fund "to facilitate the expansion and balanced growth of international trade," the Fund can consider and comment on the extent to which the policies and practices of its members conduce toward the realization of this purpose. Moreover, Article XII, Section 7 (b), provides that "the Fund may publish such . . . reports as it deems desirable for carrying out its purposes," and the first sentence of Article XII, Section 8, declares that "the Fund shall at all times have the right to communicate its views informally to any member on any matter arising under this Agreement." The broad scope of the Fund's authority under these provisions, said the Legal Department, is established by the words "purposes" in Section 7 (b) and "any matter arising under this Agreement" in Section 8. All that needed to be added—and this was then made explicit—was that the authority to publish reports and communicate views embraces authority to consider the policies and positions of members in order to decide whether to publish reports or communicate views.

Finally, Article XIV, Section 2, expected members "to develop such commercial and financial arrangements with other members as will facilitate international payments and the maintenance of exchange stability." Hence, the Fund could consider and comment on commercial and financial measures. Significantly, it was also the legal view that although this objective appeared in Article XIV, it was not confined to the period of transitional arrangements, but connoted a permanent objective.

NEED FOR CLARIFICATION

The reason why the Fund's legal position as regards trade restrictions could be established in 1960 was in part that a greater area of common ground existed between members then than in the early 1950's. But more compelling was the need, as members ceased to avail themselves of the transitional arrangements of Article XIV, to elucidate the Fund's authority under Article VIII. Not only was there the question whether the Fund should hold regular consultations with members once they had assumed the obligations of Article VIII, but also the question whether the Fund could, once a member was under Article VIII, consider and comment on its policies other than its exchange policies. Specific answers to these questions had been postponed while consultations were being conducted under Article XIV. It became especially necessary to settle the longstanding question about trade restrictions when consultations with the GATT showed that it was possible for the Fund effectively to comment on the trade restrictions of GATT members. The difficulty was that half of the Fund's members were not GATT members.

The immediate problem at hand was to work out a procedure for discussing with members under Article VIII their *import restrictions for balance of payments reasons*. The staff proposed a duality of treatment between the Fund's members which were also GATT members and those which were not. GATT members would be asked merely to send information concerning their restrictions directly to the Fund as well as to the GATT; since such information was already being sent to the Fund by most GATT members, this provision merely ensured that other members of the Fund which were also GATT members would do likewise. As regards non-GATT members, the staff proposed that the Fund should seek to "reach agreement" with those members which imposed import restrictions for balance of payments reasons, "to obtain information on these restrictions, thus facilitating the preparation of studies designed to assist members in developing principles which further the purposes of the Fund."

AGREEMENT BY THE BOARD

In 1960, the Executive Directors reached, with relative ease, a working agreement on the very question—that is, the Fund's authority on trade matters—

which had, in years gone by, provoked almost open discord. But, although a *modus operandi* could now be articulated in written agreement, some of the old concerns, long dormant, were again expressed.

Once again the Australian Director—now Mr. Garland—referred briefly to his country's well-known views about the Fund's jurisdiction over import restrictions, discriminatory or nondiscriminatory, and whether for balance of payments reasons or not. But this time he conceded that import restrictions and trade discrimination fall within the Fund's sphere of general interest and properly form the subject of general comment by the Fund. However, he was troubled about "reaching agreement" with non-GATT members; if such agreements were to vary, an unwanted differentiation between Fund members would occur.

In addition, a definition of an exchange restriction—which had been incorporated as a guiding principle in the proposed decision—caused much uneasiness among authorities of the United States. This guiding principle was that a restriction on payments and transfers for current transactions under Article VIII, Section 2, was one which involved a direct governmental limitation on the availability or use of exchange as such. It appeared to the U.S. authorities that by this definition the Fund's role in the broad field of balance of payments restrictions was reduced. Concern about explicit limitations on the Fund's "approval" jurisdiction had been abated by realization that the Fund, through its role with the GATT, could be effective in this field. However, would not non-GATT members escape a similar determination for their import restrictions? The United States, therefore, was hopeful that they would not really mind acquiescing in a Fund examination; such examination would not be for the purpose of a determination by the Fund but merely to collect and provide useful information, especially for the benefit of other Fund members which might be injured by such restrictions.

It was finally agreed that Fund members which are contracting parties to the GATT and which impose import restrictions for balance of payments reasons would continue to send information concerning such restrictions to the Fund. Such information would enable the Fund and the member to join in an examination of the balance of payments situation in order to assist the Fund in its collaboration with the GATT. It was also agreed that the Fund, by consent of its members which are not contracting parties to the GATT and which impose import restrictions for balance of payments reasons, would seek to obtain information relating to such restrictions.

BROADENING THE SCOPE OF CONSULTATIONS

The Fund's consultations on restrictions under Article XIV became, relatively quickly, a vehicle for purposes additional to an examination of restrictions.

A technique and language were soon developed for giving advice to members that was acceptable, or even desired, by them on policies that might not be strictly within the Fund's jurisdiction. The Executive Board minutes or the staff report came to be used to record comments on policies not considered appropriate to Board decisions. Some topics that were at first considered taboo or suspect by some Directors even came, within a few years, to be stressed.

As an illustration, one of the most persistent and pervasive themes to emerge almost as soon as consultations began was the need for the Fund's members to pursue what are called "sound" fiscal and monetary policies in order to overcome or to avoid inflation. In the early years the extent to which the Fund could appropriately comment and give advice on a member's domestic policies had been seriously questioned by many Directors. In the years 1952–55, for example, several Directors queried the propriety of the Fund's calling attention to the importance of fiscal and monetary policies that would maintain stability, although from the outset some other Directors had believed that the Fund might comment on purely domestic matters. Agreement was eased by the understanding that no general precedents were being set. Moreover, it was recognized that comments from the Fund might be helpful to the authorities of some countries in putting through politically unpopular policies.

Almost immediately the occasion of the consultations was used as an opportunity for the Fund and its members to work out exchange reforms. An early example of this is the agreement reached on a new exchange rate for Paraguay during the 1952 consultation with that member. Paraguay proposed a rate which corresponded quite closely to recommendations made by the Fund's staff during the discussion preceding the consultation, and the Executive Directors agreed to the proposal.

THE PROCESS ESTABLISHED

By 1955 the pattern of consultations had become firmly established. Three distinct stages had evolved: (1) preliminary work by the staff, (2) discussions between representatives of the staff and of the member country, and (3) the consultation proper, i.e., the consideration by the Executive Board of the staff report on the discussions and the taking of a Board decision on the consultation if with an Article XIV member or with an Article VIII member that maintains exchange measures requiring the Fund's approval. No decision is taken on consultations with other Article VIII members (see below).

PRELIMINARY WORK BY THE STAFF

The work of the staff proceeds according to a tentative schedule based on past experience with the particular country. The team selected generally consists of three or four professionals and a secretary. The professionals include staff members from the Area Department handling the country concerned, and from the Exchange and Trade Relations Department, although the latter is not usually involved in an Article VIII consultation. Staff members from the Fiscal Affairs Department and the Research Department may be on the team if matters relevant to these departments are to be taken up, and from the Legal Department if complex legal issues are at stake.

As a first step, the staff writes a background study of the member's economic situation and of its restrictive system. These background papers have become widely known as Part II of the Fund's consultation reports. For a few members much of the material included is available in published form. For most, however, technical discussions and policy reviews between the members and the staff result in reports and surveys with a considerable amount of information not found elsewhere. These reports contain a detailed description and analysis of internal and external economic developments and of the restrictions still in force. Systematic reviews of trends in production, of wage and price developments, of credit and monetary flows, and of the budget and fiscal situation are nearly always included. The main focus on the external side is usually the current balance of payments position and the short-run outlook for the balance of payments; but details of the magnitude and composition of exports and imports, of capital movements, of foreign indebtedness, and of foreign aid, are often included.

Differences in the situations of countries lead to variations in treatment. For example, when an exchange reform has taken place or is in process, the exchange system both before and after reform is usually described fully. Similarly, the issuance of a new long-term development plan has frequently been the occasion for a more thorough description of the country's development policies and their relation to its policies in the monetary, fiscal, and exchange fields.

As regards restrictions, the complete system—that is, all forms of restrictions, including those both within and outside the "approval" jurisdiction of the Fund—is described. Such broad coverage has been found necessary in order to relate the general level of restrictions to the balance of payments position of the country, and to the policies being used to equilibrate the balance of payments. Although the first consultations in 1952 required the use of general questionnaires to members in order to ascertain the complete nature of the restrictions actually being applied, these are no longer needed.

A preliminary version of the background paper is customarily sent to the member before discussions take place. Because of its comprehensiveness, Part II of the consultation report has proved a valuable source of information to all member governments interested in the member being consulted. At first, even Part II of a consultation report was only for the internal use of the Fund; now, however, these reports are supplied to the GATT and from time to time to some other international agencies, with the consent of the member country.

For some countries, where data have been scarce and available statistical series have not proved to be reliable indicators of significant economic trends, draft Part II reports have not been prepared in advance; sending questionnaires ahead of a staff mission has also not been found useful. In such instances the preparation of useful statistical tables has become a major concern of the mission, and has often necessitated extending the discussions or sending some staff members in advance of the policy discussions. Technical advice has also been given in the process of preparing such tables; such advice has sometimes resulted in the initiation of new statistical series or in arrangements for the Fund to give technical assistance to the member in the compilation of its statistics.

Preparations for discussions with the member include a draft agenda and a briefing paper. The latter, which is seen only by the staff concerned and the management, reviews the last consultation decision and any developments in the Fund's policy which may be of particular concern for the country being consulted, and suggests the main lines of inquiry for the forthcoming discussions, the emphasis to be placed on various subjects, and the attitudes that the staff proposes to adopt on the principal policy questions. The proposed agenda for the meetings and the briefing paper are approved by the Director of the Area Department concerned; by the Director of the Exchange and Trade Relations Department; by the Managing Director or his Deputy; and, where issues of concern to them are involved, by the Fiscal, Legal, Research, and Treasurer's Departments. The agenda is then forwarded to the member concerned.

DISCUSSIONS WITH THE MEMBER

The most important change in the consultation procedure since consultations were initiated in 1952 has been the shift in locale. Whereas in the beginning it was specified that as far as possible staff discussions with member governments should be held in Washington, such discussions today nearly always take place in the member country. The ostensible reasons for holding the discussions in Washington were the limited number of staff members available and, to some extent, the belief that the Fund should restrict expenditures in view of its low income and the budget deficits that prevailed during the early 1950's. One consequence of meetings being held in Washington was that the members tended to designate their Executive Directors or staff from their embassies in Washington to represent them, or to request that the discussions be held at the time of the Annual Meetings so that the Governors themselves or their technical advisors could attend.

The greatest disadvantage of conducting the discussions in Washington was the limited number of members' representatives who could be interviewed.

Moreover, where the representatives were Executive Directors or embassy staff, they had frequently not been in very close or recent contact with the policy-making authorities of their governments, and it was rarely possible for the Washington people to be supported by technicians from their home countries.

Furthermore, although a larger number of the Fund's staff members could attend discussions held in Washington, this advantage of acquainting more staff members with countries' problems was offset by the lack of opportunity to become well acquainted with the country itself and with a number of its officials. Also, the concentration of discussions about the time of the Annual Meetings could not help but adversely affect the efficiency of the staff; 11 of the 22 discussions held in Washington in 1953 and 10 of the 14 in 1954 took place near the time of the Annual Meeting. Subsequent experience confirmed that holding the discussions abroad reduced the burden on the senior officials of the country as well. And it permitted the Fund's staff to work closely with the country so as to produce a more authoritative report.

Consequently, although the practice of holding the staff discussions in Washington was at first closely followed, it died under the weight of its disadvantages and of a growing awareness of the usefulness of visits by Fund staff missions to member countries. While two thirds of the staff discussions with members in 1952 and 1953 were held in Washington, the proportion dropped sharply over the next three years, amounting to about one fourth in 1956. In all succeeding years, no more than two a year have been held in Washington and then, as a rule, because of unusual circumstances.

Thus, one of the features of the Fund's consultations which has come to differentiate them from the annual review techniques of a number of other international organizations is that they rely more heavily on regular staff visits to the countries concerned, and on intensive discussions in the field with officials of the member countries.

Staff teams usually stay in the country for about two weeks, but there is a wide range, from as little as four or five working days to as much as five weeks.

The member's team for the discussions includes representatives of the financial agencies of the government, e.g., the treasury, the central bank, and economic ministries; the Executive Director elected or appointed by the member often attends as an observer. These discussions have taken many forms, depending upon the problems facing the government, the working practices of the officials, the availability of statistical and other information, and the staff's familiarity with the situation. Discussions in some countries are more formal than in others. Sometimes the Minister of Finance or the Governor of the central bank attends; but in any event, the staff usually interviews these persons and often has informal discussions with them on matters outside the consultation proper. Sometimes the staff is received by the Prime Minister or the Head of State.

The staff team may also, with the knowledge and consent of the government, meet members of the parliamentary opposition, the press, the business community, and labor representatives, although this varies with the circumstances and traditions of the country.

Usually the discussions begin with a systematic review of the country's economic situation. Then the discussions center on major policies—that is, policies to promote internal financial stability and equilibrium in the balance of payments and to facilitate economic growth. With regard to the restrictive system, the staff has usually sought to understand how the restrictions operate and their principal effects, and has given special emphasis to alternative measures for correcting balance of payments difficulties.

Generally, the staff prepares detailed minutes of the discussions which, after agreement with the government concerned, are used to prepare the report to the Executive Directors. This report, which includes an appraisal of the situation in the member country, has come to be known as Part I of the consultation report. Before being circulated to the Executive Directors, this report is reviewed by a committee of representatives from several departments in the Fund and is approved by the management. During the first few years of consultations, this committee discussed and approved both the preliminary papers and the final reports, but later the practice was developed of circulating to the committee for comment only the drafts of final reports. Although the opinions expressed by the staff in the reports are attributed to the staff team, the management and staff collectively are responsible for the appraisal and the recommended draft decision.

The length of the report varies considerably, depending upon the information available and the analytic techniques that can be used effectively; in general, the more sophisticated the arsenal of economic measures available to the authorities, the longer is the description of the actual policy measures selected by the authorities, and the reasons for such choice. Part I is usually much shorter than Part II. The report is normally completed within a few weeks after the return of the mission to Washington.

Consultation in the Board

After the report has been approved, it is circulated to the Board and scheduled for consideration after a period—usually about four weeks—which permits Executive Directors to be in contact with their governments. Most consultations take only one meeting, although some have required two or more.

The decision taken by the Board represents the official views of the Fund. The Board may confirm or disagree with the views of the staff, which may have been informally communicated earlier to the country's representatives. This procedure has allowed the staff freedom while in the field to appraise or comment informally and unofficially on a country's policies or economic situation, without the need to obtain prior approval by the Board for the views expressed.

The Board's decisions have varied from country to country and from time to time. Most decisions give a capsule description of the economic situation and the current policies of the member; they sometimes indicate that excellent progress has been made, and at other times recommend that policies be changed. There is also usually a statement of the Fund's views regarding the member's monetary and fiscal policies as they relate to the country's internal financial stability and to balance of payments position. Finally, the decisions regularly comment on the country's exchange system, exchange restrictions, discrimination, and use of bilateral payments agreements. Changes in exchange systems and recent relaxations or eliminations of restrictions have often been welcomed; frequently further action has been suggested. The Fund's views on the general level of and the possibility of removing quantitative restrictions and other devices which impede the free flow of trade and payments are also included.

The decision is transmitted to the member. There is no formal follow-up. But when the country subsequently encounters serious payments problems, or requests the use of the Fund's resources, or undertakes exchange reform, further contacts take place. And in the next consultation, a review is undertaken of the progress made toward implementing the decision adopted in the previous one.

The length of time involved in the consultation process is one of the reasons, if not the principal one, why the number of consultations completed every year has been less than the number of Article XIV members, and also less than the number of Article VIII members (after they began to consult in April 1961). If a consultation has not been held with a member in the course of a given consultation year, a special effort is usually made to consult early in the following year. Details of the number of consultations held in relation to the number of members, from April 1, 1952 to March 31, 1966, are given in Table 7 at the end of this chapter.

CONSULTATIONS UNDER ARTICLE VIII

The success of consultations under Article XIV was clearly reflected in the institution in 1960 of similar consultations under Article VIII, although these are not required by the Articles. The staff suggested that such consultations should be held because they provided a method whereby the Fund could maintain contact with the officials of the countries concerned and provided also the machinery for collaboration on international monetary problems. Thoroughgoing annual reviews of economic policies were useful both to members and to the Fund. The Directors agreed on the usefulness of consultations. Some even went so far as to state that the removal of restrictions on payments created a new degree of interdependence among members and that consultations with the Fund were therefore just as important as when restrictions had been widespread. Mr. Southard stated that the U.S. Government, which had never been under Article XIV and hence not previously required to consult the Fund, was willing to consult annually with the Fund under Article VIII.

After some discussion, however, it was agreed that consultations under Article VIII would not end in formal decisions by the Board. That the Fund should not come to some conclusion about the affairs of the member concerned was in line with the philosophy that consultations under Article VIII were voluntary on the part of the member.

The Board thereupon took the following decision implementing consultations under Article VIII:

> If members at any time maintain measures which are subject to Sections 2 and 3 of Article VIII, they shall consult with the Fund with respect to the further maintenance of such measures. Consultations with the Fund under Article VIII are not otherwise required or mandatory. However, the Fund is able to provide technical facilities and advice, and to this end, or as a means of exchanging views on monetary and financial developments, there is great merit in periodic discussions between the Fund and its members even though no questions arise involving action under Article VIII. Such discussions would be planned between the Fund and the member, including agreement on place and timing, and would ordinarily take place at intervals of about one year.[2]

Consultations under Article VIII represented a new procedure that had not been contemplated at Bretton Woods. Agreement to such consultations reflected the widely held belief that the Fund's Article XIV consultations had been most helpful to members and that similar discussions with countries under Article VIII would be useful both to the Fund and to the members concerned.

In 1961–62—the first year of the new Article VIII regime—consultations under that Article were held with eleven members; these included the first consultations held with Canada, the United States, and El Salvador. The staff discussions, as in the case of Article XIV consultations, involved visits by staff missions to the capitals of the countries concerned.

In the next few years, the Article VIII consultations were found to be increasingly useful as, together with those under Article XIV, they enabled the Fund to inform itself of policy problems and attitudes throughout the world, to appreciate more fully the peculiar circumstances and needs of individual countries, and to anticipate their payments problems. It is the belief of the Fund also that these consultations serve to make members' policies more responsive to the aims of the international community.

---

[2] E.B. Decision No. 1034-(60/27), June 1, 1960; below, Vol. III, p. 261.

THE PROCESS REAFFIRMED

Between the time when the consultations started in 1952 and the end of 1965, the membership of the Fund rose from 51 to 103, and the burden of work on the staff and on the Executive Directors increased proportionately. Therefore, when the Fund reviewed its procedures late in 1965 and early in 1966, it sought ways of reducing this burden. The staff put forward proposals for abbreviating Part I of the reports, and the Board made some suggestions for shortening its consideration of the reports. It was decided that Part I of the reports should be shortened; but the basic structure of the procedures was kept intact. The opening and closing sentences of Article XIV consultations, as agreed in 1952, were dropped; instead, a simple factual statement was to be made:

> This decision is taken by the Executive Directors in concluding the [*year*] consultations with [*member*], pursuant to Article XIV, Section 4, of the Articles of Agreement.

The staff now proposed that Article VIII consultations should put forward conclusions, but the Board decided against this.

Table 7. Fund Members by Article VIII or Article XIV Status, and
Completed Consultations, April 1, 1952–March 31, 1966

Consultations Year (beginning April 1)	Number of Members at Beginning of Consultations Year				Number of Completed Consultations [1]			
					During Year			
	Total	Status Not Yet Notified	Article VIII Members	Article XIV Members [2]	Article XIV	Article VIII	Total	Cumulative Total
1952	51	—	7	44	35[3]	—	35	35
1953	54	—	7	47	35	—	35	70
1954	55	—	9	46	34[4]	—	34	104
1955	56	—	10	46	37	—	37	141
1956	58	—	10	48	36[4]	—	36	177
1957	60	—	10	50	37[5]	—	37	214
1958	65	—	10	55	38[4]	—	38	252
1959	68	—	10	58	42[4]	—	42	294
1960	68	—	10	58	44[6]	—	44	338
1961	70	1	21	48	36[4]	11	47	385
1962	76	3	21	52	38[5]	14	52	437
1963	84	4	23	57	49[5]	12	61	498
1964	102	12	25	65	40	22	62	560
1965	102	1	26	75	36	19	55	615

[1] A consultation is completed when the Board has discussed the staff report.

[2] Includes Venezuela for all years, although it did not have Article XIV restrictions and did not consult with the Fund during the years 1953–62.

[3] Includes a consultation with Germany, which did not become a member until August 1952, but excludes one with Southern Rhodesia in 1952, the only occasion on which the Board had a separate consultation with a nonmetropolitan territory.

[4] Includes two consultations with one member.

[5] Includes two consultations each with two members.

[6] Includes two consultations each with four members.

CHAPTER

12

Progress Toward Liberalization

Margaret G. de Vries

THE CONSULTATIONS PROCESS just described has become the principal instrument through which the Fund's policies on exchange restrictions have been implemented. These policies have varied a great deal—as have the Fund's policies in other fields—reflecting the ever-changing panorama of international economic and monetary conditions.

From 1946 to 1958, when external convertibility of European currencies was finally attained, the Fund's policies on restrictions were directed mainly toward the liberalization of the severe restrictions which were in force when the Fund was established. This chapter recounts the developments in those policies, and depicts also the international economic situation prevailing at the time they were formulated and which therefore influenced them. Three periods, of four to five years each, may be distinguished.

TIME PATH OF POLICY DEVELOPMENTS

The first period began in 1946, with the inception of the Fund, and lasted roughly through September 1949, when the realignment of currencies necessary to the lessening of the strict controls over international payments which prevailed after World War II took place. Apart from the working out of procedures and policies for handling multiple exchange rates, the Fund did relatively little during this period to reduce restrictions, its philosophy being that it was premature to press for any reduction.[1] Instead, it stressed to its members the importance of measures—such as exchange depreciation and domestic monetary policies—that would be likely to improve their payments positions over the longer run and would lay the basis for an *eventual* reduction of restrictions.

---

[1] *Annual Report, 1947*, pp. 2, 35, and *1948*, p. 30.

249

In the second period, 1950 to 1954, the international economic climate became propitious for some reduction of restrictions, and there was a tremendous upsurge in the Fund's activities. In March 1950 the *First Annual Report on Exchange Restrictions* appeared. Later in that year, in Torquay, England, the Fund participated in the consultations with several of the contracting parties to the GATT. The Fund's own consultations under Article XIV were begun in 1952, and within a few years were being hailed as successful points of contact between the Fund and its members. Nevertheless, the Fund continued to postulate its policies as regards restrictions on the premise that it was preferable not to push its members too hard. Recognizing that relaxation of restrictions and establishment of convertibility could be brought about only gradually, its principal aims during this period were to ensure the maintenance of the then-current momentum in the relaxation of restrictions and to prevent their reintensification.[2]

By 1955 it was evident that the abnormal postwar economic difficulties of European countries had come to an end. Large gains had been made both in productivity and in the attainment of internal financial stability. Still a third phase of the Fund's policy as regards restrictions began. Although many countries relaxed restrictions, the Fund, aware of their cautious attitudes, urged them to go further, and especially to reduce discriminatory restrictions. Western European countries undertook, under the aegis of the OEEC liberalization program, to free from restrictions most of the trade and payments which they conducted among themselves. But the Fund, anxious to hasten the convertibility of European currencies into gold and U.S. dollars, repeatedly stressed the need for an equal lessening of restrictions against imports from the dollar area. In 1955, as European countries began to take steps to widen further the transferability of their currencies, the Fund, eager to obtain greater multilateralization of world payments, also took a decision calling upon its members to reduce their use of bilateral payments agreements. By the end of 1958, external convertibility of the major European currencies had been attained.

AN INCUBATING PERIOD, 1946–49

In 1946 all the Fund's members except El Salvador, Guatemala, Mexico, Panama, and the United States had opted for the transitional arrangements of Article XIV. Although there were wide differences in the nature and severity of the restrictions maintained, most countries applied an impressive array of restrictions to virtually all foreign exchange transactions. The underlying assumption of their exchange controls was that all payments were prohibited unless specifically authorized.

[2] *Annual Report*, 1955, p. 77.

TROUBLED ECONOMIES

These restrictions mirrored the troubled economic conditions of many countries after World War II. Supply fell very much short of demand. In the countries whose economic position had been seriously impaired by the war, the amounts of goods needed for reconstruction and to meet minimum consumption requirements were in excess of their limited productive capacity. Much of the current output was being used to repair the damage and deficiencies caused by the war. Demand, however, was high as incomes were inflated by intense economic activity, including reconstruction, which did not result immediately in a flow of consumer goods. There was also a latent inflationary pressure in most countries as a result of wartime finance, the resultant build-up of liquid funds in the hands of consumers, and the sizable pent-up demand.

In these circumstances, the countries concerned, especially in Europe but also in parts of Asia and the Middle East, felt compelled to ration available supplies of domestically produced goods. The urgency of conserving foreign exchange for the most essential imports necessitated the continuation and even the extension of heavy wartime exchange restrictions. Of the alternative methods available for limiting the demand for imports, quantitative import controls and exchange restrictions appeared to most of these countries to be preferable to exchange depreciation. The disequilibrium in their balance of payments, while large, was considered to be due more to special factors connected with the war, which would in time be overcome, than to fundamental disparities in costs and prices.

Another reason for restrictions was that the pattern of world trade that emerged was seriously unbalanced. In 1947 this imbalance, which was soon to be generally referred to as the world dollar shortage, had forced many countries to change the character of their restrictions. Whereas restrictions had in general been placed on imports of certain goods—e.g., nonessential and luxury items—rather than on imports from specific currency areas, restrictions during 1947 were in most instances imposed with the intentions of reducing an existing or prospective deficit in U.S. dollars and of safeguarding gold and dollar reserves.

In many Latin American countries the huge demand for imports also necessitated the intensification of exchange restrictions after World War II, even though foreign exchange receipts were high. Their large demand for imports was a result partly of deferred wartime demand and partly of postwar inflation. In several Eastern European countries exchange restrictions, although severe, were themselves subordinated to even more direct and comprehensive state intervention through state-trading and barter arrangements.

DECIDING ON AN APPROACH

In these early years, the Fund recognized that it was not possible to effect any considerable relaxation of restrictions. The Executive Board, in fact, discussed the general problem of reducing exchange restrictions chiefly in the course of agreeing on its Annual Reports; hence, these Reports provide an indication of the Fund's attitudes during these years.

The Reports for 1946–49 were not on the whole optimistic about the possibilities for the early elimination, or even the reduction, of exchange restrictions. The severe shortages of goods of all kinds in most countries were believed to make exchange restrictions on current transactions unavoidable for some time, in order to ensure that limited foreign exchange reserves could finance imports to meet the most essential requirements for consumption and reconstruction. The first Report did, however, strike a note of optimism over the prospects of an early restoration of sterling convertibility for current transactions under the terms of the Anglo-American Financial Agreement of 1945, and the United Kingdom's intention to make agreements for early settlement of accumulated sterling balances. The Report noted that these developments would help in restoring the convertibility of currencies and freedom in current transactions in accordance with the provisions of the Fund's Agreement.[3]

By the terms of the Anglo-American Financial Agreement, the Government of the United Kingdom had undertaken that after July 15, 1947, unless an extension were agreed with the Government of the United States, it would impose no restrictions upon payments and transfers for current transactions and would permit the current sterling receipts of sterling area countries to be used in any currency area without discrimination.

During the months preceding that date the United Kingdom took a series of steps to extend the degree of transferability of sterling already existing and to fulfill its convertibility commitments; it announced from time to time the relaxation of certain wartime restrictions on the transferability of sterling. By July 1947 these arrangements covered the greater part of the trading world, negotiations being unfinished with only a few countries. Convertibility for current sterling did not, of course, obligate the United Kingdom to remove all trade and exchange controls. Exports and imports were still subject to license, and controls were retained on capital movements and on the large sterling balances which had accumulated during and immediately after the war.

Nonetheless, the deficit with the dollar area both of the United Kingdom and of the rest of the sterling area was growing as a result of the large rate of dollar expenditure by the sterling area as a whole. This deficit, the greater part being attributable to the deficit of the United Kingdom itself, was occasioning large use of reserves and dollar credits.[4]

So great was the drain on its exchange resources that on August 21, 1947 the United Kingdom, by agreement with the United States, withdrew the facility of

---

[3] *Annual Report, 1946*, p. 12.
[4] *Annual Report, 1948*, p. 31.

freely transferring sterling from Transferable Accounts to American or Canadian Accounts, and at the same time eliminated Canadian Transferable Accounts. In effect, although sterling remained transferable over a wide area, the convertibility of sterling into dollars was suspended.

ESTABLISHING THE PRECONDITIONS

The Fund's attitude toward the difficulties encountered by its members in relaxing restrictions and establishing convertibility was mixed. On the one hand, the Fund was aware that the balance of payments problems of its members were not easy of solution. But on the other, the Fund did not wish its members to abandon the objective of eventually freeing their international transactions from restrictions. It was unrealistic for the Fund to call for the abandonment of restrictions; but it was capitulation for the Fund to succumb entirely to adverse economic conditions. In these circumstances the Fund began to work out policies which stressed the need for members to lay the proper foundation for a future relaxation of restrictions. This philosophy of *establishing the preconditions* for relaxation of restrictions was exemplified by the remarks of the Managing Director, Mr. Gutt, to the Governors as he presented to them the Annual Report for 1947. The Report had been approved by the Executive Directors before failure of the attempt to restore convertibility of sterling; although the Directors considered modifying the Report to take account of this development, they decided that, instead of doing so, the Managing Director should make reference to it in his presentation of the Report to the Governors. In so doing, he commented on the difficult postwar economic and political problems, the Marshall Plan proposals of the U.S. Government, and the failure of sterling convertibility. His attitude toward restrictions was as follows:

> I have indicated . . . how much, in the monetary field as in others, the disruption of the war still makes itself felt. But that is no reason for abandoning or modifying the objectives of the Fund. Rather, concerted effort must be made to establish the conditions under which these objectives can be attained. A premature attempt to force the acceptance of exchange and trade practices suited for a balanced world economy can do much harm and even endanger the attainment of these objectives.[5]

The Annual Report for 1947 had begun to foreshadow in greater detail the main features of what would become the Fund's approaches to exchange restrictions for the next several years. First, the Fund's attitude toward restrictions would not be doctrinaire; in particular, account would be taken of the differing circumstances of member countries. Second, the criteria for judging the need for restrictions were to be whether these were warranted by balance

---

[5] *Summary Proceedings, 1947*, p. 10.

of payments considerations and whether they had harmful effects on the balances of payments of other countries. Finally, for the foreseeable future, emphasis was to be placed on the necessity of establishing the preconditions for a return to convertibility and the elimination of restrictions.[6] In the 1948 Annual Report the Executive Directors reiterated that the British experience in failing to restore convertibility showed that convertibility could succeed only when the underlying conditions were favorable to a system of multilateral trade and payments.[7]

CHARACTERISTICS OF THE PRECONDITIONS

The preconditions on which the Fund placed emphasis were the restoration of productive capacity, the establishment of a better pattern of international payments, and elimination of inflation through proper credit and fiscal policies. What was especially required was an expansion of exports in general and in particular an enhanced flow of exports in the directions most likely to diminish dollar deficits. Preference should be given to investment which would have relatively prompt effects upon the balance of payments. An improvement in the capital accounts of many countries, while not a prerequisite for the removal of restrictions from current transactions, was also considered important for strengthening their balance of payments. Changes in international indebtedness had aggravated the payments problems of several trading countries, especially those in Western Europe. In less than forty years, the United Kingdom, for example, had passed from the position of leading international creditor to that of the largest international debtor.

It also became apparent that another essential condition for the relaxation of restrictions and the restoration of currency convertibility was some building up of the non-dollar world's monetary reserves. Most of the members of the Fund that had taken advantage of the transitional arrangements did not, in 1947–48, have reserves adequate to enable them to meet large current deficits for even a short period, or to meet persistent deficits, even of a moderate size, for an extended period. By 1948, in their Annual Report, the Directors were also suggesting that some adjustments of exchange rates might sooner or later be necessary before adequate progress could be made.[8]

The Fund was also mindful that the elimination of exchange restrictions would be illusory if direct trade controls were to take their place. The mere substitution for exchange restrictions of other measures, such as direct quantitative restrictions or excessive tariffs, would not reduce the magnitude of existing restraints on international trade. Moreover, the Fund recognized that while international organizations could make an important contribution in helping to achieve these

[6] *Annual Report, 1947*, p. 35.

[7] *Annual Report, 1948*, p. 32.

[8] *Ibid.*, p. 23.

preconditions, basically it was national policies that would determine the kind of world economy which would ultimately emerge.

Dangers of prolonged restrictions

Despite the continuing consensus that early relaxation of exchange restrictions could not be expected, there was, by 1949, some change of tone in the Fund's pronouncements on restrictions. The dangers of a prolonged period of severe restrictions and inconvertible currencies began to be perceived. In discussing the transitional period, the Annual Report for 1949, for example, drew attention to the Board's view that if the earliest reasonable opportunity was not seized to modify restrictive policies, the difficulty of resuming trade under more normal conditions would be greatly aggravated and world trade would tend more and more to be conducted with inconvertible currencies on the basis of bilateral bargains.[9]

At the Annual Meeting, 1949, the Board of Governors adopted a procedure for considering selected topics, on the basis of chapters in the Annual Reports, in separate discussion groups or committees. The discussion groups at the 1949 Meeting covered two topics: (1) exchange and monetary policy, and (2) exchange restrictions and monetary reserves. The Managing Director, who chaired both discussions, noted in his report on the second discussion that the Governors generally subscribed, but with differing emphasis, to the ideas expressed by the Executive Directors in the Annual Report, that early removal of restrictions could not be expected because of difficult payments problems and low reserves, but that the improvement in the underlying economic situation over the last few years, though inadequate, provided an environment for progress toward convertibility.[10]

PROGRESS FORESEEN, 1950–54

The first signs of improving world economic conditions had appeared by 1950. The financial aid provided to European countries by the United States through the Marshall Plan had immensely facilitated the reconstruction of the economies of these countries. Production throughout Western Europe had greatly increased, exportable goods from the deficit countries had become more plentiful, and the abnormal need for imports for reconstruction had become much smaller. Inflationary pressures had, in most countries, also become more moderate. Lastly, the devaluations of September 1949 had corrected many distortions in international prices. These improvements had made it possible for some countries to achieve equilibrium in their over-all balances of payments, although not in their dollar accounts. This equilibrium was, however, maintained only with the

---

[9] *Annual Report, 1949*, p. 30.
[10] *Summary Proceedings, 1949*, pp. 37–39.

support of import and exchange restrictions and, in several countries, of extra-ordinary external financial aid.

Some countries made a start toward freeing their trade and payments from restrictions, but in general, even after the devaluations of 1949, countries moved slowly in removing restrictions. Economists debated whether, in view of the "chronic dollar shortage," substantial liberalization of restrictions would ever be feasible. Some argued that the difference in productivity between European countries and the United States was deep-seated; structural changes, including modernization of industrial techniques, were required in the economies of European countries if they were to overcome their persistent dollar deficits. Others argued that European countries needed mainly to pursue orthodox monetary policies; they contended that, with the restoration—indeed the expansion—of European productive capacity, these countries need only attain internal financial stability to be able to earn sufficient dollars to cover their outgo in dollars.

First Exchange Restrictions Report

This was the situation when the Fund, in accordance with Article XIV, Section 4, issued the first of its Annual Reports on Exchange Restrictions. That Article states in part that "not later than three years after the date on which the Fund begins operations and in each year thereafter, the Fund shall report on the restrictions still in force under Section 2 of this Article," i.e., restrictions maintained under transitional arrangements. The three-year period ended on March 1, 1950.

The first Report was drafted by the Operations Department; the Exchange Restrictions Department, which was responsible for drafting subsequent reports, was not set up until March 1950. The Report was presented in two parts. The first consisted of a general account of the forms of exchange restrictions, some historical background, and the current situation and problems; the second part was a country-by-country description of the exchange restrictions maintained by Fund members under Article XIV. The same basic structure has been followed in all subsequent reports, although in later reports the first part omitted the description of forms of exchange restrictions and historical background, and was addressed more to changes during the past year and to the current situation. The second part has also changed over the years, both in form and in countries covered, a number of nonmember countries being included in the Reports after 1951 and all Article VIII members in Reports after 1955.

The first Exchange Restrictions Report reflected the Fund's awareness of the several factors which had, since World War II, necessitated the maintenance of restrictions, and the Fund's realization that, though some of the postwar economic disturbances had been brought under control, others were still in evidence.

By 1950, the factor with which the Fund had become most concerned was continued inflation. It was apparent that increased supplies for export would shortly be forthcoming as reconstruction was completed and productive facilities were restored. However, inflation could undermine those exports: it raised internal costs and caused products to be shifted from export markets to domestic consumption.

The Fund's policy, as exemplified by this Report, was postulated on two general considerations. One, relaxation of restrictions and the establishment of convertibility should be a *progressive* action over time. Member countries could undertake gradual programs of decontrol without incurring unnecessary risks. Three ways in which restrictions could be relaxed on a step-by-step basis were specified: by categories of international transactions, by particular foreign currencies, and by types of international payments.[11] Members proceeding along these lines could test their balance of payments positions by degrees and could appropriately time the next stage of their program to remove restrictions.

Two, actions of members were interdependent: the ability of one member to eliminate restrictions was often a function of the policies and actions of other members. In many instances, members had joint responsibilities if exchange restrictions were to be effectively reduced. For example, some countries could remove their restrictions only when the main currencies which they earned had become convertible. Hence there was a need for a coordinated program so that the policies and practices of every country would, to the maximum extent, assist rather than frustrate the efforts of others.[12]

The Executive Directors had indeed agreed, when they considered the draft of this Report, that a proper and useful role for the Fund was to assist its members *to work together* in eliminating restrictions: the Fund could contribute to the progress toward relaxation of restrictions by initiating, encouraging, and coordinating appropriate concerted action among its members. Some Directors had been specific: in their view, the Fund should, as necessary, consult member countries individually as to the measures which those maintaining restrictions might take, consider with creditor countries what they might do to assist the payments position of the debtors, help to work out the proper timing of actions, and examine the possibility of making Fund resources available to cushion the shocks for countries moving toward convertibility.

Intensified Fund efforts

A few months later, when the Annual Report for 1950 appeared, the Board further clarified its specific concerns. Although the improvement in the world economic situation had been substantial, many difficulties had still to be over-

---

[11] *First Annual Report on Exchange Restrictions* (1950), p. 35.
[12] *Ibid.*, pp. 36–37.

come before countries could, without facing serious risks, remove restrictions and assume the obligations of convertibility. Inflationary pressures had been brought under more effective control by many countries, but it remained to be seen whether the stability achieved could be maintained. The correction of international price distortions was far from complete. While the strengthening of reserves was progressing, it was too early to judge whether the increase in reserves was due to permanent factors or was just a temporary aftermath of the devaluations of 1949.

Along with its concern about inflation, the Fund was anxious that countries should improve their ability to compete in the U.S. market and expand their exports to the dollar area. The reasoning underlying this position was as follows: Both the staff and the Directors recognized that the dollar reserves of most Fund members were low. But they believed that, even more than reserves, members needed to improve their *current* dollar payments position. Mindful of the large loss of reserves suffered by the United Kingdom in mid-1947 when it had attempted to make sterling convertible, both staff and Directors were cognizant of the fact that even sizable reserves might be quickly dissipated if countries relaxed restrictions before they had obtained satisfactory balance in their *current* dollar accounts. Indeed, concern with the need for countries to strengthen their current dollar earnings led several members of the staff and some of the Directors to fear that the maintenance of protected markets at home and abroad, such as was possible through the intra-European payments arrangements then being organized, would provide outlets in Europe for relatively high-cost output. The dollar positions of European countries would, in that event, remain relatively weak.

In addition, in the Annual Report for 1950, the Board was somewhat more definite on the possibilities of removing restrictions. While recognizing that it could not press members too hard, it argued that greater progress in decontrol was feasible and should be made.[13] Regretting that the 1949 devaluations had not been followed by more freeing of trade and payments, the Board warned that waiting for convertibility until all obstacles in the path had been removed might become the most effective means of ensuring that the path would always remain blocked. The danger had to be recognized that the continuation of restrictions might create a situation in which some condition for convertibility would always be absent; thereby any effective move toward the relaxation of restrictions could always be prevented.

Pointing to the further disadvantages of continuing restrictions, the Board called attention to the way in which they supported high costs and prices in the countries using them, distorted the allocation of resources, reduced competitive ability, and discouraged private capital. Accordingly, the Fund intended to press

---

[13] *Annual Report, 1950*, pp. 55–69.

forward with a continuing examination of the need for, and the effects of, existing exchange restrictions in order to make sure that no reasonable opportunity for their removal was lost.

RESTRICTIONS ON SECURITY GROUNDS

Meanwhile, the Korean conflict, which broke out in June 1950, complicated the picture by introducing strategic and military considerations into the field of restrictions. In December 1950 the United States, for reasons of national security and international emergency, placed a virtual embargo on exports to certain Far Eastern destinations and froze assets and restricted payments in the United States of residents of the Chinese mainland and North Korea. In July 1951 Cuba introduced controls similar to those of the United States. As a way of rationing scarce supplies, many other countries introduced export controls, and these became increasingly important determinants of the composition, volume, and direction of international trade.

The imposition of these restrictions raised the issue of the Fund's authority over restrictions imposed not for economic or financial reasons but on security grounds. The view of the U.S. Executive Director was that the Articles of Agreement were not explicit, and that probably the Fund would not have to act; nonetheless, the United States had informed the Fund of its measures. The Board formally noted the actions of the United States and Cuba, and deferred judgment on the questions of the Fund's authority and of how it should be exercised.

In August 1952, after extensive consideration by the staff and by the Board, the Board took a decision to the effect that Article VIII, Section 2 (a), applies to *all* restrictions on current payments and transfers, irrespective of their motivation and the circumstances in which they are imposed. However, recognizing that the Fund does not provide a suitable forum for discussion of restrictions imposed solely for the preservation of national or international security, certain policy guidelines were formulated for such situations. First, when a member proposed to impose restrictions on security grounds, it was to notify the Managing Director, preferably in advance but ordinarily not later than thirty days afterward; such notification was to be circulated to the Executive Directors. The member could assume that the Fund had no objection to the imposition of the restrictions, unless the Fund informed the member otherwise within thirty days. Second, the Fund would thereafter review the restrictions periodically and reserve the right to modify or revoke, at any time, its approval or the effect of this approval on any restrictions that might have been imposed under it.[14] The Board applied this decision retroactively to the measures taken earlier by the United States and Cuba.

---

[14] E.B. Decision No. 144-(52/51), August 14, 1952; below, Vol. III, p. 257.

This procedure was to be followed again late in 1965 when the United Kingdom, by a series of steps, subjected to exchange control all transactions with Rhodesia. Beginning on November 11, 1965, following its unilateral declaration of independence, Rhodesia was excluded from the sterling area, all transfers of capital from the United Kingdom to Rhodesia were prohibited, a stop was placed on practically all current payments from the United Kingdom to Rhodesia, imports into the United Kingdom from Rhodesia were subjected to license and virtually prohibited, and no credit was to be allowed for U.K. exports to Rhodesia.[15] In accordance with the Board's decision in 1952, the United Kingdom informed the Fund of these measures as measures solely related to the preservation of national security.

TIME TO LESSEN RESTRICTIONS

By the end of 1950, the Fund recognized that some of the essential characteristics of the problem of exchange restrictions were being altered as the largest trading countries diverted an increased proportion of their productive efforts to rearmament. For many countries, the problem had become more one of shortage of supplies and less one of inability to finance foreign expenditures. Export controls were becoming increasingly important in determining the pattern of world trade and payments. Greater attention was being given to the obtaining of strategic commodities and raw materials. Some international agreements were being worked out to ration these commodities.

At the same time the Fund continued to press for a reduction of restrictions. It was noted that during the year 1950, before the Korean hostilities, there had been a remarkable improvement in the world payments situation, especially vis-à-vis the United States, and an accelerated increase in the gold and dollar exchange reserves of countries other than the United States. The new security considerations were regarded as essentially independent of balance of payments requirements. The Fund continued to believe that the general improvement in the balance of payments positions and prospects of most of its members, stemming at least partly from the Korean crisis, justified a relaxation of restrictions, especially of discriminatory ones. Therefore, countries limiting imports of available goods for financial or protectionist reasons might well be able to relax or remove restrictions on imports despite the need for emergency measures on exports.

Not only was it feasible for countries with improved balance of payments conditions to relax restrictions, but it was in their interest as well. Relaxation of restrictions would increase the quantity of goods available for domestic consumption, and hence restrain inflation, and would permit a more economic use of resources.

---

[15] *Seventeenth Annual Report on Exchange Restrictions* (1966), pp. 588–91.

These arguments, as expressed in the Fund's public statements, reflected the concern of the Managing Director and the Governors during the Fifth Annual Meeting, held in Paris in September 1950, just three months after the outbreak of the Korean conflict. A committee of Governors was again set up to consider the Directors' views on exchange restrictions as expressed in the Annual Report and also in the first Exchange Restrictions Report. The Governor for the United States, Mr. Snyder, stressed the dangers of maintaining exchange restrictions indefinitely, their tendency to perpetuate themselves, and the desirability of the Fund's persisting in its efforts to promote relaxation of restrictions or at least to prevent unnecessary tightening, even though new difficulties would arise out of rearmament. The Governor for the United Kingdom, Mr. Gaitskell, again indicated that there was little chance of the United Kingdom's removing restrictions or dropping exchange control as a whole, but stated that the United Kingdom would remove all unnecessary restrictions. The Governor for Belgium, Mr. Frère, pointed out that the necessity for restrictions was a consequence of inadequate monetary and credit policies, and that it was idle to talk about removing restrictions if inflation was not dealt with first. The Managing Director, noting that the first Exchange Restrictions Report had been drafted before the Korean crisis, repeated in presenting the Annual Report his alarm concerning the dangers of inflation. He also expressed worry about increased restrictions as a result of the Korean hostilities. These views, except for those of the Governor for the United Kingdom, were reflected in the Report of the committee.[16]

Following its Fifth Annual Meeting, the Fund participated in the consultations held in connection with the Fifth (Torquay) Session of the CONTRACTING PARTIES to the GATT on recent changes in the import policies of Australia, Ceylon, Chile, India, New Zealand, Pakistan, Southern Rhodesia, and the United Kingdom.[17] The Fund's reports for these consultations similarly reflected a hardening of its attitude toward prolonged restrictions. These reports had concluded that it would be feasible for several countries in the sterling area to relax their restrictions, a recommendation resisted by those countries.

A START TOWARD RELAXATION

For the first time there was progress toward lessened restrictions. In Europe, after the European Payments Union (EPU) had been established, liberalization of both intra-European trade and transactions in invisibles started to move forward.[18] For example, in regard to the liberalization of intra-European visible

[16] *Summary Proceedings, 1950,* pp. 44–45.

[17] The first such consultation in which the Fund participated was on South Africa's import policy at the Fourth (Geneva) Session in the spring of 1950.

[18] Details are given in Frederic Boyer and J. P. Sallé, "The Liberalization of Intra-European Trade in the Framework of OEEC," *Staff Papers,* Vol. IV (1954–55), pp. 179–216.

trade, OEEC members agreed in 1950 to take measures for the progressive elimination of restrictions on nongovernmental imports from other members and to provide for the automatic allocation of foreign exchange to pay for such imports. This relaxation was originally (from December 15, 1949) applied to 50 per cent of imports on private account from other OEEC countries, using the year 1948 as a base. From October 4, 1950, the percentage was raised to 60 (with exceptions for certain countries); these percentages were calculated separately for each of three categories—food and feeding stuffs, raw materials, and manufactured goods. It was proposed that the 60 per cent liberalization requirement be raised, by February 1, 1951, to 75 per cent of all nongovernmental imports from participants regardless of category.

The OEEC countries varied in their ability to achieve these goals. Italy and Belgium, which had become creditors to the EPU, had, by the end of 1951, freed from restrictions commodities which in 1948 had formed over 90 per cent of their total imports on private account from other OEEC countries. But France and the United Kingdom, which had accumulated considerable deficits with the EPU, were forced during 1951–52 to reintroduce many of their import restrictions: by measures taken at the end of 1951, the United Kingdom reduced its percentage of liberalized imports to 44, and France in early 1952 again subjected all OEEC imports to quantitative restrictions.

Despite this setback, some European countries began to increase the amount of their imports not only from each other but from the dollar area as well. Some countries in the sterling area also expanded their imports, including imports from the dollar area. India, in March 1951, doubled the value of import licenses issued for the first half of 1951 and extended the validity of licenses to the end of the year. Both India and the United Kingdom placed additional raw materials under "world open general license," allowing their unrestricted import from any country. The same trend toward attempting to increase imports and relax restrictions also occurred in the Western Hemisphere and in some countries in the Middle and Far East.[19] Canada abolished its exchange control system on December 14, 1951. Some of the easing of restrictions in 1950 and 1951 took the form of formal removal or relaxation of restrictions. Much, however, was done by administrative action within existing control mechanisms: more licenses for imports were granted, for example, and some goods were freed from licensing requirements.

The Fund saw these developments as indications that the acceptance of restrictions as more or less unavoidable and well-nigh permanent features of the international economic scene was at least being challenged. Anticipating important further developments, the Fund noted that the distinction between "hard"

---

[19] *Second Annual Report on Exchange Restrictions* (1951), pp. 31–32.

and "soft" currencies had been greatly narrowed and suggested that this should lay the basis for a reduction of restrictions, and especially of discrimination. The Fund stressed an international approach to the relaxation of restrictions, as against uncoordinated and self-defeating national action.[20]

It was nonetheless apparent from the first round of the Fund's consultations under Article XIV, beginning in March 1952, that dependence on restrictions was still widespread. Most members contended that they continued to need restrictions in order to restrain aggregate import demand. The inconvertibility of many currencies, the inadequacy of reserves, the fear of capital flight, and the persistence of dollar deficits in balances of payments were repeatedly mentioned as reasons. Moreover, many members had come to regard the diminution of inflationary pressures as a very important condition for the removal of restrictions. They recognized that external balance, and particularly balance with the dollar area, could not be achieved unless the prices for their exports were competitive and unless their domestic industries could compete with imported commodities.

Thus the Fund, while recognizing the existence of other factors which still necessitated restrictions, retained its previously expressed conviction that further action in the monetary and fiscal fields was especially important if restrictions were to be reduced. Specific reference was made to monetary and fiscal policies in about two thirds of the decisions of the Executive Board in the 1952 consultations.[21]

RETENTION QUOTAS

THE NATURE OF THE PROBLEM

As supplies of goods increased, export markets gradually became more competitive. Countries were especially anxious to penetrate the heretofore difficult dollar market, especially in the United States. Hence, in the early 1950's another problem suddenly emerged, which was just as suddenly to disappear by 1954–55. This was the problem of "retention quotas." Exporters in many Western European countries were allowed to retain specified proportions of their earnings of convertible currencies, and sell them or use them to import from the dollar area commodities that could be sold profitably (usually at premium prices) in the exporter's country, where their supply was limited by discriminatory import restrictions.

There were two kinds of retention quotas, according to purpose: to foster direct exports or to promote indirect trade. The first was relatively simple in concept and operation. An exporter was induced to sell goods to the dollar area

---

[20] *Ibid.*, pp. 19–21.
[21] *Fourth Annual Report on Exchange Restrictions* (1953), p. 12.

in return for special privileges: either he could retain some of the exchange earned and sell it in a premium market or he could use such exchange to purchase imported goods which he could sell at a substantial profit. The second kind of retention quota, to boost indirect trade, had been devised to keep transit trade going in the presence of adverse conditions. Transit trade, by which traders in one country sell goods originating in another country to a third country, had tended to come to an end because of the absence of convertibility. Traders could not buy goods in a hard currency country for resale (presumably at a profit) in a soft currency country; the exchange control authorities in the trader's country would not make hard currency available for such purchases. The opposite type of transit trade transaction (buying in a soft currency country and selling in a hard currency country) would have been attractive to the exchange control authorities, but there was no profit in it for the trader at the official exchange rate.

Retention quotas made transit trade possible in these circumstances. A trader could get a license to use hard currency for the purchase of goods to be sold in a soft currency country provided that the hard currency required had been obtained as the result of a previous transit transaction effected in the opposite direction. The earlier one (sometimes called the "first leg of a switch transaction") might entail a loss; but the latter transaction (sometimes called the "second leg") yielded a profit. As the combination was attractive only if the profit on the second leg more than offset any loss on the first, the dealer who completed the unprofitable first leg of the transaction was given the right to retain part of the hard currency obtained in order to use it for the second leg. This right might or might not be negotiable. The reason why the authorities of the transit trader's country were interested in this kind of deal was that the part of the hard currency proceeds of which they demanded surrender helped to increase their hard currency holdings.

Although the Fund's staff had been concerned about retention quotas as early as 1947, it was only later, when the practice began to spread, that they became troublesome. A survey by the staff in 1952 had indicated that retention quotas were in use at least in Austria, Denmark, Finland, France, Germany, Greece, Iceland, Indonesia, Italy, Japan, the Netherlands, Norway, Sweden, Turkey, and Yugoslavia. As the Executive Board began consultations with individual countries, early in 1952, it became apparent that retention quotas were symptoms of a wider problem and that it would be desirable for the Fund to formulate a general approach to their removal. However, some countries had already indicated to the Fund that they could not see their way clear to removing such practices unless such removal was part of a general action by several countries; the Board therefore deferred any decision regarding these practices pending an over-all study.

The analysis by the staff revealed several dangers in the use of retention quotas and similar arrangements. A retention quota for the purpose of expanding direct exports was a partial *de facto* devaluation, as it made possible a cut in the price of the export product. Such devaluation might set off a chain of competitive actions. Retention quotas for transit trade were even more worrisome. Hard currency earnings were channeled from the soft currency country in which the goods originated to the country whose trader effected the final sale. The commodities marketed competed advantageously in the hard currency market with the same goods sold in that market by the original producer, since the transit trader could afford to accept a loss which the direct exporter could not. Trade was diverted, by an intermediary, from its normal channel direct from the country of production to the country of consumption; and the intermediary, not the country of production, received the precious dollar earnings.

Taking action

The importance of the retention quota problem at the time prompted the Board of Governors, at its Seventh Annual Meeting in September 1952 in Mexico City, to adopt a resolution to the effect that the Fund should make a special study of dollar retention quotas and similar practices in member countries, and make recommendations. This study was to take into account the situations which give rise to these practices, their magnitude in each country, the methods used for their application, their impact on other members of the Fund, and possible alternative measures.[22]

In judging these practices, the staff, while taking into account the point of view of the individual countries using them, employed primarily international criteria: Did they cause undue harm to the economic interests of other members? What implications did they have for international monetary cooperation? What were the consequences of these devices for existing exchange rates? Were they likely to shorten the period of inconvertibility? Essentially the staff's findings were that retention quotas constituted a break with the principle of unitary rates, that they did not add significant flexibility to the exchange rate system of the countries concerned, and that they did not help to achieve convertibility or a substantial relaxation of restrictions. Accordingly, it was suggested that the Fund should seek the simultaneous removal of these practices by all countries.

The Executive Board had considerable difficulty in agreeing on a course of action. The Directors from those countries that were condemning retention quotas and similar practices argued that such practices involved competitive exchange depreciation, undermined otherwise appropriate exchange rates, encouraged unfair commercial practices, and resulted in diverting dollar earnings from already dollar-scarce countries. On the other hand, the Directors from those countries that were using the practices argued that the real problem was the

---

[22] *Summary Proceedings, 1952,* pp. 169–70.

general dollar shortage and the fact that some countries had over-all balance of payments equilibrium while others did not. Because of the inconvertibility of currencies, the former could not use their surpluses in one currency to settle deficits in another. Meanwhile, retention quotas were useful parts of dollar export promotion programs which helped to expand dollar earnings and made the export business competitive.

This difference of view made it necessary for the Board to give intensive consideration to numerous drafts of a decision. On May 4, 1953, the following decision was taken, without dissent but with one abstention:

> In concluding consultations on restrictions on current payments and transfers as required under Article XIV of the Fund Agreement, the Fund postponed consideration of retention quotas and similar practices through which some members have sought to improve their earnings of specific currencies. The Fund has now examined these practices more fully than was possible at the consultations referred to above. The Fund has extended this examination to cover the terms of reference of the resolution adopted on September 9, 1952, by the Board of Governors, and has come to the following conclusions:
>
> 1. Members should work toward and achieve as soon as feasible the removal of these retention quotas and similar practices, particularly where they lead to abnormal shifts in trade which cause unnecessary damage to other countries. Members should endeavor to replace these practices by more appropriate measures leading to currency convertibility.
>
> 2. The Fund will enter into consultation with each of the members concerned with a view to agreeing on a program for the implementation of 1 above, including appropriate attention to timing of any action which may be decided upon.
>
> 3. The Fund does not object to those practices which, by their nature, can be regarded as devices designed solely to simplify the administration of official exchange allocations.[23]

Subsequently the Executive Board considered the retention quotas of several European countries, making suggestions where they might be reduced. During later 1953 and early 1954 the use of retention quotas declined substantially and no longer presented such an acute problem as they had a year or two earlier. They were abolished in France, Germany, the Netherlands, Sweden, and Turkey. In March 1955 Japan reduced its use of the practice.

CONVERTIBILITY OF EUROPEAN CURRENCIES CONSIDERED

PROSPECTS FOR STERLING CONVERTIBILITY

By the early 1950's the establishment by the United Kingdom of convertibility for sterling had come to be regarded by many as a necessary condition for the

---

[23] E.B. Decision No. 201-(53/29), May 4, 1953; below, Vol. III, p. 258.

introduction of convertibility by other countries where economic conditions were already favorable. Much attention, therefore, centered on the prospects for making the pound sterling convertible.

After the abortive attempt in 1947, no consideration was given to the problem of restoring sterling convertibility until the autumn of 1951, when the Conservative Party returned to power in the United Kingdom. A statement issued in London in January 1952 by the Conference of Commonwealth Finance Ministers following their discussions on the problems confronting the sterling area stated that "it is our definite objective to make sterling convertible and to keep it so." But convertibility was not imminent—rather a goal to be achieved gradually. "We intend to work towards that goal by progressive steps aimed at creating the conditions under which convertibility can be reached, and maintained." The statement noted that while the sterling area countries had the primary responsibility for creating the conditions required to reach this objective, the cooperation of other countries, especially countries in surplus, was imperative. No mention was made of the Fund or of any other international financial organization, such as the EPU.[24]

Discussions by the British Government and the Governments of the other Commonwealth countries about the prospects for convertibility were accelerated in 1952 and 1953. These discussions were more practical and pointed than those of the past: they were less in terms of whether convertibility ought to be established and more in terms of how and when the specific necessary conditions could be established and the forms which convertibility might take. Keen interest in the prospects for sterling convertibility was also expressed in meetings of the EPU and the OEEC.

In a communiqué issued at the end of the Commonwealth Economic Conference (attended by Prime Ministers) in December 1952, it was stated that the conference had agreed that it was important not only for the United Kingdom and the rest of the sterling area but also for the world that sterling should resume its full role as a medium of world trade and exchange. The communiqué reiterated that, while an integral part of any effective multilateral system was the restoration of the convertibility of sterling, this could only be achieved in progressive stages.

The stages were now made more explicit. Three conditions were outlined for the achievement of convertibility: (1) the continuing success of actions by the sterling Commonwealth countries themselves, (2) the adoption by trading nations of trade policies conducive to the expansion of world trade, and (3) the availability of adequate financial support through the Fund or otherwise.[25] Subsequent talks were held between the British Government and the new U.S. Administration

---

[24] *Third Annual Report on Exchange Restrictions* (1952), pp. 188–91.

[25] *Department of State Bulletin*, March 16, 1953, p. 399.

early in March 1953. It was agreed that while full multilateral trade and general convertibility of currencies were ultimate objectives, firm commitments on either side were then impossible.

POSITION OF OTHER EUROPEAN CURRENCIES

Meanwhile, the continental members of the OEEC had become somewhat disturbed at the prospect of sterling convertibility. They feared both that it might be established at the expense of the trade liberalization program of the OEEC and that it would mean the end of the EPU. Conceivably, a degree of convertibility might be established accompanied by the tightening of other restrictions. At the OEEC Ministerial Council Meeting held in Paris on March 23 and 24, 1953, the United Kingdom allayed these fears by supporting the consensus of the continental members that progress toward trade liberalization should proceed *pari passu* with progress toward convertibility.

During the first half of 1954, a number of official reports and statements discussed the need for, and possibilities of, establishing convertibility for several European currencies. In January the report of the U.S. Commission on Foreign Economic Policy (the Randall Commission) had stated that the general economic conditions prerequisite to currency convertibility were more nearly in prospect at that time than at any previous time since the war. The decision, the methods, the timetable, and the responsibility for introducing currency convertibility should rest with the countries concerned; the commission believed, however, that its recommendations on commercial policy and for strengthening the gold and dollar reserves of European countries, as their currencies became convertible, would assist these countries in removing restrictions.[26] These recommendations were subsequently approved by the President in his Message to the Congress on foreign economic policy on March 30. Also in March 1954 the U.S. and Canadian Ministers who had been members of the Joint United States-Canadian Committee on Trade and Economic Affairs welcomed the evidence of a desire in many countries to take decisive steps toward convertibility.[27]

Several European central banks, in the early months of 1954, pointed to the steps being taken toward convertibility.[28] On February 22, 1954, the Governor of the National Bank of Belgium, after emphasizing that convertibility required strict financial discipline, stated that the National Bank believed that Belgium had attained the necessary conditions for introducing convertibility of the Belgian franc. The Board of Governors of the Bank deutscher Länder stated that convertibility of the deutsche mark had already in large measure been established,

---

[26] U.S. Commission on Foreign Economic Policy, *Report to the President and the Congress* (January 1954), pp. 72–73.

[27] U.S. Department of State, Press Release No. 143, March 17, 1954.

[28] *Annual Report, 1954*, pp. 8–10.

expressed the opinion that the conditions for instituting a fully convertible system of payments in Europe had been better in 1953 than at any other time since the end of World War II, and urged that any monetary decisions being taken should aim at convertibility. The President of the Netherlands Bank said that the Netherlands was standing on the threshold of convertibility. The approach to convertibility had therefore been broadened to include not only sterling but the French franc, the deutsche mark, the Dutch guilder, the Belgian franc, the Italian lira, and possibly other currencies as well.

A Ministerial Examination Group on Convertibility was established at an OEEC Council Meeting in May 1954 to consider the problems that might arise for intra-European trade and payments if and when convertibility was introduced for one or more European currencies. At a meeting of this group in London in July 1954, the United Kingdom suggested the establishment of a European Fund, and this suggestion led in time to the European Monetary Agreement.

Deliberations in the Fund

As they began to consider the prospects for convertibility, both the United Kingdom and the OEEC Group on Convertibility made informal inquiries seeking the Fund's views; moreover, in their Annual Report for 1954, the Executive Directors took note of the discussions going on in Europe concerning convertibility: "Formal statements made by several Fund members in recent months have indicated a widespread interest in the possibility of more rapid movement in the direction of currency convertibility and the further removal of restrictions." [29]

While the Board welcomed both the general trend of opinion and the policy decisions made by individual countries and by groups of countries as regards convertibility, it was aware of the problems posed by the fact that not all European currencies were equally strong. Countries returning to convertibility might impose or intensify restrictions on imports from countries with weaker currencies that remained inconvertible for the time being; countries whose currencies remained inconvertible might intensify restrictions on imports from countries with newly convertible currencies in order to increase or create balances available for conversion into dollars. It was essential, therefore, that relaxation of restrictions and restoration of convertibility should go hand in hand, and that most if not all European countries should undertake convertibility simultaneously; on the other hand, the countries which had already attained strong payments positions could not wait indefinitely.

At the Ninth Annual Meeting, in September 1954, some of the Governors expressed the belief that conditions necessitating the postwar transitional

---

[29] *Ibid.*, p. 8.

arrangements of the Articles of Agreement were drawing to an end. The Governor for the United Kingdom warned that "there may well be danger in continuing for too long a transitional provision," and he asked the Fund to study the question of the best means of shifting from the transitional arrangements under Article XIV to Article VIII. The Governor for the United States supported this request.[30]

Meanwhile, the staff had been considering how the Fund might assist in a move to convertibility, both by giving financial assistance and by formulating relevant policies and procedures. Among the questions being considered was whether the Fund should announce the end of the transitional period. Did the Fund, in fact, have the power to do so? On whose initiative—the Fund's or the country's—should the decision be taken to give up Article XIV and take up the obligations of Article VIII? What restrictions, if any, might the Fund approve under Article VIII? How was Article VIII stricter than Article XIV?

From the Fund's inception, it had generally been assumed that Article XIV was somehow more permissive than Article VIII—that is, countries could presumably maintain a greater degree of restriction under Article XIV than would be permitted under Article VIII. But the precise extent to which Article VIII was stricter, and the exact nature of the restrictions that might be approved under that Article, remained uncertain. Accordingly, the policies and procedures of the Fund in these matters began to be explored.

In informal session in November 1954 the Executive Directors considered a possible shift of several member countries to Article VIII. This preliminary discussion did more to point up problems and differences among members than to resolve them. Attention tended to concentrate on two important legal issues. First, was formal notification to the Fund of acceptance of Article VIII by a member required before Article VIII could become binding on a member? Inversely expressed, could the Fund find that a member was under Article VIII by virtue of that member's having no restrictions that were maintained for balance of payments reasons? Second, did the Fund have the legal power to end the transitional period, either for all members or with exceptions for some members still in need of transitional arrangements?

Consideration of the stage at which members would come under Article VIII was also an important part of the 1954 discussions. As the staff saw it, even with the restoration of convertibility some restrictions—possibly a great many—would remain. While countries might establish "external" convertibility, it might be only at some later time that "internal" convertibility could be undertaken as well. Until then, while nonresidents could convert their earnings of a given currency, restrictions on residents would continue. The establishment of convertibility was, therefore, envisaged as occurring in two stages.

---

[30] *Summary Proceedings, 1954*, p. 44.

PROGRESS ACHIEVED, 1955–58

IMPROVED WORLD PAYMENTS SITUATION

The sudden and extensive decline in the use of retention quotas may, in part, have been occasioned by the adverse reactions of the Fund and of several of its largest members; but the virtual abolition of these practices, and the talk about prospects for convertibility, were due even more to the vast improvement in the world payments situation that had become apparent by the mid-1950's.

World industrial production was expanding rapidly and world trade even more quickly. As increased production of both agricultural and industrial commodities had made many countries less dependent on dollar imports, the volume of these imports had tended to fall despite a considerable decline in the degree of discrimination applied against imports requiring payment in dollars. The sterling area had achieved an aggregate surplus as well as a surplus with the dollar area; and several countries in Western Europe had attained, or had continued in, total balance of payments surplus. The previously difficult U.S. market had been penetrated by the exports of other industrial countries; and exporters from Western Europe and Japan were competing successfully in third markets with exports from the United States. The shares in world exports of manufactured goods of Japan, Germany, Italy, Belgium, and Sweden had sharply increased, and smaller rises had been experienced by the Netherlands, Switzerland, and France; the shares of the United States, and also of the United Kingdom, had diminished.[31]

The improvement in the international payments situation was signalized by an expansion of gold and dollar reserves outside the United States. These reserves had been rising steadily and by the end of 1954 totaled $25 billion, as against $15 billion held at the end of 1948.[32] Further testimony to the strength of the balance of payments of the non-dollar world was that the recession in the United States in 1953–54, unlike those of 1945–46 and 1948–49, did not lead to a recrudescence of payments difficulties elsewhere. In fact, the reserves of non-dollar countries in 1953 and 1954 had risen by approximately $4.8 billion.[33] In contrast, the recession of 1948–49, of about the same magnitude, had helped to precipitate the currency devaluations of September 1949.

Thus, by 1955 most of the *abnormal* postwar difficulties had faded into the past and with them had gone the acute payments problems that had given rise to severe restrictions. In addition, the improvement in the world payments situation between 1951–52 and 1954–55—in contrast to the period after the

---

[31] *Annual Report, 1957*, pp. 20–21.

[32] *Annual Report, 1955*, p. 33.

[33] *Ibid.*, p. 13.

outbreak of hostilities in Korea, when there had also been a rapid rise in the non-dollar world's reserves—was associated with stable prices and a greater freedom from inflationary pressures than in earlier years. It had been possible for countries to pursue credit policies which were more cautious than those previously employed without unduly hampering the expansion of production or creating any serious problems of unemployment.

Debates by members of the staff and by the Executive Board with representatives of member governments on the need for, and effectiveness of, anti-inflationary policies in improving balances of payments lessened in intensity and in frequency. In its 1955 consultations, for example, the Fund found in its members a much greater readiness to take measures for the correction and prevention of monetary instability. Although the authorities of practically all members made it clear that they regarded the maintenance of satisfactory levels of productive employment as a major objective of their economic policies, there was increasing recognition of the value of flexible monetary and fiscal policies as a major means of achieving stability. Differences of opinion now centered on such questions as at what point current changes in economic activity required the institution of tighter monetary, credit, and fiscal policies, the extent to which fiscal measures should be combined with monetary measures, and to which sectors of the economy stricter monetary policies should be applied.

In order to facilitate the attempts by central banks to prevent or at least counteract any inflationary or deflationary developments of sufficient magnitude to create a threat to the long-run stability of the internal and external purchasing power of their currencies, special attention was given to the problem of how to detect inflationary or deflationary developments. As part of the proceedings of the Eleventh Annual Meeting of the Board of Governors, an Informal Session on Recent Developments in Monetary Analysis was held on September 25, 1956.[34] Three papers were presented, by Dr. M. W. Holtrop, President of the Netherlands Bank, Dr. Paolo Baffi, Economic Adviser to the Bank of Italy, and Dr. Ralph A. Young, Director of the Division of Research and Statistics, Board of Governors of the Federal Reserve System of the United States.[35]

THE EASING OF RESTRICTIONS

In response to the more satisfactory balance of payments positions of many countries, notable steps were taken, particularly in Western Europe and the sterling area but also elsewhere, to accelerate the reduction of restrictions. Although the elimination of controls was sometimes delayed because authorities

---

[34] *Summary Proceedings, 1956*, p. 125.

[35] The papers presented by the principal speakers and the background paper on Monetary Analysis prepared by the Fund's staff are to be found in *Staff Papers*, Vol. V (1956–57), pp. 303–433.

hesitated to dismantle a control apparatus which they feared they might have to re-establish in the event of a deterioration of the payments situation, controls were applied less rigorously or regulations were made less rigid and formalistic. The result was a considerable relaxing of restrictions. The trade liberalization policy of the OEEC had become a driving force in the freeing of trade between Western European countries. These countries had, by January 1954, freed from quantitative restrictions three fourths of the trade conducted with each other and in 1955 they began to relax restrictions on the granting of exchange for transactions in invisibles within the OEEC. Liberalization of trade restrictions was also frequently extended to imports from other non-dollar sources. Outside Europe, where countries' policies on restrictions were not in general subject to joint agreement, there was also extensive relaxation of restrictions.

There was a tendency, as well, to give more equal treatment to imports from different countries or paid for in different currencies, i.e., to reduce the degree of discrimination. By 1955, ten members outside the dollar area (Belgium, Ethiopia, Greece, Indonesia, Luxembourg, the Netherlands, Pakistan, Peru, Thailand, and the Union of South Africa) made little significant distinction between their treatment of the dollar area and of other countries; and during the next year, dollar import lists were further enlarged by many countries, and the OEEC countries continued their efforts to extend dollar liberalization.

Moreover, in the summer of 1955 Western European countries began to terminate some of their bilateral payments arrangements with countries outside Europe and to broaden their payments arrangements with non-European countries. Under arrangements known as the "Hague Club," Belgium, Germany, Luxembourg, the Netherlands, and the United Kingdom terminated their bilateral agreements with Brazil and the degree of multilateralization of trade and payments between Brazil and their monetary areas was widened. Brazil undertook to apply to exports to the monetary areas of the participants the same exchange rate treatment as exports paid for in convertible currencies; to accept payment in any of the participants' currencies without regard to the country of destination; not to discriminate between the European currencies in respect of payments for imports; and to maintain orderly cross rates among these currencies. In addition, Brazil was permitted to transfer its earnings of these currencies to other non-dollar countries. In 1956, the arrangement was extended to include Austria, France, and Italy.

In July 1956 similar arrangements, called the "Paris Club," were established between Argentina and a number of European countries which by 1957 had increased to eleven—Austria, Belgium, Denmark, France, Italy, Luxembourg, the Netherlands, Norway, Sweden, Switzerland, and the United Kingdom. Under this regime, Argentina could freely transfer the currencies of the European participants from one participant to another.

Meanwhile, from 1955 to 1957, the areas of transferability were increasingly being extended for the pound sterling, the deutsche mark, the Belgian franc, the Italian lira, the Netherlands guilder, and the Swedish krona. There was thus a continued movement to ease the requirements of bilateral arrangements. There were new arrangements by which one partner country made its currency transferable, and arrangements in which the two partners agreed to conduct transactions in the transferable currency of a third country.

Many of these measures, considered in isolation, were of no great significance; but their result in the aggregate was an impressive relaxation of restrictions. By early in 1956, the Fund was able to report that "foreign exchange restrictions impose a less serious obstacle to international commerce today than at any time since the outbreak of World War II."[36]

CONTINUED INCONVERTIBILITY

On the other hand, relations between European currencies and fully convertible currencies, especially the U.S. and Canadian dollars, remained unchanged. It had become fairly well established that no general move to convertibility by European countries or to the Fund's Article VIII could be made before sterling became convertible. The need for countries to move together to the Fund's Article VIII had been reiterated by the Governor of the Fund for Belgium, Mr. Frère, at Mr. Rooth's luncheon for Governors at the Tenth Annual Meeting in Istanbul in September 1955, but hopes for establishment of sterling convertibility were dimming. At the Annual Meeting in Istanbul, the Governor for the United Kingdom, Mr. Butler, noted that "in the United Kingdom a too buoyant economy has called for measures to control the surge of expansion" and that "my Government has taken no decision on the timing of the convertibility of sterling." Referring to his remarks at the previous Meeting, the Governor for the United Kingdom went on to say that the Executive Directors had found that the difficulties of a move to Article VIII were considerable and that it would be a mistake "to reach a rushed decision."[37] When sterling area reserves declined in the second half of 1955, it became clear that there would be no early action by the U.K. authorities to extend general authorization to all nonresidents to convert their current sterling earnings into convertible currencies at the official rate of exchange. Thus were ended, for the time being, any expectations of an early move to convertibility for European currencies or of members shifting to Article VIII. It is noteworthy that a few months earlier, in July 1955, the Managing Director, Mr. Rooth, had recorded in his own notations his personal view that no decision should be taken at that time to end the transitional period.

---

[36] *Annual Report, 1956*, p. 89.

[37] *Summary Proceedings, 1955*, pp. 37, 39, 41.

SHAPING THE FUND'S POLICY

These were not easy years for the Fund. First, the great majority of members continued to apply restrictions under Article XIV. Second, most countries still retained some discrimination against the dollar area. Third, almost two thirds of the Fund's members had bilateral payments arrangements of some kind, though some were of little more than marginal significance. Finally, administrative machinery for applying restrictions was maintained by four fifths of the Fund's members, even though the improvements in their economic situations suggested that many could dismantle their exchange controls.

INCREASING CONCERN ABOUT DISCRIMINATION

The fact that most members, including those in Europe, still applied restrictions that discriminated against imports from the dollar area had, by the mid-1950's become of increasing concern, especially to the Directors for the United States and Canada. Part of the problem was that the way in which EPU settlements were arranged tended to encourage tighter restrictions against the dollar area. The participating countries extended credits to each other for part of the net payments due to them; consequently, they did not receive in gold or convertible currencies the full value of whatever balance of payments surplus they acquired inside the Union. They were, therefore, not able to apply the full value of surpluses within the Union to meet deficits with other areas. This settlement arrangement was of particular importance in relation to the dollar area, and, indeed, was one of the reasons given to the Fund for the retention of restrictions which discriminated against imports of dollar goods.

The U.S. and Canadian Directors were especially disturbed by discrimination against dollar imports when the country under discussion had already attained equilibrium in its aggregate balance of payments, or had achieved a surplus in its accounts with the dollar area whether or not it had reached total equilibrium. At least two of the OEEC countries which in the mid-1950's had deficits in their accounts with EPU countries were in surplus with the dollar area, and were using the resulting dollar proceeds to finance their EPU deficits. Yet these countries maintained restrictions which were more severe against imports from the dollar area than against imports from other EPU participants. Noting that other OEEC countries had liberalized to a considerable extent without discriminating between EPU liberalization and dollar liberalization, the U.S. and Canadian Directors questioned the reasons for the discriminatory restrictions given by some of the individual members of the OEEC. They disagreed, for example, with the argument presented by the representatives of one of the OEEC countries that a certain amount of discrimination against dollar imports was required if European integration was to be achieved. They doubted that the Fund could tolerate indefinitely the policy followed by EPU countries of earmarking dollar earnings for settlement of their deficits within the EPU.

In the hope and expectation that a push by the Fund against bilateral payments agreements might help to end the discrimination resulting from those agreements, and might also hasten convertibility and thus put an end to currency discrimination, the Board, in June 1955, took a decision urging members to re-examine the need for their bilateral agreements and calling upon them to reduce their use of these agreements.[38]

In addition, in September 1955, preparatory to a Board discussion of the general problem of discriminatory restrictions, the staff undertook a survey of the extent of discrimination still being applied by members. The staff study concluded that the degree of discrimination against dollar imports had diminished and was continuing to diminish, and that this was in line with the improved balance of payments and reserve positions of most members. Late in 1955 and early in 1956 the Directors held an intensive series of meetings on the topic of discriminatory restrictions. But it was evident that there remained considerable differences of opinion among them concerning whether greater progress toward reducing discrimination could be made by the majority of the Fund's members.

During the Board's discussion, Mr. Rasminsky (Canada) took strong issue with the position of the staff that some Western European countries felt obliged to maintain a significant degree of restriction because of a sense of European solidarity, or to discriminate against dollar imports in view of the nature of the EPU settlement arrangements. He believed it was becoming increasingly clear that the basic reasons for continued discrimination were commerical policy considerations, including special export advantages gained by European countries through their regional or bilateral arrangements.

DRAWINGS TO AVOID INTENSIFYING RESTRICTIONS

Meanwhile, the Fund's immediate aim was to ensure that relaxation of restrictions continued or, at a minimum, that countries avoided tightening their restrictions. The Fund was especially concerned that any retrogression would be likely to delay movements toward convertibility. To this end, it began to apply the policies regarding the use of its resources which it had been developing since 1952. These new policies, involving gold tranche drawings, stand-by arrangements, and the application of the waiver provisions of the Articles of Agreement, had been worked out so as to provide additional exchange resources to members that undertook to make their currencies convertible. The policies were also intended to assist members through renewed balance of payments crises without their having to tighten restrictions which they had previously relaxed.[39]

[38] See below, p. 304.
[39] *Annual Report, 1955*, pp. 77–78.

These policies of the Fund relating use of the Fund's resources to relaxation of restrictions and steps to convertibility proved useful in the latter part of 1956 and in 1957, when both industrial and primary producing countries experienced a new round of financial difficulties. Boom conditions and overspending, aggravated by the Suez Canal crisis, led to various strains and stresses. The Fund, in two exceptional years ending April 30, 1958, lent resources totaling $1,780 million, including substantial sums to the United Kingdom, France, India, Japan, the Netherlands, and Argentina. In general an intensification of restrictions was avoided. Countries were enabled to gain the time required for putting into effect the measures contemplated or already initiated to check deteriorations in their payments positions.

But the Fund also considered these crises as temporary and hoped to encourage greater movement toward the further relaxation of restrictions and the establishment of convertibility. It recognized that governments, anxious to avoid being compelled by unfavorable developments to reverse decisions already made, must proceed cautiously in relaxing restrictions. But at the same time, the Fund did not wish to see progress delayed unduly. Hence, in its decisions on consultations, especially in the years 1957–58, the Board pressed for more rapid progress by members in eliminating their restrictions, and especially in reducing discrimination and bilateralism.

EXTERNAL CONVERTIBILITY ATTAINED

The year 1958 witnessed the most signal achievement of the postwar period in the field of exchange restrictions. On December 29, 1958, fourteen Western European countries—Austria, Belgium, Denmark, Finland, France, Germany, Ireland, Italy, Luxembourg, the Netherlands, Norway, Portugal, Sweden, and the United Kingdom—made their currencies externally convertible for current transactions; that is, nonresidents would now be freely permitted to exchange their earnings of these currencies from current transactions into any other currency at rates within the official margins. Greece took the same step on May 25, 1959. Fifteen other countries, most of which were associated in a monetary area with one or another of these Western European countries, adjusted their exchange control regulations to the new conditions; these were Australia, Burma, Ceylon, Ghana, India, Iraq, Jordan, Libya, Malaya, Morocco, New Zealand, Pakistan, the Sudan, Tunisia, and the Union of South Africa. It thus became a matter of indifference to the exchange control authorities in what currency or to what account authorized payments to nonresidents were made by the residents of their country.

Except for Germany, however, none of the other countries with newly restored external convertibility granted nonresident convertibility, at rates within the official margins, for all payments of a capital nature. In some of the countries, a free exchange market existed in which capital transactions were unrestricted. Germany also took the opportunity provided by the moves toward nonresident convertibility—and the very strong gold and foreign exchange reserve position of Germany justified this—to announce convertibility of the deutsche mark for residents. By a series of general licenses, the German public was given complete freedom in foreign exchange transactions. The connection between licensing of imports (and of service transactions) and foreign exchange transactions was eliminated.

Before 1958 only ten member countries had been maintaining fully convertible currencies. But a number of other members had, for varying lengths of time, maintained free exchange markets in which their currencies could be converted at will into the major trading currencies. The decision taken in December 1958 was, therefore, very significant; it meant that a majority of the Fund's members now permitted nonresidents to transfer current earnings of their currencies to any other country. A system had been formally established in which the currencies used for the great bulk of international payments were convertible into other currencies or into gold. By and large, this was true whether the payments were received from residents of countries whose currencies were externally convertible or from residents of other countries, since the foreign trade of the latter was, to a very great extent, financed in currencies which were now convertible.

SIGNIFICANCE FOR THE FUND

Since none of the 30 countries that had made their currencies externally convertible was yet ready to accept the obligations of Article VIII, Sections 2, 3, and 4, of the Fund Agreement, their currencies were still inconvertible in the technical meaning of the Fund's Articles; that is, their currencies remained unacceptable to the Fund in repurchases. Nonetheless, the currency moves in Europe at the end of 1958 had immediate and long-run significance for the Fund. The introduction of external convertibility followed the substantial strengthening, during the past few years, of the reserve and balance of payments positions of the Western European countries taken as a group, and the considerable improvement in the position of sterling during 1958. External convertibility, plus the subsequent favorable developments in early 1959 in the external financial situations of the European countries concerned, reflected the fact that these countries had, on the whole, attained a balanced position internally and increased strength in relation to other countries. And it was expected that, should that improvement continue, one country after another would be able to eliminate restrictions still further.

Indeed, the Managing Director, Mr. Jacobsson, in addressing the Governors at the Fourteenth Annual Meeting in Washington on September 28, 1959, spoke of the introduction of external convertibility as "the consummation of the first stage of a process extending over many years for strengthening the economic and financial position of countries all over the world." Long an advocate of the importance of monetary and credit policies for overcoming the balance of payments deficits of European countries, Mr. Jacobsson also saw in these developments some vindication of his beliefs:

> The monetary disturbances which were brought about by the Second World War could not be easily overcome; but through increases in national income and the more effective application of flexible fiscal and credit policies, the excessive liquidity which weighed on many economies in the postwar years has gradually been worked off, so that by now the authorities in many countries have got a firm grip on the monetary position.[40]

While nonresident convertibility by itself did not necessarily produce a reduction of trade restrictions, it had important repercussions upon trade relations, and countries were thereby brought closer to the time when the Fund's objective of avoiding restrictions on current payments would be fully achieved.

All in all, the Fund warmly welcomed the establishment of nonresident convertibility, especially the remarkable cooperative effort of European countries in making a concerted move.[41]

[40] *Summary Proceedings, 1959,* p. 13.
[41] *Annual Report, 1959,* pp. 3–4.

CHAPTER

13

A Convertible Currency World

Margaret G. de Vries

AFTER EXTERNAL CONVERTIBILITY was established by the European countries at the end of 1958, another period of the Fund's policy as regards exchange restrictions began. It was the opinion of many of the Directors and staff that the time was ripe to push for the elimination of discriminatory restrictions, at least by the European members, and for the assumption of the obligations of Article VIII. To this end, two decisions were taken by the Executive Board, late in 1959 and in mid-1960. These decisions were followed by the acceptance of the obligations of Article VIII early in 1961 by 11 members. Since 10 others, all in the Western Hemisphere, had previously done so, 21 now had currencies that were fully convertible in the Fund sense of the word.

DECISION ON DISCRIMINATION

PRESSURE FOR ACTION

One of the cardinal principles on which both the Fund and the GATT had been founded was that trade and exchange restrictions, as well as any other trade barriers, should be applied in a nondiscriminatory manner.[1] However, it was generally conceded that so long as a chronic dollar shortage prevailed—that is, while many countries had serious payments deficits with the dollar area—and so long as European currencies remained inconvertible, discriminatory restrictions might have to be employed.

But while recognizing the inevitability of discrimination in the application of restrictions so long as inconvertibility prevailed, many economists feared that protected markets might thereby be developed in countries that continued, for many years, to discriminate. The industries growing up in these sheltered

---

[1] For a brief description of the origins of the principle of nondiscrimination, see Gardner Patterson, *Discrimination in International Trade*, Chap. 1. For some criticisms of this principle, see Harry G. Johnson, *The World Economy at the Crossroads*, Chap. 4.

markets would be unable to compete with the industries of countries, such as the United States, that were highly competitive. Discrimination might therefore be long lasting. In addition, producers in countries such as the United States and Canada, whose products were being discriminated against in foreign markets, were complaining about their unequal export opportunities. This concern had already found expression in statements to the Board by the Executive Directors for the United States and Canada.

Among the countries continuing to maintain discriminatory restrictions, there had been increasing recognition of the costs to their economies of such discrimination. But there were a great many anxieties about eliminating practices that had been in effect for several years. In particular, these countries were uncertain whether their industries could compete in a world without discriminatory restrictions; and, if their industries were not competitive, what would be the effects on domestic employment and on their balance of payments positions?

Once the dollar shortage was over, therefore, and after external convertibility of European currencies was established, the Fund began to examine the questions raised by the remaining discriminatory restrictions. In mid-1959, however, the Executive Directors still could not agree on just what steps against discriminatory restrictions the Fund might take. They disagreed, indeed, on whether the establishment of external convertibility meant that discriminatory restrictions for balance of payments reasons had now become unnecessary. Even if the currency inconvertibility argument for discriminatory restrictions had been destroyed, commercial reasons remained. It was also evident that, where discriminatory restrictions had been maintained for a long time, a reasonable period would have to be allowed before countries could eliminate them completely.

Hence, it was not until late in 1959 that agreement among the Directors on a general decision on discrimination could be reached. A study by the staff concentrated on two types of discrimination—that against transactions with the dollar area and that arising out of bilateral arrangements. A survey of the extent of discrimination revealed that late in 1959 about twenty of the members that were taking advantage of the transitional arrangements of Article XIV discriminated against dollar imports and also had bilateral agreements, and about twenty other members discriminated against the dollar but had no bilateral arrangements. Only about fifteen members that were still under Article XIV had neither discrimination against dollar imports nor bilateral payments agreements.

The staff study also concluded that most of the members that still maintained discriminatory restrictions could eliminate them without important repercussions on their balance of payments or reserve positions. Either the remaining discrimination was slight, or their balance of payments and reserve positions were satisfactory, or, perhaps most important of all, the existing degree of liberalization vis-à-vis other countries was so great that the impact of the removal of discrimination could not really be expected to be onerous in its effects on the balance of payments. Therefore the staff believed that these members no longer had a balance of payments reason for discrimination.

The staff, nonetheless, recognized the existence of other considerations which might cause difficulties for members in withdrawing discriminatory restrictions, particularly if those restrictions had been in force for some decades. There might be practical problems, such as the need to formulate new regulations or to dismantle administrative machinery. International commitments might have been made to import specific goods from some other country or group of countries. Alternative ways had to be found to liquidate credits built up under bilateral arrangements. Most difficult of all was likely to be the impact of the removal of discriminatory restrictions on industries that had been operating under a mantle of protection.

Consideration by the Executive Board of the problem of discrimination, and the related staff study, followed by a few weeks the Annual Meeting, 1959. At that Meeting, Mr. Jacobsson said that the essence of the problem of the remaining discriminatory restrictions was that they were now seen to be "protectionist devices." They had thus become a problem of commercial policy and were no longer to be considered a balance of payments problem. He expressed concern for future trade relations should such discrimination remain:

> The maintenance of discrimination, moreover, undoubtedly acts as a strong irritant, liable to bedevil commercial relations; it may provoke a resurgence of protectionist sentiment, especially when the business trend turns downward; and if such possibilities are not guarded against, the result might well be a dangerous disruption of trade relations in general.[2]

It was his personal conviction that for the vast majority of countries there were no longer any balance of payments reasons for the maintenance of discrimination, and he thought that the time had come when, for many reasons, the practice of discrimination should be abandoned with the least possible delay.

The Governors for Canada (Mr. Fleming) and the United States (Mr. Anderson) endorsed these views of the Managing Director.[3] They believed very strongly that the Fund should take early action to declare a position to the effect that there was no longer any balance of payments justification for discrimination.

Other Governors—for example those for Australia and the United Kingdom—while agreeing that the stage had been set for "the progressive removal of discrimination, including that arising from bilateralism," called attention to

---

[2] *Summary Proceedings, 1959*, p. 16.

[3] *Ibid.*, pp. 42, 52.

various complications. The Governor for the United Kingdom (Sir Roger Makins) stressed that discriminatory restrictions had long been maintained and that many member countries would require a reasonable time to deal with the political, social, and economic problems associated with their removal.[4] The Governor for Australia (Mr. Holt) expressed concern about the dangers of agricultural protectionism.[5]

A DECISION TAKEN

After a relatively short discussion, the Executive Board took this decision in October 1959:

> The following decision deals exclusively with discriminatory restrictions imposed for balance of payments reasons.
>
> In some countries, considerable progress has already been made towards the elimination of discriminatory restrictions; in others, much remains to be done. Recent international financial developments have established an environment favorable to the elimination of discrimination for balance of payments reasons. There has been a substantial improvement in the reserve positions of the industrial countries in particular and widespread moves to external convertibility have taken place.
>
> Under these circumstances, the Fund considers that there is no longer any balance of payments justification for discrimination by members whose current receipts are largely in externally convertible currencies. However, the Fund recognizes that where such discriminatory restrictions have been long maintained, a reasonable amount of time may be needed fully to eliminate them. But this time should be short and members will be expected to proceed with all feasible speed in eliminating discrimination against member countries, including that arising from bilateralism.
>
> Notwithstanding the extensive moves toward convertibility, a substantial portion of the current receipts of some countries is still subject to limitations on convertibility, particularly in payments relations with state-trading countries. In the case of these countries the Fund will be prepared to consider whether balance of payments considerations would justify the maintenance of some degree of discrimination, although not as between countries having externally convertible currencies. In this connection the Fund wishes to reaffirm its basic policy on bilateralism as stated in its decision of June 22, 1955.[6]

POLICY AND PROCEDURAL ASPECTS OF ARTICLE VIII STATUS

During 1959 and the early part of 1960, further substantial progress was made by many countries in reducing or eliminating their exchange restrictions. The

---

[4] *Ibid.*, p. 79.

[5] *Ibid.*, pp. 68–69.

[6] E.B. Decision No. 955-(59/45), October 23, 1959; below, Vol. III, p. 260. On the decision of June 1955, see Chapter 14 of this volume, pp. 304–305.

beneficial effects of the widening scope of external currency convertibility were felt in many areas, and there was an evolution toward freer, more orderly, and less discriminatory trade and payments. By early in 1960 the currencies of about half of the Fund's members were convertible for virtually all nonresidents. In a number of countries, the remaining restrictions on current payments had dwindled to the point of insignificance.

Under these conditions, it was becoming increasingly possible to visualize for many of the Fund's members the establishment of the multilateral system of current payments, without foreign exchange restrictions, that was foreseen in Article I of the Fund Agreement. It appeared that a number of members which had been availing themselves of Article XIV would soon be able to implement in full the obligations of Article VIII. Accordingly, the Fund began again to examine the legal, policy, and procedural aspects connected with a member's formal acceptance of the obligations of Article VIII.

SOME SUGGESTED DEFINITIONS

Answers to the questions concerning the assumption of Article VIII status which had proved controversial or difficult in the past could no longer be postponed. Accordingly, the staff prepared some suggested solutions and presented these to the Board. First came the question of whether the Fund should—or even could—announce the end of the transitional period generally. The legal staff reached the conclusion that the Fund had no such legal authority. This meant that some countries could, if they so wished, continue under Article XIV more or less indefinitely. Second, the legal staff advised the Board that the initiative to give up Article XIV and to assume the obligations of Article VIII rested solely with the member, not with the Fund. Any restrictions that the member might have would of course have to be approved under Article VIII if the member accepted the obligations of that Article. Third, a decision by a member to take up Article VIII status was irreversible: if a country moved to Article VIII, it could not revert to Article XIV should the Fund disapprove of its remaining restrictions, or should it later wish to reintroduce restrictions.

Next came the matter of the long-debated definition of a "restriction on payments" that the Fund was called upon to approve under Article VIII. The controversy was not yet dead. In January 1959—immediately after the main European currencies had become externally convertible—Mr. Callaghan (Australia) had raised the jurisdictional question once more. In calling to the attention of the Directors the need to turn their minds again toward the transition from Article XIV to Article VIII, he was interested especially in seeking to get the Fund to clarify its "approval" authority.

The staff pointed out that the language of the relevant Articles was broad and comprehensive, not narrow and restrictive. Therefore, a good case had to be made before anything that appeared to be a qualification of this general language could be accepted as having been within the intention of the drafters of the Agreement. Secondly, any doubt about the Fund's jurisdiction had to be resolved in the light of the wide purposes of Article I. Thirdly, no formula would provide automatic answers for all cases in which jurisdictional issues arise. Given these qualifications, the staff suggested that the guiding principle for determining whether a given measure was a restriction on current payments should be simply whether it "involves a direct governmental limitation on the availability or use of exchange as such." Even so, members would often need to consult the Fund, not only where it was obvious that a measure was covered by the definition, but also where this was not clear until there had been adequate study of the underlying facts.

PROPOSED STANDARDS

Next came the question of the standards which the Fund should use for approving restrictions under Article VIII: how many and which restrictions would countries be permitted to retain when they gave up Article XIV and came under Article VIII? First, noting that the use of restrictions was still widespread, the staff commented that any general move to Article VIII would create the serious dilemma discussed by the Board in the past. On the one hand, there would be pressure on the Fund to give approval to many existing restrictions. This would tend to make approval of restrictions under Article VIII a mere formality. From a practical point of view, there would also be great difficulties in the Fund's administering an "approval" jurisdiction in such conditions. Frequent changes in restrictive systems would require Board approval on the merits of particular restrictive practices, with all the difficulties of deciding in haste because of the emergency conditions in which restrictions are usually introduced. Alternatively, if strict standards were applied under Article VIII, many member countries would find themselves with restrictive practices not approved by the Fund.

The staff further noted that, in practice, the Fund had been attempting to develop the concept of Article VIII as a substantive goal—a goal which involved the *elimination* of restrictions on current payments, of multiple exchange rates, and of other practices. The Fund had been greatly facilitated in this endeavor by the fact that the ten member countries which had assumed Article VIII status prior to 1960—Canada, Cuba, the Dominican Republic, El Salvador, Guatemala, Haiti, Honduras, Mexico, Panama, and the United States—had very few or no exchange restrictions. Indeed the existing Article VIII countries had, in general, gone beyond the formal requirements of the Fund Agreement in that they had avoided capital controls as well as restrictions on current payments. Of even greater significance, Article VIII status had come to signify over the years either that a country had a sound international balance of payments position or that, if its payments position was threatened, it would avoid the use of exchange restrictions and take other corrective measures including, where appropriate, the use of the Fund's resources. The record of Article VIII countries in this respect had been remarkably good.

The Article VIII countries, with one small exception, had not introduced restrictions. The exception had been Cuba, which had introduced a new multiple rate arrangement in September 1959. Because the multiple rate measures were one of a series of tax measures adopted by the Cuban authorities to deal with their balance of payments difficulties, and because the measure was intended to be provisional, the Fund did not object; but approval was specified for a limited time (until June 30, 1960) and meanwhile the Fund was to have further discussions with Cuba.

The staff further reasoned that the achievement of Article VIII status had come to be the objective of the consultations under Article XIV. To this end, there had developed an attitude that the Fund's approval of restrictions must be based on a close scrutiny of the country's over-all economic position—domestic as well as external—and of the possibility of alternative corrective measures, particularly in the monetary and fiscal fields.

RECOMMENDED STRATEGIES

On the basis of this analysis, the staff recommended to the Executive Directors that a selective course of action be adopted for the assumption of Article VIII status. Those countries which made little use of restrictions and whose balance of payments and reserve positions and prospects were good might advantageously move to Article VIII. There were a limited number of such countries, mainly in Europe. For these countries, approval by the Fund of any existing exchange restrictions would require relatively few difficult policy decisions. Since the prospects for the removal of any remaining restrictions for balance of payments purposes would, by definition, be good, the member could commit itself to some program or time schedule for their elimination. In this way there would be a period of grace under Article VIII during which some further few restrictions might be eliminated, but that period would be short and definite. Were such countries to assume formal Article VIII status, the paradox would be ended that their currencies were treated by the Fund, for various purposes and in the technical sense of the Articles, as inconvertible, although these currencies were fully, or largely, convertible in actual foreign transactions.

This procedure would also make it clear, the staff argued, that countries having multiple exchange rates, bilateral payments arrangements, or discriminatory restrictions should not aspire to Article VIII status unless they were able to eliminate these practices promptly. Perhaps some exceptions might be made for bilateral arrangements that were maintained for other than balance of payments reasons or that discriminated solely against countries that were not members of the Fund. Furthermore, countries which had few or virtually no restrictions, but which experienced considerable uncertainty about their balance of payments outlook and reserve positions, should also refrain from undertaking Article VIII status; in their situations there would be concern about their inability to cope with deterioration in their payments positions without recourse to restrictions.

The staff further suggested that countries giving up Article XIV and coming under Article VIII should agree to periodic reviews under Article VIII similar to the consultations they had been having under Article XIV. In consultations under Article VIII there would be relatively little concern with restrictions; but, even more than in the past, attention would be devoted to the general economic and financial situation of the country. Holding consultations with countries shifting from Article XIV to Article VIII would also raise the question of holding consultations with countries already under Article VIII, such as the United States; consultations had not heretofore been conducted with countries that had never been under Article XIV.

BOARD CONCURRENCE AND DECISION

The Executive Board considered these staff suggestions at two meetings in March 1960. Most of the definitions and strategies presented by the staff were supported by the Directors. Mr. Southard (United States), Lord Cromer (United Kingdom), and Mr. Guth (Germany) were especially in agreement with the line of action proposed. Mr. de Largentaye (France) did not, however, assent to the idea that some countries, maybe even many, would continue to remain under Article XIV. In his view, Article XIV applied strictly to a postwar transitional period which, he thought, no longer existed.

With respect to the Fund's jurisdiction, Mr. Southard accepted the opinion of the legal staff that the Fund does not have "approval" jurisdiction for nondiscriminatory import restrictions imposed for balance of payments reasons. He concurred with the legal staff that where a country imposes discriminatory import restrictions for balance of payments reasons, the currency considerations are so clear that the restrictions partake of exchange as well as trade, and fall under the parallel jurisdiction of the Fund and the GATT.

Two related questions concerning the requirements which the Fund would impose for the assumption of Article VIII status were discussed in the Executive Board at this time: (1) whether a country needed to have an effective par value before assuming Article VIII status, and (2) whether consultations under Article VIII should result in conclusions. The issues involved, and the Board's decisions on both these questions in the negative, have been considered, respectively, in Chapters 4 and 11.[7]

For the next two to three months, efforts were made to draft a decision which would outline in some detail the Fund's policies and procedures on the move from Article XIV to Article VIII. On June 1, 1960 such a detailed decision was finally taken.[8]

The decision contained four basic points. The first stated that the guiding principle to determine a "restriction on payments and transfers for current transactions" under Article VIII would be that the measure "involved a direct governmental limitation on the availability or use of exchange as such." Members in doubt as to whether any of their measures did or did not fall under Article VIII were urged to consult the Fund.

The second point of the decision was that before members gave notice to the Fund that they were accepting the obligations of Article VIII, they should eliminate measures which would require the approval of the Fund and satisfy themselves that they were not likely to need to have recourse to such measures in the foreseeable future. The Fund would grant approval under Article VIII to measures for balance of payments reasons only where it was satisfied that the measures were necessary and temporary; exchange measures for other than balance of payments reasons should be avoided.

The second paragraph of the decision also stated that "members may at any time notify the Fund that they accept the obligations of Article VIII, Sections 2, 3, and 4, and no longer avail themselves of the transitional provisions of Article XIV." No mention was made of the Fund's ending the transitional period, nor was there any hint that members should be in a hurry to accept Article VIII. That countries should be cautious about undertaking the obligations of Article VIII reflected the strict standards adopted. But it also reflected the general recognition among the Directors of a difference between the industrial countries and the less developed countries—a difference in their attitudes toward policies as well as in their economic positions. Countries that found it difficult to discard restrictions would wish to remain under Article XIV. The consensus of the Board was that the wisest course would be to treat the continuation of the postwar transitional period as a sleeping dog, letting it continue without taking any action on it.

The third topic of the Article VIII-Article XIV decision concerned the matter of consultations; this is discussed in Chapter 11.[9] The fourth paragraph concerned methods of dealing with import restrictions for all members, whether or not they are also members of the GATT; this is also discussed in Chapter 11.[10]

---

[7] Above, pp. 75–76, 247.
[8] E.B. Decision No. 1034-(60/27), June 1, 1960; below, Vol. III, p. 260.
[9] Above, pp. 246–48.
[10] Above, p. 240.

IMPLEMENTATION OF DECISION ON ARTICLES VIII AND XIV

ACTIONS OF 1961

The Fund's decision on Article VIII status was followed by the acceptance of the obligations of Article VIII by nine European countries and Peru, effective February 15, 1961, and by Saudi Arabia, effective March 22, 1961. The European countries were Belgium, France, Germany, Ireland, Italy, Luxembourg, the Netherlands, Sweden, and the United Kingdom. This move resulted in all the major currencies which had been considered inconvertible in the sense of the Fund Agreement becoming convertible in the meaning of that term.

The undertaking of the obligations of Article VIII by these countries was preceded by intensive consultations and discussions, both formal and informal, between the members and the Fund. These were necessary to decide whether the arrangements for external convertibility that had been established by European countries could be maintained during the foreseeable future, and what the country's remaining restrictions were that would require, and could probably obtain, Fund approval under Article VIII. Since a notice that a member accepts the obligations of Article VIII is irrevocable, an awkward situation would have arisen if a member had given notice and then found that the Fund withheld approval of a practice that the member wished to keep. In fact, because of these consultations and discussions, and the delay in the move to come under Article VIII, by the time the move took place only four of the European countries—Belgium, France, Luxembourg, and the Netherlands—had any measures requiring Fund approval under Article VIII, and these measures were not extensive.

The precise *timing* of the move by these countries to Article VIII had also been a question of considerable importance. The staff had argued that Fund action on any measures requiring approval should be taken *before* the effective date of Article VIII status. A certain amount of time had to be allowed, therefore, for preparation of staff papers on each country's remaining exchange restrictions, if any, including the staff's recommendations to the Executive Board. These papers were also agreed by the staff with the country concerned before submission to the Board.

However, the time needed for this preparation was not the only reason for the delay of several months between the Board's general decision of June 1960 and the assumption of the obligations of Article VIII by the European countries. The staff's reports were actually agreed by the end of October 1960; the subsequent delay was due to political difficulties. First, there was the question of whether or not the undertaking of Article VIII status would be a concerted one, carried out by several European members. So far it had appeared that European countries were hesitant to be first and alone, because of the strains such a position might place on their currencies; yet none of them wished to be a laggard, for reasons of prestige and also because of intra-European ties.

By early in September 1960, before the Fund's Annual Meeting (September 26–30), the six countries of the European Economic Community (EEC) had apparently agreed to move simultaneously but had not yet agreed on the exact date. The United Kingdom, together with Ireland and Sweden, evidently intended to move when the EEC countries did. As Germany no longer had any exchange restrictions and was, it seems, the most eager of the six to come under Article VIII, the initiative for pressing for it lay with that country.[11] However, although there are indications that Germany hoped to get agreement with other countries on the exact timing of such a step at an October meeting of the EEC, no decision was reached. Other countries were not yet ready to go ahead. A press report, for example, indicated that the French Government had postponed taking the Article VIII step until after the presidential elections in the United States in November 1960.[12] By that time, the delay in making the move was causing increasing concern in the Fund, both to the staff and to certain Executive Directors, especially Mr. Southard. The fear was that the impetus toward a general shift to Article VIII status for European countries given by the Board decision of June 1960 might be lost and the decision itself might become inoperative.

However, shortly after the end of the year the difficulties that had inhibited concerted action were overcome. The Managing Director was informed between January 27 and February 2 by the Executive Directors of the countries concerned of these countries' intentions to assume the obligations of Article VIII on February 15, 1961. The Board's discussions of the countries' intentions and remaining restrictions, if any, took place on February 6 and 8. As had been expected, Peru joined the nine European members. A few weeks later, in March 1961, Saudi Arabia also assumed the obligations of Article VIII. This brought the number of members that had achieved formal convertibility under the Fund Agreement to 21.

This widening of the area of formal convertibility had implications of consequence for the Fund's general activities. Although drawings from the Fund had, from 1959 to 1961, included the use of the currencies of some of the countries which, in 1961, assumed the obligations of Article VIII, it had not been permissible under the Fund Agreement to use such currencies to make repayments to the Fund. The removal of this limitation proved an added encouragement to the use of a larger number of currencies in Fund transactions. Indeed, the

---

[11] See, for example, the statement by Mr. Blessing, Governor for Germany, in *Summary Proceedings, 1960*, p. 65.

[12] *Agence Economique et Financière* (Paris), October 28, 1960.

question of which particular currencies should be drawn from the Fund was to become a vital one in the next few years.[13]

As stated above, the member countries that assumed Article VIII status early in 1961 had by that time eliminated all, or nearly all, restrictions on current payments and transfers. However, these countries in most cases restricted the making of some capital payments at official rates of exchange. Only Germany and Saudi Arabia permitted all current and capital payments to be made at market rates of exchange maintained within the limits permitted by the Fund Agreement. Peru had similar arrangements except that the exchange rate was a unitary fluctuating one.

By 1961 the European countries that had established external convertibility—and defended it against something of a crisis in 1960–61—had been joined by others. The Exchange Restrictions Report for 1961 recorded that two thirds of the Fund's members permitted nonresidents to transfer freely to other nonresidents the local currency they acquired from current transactions.[14] Most of these countries believed that their balance of payments prospects or remaining restrictions, or both, made it advisable for them to await further developments before assuming formal Article VIII status. Nevertheless, virtually every currency used in financing international trade was now convertible in terms of the Fund Agreement, and virtually all of the trade of the other Fund members was conducted in these convertible currencies. Thus, while important obstacles to international trade persisted, relatively few impediments remained to conducting that trade on the basis of a multilateral payments system.

CONTINUED RELAXATION OF RESTRICTIONS

The successful maintenance of widespread convertibility provided, in the next few years, the basis and incentive for further reductions in restrictions. Import restrictions were reduced or simplified in many countries in addition to those that had moved to Article VIII in 1961. Countries relaxing their import restrictions included Austria, Burma, Finland, Pakistan, Portugal, Spain, Turkey, and Yugoslavia. Discrimination against imports from Canada and the United States was eliminated, or virtually eliminated, by Australia, Austria, Finland, France, Greece, Italy, Japan, Malaysia, Norway, and Sweden. Several countries—France, Iceland, Italy, Japan, the Netherlands, Pakistan, Spain, Sweden, and the United Kingdom—were able to liberalize further the granting of exchange for payments for invisibles. By 1962, restrictions on trade and payments for the world as a whole were less than they had been for some decades.

---

[13] See below, Chapter 19, p. 451.

[14] *Twelfth Annual Report on Exchange Restrictions* (1961), pp. 4–5.

Other members also accepted Article VIII status. In 1962–63 Austria, Jamaica, and Kuwait came under Article VIII. Japan and Nicaragua joined the list in 1964 and Australia and Costa Rica during 1965. Meanwhile, Cuba— an Article VIII member—had withdrawn from Fund membership. Thus, 27 countries had made their currencies convertible under the Articles of Agreement by the end of 1965; these are listed in Table 8.

As the decade of the 1960's got under way, many countries went even further in reducing their restrictions on payments than they were obliged to do under the Articles: although the Articles permitted controls on capital movements,

Table 8. Countries with Article VIII Status, as at December 31, 1965

Member	Date [1]	Member	Date [1]
Australia	July 1, 1965	Jamaica	Feb. 22, 1963
Austria	Aug. 1, 1962	Japan	Apr. 1, 1964
Belgium	Feb. 15, 1961	Kuwait	Apr. 5, 1963
Canada	Mar. 25, 1952	Luxembourg	Feb. 15, 1961
Costa Rica	Feb. 1, 1965	Mexico	Nov. 12, 1946
Dominican Republic	Aug. 1, 1953	Netherlands	Feb. 15, 1961
El Salvador	Nov. 6, 1946	Nicaragua	July 20, 1964
France	Feb. 15, 1961	Panama	Nov. 26, 1946
Germany	Feb. 15, 1961	Peru	Feb. 15, 1961
Guatemala	Jan. 27, 1947	Saudi Arabia	Mar. 22, 1961
Haiti	Dec. 22, 1953	Sweden	Feb. 15, 1961
Honduras	July 1, 1950	United Kingdom	Feb. 15, 1961
Ireland	Feb. 15, 1961	United States	Dec. 10, 1946
Italy	Feb. 15, 1961		

[1] I.e., the date on which the country's acceptance of the obligations of Article VIII became effective.

liberalization was gradually extended even to these. A view that had been dominant before 1930 began to gain ground, namely, that freedom of capital movements was highly desirable in itself: the movement of short-term funds might be regarded as an equilibrating factor in international payments, diminishing the need for reserves.

Liberalization of capital movements, both for direct investment and for portfolio investment, was therefore undertaken in the countries of Western Europe and certain others, including Japan, New Zealand, and South Africa. Complete freedom to transfer capital among the member countries of the EEC, for example, was achieved in 1963 for direct investments, personal transfers, short- and medium-term commercial loans, and operations in marketable securities. Also, the United Kingdom permitted transactions in foreign securities, and in domestic securities by nonresidents, to be carried out in exchange markets separate from the market for current transactions. In 1964 restrictions on outward capital transfers were further relaxed by European countries. In most

OECD countries, direct investment (both incoming and outgoing) was completely, or almost completely, liberalized or was treated liberally in practice; much the same was true of portfolio investment, other than new issues of securities.

The reductions in restrictions that had taken place were mirrored even in changes in the internal organization of the Fund's staff. In 1965, the Exchange Restrictions Department, which had been set up in 1950 especially so that the Fund might center its attention on the problems of restrictions, became the Exchange and Trade Relations Department. Its functions were now broadened to include assessments of the aggregate international trade and payments situation and of programs for stabilizing the economies of Fund members.

RESTRICTIONS OF LESS DEVELOPED COUNTRIES

Nonetheless, problems of restrictions were not entirely ended. In fact, the elimination of restrictions and even the dismantling of controls that occurred laid bare one problem and created another. The problem that remained concerned the general persistence of restrictions among the less developed countries, which were now generally called developing countries. Several of these countries shared in the progress made between 1955 and 1965 toward the establishment and maintenance of a relatively free international payments system. Of the 27 members that had by 1965 accepted the obligations of Article VIII, about one half were among the developing countries.

Most developing countries, however, still had serious balance of payments problems, and continued to apply an extensive array of restrictions. In addition, from 1960 to 1965, 35 new members, practically all of which were newly independent states and in the early stages of economic development, joined the Fund; all but one chose to avail themselves of the provisions of Article XIV (the transitional arrangements).

The developing countries also began to use a greater range of practices. The use of advance import deposit requirements spread, and more countries applied surcharges to imports. A wide variety of arrangements began to be used to encourage exports—the granting of export credits on concessionary terms, refunds of import duties paid on materials imported for use in the production of exports, certain fiscal measures (including tax refunds and rebates), and export subsidies. A number of countries supported exports through export bonus schemes, whereby exports were granted import entitlements; these arrangements were, in many respects, similar to the retention quotas employed earlier by some of the industrial countries, discussed in the preceding chapter. While in some countries these techniques for exports were introduced as an alternative to other practices, in many countries they supplemented restrictions already in force.

Although many of the developing countries requested and received assistance from the Fund in order to avoid intensification of exchange restrictions, some, in an attempt to avoid undue pressure on their exchange rates and drains on their reserves, did intensify restrictions. In sum, while the industrial countries were able to maintain their external economic relations with few limitations on the acquisition or use of foreign exchange, many of the developing countries continued to rely on restrictions, sometimes in combination with multiple exchange rates. Possibly worst of all, in some of the developing countries restrictions seemed so entrenched as to offer little prospect of rapid removal.

As the Fund explored the trade and payments problems of the developing countries in greater depth, it increasingly recognized that there was no simple solution for the continuing restrictions of these countries. Their situations were very diverse. Many were primarily dependent on the export of a few commodities to provide the imports which accounted for a large part of their consumption and investment, but others had already achieved a high degree of self-sufficiency. Some were faced with serious population pressures, whereas others were able to absorb a fairly large number of immigrants. In many, export products were subject to wide price fluctuations, which made the determination of the prospective profitability of investment uncertain and the maintenance of balance of payments equilibrium difficult. Many had attained internal financial stability, but for a few inflation was almost endemic. By 1964, moreover, increasing international indebtedness and difficulties in servicing existing debt had added to the payments burdens of these countries.

The Fund's policies toward restrictions reflected its awareness of the complexity of the problems of developing countries. Some years earlier (in 1955) the Executive Directors, in considering the impact that the restoration of the convertibility of European currencies would have on the developing countries, had been mindful that these countries might continue to apply restrictions for a long time despite the convertibility of European currencies. Although the revision of the GATT then being discussed contemplated more lenient treatment of restrictions imposed for purposes of speeding up economic development by "countries which can only support low standards of living and are in the early stages of development," the Executive Directors of the Fund had attached significance to the fact that no such distinction had been made in the Fund's Articles, which contemplated the use of generally applicable criteria. Nonetheless, in implementing its policies, the Fund was careful to take into consideration the particular problems of individual countries; these included problems related to economic development.

The staff and the Directors, therefore, stressed alternative measures to restrictions and put considerable effort into working out specific alternatives. In brief, in its consultations with individual members and in its technical assistance, the

Fund argued against temporary expedients—such as price controls, import restrictions, currency overvaluation, multiple rates, and protectionist devices—and in favor of exchange rate adjustment, internal stabilization programs, freer trade and payments, and export promotion and diversification.

There was also, by the 1960's, an enhanced appreciation by the Fund that financial problems—in which the Fund is necessarily most directly interested—account for only part of the difficulties of the developing countries. The Fund recognized, for example, that the search for broader solutions to their trade and payments problems had to include action by the industrial countries: industrial nations had to maintain a high level of economic activity and to reduce their own trade barriers, both tariff and nontariff restraints, against imports from developing countries, as well as export capital to the developing nations.[15]

NEED TO RESTRAIN CAPITAL MOVEMENTS

The second problem of the mid-1960's concerned the massive revival of capital movements among the industrial countries which took place once European currencies had become convertible and restrictions on these movements had been eased. Prior to the late 1950's any capital movements that might have been induced by international monetary developments, such as the emergence of differences in interest rates between countries, had been restrained by restrictions or by special exchange rates applied to capital transfers. But by the early 1960's, either differential interest rates or the prospect of a change in the foreign exchange value of any leading currency—or even political changes—tended to cause large movements of capital. Transfers of short-term capital, in particular, became large and frequent. As these short-term capital movements were often speculative and disequilibrating, they presented the financial authorities, especially in industrial countries, with new problems. Sterling, for example, from time to time in the 1960's was subjected to severe strains in the world's exchange markets, at least partly because of rather sharp movements of short-term capital. For a while in 1962, severe pressures on Canada's balance of payments could be traced mainly to capital flows. The unexpected magnitudes of capital flows from the United States were also responsible in part for the emergence and persistence of a sizable deficit in the balance of payments of that country.

These disturbing occurrences often necessitated official intervention—sometimes on a large scale—to enable countries to maintain their exchange rates within the margins specified in the Articles of Agreement. In order to avoid impairing the freedom already allowed to foreign payments, large amounts of reserves were utilized. There was heavy resort to the Fund. New forms of cooperation arose among the monetary authorities of the industrial countries,

[15] *Annual Report, 1963*, p. 71, and *1964*, pp. 68–69.

including mutual assistance to support each other's currencies and the setting up in the Fund of the General Arrangements to Borrow (GAB).[16]

Despite these arrangements, the principal industrial countries had, by 1964, to take special measures to curb capital flows. On September 2 of that year, the United States enacted a tax to be applied to purchases by U.S. residents of foreign stocks and bonds. Only a relatively few transactions—such as direct investments, investments in less developed countries, purchases of stocks and bonds from other U.S. holders, and purchases of Canadian stocks and bonds— were exempted. In February 1965, this tax was extended to bank loans with a maturity of one year or more made to residents of countries other than the developing countries; and still later, the tax was further extended to nonbank lending of one to three years' maturity. The United States also introduced a voluntary program to discourage capital exports by banks and other financial institutions.

As part of a series of steps to correct its balance of payments in 1964–65, the United Kingdom made changes in its exchange control regulations affecting capital movements. These included making slightly more stringent the criteria for the use of official exchange for direct investment outside the sterling area, and a strengthening of controls on travel expenditure so as to prevent evasion of the controls on capital movements.

True, the major industrial countries, while resorting to controls on capital movements, had avoided recourse to restrictions on current payments and transfers. Nonetheless, as 1965 came to a close there were evidences of continuing difficulties in the international monetary system. Some searching questions were being asked. Was there a risk that the large trading nations would go their own separate ways, introducing controls as needed? Might not the international monetary system thus even "collapse"? How could the functioning of the international monetary system best be improved? Would the introduction into the system of new liquidity solve the problems arising from capital movements? Should some procedure be arranged for enhancing the flexibility of exchange rates?

Debates on these, and similar questions, become more intensive after 1965, when the United Kingdom and the United States further tightened controls on capital movements and when other industrial countries—for example, France—began to reinstitute controls on capital movements.

---

[16] See below, pp. 375–76.

14

The Retreat of Bilateralism

Margaret G. de Vries

WHEN THE MACHINERY for international monetary cooperation was being set up in 1943 and 1944, bilateral trade and payments agreements were not as extensively used as they were later to be. During the interwar period, these kinds of agreement had been employed mainly by Germany and by countries in Central and Eastern Europe.[1] However, because bilateral agreements had been manipulated so as to promote exports, and hence domestic employment, and to protect agriculture and manufacturing industries against imports that threatened to increase domestic unemployment, bilateral agreements had come to be regarded as synonymous with aggressive commercial policies. Another difficulty with bilateral agreements, as revealed by earlier international experiences, was that imports might be curtailed in order to force the partner to repay past debts.[2] A few economists, anticipating in the postwar period the widespread unemployment that had prevailed before the war, were fearful that bilateralism might become more prevalent.[3] Consequently, one of the major purposes of the Fund, as noted in Chapter 2, is to assist in the establishment of a multilateral system of payments in respect of current transactions between members.

THE EXTENSION OF BILATERALISM

RAPID SPREAD AFTER WORLD WAR II

Because virtually all non-dollar countries had balance of payments difficulties in the late 1940's and early 1950's, bilateral payments arrangements spread more rapidly and became much more widespread than in the 1930's. Such arrangements provided a mechanism by which the partner countries could effect their

---

[1] The bilateral arrangements of the interwar period are described in Margaret S. Gordon, *Barriers to World Trade*, and Howard S. Ellis, *Exchange Control in Central Europe*.

[2] See, for example, Henry J. Tasca, *World Trading Systems*, Chaps. IX and X.

[3] See, for example, Howard S. Ellis, *Bilateralism and the Future of International Trade*.

reciprocal current settlements with a minimum use of convertible exchange and gold. In a typical case, the two central banks opened accounts in their respective currencies in each other's name, and all permitted payments were channeled through these agreement accounts; settlements in convertible currencies or gold had to be made only for balances within limits agreed in advance, that is, for amounts specified in what were called the "swing." [4]

The models for postwar payments agreements were the Belgo-Dutch (1943) and the Anglo-Belgian (1944) agreements.[5] Toward the end of 1944, the United Kingdom started negotiations with a number of continental countries with a view to the signing of payments agreements. Several of these were concluded between October 1944 and May 1946, with—in chronological order—Belgium, Sweden, France, Denmark, the Netherlands, Czechoslovakia, Norway, Switzerland, and Portugal.

What happened to the number of agreements into which Switzerland entered serves as an illustration. At no time before World War II did Switzerland have more than 14 clearing systems in force; but in 1945 and 1946 alone Switzerland signed 12 new payments agreements, and by the end of May 1947 it had 19 such agreements. Other countries had similar experiences. By the end of 1946 France was already a partner to 20 payments agreements, Belgium to 17, and the Netherlands to 14. By June 1947, the number of bilateral payments agreements in effect was estimated at 200.[6]

Shortly thereafter came a further series of agreements by the United Kingdom. While using bilateral payments agreements after the war, the United Kingdom had at first made little use of bilateral trade agreements. However, following the failure to establish sterling convertibility in mid-1947, it concluded bilateral trade agreements with countries with which it already had payments agreements. In 1948, Germany started to enter into trade and payments agreements with Latin American countries. Also in 1948, the Supreme Commander for Allied Powers in Japan embarked on a policy of bilateralism. A number of agreements were concluded between Japan and European countries, followed in 1949 by the first series of trade and payments agreements between Japan and Latin American countries.

In addition, in the late 1940's European countries rounded out their systems of agreements by concluding agreements with their smaller European trading

[4] The main features of postwar bilateral payments agreements, their purposes, and how they operated, are described in considerable detail by Johan H. C. de Looper in "Current Usage of Payments Agreements and Trade Agreements," *Staff Papers*, Vol. IV (1954–55), at pp. 339–50.

[5] The contrast between the type of bilateral agreements used after World War II and those used earlier is described by J. W. Beyen in *Money in a Maelstrom*. The genesis and spread of postwar agreements is recounted by Judd Polk and Gardner Patterson in "The Emerging Pattern of Bilateralism," *Quarterly Journal of Economics*, Vol. 62 (1947–48), pp. 118–42.

[6] Bank for International Settlements, *Seventeenth Annual Report* (Basle, 1947), p. 75.

partners. The establishment of the sovereign states of Israel in 1948 and Indonesia in 1949 also led to a series of bilateral payments agreements.

Similarly, the number of payments agreements of the Latin American countries gradually became larger than the number of agreements which they had had before World War II. European countries arranged a number of payments agreements with those Latin American countries that were *not* in the dollar area— that is, with Argentina, Brazil, Paraguay, and Uruguay. (The dollar area included the Republics of Central America and the Caribbean, and Bolivia, Chile, Colombia, Ecuador, Mexico, Peru, and Venezuela.) European countries were also anxious to enter into payments agreements with Latin American countries that *were* in the dollar area, as these enabled European countries to purchase, for inconvertible currencies, commodities for which they previously had been paying dollars, and facilitated their exports to these countries. The Latin American countries in the dollar area, in turn, were induced to enter into agreements with European countries in order to overcome the effects of discriminatory import licensing in countries with inconvertible currencies, and thus to recapture or to expand markets in Europe. European countries tended to discriminate against any Latin American country that did not enter into a payments agreement, particularly with regard to commodities which the former were able to obtain without financial problems from their dependent or associated territories. There were relatively few intra-Latin American bilateral trade and payments agreements.[7]

Not only did inconvertibility and the virtually universal existence of balance of payments deficits induce the onset of so many bilateral agreements, but bilateralism, once started, tended to generate more bilateralism. Once a number of important payments agreements had been signed, countries had an incentive to conclude additional agreements. First, because of the "swing" arrangements, bilateral agreements offered a means of obtaining or giving a tied credit. Second, countries that already had payments agreements adopted import licensing techniques and policies discriminating against the dollar area and favoring their bilateral payments and trade agreement partners; hence rather than be discriminated against, even some countries in the dollar area became partners to new agreements.

Dimension of the problem by 1954

At the end of 1954, the Fund began to take measures to reduce the use of bilateral agreements by its members. At the time, over 400 bilateral payments and similar arrangements were believed to be in force. Of these, approximately

---

[7] Latin America's bilateral arrangements after World War II are described by Johan H. C. de Looper in "Recent Latin American Experience with Bilateral Trade and Payments Agreements," *Staff Papers*, Vol. IV (1954–55), pp. 85–112.

235 were between pairs of European countries. Next in numerical importance was the network of approximately 100 agreements between European and Latin American countries. European countries also had about 60 agreements with countries in the Middle East and the Far East. Finally, a much smaller number of intraregional agreements existed within Latin America and among the Middle Eastern and Far Eastern countries. At least 18 countries were maintaining 15 or more bilateral payments agreements each: Argentina, Belgium-Luxembourg, Brazil, Denmark, Egypt, Finland, France, Germany, Greece, Israel, Italy, Japan, the Netherlands, Spain, Turkey, Uruguay, and Yugoslavia.

The number of agreements alone is not, however, a sufficient measure of their importance. The estimated amount of trade affected is perhaps even more indicative. The total value of exports in 1954 by members of the Fund with countries with which they had bilateral agreements reached $6.4 billion, which was about 8.5 per cent of aggregate world exports. For some individual countries, the significance of bilateralism for their exports was much higher. Over half of the exports of Argentina, Brazil, China, Egypt, Finland, Uruguay, and Yugoslavia were conducted with countries with which they had bilateral agreements. From one quarter to one half of the exports of Chile, Iceland, Indonesia, Iran, Israel, Japan, Korea, Spain, and Turkey, and from 10 to 25 per cent of the exports of another 15 countries—including several large ones in Western Europe (Austria, Denmark, France, Germany, Italy, the Netherlands, and Norway)—were with bilateral partners.

At the end of 1954, 41 out of the 56 members of the Fund conducted at least 10 per cent of their exports under bilateral arrangements. Much of the trade between Western European countries and the Soviet bloc in Eastern Europe was still conducted bilaterally, as well as a large part of the trade between Western Europe and Latin America and a substantial part of the trade between Latin America and Asia.

On the other hand, there was evidence that some bilateral arrangements tended to be construed less strictly. European countries had developed techniques to widen the scope of their payments arrangements. Although the United Kingdom had been a partner to many bilateral agreements, these usually gave the partner access to the whole sterling area. The existence of the sizable sterling area, the wide international use of sterling, although inconvertible, for financing trade and payments between countries unwilling or unable to finance their trade or payments in dollars, and the widening transferability of sterling, accordingly made the payments agreements of the United Kingdom much more plurilateral than bilateral.

In addition, with the establishment in 1950 of the European Payments Union (EPU),[8] the payments agreements between pairs of participating European coun-

---

[8] See Chapter 15 below.

tries were left with nothing but a technical function.[9] Since all member currencies had become transferable among EPU members, they were all equally "hard"
(or "soft") to any one of them. In these circumstances, while some European
countries were concluding new bilateral payments agreements, the general
tendency after 1953 was for the important trading countries to place a decreasing reliance upon bilateralism.

PROPITIOUS CIRCUMSTANCES FOR FUND ACTION

Not only had European countries, by 1954, decreased their reliance on bilateral
agreements, but other circumstances were also propitious for the Fund to take
action against bilateralism. By 1953–54, the balance of payments positions of
the European countries vis-à-vis their bilateral partners outside Europe, including
Latin America, the Middle East, and the Far East, had become very different
from that immediately after the war. Whereas earlier the Latin American and
other countries had acquired substantial balances of European currencies, especially sterling, and their inability to convert these currencies had given them a
strong incentive to form bilateral arrangements with Europe, by 1953–54 accumulated balances had been used up.

Additionally, there were limits to the amount of bilateral credits that European
countries were willing to grant to countries outside Europe. When these limits
were reached, their bilateral partners had either to restrict imports under their
agreements or to pay acceptable currencies, such as U.S. dollars. When bilateral
credit margins were exhausted and settlements with the bilateral partner had
to be made in dollars, the inducement on the part of countries outside Europe
to discriminate against dollar imports through bilateral agreements with European countries was greatly reduced.

At the same time, the more liberal trade policies emerging in Western Europe,
as described in Chapter 12, made less acceptable the artificial and noncompetitive
prices which frequently had to be paid for the commodities which the European
countries imported under bilateral agreements. Many creditor countries started
to restrict their exports, and sometimes refused to convert export proceeds into
local currency. Furthermore, the reduced scope of government purchasing and
the relaxation of restrictions on imports into certain countries increased the
difficulties of operating some payments agreements.[10] Bilateral agreement currencies were being sold at discounts in an effort to evade the strict bilateral
balancing of accounts.[11]

---

[9] European experience with trade and payments agreements prior to the EPU is described
in William Diebold, *Trade and Payments in Western Europe.*

[10] The ways in which it gradually become more difficult for countries to operate bilateral
agreements are spelled out in *Fifth Annual Report on Exchange Restrictions* (1954), pp. 17–18.

[11] See Barend A. de Vries and F. A. G. Keesing, "The Use of Bilateral Agreement Currencies
for Trade with Third Countries," *Staff Papers,* Vol. V (1956–57), pp. 170–79.

All these developments had begun to reduce the flow of trade taking place under bilateral arrangements.

At the same time, it could not be assumed that bilateralism would come to an end easily, even though convertibility might be imminent. The Japanese authorities had, for example, already suggested to the staff of the Fund that a return to convertibility might decrease rather than increase the volume of world trade; therefore, bilateral agreements would be necessary to prevent increased unemployment. The subsequent discussion in the Executive Board on the occasion of the annual consultation with Japan had revealed that Japan was not alone in such fears. In several countries bilateral agreements had become motivated more by the desire to safeguard export industries than by balance of payments considerations.

FORMULATION OF THE FUND'S POLICY

STAFF INITIATIVE

In these circumstances the staff of the Fund, toward the end of 1954, decided that it was time to bring to the Executive Board the general issue of bilateral payments agreements. This staff action may have been prompted in part by the facts that the United Kingdom had, in June 1954, suggested to the OEEC Ministerial Group on Convertibility a concerted move by OEEC countries to abolish bilateral agreements and that the United Kingdom's paper had been accepted by the Group in September 1954 as a basis for study. But a stronger reason for the decision of the Fund staff to suggest that the Fund take action against bilateralism was that, in the improving world payments situation, bilateralism seemed to be much less warranted than it had been earlier. Even more compelling was the belief, held by some members of the staff and by some Executive Directors, that a stronger line by the Fund against bilateralism might hasten the establishment of convertibility of European currencies.

The staff first suggested a three-phase policy, the timing of which would depend on the progress made by the major countries toward the convertibility of their currencies. The first phase was to extend from 1954 until the several countries then approaching convertibility had actually taken this decisive step. In this phase, the Fund would use its annual consultations to explore in greater detail than hitherto the scope and content of bilateral agreements and the reasons for their retention. Such action, it was argued, not only might help to shorten the life of some agreements, but also would build up an important body of experience, and enable the Fund to move effectively in the following phases.

The second phase would arise if not all the main currencies became convertible. In these circumstances some of the countries whose currencies were newly convertible might be faced with new restrictions by other industrial countries, with currencies still inconvertible, which continued to practice discrimination. The former might then feel the need to enter into some bilateral agreements. The Fund would have to pay careful attention to any restrictions which it was asked to approve under Article VIII by countries opting to accept the obligations of this Article. The reasons given by countries for not making their currencies convertible would also have to be carefully scrutinized. But it was recognized that this second phase might never occur.

The third phase would be reached when the largest members of the Fund—and particularly all the industrial countries—had convertible currencies. The countries whose currencies remained inconvertible might still find it useful in certain instances to conclude bilateral agreements among themselves, but these were expected to be of minor importance in world trade. During this third phase the Fund would have to ensure that, except for such minor exceptions, bilateralism would be abandoned by all countries; its jurisdiction under Article VIII would provide it with the necessary means.

The Board had no difficulty in accepting that bilateral payments agreements, having a restrictive character and an inherent bias toward discrimination, clearly fell within the Fund's jurisdiction. However, the emphasis to be given to bilateralism was subject to considerable debate. A few Directors believed that the staff's approach, which based the need for bilateralism on the absence of convertibility and which would intensify the Fund's action against bilateralism as steps were taken toward convertibility, was too narrow. These Directors pointed to additional reasons why countries resorted to bilateralism. Primary producing countries used bilateral agreements because they had special problems in sustaining their basic exports or stabilizing their export earnings, or both. Other agreements were used to avoid or to repay commercial debts. Bilateral agreements also had a function for trade with countries which were not members of the Fund, such as state-trading countries.

The majority of Directors—including those from the United States, Canada, the United Kingdom, and Germany—believed, nonetheless, that the only practical course for the Fund was the pursuit of the aims of the Articles, including that of multilateralism. They advocated an even stronger line against bilateralism than that proposed by the staff. The Directors therefore agreed that the staff should ascertain the nature and extent of the bilateral arrangements then prevailing and draft a decision for the consideration of the Board.

Decision of 1955

The staff reported back to the Directors in May 1955. The Western European countries had been found to be in the process of multilateralizing their bilateral payments relationships by resort to transit trade, by acceptance of third currencies such as transferable sterling and transferable deutsche mark, and by granting permission to effect transfers to and from certain payments agreement partners through the accounts established under payments agreements with other countries. However, a significant measure of bilateralism remained in the Eastern European countries, the Latin American non-dollar countries, and the Far Eastern and Middle Eastern countries. The staff still related the proposed policy of the Fund to convertibility. With the attainment of convertibility of the major European currencies, the balance of payments justification for bilateralism would diminish, if not disappear. Another reason why the staff tied the proposed policy against bilateralism to the prospects for convertibility was its belief that countries with newly convertible currencies would require safeguards against the use of bilateral arrangements by other countries.

The ensuing discussion in the Executive Board revealed that many Directors did not accept the staff's view that convertibility would result in the abolition of bilateral agreements by members. These Directors feared that members would still retain bilateral agreements for commercial reasons. Since members would always defend bilateralism on balance of payments grounds, would not an emphasis by the Fund on the balance of payments justification for bilateralism in effect make all bilateralism defensible? What criteria could be used to determine a "balance of payments need"? What would be accomplished if the Fund's efforts to wipe out bilateral *payments* agreements were accompanied by an intensification of bilateral *trade* agreements? Was it not necessary for the Fund and the GATT to work together? Could not the Fund do more than merely explore with members their need to continue bilateral arrangements and the possibilities of removing these arrangements? Should not countries in surplus as well as those in deficit review their policies so as to improve the system of multilateral payments?

On the other hand, a number of Directors were concerned about too strong a push against bilateralism. They reiterated their view that the composition of the exports of a number of the less developed countries made them particularly dependent on bilateralism, and that trade with state-trading countries posed some special problems. These concerns led to the inclusion in the decision finally taken of a statement that

> in its examination of the justification for reliance on such bilateral arrangements the Fund will, without excluding other considerations, have particular regard to the payments position and prospects of the members concerned.

The decision against bilateralism was adopted in June 1955.[12] The Board strengthened the text suggested by the staff. Where, for example, the draft had called on members "eventually" to eliminate bilateral arrangements, the Board substituted "as rapidly as practicable."

---

[12] E.B. Decision No. 433-(55/42), June 22, 1955; below, Vol. III, p. 258.

The essential elements of the decision were that the Fund's policy on bilateralism was an integral part of its policy on restrictions, that the Fund urged the full collaboration of all its members to reduce, and to eliminate as rapidly as practicable, reliance on bilateralism, and that the Fund would explore with all countries which were parties to bilateral arrangements which involved the use of exchange restrictions the need for continuation of these arrangements, the possibilities of their early removal, and ways and means, including the use of the Fund's resources, by which the Fund could assist in this process. A letter from the Managing Director transmitting the decision to members indicated that bilateral payments agreements would receive special attention in the forthcoming round of Article XIV consultations; as a preparation, members were requested to review their bilateral agreements.[13]

REAFFIRMATION OF POLICY

On three subsequent occasions the Fund reaffirmed that it would persist in its efforts to secure the speedy elimination of bilateral arrangements. Further ways in which this elimination might be accomplished were made explicit.

SPECIFICATION OF IMMEDIATE GOALS

The first reaffirmation of the Fund's general policy against bilateralism came in mid-1956, when the Directors reviewed the progress that had been made since the general decision of the year before. The staff was able to report that there had been considerable progress in widening the payments arrangements under existing bilateral agreements in the intervening year. The United Kingdom and Germany had, for example, facilitated the use, under their bilateral payments agreements, of certain inconvertible currencies of third (nonpartner) countries. The "Hague Club" had been formed to multilateralize the payments relations of most Western European countries with Brazil. The "Paris Club," just being instituted, would effect virtually the same multilateralization of payments between Europe and Argentina (Chapter 12).

Nonetheless, in their consultations with the Fund several member countries were advancing a number of reasons why they had to go slowly in abolishing their bilateral arrangements. Some argued that they needed special arrangements vis-à-vis the state-trading countries of Eastern Europe. Even more common was the contention that bilateral arrangements were necessary to protect or promote exports. Some countries feared that the elimination of a bilateral agreement with a specific partner would put them at a disadvantage compared with other suppliers which still maintained preferential access to the markets of

---

[13] The letter was published in *Annual Report, 1955*, Appendix I, p. 123.

that partner. For a few countries, the inadequacy or unsatisfactory composition of foreign exchange reserves made bilateral swing credits still of some importance. For one or two others, bilateral agreements were the means for the gradual unfreezing of capital claims.

In these circumstances the staff proposed, and the Board agreed, that during the 1956 round of consultations the Fund should continue to press the issue of bilateralism. Specific goals were to be the termination of those bilateral arrangements which no longer seemed essential; the renegotiation of unnecessarily restrictive or discriminatory agreements; the replacement of bilateral swing credits by other forms of credit, including the Fund's resources; and the abandonment of bilateralism as the use of transferable currencies became possible. It was also agreed that, where the situations so merited, the Fund would make a simultaneous approach to two or more member countries, perhaps through their Executive Directors, to end a particular agreement.

THE POLICY FURTHER ELABORATED

Some three and a half years later, in October 1959, the Fund's policy on bilateralism was again restated. The occasion was the decision on discrimination for balance of payments reasons (Chapter 13). By then bilateral payments agreements had been considerably reduced, and in the Western European countries virtually eliminated except for those with state-trading nations. It had become the Fund's view that there was no longer any justification for bilateral agreements between countries having externally convertible currencies. However, several countries—although by no means all—were still using bilateral payments agreements for trade with Soviet bloc countries, and with other state-trading countries, most of which were not members of the Fund.

This situation called for a new elaboration of the Fund's policy. The original decision in 1955 had not differentiated those bilateral payments agreements arranged between two members of the Fund from those agreements arranged by a Fund member with a nonmember. This distinction had now become important. The Board decision on discrimination of October 1959, therefore, clarified the Fund's position on bilateral payments agreements between members and nonmembers. Member countries were expected to proceed with all feasible speed to eliminate discrimination against other members, including discrimination arising from bilateralism. However, some concession was thought necessary regarding the bilateral arrangements of members of the Fund with nonmembers. For such arrangements the Fund stated that it would be "prepared to consider whether balance of payments considerations would justify the maintenance of some degree of discrimination, although not as between countries having externally convertible currencies." [14]

[14] E.B. Decision No. 955-(59/45), October 23, 1959; below, Vol. III, p. 260. .

This specification represented an elaboration—not a change—in the Fund's attitude toward bilateral payments arrangements. As expressed by the Chairman of the Executive Board at the time, the statement being made by the Fund in 1959 was that those members still engaging in bilateralism should be mindful of the fact that many other members had been able to eliminate reliance on bilateralism, and aware also of their obligation not to harm the interests of other members of the Fund by their bilateral arrangements, including those with nonmembers.

At the same time the Fund would not concern itself directly with bilateral payments agreements with nonmembers; the 1959 decision did not condemn such agreements. Rather, stress was laid on the *discrimination against other members of the Fund* that might be involved in any bilateral arrangements with nonmembers. The question whether bilateral agreements with state-trading countries did or did not actually involve discrimination against members remained open and, as discussed below, was to come up on various occasions in the next few years.

The third occasion on which the general problem of bilateralism was reviewed by the Executive Board was in June 1960, when the Board determined the conditions necessary for a country to accept the obligations of Article VIII (Chapter 13). Bilateralism was specifically covered by the preamble to the decision on Articles VIII and XIV, which states that

> previous decisions taken by the Fund, such as those on multiple currency practices, bilateral arrangements, discriminatory restrictions maintained for balance of payments purposes, and payments restrictions for security reasons, indicate the Fund's attitude on these matters.[15]

It was further agreed that bilateral payments agreements were included as "measures" in the statement in paragraph 2 of that decision:

> As regards measures requiring approval under Article VIII and maintained or introduced for nonbalance of payments reasons, the Fund believes that the use of exchange systems for nonbalance of payments reasons should be avoided to the greatest possible extent, and is prepared to consider with members the ways and means of achieving the elimination of such measures as soon as possible.[16]

Even more significant was the consensus of the Directors that, because bilateral payments agreements involved both restrictions and discrimination, members should have eliminated all such arrangements before moving to Article VIII status, or should be prepared to get rid of them within a stated time, e.g., at the expiry of the current agreement.

---

[15] E.B. Decision No. 1034-(60/27), June 1, 1960; below, Vol. III, p. 260.
[16] *Ibid.*

IMPLEMENTATION OF POLICY

The general policy of the Fund against bilateral payments agreements, like other policies of the Fund, has been implemented on a case-by-case basis. In particular, as countries consulted the Fund under Article XIV, the Fund has been able to apply the above pronouncements to specific country situations. Since 1955 the reports on the staff's discussions with member countries have regularly contained descriptions of bilateral payments agreements, the results of the discussions pertaining to bilateralism between the representatives of the member government and the staff, and a staff appraisal of the possibilities of ending any bilateralism still remaining.

The Executive Board decisions in Article XIV consultations have also usually included recommendations as regards the member's bilateral payments agreements. During 1964 and 1965, for example, out of 62 countries for which Article XIV consultations were concluded, 42 had some bilateral agreements; of these the Fund made recommendations on bilateralism to 27. The countries for which no recommendations were made were mainly those with only one or two agreements, sometimes involving an element of doubt about whether the arrangements could be considered as bilateral payments agreements, and sometimes covering a negligible volume of transactions. There were also a few countries which had agreements only with nonmembers and these were not important in terms of the total amount of trade.

The recommendations made to members have varied, depending on the number of agreements, the proportion of trade financed under them, the possibility of alternative outlets for exports, the degree of discrimination practiced on the import side, and the size of the accumulation of inconvertible balances. Consideration has also been given to the measures which the government was taking to deal with the problems which gave rise to the reliance on bilateralism. When there were objectionable features in the exchange systems—for example, an unrealistic exchange rate supported by heavy dependence on restrictions— the recommendations have frequently put major emphasis on these factors, and the removal of bilateralism has been linked to the need for more fundamental reform. Where progress has already been made in removing bilateral agreements, the recommendation for further action has been less forceful.

A second way in which the Fund's general policy on bilateralism has been implemented is through the exercise of the Fund's powers of approval under Article VIII. As countries have assumed the obligations of Article VIII, additional pressure has been applied. When the European countries began to undertake the obligations of Article VIII in the early 1960's, the number of bilateral payments agreements which they still retained were few, and these agreements no longer reflected inconvertibility or balance of payments problems. The arrangements being maintained between Belgium-Luxembourg and the Congo, Rwanda, and Burundi, and those between the Netherlands and Indonesia, for example, were outgrowths of past relations with former overseas territories. When Belgium and the Netherlands accepted Article VIII obligations, the Fund approved these agreements.

When discussing members' plans to move to Article VIII, the Fund also reviewed the bilateral payments arrangements maintained by some of these countries with nonmembers. Austria, Belgium-Luxembourg, France, Italy, the Netherlands, and Sweden all argued that their bilateral arrangements with non-members did not result in restrictions or discrimination against any member of the Fund. Sweden argued that its payments arrangements were, in fact, sup-plementary to parallel bilateral trade agreements, and that most imports from nonmembers were subject to licensing requirements while most imports of similar goods from other countries were free from such requirements. As a consequence, there was no mechanism by which the authorities could favor imports from bilateral countries to the detriment of imports from Fund members.

Still a third way in which the Fund has implemented its policy on bilateralism has been through stand-by arrangements. These arrangements have involved commitments to carry out the Fund's policy regarding the use of bilateral agree-ments; however, in all but those exceptional cases where bilateral payments agreements have dominated the restrictive system, commitments concerning bilateralism have been of the second order of priority and not central elements in the program for which the stand-by arrangement was granted.[17] Frequently the Fund has expected that general programs for achieving internal and external equilibrium would ensure a substantial improvement in the balance of payments and would, in due course, permit elimination of undesirable restrictive practices, including bilateral agreements.

By the end of 1965, the Executive Board had approved 167 stand-by arrange-ments with 50 governments; 104 of these had been concluded with 37 member countries maintaining bilateral payments agreements, some of which still had several agreements. There had also been 31 letters of intent from 17 countries, submitted in support of requests for stand-by arrangements, which contained specific policy statements regarding bilateral payments agreements. Some of these stated the government's intent to eliminate bilateral agreements "shortly" or within a specified time period; more stated "as soon as possible," or words to that effect. In 1965 two stand-by arrangements had "binding commitments" on bilateralism; many have included binding commitments with respect to the introduction of exchange restrictions, which have thus inhibited the introduction of bilateral agreements.

---

[17] The provisions of stand-by arrangements are described below in Chapter 20.

BILATERALISM DUE TO INCONVERTIBILITY DIMINISHED

Well before the end of 1965 the use of those bilateral payments agreements which stemmed from the inconvertibility of major currencies had all but disappeared. This elimination of bilateralism had come in surges. By the mid-1950's, European bilateralism was on the wane. The establishment of the "Hague Club" and the "Paris Club" in 1955 and 1956 led soon after to the elimination of a group of bilateral agreements between Brazil and Argentina, on the one side, and European countries on the other. By the late 1950's other Latin American countries had also reduced their agreements. The remaining European bilateralism had greatly diminished as the countries moved to Article VIII status in 1960 and 1961.

Statistically, by the end of 1964 more than 80 per cent of the total number of bilateral payments agreements that had been in effect in 1955 when the Fund's decision was taken had been abolished. The number of agreements abandoned by individual countries was impressively large. From 1955 to 1964 Argentina, Belgium-Luxembourg, Finland, Germany, Italy, Japan, the Netherlands, and Uruguay eliminated 15 or more agreements each; and at least 6 agreements each were given up by a number of other countries, including Brazil, Chile, Denmark, Norway, Paraguay, Spain, Sweden, and Turkey.

Looked at more generally, rather than in terms of the number of agreements that individual countries had given up, in 1955 some 165 bilateral payments agreements were maintained by those 26 countries that had, by the end of 1964, accepted the obligations of the Fund's Article VIII; but by the end of 1964 these countries had only 16 such agreements. In other words, they had eliminated over 90 per cent of their agreements. The agreements still remaining were maintained by only 7 of the 26 countries concerned, 4 of which had agreements exclusively with state-trading countries. Taking the whole of the Fund's membership into account, by the end of 1964 more than one third had no bilateral payments agreements at all and nearly one half had no agreements with other members of the Fund.

The value of exports being conducted under bilateral payments agreements had, of course, also fallen—by about one half between 1954 and 1964—so that only 2 per cent of world exports, instead of 8.5 per cent, was involved.

Usually a country gave up its bilateral payments agreements prior to assuming Article VIII status. But in a few instances agreements were maintained which were eliminated later. For example, in 1964 France and Japan gave up the last of their agreements and Sweden ended two of its remaining agreements.

The elimination in 1965 of an agreement between Argentina and Uruguay left only two intra-Latin American agreements. One of these, between Bolivia and Brazil, was little used in practice; however, a new one between Mexico and Argentina had come into effect.

CONTINUED RELIANCE ON BILATERALISM BY LESS DEVELOPED COUNTRIES

Despite the sharp drop in the use of bilateral payments agreements, especially by Western European countries, Japan, and Latin American countries, some other less developed countries have continued to arrange bilateral payments agreements, especially among themselves. A tendency to conclude bilateral payments agreements, even though little trade was covered, has been particularly prevalent among the newly independent countries in Africa. In addition, many less developed countries still conduct much of their trade with state-trading countries under bilateral arrangements.

As a result, the total *number* of bilateral payments agreements in the world declined little from 1954 to 1964. While four fifths of the agreements that had been in effect in 1954 had disappeared by 1964, many new agreements had come into being, and in December 1964 there were still 322 agreements in force. The number of bilateral payments agreements within Africa (including those of the United Arab Republic) had risen from nil to 20; and the number of agreements between African countries and state-trading countries had increased from 7 to 81. No agreements had been signed between African countries and Latin American countries or the European countries that had moved to Article VIII.

As did the African countries, so less developed countries in other regions entered into new bilateral agreements. A number of such countries (for example, Ceylon, India, Portugal, Spain, and the Syrian Arab Republic) which had had no agreements with state-trading countries in 1954, subsequently concluded several. At the end of 1964, seven Fund members—Brazil, Ghana, Guinea, Mali, Spain, the United Arab Republic, and Yugoslavia—still had 15 or more bilateral payments agreements each.

The implications of these agreements for the volume of trade conducted under bilateral arrangements were not uniform among the countries concerned. Many of the countries that had joined the Fund after 1954 and that had entered into new bilateral payments agreements had previously used the payments arrangements provided by their metropolitan centers in Europe, which, except for the United Kingdom, had been using some bilateral agreements in 1954. Hence, many of the new agreements of the African countries—e.g., those of Algeria, Burundi, Cameroon, the Central African Republic, Congo (Brazzaville), Dahomey, Laos, Mauritania, Niger, Senegal, Somalia, and Tunisia—did not necessarily involve an expansion of bilaterally conducted trade.

For other countries, however, including Afghanistan, Ceylon, Ghana, Guinea, India, Jordan, Mali, Morocco, the Syrian Arab Republic, and Upper Volta, trade under bilateralism had risen sharply. Most important of all, in 1964 more than

25 per cent of the total exports of some nine countries—Afghanistan, Greece, Guinea, Korea, Mali, the Syrian Arab Republic, the United Arab Republic, Upper Volta, and Yugoslavia—were still being sold to bilateral partners.

CHANGED CHARACTER OF BILATERALISM

This marked change in the *distribution* of bilateral agreements from early 1955 to late 1964—which was to have implications for the Fund's policies—is shown in Table 9. While there was a reduction of one half in the arrangements between Fund members, bilateral payments agreements between members of the Fund and nonmembers (primarily state-trading countries) rose by more

Table 9. Bilateral Payments Agreements Maintained by
Fund Members in 1955 and 1964

	Number of Agreements	
	April 1955	December 1964
Agreements with other members	189	95
Agreements with nonmembers	146	227
Total	335	322

than 50 per cent. Agreements with nonmembers, which had constituted 44 per cent of the total number of agreements in April 1955, had become 70 per cent of the total remaining agreements in December 1964.

The important increase in bilateral payments agreements between members of the Fund and state-trading countries had to some extent been the result of new agreements with state-trading countries by Western European countries. But to a much larger extent it had been the less developed members in Africa, Asia, and the Middle East that had been partners to the new agreements. A few statistics suggest the magnitudes involved. At the end of 1964, bilateral payments agreements between European members of the Fund—which here include Cyprus—and state-trading countries totaled 74; eight European members—Austria, Cyprus, Finland, Greece, Iceland, Spain, Turkey, and Yugoslavia—each maintained more than 5 agreements apiece. Less developed countries elsewhere had some 140 agreements with state-trading countries. Several of these countries—Algeria, Brazil, Ceylon, Colombia, Ghana, Guinea, India, Morocco, Tunisia, and the United Arab Republic—still maintained a number of agreements.

REASONS FOR PERSISTENCE OF BILATERALISM

The Fund's consultations with members have revealed three main reasons why the less developed countries have continued, in the 1960's, to arrange bilateral agreements despite the absence of a currency convertibility problem such as had prevailed in the 1950's.

First, one of the principal motivations impelling the less developed countries to enter into bilateral payments agreements has been their need to promote additional exports of primary products. Brazil, Ceylon, Colombia, Ghana, India, and the United Arab Republic, for example, have maintained agreements to boost sales of coffee, cocoa, tea, or cotton. Certain countries—for instance, Denmark, Finland, Spain, Yugoslavia, and most state-trading countries—purchased coffee under bilateral arrangements as late as 1964–65. Since many of the producing countries have exportable supplies in excess of their quotas under the International Coffee Agreement, since attempts to reach an international commodity agreement for cocoa have been unsuccessful, and since storage is costly and has inflationary implications, the pressure on exporters of primary products, such as coffee and cocoa, to enter into bilateral arrangements has been strong.

The main argument of Fund members which have been relying on bilateral arrangements with state-trading countries has been that sales to these countries must be made bilaterally because commodities such as coffee and cocoa are given low priority in the plans of state-trading nations. But the member governments concerned have also argued that to open up important new markets by fostering changes in consumption patterns in these countries will make easier of solution the structural problem of excess supplies of primary products in world markets. Moreover, imports from bilateral partners, even if obtained on unfavorable terms, are considered a net gain to the economies of the less developed countries so long as these countries are themselves unable to produce the kind of products imported. In other words, as long as the factors of production are fairly immobile, and in particular cannot be moved out of the major export industries, less developed countries have considered bilaterally conducted trade as useful for disposing of surplus exports in return for needed imports.

The magnitudes involved in such bilateral trade, although marginal, have not been unimportant. In 1964, for example, Brazil and Colombia, which together accounted for about 60 per cent of world exports of coffee, sold 9 per cent and 7 per cent, respectively, of their total exports to countries with which they had bilateral agreements; and Brazil and Ghana, which accounted for almost half of the world's cocoa exports, sold about 20 per cent of their cocoa exports under such agreements. Exports of tea by Ceylon and India under bilateral agreements, however, involved less than 3 per cent of India's exports of tea in 1964 and less than 2 per cent of Ceylon's.

A second reason for prolonged bilateralism, according to the authorities of a number of Fund members, is to assist the minor exports of the less developed countries. Some less developed countries have argued that they need the special export arrangements provided by bilateralism because of the trade barriers against their products, especially nontariff restrictions, prevailing in several industrial nations of the West. The Tunisian and Jordanian authorities have, for example, used bilateral agreements for exports of phosphates. Chilean nitrates have also been exported bilaterally, as have fruits, nuts, and tobacco by a number of Mediterranean countries. A few of the less developed countries which have traditionally sold manufactured goods to markets in state-trading countries have financed that trade through bilateral agreements in an effort to avoid the difficult processes of finding alternative markets or of shifting productive factors.

Finally, the increased use of bilateral arrangements to finance mutual trade among the less developed countries has reflected the desire, partly for political reasons, for some type of regional cooperation. Not only have agreements been fostered by the central banks concerned with international payments, and by the trade ministries interested in promoting exports, but the ministries of foreign affairs of the countries concerned have often also urged bilateral agreements in order to foster political or diplomatic ties between countries. Thus, for several of the less developed countries bilateral payments agreements have been only one part of a complex of arrangements.

FUND'S REACTION TO CONTINUED BILATERALISM

The Fund's general policy decisions of 1955–60 foreshadowed the changing character of bilateralism, and hence have continued to be relevant to the altered circumstances. Thus the Fund has continued to try to reduce the use of bilateral agreements by individual members when annual consultations have been undertaken and when stand-by arrangements have been agreed.

STRESSING DISCRIMINATION AGAINST MEMBERS

Immediately after the Board's decision on discrimination in October 1959, the Fund's primary concern as regards the bilateral agreements of some of its members with state-trading countries centered on the possible harm to other members. The Directors, however, had differing opinions about whether the agreements of Fund members with state-trading countries really did discriminate against other members of the Fund.

The Board's concern with such agreements may be illustrated by its discussion in 1960 of the agreements maintained by Ceylon. These were all with nonmembers and affected mainly food items imported by the Government. The most important agreement was with mainland China; under this agreement, the two countries had undertaken to import certain items up to specified quotas and to endeavor to keep the balance of trade and payments between them as nearly equated as possible. Mr. Jayarajan (Ceylon), Alternate to Mr. Watanabe, stated that his Government believed that the bilateral agreements of Ceylon with state-trading countries did not conflict with the Fund's objectives; in particular, these agreements did not contain any discriminatory features. Ceylon's view was that bilateral trade agreements continued to be the only way in which Ceylon could maintain and foster trade with state-trading countries until these countries were willing to pay for their imports in convertible currencies.

Both Lord Cromer (United Kingdom) and Mr. Southard (United States), nonetheless, had reservations about the inoffensiveness of these agreements. In their view, some kind of *de facto* discrimination against private traders might well arise from these arrangements. Bilateral agreements of this type, they thought, gave rise to discrimination against other members of the Fund by requiring Ceylon to import from partner countries certain quantities of goods which could not therefore be imported from other countries. Mr. Southard wished to retain in the Board's decision on the consultation with Ceylon a sentence urging Ceylon to re-examine the need for its bilateral agreements. Mr. Jayarajan argued against the inclusion of this sentence on the grounds that, as there had been no increase in the scope of bilateralism since the previous year's consultation, and as no mention of Ceylon's bilateralism had then been made, it was unnecessary for the Fund to say anything now. After considerable discussion, in which it was noted that Ceylon had declared its willingness to re-examine its agreements, the Directors agreed on a sentence for the decision as follows: "The Fund notes the intention of Ceylon to keep under review its bilateral trade and payments arrangements, especially as to their possible discriminatory aspects."

EMPHASIZING THE COSTS OF BILATERALISM

In more recent years the Fund has taken special pains to point out to the individual countries concerned the economic disadvantages likely to flow from bilateral agreements. In general the Fund has conceded that, in the short run, such agreements often seem to achieve the objectives sought, which may include economizing convertible exchange, seeking more outlets for traditional exports or opening up markets for new ones (e.g., manufactures produced by emerging industries), or merely postponing settlements in convertible currencies until swing credits are overdrawn. The Fund has stressed, however, that in the longer run serious drawbacks become apparent where an attempt is made to divert trade into new channels. The most common and most obvious one is that it is difficult to find in the partner country a sufficient variety of goods of the right qualities, at attractive prices, and on acceptable delivery terms, to avoid a one-way development of the clearing account to the point where an excessive bilateral claim arises. Thus, less developed countries may find themselves granting credits which they cannot afford, rather than receiving them; alternatively, trade under the agreement may stagnate.

A less apparent drawback that the Fund has pointed out is that, in the longer run, bilateralism actually tends to harm the exports of a less developed country. Exports effected bilaterally may cause upward pressures on prices, wages, and costs; or may distort the structure of domestic production. What is more, the Fund has argued, the other party to the bilateral agreement may well experience similarly adverse economic effects, and is likely to feel obliged to maintain more discriminatory trade and exchange policies than would be required in the absence of the agreement.[18]

The Fund has often pointed out to members that it is doubtful that imports by other Fund members of products such as cocoa and coffee are determined by the availability of bilateral financial arrangements or by preferential access to the import markets of the producing countries. Such small amounts of trade are involved, so the Fund's argument has run, that they could readily be handled on a convertible basis. As regards sales to state-trading countries, the Fund has also noted that the actual increase in exports by primary producers may be exaggerated; time and again evidence has been found of substantial re-exports of these commodities by state-trading countries to established markets, often with unfavorable effect on the prices of the commodities. As regards the problem of bilaterally conducted sales by member countries of minor exports, the staff of the Fund has used mainly the approach of suggesting to members alternative ways to promote minor exports.

Thus the Fund's efforts to diminish the use of bilateral agreements, even those of members of the Fund with state-trading countries, have continued. Members have been encouraged to implement the Fund's general policy whenever the opportunity to dispense with bilateral agreements arises.

---

[18] See, for example, *Annual Report, 1963*, pp. 69–70.

CHAPTER

15

The Fund and the EPU

Margaret G. de Vries

THE STORY OF THE FUND'S REACTIONS to plans in the late 1940's for European payments arrangements, and of its relations with the European Payments Union (EPU) which was formed in 1950, belongs to an era of the Fund's history which has little relevance to the present. The EPU was terminated in 1958, and long before that—in fact after 1952—relations had distinctly improved.

However, this period of the Fund's history has, time and again, been the subject of possibly the severest attacks that the Fund has experienced. It has been contended, for example, that as the EPU became the main instrument by which the trade and exchange restrictions of European countries were reduced, the Fund, by failing to organize under its own aegis a multilateral system of European settlements, "missed the bus."[1] And the Fund has been characterized as having been thenceforth outside the principal stream of important international economic events.[2]

The critics stress that, once European countries had developed the habit of intraregional cooperation on economic questions, they continued to make their most crucial financial and monetary decisions in small meetings among themselves rather than through the wider framework of the Fund. In some respects, the EPU thus formed the nucleus of the Group of Ten.

Whether or not these criticisms are wholly valid, it did appear to many observers that for some years following the establishment of the EPU the focal point of important monetary decisions was that organization rather than the Fund. Only after the Fund commenced to have large-scale financial operations with European countries in 1956 did this impression begin to change.

---

[1] See, for example, Robert Triffin, *The World Money Maze*, p. 406.
[2] Harry G. Johnson, *The World Economy at the Crossroads*, Chap. 3.

Accordingly, it is worthwhile to take a brief look at what the Fund's records show about its reactions to proposals for intra-European payments arrangements, including the EPU itself. A reading of these records suggests that the story was neither so simple nor so one-sided as the one heretofore publicly revealed.

THE NEED FOR INTRA-EUROPEAN CLEARING [3]

The EPU, established in September 1950, was the outgrowth of discussion and experimentation from 1947 to 1950 among European countries, looking to some sort of clearing union to facilitate trade and payments between them. Meetings to explore European payments arrangements were held as early as August 1947, shortly after General George C. Marshall (in June 1947) proposed that the U.S. Government should undertake a special program to help in reconstructing the economies of Europe. Although intra-European trade had made a remarkable recovery after World War II, that trade had expanded much less rapidly than either the industrial or the agricultural output of most European countries; and a much greater expansion of trade was considered necessary for the general economic recovery of Europe.

A number of officials, both in the U.S. Government and in several of the governments in Europe, had come to the conclusion that, although the bilateral payments agreements established among European countries immediately after the war had facilitated the restoration of intra-European trade, these payments arrangements were preventing further increases in that trade. Trade deficits in excess of the credit limits specified in bilateral payments agreements had to be financed with gold or convertible currencies. European countries with such deficits tended to restrict imports from other European countries in order to conserve their scarce supplies of gold and convertible foreign exchange for payments to the dollar area.

These misgivings about the existing payments arrangements were reinforced by developments in the fall of 1947. By that time, the effective credit or debit balances under existing payments agreements were tending more and more to exceed the bilateral ceilings, and had forced a resumption of gold settlements. Simultaneously, there had been an actual decline in the volume of intra-European trade. Illustrative of the thinking which related these two events was that of Mr. Robert Triffin, a staff member, who in July 1948 was to take charge of the Fund's Paris Office; Mr. Triffin regarded the decline in European trade as

---

[3] A comprehensive description of the development of the EPU can be found in William Diebold, *Trade and Payments in Western Europe*, and in Raymond F. Mikesell, *Foreign Exchange in the Postwar World*. The first three sections of this chapter are based largely on Mikesell's volume, Chap. 6, pp. 100–102, 108–23.

probably due in part to the progressive paralysis of the payments agreements mechanism.[4]

A number of officials believed that intra-European trade could be expanded by the institution of some system of multilateral compensation and a multi-lateralization of credits among European countries. What was required was a mechanism by which European countries having bilateral surpluses with other European countries could use these surpluses to finance (or to offset) their deficits with third countries in Europe. Payments in gold and convertible currencies between European countries could thereby be held to a minimum.

In addition, some way was needed to finance any over-all deficit a European country might have with its European trading partners as a group. The fact that some European countries, such as France and the Netherlands, had tended to have deficits with nearly all their European trading partners, while other countries, such as Belgium, tended to have surpluses, made it extremely difficult to establish a payments system through which even the bilateral positions that in theory could be offset against one another could, in practice, be cleared. Since all European countries had deficits with the dollar area, there were no dollar surpluses with which a European country could finance its deficit on intra-European account. By the same token, creditor countries, such as Belgium, that tended to have persistent surpluses with their European partners were anxious to receive convertible exchange with which to cover deficits with the Western Hemisphere.

FORERUNNERS OF THE EPU

Following meetings in London and Paris in the late summer and early fall of 1947, Belgium, France, Italy, Luxembourg, and the Netherlands signed a five-nation agreement on multilateral compensations in November 1947. The successful operation of compensation machinery of this kind was dependent, however, upon the balance of creditor-debtor relations between the participants in the system. The predominant creditor position of Belgium among European countries at the time, and the few participants in the scheme, narrowly limited the scope for compensation. It became apparent before long that, if any clearing system was to succeed, all the sixteen countries that had by then formally come together in the Organization for European Economic Cooperation (OEEC) would have to be brought into the system. Further, some way would have to be found to deal with those countries that were predominantly creditors or debtors of most of the other European countries.

There was considerable divergence of opinion among European countries as to what arrangements for multilateral clearing were preferable. Differences of

---

[4] Triffin, *World Money Maze*, p. 408.

view prevailed as well between European countries and officials of the Economic Cooperation Administration (ECA), an arm of the U.S. Government that had been set up in April 1948 to administer the European Recovery Program (ERP) on the U.S. side. Much debate concerned, for example, the arrangements to be made for the settlement of payments between debtors and creditors that were in excess of agreed limits. Especially basic was the question of how liberal should be the terms under which credits to debtors would be extended. If credit terms were too liberal, the pressure on debtor countries to correct the causes of their balance of payments deficits might not be sufficient.

In addition, creditor countries did not like the prospect of extending further substantial credits to their European neighbors; such credit extension not only entailed the loss of current receipts of convertible exchange, but also had an inflationary impact on the economies of the creditors. Belgium, therefore, as well as some other countries—including France, Italy, Luxembourg, and the Netherlands—favored a completely multilateral payments system, with excess credit positions being covered by an arrangement for U.S. aid. Belgium in fact did not like any arrangement which did not provide for the conversion of credit positions into gold or dollars. The United Kingdom and the other OEEC countries, however, hesitated to adopt such a scheme, on the ground that it would introduce too much dollar competition into intra-European trade.

The United States, for its part, was unwilling in the initial stages of the ERP to allocate aid to a special clearing fund from which it would be used automatically. The intent of the U.S. Congress in passing the Economic Cooperation Act in April 1948 had been that ECA aid should cover specific dollar deficits of European countries for programs to achieve particular recovery goals. Moreover, the ECA wished to stimulate competition in intra-European trade, so that European industries would be induced to improve their productivity vis-à-vis both the industries of other European countries and the industries of the Western Hemisphere.

On October 14, 1948, the sixteen OEEC countries signed an Agreement on Intra-European Payments and Compensations, covering the year July 1948 to June 1949. This agreement had been made possible by the adoption by the ECA of a new arrangement for the settlement of intra-European deficits. Under a system of "conditional aid," part of the ECA's assistance to European countries was based upon the amount of each country's planned bilateral surplus with each of the other members. Recipients of conditional aid were, in turn, required to provide drawing rights to each bilateral partner with whom they expected to have a surplus during a specified period. Thus each ERP country would receive drawing rights on the member countries with which they were expected to have bilateral deficits, entitling them to incur a given amount of deficit without being required to pay gold or to accumulate an indebtedness. By this device, nearly every country entitled to ECA aid both extended drawing rights to other members (equal to the amount of conditional aid received) and received drawing rights from others.

With some relatively minor changes, a second such agreement was adopted in September 1949, for the year ending June 30, 1950. But, because these agreements did not permit the full offsetting of deficits against surpluses among participating countries, and because their operation required estimating the anticipated bilateral surpluses and deficits, they, like the earlier five-nation clearing scheme of 1947–48, were not wholly satisfactory. The system remained basically bilateral.

ESTABLISHMENT OF THE EPU

Late in 1949, at the suggestion of the ECA, the countries in the OEEC began to discuss again ideas for a payments arrangement for Western European and related currencies that would provide a better solution to intra-European trade and payments problems. In December 1949, the ECA and a number of European countries submitted to the OEEC proposals for a European clearing union.

There were long negotiations over numerous difficult problems. One problem, for example, concerned the treatment of the pound sterling. Should sterling be treated differently from other European currencies because of its international character—that is, because sterling was widely used in third country settlements and as a form in which monetary reserves were held? Additional complications arose from the fact that the sterling area encompassed a large number of independent monetary authorities, whereas each of the continental European currencies was controlled by a single monetary authority. What, for example, would be the relations between an independent country like Australia and the European members of the EPU? Accounts within the sterling area were already settled between the member countries; if the sterling area settled its accounts with the EPU on an aggregated net basis, the United Kingdom would have to cover with gold and dollar payments the EPU deficits of the rest of the sterling area as well as those of Britain alone.

There was also the problem that some OEEC members held sizable accumulated sterling balances. If these countries were permitted to use such balances to settle EPU deficits, Britain might be required to pay gold to the EPU on account of large transfers of sterling to the EPU by these OEEC members. To settle these difficulties, the ECA agreed to reimburse the United Kingdom for any net payment of dollars to the EPU which might result from the use of accumulated sterling holdings by participating EPU countries to cover their deficits with the Union.

The agreement setting up the EPU was finally signed on September 19, 1950, to be effective for a period of two years from July 1, 1950 to June 30, 1952. The new Union was designed to facilitate liberalization of intra-European trade on a nondiscriminatory basis; to assist its members in their progress toward viable economies, especially by supplying credit and providing incentives; and to encourage them to achieve or maintain high and stable levels of trade and employment. Like the Fund, the EPU also stood for the maintenance of internal and external financial equilibrium and the need for European countries to return to full multilateral trade and to currency convertibility.

There were two important features of the arrangements: the full multi-lateralization of payments among members of the OEEC and their associated monetary areas through a compensation mechanism, and a means of facilitating the net payments due from debtors after the compensations were effected. The first feature came from provision for a complete netting of all bilateral payments positions at the end of each accounting period. Each member country was to report its position with every other member to the Bank for International Settlements (BIS) at the end of each month. The BIS was then to determine for each country its "accounting surplus or deficit" for that month. The bilateral positions with other members were thus eliminated in exchange for a position with the EPU.

The complicated nature of the EPU derived from the method of net settlement—not from the clearing operation. Within certain limits, the settlement of accounting surpluses and deficits was to consist merely of the crediting or debiting of each member's account. EPU credits were to be available for use in covering a deficit with other EPU members, since each member agreed to accept EPU credits in settlement of a credit against any other member. When a member's accounting credit or debit reached a certain level, additional amounts had to be settled partly in gold. Schedules fixing the proportions of the monthly settlements to be made in gold by debtors and to be received in gold by creditors provided for the payment of an increasing proportion by debtors as their cumulative deficits rose and the receipt of a decreasing proportion by creditors as their cumulative surpluses, for which a quota was set, rose.

While most of the liquidity of the payments system was provided by the members themselves through the extension of credits, some working capital was provided by the ECA. At the beginning of the EPU's operations in the middle of 1950, the ECA made available to the EPU $350 million to be used in the event that gold payments to creditor countries exceeded gold receipts from debtors.

The EPU was to be administered by a Managing Board, whose policymaking power was, however, limited to making proposals to the OEEC Council, by which it was appointed. The EPU remained in existence until December 1958, when it was terminated following the establishment of external convertibility for the major European currencies. In accordance with an agreement reached by the OEEC in July 1955, the European Monetary Agreement (EMA) then came into force.

THE FUND'S INITIAL REACTIONS [5]

In view of the similarity of the objectives of the European payments arrangements, and those of the EPU as established, with those of the Fund, it might have been expected that the Fund's reactions to these arrangements would have been at least favorable, if not enthusiastic. Indeed, in the early stages, the Board agreed to send observers to the meetings of the Financial Committee of the Committee on Cooperation of European Countries, held in London in the fall of 1947. However, several Directors were anxious that the Fund should not become committed to any particular clearing scheme, especially as a number of proposals were just beginning to be discussed among the European countries.

Fund observers did attend meetings in London. However, although the report of the participants in the London meetings had indicated that the Fund was invited to send an observer to the next series of meetings in Paris in October 1947, the Fund was not in fact represented. The absence of a Fund observer at these meetings was to have lasting consequence. For it was then and there that Belgium, France, Italy, Luxembourg, and the Netherlands signed the first European payments agreement. While the Fund was not represented, the BIS was. The first draft of the payments agreement signed by these five nations had provided for the Fund to act as a clearing agent, but, in the absence of a representative from the Fund, the BIS's offer of its services as a clearing agent was accepted. The BIS remained the agent for all later intra-European payments organizations, including the EPU and the subsequent EMA.

The Fund has at times been criticized for failing to become at least the clearing agent for the EPU. However, as far as the Fund's records show, its absence from the Paris meeting in October 1947 was accidental, although how the accident happened is not clear. In a statement to the Board on November 12, 1948, the Managing Director stated that it had been due to a "genuine misunderstanding." Actually, the Managing Director, some Executive Directors, and most staff members were inclined to advocate a stronger role for the Fund than that of clearing agent. As early as December 1947 the staff suggested to the Executive Board that additional credits were essential to enable a European clearing mechanism to work and that the Fund could and should provide them. In May 1948, the Board discussed a specific staff plan for the Fund's participation in European multilateral clearing arrangements; this plan would have had the

---

[5] Details of the Executive Directors' discussions of the various plans for European payments arrangements may be found in Vol. I above, pp. 212–23, 288–90.

Fund make available resources of $338 million, in the form of drawings of Belgian francs or other European currencies.

But, although some Directors believed that the aims of multilateral clearing in Europe were in accord with the Fund's objectives, other Directors had misgivings. Would European payments schemes, in fact, help to lay the basis for eventual convertibility of European currencies? Would a clearing arrangement not tend to postpone the solution of Europe's problems rather than help to solve them? Was there not a danger that increasing the means of payment in Europe would encourage nonessential and luxury imports more than essential trade? In addition, since the Fund had in the previous month taken a decision (the "ERP Decision" of April 1948) limiting European members' access to the Fund's dollar resources during the life of the ERP, several Directors inquired specifically about those portions of any plan which called for use of the Fund's dollar resources.[6] Would not a contribution from the Fund to clearing arrangements be counter to the Fund's "ERP Decision"? What guarantee could there be that the Fund's commitments under the clearing arrangements proposed would not be excessive, using up in a few months resources which should be made available over several years?

Concern of the kind indicated by these questions led the Directors to take, on June 4, 1948, a decision which limited the Fund's involvement in European payments arrangements.[7] The decision stated that the Fund hoped that an arrangement could be made for multilateralizing European payments. The Fund also hoped that a revision of and a moderate rise in credits could be agreed for use in multilateral payments and, reiterating the Fund's "ERP Decision" on the use of its own resources, hoped that any increase in credits could be financed by the creditor countries. The Fund was also willing to place its advice and technical facilities at the disposal of its members in connection with the formulation and administration of any multilateral payments arrangements and for other purposes related to their payments problems.

Mr. Triffin, as head of the Fund's Paris Office, strongly advocated participation by the Fund in European multilateral clearing arrangements. Early in 1949 he submitted to the Executive Board a second specific proposal for a modification of the European payments arrangements then being discussed; this proposal again envisaged the possible use of the Fund's resources as an aid to multilateralizing payments in 1949–50. However, the proposal was not accepted by the Board.

The Managing Director of the Fund, Mr. Gutt, was also very much in favor of the Fund's cooperating actively with the plans for multilateral clearing which

---

[6] The "ERP Decision" is reproduced in Chapter 18 below (pp. 395–96). Other implications of the decision are discussed later in this chapter (p. 328).

[7] See above, Vol. I, p. 221.

were continuing to go forward in Europe. On one occasion, in November 1948, he made a powerful plea to the Executive Board for the Fund to take an active share in these plans. He was concerned, inter alia, that if the sixteen nations assembled together in Europe did not have enough contact with the rest of the world, they might tend to build up a so-called European monetary policy, which might be different from, or opposed to, an international monetary policy. Again in January 1950 he recommended to the Board that the Fund participate in the discussions for the setting up of the EPU.

Anticipating that the Managing Director's appeal might bring favorable response from the Board, the staff came up with new suggestions as to how European clearing could be conducted through the Fund. While recognizing that the Fund had been used very little for the purchase of European currencies, the staff believed that the Fund constituted suitable machinery to facilitate payments within Europe if a large group of European countries decided jointly to use the Fund for this purpose. However, for reasons discussed in the next section the Board was unwilling to proceed along these lines.

SOME DIFFERING OPINIONS

Throughout these years, the Board was kept informed by the Paris Office of the various proposals for clearing arrangements which were put forward in Europe. After studying these, however, the staff formed the view that the clearing mechanisms being considered would be more likely, at least in the short run, to impede than to advance convertibility and a solution of the dollar problem. The argument was that, while the progressive removal of trade and payments restrictions within Europe as called for by the planned arrangements was an objective of great importance, it could not be regarded as transcending the basic need that must dominate European policy: a tenable *dollar* payments position.

It was pointed out that even for the countries participating in the OEEC, intra-European trade as measured by imports was only 46 per cent of their total trade; and that the magnitudes of the payments deficits within Europe were quite small compared to the dollar deficits. The staff stressed that the restrictions from which European countries suffered most were not those against one another, but those which they had to impose on their dollar imports because of their own inadequate dollar earnings, and concluded that it was in the interest of European countries to reduce restrictions on trade and payments between them to that minimum *which was consistent with positive progress in the solution of the dollar problem.*

Elaborating this argument, the staff reasoned that before September 1949 Fund members had tended to concentrate on exporting to the high-priced markets of Europe. This was because inflated demand within Europe had made these markets, despite restrictions, more attractive than dollar markets. Under such conditions, the general removal of trade and payments restrictions within Europe could only have added to the difficulties that European countries already faced in instituting positive measures to meet their dollar problems. Since the devaluations of September 1949, there had been a great change in the relative attractiveness to exporters of dollar markets and of markets in Europe and associated currency areas. If the active and latent inflation within Europe and in the associated currency areas could be eliminated, the case would be exceptionally strong for the removal of nearly all trade and payments restrictions in the countries participating in any intra-European payments scheme. But until inflation had been at least sharply reduced, liberalization of European trade would not be likely to solve the dollar problem.

Recognizing that their conclusions were contrary to the usual opinions about European clearing arrangements and the liberalization of intra-European trade, staff members added some qualifications to their analysis. Their conclusions would be affected if the tendency that had been occurring among European countries for exports to the dollar area to be reduced were to be reversed after a new payments scheme had gone into effect. Furthermore, their conclusions could be altered depending on what happened to the productivity of European industries as trade barriers were relaxed and greater competition among European countries was induced. In the longer run, greater productivity might result in lower costs and prices which, in turn, would help to solve Europe's dollar problem.

Thus there were genuine differences of opinion, both in the staff and in the Executive Board, from the views being expressed in Europe concerning the advantages and disadvantages of the various proposed mechanisms.

The official policy of the Fund early in 1950 was exemplified by the Board's instructions to a staff mission which was to participate in discussions in Europe on the proposals for an EPU. The position of the Fund was that European countries needed primarily to overcome their inflationary difficulties and that, while inflation remained a threat, the role of credit, particularly of long- and medium-term credit, in the settlement of intra-European current balances should be restrained. Settlement in gold or dollars should be relatively large and should become the rule whenever possible.

The Fund considered that, in any European payments arrangement, credit had two functions as regards debtors and one as regards creditors. As regards debtors, credits were a substitute for grants insofar as they tended to undo the deterrent effect of any payments scheme on a debtor's building up of deficits. On the other hand, if credits were a substitute for required gold payments, they acted as a safety valve to prevent a scheme from acting too rigorously and perhaps from breaking down. As regards creditors, the function of credit was to make earnings inside Europe less attractive than gold, in order to discourage undue attempts by creditors to earn dollars by trading with European countries rather than by exporting to the dollar area. Moderate amounts of credit, with large amounts of settlements required in gold or dollars, would best reconcile these conflicting functions of credit.

THE QUESTION OF LIAISON

Apart from the merits of European clearing arrangements, the question of liaison with any European organization that might be established was also carefully weighed in the Fund. Once it had become evident that the EPU was to come into being, the question of liaison became, for the Fund, a more pertinent issue than the nature of the particular clearing mechanism to be set up.

NEED FOR COLLABORATION

Many, both among the Fund staff and on the Board, believed that the closest possible relationship should be established between the Fund and the EPU. The fact that the EPU involved a number of the Fund's members was itself sufficient, several thought, to argue for close collaboration. The provisions agreed upon by the OEEC Council could lead to actions by European members of the Fund which would be inconsistent with their obligations under the Fund Agreement. To avoid such situations, and to protect other members of the Fund from the consequences thereof, the Fund should be in close touch with the EPU and make its views known to its European members. Moreover, the shape which the EPU had taken might be changed from time to time, and the Fund had a duty to all of its members, including those in Europe, to do its best to assist in improving the system and in bringing about as rapidly as possible conditions under which the purposes of the Fund Agreement could be achieved.

The Fund also believed that it had a vital stake in any decisions taken by the EPU Managing Board. The Fund's attitude, prior to the establishment of the EPU, had been that the degree of its interest in the management of any European clearing arrangement depended greatly on the purposes of that management. If such management was to deal only with the financial terms on which credits were extended, such as the conditions for repayment and the rate of interest, the Fund had no concern with it. The Fund would have some concern if an EPU management was to deal with the amounts of credit granted; and if that management was to prescribe the policy conditions on which credits were granted, the Fund believed it was vitally concerned.

Once it was evident that the Managing Board of the EPU would have broad powers and would be discussing the policies of the OEEC members, the Fund believed its interests were definitely involved and that collaboration was important. The Board decided that, although the Fund's representatives should not seek to secure any special arrangements with the EPU, these representatives might ask to attend meetings of the EPU Managing Board. The Managing Director, Mr. Gutt, and the Deputy Managing Director, Mr. Overby, visited Paris several times in the last planning stages of the EPU in April, May, and June, 1950. The Managing Director went to Europe again prior to the Annual Meeting in Paris in September 1950, and simultaneous and subsequent visits to European countries were also made by the staff. The suggestions made by these Fund representatives were that the Fund might have a permanent observer on the EPU Board; then, after experience in Fund-EPU cooperation had been gained, a more formal relationship between the two organizations might be established.

OPPOSITION TO THE FUND'S PARTICIPATION

Several circumstances, however, operated against the possibilities of close cooperation, at least in the early years, between the Fund and the EPU. European countries were not necessarily eager for the Fund to have much, if any, participation in their arrangements. European countries had, to some extent, been disturbed by the Fund's "ERP Decision" on the use of its resources. They apparently did not take seriously the possibility, which was mentioned during the Board's discussions, that the amount of ERP aid might be reduced to the extent that Europe received dollar resources from the Fund. They therefore viewed the Fund's decision as a curtailment of the amount of dollar resources that might have been available to Europe. The Fund's non-dollar resources were of less interest to them, because these currencies were inconvertible at that time and repurchases would have to be made in gold or dollars. There was also some feeling in Europe that the Fund was dominated by the U.S. Government, with which the Europeans already had to deal through the ECA.

That the European countries hesitated to have close participation by the Fund in their arrangements was manifested as early as the summer of 1948, when the Fund's representative in Paris was endeavoring to obtain representation for the Fund in the OEEC and a role in the proposed first Intra-European Payments Agreement. He was then told by Mr. Hubert Ansiaux, Chairman of the Financial Committee of the OEEC as well as an Executive Director of the Fund, that there was a great deal of resistance in the OEEC toward inviting international organizations to be represented officially at its regular meetings, as the OEEC considered itself primarily a European organization. Again, at the end of January 1950, Mr. Ansiaux wrote to the Managing Director about the EPU proposals and, especially, about European attitudes toward the Fund's participation in such a Union and in the OEEC. He indicated that while it would be possible for the Fund to have an observer to follow the discussions in the OEEC on the EPU proposals, it appeared impossible, for both political and practical reasons, that the Fund should participate either in the discussions of the plans or in their implementation.

Later in 1950, discussions with the continental European countries showed that they were willing to have an observer from the Fund on the EPU Board. However, discussions with the British representative in the OEEC and the EPU showed that the United Kingdom opposed the idea of any Fund observer. The reasons given were as follows: First, the United Kingdom wanted to keep the number of people around the table very small. Second, the discussions of the EPU Board were confidential even vis-à-vis members of the EPU not represented on the EPU Board. Third, some countries in the EPU were not members of the Fund. Finally, the British representative argued that the Fund was unable to maintain the necessary confidentiality in view of the insistence of its Board on receiving all information given to the staff and of the right of the Executive Directors to report to their governments.

Still another political consideration militated against the Fund, with its world-wide membership, taking much of a role in European arrangements. The U.S. Government, in particular the ECA and the State Department, had become committed to an independent EPU as an essential means of promoting European political integration. Integration was expected to be furthered principally by getting the European countries to coordinate their monetary policies toward the common end of balance of payments equilibrium.

In addition to the political considerations that made it difficult for the Fund to participate effectively either in the discussions for European clearing or in their implementation, there were two practical difficulties which precluded any effective role for the Fund. One was that it appeared inconceivable that decisions taken at a ministerial level in the OEEC should be subject to review by the ministers' own representatives on the Fund's Board. The other was that EPU operations had to be directed from Paris, not from Washington, and if decisions made in Paris had to be approved by the Fund's Board, there would inevitably be delays.

All these circumstances, taken together, had the result that a representative from the Fund was not invited to attend meetings of the EPU Managing Board until 1952.

IMPROVEMENT IN RELATIONS

Improvement in Fund-EPU relations, when it came, resulted not from any formal decisions but rather from the more favorable attitudes in Europe toward cooperation with the Fund which followed the Fund's agreement in June 1952 to a request from Belgium for a stand-by arrangement.

In June 1952, the OEEC Council agreed to extend the EPU for another year, until June 30, 1953. But among the problems that had to be solved was the emergence of Belgium as a large creditor. It was necessary for the EPU to reach agreement concerning payment to Belgium for its past surplus and to arrange for new credits for the coming year. Part of the settlement worked out between the EPU and Belgium was that $50 million would be paid to Belgium in five annual installments. But Belgium was reluctant to agree to this arrangement unless it was, meanwhile, safeguarded against a possible dollar drain, and the U.S. Government had decided not to commit any more funds to the EPU. A way was found around this impasse when the Fund agreed to a stand-by arrangement with Belgium for $50 million which was automatically renewable for five years unless canceled by either party. The commitment from the Fund gave the National Bank of Belgium assurance that, if necessary, it could mobilize in advance the dollar debt owed to Belgium by the EPU.

The OEEC Council, in its meeting of July 11, 1952, formally expressed its appreciation of the prompt and favorable response of the Fund to the Belgian request, and declared its hope that "it may also be possible to have fruitful collaboration in the future between the Fund and the Organization in connection with problems of mutual concern." As a result, members of the Fund's Office in Paris were invited with increasing frequency to meetings of the EPU Managing Board.

In the spring of 1953, the EPU Managing Board's recommendations for the extension of the Union contained three paragraphs on relations with the Fund. It was stated that close cooperation with the Fund was increasingly necessary and practical, especially as European countries needed more reserves to continue their progress toward derestriction. Examples were listed of circumstances in which EPU members could usefully draw on the Fund, which seemed to raise no problems except for one which suggested the possibility that the Fund and the EPU open joint credits for European countries so as to stabilize their currencies. Also suggested were a joint examination of problem countries and coordinated decisions on the measures to be taken. These suggestions were discussed by the two staffs, but no formal proposals were made to the Fund.

In the summer of 1953, the Fund staff suggested, and the Executive Board approved, the formal transmittal of certain Fund documents, including Part II of the Fund's consultation reports, for the use of the OEEC, subject to approval in each case by the Executive Director concerned. In April 1956, the Board also agreed to transmit to the OEEC Part I of the Fund's consultation reports, again subject to the right of any Executive Director to object to the transmission of any report in which he was interested.

Closer liaison between the Fund and the OEEC also developed as the latter assumed responsibilities for supervising the progress of its members toward liberalization of trade. As the trade of OEEC countries began to be freed from restrictions, the objectives of the OEEC and of the EPU came closer to those of the Fund than had been thought likely when the EPU was set up. The result was that Fund-EPU relations steadily improved.

Some doubts remained as to whether the EPU made restrictions against dollar area imports more discriminatory than they would otherwise have been. A few Directors argued that the EPU actually contributed to reduce such discrimination, but others continued to have misgivings. After the EPU had come to an end, the Managing Director of the Fund, Mr. Jacobsson, stated that "the European Payments Union, for eight and a half years up to the end of 1958, made a most useful contribution to progress in Europe by assuring prompt payments and by giving an impetus to the relaxation of trade restrictions."[8]

One final word may be added about the Fund's reactions in 1947–50 to European payments arrangements. The Fund itself was a young institution. It was just beginning to formulate general policies to guide it in its relations with members. Moreover, it was having difficulty in establishing its own authority, especially in the field of exchange rates. In these circumstances, it is understandable that the prospect of a European financial organization dealing with many of the subjects in the Fund's field, and including many of the Fund's important members, was viewed with some anxiety.

During the next several years the Fund was able to work out the policies it would pursue—toward exchange rates, the use of its resources, the transitional period, restrictions, and the restoration of convertibility. By 1952 its own consultation program with its members had also commenced. Hence it is not unlikely that, had the whole matter of European payments arrangements come up five years later than it did, the outcome might have been quite different from what it was.

---

[8] *Summary Proceedings, 1959*, p. 15.

16

Collaborating with the GATT

Margaret G. de Vries

WHEN THE FUND WAS PLANNED it was expected that there would be some international body responsible for trade relations. Resolution VII passed at Bretton Woods recommended to the governments participating in the Conference that they seek to reach agreement as soon as possible on ways and means to reduce obstacles to international trade and in other ways to promote mutually advantageous international commercial relations.[1] Originally it had been thought that the Fund and the proposed International Trade Organization (ITO) would have a common membership.

Thereafter—in the planning for an ITO, in the provisions of the General Agreement on Tariffs and Trade (GATT), and in the GATT's subsequent activities—the Fund has continuously and overtly recognized that it has a vital stake in the regulation of barriers to world trade in any form. The attainment of the Fund's own objectives has been regarded as intertwined with the successful operation of some international mechanism for achieving the same freedom from restrictions in relation to international trade as the Fund seeks to achieve with respect to international payments. In its relations with the GATT, therefore, the Fund has been guided by a conviction that the freeing of trade and the freeing of exchange are complementary, if not interdependent, objectives.

The GATT provides that any contracting party to it that is not a member of the Fund must enter into a Special Exchange Agreement with the Fund so that the Fund can, for those countries, fulfill its responsibilities to the GATT. Such Special Exchange Agreements were used for a time for one or two countries, notably for New Zealand until that country joined the Fund in 1961. More recently, contracting parties to the GATT that are not Fund members have been given waivers of the applicability of the relevant provisions of the GATT, and have agreed to provide the Fund with the information and documentation

---

[1] *Proceedings*, p. 941.

necessary for the Fund to make its presentation to the GATT, should such presentation be required.

FUND PARTICIPATION IN SETTING UP THE GATT

MEETINGS FOR THE PROPOSED ITO

Shortly after its establishment, the Fund participated in the meetings which were called by the United Nations in 1946 to plan for the ITO. The Preparatory Committee for an International Conference on Trade and Employment had two meetings, one in London from October 15, 1946 to November 20, 1946, and a second in Geneva from April 10, 1947 to August 25, 1947. Between these periods a drafting committee met in Washington from January 20 to February 25, 1947. In the following winter a third session of the Preparatory Committee was held in Havana.

The Fund's acute interest in whatever plans were drawn up was immediately made clear by the Executive Directors. The field of activity of the proposed ITO would, at the least, run parallel to that of the Fund. It might even be so formulated as to encroach upon the Fund's responsibilities; indeed, the rules of the ITO might provide for its members a means of escape from the jurisdiction of the Fund. In either case, the Fund's influence would be impaired. How to prevent this formed a major preoccupation of the Executive Directors as they considered the Fund's participation in the Preparatory Committee's sessions. The Directors were especially mindful of the wide differences in attitude among the major countries planning the trade organization. While the United States sought, for example, the outright prohibition of trade restrictions, especially discriminatory ones, except when members had large or prolonged balance of payments deficits, the United Kingdom and Australia were less desirous of erecting a strong trade organization. At the same time, the Executive Board wished to assert the Fund's right under its Articles to supervise any issues pertaining to exchange rates, multiple rates, exchange restrictions, or exchange controls, regardless of the purpose for which they were used.

At the first session of the Preparatory Committee in London, the Fund's representative, Mr. Luthringer (United States), Alternate to Mr. White, made several suggestions: that in the charter being drafted the use of quantitative restrictions under the ITO should be subject to provisions similar to those of Article XIV of the Fund Agreement; that the charter should seek, once the transitional period had been passed, to limit the use of quantitative restrictions to circumstances in which other techniques had been exhausted; and that, in these conditions, the ITO should request the Fund to make a finding as to whether the member's foreign exchange reserves warranted the imposition of the proposed restrictions, and should subsequently consult the Fund on the possibilities for the progressive removal of restrictions that had been authorized.

At the session in Geneva, the Fund's representative, Mr. Saad (Egypt), saw to it that the provisions concerning multiple exchange rates and control of capital movements which were in the draft ITO charter were in accord with the Fund Agreement, and that the draft charter for the ITO provided for close coordination of policy between the two organizations, both on exchange questions and on quantitative restrictions. The activities of the Fund's representatives at these preparatory sessions helped to ensure that the charter of the ITO would be compatible with the Fund's interests.

Following the Havana Conference of 1947–48, Mr. Saad emphasized to the Fund's Board that the interdependence of the roles of the Fund and the ITO made it imperative that there should be full cooperation between the two bodies. He suggested that the Fund's Board should immediately consider the terms of a possible agreement for cooperation with the ITO. Hence, in July 1948 a Committee of Directors on Liaison with the ITO, with Mr. Saad as its first chairman, was formed. When the ITO failed to materialize, this committee was reconstituted as the Committee on Liaison with the CONTRACTING PARTIES to the GATT, and in that form has continued to be one of very few standing committees of the Executive Board.

THE GATT EMERGES

Pending action by the prospective members of the ITO, a multilateral trade agreement, called the General Agreement on Tariffs and Trade, which had been agreed at the second session in Geneva, was put into provisional application during the summer of 1948. Fortunately for the Fund, many of the relationships with the Fund that had been so carefully defined for the proposed ITO were contained in the GATT.

The GATT consists of tariff provisions and of regulations concerning general commercial policy. A multilateral trade agreement of such comprehensive scope, covering not only tariffs but also the general principles of commercial policies, is without precedent. The participating governments deliberately avoided the traditional pattern of an international organization; they merely established contractual relations among themselves. The participants in the GATT attempt to achieve their purpose of reducing excessive trade barriers through a number of consultative arrangements.[2] In September 1948, the Board of the Fund approved proposals by the Chairman of the CONTRACTING PARTIES for informal cooperation between the GATT and the Fund. Between 1948 and

---

[2] For a detailed explanation of how the GATT is organized and how it works, see Gerard Curzon, *Multilateral Commercial Diplomacy*, Chap. II, p. 53.

1950 thirty-one countries, most of which were members of the Fund, became contracting parties to the GATT.

PROVISIONS OF THE GATT RELATING TO THE FUND

The Fund's close ties with the GATT are made explicit by three basic provisions contained in Article XV of the GATT. Paragraph 1 provides:

> The CONTRACTING PARTIES shall seek co-operation with the International Monetary Fund to the end that the CONTRACTING PARTIES and the Fund may pursue a co-ordinated policy with regard to exchange questions within the jurisdiction of the Fund and questions of quantitative restrictions and other trade measures within the jurisdiction of the CONTRACTING PARTIES.

The first sentence of paragraph 2 states:

> In all cases in which the CONTRACTING PARTIES are called upon to consider or deal with problems concerning monetary reserves, balances of payments or foreign exchange arrangements, they shall consult fully with the International Monetary Fund.

Later in the same paragraph the CONTRACTING PARTIES are required

> in cases involving the criteria set forth in paragraph 2 (a) of Article XII or in paragraph 9 of Article XVIII [to] accept the determination of the Fund as to what constitutes a serious decline in the contracting party's monetary reserves, a very low level of its monetary reserves or a reasonable rate of increase in its monetary reserves, and as to the financial aspects of other matters covered in consultation in such cases.

In sum, the general effect of the GATT is that countries are to coordinate their exchange policies (under the jurisdiction of the Fund) and their trade policies (under the jurisdiction of the GATT). The CONTRACTING PARTIES must consult the Fund on all matters dealing with reserves and balances of payments and must accept the Fund's findings. The CONTRACTING PARTIES themselves, of course, determine whether or not the subject with which they are dealing involves monetary problems, and consequently whether consultations with the Fund are required. Legal opinion is that, in the final analysis, the GATT is sovereign in these matters. Moreover, the Fund's findings are only part of the material on which the GATT's decisions are taken.[3]

The provisions of the GATT relating to the Fund are the more significant because the GATT bases any permission given to a contracting party to institute or maintain import restrictions on the state of that country's reserve and balance of payments positions. The specific provisions of the GATT governing the use of import restrictions were revised in 1954–55 during a

---

[3] Ervin Hexner, "The General Agreement on Tariffs and Trade and the Monetary Fund," *Staff Papers*, Vol. I (1950–51), pp. 448–52.

Review Session of the CONTRACTING PARTIES; the improvement in the balances of payments of most countries by the mid-1950's had produced a desire to put an end to the provisional character of the GATT and to transform it into a permanent international organization.[4] It is the revised rules, operative since October 1957, to which we refer in this chapter.[5]

All restrictions are subject to a system of periodic consultations, based on a detailed examination by the CONTRACTING PARTIES of the level, methods, and effects on trade of the restrictions in use by the various countries. The General Agreement also makes the purpose of these consultations fairly explicit. The CONTRACTING PARTIES, finding that a country's restrictions are inconsistent with the provisions of the GATT, can advise that the restrictions be suitably modified. They can even make appropriate recommendations for securing conformity with GATT provisions within a specified period, and sanctions against noncompliance with such recommendations are provided for in the form of a suspension of obligations by any adversely affected contracting party.

More specifically, provision is made for the introduction or maintenance of restrictions to safeguard a contracting party's balance of payments at two points—in Article XII, and in Section B of Article XVIII, the latter applying to less developed countries. By paragraph 2 (a) of Article XII, import restrictions imposed by a contracting party under that Article may not exceed those necessary

> (i) to forestall the imminent threat of, or to stop, a serious decline in its monetary reserves, or
> (ii) in the case of a contracting party with very low monetary reserves, to achieve a reasonable rate of increase in its reserves.

Paragraphs 9 and 11 of Article XVIII:B provide broadly the same facilities, but with some changes in phraseology, such as the elimination of the word "imminent" from clause (i), and the replacement of "very low" in clause (ii) by the word "inadequate."

The two Articles go on to provide for consultations on restrictions imposed or maintained. The text in Article XII is:

> 4. (a) Any contracting party applying new restrictions or raising the general level of its existing restrictions by a substantial intensification of the measures applied under this Article shall immediately after instituting or intensifying such restrictions (or, in circumstances in which prior consultation is practicable, before doing so) consult with the CONTRACTING PARTIES as to the nature of its balance of payments difficulties, alternative corrective measures which may be available, and the possible effect of the restriction on the economies of other contracting parties.
>
> (b) On a date to be determined by them, the CONTRACTING PARTIES shall review all restrictions still applied under this Article on that date. Beginning one year

---

[4] Curzon, *Multilateral Commercial Diplomacy*, p. 136.

[5] The provisions of the earlier rules can be found in Hexner, "General Agreement on Tariffs and Trade and the Monetary Fund," pp. 436–43, 445–48.

after that date, contracting parties applying import restrictions under this Article shall enter into consultations of the type provided for in sub-paragraph (*a*) of this paragraph with the CONTRACTING PARTIES annually.

Similar provisions are included in Article XVIII: 12 (relevant to less developed countries), except that the consultations provided for in subparagraph (*b*) are to take place at intervals of two years instead of annually.

QUESTIONS CONCERNING THE FUND'S ROLE

At first the Executive Directors had doubts about the precise way in which the Fund should implement the provisions called for by the GATT. In May 1949 South Africa sought approval under the GATT for some new import restrictions, and the CONTRACTING PARTIES consulted the Fund on the question whether these restrictions were justified by South Africa's balance of payments. The request for the Fund's advice led some Executive Directors to inquire into the extent of the Fund's responsibility. Specifically, the question was raised whether the Fund should merely report facts to the GATT, or whether the Fund should also provide an evaluation of the facts. Mr. Southard (United States) thought that full consultation, such as the agreement with the GATT visualized, necessarily implied an evaluation. On the other hand, Mr. McFarlane (Australia), who had been elected by South Africa, suggested that only the GATT could decide on the implications of import restrictions for its other members; the Fund should not risk an independent opinion which might clash with that of the GATT.

Since the exact nature of the South African proposals was not made clear at first, and since the issue of discriminatory restrictions was involved and several Directors doubted whether enough data was available to conclude that discrimination was justified, the issue was not really resolved. Rather, it was decided to transmit to the GATT a staff study of the balance of payments of South Africa, which justified import restrictions, but to omit the last paragraph of the study, which would have advised the GATT that some discrimination was not unreasonable.

Something of a major conflict on these issues was still to come. Mr. McFarlane continued to urge that the Board should be very cautious in such matters. As the representative of Australia, he stated that his Government had understood when joining the Fund that the Fund would not intervene in matters of import restrictions. But Mr. Saad, who had been representing the Fund at the consultations with the GATT, pointed out that, where import restrictions were imposed for balance of payments reasons, the responsibilities of the Fund and the GATT were necessarily interlocked. No final decision on this issue was reached during the year, and the discussion was resumed in 1950, when further restrictions were submitted by South Africa for approval under the GATT and a fresh consultation took place.

There were various reasons why countries, such as Australia, that were apprehensive about subjecting their import restrictions to international review tended to fear the Fund's scrutiny more than they did that of the CONTRACTING PARTIES to the GATT. For one thing, the Fund had a large professional staff to prepare for consultations whereas the GATT did not. For another, since the Board of the Fund was in continuous session, while the CONTRACTING PARTIES met only periodically in General Session, the Fund's Directors had frequent opportunity to review and comment on the restrictions of its members. More importantly, the Fund's system of weighted voting gave such countries less of a vote in the decision-making process than did the GATT's one country, one vote system. Finally, until the GATT was revised in the middle 1950's, its powers were clearly less than those of the Fund: no provision was made in the GATT for the organization to make representations to its members and it had no financial resources of which to dispose. After all, the GATT had come into being because countries had not been able to agree on an international trade organization. For all these reasons, the GATT was less able than the Fund to take action against the restrictions of its members. There were some observers who went even further, believing that the role of the Fund as a fact-finding agency for the GATT would have little influence on the attitudes of the CONTRACTING PARTIES.[6]

CONTROVERSY AT TORQUAY

The controversies concerning the Fund's role in the consultations under the GATT came to a head in 1950, when several countries in the sterling area undertook such consultations. In July 1949 the Commonwealth Finance Ministers had agreed that, because of a continuing and growing drain on the dollar reserves of the sterling area,[7] each member of the sterling area would reduce its dollar expenditures by 25 per cent of their total in calendar 1948. The GATT permitted contracting parties temporarily to *intensify* restrictions—including making their restrictions more discriminatory—in order to forestall or stop a serious decline in monetary reserves or to permit a reasonable rate of increase in reserves; consultations were, however, required. The CONTRACTING PARTIES, therefore, in accordance with Article XV of the GATT, invited Australia,

---

[6] Michael A. Heilperin, *Answer to the State Department's Comments on the Document, Basic Criticisms of the Havana Charter* (October 1948), as cited in Curzon, *Multilateral Commercial Diplomacy*, pp. 134–35.

[7] See Chapter 4 above, pp. 97–98.

Ceylon, India, New Zealand, Pakistan, South Africa, Southern Rhodesia, and the United Kingdom (as well as Chile, which had also intensified its restrictions) to consult. The Fund was invited by the GATT to take part in these consultations, which took place at the Fifth Session held at Torquay, England, in the autumn of 1950.

DEBATES WITHIN THE FUND

As the Fund's staff began to prepare the documentation for these consultations, the deep differences of opinion among the Executive Directors on just what the Fund should submit to the GATT came to the surface. Should the Fund's documentation focus only on the justification for the restrictions when they were initially imposed—that is in July 1949—or should emphasis be placed on the need for the restrictions at the time of the consultations, that is, late in 1950? (Since the devaluations of September 1949 had occurred in the meantime, and presumably alleviated the need for some of the restrictions, the difference in the date to be used was significant.) Should the Fund supply to the GATT only facts, especially statistical material, or should an evaluation and conclusions, particularly conclusions passed by the Fund's Board, be transmitted as well?

Eventually these questions had to be answered by vote.[8] The Board decided that the Fund was to supply to the GATT not only relevant statistical data but also conclusions as to the current need for restrictions. The information supplied to the GATT on behalf of the Fund thus covered the restrictive systems and the balance of payments and presented analyses of the causes and effects of the import restrictions in the light of the existing situation. Separate reports to the GATT contained the Fund's conclusions with respect to the import restrictions of each country. The results of the Fund's analyses varied from case to case. For some countries, balance of payments conditions did not seem to warrant further relaxation of import restrictions. For others, the conclusion was that circumstances were such that a progressive relaxation of discriminatory import restrictions could begin, having due regard to the uncertainties of the situation.

That separate reports and conclusions were prepared for each country was significant in itself. By judging the need for restrictions of each sterling area country in the light of its own balance of payments situation, the Fund was in effect challenging the principles by which the sterling area hung together. The two basic tenets of the sterling area were the institution of common policies by all its members and the combining of dollar reserves in a central pool, regardless of the balance of payments position of the individual sterling area member. Sterling area members, especially the United Kingdom, were anxious to preserve the sterling area for both economic and political reasons. For all members it

---

[8] See Chapter 11 above, pp. 230–31.

provided a sheltered export market; for the United Kingdom it helped to provide non-sterling earnings, and for the "outer sterling area," easy access to the London capital market. In addition, the sterling area preserved political ties within the British Commonwealth. The Fund's position was the same as it was later to take in its own consultations, as regards members both of the sterling area and of the EPU—namely, that groupings of these types were not members of the Fund or of the GATT, and that each member of these groupings as a member of the Fund (or a contracting party to the GATT) was individually responsible for its international commitments.

DELIBERATIONS AT TORQUAY

Mr. Saad led the Fund's delegation to Torquay. The actual consultations with the GATT were protracted and at times acrimonious. The method, the findings, and the recommendations of the Fund were supported in the GATT by the delegates of Belgium, Cuba, Canada, and the United States—mainly nations whose exports were the subject of discrimination. But the Fund's findings were bitterly contested by representatives of the United Kingdom, Australia, and New Zealand. They argued that the Fund had to recognize the existence of the sterling area and that it was unrealistic and unhelpful to look at individual nations apart from their membership in the regional system. Beyond this, they asserted that the discrimination resulting from the dollar pool was defensible because such discrimination enhanced the hard currency reserves of the sterling area and thereby helped to create conditions under which sterling could be made convertible and discrimination eventually eliminated. Australia also continued to argue, with considerable acerbity, that the Fund's concern was exclusively with exchange and other financial matters, and not at all with import restrictions or trade controls; that the Fund's advice should have been directed only to the need for intensifying restrictions at the time that the step was taken and not with the current position; and that the Fund's contribution to GATT consultations should be limited to detailed factual information.

Gradually, debates over these issues tended to subside, especially after the Fund began its own annual consultations program in March 1952. The Fund continued to be concerned that temporary regional arrangements, such as the sterling area and the EPU, might not be the road to convertibility and might become permanent economic blocs, but it confined itself to pointing out the dangers, such as prolonged inconvertibility, that could result from regional arrangements and to urging countries individually to reduce their restrictions. The Australian representatives did not push their position as strongly as before. A working party set up in Geneva in October 1951, under Australian chairmanship, to draft a procedure for consultations in and after March 1952 recommended only that a consultation under the GATT should not take place until the Fund had completed its consultation under Article XIV with the same country, and that the Fund should make available to the CONTRACTING PARTIES the results of its consultation with that member. In later years, in recognition of Australia's interest in GATT matters, the Australian Executive Director was appointed chairman of the Fund's Board Committee on Liaison with the CONTRACTING PARTIES to the GATT.

THE PROCEDURES REGULARIZED

Over time a regular procedure emerged for the Fund's participation in the GATT's consultations. Significantly, one of the reasons why the Fund wished to retain annual consultations with its members even after they had given up Article XIV of the Fund Agreement was that the Fund could implement its responcibilities to the CONTRACTING PARTIES to the GATT. Moreover, the Fund's decision of 1960 on the transition from Article XIV to Article VIII had a fourth paragraph concerning the Fund's coordination with the GATT.[9] In the interest of Fund-GATT collaboration, those Fund members which were also contracting parties to the GATT were requested to continue to send to the Fund information about their import restrictions maintained for balance of payments reasons. For countries which were not parties to the GATT, the Fund would seek to obtain information about such restrictions.

Certain changes in the GATT rules concerning discriminatory restrictions also came into effect as countries which were members of the Fund assumed the obligations of Article VIII. In general, the rules under which a contracting party could continue to have discriminatory restrictions were greatly simplified. A contracting party was now allowed to have discrimination in the application of its balance of payments restrictions only in a manner having equivalent effect to its restrictions maintained under the Fund Agreement, either Article XIV or Article VIII. These changes in the GATT rules took effect in February 1961. However, the practical significance of these changes in GATT rules was limited, since no contracting party had had discriminatory restrictions since October 1960.

GATT PROCEDURE

The actual process by which the CONTRACTING PARTIES conduct their consultations is different from that of the Fund.[10] Under the GATT, consultations are typically conducted by a working party or committee consisting of representa-

---

9 E.B. Decision No. 1034-(60/27), June 1, 1960; below, Vol. III, p. 261.

.10 The process of Fund consultations is described in detail in Chapter 11 above. A brief statement contrasting Fund and GATT consultations procedures can also be found in Gardner Patterson, *Discrimination in International Trade*, footnotes 77 and 78 on pp. 62–63.

tives of individual contracting parties. Recently, this has been the Committee on Balance of Payments Restrictions.

To facilitate the conduct of the consultations provided for in the GATT, the CONTRACTING PARTIES agree from time to time on certain plans, on the basis of which the consultations are conducted. Generally the plan for consultations under Articles XII:4 (*b*) and XVIII:12 (*b*) contains the following major headings:

    I. Balance of payments position and prospects
    II. Alternative measures to restore equilibrium
    III. System and methods of restrictions
    IV. Effects of the restrictions

Also considered under the heading "Balance of payments positions and prospects" are the level of and expected movements in monetary reserves, and any special factors affecting the availability of or the need for reserves. Under the topic "Alternative measures to restore equilibrium" are examined the internal monetary and fiscal situation and other relevant matters which may affect the balance of payments, and any internal action necessary to preserve or restore equilibrium. Such action may include long-term measures designed to raise productivity and expand capacity or to reduce structural rigidities. In discussing the "System and methods of restrictions" the legal and administrative bases for the restrictions are examined, as well as the particular categories of goods and the proportion of imports restricted. Variations in the treatment given to imports from different countries or currency areas are given special attention. Finally, under the last heading, the protective effects of restrictions on domestic production are closely considered, as well as the difficulties that may be expected upon relaxation or elimination of the restrictions.

Written material on these topics, or on other topics considered relevant, is examined by the Committee on Balance of Payments Restrictions; high-level technicians from the contracting party having the consultation are then expected to explain at some length to the committee their country's position. Finally, the GATT secretariat prepares a draft report on the committee's discussion with respect to each consultation; after agreement by the committee on a final version, the report is submitted to the CONTRACTING PARTIES for adoption.

FUND PROCEDURE

Under the procedure which has been evolved in the Fund, and by agreement with the GATT, the Fund provides for each GATT consultation, when notified of it, background material (such as Part II of a Fund paper prepared for a recent consultation under Article XIV or Article VIII with the country concerned, if this is available) together with the recent Article XIV consultation decision, if there is one. The right of any Executive Director concerned to object to the transmission of any of these documents is reserved. Supplementary or special background papers are transmitted only with the agreement of the Executive Board.

In addition to the provision of this background material, the Fund representative at a GATT consultation (nowadays always a member of the staff) is customarily invited by the chairman of the GATT Committee on Balance of Payments Restrictions to make a statement supplementing the documentation with respect to the position of the consulting country. This statement, which is approved by the Board in advance, is in two parts. The first relates to the balance of payments need for, and to the form of, the restrictions, i.e., to items I and III of the plan for the GATT consultations. The second part of the statement relates to "Alternative measures to restore equilibrium," in the language of item II of the plan, or to "alternative corrective measures which may be available" in the language of Article XII:4 (a) or Article XVIII:12 (a).

Somewhat different statements are made on behalf of the Fund at GATT consultations under Articles XII:4 (a) and XVIII:12 (a)—"intensification" consultations—on the one hand, and at annual or biennial consultations under Articles XII:4 (b) and XVIII:12 (b), on the other. For the former, the formula which has been evolved to present the Fund's views, if it is of the opinion that the level of restrictions is not excessive in relation to the balance of payments and reserve developments (the normal case), is:

> The general level of restrictions of [country] which are under reference does not go beyond the extent necessary at the present time to stop a serious decline in its monetary reserves.

When an earlier version of this statement was being worked out in 1952, the staff and the Board of the Fund believed that a determination in terms only of the last sentence of Article XV:2 (i.e., "as to what constitutes a serious decline in the contracting party's monetary reserves, a very low level of its monetary reserves or a reasonable rate of increase in its monetary reserves") would be difficult to formulate and probably not very helpful if it were presented in a flat, absolute form without a reference to the impact of the restrictions under consideration. Thus an attempt was made to relate the level of restrictions to the balance of payments or reserve problem, but still to keep as close as possible to the GATT criteria.

At the regular annual or biennial consultations, the statements made have varied according to circumstances. Some have been in terms similar to the one quoted above, while some have drawn attention to recent decisions taken in connection with Fund consultations under Article XIV and quoted passages from these decisions. These passages range from expressing the Fund's hope that progress in reducing discrimination and bilateralism will continue and that progress in reducing restrictions will be resumed as soon as practicable, to stating that the Fund considers that restrictions on a country's imports are no longer necessary to safeguard a country's monetary reserves and balance of payments.

The quotation of passages from Article XIV consultation decisions is particularly appropriate if the Fund wishes neither to suggest that the country has no balance of payments need for restrictions nor that its situation is such as to warrant the retention of restrictions. In such circumstances the standard form quoted above ("The general level . . . does not go beyond the extent necessary . . .") is clearly inappropriate, and the exact nuance of the Fund's views can best be conveyed by using the words of the Article XIV decision.

A third type of statement has been necessary where the Fund is not in a position to offer firm advice, either because the current year's consultation with the country under Article XIV has not been completed, or because the situation in the country has recently changed so substantially that a judgment on it is not yet possible.

As regards alternative measures (item II of the plan of the GATT consultations), the practice has been to notify the GATT that the Fund has no alternative measures to suggest. This wording has been taken to mean "no measures additional to the whole complex of measures discussed in the documentation" and not just the restrictions maintained by the country.

The provision of advice to the GATT is thus greatly dependent upon the smooth progress of the Fund's own program of consultations under Article XIV or Article VIII. The GATT secretariat seeks, after informal contact with the Fund staff, to arrange the CONTRACTING PARTIES' consultation schedules so that GATT consultations follow with a minimum of delay those which the Fund conducts with the same countries. Despite these efforts, however, GATT consultations sometimes take place without a recent Fund consultation decision and related background material being available. There are two main reasons why the Fund may not have completed a consultation with the country in question in the year since the preceding GATT consultation: (1) GATT consultations normally take place in brief semiannual meetings of the Committee on Balance of Payments Restrictions; (2) the contracting party may wish to have its GATT consultation scheduled at a particular time which does not fit the Fund's schedule. For these reasons, the Fund has devised a variety of "holding" or "delaying" statements.

The preparation of advice to be given to the GATT can therefore not be a routine matter. It is handled at Executive Director level by the Committee on Liaison with the CONTRACTING PARTIES to the GATT. As meetings of this committee are in practice attended by all Executive Directors with an interest in the matters on its agenda, it is usually possible to dispose of the committee's reports, when they reach the Board, under the lapse of time procedure.

CONSULTATIONS HELD AND THEIR SIGNIFICANCE

By the process described above, the CONTRACTING PARTIES undertook well over a hundred consultations from 1949 to 1965. After those in Torquay in November 1950, the next were held in Geneva in October-November 1952. These included consultations with Italy and the Netherlands on the continuance of discrimination, with France and Pakistan on the intensification of restrictions, and with Australia, Ceylon, and the United Kingdom on both discrimination and intensification. The revision in 1954–55 of the provisions of the GATT governing the use of import restrictions was undertaken principally to meet the emerging situation in which most countries no longer had balance of payments deficits of any consequence. But these provisions did not come into force until late in 1957 because the necessary number of acceptances had not been received earlier. Since several countries still maintained various import restrictions despite their strong balance of payments positions, the CONTRACTING PARTIES made use of a clause in the old provisions, and in 1956 invited twenty-one countries to consult: Australia, Austria, Brazil, Ceylon, Denmark, Finland, France, Germany, Greece, India, Italy, Japan, the Netherlands, New Zealand, Norway, Pakistan, the Federation of Rhodesia and Nyasaland, Sweden, Turkey, the Union of South Africa, and the United Kingdom. These consultations took place in the second half of 1957.

After the revised rules had come into effect, a broad general review of outstanding quantitative restrictions was initiated in 1958, and the first annual consultations under the new rules took place with thirteen countries in 1959. Biennial consultations were begun in 1960 with several less developed countries that maintained import restrictions for balance of payments reasons under Article XVIII of the GATT.[11]

Inasmuch as the Fund has assisted the GATT in all these consultations, Fund collaboration with the GATT has become a significant part of the Fund's work on restrictions. Cooperation between the two organizations has been close from the beginning, and the Fund's findings have always been accepted. Staff of the Fund have not only participated in the General Sessions but also have frequently attended meetings of the Committee on Balance of Payments Restrictions and of various working parties. To facilitate the Fund's participation in these various GATT activities, as well as to establish close contact with the UNCTAD, the Fund in 1965 set up its own office in Geneva.

This is not the place to consider just how effective the consultations held under the GATT have been in eliminating restrictions; but in view of the Fund's interest, a few observations may be made. An independent appraisal of the

[11] A list of the countries involved in GATT consultations from 1949 to 1963 is to be found in Curzon, *Multilateral Commercial Diplomacy*, Table 10, pp. 141–43.

GATT consultations held up to 1963 has come to the conclusion that they were blunt and hard-hitting, that they made European countries accountable for significant restrictions left untouched by the OEEC code of liberalization, and that they served to bring pressure on some European countries to remove import restrictions no longer needed in view of their balance of payments positions.[12] From the Fund's point of view, the last conclusion is the most important one: it seems safe to infer that, for the most part, countries which had relaxed restrictions covered by the Fund's Articles did not substitute restrictions falling under the jurisdiction of the GATT.

---

[12] Curzon, *Multilateral Commercial Diplomacy*, pp. 145–65.

PART IV

The Fund's Resources and Their Use

17

Derivation and Significance of the Fund's Resources

J. Keith Horsefield

THE FINANCIAL RESOURCES which the Fund can make available to its members originate in three ways. The first and largest source is the subscriptions paid by members when they join the Fund; the second is the excess of the Fund's income—mainly consisting of charges levied by the Fund for the use of its resources plus its income from investments—over its expenditures; the third is borrowing from members. For the purposes of the present chapter it is the total rather than the constitution of the Fund's holdings of members' currencies that is relevant. The replenishment of the Fund's holdings of individual currencies by the sale of gold is reviewed in Chapter 19.

QUOTAS AND SUBSCRIPTIONS

PROVISIONS OF THE ARTICLES

The principal Article in connection with quotas and subscriptions is Article III, of which the contents, partly summarized (in brackets), follow:

> SECTION 1. *Quotas.*—Each member shall be assigned a quota. [Members represented at Bretton Woods have quotas set out in Schedule A to the Articles.] The quotas of other members shall be determined by the Fund.

> SEC. 2. *Adjustment of quotas.*—The Fund shall at intervals of five years review, and if it deems it appropriate propose an adjustment of, the quotas of the members. It may also, if it thinks fit, consider at any other time the adjustment of any particular quota at the request of the member concerned. A four-fifths majority of the total voting power shall be required for any change in quotas and no quota shall be changed without the consent of the member concerned.

> SEC. 3. *Subscriptions: time, place, and form of payment.*—(*a*) The subscription of each member shall be equal to its quota and shall be paid in full to the Fund

at the appropriate depository on or before the date when the member becomes eligible under Article XX, Section 4 (c) or (d), to buy currencies from the Fund.

(b) Each member shall pay in gold, as a minimum, the smaller of

(i) twenty-five percent of its quota; or

(ii) ten percent of its net official holdings of gold and United States dollars as at the date when the Fund notifies members under Article XX, Section 4 (a) that it will shortly be in a position to begin exchange transactions.

Each member shall furnish to the Fund the data necessary to determine its net official holdings of gold and United States dollars.

(c) Each member shall pay the balance of its quota in its own currency.

(d) [Provision for countries occupied by the enemy]

SEC. 4. *Payments when quotas are changed.*—(a) Each member which consents to an increase in its quota shall, within thirty days after the date of its consent, pay to the Fund twenty-five percent of the increase in gold and the balance in its own currency. If, however, on the date when the member consents to an increase, its monetary reserves are less than its new quota, the Fund may reduce the proportion of the increase to be paid in gold.

(b) [Provision for reduction in quota]

SEC. 5. *Substitution of securities for currency.*—[The Fund must accept nonnegotiable noninterest-bearing securities in place of currency to the extent that it deems the currency not to be needed for its purposes.]

Two provisions elsewhere in the Articles safeguard members' rights in relation to quotas. By Article XII, Section 2 (b) (ii), only the Governors (not the Executive Directors) can approve a revision of quotas. By Article XVII (b) (ii), the provision in Article III, Section 2, that no change in a quota shall be made without the consent of the member concerned, can be revoked only with the consent of every member.

The only interpretation that the Board has found it necessary to give in connection with the foregoing provisions was the following, decided on July 20, 1950:

It is determined as a matter of interpretation that Article III, Section 4, and not Article III, Section 3, applies to all changes in quotas.[1]

The occasion for this interpretation arose when France received an increase in its quota before it had paid its subscription. Because of the low level of its reserves, its gold subscription was to be 10 per cent of its net official holdings of gold and dollars instead of 25 per cent of its quota. The question was whether this subscription would suffice for the enlarged quota, or whether 25 per cent of the increase would have to be paid in gold. The Board decided, in principle, that the latter was right; but as France had been given to understand the contrary, it accepted 10 per cent of France's net official holdings of gold and

---

[1] E.B. Decision No. 595-3, July 20, 1950; below, Vol. III, p. 222.

dollars as sufficing for the whole gold subscription. (Subsequently France reduced the Fund's holdings of its currency to 75 per cent of its quota, as has been done by most members that originally subscribed less than 25 per cent of their quotas in gold.)

BASIS OF QUOTAS

The quotas negotiated at Bretton Woods and listed in Schedule A to the Articles of Agreement bore some relation to a formula devised by the U.S. Treasury, as follows:

> 90 per cent of
>> 2 per cent of national income, 1940,
>
> *plus* 5 per cent of gold and dollar balances on July 1, 1943,
> *plus* 10 per cent of maximum variation of exports, 1934–38,
> *plus* 10 per cent of average imports, 1934–38,
>
> increased for each country in the same ratio as average
> exports, 1934–38, bore to national income.

The extent to which the quotas negotiated actually conformed to this formula has been discussed in Volume I.[2] It is sufficient here to note that when considering quotas for new members in the early years of the Fund, the data yielded by this formula were used as a starting point for the discussion. Some anomalies produced by the formula were reviewed in 1962, and are considered below.

In accordance with Article III, Section 2, a general review of quotas took place in 1950, 1955, 1960, and 1965. Although there have been only two general revisions of quotas during the twenty years covered by this volume, and one of these did not coincide with the date for a general review, it will be convenient to divide our study of quotas into four parts corresponding to the periods between the general review dates.

Table 14 at the end of this chapter lists the quotas for all member countries as shown in Schedule A to the Articles of Agreement and as they stood at the end of 1950, 1955, 1960, and 1965.

SIGNIFICANCE OF QUOTAS [3]

For the Fund as a whole, the size of quotas determines the volume of currencies and of gold which is available to it. Quotas have two other functions, both applying to individual members: they determine the member's basic voting rights and they influence the amount that it can draw from the Fund.

---

[2] See above, Vol. I, pp. 97–98.

[3] See also Oscar L. Altman, "Quotas in the International Monetary Fund," *Staff Papers*, Vol. V (1956–57), pp. 129–50.

A member's basic votes comprise 250 votes plus one additional vote for each part of its quota equivalent to $100,000 (Article XII, Section 5 (a)). For the purpose of voting under Article V, Sections 4 and 5, relating to the use of the Fund's resources (waiver of conditions and declaration of ineligibility), these votes are increased by one for each $400,000 of net sales by the Fund of the member's currency, or decreased by one for each $400,000 of its net purchases from the Fund, as the case may be (Article XII, Section 5 (b)).[4] Executive Directors cast the votes of the members that have appointed or elected them. They must cast these votes as a unit (Article XII, Section 3 (i)). On most matters, a majority of votes is sufficient to carry a Board decision. In recent years votes have seldom been formally counted, except where required by the Articles in connection with changes in the scale of charges. Nevertheless, the voting power of Executive Directors still operates as the means by which a consensus is arrived at.

Table 10 shows the proportion of the total votes that could be cast, at five selected dates, by each Executive Director. The changes between the columns reflect principally the effects of (a) the quotas of countries joining the Fund, and (b) disproportionate changes in members' quotas, particularly the special increases approved by the Governors in 1959 and the increases granted under the decision on the compensatory financing of export fluctuations.[5] As new countries have joined the Fund the number of Executive Directors has increased, although not in proportion to the growth in total membership or total quotas. As a result of all the foregoing, the proportion of total votes which can be cast by the five appointed Executive Directors declined from 67.33 per cent in 1946 to 45.67 per cent in 1964.

The stability of the Executive Board in terms of the nationality of the Directors is indicated in Table 10 and shown in more detail in Appendix A to Volume I. The latter also shows the stability of the groupings of countries electing Directors, which has been almost complete since 1954. The lack of change in these respects reflects the interweaving of four factors: (1) the relative sizes of members' quotas; (2) the rules of election laid down in the Articles of Agreement (Schedule C), as modified from time to time by the Board of Governors; (3) economic, political, social, and cultural affinities; and (4) pre-election negotiation among members and Executive Directors, influenced by the relative voting powers of the members.

Two limits are imposed by Article V, Section 3 (a) (iii), on the amounts that a member may draw from the Fund. Unless the Fund agrees to waive these limits, the member may not draw in any twelve months more than 25 per cent of its quota plus any amount needed to increase the Fund's holdings of its

---

[4] For a discussion of the interpretation of this provision, see above, Vol. I, pp. 367–68.

[5] See Chapter 18 below, pp. 421–22.

Table 10. Voting Power of Executive Directors as Percentage of Total Votes,
at Selected Election Dates

	Years in Which Elections Held				
	1946	1950	1956	1960	1964
	Number of Executive Directors				
Executive Directors	12	14	16	18	20
Appointed by:					
United States	33.52	30.46	26.62	25.63	22.63
United Kingdom	16.00	14.54	12.71	12.18	10.77
China	6.95	6.31	5.52	—	—
France	5.73	6.04	5.28	5.02	4.43
India	5.13	4.66	4.08	3.86	3.41
Germany	—	—	—	5.02	4.43
Elected from: (Article XII, Section 3 *(b)* (iii))					
Belgium	3.75	4.84	4.46	4.03	3.58
Canada	4.83	3.85	3.12	3.98	3.76
Czechoslovakia/Yugo-slavia/Germany	4.65	2.53	3.41	—	—
Netherlands	5.13	4.12	3.98	3.57	3.78
United Arab Republic	3.48	4.77	4.78	4.86	5.20
Australia	—	3.84	3.72	3.95	4.35
Italy	—	3.79	3.88	3.43	4.74
Denmark/Iceland/Sweden	—	—	3.66	3.54	3.13
Japan	—	—	3.77	4.36	4.10
China	—	—	—	3.55	3.14
Indonesia	—	—	—	2.81	2.90
Senegal	—	—	—	—	2.74
Uganda	—	—	—	—	3.09
Elected from: (Article XII, Section 3 *(b)* (iv))					
Brazil	5.53	5.33	3.72	3.61	3.30
Mexico/El Salvador/Venezuela	5.28	4.92	3.57	3.08	3.17
Argentina/Chile	—	—	3.73	3.50	3.35
Total [1]	100.00	100.00	100.00	100.00	100.00
Number of members	38	49	60	68	101
Total quotas *($ million)*	7,329.5	8,036.5	8,750.5	14,740.7	15,849.5

[1] The sums of the items may not equal the totals because of rounding.

currency to 75 per cent of its quota; and the Fund's holdings may not exceed 200 per cent of the quota.

QUOTAS, 1946–50

Among the earliest tasks undertaken by the Executive Board when it began work in 1946 was to review the quotas of certain members that had protested at Bretton Woods that the amounts allotted to them were too small. One of these members was Paraguay, which had been allotted $2 million at Bretton Woods but sought a quota of $5 million. Its representative argued that the formula showed that $5 million would have been the correct figure, but the Board, viewing the formula as having no official standing, decided to increase Paraguay's quota to $3.5 million only.

A request by France for an increase from $450 million to $675 million was also supported by a reference to the formula. This request, however, would have raised the French quota above that of China, whereas it had been understood between the U.S. and Chinese delegations at Bretton Woods that China should have the fourth largest quota (after the United States, the United Kingdom, and the U.S.S.R.). China therefore made a counter-request for an increase in quota from $550 million to $715 million. The Governors decided to increase the French quota only to $525 million,[6] and China then withdrew its request.

Australia, which had been allotted a quota of $200 million at Bretton Woods, delayed its application for membership until 1947. When this came before the Board, Mr. Saad (Egypt) pointed out that the formula would have yielded a quota for Australia of $134 million only. He was reminded that the formula had no binding force, and that Australia's quota had been settled at the same time as those of the other original members. He suggested, however, that if Australia was to receive a quota so appreciably larger than that yielded by the formula, Egypt and Iran, which had protested at Bretton Woods against the amounts allotted to them, should also be given larger quotas. The Executive Directors therefore considered the cases of these two members, and recommended to the Governors that their quotas should be revised. The Governors agreed, and accordingly the quota for Egypt was increased from $45 million to $60 million and that of Iran from $25 million to $35 million.[7]

There were no further increases in quotas during the years 1946 through 1950. However, on the partition of India in 1947 the quota for India was maintained unaltered, thus affording the member, in effect, an increase in quota per capita;[8] India had protested at Bretton Woods that its quota was too small. Honduras, because of a difficulty in providing its gold subscription, asked that

---

[6] Resolution 1-13, *Summary Proceedings, 1946*, p. 56.

[7] Resolutions 2-3 and 2-4, *Summary Proceedings, 1947*, pp. 35–36.

[8] *Summary Proceedings, 1947*, p. 20.

its quota should be reduced from $2.5 million to $0.5 million. The Governors agreed.[9]

Rule D-3 requires the Board, at least one year before the time when a quinquennial review of quotas is due, to appoint a committee to study what should be done and prepare a written report. Accordingly, in December 1949 the Board agreed, on the proposal of the Managing Director, to set up a Committee of the Whole on Review of Quotas. A staff committee, appointed to advise the Committee of the Whole, recommended that quotas should be doubled to correspond to the general economic growth since the dates on which the formula was based. However, the Managing Director suggested to the Board that, in view of the uncertain conditions prevailing in the world late in 1950, the time was inopportune to make any change. The Committee of the Whole agreed with the Managing Director, and the Board formally closed the general review in March 1951 with a decision that no increase should be proposed at that time.

The total of quotas, which in Schedule A was $7,600 million (excluding the U.S.S.R.), had risen by the end of 1950 to $8,036.5 million, principally because of the addition of nine new members, offset by one (Poland) that left the Fund.

Proposals to entrust the Fund with additional resources were made by a group of experts appointed by the United Nations in 1949 to recommend national and international measures to achieve full employment. The inflationary dangers inherent in their proposals, however, caused these to be disregarded.

QUOTAS, 1951–55

A second group of experts, asked by the United Nations to propose measures to achieve international economic stability, including the reduction of fluctuations in primary product markets, reported late in 1951.[10] The report included a number of proposals affecting the Fund, including a recommendation that its resources should be increased to the point at which it could meet its share of a decline in the supply of dollars which might amount to $10 billion over two years. The Board considered this report in April 1952, and decided that the Fund's representatives to the meeting of ECOSOC at which the report was to be presented should make two points that concern the subject of this chapter. One was that the Fund regarded it as its function to make its resources available, to make known that they were available, and to provide a forum for the discussion of economic problems. A second point was that the Fund's resources were limited, and although there had for some time been discussions of the possibility of increases in quotas, these seemed likely to be frustrated by members' inability to find the necessary 25 per cent of any increase in gold.

---

[9] Resolution 3-5, *Summary Proceedings, 1948*, p. 48.

[10] *Measures for International Economic Stability.*

Toward the end of 1952 the Board discussed a request from Ethiopia for an increase in its quota (which was not, however, proceeded with). At the request of Directors, the staff then prepared a general study of the adequacy of quotas. Because it was less than two years since the Board had decided that no general increase was needed, the staff concentrated on a possible need for relative increases. In a report to the Board in January 1953 the staff pointed out that, while the value of world trade in general had increased by approximately three times since 1937–38, there were eleven members whose trade had increased by more than four times in the interval. The staff also pointed to three members whose quotas as fixed at Bretton Woods appeared to be badly out of line with the formula. To amend these discrepancies an increase in aggregate quotas of some $250 million would be needed. The Managing Director commented, however, that it appeared from the staff's inquiries that the quota structure as a whole was not badly distorted, and for this reason, and because quotas could not be fixed on statistical grounds alone, he proposed that no action should be taken. The Board tacitly agreed.

The Fund's views were noted at the meeting of ECOSOC at which the report on measures for international economic stability was considered, and the Fund was invited to keep under review the adequacy of monetary reserves and to furnish a report on the subject for the meeting of ECOSOC in 1953.[11] In response to this invitation the staff prepared in April 1953 a draft study which, after discussion in the Board and some consequential revision, was forwarded to ECOSOC in June 1953.[12] Its conclusions were presented in the form of four alternative definitions of "adequacy," coupled with the statement that while many countries would have adequate reserves on the least exacting definition, only a few would do so if reserves were to be expected to maintain currency stability without restrictions even in a severe depression—falling short, however, of the severity of the 1930's.

Thereafter the staff continued to study the subject, with particular reference to a possible need to expand the Fund's resources in order to enable it adequately to supplement members' owned reserves.

In December 1954 the Board set up a Committee of the Whole to undertake the Second Quinquennial Review of quotas, due in 1955. It became clear at an early meeting of the committee that some of the primary producing countries, especially in Latin America, were seeking increases in their quotas. Mr. Southard (United States), however, suggested that no over-all increase in quotas was justified because the Fund's resources were already large and had remained relatively unused. He and Lord Harcourt (United Kingdom) announced that their

---

[11] Resolution 427(XIV), July 8, 1952.

[12] An updated version was printed in *Staff Papers*, Vol. III (1953–54), pp. 181–227, and is reproduced below, Vol. III, pp. 311–48.

Governments were unwilling to increase their quotas. As this meant that the necessary 80 per cent majority for an increase in quotas would not be forthcoming, the Board decided instead to invite individual member countries to approach it if they wished their quotas increased.

Meanwhile several attempts were made to evolve a formula which would permit members with the smallest quotas to increase them, although any such formula was opposed by some Directors as tending to impair the liquidity of the Fund by increasing only its supply of currencies not likely to be needed for drawings. The Committee of the Whole was reluctant, in any case, to suggest an increase in any quota that already exceeded $20 million, and as it turned out a number of Latin American countries seeking increases had quotas in that category. Taking everything into account, the committee recommended in January 1956 that there should be no general increase in quotas, but that the Board should look with favor upon requests by members with small quotas to increase them. The Board accepted this recommendation, thereby ending the Second Quinquennial Review. Within the five years 1951–55 only one increase in quota was granted, Honduras being permitted to restore its quota from an initial figure of $0.5 million to the $2.5 million agreed at Bretton Woods.

During the five years 1951–55 the aggregate of quotas increased by $714 million as the result of the addition of ten new members, offset by the departure of Czechoslovakia.

QUOTAS, 1956–60

In contrast to the preceding five years, the quinquennium 1956–60 saw major changes in quotas. During 1956 and 1957 a number of increases were granted, following the recommendation of the Committee of the Whole in January 1956. These were based on a scale which was worked out in the course of informal discussions among Executive Directors and was officially known as the "Small Quotas Policy." It provided that quotas below $5 million could be increased, on request, to $7.5 million, those of $5–8 million to $10 million, those of $10 million to $15 million, and those of $15 million to $20 million.

First signs of pressure on the Fund's resources also developed in 1957. The Managing Director and some Governors at the Annual Meeting, 1957, pointed out that almost all drawings during the year had necessitated waivers of the quantitative limits set by Article V, Section 3 (a) (iii), and suggested that this implied that quotas were too small.[13] Pursuing this point, the staff provided the management in April 1958 with an interim report on a possible need to increase quotas. This argued that the recession in the United States, and the related decline in raw material prices, were likely to induce primary producing

[13] *Summary Proceedings, 1957*, pp. 22, 42, 62, 86, 139.

countries to seek drawings from the Fund on a scale which it might be difficult for the Fund to meet. After further review, the staff produced in August 1958 a report entitled *International Reserves and Liquidity*, which concluded that it was doubtful whether the Fund's resources were adequate fully to perform its duties under the Articles in the conditions likely to be met in coming months.[14]

Meanwhile a decision was reached in the U.S. Government on the basis of which the President instructed the U.S. Governor to propose, at the forthcoming Annual Meeting in New Delhi, that prompt consideration should be given to a general increase in quotas. A resolution to that effect was adopted on October 7,[15] and on the Board's return to Washington from New Delhi consideration was given to it.

The outcome of the Board's deliberations was a report to the Governors entitled *Enlargement of Fund Resources Through Increases in Quotas*, which was printed and distributed at the end of December 1958. In this, the Directors announced their conclusion that an increase in quotas was highly desirable, and suggested that an increase by 50 per cent was a reasonable basis for a general increase.[16] At the same time, the Board proposed that special increases should be given to Canada, Germany, and Japan, and to members with particularly small quotas. The report concluded with three draft resolutions, the first providing for a general increase of 50 per cent in quotas, the second for increasing the quotas of twenty-four members to which the Small Quotas Policy applied to levels 50 per cent above those provided by that formula, and the third for special increases for Canada, Germany, and Japan. At the time that this report was completed the Board had not finished reviewing the requests for special increases submitted by some other members, and in February 1959 the Governors were invited to consider a fourth resolution providing for such increases for fourteen members other than those covered by the second and third resolutions.

The justification for these special increases rested on two alternative arguments. Some members sought such increases because at Bretton Woods they had been offered smaller quotas than they wished for, or quotas not in line with the formula, or quotas based on incomplete or inaccurate data. Other members requested increases because their economies had grown appreciably faster than the general run in the postwar period.

The difficulty expected to be experienced by some members in finding gold to pay for 25 per cent of the increase in their quotas, mentioned to ECOSOC in 1952, was met by the offer of two concessions. Members in that position were

---

[14] The report was published on September 16; see below, Vol. III, pp. 349–420.

[15] Resolution 13-10, *Summary Proceedings, 1958*, p. 178.

[16] *Enlargement of Fund Resources Through Increases in Quotas*, pp. 11, 12; below, Vol. III, p. 427.

to be allowed to increase their quotas by installments over five years, paying in gold 25 per cent of each installment annually; or, if they preferred, they might provide the gold subscription by making a special drawing, which would have to be repurchased in three annual installments. These arrangements applied only to the general increase in quotas; members having special increases were expected to pay 25 per cent of their increases in gold.

All four resolutions were adopted by the Governors, the first three on February 2, 1959 and the fourth on April 6.[17] The new quotas became operative on September 9, when members aggregating more than 75 per cent of total quotas had accepted their increases.

During 1960 special increases were approved for four other countries, Australia, Chile, Colombia, and Yugoslavia.[18]

A Committee of the Whole appointed by the Board in December 1959, in preparation for the quinquennial review of quotas due in 1960, recommended that no further increases were necessary. The Board agreed on December 16, 1960.

As a result of the foregoing changes, and of the addition of eleven new members, the total of quotas at the end of 1960 was $14,740.7 million, an increase of almost $6 billion compared with five years earlier.

QUOTAS, 1961–65

During the Fund's fourth quinquennium, as during the preceding one, much attention was focused on small quotas. The period ended with a recommendation for a second general increase in quotas, together with a further group of special increases, all of which took effect after 1965.

Apart from one or two belated increases stemming from the general review described in the previous section, the first occasion when the Board's attention was directed to quotas during the period 1961–65 was in April 1962, when the United Arab Republic sought an increase from $90 million to $120 million. Among the reasons which the member cited for the increase was the instability of its export receipts, and the same reason was given three months later when the Syrian Arab Republic asked for an increase from $15 million to $25 million. The United Arab Republic's request was approved by the Board and in due course by the Governors.[19] When that of the Syrian Arab Republic was discussed by the Board, Mr. Southard said that he understood that many countries in the same quota range desired increases in their quotas, and the increase sought therefore raised very broad questions. Shortly afterward, El Salvador asked for its quota to be increased from $11.25 million to $15 million.

---

[17] Resolutions 14-1, 14-2, 14-3, 14-4, *Summary Proceedings, 1959*, pp. 158–62.

[18] Resolutions 15-2, 15-3, 15-4, 15-11, *Summary Proceedings, 1960*, pp. 158–60, 169.

[19] Resolution 17-2, *Summary Proceedings, 1962*, p. 221.

During the Annual Meeting, 1962, the Managing Director discussed the problem of small quotas with a number of Governors, and subsequently reported to the Board that he believed that increases in such quotas might be a useful way in which the Fund could assist the members concerned. The staff was asked to prepare a study suggesting the lines along which the Board might proceed.

In the meantime the Board had before it an invitation from the UN Commission on International Commodity Trade to consider whether the Fund could play a larger part in providing compensatory financing for export fluctuations, and if so in what way. By the time that the staff study just mentioned was ready, the Board was engaged in considering its reply to the UN Commission, and the two subjects thereafter were dealt with together.

The staff analysis divided members into four groups, (1) those having quotas of $30 million and under, (2) those having quotas between $31 million and $60 million, (3) the ten industrial countries, and (4) the remainder (excluding China). Comparisons of existing quotas with the Bretton Woods formula applied to 1955–59 data, with average exports for 1955–59, and with the variation of exports from trend in 1950–61, showed that the quotas of the second group of countries compared unfavorably with those of the countries in the other three groups. Using the comparison with variation of exports from trend, the under $30 million group also appeared to have quotas that were too small in relation to the ten industrial countries and the remainder. Fresh calculations, made a little later with more up-to-date data, confirmed these results.

The staff then undertook extensive research into possible variations in the formula underlying quotas, in the hope of discovering a version of it which would avoid certain unsatisfactory features. A first report pointed out that the inclusion of the ratio between exports and national income in the formula had the effect, if quotas were plotted on a graph measuring quotas vertically and national income horizontally, of producing a U-shaped curve instead of one that rose consistently from left to right. The staff also commented that if the weights allotted to national income and to reserves in the formula were lessened, the quotas for small countries would be increased relative to those of large countries. The Board considered with interest these results of the staff's work, but was unwilling to accept any alternative formula, preferring to continue to regard the original one as a point of reference when the calculation of quotas was being undertaken.

It may be noted here that a substantial departure from the formula as applied to small countries followed from the resolutions taken in 1959 and reported above. The combined effect of the Small Quotas Policy and the 50 per cent general increase in quotas in 1959 was to raise the minimum quota to $11.25 million. This, however, was greatly in excess of the figure reached by applying the Bretton Woods formula to data for a large number of the newly established

African countries which joined the Fund in 1963. It was accordingly suggested to some of these countries that they might prefer to accept a quota of $7.5 million, and nine of them did so, as Laos and Nepal had done in 1961.

Meanwhile the Fund's reply in February 1963 to the inquiry from the UN Commission included a statement that consideration would be given to increases in quotas if members felt that their existing quotas were inadequate to enable them to deal with fluctuations in export proceeds, or in their balances of payments generally.[20]

Any increases in quotas, and particularly those of small countries, were likely to raise again the question whether the members concerned were able to contribute 25 per cent of the increases in gold. The Board accordingly offered again the options of increasing the quotas by installments over five years or of taking special drawings from which to provide the needed gold.[21] It considered, but rejected, a suggestion by the staff that the Fund might also be prepared to reduce the proportion of increases required to be provided in gold, as contemplated by Article III, Section 4 (*a*).

The increase requested by the Syrian Arab Republic, that by El Salvador (which had since been revised upward to $20 million), and one asked for by Honduras (from $11.25 million to $15 million) were recommended to the Governors under the terms of the compensatory financing facility, and were approved.[22] Six similar increases were approved in 1964, and a further five in the first two months of 1965.[23]

Apart from these increases under the compensatory financing facility, the quotas of four countries were enlarged in the latter part of 1963 and the early part of 1964—those of Israel ($25 million to $50 million), Italy ($270 million to $500 million), Malaysia ($37.5 million to $100 million), and Panama ($0.5 million to $11.25 million).[24]

In March 1964, as part of its study of the problems of international liquidity, the staff prepared a study of quotas which suggested that substantially larger ones would be appropriate in 1964–65. An increase of the general order of 50 per cent was suggested, together with special increases larger than this for certain members in order to reduce disparities between the existing quotas. This recommendation was discussed by the Board in April, and again in connection with the drafting of the Annual Report in June. In the Annual Report the

---

[20] *Compensatory Financing of Export Fluctuations: A Report by the International Monetary Fund;* below, Vol. III, pp. 442-57.

[21] E.B. Decision No. 1529-(63/33), June 14, 1963; below, Vol. III, p. 222.

[22] Resolutions 18-19, 18-20, 18-21, *Summary Proceedings, 1963,* pp. 264–65.

[23] Resolutions 19-1, 19-4, 19-5, 19-16, 19-17, 19-19, *Summary Proceedings, 1964,* pp. 254, 256–58, 266–67, 268; Resolutions 20-1 through 20-5, *Summary Proceedings, 1965,* pp. 241–45.

[24] Resolutions 19-2, 19-3, 19-7, 19-18, *Summary Proceedings, 1964,* pp. 255–56, 259, 267–68.

Directors commented that increases in quotas were the normal way to expand the operations of the Fund, and suggested that it would be advantageous to consider quotas as promptly as possible after the Annual Meeting.[25]

Once more the problem of the payment in gold for 25 per cent of any increase came to the fore. On this occasion the Annual Report distinguished two types of difficulty.[26] One, which had previously been provided for, was that some members' reserves of gold and foreign exchange were too low for them to be able to afford the gold payment. The other, which was considered for the first time, was that other members having reserves of convertible currencies but not gold would be apt to request the issuers of these currencies (mainly the United States and the United Kingdom) to convert appropriate amounts into gold for use in providing the necessary 25 per cent of quota increases. While gold found from a member's own reserves entailed only an exchange of one type of reserve for another (an improved position in the Fund), gold provided by the issuers of reserve currencies in exchange for their currencies would adversely affect their reserve positions.

On the invitation of the Executive Board, the Governors passed a resolution instructing the Executive Directors to consider adjusting members' quotas and to submit an appropriate proposal to the Board of Governors at an early date.[27] Pursuant to this resolution there was prolonged consideration in the Executive Board [28] which culminated in a recommendation for a general increase of 25 per cent all round, together with special increases for sixteen countries whose quotas were disproportionately small.[29] Provision was made for the increases in quotas to be taken in installments, and for special drawings, as on previous occasions. In addition the Board, after much debate, proposed two procedures to mitigate the drain on those members whose currencies were converted to provide gold. One was that certain of the special drawings, up to the equivalent of $150 million, would be directed by the Fund to specific members' currencies; the Fund would then replenish its holdings of these currencies by the sale of gold to the members concerned. The second was that the Fund would make general deposits of gold with the United States (maximum $250 million) and the United Kingdom (maximum $100 million) in respect of gold sold by those countries. The deposits would be demand deposits, and the Fund would propose to draw on them and on earmarked gold, in appropriate proportions, when it had need of gold.

Resolutions embodying the Directors' proposals were submitted to the Governors for a vote without meeting and by April 1, 1965 had been approved by

---

[25] *Annual Report, 1964*, pp. 35–36.
[26] *Ibid.*, pp. 36–37.
[27] Resolution 19-20, *Summary Proceedings, 1964*, p. 269.
[28] See Vol. I above, pp. 579–83.
[29] *Annual Report, 1965*, pp. 124–32. See also below, Vol. III, pp. 458–65.

the necessary 80 per cent of votes.[30] However, the acceptance of individual increases, which in many countries required legislative action, was protracted, and it was not until February 23, 1966 that the Directors were able to decide that members holding two thirds of the total votes had notified their acceptance, this being the minimum stipulated in the resolutions to bring the increases into effect. Shortly afterwards the Fourth Quinquennial Review was formally terminated.

The concessions offered in connection with the 25 per cent gold subscription were utilized by forty-two members; of these, twenty-three took special drawings totaling $246 million and nineteen opted for increases by installments. Gold deposits of $289.1 million were made, of which $244.7 million were in the United States and the remainder in the United Kingdom. Gold to the value of $148 million was used to replenish currencies. Four members declined the offered increases, and three others had not decided whether to accept at the expiration of the period allowed for the purpose.

Seven members that applied for increases under the compensatory financing facility after the Directors' recommendations had been submitted to the Governors were permitted to superimpose the general increase upon the special increases which they sought.[31]

As a result of the influx of new members and of the various special increases (including compensatory financing increases) mentioned above, the aggregate of quotas rose between 1961 and the end of 1965 to $15,976.6 million, an increase of $1,236 million. But the effect of the general increase was felt progressively after 1965. By the end of 1968 the total had risen to $21,198.4 million; and it continues to rise as the quotas being increased by installments progressively attain higher levels.

INCOME AND EXPENDITURE

The Fund's income is mostly derived from charges, and is therefore closely related to the volume of transactions. It will be convenient to summarize the figures (set out in Table 11) by the same five-year periods as were used in the previous section.

During the first five years of the Fund's life drawings were small, except in 1947. Correspondingly, the addition to its resources arising from charges was also small. For the five financial years 1946/47 through 1950/51 the Fund's income totaled $11.4 million, of which $9.3 million was paid in gold and the

---

[30] Resolutions 20-6 and 20-7, *Summary Proceedings, 1965*, pp. 245–49.

[31] Resolutions 20-9 through 20-13, *Summary Proceedings, 1965*, pp. 252–57; Resolutions 21-1 and 21-2, *Summary Proceedings, 1966*, pp. 236–38.

Table 11. International Monetary Fund: Income, Expenditure, and Reserves, Fiscal Years 1947–66

(In millions of U.S. dollars)

Fiscal Year [1]	Income Excluding Investments				Expenditure	Investment Income		Accumulated Deficit (−) or General Reserve	Accumulated Total of Special Reserve
	Charges on Drawings		Other [2]	Total		Applied to Deficit	To Special Reserve		
	Paid in gold	Paid in currencies							
1946/47	0.47	—	—	0.47	2.17[3]	—	—	−1.70	—
1947/48	4.16	0.03	—	4.19	2.63	—	—	−0.15	—
1948/49	1.38	0.41	0.01	1.80	3.81	—	—	−2.16	—
1949/50	1.59	0.72	0.01	2.32	3.97	—	—	−3.81	—
1950/51	1.76	0.90	0.01	2.68	4.60	—	—	−5.72	—
1951/52	2.52	0.71	0.02	3.25	4.77	—	—	−7.24	—
1952/53	2.96	0.92	0.28	4.16	4.89	—	—	−7.96	—
1953/54	4.41	0.51	0.07	4.99	5.01	—	—	−7.99	—
1954/55	2.16	0.13	0.06	2.47	4.99	—	—	−10.51	—
1955/56	1.30	0.02	0.23	1.53	5.35	0.12	—	−14.21	—
1956/57	4.63	3.57	0.19	8.40	5.38	4.90	—	−6.30	—
1957/58	13.47	5.50	1.29	20.30	11.34[4]	3.33	2.83	5.99	2.83
1958/59	20.57	4.55	2.05	27.17	6.68	—	4.11	25.58	6.94
1959/60	12.57	5.16	3.27	21.00	6.88	—	15.36	39.76	22.30
1960/61	10.72	3.18	0.65	14.55	7.36	—	19.87	46.99	42.16
1961/62	20.59	11.98	0.54	33.11	8.16	—	22.78	71.81	64.94
1962/63	22.72	4.66	3.66	31.04	9.57	—	25.09	93.29	90.04
1963/64	27.95	6.68	1.72	36.35	13.12[5]	—	27.49	116.52	117.52
1964/65	27.36	18.03	2.36	47.75	22.20[6]	—	30.75	141.81	148.27
1965/66	27.65	52.18	1.49	81.32	36.77[7]	—	33.91	186.36	182.18
Totals [8]	210.94	119.84	17.91	348.85	169.65	8.35	182.19		

[1] Ending June 30 for 1946/47 and April 30 for 1947/48–1965/66.
[2] Mainly charges on stand-by arrangements, and mainly paid in currencies.
[3] Includes excess of expenditure over income from inception to June 30, 1946, amounting to $0.10 million.
[4] Includes building costs to end of fiscal year 1957/58 ($5.62 million).
[5] Includes building costs, $2.18 million.
[6] Includes building costs, $4.64 million, and payments under the GAB, $4.56 million.
[7] Includes building costs, $5.66 million, and payments under the GAB, $16.07 million.
[8] Totals do not exactly agree because of rounding and of certain administrative adjustments.

remainder in drawing members' currencies. As total expenditure in the five years was over $17 million, the Fund's resources were reduced, on income and expenditure account, by some $5.7 million.

During the five financial years 1951/52 through 1955/56, income totaled $16.4 million and expenditure amounted to $25 million. By the end of the Fund's first ten years, therefore, there had been a net loss of resources on income and expenditure account of $14.2 million.

The year 1956 was, however, the turning point. Since then much greater drawings have produced a large increase in the Fund's income. During the five financial years 1956/57 through 1960/61 charges totaled almost $84 million, of which three fourths was paid in gold. Total income apart from that derived from investments was over $91 million, and as expenditure was only $37.3 million a substantial increment to the Fund's resources resulted. During the same period the income from the Fund's investments (see the immediately following section) totaled $50.5 million.

During the five financial years 1961/62 through 1965/66, the Fund's income rose steeply to a total of $229.6 million, exclusive of $140 million from investments. Charges totaled $220 million, of which $126 million was paid in gold. Expenditure was $88 million. At the end of the five years the General Reserve amounted to $186.4 million and the Special Reserve (resulting from investment income) to $182.2 million.

INVESTMENT OF THE FUND'S ASSETS

PROVISIONS OF THE ARTICLES

Article XII, Section 2 (g), provides that

> The Board of Governors, and the Executive Directors to the extent authorized, may adopt such rules and regulations as may be necessary or appropriate to conduct the business of the Fund.

This has been held to recognize the principle of implied powers, by virtue of which the Executive Board may perform any act that it judges to be necessary or appropriate to the proper administration of the Fund's assets, unless a specific provision of the Articles prohibits it.

Article IX, Section 2, states in part that "the Fund shall possess . . . the capacity . . . to acquire and dispose of immovable and movable property," and Article IV, Section 8 (a), provides that "the gold value of the Fund's assets shall be maintained notwithstanding changes in the par or foreign exchange value of the currency of any member." It should be noted that the latter provision covers not only the Fund's holdings of currencies but all its assets.

A limit to the Fund's operations is set by Article V, Section 2, which reads:

> Except as otherwise provided in this Agreement, operations on the account of the Fund shall be limited to transactions for the purpose of supplying a member, on the initiative of such member, with the currency of another member in exchange for gold or for the currency of the member desiring to make the purchase.

This has been held to limit operations to those specifically provided for in the Articles, but not to prohibit transactions of an administrative character.

EARLY PROPOSALS

In October 1946 Mr. White (United States) sent to the Board a memorandum stating that he had asked the Legal Department to investigate whether the Articles would prohibit investment by the Fund in U.S. Government securities. The Legal Department's reply to this inquiry contained the explanation of Article XII, Section 2 (g), and of Article V, Section 2, and drew attention to the significance of Article IX, Section 2, and Article IV, Section 8 (a). It suggested that in the light of these provisions the Executive Directors were entitled to invest the Fund's assets and to use the income from the investment for administrative purposes. However, a prior understanding with the United States concerning the application of Article IV, Section 8 (a), would be advisable. If possible, any arrangements for an investment should include a guarantee of conversion into gold at the price received by the Fund for its gold.

Mr. White's proposal, and the Legal Department's comments, were considered by the Board in November 1946. Directors accepted the legal arguments that an investment in short-term U.S. Government securities, such as Mr. White proposed, could be made by the Fund, and agreed that it could be so arranged as to be practically riskless. Some Directors, however, deprecated an investment on the grounds that it might be misunderstood and even impair confidence in the Fund. The Board accordingly decided not to take any decision at that time.

During the discussion the Research Department was asked to review the possible effects on the U.S. money market of the suggested investment. In a memorandum distributed shortly afterward, the Department replied that an investment of a substantial size, and its subsequent liquidation, would have important effects on money and credit in the United States—which effects could, however, be offset by the Federal Reserve System.

Four years later Mr. Overby, Deputy Managing Director, asked the Legal Department for an opinion on the legality of investing in U.S. Government securities (a) part of the Fund's gold holdings and (b) part of the dollar subscription of the United States. The Legal Department's reply was confined to the question of investing gold. After confirming the opinion that it had expressed in reply to Mr. White, the Legal Department proposed three safeguards to which any investment should conform:

(i) The amount of the investment should be reasonably proportioned to the expenditures for which income was intended to be produced;

(ii) the amount and duration of the investment should be such as not to hamper sales of currencies by the Fund to its members; and

(iii) risks of loss should be avoided by a U.S. guarantee that the Fund could reacquire at any time the same amount of gold, and by an interpretation of the Articles that would establish the responsibility of the United States to maintain the gold value of the investment should the par value of the dollar be changed.

In April 1951 the Board again considered the question of investment, and this time appointed an Ad Hoc Committee consisting of Mr. Martínez-Ostos (Mexico), chairman, Mr. Beyen (Netherlands), Sir George Bolton (United Kingdom), Mr. Melville (Australia), and Mr. Southard to investigate the possibilities of investing some of the Fund's assets in order to yield an income to offset the operating deficit. This committee met for the first time in May 1951. Mr. Southard then said that he could not state the U.S. Government's position on either the legal or the policy issues involved, since the U.S. legal advisors were still reviewing the matter. For himself, while he agreed with the staff that legally the Fund could make such an investment, he had doubts about the wisdom of doing so. He also doubted whether the U.S. Government would be willing to give a repurchase guarantee, or would accept that it was obliged to maintain the gold value of the investment. Other members of the committee also expressed doubts on both the legal and the policy issues.

The committee did not meet again until July 1952. The chairman then reported that the U.S. Government had still not reached any definite decisions. He had examined the possibility that the Fund might purchase government bonds from some members' central banks, with a guarantee of the convertibility of the earnings, but the interest shown earlier by some Latin American banks in such a proposal had waned. He had also looked into a suggestion that the Fund might acquire World Bank bonds, but discussions with the World Bank had shown that this would not be feasible. In view of these negative results, and of the continuing differences of view among Directors, the committee recommended to the Board that no action be taken and that it be discharged; this was done in August 1952.

First investment

In April 1955 Mr. Southard suggested that, in view of the Fund's growing deficit, further consideration should be given to investing part of its gold. When this was discussed at three meetings in May, the legality of an investment was debated but no decision was reached. Mr. Southard indicated that the U.S. Government was willing to accept $200 million of the Fund's gold for investment in U.S. securities, but while Lord Harcourt expressed appreciation of this offer and said that in the British view the Fund could legally make such an investment, he reported that the British Government doubted the wisdom of making one: the Fund's prestige might be damaged, and its influence impaired, if the impression was given that it was not functioning as had been intended. Other Directors, including Mr. Crena de Iongh (Netherlands), Mr. van Campenhout (Belgium), and Mr. de Largentaye (France), also opposed an investment, citing both legal and policy objections. However, at a fourth meeting, in July, some change of view appeared. Mr. Southard and Mr. Rasminsky (Canada) urged that a favorable decision should be taken because it was vital that the Fund should not continue to run a deficit. Lord Harcourt agreed to take the matter up again with his authorities.

One of the reasons urged at these meetings against making an investment was that there was a possibility that in the near future convertibility of some of the major non-dollar currencies would be restored, which might alter the Fund's situation in an unforeseeable way. This reason was undermined at the Annual Meeting, 1955, when the Governor for the United Kingdom announced that for the time being sterling would not be made convertible. After the Meeting, Lord Harcourt informed the Managing Director that the United Kingdom was now willing to agree to the Fund's investing part of its gold on the conditions that (1) the amount and terms of the investment must be such as not significantly to impair the Fund's liquidity; (2) the U.S. Treasury must recognize the Fund's right to repurchase the gold; (3) the Fund must not bear an exchange risk on the dollars that it acquired; and (4) the amount to be invested should be subject to review by the Board from time to time. Some two months later, in December 1955, Mr. Southard notified the Board that he was now in a position to return to the question of investment, and Lord Harcourt then repeated these conditions to the Board.

Three further meetings were needed before Executive Directors were satisfied that the proposal should be implemented. Mr. de Largentaye still contended that the investment was *ultra vires* because of Article V, Section 2, but he was alone in dissenting from the eventual decision, which set out the purposes and the rationale of the investment in the following terms:

> The Executive Board, observing that the Fund has had and may continue to have an excess of expenditure over income and that the greater part of the Fund's administrative expenditures has been and will continue to be in United States dollars, considers that in the interest of good administration and conservation of the Fund's resources it would be appropriate to raise income towards meeting the deficit by the investment of a portion of the Fund's gold. . . .[32]

The decision also noted the willingness of the United States to consent to the investment, and embodied two interpretations under Article XVIII (*a*) of the

---

[32] E.B. Decision No. 488-(56/5), January 25, 1956; below, Vol. III, p. 275.

Articles of Agreement. The first of these specified the conditions under which the sale of gold for investment would be legal:

(1) The amount of gold to be sold for investment:

(a) will not be such as to limit the ability of the Fund to make its resources available to members in accordance with the Articles of Agreement; and

(b) will be such as to produce an amount of income reasonably related to the deficit of the Fund;

(2) Whenever the Fund decides to reacquire gold after the sale or maturity of any United States Treasury bills invested in, it will be able to reacquire the same amount of gold as was sold for investment in such bills; and the United States, at the request of the Fund, will sell the said amount of gold to the Fund for U.S. dollars at the United States selling price at the time of the sale to the Fund;

(3) In any computations for the purpose of applying the provisions of the Articles of Agreement the Fund will treat the following assets as representing gold and not as holdings of United States currency;

(a) the dollar proceeds of the sale of gold before investment in the United States Treasury bills; and

(b) the United States Treasury bills invested in; and

(c) the dollar proceeds resulting from the sale or maturity of any such bills before the purchase of gold therewith.[33]

The second interpretation was to the effect that Article IV, Section 8 (a), required the United States to maintain the gold value of the assets mentioned in paragraph (3) above, notwithstanding changes in the par or foreign exchange value of the U.S. dollar. It continued:

This obligation of the United States shall be fully discharged by its maintaining the gold value of the dollar proceeds resulting from the sale of the gold or from the sale or maturity of the U.S. Treasury bills purchased therewith.

Mr. Southard had indicated earlier that the U.S. Secretary of the Treasury was prepared to give the assurances required by this interpretation, and also to recommend to the President a waiver of the customary ¼ of 1 per cent handling charge on the sale and ultimate repurchase of gold. Both of these arrangements were carried through.

When it became evident in December 1955 that the Board would probably approve the investment, the staff began to make arrangements for the gold to be sold and the resulting investment to be made through the Federal Reserve Bank of New York. The latter approached the transaction with some reluctance. Its President, Mr. Allan Sproul, looked on it unfavorably, believing that the investment would be more severely criticized in Congress than the Fund's deficit had been. The Federal Reserve Bank's advisors were also apprehensive that the

---

[33] *Ibid.*, pp. 275–76.

Bank might be subjected to lawsuits on the ground that the investment was illegal. Although the advisors of the Fund and of the U.S. Treasury held that the legality of the transaction was fully established, the Fund's letter to the Federal Reserve Bank of New York instructing it to carry out the operation—the terms of which were agreed with the Bank—stated that the Fund would indemnify the Bank for any claims, losses, damages, or charges that it might incur or for which it might become liable in connection with the operation.

The Federal Reserve Bank's letter to the Fund included the following paragraph, accepted by the Fund in recognition of the Federal Reserve System's responsibilities in the monetary field:

> We hold to the principle that in this market operations of foreign central banks and international organizations should conform in a general way to the monetary and credit policy of the Federal Reserve System, as otherwise it might be necessary for us at times to magnify our own operations in order to offset those here of such banks and organizations. Accordingly, we are sure that you will understand that, if at any time in the future the investment of your dollar balances should run counter to the Federal Reserve System policy, we would wish to feel free to advise you to that effect and, if we deem it necessary, to request that you allow your investments to run off at maturity.

To comply with the Federal Reserve Bank's wishes, the investment of the Fund's gold was made gradually, being completed in October 1956.

Change of purpose

A sharp increase in drawings during the winter of 1956–57 produced a steep rise in the Fund's income, and by the middle of August 1957 it became clear to the staff that the Fund's accumulated deficit was likely to be eliminated by the time of the Annual Meeting. As the decision taken in 1956 restricted the investment to the purpose of dealing with the accumulated and current deficit, the Acting Managing Director, Mr. Cochran, decided that the cost of the new Fund building, then under construction, should be charged to income instead of to a special account as had been done previously. This delayed the elimination of the deficit on income account until November 1957.

After the Annual Meeting, 1957, the Managing Director submitted to the Board a proposal that the investment should be continued to provide a reserve against possible future deficits. He pointed out that there could be no guarantee that drawings would continue at the level they had reached, so that the Fund's future income could not be relied upon to cover expenditure. He recommended that the purpose of the investment be altered from "to raise income towards meeting the deficit" to "to raise income and provide a reserve towards meeting possible future deficits." The income from the investment should be placed in a special reserve. It was unnecessary to set a limit to the size of the reserve.

This proposal was discussed by the Board at the end of November 1957 and approved, Mr. de Largentaye being the only dissentient. Mr. Southard expressed the view that a reserve of at least $100 million would be sensible, and that the program should be reviewed annually. Following this decision, the Special Reserve was set up (see Table 11).

Other possible purposes for an investment were discussed in a memorandum prepared by the Director of Research and the Deputy General Counsel in February 1959 which suggested that the Fund should embark upon a long-term policy of investing a substantial amount of the Fund's gold, not limited to U.S. securities. The memorandum pointed out that the Fund's gold holdings would increase substantially as a result of the general quota increase just then approved by the Governors, and suggested that the disadvantages of the resulting decrease in members' owned reserves could be counteracted if the Fund were able to channel back some of the gold to them by means of an investment. However, the memorandum recognized that an investment for this purpose would be *ultra vires*, because of the prohibition in Article V, Section 2.

One particular aspect of members' loss of gold was the subject of a further memorandum in June 1959. In this, the Deputy General Counsel pointed out that the gold holdings of the United States had been declining sharply, and he observed that if the Fund were to make a further investment of gold in U.S. securities—perhaps increasing the existing $200 million to $500 million—this would ease for the United States the payment of $343.75 million in gold due in connection with the increase in the U.S. quota.

INCREASE IN AMOUNT AND MATURITY

In July 1959 the Managing Director proposed to the Board that the amount of gold invested should be increased from $200 million to $500 million, and that part of the larger sum should be invested in securities having a term to maturity of more than three months but not more than twelve months. He pointed out that the effect of the increases in quotas then being implemented would be to reduce the Fund's income (1) by relating existing drawings to lower tranches of the quotas and (2) in particular, by shifting some drawings into the gold tranche, thereby ending charges on that drawing. Such changes were expected to lower income by $10 million a year. Income might also be expected to decline as the large drawings then outstanding were repurchased. The result would be a decline in the rate of growth of the General Reserve, to which the operating surplus was carried. This Reserve totaled about $26 million at that time. In relation to the Fund's capital, increased by the changes in quotas to about $15 billion, total reserves (General and Special together) of $100–200 million would not be excessive. In these circumstances an increase in the rate of growth of the Special Reserve was desirable. At that time the Special Reserve totaled about

$8 million and was increasing at a rate of $4–6 million a year, depending on the rate of interest earned. Under the new proposal it would increase by $10–15 million a year. This figure resulted partly from the larger amount of the investment and partly from the higher rate of interest which would be obtainable on securities with a longer term than three months; recourse to the latter would require an amendment to the interpretation of the Articles set out in the first decision on investment, and a draft decision provided to the Board embodied this.

When this proposal came before the Board, Mr. Southard said that the U.S. Government was willing to extend its guarantee of the gold value of the investment to cover the enlarged sum. Mr. Rasminsky stressed the desirability of cooperation with the U.S. monetary authorities, and commented that since the investment was useful to the Fund, advantage should be taken of the authorities' willingness so long as this continued. Mr. Feuché (France) again stated the French objections, explained on previous occasions by Mr. de Largentaye. Messrs. Lieftinck (Netherlands) and Toussaint (Belgium), while not objecting to the proposal, expressed concern at the proposed size of the reserves in relation to the Fund's prospective expenditure, and also questioned the wisdom of increasing the investment in a period of boom. The investment was, however, approved.

Second increase in amount

In November 1960 the Managing Director proposed to the Board that the amount invested should be further increased, from $500 million to $800 million. His reasons were that the continuous growth in the number of Fund members was necessarily expanding the Fund's expenditure, while its operating income had been declining. Further, the rate of interest earned on the investment was appreciably less than it had been at the time of the increase from $200 million to $500 million. The increase in the Special Reserve (then about $32 million) which would result from a larger investment would give greater assurance that the whole of the General Reserve (then about $43 million) would be available for purposes other than financing administrative deficits.

Mr. Southard told the Board that the U.S. authorities would agree to the proposed increase in the investment, and would give the necessary guarantee. While the continued decline in the U.S. gold reserves (from $20.58 billion at the end of 1958 to $18.44 billion in October 1960) was not mentioned in the discussion, it may be assumed that this played a part in influencing the U.S. Government's decision.

The Board accepted the Managing Director's proposal. On this occasion Mr. de Largentaye agreed with the decision, on the footing that the Board's interpretations had made the investment legal. Mr. Reid (Canada) suggested that it might be desirable to give some consideration in the future to permitting investment in longer-term (say 3-year) securities. The Managing Director undertook that the suggestion would be borne in mind, and that if such an investment seemed desirable a recommendation would be made to the Board. However, no general recommendation has been made, and the only securities for longer than 12 months that have been held by the Fund have been U.S. Treasury notes in which investments of about $62 million were twice authorized, in July and November 1961. Both investments were suggested by the U.S. authorities, the first in 15½-month notes to facilitate a Treasury refinancing operation, and the second in 15-month notes because no 12-month securities were being issued at a time when the Fund had $62 million of 12-month securities coming to maturity.

BORROWING BY THE FUND

The powers of the Fund to borrow currencies that it needs for its operations are contained in Article VII, Section 2—which forms part of the Article making provision for action by the Fund should a currency become scarce, and is the only part of that Article of which the Fund has so far made use. Section 2 reads as follows:

> The Fund may, if it deems such action appropriate to replenish its holdings of any member's currency, take either or both of the following steps:
>
> (i) Propose to the member that, on terms and conditions agreed between the Fund and the member, the latter lend its currency to the Fund or that, with the approval of the member, the Fund borrow such currency from some other source either within or outside the territories of the member, but no member shall be under any obligation to make such loans to the Fund or to approve the borrowing of its currency by the Fund from any other source.
>
> (ii) Require the member to sell its currency to the Fund for gold.

The provisions of Section 2 (ii) involve, of course, the exchange by the Fund of one type of asset for another. They are accordingly dealt with in Chapter 19 below. In the present chapter we shall be concerned only with Section 2 (i).

Very soon after the first general increase in quotas had taken effect in 1959, the increasing volatility of balances of payments resulting from the restoration of external convertibility by European countries began to make the staff question whether the Fund's resources would be adequate for the greater demands likely to be made upon them. Outside the Fund also, questions of the same sort were being raised. In testimony before the U.S. Congress in January 1960 Mr. Bernstein (former Director of the Fund's Research Department) suggested that the Fund should take steps to issue debentures for, say, $6 billion to add to the resources available to it in case of emergency.

In February 1961 the Managing Director presented to the Board three proposals for enhancing the Fund's ability to serve the purposes of the Articles; one
of these was a suggestion that use might be made of Article VII, Section 2 (i), to
borrow currencies likely to be needed in the event of large drawings. Following
up this proposal, the staff submitted to the Board in April a detailed memorandum on the need to borrow currencies, on the amounts likely to be required, and
on the conditions under which such borrowings might be made.

Two meetings in May 1961 were devoted to a discussion of these proposals,
and showed that the Board was in general favorably disposed toward them but
that some Directors felt that it would be important to stress that drawings
involving the use of borrowed currencies should be made on terms no less strict
than those applied to drawings on the Fund's own resources. Inquiries made by
the staff in continental European countries during the summer showed that there
was considerable anxiety on this point, and that the members concerned feared
that if their currencies were lent to the Fund, and by the Fund lent, for example,
to the United Kingdom, the latter might obtain them on less stringent terms than
if it had had recourse to the European Fund controlled by its partners in the
OEEC.

The Annual Report for 1961 referred to the possible need for the Fund to
utilize Article VII, Section 2 (i); [34] and in his speech at the Annual Meeting the
Managing Director expanded at some length on the possibility. [35] At the same
Meeting, however, a discussion among representatives of the main industrial
powers, convened by the Secretary of the U.S. Treasury, Mr. Dillon, showed that
the apprehensions detected by the staff in Europe were likely to influence the
terms on which the members whose currencies would be most needed would be
willing to make them available to the Fund. These terms were likely to include
a measure of control over the use to which the borrowed funds were put. [36]

During the last quarter of the calendar year 1961, negotiations for a borrowing
arrangement—involving Belgium, Canada, France, Germany, Italy, Japan, the
Netherlands, Sweden, the United Kingdom, and the United States—were undertaken by the Managing Director and members of the staff at a series of meetings
with representatives of these countries in Paris. Some difficulty was found in
reconciling the philosophy behind the plan, as originally conceived and
expressed in a Franco-American draft handed to the Managing Director on
November 17, with the provisions of the Fund Agreement. The Franco-American
draft would have transferred from the Fund to the member providing borrowed
funds the responsibility for deciding whether to permit the use of the Fund's
resources, if borrowed funds were involved. It would also have permitted the

[34] *Annual Report, 1961*, p. 19.
[35] *Summary Proceedings, 1961*, pp. 27–29.
[36] *Ibid.*, pp. 54–55, 64, 117.

member requesting the drawing, and not the Fund, to decide whether the member's needs should be met from borrowed funds or from the Fund's own resources. Both these provisions were inconsistent with the principles of the Fund, and were rejected by the Managing Director.

Subsequent drafts of a borrowing arrangement were prepared by the Fund staff. They were communicated to the Executive Directors, but the exclusion of the latter from the actual negotiations was regarded as unfortunate, and the eventual text, although accepted as containing probably the best conditions that could be arranged, still seemed to some Directors to fall short of what was desirable. The General Arrangements to Borrow (GAB), as they were termed, are set out in full in Volume III.[37] Here it will suffice to note the main features.

(1) The Arrangements were to be implemented only "to forestall and cope with an impairment of the international monetary system" and only for the purpose of meeting a request to draw on the Fund by one of the participants in the Arrangements.

(2) A participant that proposed to make a drawing, or to seek the repayment of a loan made previously under the Arrangements, if either might necessitate activating the Arrangements, would consult the Managing Director first and then the other participants.

(3) Before making a call on the other participants, the Managing Director would consult the Executive Directors and the participants.

(4) The amount that each participant would lend on a given occasion would be based on its (or its country's) existing and prospective balance of payments and reserve position.

(5) When the Managing Director made a call on the participants, they would consult and inform him of the amounts of their currencies that they were prepared to lend. If they could not agree on the distribution proposed by the Managing Director, they would propose an alternative one of the same order of magnitude as his call.

(6) Each request for a drawing which would require the activation of the Arrangements would be dealt with in accordance with the Fund's established policies.

(7) When such a drawing was repurchased, the Fund would repay the countries from which it had borrowed; in any event it would repay them within five years of the transfer of funds by them for that drawing.

(8) A participant that had lent to the Fund could receive early repayment should it need and request this because its own payments position had deteriorated.

---

[37] E.B. Decision No. 1289-(62/1), January 5, 1962; below, Vol. III, pp. 246–52.

(9) Interest would be payable on sums borrowed, in accordance with a formula which initially yielded a rate of 1½ per cent per annum. The Fund would also pay a charge of ½ of 1 per cent on each borrowing transaction.

Not all these provisions were spelled out in the Arrangements themselves; those summarized in paragraphs (2) and (5) above were contained in a letter sent to the other participants by Mr. Baumgartner, the French Minister of Finance.

The commitments which the participants undertook, adjusted to allow for two minor changes effected in 1962, are set out in Table 12.

The plan was formally adopted by the Board on January 5, 1962. By October 24, 1962, enough of the participants had acceded to it to bring the Arrangements into operation. The last country to adhere was Canada, which notified the Fund of its agreement in January 1964. The Managing Director subsequently negotiated an arrangement with Switzerland, which is not a member of the Fund, by which Switzerland undertook to lend to a country

Table 12. General Arrangements to Borrow: Participants and Commitments
as at December 31, 1965

Participant	Units of Participant's Currency		Equivalents in Millions of U.S. Dollars at 1962 Rates
United States	US$	2,000,000,000	2,000
Deutsche Bundesbank	DM	4,000,000,000	1,000
United Kingdom	£	357,142,857	1,000
France	F	2,715,381,428	550
Italy	Lit	343,750,000,000	550
Japan	¥	90,000,000,000	250
Canada	Can$	216,216,216	200
Netherlands	f.	724,000,000	200
Belgium	BF	7,500,000,000	150
Sveriges Riksbank	SKr	517,320,000	100
Total			6,000

drawing on the Fund on occasions when the General Arrangements were activated, subject to the completion of an agreement with that participant.[38]

The first occasion on which the General Arrangements were activated was in December 1964, when the United Kingdom drew under its stand-by arrangement for $1 billion. The amounts borrowed then and for another drawing by the United Kingdom in May 1965 are summarized in Table 13.

The Arrangements were originally introduced for four years, with the proviso that they could be renewed if the decision to this effect was taken by October 23, 1965. The question of renewal was discussed in the Board on April 28, 1965. A number of changes were then mentioned as desirable, including the elimination

[38] E.B. Decision No. 1712-(64/29), June 8, 1964; below, Vol. III, p. 254.

of the requirement that the international monetary system should be in danger of impairment and of the limitation of borrowings to drawings by participants. Some simplification of the method of activating the Arrangements was also suggested. As, however, it seemed likely that such changes would not be approved by the participants, the Chairman proposed, and the Board approved,

Table 13. General Arrangements to Borrow: Borrowings by the Fund, 1964–65
(In millions of U.S. dollars)

| Participant | Amounts Borrowed | | Amount Still Available |
	Dec. 1964	May 1965	Dec. 1965
Belgium	30.0	37.5	82.5
Canada	15.0	35.0	150.0
France	100.0	140.0	310.0
Deutsche Bundesbank	180.0	167.5	652.5
Italy	5.0	65.0	480.0
Japan	20.0	25.0	205.0
Netherlands	40.0	37.5	122.5
Sveriges Riksbank	15.0	17.5	67.5
United Kingdom	—	—	1,000.0
United States	—	—	2,000.0
Totals	405.0	525.0	5,070.0

that the Fund should seek a continuation of the Arrangements without amendment.

After consultation with the participants, it was agreed that the Arrangements should continue until October 23, 1970, subject to a review within two years from the expiry of the original four years (October 23, 1966), and subject to the right of any participant to withdraw at any time during the three months ending October 23, 1968.

Table 14. Quotas of Members at Selected Dates [1]
(In millions of U.S. dollars)

Member Country	Dec. 31 1945	Dec. 31 1950	Dec. 31 1955	Dec. 31 1960	Dec. 31 1965
Afghanistan	•	•	10.0	22.5	22.5
Algeria	•	•	•	•	60.0
Argentina	•	•	150.0[2]	280.0	280.0
Australia	200.0	200.0	200.0	400.0	400.0
Austria	•	50.0	50.0	75.0	75.0
Belgium	225.0	225.0	225.0	337.5	337.5
Bolivia	10.0	10.0	10.0	22.5	22.5
Brazil	150.0	150.0	150.0	280.0	280.0
Burma	•	•	15.0	30.0	30.0
Burundi	•	•	•	•	11.25
Cameroon	•	•	•	•	15.0
Canada	300.0	300.0	300.0	550.0	550.0
Central African Rep.	•	•	•	•	7.5
Ceylon	•	15.0	15.0	45.0	62.0
Chad	•	•	•	•	7.5
Chile	50.0	50.0	50.0	100.0	100.0
China	550.0	550.0	550.0	550.0	550.0
Colombia	50.0	50.0	50.0	100.0	100.0
Congo (Brazzaville)	•	•	•	•	7.5
Congo, Dem. Rep.	•	•	•	•	45.0
Costa Rica	5.0	5.0	5.0	5.5	20.0
Cuba	50.0	50.0	50.0	50.0	•
Cyprus	•	•	•	•	11.25
Czechoslovakia	125.0	125.0	•	•	•
Dahomey	•	•	•	•	7.5
Denmark	•	68.0	68.0	130.0	130.0
Dominican Rep.	5.0	5.0	5.0	15.0	25.0
Ecuador	5.0	5.0	5.0	15.0	20.0
El Salvador	2.5	2.5	2.5	11.25	20.0
Ethiopia	6.0	6.0	6.0	9.6[3]	15.0
Finland	•	38.0	38.0	57.0	57.0
France	450.0	525.0	525.0	787.5	787.5
Gabon	•	•	•	•	7.5
Germany	•	•	330.0	787.5	787.5
Ghana	•	•	15.0[4]	35.0	55.0
Greece	40.0	40.0	40.0	60.0	60.0
Guatemala	5.0	5.0	5.0	15.0	20.0
Guinea	•	•	•	•	15.0
Haiti	5.0	•	2.0	11.25	11.25
Honduras	2.5	0.5	2.5	11.25	15.0
Iceland	1.0	1.0	1.0	11.25	11.25
India	400.0	400.0	400.0	600.0	600.0
Indonesia	•	•	110.0	165.0	•
Iran	25.0	35.0	35.0	70.0	70.0
Iraq	8.0	8.0	8.0	15.0	64.0

Footnotes on page 380.

Table 14 *(continued).* Quotas of Members at Selected Dates [1]
(In millions of U.S. dollars)

Member Country	Dec. 31 1945	Dec. 31 1950	Dec. 31 1955	Dec. 31 1960	Dec. 31 1965
Ireland	•	•	30.0[5]	45.0	45.0
Israel	•	•	4.5	25.0	50.0
Italy	•	180.0	180.0	270.0	500.0
Ivory Coast	•	•	•	•	15.0
Jamaica	•	•	•	•	20.0
Japan	•	•	250.0	500.0	500.0
Jordan	•	•	3.0	4.5[3]	12.25[3]
Kenya	•	•	•	•	25.0
Korea	•	•	12.5	18.75	18.75
Kuwait	•	•	•	•	50.0
Laos	•	•	•	•	7.5
Lebanon	•	4.5	4.5	4.5	6.75
Liberia	0.5	•	•	11.25[6]	16.0
Libya	•	•	5.0[7]	9.0	15.0
Luxembourg	10.0	10.0	10.0	11.0[3]	15.0
Malagasy Rep.	•	•	•	•	15.0
Malawi	•	•	•	•	11.25
Malaysia	•	•	25.0[8]	30.0[3]	58.33[3]
Mali	•	•	•	•	13.0
Mauritania	•	•	•	•	7.5
Mexico	90.0	90.0	90.0	180.0	180.0
Morocco	•	•	35.0[9]	52.5	72.0
Nepal	•	•	•	•	7.5
Netherlands	275.0	275.0	275.0	412.5	412.5
New Zealand	50.0	•	•	•	125.0
Nicaragua	2.0	2.0	2.0	11.25	11.25
Niger	•	•	•	•	7.5
Nigeria	•	•	•	•	50.0
Norway	50.0	50.0	50.0	100.0	100.0
Pakistan	•	100.0	100.0	150.0	150.0
Panama	0.5	0.5	0.5	0.5	11.25
Paraguay	2.0	3.5	3.5	10.0[3]	11.25
Peru	25.0	25.0	25.0	30.0[3]	37.5
Philippines	15.0	15.0	15.0	75.0	75.0
Poland	125.0	•	•	•	•
Portugal	•	•	•	•	60.0
Rwanda	•	•	•	•	11.25
Saudi Arabia	•	•	10.0[5]	55.0	72.0
Senegal	•	•	•	7.5[10]	25.0
Sierra Leone	•	•	•	•	11.25
Somalia	•	•	•	•	11.25
South Africa	100.0	100.0	100.0	150.0	150.0
Spain	•	•	100.0[7]	150.0	150.0
Sudan	•	•	10.0[4]	15.0	45.0
Sweden	•	•	100.0	150.0	150.0

Table 14 *(concluded).* Quotas of Members at Selected Dates [1]
(In millions of U.S. dollars)

Member Country	Dec. 31 1945	Dec. 31 1950	Dec. 31 1955	Dec. 31 1960	Dec. 31 1965
Syrian Arab Rep.	•	6.5	6.5	11[11]	25.0
Tanzania	•	•	•	•	25.0
Thailand	•	12.5	12.5	45.0	76.0
Togo	•	•	•	•	11.25
Trinidad & Tobago	•	•	•	•	20.0
Tunisia	•	•	12.0[9]	14.1[3]	22.5
Turkey	•	43.0	43.0	86.0	86.0
Uganda	•	•	•	•	25.0
United Arab Rep.	45.0	60.0	60.0	105.0[12]	120.0
United Kingdom	1,300.0	1,300.0	1,300.0	1,950.0	1,950.0
United States	2,750.0	2,750.0	2,750.0	4,125.0	4,125.0
Upper Volta	•	•	•	•	7.5
Uruguay	15.0	15.0	15.0	15.0	30.0
Venezuela	15.0	15.0	15.0	150.0	150.0
Viet-Nam	•	•	12.5[2]	16.5[3]	22.5
Yugoslavia	60.0	60.0	60.0	120.0	120.0
Zambia	•	•	•	•	50.0
Totals	7,600.0[13]	8,036.5	8,750.5[14]	14,740.7[15]	15,976.6[16]

[1] The column headed Dec. 31, 1945 lists the quotas decided on at Bretton Woods and listed in Schedule A to the Articles of Agreement. The other columns show the quotas at the end of each year in which there was a quinquennial review of quotas. A dot (•) indicates that the country was not a member at the time.

[2] Initial quota (September 1956).

[3] Increasing quota by installments; not yet completed.

[4] Initial quota (September 1957).

[5] Initial quota (August 1957).

[6] Initial quota (March 1962).

[7] Initial quota (September 1958).

[8] Initial quota (March 1958).

[9] Initial quota (April 1958).

[10] Initial quota (August 1962).

[11] At this date Syria was part of United Arab Republic.

[12] Including Syria.

[13] Excluding U.S.S.R.

[14] Excluding the eleven countries designated by footnotes 2, 4, 5, 7, 8, and 9.

[15] Excluding Liberia and Senegal.

[16] The Fourth Quinquennial Review was not formally terminated until early in 1966 (see p. 363 above), so that the resulting increase in quotas is not reflected in the December 31, 1965 total. On December 31, 1968 the total of quotas was $21,198.4 million.

CHAPTER

18

Evolution of the Fund's Policy on Drawings

J. Keith Horsefield and Gertrud Lovasy *

THE ORIGIN AND MAGNITUDE of the Fund's resources (which are so far derived mainly from subscriptions) were described in Chapter 17. For the purpose of the following discussion it should be kept in mind that each member has a quota in the Fund; that its subscription, which is paid partly in gold and partly in the member's own currency, is equal to its quota; and that the normal quantitative limitations on the use of the Fund's resources by each member are determined by its quota.

The basic mechanism of a drawing from the Fund consists of an exchange of the drawing member's currency for an equivalent amount of other currencies. The effect is therefore to increase the Fund's holdings of the drawing member's currency and to decrease its holdings of the currencies that are drawn. The Articles contain provisions the effect of which is to tend to restore the Fund's holdings of each member's currency to a level equal to 75 per cent of that member's quota—i.e., to the level at which the Fund's holdings would stand if the member had paid the required 25 per cent of its subscription in gold, and the Fund had effected no transactions in that currency (or any transactions effected had canceled one another out).

Annual figures for drawings are given in Table 22 at the end of Chapter 19.

LEGAL PROVISIONS

The provisions in the Articles of Agreement governing the use of the Fund's resources are extensive and complicated. Since much of the evolution of the

---

* The first three sections of this chapter were written by Mr. Horsefield; the last section, on the Compensatory Financing of Export Fluctuations, by Miss Lovasy. In the earlier parts of the chapter, use has been made of an article by Mr. Subimal Mookerjee entitled "Policies on the Use of Fund Resources," *Staff Papers*, Vol. XIII (1966), pp. 421–42.

relevant policies hinged on the text of these Articles, it is necessary to start by setting them out in some detail. The reader will need to refer back to the following extracts as the argument proceeds.[1]

ARTICLES OF AGREEMENT

The Fund's resources are to be used in accordance with the purposes of the Fund, which are set out in Article I of the Fund Agreement. Among these purposes are:

(v) To give confidence to members by making the Fund's resources available to them under adequate safeguards, thus providing them with opportunity to correct maladjustments in their balance of payments without resorting to measures destructive of national or international prosperity.

(vi) In accordance with the above, to shorten the duration and lessen the degree of disequilibrium in the international balances of payments of members.

The conditions governing the use of the Fund's resources are set out more precisely in Article V, Section 3, which reads as follows:

(a) A member shall be entitled to buy the currency of another member from the Fund in exchange for its own currency subject to the following conditions:

(i) The member desiring to purchase the currency represents that it is presently needed for making in that currency payments which are consistent with the provisions of this Agreement;

(ii) The Fund has not given notice under Article VII, Section 3, that its holdings of the currency desired have become scarce;

(iii) The proposed purchase would not cause the Fund's holdings of the purchasing member's currency to increase by more than twenty-five percent of its quota during the period of twelve months ending on the date of the purchase nor to exceed two hundred percent of its quota, but the twenty-five percent limitation shall apply only to the extent that the Fund's holdings of the member's currency have been brought above seventy-five percent of its quota if they had been below that amount;

(iv) The Fund has not previously declared under Section 5 of this Article, Article IV, Section 6, Article VI, Section 1, or Article XV, Section 2 (a), that the member desiring to purchase is ineligible to use the resources of the Fund.

(b) A member shall not be entitled without the permission of the Fund to use the Fund's resources to acquire currency to hold against forward exchange transactions.

Other relevant provisions of the same Article are as follows:

SEC. 4. *Waiver of conditions.*—The Fund may in its discretion, and on terms which safeguard its interests, waive any of the conditions prescribed in Sec-

---

[1] In what follows no account is taken of the amendments to the Articles effected in 1969, of which a summary appears in Part V of this volume. The full text of the Articles of Agreement as approved at Bretton Woods is reproduced below, Vol. III, pp. 185–214. The amendments to the Articles are reproduced in Vol. III, pp. 521–41.

tion 3 *(a)* of this Article, especially in the case of members with a record of avoiding large or continuous use of the Fund's resources. In making a waiver it shall take into consideration periodic or exceptional requirements of the member requesting the waiver. The Fund shall also take into consideration a member's willingness to pledge as collateral security gold, silver, securities, or other acceptable assets having a value sufficient in the opinion of the Fund to protect its interests and may require as a condition of waiver the pledge of such collateral security.

SEC. 5. *Ineligibility to use the Fund's resources.*—Whenever the Fund is of the opinion that any member is using the resources of the Fund in a manner contrary to the purposes of the Fund, it shall present to the member a report setting forth the views of the Fund and prescribing a suitable time for reply. After presenting such a report to a member, the Fund may limit the use of its resources by the member. If no reply to the report is received from the member within the prescribed time, or if the reply received is unsatisfactory, the Fund may continue to limit the member's use of the Fund's resources or may, after giving reasonable notice to the member, declare it ineligible to use the resources of the Fund.

Article V, Section 7, contains provisions designed to restore a member's position in the Fund after it has made use of the Fund's resources. These are set out in full in Chapter 19. They may be summarized as follows:

(1) At the end of each of the Fund's financial years each member must use in repurchase of its own currency from the Fund an amount of its monetary reserves equal in value to one half of any increase that has occurred during the year in the Fund's holdings of its currency plus one half of any increase, or minus one half of any decrease, that has occurred during the year in the member's monetary reserves (Section 7 *(b)* (i)).

(2) But repurchases are *not* to be made at all if the member's monetary reserves have decreased more than the Fund's holdings have increased during the year (Section 7 *(b)* (i)); or to an extent that would *(a)* reduce the member's monetary reserves below its quota (Section 7 *(c)* (i)); *(b)* reduce the Fund's holdings of the member's currency below 75 per cent of its quota (Section 7 *(c)* (ii)); *(c)* increase the Fund's holdings of any other member's currency above 75 per cent of that member's quota (Section 7 *(c)* (iii)).

The make-up of repurchase requirements, in terms of gold and particular currencies, is stipulated in detail in Schedule B.

Article V, Section 8, details the charges which the Fund makes for the use of its resources. These are discussed in Chapter 19, but mention must be made here of Section 8 *(d)*, which reads in part:

> Whenever the Fund's holdings of a member's currency are such that the charge applicable to any bracket for any period has reached the rate of four percent per annum, the Fund and the member shall consider means by which the Fund's holdings of the currency can be reduced.

Elsewhere in the Articles there are a number of other provisions relevant to the use of the Fund's resources, as follows:

(a) Drawings to finance capital transfers are subject to limitations (Article VI). This is the subject of a later section in this chapter.[2]

(b) The Fund was not intended to provide facilities for relief or reconstruction or to deal with the international indebtedness arising out of World War II. (Article XIV, Section 1).

(c) The Fund may postpone exchange transactions with any member if its circumstances are such that, in the opinion of the Fund, they would lead to use of the resources of the Fund in a manner contrary to the purposes of the Fund Agreement or prejudicial to the Fund or its members (Article XX, Section 4 (i)).

(d) If a member changes the par value of its currency despite the objection of the Fund, in cases where the Fund is entitled to object, the member shall be ineligible to use the resources of the Fund unless the Fund otherwise determines (Article IV, Section 6).

(e) If a member fails to fulfill any of its obligations under the Articles of Agreement, the Fund may declare the member ineligible to use the resources of the Fund (Article XV, Section 2 (a)).

(f) In its relations with members, the Fund was enjoined to recognize that the postwar transitional period would be one of change and adjustment, and in making decisions on requests occasioned thereby which were presented by any member it must give the member the benefit of any reasonable doubt (Article XIV, Section 5).

(g) In the event of an emergency or the development of unforeseen circumstances threatening the operations of the Fund, the Executive Directors by unanimous vote may suspend for a period of not more than one hundred and twenty days the operation of certain provisions, including those in Article V, Sections 3 and 7. Such suspension may be extended by not more than two hundred and forty days by the Board of Governors, by a vote of four fifths of the total voting power (Article XVI, Section 1 (a) and (c)).

INTERPRETATIONS

Over the years, these provisions of the Articles of Agreement have been the subject of much discussion in the Executive Board, and many of the relevant phrases have had to be interpreted by decisions of the Executive Directors. Some, but not all, of these were formal interpretations under Article XVIII.[3] The most important of these decisions may be summarized as follows:

---

[2] Below, pp. 410–16.

[3] For an explanation of the Fund's powers of interpretation, see below, pp. 567–73.

General purposes of provisions

The U.S. Bretton Woods Agreements Act required the Governor of the Fund for the United States

> to obtain promptly an official interpretation by the Fund as to whether its authority to use its resources extends beyond current monetary stabilization operations to afford temporary assistance to members in connection with seasonal, cyclical, and emergency fluctuations in the balance of payments of any member for current transactions, and whether it has authority to use its resources to provide facilities for relief, reconstruction, or armaments, or to meet a large or sustained outflow of capital on the part of any member.[4]

This question was put by the Governor for the United States to the Governors at the Inaugural Meeting at Savannah, and was by them referred to the Executive Directors.[5] The Directors discussed it in September 1946. The answer was complicated by the consideration that the Articles of Agreement provided for the Fund to finance balance of payments deficits as a whole, and not particular types of imports. However, the Directors agreed to report to the Governors at the First Annual Meeting that

> authority to use the resources of the Fund is limited to use in accordance with its purposes to give temporary assistance in financing balance of payments deficits on current account for monetary stabilization operations.[6]

The key words in this interpretation were "temporary" and "current account." The significance of the former will become apparent in the next section of this chapter; the latter assumed importance, after some years, in connection with the possible use of the Fund's resources to cope with deficits due to capital transactions, and is discussed in that connection in the next section but one.

Meaning of "the member . . . represents" (Article V, Section 3 (a) (i))

That the Fund was not obliged to accept the representation of a member had been the view of the U.S. delegation at Bretton Woods.[7] The point was discussed in the Board on May 6, 1947, and the conclusion reached (after a slight change of wording on May 29) was as follows: [8]

> The word "represents" in Article V, Section 3 (a) (i), means "declares." The member is presumed to have fulfilled the condition mentioned in Article V, Section 3 (a) (i), if it declares that the currency is presently needed for making payments in that currency which are consistent with the provisions of the Agreement. But the Fund may, for good reasons, challenge the correctness of this declaration, on the grounds that the currency is not "presently needed" or because

---

[4] Public Law 171, 79th Cong., 1st sess., Sec. 13.(a); *Selected Decisions*, p. 155.

[5] Resolution IM-6, *Selected Documents*, p. 19.

[6] E.B. Decision No. 71-2, September 26, 1946; below, Vol. III, p. 245.

[7] See above, Vol. I, p. 72.

[8] E.B. Decision No. 284-4, May 29, 1947, reaffirmed March 10, 1948; below, Vol. III, p. 227.

the currency is not needed for payment "in that currency," or because the payments will not be "consistent with the provisions of this Agreement." If the Fund concludes that a particular declaration is not correct, the Fund may postpone or reject the request, or accept it subject to conditions. . . .

Meaning of "presently needed" (Article V, Section 3 (a) (i))

The decision just quoted concludes with the following sentence:

> The phrase "presently needed" cannot be defined in terms of a formula uniformly applicable to all cases, but where there is good reason to doubt that the currency is "presently needed," the Fund will have to apply the phrase in each case in the light of all the circumstances.

This pronouncement followed a short discussion of the meaning of the phrase, during which it was stated that it implied an intent by the drafters of the Articles of Agreement that members should draw in limited amounts as necessary for immediate payments. When, on April 23, 1947, the first member to apply for a drawing, Ethiopia, sought to obtain $900,000, some Directors thought that since this amount was 15 per cent of the member's quota, it was more than could be "presently needed," and Ethiopia was asked to justify the request. As, instead, the request was withdrawn, the point was never cleared up. However, since then the Board's views on what can be "presently needed" have undergone much change, so that, when in February 1956 Burma asked to draw $15 million (100 per cent of its quota), this was allowed, the question whether the amount was "presently needed" not being raised.

Meaning of "making in that currency" (Article V, Section 3 (a) (i))

The question raised by this phrase was whether a member that conducted its international transactions wholly in terms of a reserve currency could be allowed to draw some other currency from the Fund, in order to convert this other currency into the reserve currency which it needed to settle its international accounts. This question was considered by the Board in April 1961, and although the point was not formally decided, the practice of the Fund has since conformed to the view of the Legal Department that the meaning of Article V, Section 3 (a) (i), is that a member may draw from the Fund any currency which it uses, directly or indirectly, to support its exchange market.

Meaning of "consistent with the provisions of this Agreement" (Article V, Section 3 (a) (i))

The Board decided in March 1948 that the phrase meant

> consistent both with the provisions of the Fund Agreement other than Article I and with the purposes of the Fund contained in Article I.[9]

---

[9] E.B. Decision No. 287-3, March 17, 1948; below, Vol. III, p. 228.

The significance of this decision, as is explained below, was that it required that a member seeking to draw from the Fund should not only fulfill the specific stipulations of Article V, Section 3, but also be conforming to the general purposes of the Fund, as set out in Article I.

Meaning of "twenty-five percent" (Article V, Section 3 (a) (iii))

In 1955 the Board interpreted the quantitative limit of 25 per cent of quota in relation to drawing rights under Article V, Section 3 (a) (iii), as follows:

> Where the Fund's holdings of a member's currency are not less than seventy-five per cent of its quota, and to the extent that such holdings would not be increased above two hundred per cent of its quota, the purchases which the member may make during a period of twelve months ending on the date of a proposed purchase shall be determined as follows:
>
> (a)   The total purchases shall not exceed twenty-five per cent of its quota;
>
> (b)   Provided that, if the member has made purchases during the period, it may then purchase an amount equal to the difference between twenty-five per cent of its quota and the total of such purchases adjusted on the basis that a repurchase by the member or sale of its currency during the period is deducted from a previous, but not subsequent, purchase or purchases during the period.[10]

Meaning of "is using" (Article V, Section 5)

In March 1948 the Board decided that

> a member "is using" the resources of the Fund within the meaning of Article V, Section 5, where it is either actually disposing of the exchange purchased from the Fund, or, having purchased exchange from the Fund, the Fund's holdings of its currency are in excess of 75 per cent of its quota.[11]

There have been two decisions explaining the Fund's right to use the powers provided by Article V, Section 5. Three weeks before the decision just quoted, the Board affirmed that

> The Fund has, in the case of a member which has had a previous exchange transaction with the Fund, power to declare the member ineligible or limit its use of the resources of the Fund if the member is, in the opinion of the Fund, using the resources of the Fund in a manner contrary to the purposes of the Fund.[12]

Two meetings later, the Board decided that

> if the Fund receives a request from a member to purchase exchange and either, (1) the Fund is considering sending the member a report pursuant to Article V, Section 5, or (2) the Fund finds when the request is before it that action pursuant to that Section should be considered; then the Fund has the authority, pursuant

---

[10] E.B. Decision No. 451-(55/52), August 24, 1955; below, Vol. III, p. 228.

[11] E.B. Decision No. 292-3, March 30, 1948; below, Vol. III, p. 235.

[12] E.B. Decision No. 284-3, March 10, 1948; below, Vol. III, p. 234.

to Article V, Section 5, of the Fund Agreement, to postpone the transfer as permitted under the provisions of Rules and Regulations G-3 for such time as may reasonably be necessary to decide the question of applying Article V, Section 5, and, if it decides to apply it, to prepare and send to the member a report and subject its use of the Fund's resources to limitations. Under such circumstances the limitations imposed will apply to the pending request for the purchase of exchange as well as to future requests.[13]

Nevertheless, the Board was reluctant to apply Article V, Section 5, considering this rather a drastic sanction. It had in any case provided, by Rule K-2, that whenever the Board would be authorized to declare a member ineligible to use the Fund's resources, it could exercise less extreme powers—i.e., it could "indicate the circumstances under which, and/or the extent to which" drawings would be permitted.

Use for "reconstruction" (Article XIV, Section 1)

In July 1947 the Board agreed that

the prohibition in the Fund Agreement, Article XIV, Section 1, was not meant to prevent countries which were undergoing reconstruction from using the Fund's resources.[14]

It should be noted that the prohibitions in Article XIV, Section 1, were based on two considerations discussed at Bretton Woods. The first was that long-term tasks of reconstruction were to be undertaken by another agency than the Fund, viz., the World Bank. The second was that the United Kingdom had asked that the possibility of using the Fund's resources to repay blocked sterling balances should be omitted from the Fund Agreement.[15]

Postponement under Article XX, Section 4 (i)

The Board has interpreted its powers under Article XX, Section 4 (i), as follows:

The Fund has, in the case of a member which has had no previous exchange transaction with the Fund, the power to postpone exchange transactions with it if its circumstances are such that, in the opinion of the Fund, they would lead to the use of the resources of the Fund in a manner contrary to the purposes of the Agreement or prejudicial to the Fund or its members. This power did not lapse as of the date the Fund began exchange transactions.[16]

This conclusion was reached in two stages. In February 1947 the Board agreed, in effect, on the decision embodied in the last sentence quoted above;

---

[13] E.B. Decision No. 286-1, March 15, 1948; below, Vol. III, p. 234. For Rule G-3 see below, Vol. III, p. 292.

[14] E.B. Decision No. 196-2, July 31, 1947; below, Vol. III, p. 268.

[15] See discussion in Vol. I above, p. 52.

[16] E.B. Decision No. 284-2, March 10, 1948; below, Vol. III, p. 272.

a year later the Directors considered the related problem whether the Fund's powers lapsed once a member had drawn on the Fund, and decided by a majority that they did.

Use of ineligibility provisions

It will be convenient to note here the few occasions on which members have become ineligible to use the Fund's resources, or the Board has considered using the provisions of the Articles to render them ineligible.

Before beginning transactions, the Board considered whether to invoke its powers under Article XX, Section 4 (*i*), to restrain members from drawing if their circumstances were such as to make the short-term use of the Fund's resources by them unlikely. The Board decided not to invoke its formal powers, but to notify the affected members informally. Ten members were so notified in the winter of 1946–47, although the ban was removed from three of them after a short time.

The first occasion on which a member became ineligible to use the Fund's resources was in January 1948, when the French Government devalued the franc and introduced measures which created multiple currency practices. The Board was unable to approve these measures and accordingly, under the terms of Article IV, Section 6, France became ineligible to draw upon the Fund. Eligibility was restored by a decision of the Board in October 1954.[17]

The next occasion was in October 1953, when Czechoslovakia's unauthorized change in the value of the koruna, and its failure to cooperate with the Fund in other ways, led the Board to invoke Article XV, Section 2 (*a*), and declare Czechoslovakia ineligible to use the Fund's resources.[18] The ban had not been removed when Czechoslovakia left the Fund early in 1955.

The use of Article XV, Section 2 (*a*), was again considered by the Board in January 1964, in connection with Cuba's failure to repurchase a drawing within five years, its failure to supply essential data, and its continuance of exchange restrictions which the Fund had disapproved. However, the provisions of the Article were not, in fact, applied, because Cuba resigned from the Fund before the date set for a meeting at which it was to be given the opportunity to answer the Fund's complaints.[19]

In September 1958 Bolivia found itself unable to carry out the conditions under which it had been granted a stand-by arrangement. By that time $2 million out of a total of $3.5 million authorized by the stand-by arrangement had been drawn. The staff recommended to the Board, which agreed, that in the

[17] See above, Vol. I, pp. 202, 412.
[18] See above, Vol. I, p. 361.
[19] See above, Vol. I, p. 549.

circumstances Bolivia should not be allowed to draw further until it had agreed with the Fund on revised conditions for the stand-by arrangement. Satisfactory new undertakings were given by the member in November, and it was authorized to resume drawing.

The Fund's powers under Article V, Section 5, and Article XX, Section 4 (i), have never been used expressly, although, as noted above, they have been regarded as authorizing the Fund to impose less drastic conditions than the exclusion of a member from the use of its resources.

FORMATION OF POLICY

BACKGROUND

The difference of view between Keynes and White on the attitude of the Fund toward applications to draw has been examined in detail in Volume I, and need not be recapitulated here.[20] It will suffice to say that White was convinced that the Fund must have the power to question any request to draw on its resources, in order to prevent unjustified drawings which, in the circumstances of 1945, would necessarily have been drawings of U.S. dollars. Keynes, on the other hand, sought to ensure that members would have the right (at least, once convertibility had been achieved) to draw from the Fund, without question, the equivalent of 25 per cent of their quotas annually, up to the point at which the Fund's holdings of their currencies were equal to 200 per cent of their quotas.

This difference of view found expression in the Articles of Agreement in juxtaposition of Article V, Section 3 (a) (i) and (iii), which are permissive, and Article V, Section 3 (a) (iv), which gives the Fund power to declare a member ineligible to use its resources. The latter subsection was reinforced, among other provisions, by Article XX, Section 4 (i), which empowers the Fund to postpone transactions before a member has drawn, and by Article V, Section 5, which elaborates the powers in Article V, Section 3 (a) (iv), for application once a member has used the Fund's resources.

After the Board had begun work, the significance of the Sections just quoted led to extensive discussions, in the course of which the issue came to be seen as one between automatic rights to draw on the one hand and conditional rights on the other. Those Directors who took the point of view of Keynes protested that members should be able to draw without question the annual 25 per cent of quota provided by Article V, Section 3 (a) (iii); those who were of White's opinion claimed that no member should be able to draw from the Fund without the Fund's explicit consent.

---

[20] See above, Vol. I, pp. 67–77.

For a short time in 1947 it became the practice for a member to be allowed to draw without the Board's specific approval sums not exceeding 5 per cent of its quota in any thirty days.[21] However, for reasons discussed below, this practice did not last.

The stumbling block which eventually frustrated the application of the principle of automaticity to drawings was the ineffectiveness of repurchase obligations.[22] It was generally agreed by Executive Directors that the Fund's resources were to be used for short-term advances, unlike those of the World Bank. But the provisions of Article V, Section 7, and Schedule B proved inadequate to ensure the brevity of use which was desired.[23] The main cause of this was the limitations set out in Article V, Section 7 (c), and especially, at first, the elimination of any repurchase obligation which would bring the member's monetary reserves below its quota. In the early postwar period many members' reserves were already below their quotas. This was particularly true of the United Kingdom, whose reserves were offset by such large liabilities that the net amount was below its quota. It was also true of the other countries in the sterling area, because most of their monetary reserves were held in sterling, which was not (until 1961) convertible and so was not included in reserves calculated for the purposes of the Fund.

The Board also realized that the size of a member's monetary reserves was to a considerable extent within its own power to determine, and accordingly, if a member wished to avoid a repurchase obligation, it had a fairly ready method of doing so.

It was true that the Articles of Agreement provided, in Article V, Section 8 (d), for consultation between the Fund and the member as a means of reducing the Fund's holdings of the member's currency after charges had reached 4 per cent. Quite apart from uncertainty as to the outcome of such consultations, however, 4 per cent would not be payable for drawings in the lower credit tranches until they had been outstanding for 6–7 years, and the provision cited would not apply at all to drawings in the gold tranche. The Section was therefore not regarded as adequately ensuring that the Fund's resources would be revolving.

THE FIRST YEAR

Before the Fund could begin transactions, a number of preliminary procedures had to be gone through. Among these was the determination of par values for countries having at least 65 per cent of the total of quotas. For this and other

---

[21] See above, Vol. I, pp. 190–92.

[22] See above, Vol. I, pp. 276–77.

[23] See below, pp. 441–43.

reasons,[24] it was not until March 1, 1947 that the Fund was ready to begin to permit the use of its resources. During the previous ten months, two points calling for comment arose in connection with the formation of policy.

In the Annual Report for 1946 (the Board's first report, which was written in September 1946) emphasis was laid on the temporary nature of the assistance which the Fund could give:

> The essential test of the propriety of use of the Fund's resources is . . . whether the prospective balance of payments position of the country concerned (including long-term capital movements) will be such that its use of the Fund's resources will be of relatively short duration.[25]

At the same time, the Fund would run the risk that some of its resources would be used for other than temporary assistance, and the Directors considered it their duty to bring this risk to the notice of the Board of Governors. This did not, however, mean that the Fund would be undiscriminating. On the contrary, the Directors remarked that "there are certain to be disappointments because of the restraints placed on use of the Fund's resources by some members." [26] (The ambiguity of this sentence was resolved by the context, which referred to restraints placed by the Fund, not by members.) Mention of these "restraints" was made earlier in this chapter.

References to the Fund's policy on the use of its resources in the Annual Report for 1947 were confined to two points. One was an exposition of the decision about the meaning of "the member . . . represents," which stated that the Board would implement its responsibility for adjudicating on the correctness of representations by keeping itself closely informed at all times of developments in each member country.[27] The other pointed out that the Fund was not intended to give assistance for reconstruction, and that, while it could and would provide temporary assistance to members even during the transitional period, in order to attain the objectives of the Fund it must be in a position to provide financial assistance after the transitional period.[28] The implicit suggestion that the Fund should meanwhile conserve its resources assumed greater importance six months later.[29]

EARLY DISAGREEMENTS

The interpretation by the Board of a number of phrases in Articles V and XX, summarized in an earlier section of this chapter, was not achieved without

---

[24] See details in Vol. I, pp. 157–60.

[25] *Annual Report, 1946*, p. 13.

[26] *Ibid.*

[27] *Annual Report, 1947*, p. 31.

[28] *Ibid.*, p. 18.

[29] See below, pp. 394–96.

dissent being expressed. Mr. de Largentaye (France) challenged the advice given by the staff to the Board on the subject of the meaning of "consistent with the provisions of this Agreement" (Article V, Section 3 (a) (i)); he and Mr. de Selliers (Belgium) did not see how a member could be required to make a representation that a drawing was for the purpose of making payments which would be consistent with the purposes of the Fund when it did not know how the Fund would interpret Article I. Mr. de Largentaye also believed that Article V, Section 5, could not be used to postpone a drawing once the member had made application for one. Mr. Overby (United States), on the other hand, could not accept that the Fund's powers were so limited. The view which the Board adopted of Article XX, Section 4 (i)—that its powers under this Section lapsed when a member drew—was also disputed; Messrs. Overby and Saad (Egypt) argued that the Section remained in force, and was a more suitable sanction for the Board to use than Article V, Section 5.

It was problems like these which the Managing Director had in mind when in January 1948 he sent to the Board a memorandum on the interpretation of the Articles of Agreement. He referred to the ambiguities and inconsistencies that could be found in them, and urged the Board to resolve such questions (where appropriate) by interpretations. His view, as he explained it to the Board, was that where the wording of the Agreement was clear it had to be applied or else a constitutional change had to be sought. However, where the text was ambiguous or even inconsistent, the interpretation should be guided by common sense and the broad principles and purposes of the Fund such as were expressed in Article I.

A similar view was expressed by Mr. Rasminsky (Canada). The minutes of the meeting report him to have said that

> he had been Chairman of the Drafting Committee at Bretton Woods. Because of the shortage of time and the conditions of work at the Conference, the result had not always been the optimum. He would be the first to admit that there were ambiguities in the text, some intended and others not. There also were inconsistencies. Hence, he thought, to a greater degree than usual the meaning had to be interpreted in terms of the general principles underlying the Fund. He pointed out the undesirability of reliance on shaky legal interpretations to secure action by members. In such cases, he thought, general statements of the Fund's policy on nonlegal bases would be preferable as means of securing member support.

These ideas were not, however, shared by all Executive Directors. One view was that

> in some cases of interpretation by the Executive Board there had been a tendency to overrule the evident meaning of precise provisions in favor of some general provision in Article I. This was not proper, especially since there might even be conflicts between certain of the enumerated purposes in Article I, such as high levels of employment and expanded international trade.

It was also pointed out that

> some members had thought their particular needs had been safeguarded by one
> specific provision or another in the Agreement. They would be alarmed if they
> found these particular provisions being overturned by some general phrasing.

Mr. Gutt's memorandum had stressed the significance of inflation as evidence
of a member's likely inability to qualify for a drawing from the Fund. This
point was also made by Mr. Overby in a contemporary memorandum, in which
he proposed that four specific questions should be asked when a member
sought to draw from the Fund: (a) Is its exchange rate increasing its balance of
payments difficulties, and would an adjustment of the rate reduce them?
(b) What are the prospects of the member's repurchasing? (c) Will the drawing
be used for relief, reconstruction, or development? (d) Are the member's
monetary or fiscal policies leading to fundamental disequilibrium? This attempt
to categorize the conditions under which a member might have access to the
Fund's resources led to a debate on whether the Board should attempt to
establish general policies to follow when considering members' requests to use
the Fund's resources, or should base its determination on the particular circumstances of the member concerned. The decision reached was that certain broad
considerations—such as the existence of inflation and the current general disequilibrium—would in all probability influence the Executive Board's opinion
as to the use of the Fund's resources by particular members. However, in any
case, the particular position of the member would have to be examined. It was
probable, the Board concluded, that policies on general aspects would tend to
develop as the individual reviews proceeded.

The foregoing discussions, which took place early in 1948, led to a number
of interpretations set out at the beginning of this chapter. In reaching these
decisions, the Board as a whole moved further away from the concept of an
automatic right to the use of the Fund's resources—a movement that had been
started by the interpretation of the phrase "the member . . . represents" in
May 1947.

ERP Decision

The elucidation of general principles was, however, interrupted shortly afterward by the intervention of U.S. aid to Europe through the European Recovery
Program (ERP). Expounding the Program to the Board, the U.S. Executive
Director and his Alternate explained that the data upon which the U.S. proposals
for the ERP had been predicated did not assume any assistance from the Fund
to European participants during the four-year period which it covered, chiefly
because the data were concerned with the needs of Europe for relief and reconstruction, for neither of which the Fund was intended. They cited several

reasons why, in their view, the Fund's resources should not be used, during the course of the Program, by the countries assisted:

(a) By making dollars available, the ERP would substantially reduce the pressure for dollar currencies to balance the international payments of the receiving countries.

(b) The determination by Congress of the dollar limits of ERP aid implicitly indicated the amount of U.S. production which should be shipped to Europe during the program. Any substantial provision of dollars through the Fund might result in a reconsideration of the amount of ERP aid.

(c) The balance of payments estimates for Europe showed a dollar disequilibrium of $3.5 billion still to be expected in 1952, so that the prospects for repurchase within five years were not bright. (This seems to have been the first occasion on which repurchase within five years was assumed to be normal.)

These arguments were countered by other Directors, who appealed to general principles. Even if the ERP would tend to reduce the need for members to call on the Fund for dollars, these Directors doubted whether this justified a policy limiting the members' access to the Fund. They believed that under the Articles of Agreement members had certain rights to purchase exchange, and the existence of programs such as the ERP could not diminish members' legal rights to use the Fund's resources. Moreover, because the ERP was assisting all European countries, it did not follow that each of them would be in deficit in 1952.

Nevertheless, Mr. Overby pressed the point that the Board's decision on any request to draw must take into account all the circumstances, and the existence of the ERP was a factor which could not be ignored. While there might be individual circumstances in which a drawing could be justified, he felt that the general effect of the new situation in Europe must be to tighten the Fund's evaluation of "reasonable doubt."

The formal decision of the Board was deferred until the ERP was actually in operation, and was then taken in the following terms, Mr. Tansley (United Kingdom) alone dissenting:

> Although the Fund recognizes that a general rule is not sufficient basis for all cases, the Fund must, in examining requests for the use of its resources, take into account the European Recovery Program. . . . Since the ERP is to be handled year by year, related policies on use of the Fund's resources should be developed at similar intervals. For the first year the attitude of the Fund and ERP members should be that such members should request the purchase of United States dollars from the Fund only in exceptional or unforeseen cases. The Fund and members participating in ERP should have as their objective to maintain the resources of the Fund at a safe and reasonable level during the ERP period in order that at the end of the period such members will have unencumbered access to the resources of the

Fund. This objective conforms with the intention of Article XIV, Section 1, that during the transitional period members should not impair the capacity of the Fund to serve its members or impair their ability to secure help from the Fund after the transitional period.[30]

At the same meeting as that at which the foregoing decision (generally known as the "ERP Decision") was adopted, Mr. de Selliers asked what would be the Fund's view of drawings of currencies other than the U.S. dollar. Mr. de Selliers was concerned about this because Belgium was the principal European creditor. The Belgian franc was therefore most likely to be in demand, but extensive drawings of that currency might place a severe strain on Belgium's balance of payments. Taking this into account, the Board decided as follows:

> During the European Recovery Program members of the Fund may wish to use the Fund's holdings of the currency of a country participating in ERP. No member has the right to veto or limit the Fund's sales of its currency to other members for use in accordance with the Fund Agreement. The Fund recognizes, however, that such sales should not have the effect of compelling a country to finance a large bilateral surplus with some countries, while it has to make net drawings on its gold and convertible currency reserves for current payments. Such circumstances would fall within the meaning of the "exceptional or unforeseen cases" mentioned in the policy decision of April 5, 1948, made by the Fund concerning the use of the Fund's resources by ERP countries and would justify requests by a country to purchase foreign exchange from the Fund to make to other members current payments or payments authorized by Article VI, Section 2, but not to build up its monetary reserves. This is in fact the manner in which the Fund is intended to facilitate a system of multilateral payments.[31]

The foregoing decisions were reproduced in full in the Annual Report for 1948, and the Board took the opportunity to make some general statements bearing on its attitude toward requests to use the Fund's resources. Having explained that certain members had been asked to refrain from seeking to draw because their situation was "not conducive to the proper use of the Fund's resources," and that judgment was necessary to determine whether a particular drawing was likely to be outstanding for a relatively short or a relatively long period, Directors went on:

> The Board has had, moreover, within the limits of the Fund Agreement, to weigh the advantages from both its own point of view and the point of view of its members of conserving the resources of the Fund for use in the post-transitional period against the advantages which members could derive from some immediate use of the Fund's resources. In the grave and unsettled conditions which prevailed, the Fund reached the conclusion that in some doubtful cases there were in general more disadvantages involved in denying members access to its resources than in allowing them such access.[32]

---

[30] *Annual Report, 1948*, p. 74.

[31] *Ibid.*, p. 75.

[32] *Ibid.*, p. 47.

The last sentence of this quotation was addressed to the point that the Fund was prepared to take risks—a point which, it will be recalled, was made in its first Annual Report. It did not imply that the Board's attitude to drawings by members in receipt of ERP aid would similarly give them the benefit of the doubt, for immediately after this statement the Board explained its attitude to such drawings along the lines of the U.S. arguments mentioned above, and of the terms of the ERP Decision.[33]

Formulating criteria

As a result of the ERP Decision, the volume of Fund transactions, which had totaled $606.0 million in the financial year 1947/48, fell in the three ensuing years to $119.4 million, $51.8 million, and $28.0 million, respectively. Such requests as were made by European countries to draw on the Fund while the ERP was in force gave rise to sharp differences of opinion in the Board. The first occasion for such a discussion was a preliminary inquiry from the Netherlands, in October 1948, as to the possibility of drawing Belgian francs. Mr. Beyen (Netherlands) explained that if the Fund's resources were used in this way it would be to tide his country over temporarily in anticipation of U.S. aid.

Mr. Overby then raised two questions: (1) whether the Fund could properly provide "temporary" financing to a country whose payments deficit arose essentially from a large reconstruction program and other nontemporary needs, and (2) whether a drawing could be considered as being for a relatively short term when all the indications were that the Netherlands' balance of payments deficit, particularly in convertible currencies, would continue long after 1952. Mr. Beyen's response was that if the Netherlands did apply to the Fund for a drawing it would be for purposes in accordance with the Articles of Agreement; should the Netherlands wish to finance reconstruction, it would seek assistance elsewhere.

The Director of Research, intervening, drew attention to the fact that the Fund's decision on dollar drawings by ERP countries indicated that the proper test would be quantitative. So far the drawings by the Netherlands had been very limited, and any need for Belgian francs should be small—probably not over 6 per cent of quota. As for repayment, he believed that the Netherlands' international accounts would be in balance long before 1955; while they would probably still be short of dollars, they would be long of other currencies which would be convertible for the Fund's purposes. Some Executive Directors pointed out that in the past the Fund had never required a precise demonstration of the arrangements for repayment; they felt that the burden of proof concerning the prospects of repurchase would be on the Fund. Mr. Ansiaux (Belgium)

---

[33] *Ibid.*, pp. 48–50.

said that he agreed with that view and noted that Belgium would not object to drawings of its currency from the Fund for the purpose indicated. Mr. Bolton (United Kingdom), expressing his views on the Fund's policy in more general terms, opposed the increasing number of interpretations reading into the Fund Agreement limitations which were not in the text. Because of such limitations, he said, the Fund was now of no use to its European members; it carried obligations but no benefits.

The occasion for the Netherlands' request was that it had given an informal undertaking not to draw on the Fund, which it now wished to withdraw. At the conclusion of the discussion Mr. Overby agreed to this course, on the understanding that if a request for a drawing from the Netherlands reached the Board, Executive Directors would be free to challenge it in accordance with Article V, Sections 3 and 5. However, he intervened also when some subsequent requests for drawings, not connected with the ERP, were made (e.g., by Nicaragua and South Africa), questioning either the temporary character of these drawings or the prospects for repurchase.

The differences of opinion which had emerged in the discussions of these transactions contributed to a growing feeling in the Executive Board that a further clarification of the Fund's policy on the use of its resources was urgently needed. It was obviously desirable that members should know how they stood with the Fund. It was also clear that the confidence which the Fund intended to give to its members would not be assured if the fate of a request for use of its resources were left uncertain while the Fund engaged in a lengthy review of the member's position.

For the moment, however, the clarification took the form of a restatement of the U.S. position. In a memorandum circulated to the Executive Directors on May 20, 1949, Mr. Southard, who had succeeded Mr. Overby as Executive Director for the United States, reported on the outcome of a review within the U.S. Government of the Fund's policy and practices on the use of its resources. The position of the United States was that

> the use of the resources of the Fund by any member should be subject to close scrutiny to assure that any purchases conform strictly to the general principles and purposes of the Fund, as well as to the specific provisions of the Articles of Agreement. Any doubt should be resolved in favor of the Fund rather than in favor of the member.

The practical principles and criteria which the U.S. authorities had evolved from this position were that drawings by a member which applied exchange restrictions on current transactions or quantitative import controls should not be permitted without four specific determinations by the Fund: (a) that the par value of the member was appropriate; (b) that the circumstances which gave rise to the proposed drawing were due to a temporary rather than to a fundamental disequilibrium; (c) that the proposed drawing could not primarily be attributed, directly or indirectly, to requirements engendered by programs of rehabilitation or development; and (d) that the member was taking all the steps essential to assume, as soon as possible, its full obligations under the Articles of Agreement.

The first occasion on which these tests were applied to a prospective drawing occurred on May 31, 1949, when Brazil sought to draw $15 million. Mr. Southard then accepted that the first of his criteria was satisfied, but said that he wished to be assured that Brazil's request was prompted neither by a fundamental disequilibrium nor by the requirements of development. Other Executive Directors deprecated this approach, believing that Brazil was entitled to the benefit of "any reasonable doubt" during the transitional period, and questioning whether Mr. Southard's tests were justified in terms of the Articles of Agreement. At the end of the discussion, Mr. Paranaguá (Brazil) said that Brazil would defer its request.

In the middle of July an application by the Netherlands to purchase Belgian francs was deferred after Mr. Southard said that he doubted whether the circumstances satisfied the criteria which he had laid down. By then the probability that European currencies would have shortly to be devalued was becoming increasingly recognized, and this underlay the Board's attitude not only to the Netherlands' request but to drawings in general.

In these conditions the Directors did not attempt any fresh description of the Fund's policies on the use of its resources when they came to write the Annual Report for 1949; they contented themselves with referring to the passage in the Annual Report for 1948 cited above.[34]

Counterproposals, 1949–51

After the Annual Meeting and the group of major devaluations which immediately followed, Mr. Southard again took the initiative. In a memorandum to the Managing Director dated October 17, 1949, he requested that the following proposal should be placed on the Board's agenda:

> ... in the future dollar drawings should be objected to unless the member proposing to draw on the resources of the Fund is willing to make an agreement, or to give a firm commitment, to repurchase its currency from the Fund within a maximum period of five years, preferably according to a definite schedule of repayment.

Underlying this proposal was the realization, explained earlier, that the repurchase provisions in the Articles of Agreement were inadequate to ensure the prompt repayment of sums drawn from the Fund. Mr. Southard called attention in particular to the position in the sterling area and in member countries with

---

[34] *Annual Report, 1949*, p. 43.

centrally planned balances of payments. He agreed that his proposal would apply logically to drawings in all currencies, and not only in dollars, and suggested that it should be considered in those terms.

A counter memorandum by Mr. Beyen pointed out that while the Articles of Agreement defined, although negatively, the purposes for which drawings might be made, they said nothing about the period for which they might be held by the member. Mr. Southard's proposal therefore, in Mr. Beyen's view, cut right across the provisions of the Agreement. Mr. Beyen also argued that the repurchase provisions of Article V, Section 7, and Schedule B were not meant to be the normal mechanism for securing repurchases, but rather to become operative if members failed to repurchase spontaneously.

A discussion of Mr. Southard's and Mr. Beyen's memoranda on December 19, 1949 showed that most Executive Directors shared Mr. Beyen's point of view. Several questioned the legality and propriety of the Fund's imposing requirements as to the time of repurchase. Some went further, and believed that most members would be much concerned at a proposal like Mr. Southard's. Before accepting the Articles of Agreement, members had carefully weighed the benefits and obligations which were entailed, and many, at least, had never believed that the Articles involved such a severe limitation of drawing rights as was suggested. While agreeing that the use of the Fund's resources should be temporary, Directors thought that the proper course was for the Fund to work out ways to ensure this without imposing conditions which might force members, in order to repurchase drawings, to introduce measures which would be inimical to the Fund's basic aims. The debate was continued at two further meetings in January 1950.

Early in December the staff had put before the Board a recommendation that a circular letter should be sent to all members pointing out that proper use of the Fund's resources required that members should adopt corrective measures to ensure repayment. The staff suggested that as a general rule members should consult the Fund before drawing; however, the Board should as soon as possible review each member's prospects, and if these were satisfactory the request to consult before drawing could be canceled. This proposal was refined and elaborated by a staff Working Party which reported in May 1950. The Working Party emphasized the need for member countries to know in advance whether they could draw on the Fund. To enable the Board to inform them on this point, the Working Party proposed a system of prior review and assessment of the eligibility of each member, coupled with criteria on the basis of which it could be determined whether the member was following appropriate policies with regard to its exchange rate, etc.

The Board discussed this report at several informal sessions, but it was not favorably received. Objections were raised on various grounds. It was argued, in particular, that the procedure might lead to a kind of blacklisting of members, and that unless the reviews were frequently repeated they would be ineffective. In July the Board agreed to resume discussion of the problem after the Annual Meeting. No reference to the controversy was made in the Annual Report for 1950. A further informal session held in October showed that the Directors' views were unchanged.

In an attempt to break the deadlock, the Managing Director proposed early in November a procedure which would tie drawings to programs of action by the drawing members. He suggested that where a member was in difficulties the staff might assist it to work out a suitable policy for the recovery of equilibrium, and that this policy might then be supported by a drawing. This was discussed at several meetings during the ensuing six months and eventually accepted by the Board for use "in addition to and without prejudice to existing procedures, or policies." Objections to it were, however, maintained by Mr. de Largentaye and by Mr. Stamp (United Kingdom), the former on both legal and practical grounds, and the latter because the British Government objected to "any suggestion that the right of members to come to the Fund would in any way depend upon their carrying out policies with which they did not agree." As it turned out, the new procedure had little practical result, partly because discussions aimed at designing a program of action for a member in difficulties were bound to be lengthy.

The change of attitude toward drawing rights which was implicit in the Managing Director's proposal was brought into the open by Mr. Beyen. In the discussion in the Board in November 1950, and again in a memorandum three months later, he pointed out that the plan to tie drawings to programs of action involved changing the concept of eligibility from automaticity to conditionality. It was on this note that Mr. Gutt's tenure of the Managing Directorship ended.

THE ROOTH PLAN

After the arrival of Mr. Rooth as Managing Director, the search for an effective policy for the use of the Fund's resources was actively resumed. On October 19, 1951, Mr. Rooth proposed to the Board a revision of the scale of charges for drawings. These changes, and the resulting new scale, are discussed in Chapter 19; here it will suffice to say that the general effect of the changes proposed was to emphasize the short-term character of drawings by reducing the cost of using the Fund's resources for a very short period, and increasing the cost for longer periods. It was even more important that the changes also reduced the length of time for which a drawing could remain outstanding before the member was required to consult the Fund about ways of reducing the Fund's holdings of its currency.

Three weeks later Mr. Rooth outlined to the Board some principles which in his view would enable the Fund to make its resources more readily available. He suggested that, in order to preserve the revolving character of the Fund, the time limit for repurchases should normally be three years, with an outside limit of five years. He proposed also that there should be special terms for drawings within the gold tranche (i.e., drawings which increased the Fund's holdings of the member's currency to not more than 100 per cent of its quota), and for very short-term drawings (i.e., drawings for not more than eighteen months).

In the discussion that followed, most Executive Directors commented favorably on Mr. Rooth's proposals. The only strong objection came from Mr. de Largentaye, who argued that the Articles of Agreement permitted the imposition of special conditions as to repurchases in accordance with Article V, Section 4, only for drawings above the limits of 25 per cent of quota a year and 200 per cent of quota in all. Where such special circumstances did not exist, members would find it very difficult to give up their rights under Article V, Section 3. Mr. de Largentaye also made a comment on the Managing Director's proposal for special terms for drawings in the gold tranche; while he regarded these as commendable, his own view was that such drawings were a matter of right, and not one of special privilege.

Encouraged by the general support of the Board, the Managing Director appointed a new staff Working Party to make definite recommendations. This Working Party's report was circulated on January 19 and was debated at two informal and two formal sessions of the Board, resulting on February 13, 1952 in a decision approved by all the Directors present except Mr. de Largentaye, who abstained on legal grounds. This decision became known as the Rooth Plan, and with only minor changes it has governed the use of the Fund's resources ever since. The text will be found in Volume III.[35] The following features of the decision should, however, be specially noted:

(1) An introductory statement by the Managing Director suggested that sometimes "discussions between the member and the Fund may cover its general position, not with a view to any immediate drawing, but in order to ensure that it would be able to draw if, within a period of say 6 or 12 months, the need presented itself." This proposal contained the germ of the stand-by arrangements which have since become one of the most important features of the Fund's work; these arrangements are discussed in detail in Chapters 20 and 21.

(2) By paragraph 2.a., "exchange purchased from the Fund should not remain outstanding beyond the period reasonably related to the payments problem for which it was purchased from the Fund. The period should fall within an outside range of three to five years."

---

[35] E.B. Decision No. 102-(52/11), February 13, 1952; below, Vol. III, p. 228.

(3) By paragraph 3, a "member can count on receiving the overwhelming benefit of any doubt respecting drawings which would raise the Fund's holdings of its currency to not more than its quota"—i.e., for drawings in the gold tranche.

(4) By paragraph 2.e., a member seeking to draw from the Fund "will be expected to include in its authenticated request a statement that it will comply" with the principles of the decision.

WAIVERS

Six months later, on October 1, 1952, the Board adopted a decision which made detailed provision for stand-by arrangements.[36] The details of this decision are discussed in Chapter 20. Here it need only be noted that while such arrangements were expected to be, in general, for not more than a quarter of the member's quota—the limit mentioned in Article V, Section 3 (a) (iii)—the decision provided that the Fund would not regard itself as precluded from granting stand-by arrangements for a larger proportion of the quota. This would be done, of course, by invoking the provisions in Article V, Section 4, for a waiver.

The first waiver granted was to Turkey in August 1953, in connection with a drawing equivalent to 47 per cent of its quota. At first, recourse to a waiver was regarded as exceptional, and indeed as late as December 1954 the granting of a waiver was described as "unusual in itself." But in 1956 waivers were granted for all the 8 stand-by arrangements approved, and for all the 8 drawings not made under stand-by arrangements, and during the ten years 1956 through 1965 only 11 out of 157 stand-by arrangements and 32 out of 76 direct drawings did not involve a waiver.

The first drawing equivalent to 100 per cent of quota was made, as already mentioned, by Burma in 1956.[37] In 1961 Chile was given a drawing and stand-by arrangement which together committed the Fund, for the first time, to increase its holdings of a member's currency beyond 175 per cent of the member's quota. In October 1963 the United Arab Republic, by drawing $16 million, increased the Fund's holdings of its currency to 215 per cent of quota. This was the first time that the limit of 200 per cent had been exceeded, and resulted from the Fund's new policy for the compensation of export fluctuations, described in the final section of this chapter. The largest drawing by any member down to the end of 1965 was one of $1,400 million (72 per cent of quota) by the United Kingdom in May of that year.

CREDIT TRANCHE POLICY

The decision of February 13, 1952 differentiated only between drawings in the gold tranche and all other drawings. During the next three years the Board

---

[36] E.B. Decision No. 155-(52/57), October 1, 1952; below, Vol. III, p. 230.

[37] See above, p. 386.

was cautiously exploring the possibilities opened up by the decision, and especially by the introduction of stand-by arrangements. By 1955, sufficient experience had been gained to enable the Board to begin to refine upon its policies in respect of drawings beyond the gold tranche. In its Annual Report for 1955 the Board first stated that "unless there are overwhelmingly strong reasons for not doing so, the Fund will invariably grant members' requests for gold tranche drawings,"[38] and then went on to distinguish among larger drawings, as follows:

> . . . The larger the drawing in relation to a member's quota the stronger is the justification required of the member.
>
> In practice, the Fund's attitude toward applications for drawings within the first credit tranche (i.e., drawings that raise the Fund's holdings of a member's currency above 100 per cent but not over 125 per cent of its quota) is a liberal one. Members are aware that, if they face balance of payments problems of a temporary nature, they may confidently expect a favorable response from the Fund to a request for a drawing within the first credit tranche, provided they are themselves making reasonable efforts to solve their problems.[39]

For drawings beyond the first credit tranche, the Report explained, there was not as yet the same body of precedent, but "should the need arise, and should the justification be substantial, members need not doubt that drawings on subsequent tranches will be permitted."[40]

By 1958 the necessary experience had been gained, and in the Annual Report for that year the Board set out its policy toward drawings beyond the first credit tranche. This was repeated in the following year in a recapitulation which has since served as the classic statement of policy on the use of the Fund's resources:

> Members are given the overwhelming benefit of the doubt in relation to requests for transactions within the "gold tranche". . . . The Fund's attitude to requests for transactions within the first credit tranche . . . is a liberal one, provided that the member itself is also making reasonable efforts to solve its problems. Requests for transactions beyond these limits require substantial justification. They are likely to be favorably received when the drawings or stand-bys are intended to support a sound program aimed at establishing or maintaining the enduring stability of the member's currency at a realistic rate of exchange.[41]

The undertaking to give gold tranche drawings "the overwhelming benefit of any doubt" was intended to encourage members to regard the right to draw in the gold tranche as part of their reserves. In the Annual Report for 1963, in a table showing monetary reserves, the Board included for the first time members' gold tranche drawing rights as part of these reserves.[42] Some mem-

---

[38] *Annual Report, 1955*, p. 84.

[39] *Ibid.*, pp. 84–85.

[40] *Ibid.*, p. 85.

[41] *Annual Report, 1959*, p. 22.

[42] *Annual Report, 1963*, pp. 40–41.

bers were, however, unable to accept this concept; opposition to it was expressed on several occasions, notably by Mr. van Campenhout (Belgium)—chiefly on the ground that requests to draw in the gold tranche were not legally immune from challenge.

Considering what could be done to strengthen the claim of gold tranche drawing rights to be regarded as reserves, the staff suggested in December 1963 that steps should be taken to streamline the procedure for such drawings. Up to that time they had been handled by the normal drawing procedure, which involved the preparation of a staff recommendation to the Board, its consideration at a Board meeting, and the subsequent giving of instructions to the relevant depositories to transfer the required currencies to the drawing member. The whole procedure took about a week.

As the General Counsel pointed out at an informal session in January 1964, to go further and make such drawings wholly automatic (as was suggested by Mr. Saad) would conflict with the tradition, founded on the interpretation of "the member . . . represents," that the Fund had the right to challenge any request for a drawing. However, the opportunity for a challenge could be given by a brief notification by the Managing Director to Executive Directors that a request for a gold tranche drawing had been received, on the understanding that if no objection was raised within, say, twenty-four hours, the drawing would proceed. This proposal was further considered by the Board in August 1964 and was approved. The decision was:

> When a duly authenticated request to draw in the gold tranche is received from a member, the request shall be notified to the Executive Board on the day it is received, whenever possible, or on the next business day, and unless, by the close of that business day, the Managing Director decides or an Executive Director requests that the matter be placed on the Board's agenda for discussion, the Fund shall, at the close of the first business day following the date of the receipt of the request, instruct the appropriate depository to make the transfer on the next business day after the instruction or as soon as possible thereafter.[43]

It should be added that while this change in procedure shortened the time needed to effect a gold tranche drawing to about three days, it did not satisfy those members that had hesitated to regard the rights to such drawings as reserves. Their doubts were expressed, for example, by Mr. Ansiaux, Governor for Belgium, at the Annual Meeting in 1965. As will be seen, these doubts expressly included drawings that raised the Fund's holdings of the member's currency from below 75 per cent to 75 per cent of quota (sometimes known as the "super gold tranche"). Mr. Ansiaux said:

> . . . The use of the gold tranche and even of the super gold tranche remains juridically and, therefore, potentially in fact, conditional. . . . It is, therefore,

[43] E.B. Decision No. 1745-(64/46), August 3, 1964; below, Vol. III, p. 243.

impossible for central banks to incorporate them in their reserves on the same footing as gold or convertible currencies.[44]

It was a recognition of this difficulty that prompted the change in the Articles of Agreement, effected in 1969, which made gold tranche drawings legally immune from challenge.[45]

There was, as time went on, a natural tendency for drawings to reach higher tranches in members' quotas—i.e., for the Fund's holdings of the members' currencies to increase relative to quotas. On the other hand, in 1961, 1962, and 1964, there were drawings in the "super gold tranche." These tendencies are summarized in Table 15.

Table 15. Fund Transactions by Tranches, 1947–65
(In per cent)

Calendar Years	Annual Average of Amounts Drawn ($ million)	Percentage of Amounts Drawn That Increased the Fund's Holdings to the Following Percentages of Quotas				
		0–100	101–125	126–150	151–175	Over 175
1947–51	162	68	32	—	—	—
1952–56	219	48	45	6	1	—
1957–61	851	31[1]	36	30	2	—
1962–65	1,325	38[2]	16	20	14	12[3]

Source: Mookerjee, *op. cit.*, p. 430, supplemented by *IFS*, December 1965–February 1966.
[1] Includes 1 per cent in the member's "super gold tranche."
[2] Includes 3 per cent in the member's "super gold tranche."
[3] Includes 0.3 per cent, raising the Fund's holdings above 200 per cent of quota.

DRAWINGS AGAINST GOLD COLLATERAL

It will be remembered that Article V, Section 4, requires that the Fund, when deciding whether to waive any of the requirements for a drawing set out in Section 3 (*a*), shall take into consideration "a member's willingness to pledge as collateral security gold, silver, securities, or other acceptable assets having a value sufficient in the opinion of the Fund to protect its interests," and empowers the Fund to require such collateral security if it so wishes. The power to require collateral security has never been exercised. When the request by Burma to draw the equivalent of 100 per cent of its quota was being considered, Mr. Lieftinck (Netherlands) suggested that the Fund should call for collateral security to cover one third of the sum, but this was not adopted by the Board.[46] This appears to have been the only time that an Executive Director has suggested that the Board should require the deposit of collateral security. However, a deposit of gold as security has on four occasions been offered by members wishing to draw from the Fund, and such a deposit has three times been accepted.

---

[44] *Summary Proceedings, 1965*, pp. 131–32.
[45] See below, p. 601.
[46] See above, p. 386.

On the first occasion when an offer was made, by Iran in February 1953, it was withdrawn before a decision had been reached in the Board. In the three other instances, the proposal was made by the United Arab Republic. The first time was in December 1958, but the member then decided, after its offer had been accepted by the Board, to withdraw its request for a drawing. The other two offers were made in 1962, and both were carried through. The relevant drawings increased the Fund's holdings of Egyptian pounds to 155 per cent of the member's quota.

It was, however, not without some hesitation that the Board approved the United Arab Republic's proposals. In the first place, Directors considered that gold collateral was not an adequate substitute for a stabilization program, such as would normally have been required as a condition for permitting a drawing reaching into the third credit tranche. Secondly, the offer made by the member was to earmark gold in Cairo, whereas the Board felt that gold accepted as collateral should be deposited in one of the Fund's own gold depositories (which did not include Cairo). The Board therefore readily agreed to the release of the gold when in April 1962 the United Arab Republic sought a stand-by arrangement in connection with which it undertook to implement a stabilization program.

As a result of the foregoing experience, the staff was asked to draft standard terms for drawings against gold collateral. Proposing these to the Board in March 1963, the staff suggested that such drawings should be regarded as exceptional, but that they might have a value in special circumstances, as for example if the member was planning a stabilization program but had not yet been able to bring it into effect and needed assistance meanwhile. The terms for a drawing against gold collateral should be the same as for an ordinary drawing, except that the drawing would normally be expected to be repurchased within six months. The member should pay any incidental charges in connection with the transfer of the gold to a depository named by the Fund, where it should be retained until the drawing was repurchased. If the repurchase was not completed in the agreed time, the gold would be used by the Fund to repurchase the drawing. These proposals were accepted by the Board and embodied in a decision taken on July 1, 1963.[47] There was, however, no other drawing against gold collateral during the period covered by this volume.

DRAWINGS BY NEW MEMBERS

On three occasions during the twenty years 1945–65 the Board reviewed the link between the establishment of a par value and the right to use the Fund's resources. This link, and in particular the problems of new members in this respect, have been discussed in detail in Chapter 4 of this volume (pages 65–73).

[47] E.B. Decision No. 1543-(63/39), July 1, 1963; below, Vol. III, p. 240.

A brief recapitulation here will be sufficient to round out the discussion of the Fund's policy on the use of its resources. It will be remembered that the link in question was created by Article XX, Section 4 (c), which reads, in part:

> When the par value of a member's currency has been established . . . the member shall be eligible to buy from the Fund the currencies of other members to the full extent permitted in this Agreement. . . .

This is modified by Article XX, Section 4 (d) (ii), to permit members that had been occupied by the enemy to use the Fund's resources after they had proposed a par value, even though this had not been accepted by the Fund. Original members—that is, countries that had signed the Articles of Agreement by December 31, 1946—could utilize Article XX, Section 4 (d) (ii), automatically, but new members could do so only if an appropriate reference was made, in the Membership Resolution admitting them to the Fund, to the privileges accorded by that Section. Such a reference was made in the Membership Resolution for Italy, but it was thought cumbersome to repeat it for members joining later, and this was not done. This omission gave rise to the first review by the Board of the conditions under which new members might draw on the Fund.

The occasion for this review arose in 1952, when at the Annual Meeting the Governor for Thailand asked that consideration should be given to permitting his country—which was not an original member—to draw on the Fund even though it did not have, and was not able to propose, a par value.[48] When the Board looked into the matter, it appeared that Thailand and Indonesia were unique in that their Membership Resolutions made no provision for utilizing Article XX, Section 4 (d) (ii). (Burma would have been in a similar position except that it was on the point of agreeing with the Fund a par value for the kyat.) The Board accordingly decided to invite the Governors to amend the Membership Resolutions for Thailand and Indonesia so as to include a reference to Article XX, Section 4 (d) (ii), and this was done.[49]

Ten years later a new point arose. The Membership Resolutions for all members from 1947 onward had provided that the member should not draw until thirty days after a par value for its currency had been agreed. The original purpose of this provision had been to allow time for the completion of formalities, such as the calculation of the member's net official holdings and of its gold and currency subscriptions, the last of which could not be determined until the par value was known. When, however, Afghanistan sought the Fund's agreement to a par value at the beginning of 1963, and wished also to draw from the Fund, Executive Directors questioned whether the interval of thirty days was necessary. The staff then agreed that since 1947 it had become the custom to

---

[48] *Summary Proceedings, 1952,* p. 65.
[49] Resolutions 8-4 and 8-5, *Summary Proceedings, 1953,* pp. 96–97.

settle all technical points before a par value was actually agreed, so that the need for the interval no longer existed. The Board accordingly recommended to the Governors that the Membership Resolutions should be amended so as to permit members to draw as soon as a par value had been agreed and put into operation. The Governors agreed.[50]

So far, it will be observed, eligibility to draw on the Fund remained linked to at least the proposal of a par value; members that had not been occupied by the enemy had to have a par value established before a drawing could be permitted. The third review by the Board of this subject was concerned with the necessity for retaining this link at all.

The proposal that it should be discarded was made by the staff early in 1964. There were then 28 members, including most of the newly joined African members, that had not established a par value, and the staff suggested that it was anomalous that such members might not draw from the Fund, even if they had a stable exchange rate, while other countries, having par values, were permitted to do so, even though their effective exchange rates departed widely from their par values. The staff also believed that there would be positive advantages in severing the link between par values and eligibility to draw on the Fund. For one thing, it would discourage members from proposing possibly unrealistic exchange rates as par values in order to qualify for a drawing; for another, a drawing might in some instances assist a member to achieve a stable exchange rate, and a viable par value, which might otherwise be beyond its power to attain.

Preliminary discussions of the matter with Executive Directors showed that the Board was sensitive to the need to avoid diminishing the importance which the Fund attached to the establishment and maintenance of par values. The staff therefore amended its proposal by adding to the proposed decision a declaration safeguarding this point. In this amended form the Board accepted the staff's recommendation, and decided as follows:

> (a) Where the Fund prescribes the conditions and amount of an exchange transaction by a member before the establishment of an initial par value, the member will be required to complete the payment of its subscription on the basis of a provisional rate of exchange for its currency proposed by the member and agreed by the Fund.

> (b) In deciding whether to permit exchange transactions before the establishment of an initial par value, the Fund, in accordance with the last sentence of Article I, will be guided by the purposes of the Articles; the Fund will encourage members to follow policies leading to the establishment of realistic exchange rates and to the adoption at the earliest feasible date of effective par values, and will take into account the efforts that are being made to achieve this objective. . . .[51]

---

[50] Resolution 18-2, *Summary Proceedings, 1963*, pp. 227–29.

[51] E.B. Decision No. 1687-(64/22), April 22, 1964; below, Vol. III, p. 243.

The decision concluded with an assurance that the Fund would give the over-whelming benefit of any doubt to a request for a gold tranche drawing, and would implement drawings under the compensatory financing decision (see the final section of this chapter). Appropriate amendments to the Membership Resolutions of members without par values were proposed to the Governors and accepted on June 1, 1964.[52]

THE FUND'S ATTITUDE TODAY

It is right to conclude this description of the evolution of the Fund's policy on drawings by saying that in recent years the legal limitations on members' rights to draw have ceased to preoccupy the Board. This development has been made possible by three things: the decision of February 13, 1952, with its specific provisions for repurchases within three to five years; the increasingly detailed knowledge of members' situations which has been built up over the years; and the emergence of unwritten but clearly understood guidelines as a result of the Board's consideration of the several hundred drawings already made. The existence of these guidelines has enabled the staff to advise member countries, when they wish to draw, what steps they should take in order to ensure favorable consideration for their requests. This in turn enables members to make formal requests for drawings with confidence that they will not be rejected. It can be fairly said that in present circumstances the Board would wish never to withhold approval of a drawing; at the most, Directors would criticize during the dis-cussion any features which they considered to be unsatisfactory, in order to guide the staff in its future advice to members.

DRAWINGS FOR CAPITAL TRANSFERS

THE TERMS OF THE ARTICLES

The principal provisions of the Articles of Agreement on the subject of capital transfers are as follows:

Article VI. Capital Transfers

SECTION 1. *Use of the Fund's resources for capital transfers.*—(a) A member may not make net use of the Fund's resources to meet a large or sustained outflow of capital, and the Fund may request a member to exercise controls to prevent such use of the resources of the Fund. If, after receiving such a request, a member fails to exercise appropriate controls, the Fund may declare the member ineligible to use the resources of the Fund.

(b) Nothing in this Section shall be deemed

(i) to prevent the use of the resources of the Fund for capital transactions of reasonable amount required for the expansion of exports or in the ordinary course of trade, banking or other business, or

---

[52] Resolution 19-8, *Summary Proceedings, 1964*, pp. 260–61.

(ii) to affect capital movements which are met out of a member's own resources of gold and foreign exchange, but members undertake that such capital movements will be in accordance with the purposes of the Fund.

SEC. 2. *Special provisions for capital transfers.*—If the Fund's holdings of the currency of a member have remained below seventy-five percent of its quota for an immediately preceding period of not less than six months, such member, if it has not been declared ineligible to use the resources of the Fund under Section 1 of this Article, Article IV, Section 6, Article V, Section 5, or Article XV, Section 2 (*a*), shall be entitled, notwithstanding the provisions of Section 1 (*a*) of this Article, to buy the currency of another member from the Fund with its own currency for any purpose, including capital transfers. Purchases for capital transfers under this Section shall not, however, be permitted if they have the effect of raising the Fund's holdings of the currency of the member desiring to purchase above seventy-five percent of its quota, or of reducing the Fund's holdings of the currency desired below seventy-five percent of the quota of the member whose currency is desired.

SEC. 3. *Controls of capital transfers.*—Members may exercise such controls as are necessary to regulate international capital movements, but no member may exercise these controls in a manner which will restrict payments for current transactions or which will unduly delay transfers of funds in settlement of commitments, except as provided in Article VII, Section 3 (*b*), and in Article XIV, Section 2.

Article XIX (*i*) defines, though not exhaustively, payments for current transactions as "payments which are not for the purpose of transferring capital," and includes certain items which in ordinary parlance would be regarded as capital transactions, viz., "payments of moderate amount for amortization of loans or for depreciation of direct investments." The paragraph also empowers the Fund to determine, after consultation with the members concerned, whether certain specific transactions are to be considered current transactions or capital transactions.

We are not here concerned with the main purpose of this definition, which was to clarify the obligations of members, set out in Articles VIII and XIV, in connection with exchange restrictions. It is sufficient to note that the special definition of current transactions given in Article XIX (*i*) does not invalidate the prohibition, in Article VI, Section 1, on the use of the Fund's resources to meet large or sustained outflows of capital.

APPLICATION OF THE ARTICLES

The Board has not formally adopted any rules or guiding principles to help it to apply the prohibition in Article VI, Section 1, or the interpretation given, in response to the United States in 1946 (quoted above), to requests to use the Fund's resources. In practice emphasis has been laid, in discussing requests for drawings, upon the existence of a current account deficit, whether or not a capital account deficit also existed. In 1961 the position was transformed, as described below, by the clarification of the interpretation given in 1946. Before then there had been a number of transactions where the presence of a capital account deficit was taken into consideration in reaching the Board's decision.

The first example of such a transaction was one with Mexico in connection with the devaluation of the peso in 1954. Mexico had never employed exchange controls, and its representatives had several times informed the Board that it would be impracticable to do so. As a result, when a strong speculative outflow of capital funds was added in 1954 to the current account deficit which had persisted since 1951, an exchange crisis developed. It was at this point that Mexico approached the Fund with a proposal to devalue the peso by 30 per cent in order to correct a fundamental disequilibrium, and asked at the same time for a stand-by arrangement for $50 million (about 55 per cent of Mexico's quota at that time).

During the discussion of this request, Mr. Southard observed that the degree of devaluation had to be large enough to provoke a backflow of capital (thus implying that the Fund's resources would not be used to finance a further capital outflow), and supported the stand-by request in view of the assurances given by Mexico with regard to the financial policies it would pursue. When some other Directors questioned the need for a stand-by arrangement as well as the devaluation, the representative of Mexico explained that the authorities believed that a second line of reserves was needed to strengthen the exchange position. Mr. Saad supported the request for a stand-by arrangement because, as he said, he had always understood that one of the purposes to be served by such an arrangement was to provide psychological assistance to a member in circumstances such as those of Mexico. The approval of the stand-by arrangement thus appeared to establish the principle that such arrangements could assist a member in dealing with the problems of capital outflow by helping to restore and maintain confidence in its currency.

Somewhat similar considerations arose when Cuba came to the Fund for a gold tranche drawing and a stand-by arrangement in December 1956. Cuba, which was also without exchange controls at that time, feared that too large a decrease in reserves, which might result from the imminent settlement of some short-term and medium-term debts incurred to meet past deficits on current account, would lead to capital flight. Some doubts were expressed by members of the Board as to the need for the stand-by arrangement, but it was in fact approved.

Four days later the United Kingdom came to the Fund for a drawing of $561.47 million and a stand-by arrangement for $738.53 million, amounting together to 100 per cent of the British quota. The request was prompted by the crisis of confidence in sterling which resulted from the Suez Canal conflict.

While the British authorities believed that measures already taken should ensure a satisfactory current account balance for 1956–57, they were afraid that this result would be endangered if the loss of confidence in sterling were not overcome. Both in the staff's memorandum to the Board and in the discussion of it by Executive Directors, the need to restore confidence in sterling was cited as the most cogent justification for the drawing and the stand-by arrangement, which were approved.

In March 1958 the Union of South Africa approached the Fund for a gold tranche drawing and a stand-by arrangement covering the first credit tranche. At that time, South Africa's reserves had been drawn down because of balance of payments deficits on both current and capital account, that on capital account being the more important. The current account deficit resulted mainly from a sharp expansion of imports, which had reached a high stage of liberalization following relaxation of import restrictions in 1957. The capital outflow was primarily connected with a reduction in the intake of foreign investments and the sharp increase in interest rates abroad, particularly in the United Kingdom. Mr. Fleming (Australia), Alternate to Mr. Callaghan, who had been elected by South Africa, explained that the drawing and stand-by arrangement were needed to enable the South African Government to avoid reimposing import restrictions. The request was approved on these grounds.

In March 1960 the Fund agreed to a one-year stand-by arrangement for Venezuela which would, if fully utilized, raise the Fund's holding of bolívares to 142 per cent of Venezuela's quota, as this would be when the first general increase in quotas took effect.[53] Venezuela's international reserves had been drawn down by substantial amounts in 1958 and 1959, in contrast to large gains in 1956 and 1957. However, the deficits on current account in its balance of payments were not large, the principal cause of the decline in reserves being a substantial outflow of capital. This was due in part to repayment of foreign-held floating debt created by the preceding Government.

On this occasion the prohibition in the Articles against financing "large or sustained" outflows of capital was expressly introduced into the discussion in the Board. Mr. Toussaint (Belgium) pointed out that if a continuation of such substantial capital exports as had been observed recently was to be expected in the coming months, it would not be appropriate, in view of the language of Article VI, Section 1 (a), that the Fund's resources should be used to cover the deficit. However, he took note of the special and nonrecurrent character of a large part of the capital outflow over the previous two years, and of the staff's judgment that the effect of the stabilization measures then being taken by the Venezuelan authorities would be to reduce the net sales of exchange by the

---

[53] On the first general increase in quotas, see above, pp. 358–59.

Central Bank in the coming months to an amount which could be financed from foreign bank credits then under negotiation.

It will be observed that Mr. Toussaint's intervention was based on Article VI, Section 1 (a), and not on the interpretation given in response to the request from the U.S. Government in 1946. The General Counsel commented on this in a memorandum to the Managing Director later in 1960. Surveying the Board's practice in connection with drawings which involved consideration of capital transfers, he said:

> It has been the growing tendency of the Fund not to examine closely whether there exists a current account deficit in the case of drawings within the gold tranche or, to some extent, in the first credit tranche. However, the Board has never said that the [1946] interpretation does not apply to such drawings. In the case of Venezuela, on the other hand, where drawing rights in upper tranches were involved, the question of capital outflow was raised.

By the time that this memorandum was written, international short-term capital movements were again threatening to cause serious dislocation on the international monetary scene. The restoration of external convertibility for European currencies at the end of 1958 had partially opened the way for such movements, and it was apparent that when the major countries which were relying on Article XIV came to accept the obligations of Article VIII, Sections 2, 3, and 4 (as they were shortly expected to do), the risk of such movements would be enhanced. It was, indeed, very shortly after ten countries had accepted these obligations, in February 1961, that the problem created by the 1946 interpretation was raised in the Board.

Before then there was one more transaction which involved a deficit on capital account. Late in December 1960 South Africa, which had repaid its earlier drawing from the Fund, sought to draw $18.75 million, which would raise the Fund's holdings of its currency from 75 per cent to 87.5 per cent of its quota. On this occasion, South Africa's balance of payments on current account was in surplus, and the large decline in reserves which prompted the member's request was caused by a substantial outflow of capital. A large part of the outflow consisted of the withdrawal of foreign capital invested in South Africa, both portfolio and direct investment, and of contractual repayments on loans. It appeared doubtful whether the capital outflow would end during the ensuing year, especially in view of further contractual repayments falling due. As the Managing Director pointed out to the Board, such repayments would count as current transactions under the definition in Article XIX (i).

Commenting on the request, Mr. Lieftinck said that everyone would agree that the case would have been stronger if the strain on the balance of payments had been concentrated on the current account instead of the capital account. However, the drawing would be within the gold tranche, which the Fund had agreed belonged to the free reserves of the member countries. For that reason he supported the drawing, which was approved. It would appear that the consideration which Mr. Lieftinck advanced was regarded as decisive.

CLARIFICATION OF 1946 DECISION

On February 10, 1961, the Managing Director proposed to the Board for consideration five issues concerned with the future activities of the Fund. The fifth of these was set out by Mr. Jacobsson as follows:

> In recent years there have been a number of movements of international reserves between monetary centers, for which capital as well as current transactions have been responsible. Some of these movements are a normal feature of international business under conditions of widespread convertibility and freedom of transfers, which are most certainly welcomed by the Fund. The manner in which the Fund's resources can be made available to countries whose reserves are temporarily reduced by certain of these movements involves a number of questions. Some of these questions have arisen from time to time during discussions in the Board and it has been pointed out that the concept of "current" transactions under the Articles is a good deal wider than it is in common statistical usage. These questions merit examination in the light of the needs of the member countries under present-day circumstances.

In two informal sessions, on February 24 and 27, the Board discussed the Managing Director's statement. It was generally agreed that the Fund should consider the problem of capital transfers, and several Directors expressed the view that the use of the Fund's resources in the conditions described by the Managing Director would be proper and useful. However, the three Executive Directors who had been on the Board when the 1946 interpretation was given— Messrs. de Largentaye, Rasminsky, and Saad—drew attention to the legal difficulties which would arise if it was proposed to change that interpretation. The Legal Department was therefore asked to prepare a memorandum on the subject.

The results of the Legal Department's researches were distributed to the Board on May 24, 1961. The Department's memorandum threw doubt on the adequacy of the 1946 interpretation, since this ignored the provisions in Article VI, Section 1 (b) (i), permitting the use of the Fund's resources for certain capital transfers. The interpretation also failed to allow for the fact that Article V, Section 3 (a), did not specifically limit the use of the Fund's resources to the financing of current account deficits, but permitted them for payments "which are consistent with the provisions of this Agreement." These provisions included Article VI, Section 1, which barred only drawings to meet a "large or sustained outflow of capital." Thirdly, the interpretation overlooked that Article VIII, Section 4, implied that it was permissible to use the Fund's resources for capital transfers, since it provided that a member might be required to convert foreign-held balances of its currency subject to certain conditions, one of which was that the holder of the balances was entitled to use the Fund's resources (and therefore presumptively to draw from the Fund to finance the conversion of its balances).

Taking into account all the provisions in the Articles, the staff concluded that there were three purposes for which the Fund's resources might be used: (1) to meet current account deficits; (2) to meet deficits on capital account that were neither large nor sustained; and (3) to meet deficits stemming from the special types of capital transaction mentioned in Article VI, Section 1 (b) (i).

A second memorandum, submitted to the Board by the Exchange Restrictions Department and the Research Department, pointed out the desirability, from the Fund's point of view, of its resources being available to meet deficits caused by international capital movements. The two Departments proposed that such drawings should be approved on the same terms as had been established for other drawings; and that whether the capital outflow was "large" should be judged in relation to the Fund's resources, possibly augmented by borrowing, rather than in relation to the member's balance of payments.

The Board devoted five meetings to a consideration of these memoranda. Four different solutions to the problem created by the 1946 interpretation were suggested: (1) widening the definition of current transactions; (2) amending the Articles of Agreement; (3) revising or repealing the interpretation by a new decision; and (4) adding a sentence to the interpretation to clarify the Board's understanding of what it meant. The first three of these were rejected. Little reference was made to the first possibility, but the Board appears to have felt that any distinction between current and capital transactions would be difficult to apply. The second was discarded because, in the words of Mr. Pitblado (United Kingdom), "there appeared to be no desire on the part of anyone to change the Articles of Agreement." The third possibility—revising or repealing the earlier interpretation—was regarded as impracticable, if only because there was no agreement whether the powers of the Board would permit it to amend an interpretation. This left the solution that was ultimately adopted—the clarification of the interpretation.

A proposal to this effect was tabled by Mr. Saad at the first of the five meetings, and a streamlined version of it was eventually accepted. The Board's decision was:

> After full consideration of all relevant aspects concerning the use of the Fund's resources, the Executive Directors decide by way of clarification that Decision No. 71-2 [the 1946 interpretation] does not preclude the use of the Fund's resources for capital transfers in accordance with the provisions of the Articles, including Article VI.[54]

---

[54] E.B. Decision No. 1238-(61/43), July 28, 1961; below, Vol. III, p. 245.

COMPENSATORY FINANCING OF EXPORT FLUCTUATIONS

The term "compensatory official financing" was originally used by the Fund to mean transactions undertaken by monetary authorities for the purpose of meeting temporary balance of payments disequilibria regardless of their origin.[55] In this sense it covers, for example, reserve movements, drawings from the Fund, and official borrowing from official or private sources. Compensatory financing of this kind has been the domain of the Fund since its inception. The present section, however, refers to the narrower concept of compensatory financing provided by the Fund and intended specifically to offset the effects of fluctuations in export earnings of primary producing countries.

EARLY PLANS

Efforts to deal with instability of exports of primary products have a long history; the traditional means to cope with the problem have been commodity agreements designed to maintain prices and/or export receipts within agreed ranges. The fact that such agreements could be applied to a limited number of commodities only, that negotiations have generally proved difficult and often abortive, and that even where established such agreements have not always been successful, has prompted the search for a different approach. Reducing the effects of export fluctuations by compensatory financing could take the place of, or could supplement, commodity agreements. Discussions along these lines have been held, and various proposals have been made, within the framework of the United Nations and that of the Organization of American States, in both instances with the active participation of the Fund itself. What emerged in the end was what has become known as "the special compensatory facility" established in 1963 by the Fund—less ambitious than some of the schemes proposed, but readily available to member countries experiencing export shortfalls which endanger their balance of payments.

Establishment of the "facility" came just one decade after the first suggestion for compensatory financing had been made by a group of experts convened by the United Nations in 1953. This group, in its report,[56] proposed compensatory financing in the form of countercyclical lending, intended to avoid disturbances arising from fluctuations in industrial countries' import demand. The authors suggested that such lending might be channeled through the Fund; though conceptually not distinct from current operations by the Fund, it "would involve

---

[55] For a discussion of this concept, see above, Vol. I, pp. 345–47.

[56] *Commodity Trade and Economic Development*; Submitted by a Committee appointed by the Secretary General, United Nations, Department of Economic Affairs (New York, 1953), pp. 67 ff.

a radical change in scale of action" and would necessitate extension of the Fund's resources.

The Board of the Fund responded to this suggestion by confirming that it was one of the Fund's "important functions to make available to its members temporary assistance in meeting a decline in their international receipts arising out of a fall in the value of their exports in time of depression." [57] This was consistent with the Articles of Agreement; rules and procedures governing transactions were intended to allow countercyclical lending. While there were various other important uses for the Fund's resources, these resources could be a significant factor in connection with a (world) depression; moreover, it might be expected that in the case of a severe depression the Fund would consult with its members on the desirability of additions to its resources.

THE FUND'S FIRST REPORT

Postwar recessions have so far been mild, and the need for countercyclical lending on a wide scale has not arisen. But fluctuations in export proceeds resulting from various other causes have continued to plague primary producing countries. The general decline in the prices of primary products, which started in the second half of the 1950's, aggravated their problems. The question of providing compensatory financing in order to alleviate the effects of export shortfalls was taken up again, in March 1959, by the UN Commission on International Commodity Trade (CICT). It was decided, as a first step, to explore the role of the Fund in this connection, and the Fund was invited to inform the Commission about its policies and procedures as they bore on the subject.[58] In response to this request the staff prepared a report, "Fund Policies and Procedures in Relation to Compensatory Financing of Commodity Fluctuations." [59] Though this report has been superseded by later documents announcing the Fund's decision to establish a special compensatory facility, it contributed much by way of clarifying issues and explaining the Fund's attitude; it also laid the foundation for methods of measuring export shortfalls. It is, therefore, worthwhile to recall here some of its findings and conclusions.

In the first part of the report attempts were made to determine the magnitude of fluctuations in export receipts of primary producing countries in the interwar and postwar (1948–58) period; for that purpose deviations were measured relative to a five-year moving average centered on the current year. However, the report recognized that for practical purposes of compensatory financing this norm cannot be derived from export data known at the time action has to be taken. In consequence, subsequent studies have attempted to develop statistical approaches for estimating the norm on the basis of exports in past years.

---

[57] ECOSOC: Official Records, 17th Session, 765th meeting, April 7, 1954, p. 55.
[58] ECOSOC: Official Records, 28th Session, Supplement No. 6 (E/3225), p. 15.
[59] Reproduced in *Staff Papers*, Vol. VIII (1960–61), pp. 1–76.

Part II of the report discussed the concept of compensatory financing in the broad sense, as understood by the Fund, and its implications for the policies of countries making use of it; the principles guiding the use of the Fund's resources; and the attitude of the Fund to automatic access to these resources in the event of export shortfalls. The report explained that compensatory financing, as understood by the Fund, was not confined to international transfers in the form of loans or grants, but encompassed, in addition, the use of a country's own reserves. The need for compensatory financing did not stop at export shortfalls; it applied to the balance of payments as a whole. If countries wished to mitigate the effect of short-term fluctuations in their exports, they could do so by drawing on their reserves, supplemented by short-term borrowing; the Fund was among the principal sources for such temporary assistance. But reserves have to be replenished and loans have to be repaid. Hence countries needed to aim at maintaining approximate equilibrium in their international accounts over a reasonable period of time. The report then described the criteria for the use of the Fund's resources which had been developed in the course of the years: the larger the drawing in relation to the member's quota, the higher the degree of justification for it that was expected. This policy constituted one reason for rejecting automatic access to the Fund's resources in the event of export shortfalls: the causes of such a shortfall, as well as the country's balance of payments situation as a whole, had to be taken into account.

However, in its concluding remarks the report stressed that member countries that were taking appropriate steps to preserve internal financial stability and to maintain their balance of payments in equilibrium, taking good years with bad, and that were otherwise making satisfactory progress toward the fulfillment of the Fund's purposes, could anticipate with confidence that financing would be available from the Fund which, in conjunction with a reasonable use of their own reserves, should be sufficient to enable them to overcome temporary payments difficulties arising from export fluctuations.

The report was presented to the May 1960 session of CICT. Discussions at this session centered around the question whether assistance by the Fund could adequately solve the problem arising from export fluctuations. Doubts were expressed in various respects: the Fund was limited to short-term operations; a country might be ineligible on account of earlier drawings or because it was not fulfilling Fund requirements concerning internal stability; the resources the Fund could devote to compensation of export fluctuations might not be adequate.

UN and OAS proposals

A group of experts appointed for the purpose of "assisting CICT in its consideration of commodity problems . . . with special reference to compensatory financing" [60] suggested that enhancement of the compensatory role of the Fund was desirable; member countries had not fully tested the Fund's willingness to provide resources in order to meet difficulties arising from commodity fluctuations and should be encouraged to do so. But, unless the basic structure of the Fund was altered, a large increase in automatic drawing rights was not practicable. One of the experts added a note which suggested that primary producing countries should be entitled to look to the Fund for automatic compensation of export shortfalls, determined by a formula estimating the trend on the basis of a moving average of the preceding three years. In that event the Fund should make available resources up to "say, an amount which causes the Fund's holdings of the country's currency to equal 125 per cent of its quota." [61] When, subsequently, export proceeds were above trend, the excess earnings should be used automatically to repay the drawings. Nevertheless, the group as a whole shared the doubts expressed by CICT members and proposed the setting up of a special scheme called a Development Insurance Fund (DIF) which would provide automatic compensation to countries experiencing export shortfalls. Compensation would take the form of loans, repayable if (and within the limits to which) exports within the next three years exceeded the trend; any balance outstanding after three years would be written off. An alternative variant of the scheme would give compensation in the form of outright grants. [62]

The Conference of the Organization of American States (OAS), held in Punta del Este in August 1961, also concerned itself with compensatory financing and the Fund's possible contribution to the problem. In pursuance of a resolution taken by this Conference, an expert group developed yet another scheme for automatic compensation of export shortfalls, in the form of loans to be repaid not later than five years from the date of extension.

Both the DIF and the OAS schemes were discussed by CICT [63] and were referred for further study to a technical working group with which the Fund would be closely associated. At the same time, the Fund was requested to prepare a report on any possible expansion of its own role with respect to compensatory financing. Hope was expressed that the Fund might be persuaded to play a more active part in the compensation of export shortfalls.

The Board had closely followed the emergence of the schemes developed and the staff undertook extensive studies on their technical aspects. [64] Statistical

---

[60] General Assembly Resolution 1423 (December 1959).

[61] *International Compensation for Fluctuations in Commodity Trade*, United Nations (New York, 1961), p. 81.

[62] *Ibid.*, pp. 39 ff.

[63] Tenth Session of CICT, held in Rome in May 1962.

[64] The main results of these studies have been reported in Marcus Fleming, Rudolf Rhomberg, and Lorette Boissonneault, "Export Norms and Their Role in Compensatory Financing," *Staff Papers*, Vol. X (1963), pp. 97–149.

methods of estimating the medium-term trend value of exports in any given year, with a view to measuring shortfalls from this trend, were explored in great detail and a number of variants of repayment conditions were analyzed, with regard to their bearing on both benefits derived and cost involved. Experience gained in the course of these studies proved valuable not only for appraising the proposed schemes but also for revising the Fund's own policy.

ESTABLISHMENT OF FUND FACILITY

While the Fund staff was actively participating in the work of the technical working group, the Board proceeded to consider ways in which it could extend special assistance to members experiencing balance of payments difficulties arising from temporary export shortfalls. The result was the development of what has become known as the Fund's "compensatory financing facility." The Fund report announcing its establishment, with immediate effect, was issued late in February 1963 and presented to CICT at its meeting in May 1963.[65]

In essence the new facility, set out in Part V of the report, provided that a compensatory drawing would be made available where (a) a shortfall in export receipts was of short-term character and largely caused by circumstances beyond the member's control, and (b) the member was willing to cooperate with the Fund in an effort to find appropriate solutions for its balance of payments difficulties, where such solutions were needed.

In order to identify shortfalls of a short-term character, the Fund, in conjunction with the member concerned, would seek to establish reasonable estimates of the medium-term trend of the country's exports; such estimates would be based partly on statistical data and partly on qualitative information regarding export prospects.

Provided conditions (a) and (b) above were satisfied, a country was assured that its request for a compensatory drawing would be met in amounts not normally exceeding 25 per cent of its quota. Such drawings would be subject to the Fund's established policies and practices on repurchase, i.e., exchange purchased from the Fund should not remain outstanding beyond a period reasonably related to the payments problem for which it was purchased, which period should normally fall within an outside range of three to five years.

In order to enable members to have the full benefit of the facility, the Board declared its willingness to waive the provision in the Articles limiting the Fund's holdings of a member's currency to 200 per cent of quota.

The report also announced that in those instances where adjustments of quotas would be appropriate to make them more adequate in the light of fluctua-

---

[65] *Compensatory Financing of Export Fluctuations*, February 1963 (E.B. Decision No. 1477-(63/8)); below, Vol. III, pp. 238, 442–57.

tions in members' export proceeds, the Fund would be willing to give sympathetic consideration to requests for such adjustments.

REFLECTIONS ON THE DECISION

Over the previous decade the Fund had been dealing increasingly with the specific problems of primary producing countries. The establishment of the compensatory facility marked a further step in that direction. It has been said that the Fund's decision represented a development in thought but not a departure from its major principles.[66] The report repeated the Fund's rejection of automatic recourse to its resources. It explained that the exercise of judgment based on an analysis of causal factors was required when appraising the nature of a shortfall and deciding whether it was temporary. Moreover, the country's balance of payments position as a whole had to be examined. Automatic access to the Fund's resources in case of an export shortfall would ignore such requirements. Hence the indication of an export shortfall by a mathematical formula could not, per se, entitle a member to make a drawing.

The report also reiterated that the Fund's resources should supplement the use of domestic reserves and should not be regarded as the sole source of finance to meet short-term needs. However, the Board recognized that declining trends in the prices of primary products over a number of years had adversely affected the export earnings of many of the Fund's members and thus increased the strain on their reserves. The special facility was designed to assure effective support to members faced with fluctuations in exports.

The main respects in which the new facility involved a change in established procedures were the following: (1) A member with an export shortfall due mainly to factors beyond its control might draw on the Fund, if it was willing to cooperate with the Fund in an effort to find solutions, where required, to its balance of payments difficulties. It would not be necessary for such a country, even if it had already drawn the equivalent of a substantial part of its quota, to have an approved program worked out and agreed with the Fund before the drawing took place, as would be required under the Fund's normal policies for drawings in higher tranches. (2) The Board's willingness to waive the 200 per cent limit on drawings would permit a member to obtain compensatory financing of an export shortfall even if the Fund's holdings of its currency had already reached that limit.

EXPERIENCE WITH THE FACILITY

Up to the end of 1965 experience with the new facility was limited. Export developments for primary producers were favorable. Prices rose through 1963

---

[66] Statement of the Fund observer in presenting the report to CICT.

and well into 1964; in spite of a subsequent downturn, part of the previous gain was still maintained in 1965. As a result, only three countries—Brazil, the United Arab Republic, and the Sudan—applied for and made compensatory drawings. Export shortfalls were calculated *ex post* for the latest twelve-month period for which, at the time of the request, relevant data were available. The trend value against which shortfalls were measured has been defined as the five-year moving average of exports, centered on the shortfall year. This trend value was estimated, in part, by forecasting exports in the two years following the shortfall year and, in part, on the basis of a formula developed by the Fund, using a weighted average of exports in the shortfall year (with a weight of 50 per cent) and in the preceding two years (each with a weight of 25 per cent). For two of the three members the shortfall so derived was less than 25 per cent of the country's quota and was met in full; for the third, where the shortfall exceeded the limit, compensation was confined to 25 per cent of the country's quota.

Sixteen countries applied for quota increases so as to make their quotas more adequate, as suggested in the Fund's report. In all cases the increase was granted.

REACTIONS TO THE FACILITY

The new facility attracted many comments and some suggestions. It was hailed by CICT as a significant contribution toward the problems arising for primary producing countries through short-term fluctuations in their export proceeds. Similarly the OAS Committee on Basic Products welcomed the facility, although it suggested that it should be widened and further liberalized. The facility was again discussed in the wider framework of compensatory financing at the UN Conference on Trade and Development (UNCTAD) in 1964; earlier proposals were reiterated and a resolution was passed suggesting to member governments of the Fund that consideration should be given to revising the decision along the following lines: (1) increasing the amount allocated to compensatory financing from 25 per cent to at least 50 per cent of quota; (2) placing compensatory credits entirely outside the structure of the gold and credit tranches, ensuring that such credit would in no way prejudice a member's ability to make an ordinary drawing; (3) exploring ways of possible refinancing of drawings in the event of a persistent export shortfall beyond the control of the country affected; (4) giving greater weight to the country's actual experience in the preceding three years when determining the export shortfall.

Suggestions along similar lines, particularly with respect to raising the amount allocated for compensatory financing and to placing drawings under that title entirely outside the tranche structure, were put forward at the Annual Meeting in 1965. It also was suggested, in the course of this Meeting, that compensatory assistance should be tied to a deterioration in the terms of trade rather than to an export shortfall.

REVIEW AND SUGGESTIONS BY THE STAFF

In the course of 1965 the staff reviewed the experience gained so far, as well as problems deemed likely to arise in the future. Policies and procedures embodied in the decision of 1963 were re-examined and various possible alterations were considered, taking into account the suggestions made at the Annual Meeting and at the UNCTAD Conference. As a result, a memorandum entitled "The Fund's Compensatory Financing Facility Reconsidered" was prepared and sent to the Board on December 10, 1965. The main changes suggested concerned (1) the relationship of compensatory to other drawings and (2) the limit of compensation in relation to quota.

(1) The separation of compensatory from other drawings, in a quantitative sense, had already been provided for under the decision; as pointed out earlier, the Fund had declared its willingness to waive the 200 per cent limit on holdings of a member's quota in order to accommodate compensatory drawings above that limit. However, such drawings, which were likely to be made after a country had used its gold tranche, and probably its first credit tranche, would be taken into account when subsequent requests for drawings were received. Accordingly, these further requests would be subject to the increasingly stringent criteria applicable to drawings in the higher tranches. To follow the suggestion made by UNCTAD, and again at the Annual Meeting, that compensatory drawings should be treated as entirely outside the tranche structure, would eliminate this effect, so that compensatory drawings would become additional in both a quantitative and a qualitative sense. Even though such a concession would obviously weaken somewhat the Fund's ability to secure satisfactory corrective programs in connection with ordinary drawings, the staff expressed itself in favor of accepting this proposal.

(2) The second suggestion made by UNCTAD and at the Annual Meeting was to extend the limit on compensatory drawings from (normally) 25 per cent of a member's quota to a straight 50 per cent of the quota. Commenting on this proposal, the staff pointed to the qualifying word "normally" in the decision, which would permit the Board at its discretion to exceed the limit of 25 per cent of quota. This was not, however, sufficient to assure a country that it could depend on compensatory drawings beyond that limit. That a larger drawing might sometimes be desirable was shown by the experience of the three drawings made before the end of 1965. In connection with one of these, as mentioned above, the shortfall as determined by the Fund actually exceeded the limit of 25 per cent of the member's quota; in one of the other two 86 per cent of that limit was absorbed, and in the other 71 per cent.

Moreover, larger drawings might bring "export availabilities," defined as export proceeds plus compensatory drawings or minus repurchases, closer to the desired goal, the true trend value; statistical tests covering 48 countries and 15 years (1951–64) showed that schemes allowing drawings up to 50 per cent of quota would be superior in this respect. On the other hand, to extend the maximum from 25 per cent of quota to 50 per cent would further weaken the "conditionality" of drawings, which would already be somewhat reduced by placing compensatory drawings outside the ordinary tranche structure.

The staff nevertheless suggested that the limit should be extended to 50 per cent of quota, subject to the following two qualifications: (a) the net expansion of compensatory drawings outstanding should not, in any twelve-month period, exceed 25 per cent of quota, and (b) a compensatory drawing which would raise the increase in the Fund's holdings of a member's currency, caused by compensatory drawings, beyond 25 per cent of quota, would be granted only if the member had been following policies "reasonably conducive to the development of its exports."

The foregoing recommendations by the staff were both adopted, and were incorporated, with some minor modifications in wording, in *Compensatory Financing of Export Fluctuations: A Second Report by the International Monetary Fund*, published in September 1966.[67]

A third suggestion put forward by UNCTAD was that the Fund should give consideration to ways of refinancing members' obligations in the event of a persistent shortfall in export receipts beyond the country's control. In this connection the staff pointed out that refinancing was entirely possible under existing procedures: repurchase at any time would restore the compensatory facility, and if an export shortfall of the type mentioned persisted, the member would be able to apply immediately for a new drawing.

In the broader context of repayments provisions, the staff raised the more fundamental issue whether repayment should be requested in any year in which exports exceeded the estimated trend value. Under such a system repurchases might be made exclusively in years (and to the extent) of such excesses; alternatively, under a "mixed" system any outstanding balance would have to be repaid before the end of the fifth year. In testing these two variants—a fully and a partially "compensatory" repayment system—it was assumed that for the purpose of repurchases the trend value would be determined by the mathematical formula only; that the full amount of an excess (unless it exceeded the outstanding drawing) would be used for repurchase and, in the second variant, that amounts outstanding after three years (if any) would be repaid in the fourth and/or fifth year. The statistical tests indicated that the results of either variant would be superior to those under existing repurchase provisions—superiority

---

[67] Reproduced below, Vol. III, pp. 469–96.

being again measured by success in bringing export availabilities closer to the trend value.

This concept of "compensatory" repurchases, and the statistical evidence in its favor, were brought to the attention of the Board, but no specific recommendation was made by the staff. The Board decided not to include any mandatory provision along these lines, but to suggest that exports in excess of the trend value should in fact be used for the repurchase of compensatory drawings. A recommendation to that effect was included in the second report.

A fourth recommendation made by UNCTAD, that in the formula for calculating the trend greater weight should be given to the three years preceding the shortfall, was also examined by the staff. Statistical tests, however, indicated that the formula devised by the staff was superior, and no change was suggested.

The related issue, of substituting fully automatic determination of the trend value for a combination of statistical and qualitative estimation, was not re-examined. However, the staff gave some thought to the problem of the relative weight to be given to the statistical evidence and to the element of judgment when determining the trend. It was found by experience that short-term forecasts by the Fund and by other expert bodies had yielded results that were closer to the truth than even the best statistical formula. On the other hand, statistical calculations, if taken by themselves, would enable member countries to foresee more accurately what compensatory financing they would be able to rely upon. Thus the weight to be given to the automatic element would itself be a matter of judgment, and might well differ in individual cases.

Commenting on the suggestion that compensation should be provided for a deterioration in the terms of trade rather than in export proceeds, the staff pointed out that such compensation would not cover changes in the volume of exports, such as those arising, not infrequently, from crop failures. Such a change might, therefore, do more harm than good. It was true that there was much to be said for taking account of variations in import prices in the determination of export shortfalls, thus aiming at compensating for a decline not in their money value but in their real value. This was not, however, practicable; for a number of countries import price indices are lacking, for others they are not reliable, and for yet others they become available only after great delay.

For the reasons given in the preceding paragraphs the staff suggested no changes in the procedure for determining the magnitude of shortfalls, or in the nature of the shortfalls to be compensated.

One further point taken up by the staff concerned the problem of double compensation for shortfalls. This might arise in the event of a country making two consecutive compensatory drawings or, more probably, making an ordinary drawing, perhaps under a stand-by arrangement, followed within less than twelve months by a drawing under the compensatory financing decision. It was conceivable, under these conditions, that the payments situation leading to the first drawing was caused, in part, by a shortfall in exports for which a compensatory drawing was subsequently claimed. The staff pointed out that there was no way of determining to what extent such a shortfall had been responsible for the payments difficulties experienced; or, consequently, what proportion of the shortfall should be regarded as met by the original drawing. For practical purposes, however, standard procedures have been laid down which provide guidelines for determining what part of such a shortfall should be deemed to have been covered by the original drawing, and not eligible for additional compensation.

It may be added, in conclusion, that the years 1963 to 1965 were the formative years of the compensatory financing facility. It was not until after the end of 1965 that this type of financial assistance from the Fund became a routine source of drawings, widely used by member countries.

CHAPTER

19

Charges, Repurchases, Selection of Currencies

J. Keith Horsefield

THE MAIN LINES OF THE FUND'S POLICIES on the use of its resources were discussed in Chapter 18; those for stand-by arrangements are dealt with in Chapters 20 and 21. Incidental references have necessarily been made already to charges on drawings and to the repurchase obligations. These subjects are more fully discussed in the present chapter, which also describes the Fund's policy for the selection of currencies to be used in purchases and repurchases. A statistical section is appended.

CHARGES

When a member uses the resources of the Fund, it becomes subject to certain charges which are uniform for all members. These charges provide the Fund with an income. At the same time, they are designed to act as a deterrent against excessive or prolonged use of the Fund's resources.

NATURE OF CHARGES

Article V, Section 8, the relevant provisions of which are reproduced below, provides for two kinds of charges on drawings, viz.: (1) A service charge which is levied on the amount drawn without reference to the time that a drawing remains outstanding; this may be varied within narrow limits and was in fact reduced from ¾ of 1 per cent to ½ of 1 per cent in 1951. (2) Periodic charges on the Fund's holdings of a member's currency in excess of the member's quota, varying with the relation of the holdings to quota and with the length of time that the drawings have been outstanding; these may also be varied, and were in fact altered in 1951, 1953, and 1963. There are supplementary provisions for the calculation of charges in Rules and Regulations I-4 and I-5.

428

The pertinent provisions of Article V, Section 8, are as follows:

(*a*) Any member buying the currency of another member from the Fund in exchange for its own currency shall pay a service charge uniform for all members of three-fourths percent in addition to the parity price. The Fund in its discretion may increase this service charge to not more than one percent or reduce it to not less than one-half percent.

(*c*) The Fund shall levy charges uniform for all members which shall be payable by any member on the average daily balances of its currency held by the Fund in excess of its quota. These charges shall be at the following rates:

(i) *On amounts not more than twenty-five percent in excess of the quota:* no charge for the first three months; one-half percent per annum for the next nine months; and thereafter an increase in the charge of one-half percent for each subsequent year.

(ii) *On amounts more than twenty-five percent and not more than fifty percent in excess of the quota:* an additional one-half percent for the first year; and an additional one-half percent for each subsequent year.

(iii) *On each additional bracket of twenty-five percent in excess of the quota:* an additional one-half percent for the first year; and an additional one-half percent for each subsequent year.

(*d*) Whenever the Fund's holdings of a member's currency are such that the charge applicable to any bracket for any period has reached the rate of four percent per annum, the Fund and the member shall consider means by which the Fund's holdings of the currency can be reduced. Thereafter, the charges shall rise in accordance with the provisions of (*c*) above until they reach five percent and failing agreement, the Fund may then impose such charges as it deems appropriate.

(*e*) The rates referred to in (*c*) and (*d*) above may be changed by a three-fourths majority of the total voting power.

(*f*) All charges shall be paid in gold. If, however, the member's monetary reserves are less than one-half of its quota, it shall pay in gold only that proportion of the charges due which such reserves bear to one-half of its quota, and shall pay the balance in its own currency.

In computing charges on drawings, the Fund treats reductions in its holdings of a member's currency as canceling the portions of these holdings that have most recently accrued—i.e., those resulting from the member's most recent drawing. The Fund thus applies the LIFO (last in, first out) principle to the calculation of charges. If it did not do this, a member that obtained a succession of drawings from the Fund could in effect acquire very cheaply a continuously revolving sum. The effect of this procedure is that charges on the portions of a member's currency that the Fund has held longest continue to rise in accordance with the scale of charges, even though for the purpose of allocating reductions in the Fund's holdings (to which, as mentioned in the next section of this chapter, the FIFO principle applies) those holdings are considered to have been repurchased. Not until the Fund's holdings of a currency have been reduced to the level of the member's quota for at least one calendar month is the progression of charges broken. Once that has been done, any subsequent drawing attracts charges at the lowest end of the scale once more.

Stand-by arrangements are not expressly provided for in the Articles, but when these are approved the Fund makes a commitment charge similar to a service charge, acting under its general powers (Article XII, Section 2 (g)). This charge (¼ per cent per annum) has to be paid in gold or U.S. dollars, except that where Article V, Section 8 (f), would permit a member to pay in its own currency part of the charges for a drawing, the commitment charge may similarly be paid partly in a member's own currency. No commitment charge is made for such part of a stand-by arrangement as would permit the member to make drawings within the gold tranche.

CHANGES IN CHARGES

The charges originally imposed by the Fund were those laid down in Article V, Section 8, but on three occasions the Board has exercised its powers to alter the rates contained in this schedule. Table 16 summarizes the changes made. As a consequence of the system of progressively rising charges, there is a spread between the rate currently being paid on the Fund's holdings resulting from any drawing and the average rate which has been paid on those holdings during the time that they have been outstanding. The lower half of the table shows the latter average (which includes the service charge) corresponding to each rate in the upper half. For example, if since May 1, 1963 the Fund's holdings of a member's currency have for three years been between 100 per cent and 150 per cent of the member's quota, the charge payable will have risen to 3.5 per cent per annum on the amount drawn. The table shows that the average rate which the member will have paid during the three years was 2.5 per cent. On any part of the Fund's holdings of the member's currency which exceeds 150 per cent but is not over 200 per cent of the member's quota, the corresponding figures will be 4.0 per cent and 2.83 per cent.

The first occasion on which a change was introduced in the schedule of charges was in November 1951, as the first step toward a policy of encouraging the short-term use of the Fund's resources. The changes made were as follows: (a) The service charge was reduced from ¾ per cent to ½ per cent. (b) The charge on the Fund's holdings of a member's currency lying between 100 per cent and 125 per cent of quota and maintained for between three and six months was deleted. (c) The intervals at which the charges rose by ½ of 1 per cent per annum were reduced from a year to six months, so that the charges on all other holdings maintained for periods longer than six months were increased by progressively larger amounts. (d) The point at which it becomes obligatory for the Fund and the member to discuss means of reducing the member's outstanding drawings was lowered from that at which the charge reached 4 per cent to that at which it reached 3½ per cent. (e) The point at which charges ceased to be expressly prescribed and were left to the discretion of the Fund was put at 4 per cent, not 5 per cent. There was, however, a limit of 4½ per cent to the rate which might be charged during the ensuing six months, and a limit of 5 per cent to the rate for the six months after that.

As will be seen from the lower half of Table 16, the effect of these changes was as follows: For a drawing which increased the Fund's holdings of the member's currency to not more than 125 per cent of quota, the average rate of charge was reduced if these holdings were maintained for not more than a year. For drawings in higher tranches, the average rate of charge was reduced if the Fund's holdings were maintained for not more than six months. If the Fund's holdings of the member's currency remained above the member's quota for eighteen months or longer, the average rate of charge was increased. This effect was designed: it was related to the Managing Director's wish to encourage small and ultra short-term drawings, and to discourage long-term drawings. Moreover, the shortening of the period before the member was required to consult the Fund about ways of reducing the Fund's holdings of its currency was deliberately intended to ensure that repurchases were made sooner than was implicit in the schedule adopted at Bretton Woods.

In accordance with the requirements of Article V, Section 8 (e), the minute recording the foregoing decision noted that a vote was taken. The decision was supported unanimously by the Directors present at the meeting, who cast 78,455 votes out of a possible maximum for the whole Board of 91,115 votes. Similar votes were taken on the occasion of all the later changes noted below.

The decision taken in November 1951 determined the new schedule only for the period ending December 31, 1952. In November 1952 its currency was extended to June 30, 1953; in June 1953 it was further extended to the end of October 1953; and in October it was again extended to December 31, 1953.

The reason for these piecemeal prolongations was that some Executive Directors, and notably Mr. Southard (United States), were dissatisfied with the schedule but were unable to reach agreement with their colleagues on a new set of charges. Some Directors believed that the charges were too high. The U.S. view was that the rate of charge arranged in 1951 on drawings which raised the Fund's holdings of the member's currency to 125 per cent of quota was too low, but that some reduction would be practicable in charges on drawings in higher tranches. Eventually, after negotiations lasting several months, Mr. Southard proposed to the Board a new scale which represented a compromise between the views of his Government and those of other members. The principal feature of his proposal was the abandonment of a separate rate of charge for holdings in the 100–125 per cent bracket, and the application to such holdings of the charge

Table 16. Charges on the Fund's Holdings of a Member's Currency in Excess of the Member's Quota Resulting from Transactions Effected

Holdings Equivalent to the Following Percentages of Quota

	Prior to December 1, 1951				From December 1, 1951 through December 31, 1953				From January 1, 1954 to April 30, 1963			From May 1, 1963 to December 31, 1965		
More than	100	125	150	175	100	125	150	175	100	150	175	100	150	200
But not more than	125	150	175	200	125	150	175	200	150	175	200	150	200	

Charges in Per Cent Per Annum [1]

	Prior (100–125)	(125–150)	(150–175)	(175–200)	Dec 1951 (100–125)	(125–150)	(150–175)	(175–200)	Jan 1954 (100–150)	(150–175)	(175–200)	May 1963 (100–150)	(150–200)	(>200)
Service charge	0.75	0.75	0.75	0.75	0.5	0.5	0.5	0.5	0.5	0.5	0.5	0.5	0.5	0.5
Duration:														
0–3 months	0.0	0.5	0.5	1.0	0.0	0.5	1.0	1.5	0.0	0.0	0.0	0.0	0.0	0.0
3–6 "	0.5	0.5	1.0	1.0	0.5	1.0	1.5	2.0	2.0	2.0	2.0	2.0	2.0	2.0
6–12 "	0.5	1.0	1.0	1.5	1.0	1.5	2.0	2.5	2.0	2.0	2.0	2.0	2.0	2.5
1–1½ years	1.0	1.0	1.5	1.5	1.5	2.0	2.5	3.0	2.0	2.5	3.0	2.0	2.5	3.0
1½–2 "	1.0	1.5	1.5	2.0	2.0	2.5	3.0	3.5[2]	2.5	3.0	3.5	2.5	3.0	3.5
2–2½ "	1.5	1.5	2.0	2.0	2.5	3.0	3.5[2]	4.0	3.0	3.5	4.0[2]	3.0	3.5	4.0[2]
2½–3 "	1.5	2.0	2.0	2.5	3.0	3.5[2]	4.0	4.5[3]	3.5	4.0[2]	4.5	3.5	4.0[2]	4.5
3–3½ "	2.0	2.0	2.5	2.5	3.5[2]	4.0	4.5[3]	5.0[3]	4.0[2]	4.5	5.0[3]	4.0[2]	4.5	5.0
3½–4 "	2.0	2.5	2.5	3.0	4.0	4.5[3]	5.0[3]		4.5	5.0[3]		4.5	5.0	
4–4½ "	2.5	2.5	3.0	3.5	4.5[3]	5.0[3]			5.0[3]			5.0		
4½–5 "	2.5	3.0	3.5	4.0[2]	5.0[3]									
5–6 "	3.0	3.5	4.0[2]	4.5										
6–7 "	3.5	4.0[2]	4.5	5.0										
7–8 "	4.0[2]	4.5	5.0											
8–9 "	4.5	5.0												
9–10 "	5.0													

Average Effective Rates in Per Cent Per Annum [4]

Duration:												
3 months	3.00	4.00	4.50	5.00	2.00	3.00	3.50	4.00	2.00	2.00	2.00	2.00
6 "	1.75	2.50	3.00	3.50	1.00	2.00	2.50	3.00	2.00	2.00	2.00	2.00
1 year	1.12	1.75	2.25	2.75	1.00	1.75	2.25	2.75	2.00	2.00	2.00	2.25
1½ years	1.08	1.67	2.17	2.67	1.17	1.83	2.33	2.83	2.00	2.00	2.17	2.50
2 "	1.06	1.62	2.12	2.62	1.38	2.00	2.50	3.00	2.12	2.12	2.38	2.75
2½ "	1.15	1.70	2.20	2.70	1.60	2.20	2.70	3.20	2.30	2.30	2.60	3.00
3 "	1.21	1.75	2.25	2.75	1.83	2.42	2.92	3.42	2.50	2.50	2.83	3.25
3½ "	1.32	1.86	2.36	2.86	2.07	2.64	3.14	3.64	2.71	2.71	3.07	3.50
4 "	1.41	1.94	2.44	2.94	2.31	2.88	3.38		2.94	2.94	3.31	
4½ "	1.53	2.06	2.56	3.06	2.56	3.11			3.17	3.17		
5 "	1.62	2.15	2.65	3.15	2.80							
6 "	1.85	2.38	2.87	3.38								
7 "	2.09	2.61	3.11	3.61								
8 "	2.33	2.84	3.34									
9 "	2.57	3.08										
10 "	2.81											

[1] Except for the service charge, which is payable once per transaction and is expressed as a percentage of the amount of the transaction.

[2] Point at which consultation between the Fund and the member becomes obligatory.

[3] Maximum charges.

[4] Total charges payable by the member over the stated period, expressed as a percentage and divided by the number of years of the period. Includes service charge.

on holdings in the 125–150 per cent bracket. Another change was the abandonment of any charge except the service charge on holdings maintained for not more than three months; this overcame the difficulty that under the earlier scales the annual rate of charge (including the service charge) was greater on holdings maintained for not more than three months than on holdings maintained for substantially longer periods. At the same time, the point of time at which a member was required to consult the Fund about ways to reduce the Fund's holdings of its currency was left unaltered. Because charges had risen, this point again became that at which the rate of charge reached 4 per cent. The new scale was approved on December 23, 1953, to be applied to drawings on or after January 1, 1954.

The discussion of Mr. Southard's proposal raised a question which was subsequently to feature in most discussions of charges: Should the rates take account of the rates of interest ruling in the world's principal money markets? Executive Directors' views on the point have continued to differ, and the lack of unanimity has contributed to the subsequent stability of charges. While the schedule of rates has been reviewed annually since 1954, the only change introduced has been necessitated by the emergence of a new factor. This was the decision that a drawing under the compensatory financing plan might be permitted to increase the Fund's holdings of a member's currency beyond 200 per cent of quota,[1] whereas the scale previously in force made no provision for such drawings.

The staff recommended in April 1963 that for the future the charges applicable to holdings in the 175–200 per cent bracket should be applied to drawings which raised the Fund's holdings above 200 per cent of quota. Drawings which raised the Fund's holdings to between 175 per cent and 200 per cent of quota should in future attract the rate charged in the next lower bracket (150–175 per cent of quota). One argument for the proposal not to charge more on holdings above 200 per cent of quota than had previously been charged on holdings in the 175–200 per cent bracket was that under the previous scale the point at which the Fund and the member had to discuss ways to reduce the Fund's holdings of the member's currency was reached after only two years; there seemed to be no point in setting rates of charge which would shorten even more the time before such discussions became obligatory. The Board approved the proposal, with effect from May 1, 1963.

It will be observed that the maximum rate of charge shown in Table 16 is 5 per cent per annum. This would be reached, for drawings effected after January 1, 1954, one year after the point at which the Fund and the member were required to enter into discussions. Neither Article V, Section 8, nor the relevant Rule prescribed what rate of charge was to be levied on drawings held still longer. This deficiency was remedied in two stages.

---

[1] See above, pp. 421–22.

In April 1959 the Board decided that if the member agreed with the Fund on a schedule which would complete repurchases within five years of the date of a drawing, the maximum rate of charge should be 5 per cent. If agreement on a schedule was reached, but repurchases under this schedule would not extinguish the drawing within the five years, the Fund might adopt higher maximum rates. If no agreement was reached with the member at all, the Fund might impose such charges as it deemed appropriate, after the 5 per cent rate had been reached.

Four years later the question of such charges became an imminent one, as Cuba had failed to agree on a schedule of repurchases which would extinguish a drawing which it had had five years earlier. The staff then proposed that so long as a member in Cuba's position failed to reach an agreement, the charge should continue to rise by ½ of 1 per cent each six months; but it also suggested that the Board might wish to consider imposing a maximum rate of charge. The staff also proposed a procedure to deal with the case, hitherto unprovided for, of a member that agreed to a schedule which would complete repurchase within five years, but failed to keep the agreement. The staff suggested that for such a member the rate of charge should rise to 5½ per cent six months after it had reached 5 per cent, and thereafter increase by ½ of 1 per cent each six months; except that if the member broke the agreement at a time when it had already been paying 5 per cent for more than six months, the rate should rise to 5½ per cent immediately. These recommendations were approved when they came before the Board, and at the instance of Mr. Saad (United Arab Republic) provision was made for reviewing the rate of charge when this had reached 6 per cent.

Also in 1959 a change was made in the rules governing the commitment charge on stand-by arrangements, as a result of which it was made payable in advance but became available to be offset against the service charge on any drawing made while the stand-by arrangement was in force.[2] (Previously the commitment charge had been payable in half-yearly installments, and that for the second half of a year had not been available to be offset against a drawing in the first half of the year.) At the same time, appropriate arrangements were made to cover such complications as arose if a member (a) made a drawing under a stand-by arrangement, as a result of which it was credited with a pro-portionate part of the commitment charge, (b) subsequently repurchased all or part of the drawing, and (c) wished to reconstitute a commensurate part of the drawing rights conferred by the stand-by arrangement. It was also decided that when a member canceled a stand-by arrangement it should be entitled to a refund of the commitment charge proportionate to the unexpired period of the arrangement in respect of the part of the drawing rights under the arrangement (if any) which could still be drawn when the arrangement was canceled, and in respect of which the member had paid a charge.

---

[2] E.B. Decision No. 876-(59/15), April 27, 1959; below, Vol. III, p. 232.

The reason for the final clause of the last-mentioned decision was that commitment charges are not levied in respect of such part of a stand-by arrangement as covers the member's gold tranche. In the same decision, the Board agreed that where the Fund's holdings of the currency of a member that had a stand-by arrangement were reduced, so that the excess of these holdings over the member's quota was less than the undrawn amount of the stand-by arrangement, the commitment fee would be pro rata refunded. Three years later, this was modified to exclude changes in the Fund's holdings of a member's currency in a special account for administrative expenditures, provided that these did not exceed 1/100 of 1 per cent of the member's quota.[3] This avoided trifling refunds which became due if the Fund or a member made a small payment (e.g., for a book) at a time when the member had a stand-by arrangement straddling its quota.

REPURCHASES [4]

PROVISIONS IN ARTICLES OF AGREEMENT

The provisions in the Articles of Agreement that relate to repurchases may be divided into six categories, as follows:

(1) Provision for the automatic repurchase of the Fund's holdings of the member's currency in excess of 75 per cent of its quota (Article V, Section 7 (b) (i)).

(2) Provision for the automatic repurchase of additional segments of the Fund's holdings in excess of 75 per cent of the member's quota, in particular circumstances (Article V, Section 7 (b) (ii)).

(3) Limitations on the foregoing (Article V, Section 7 (c)).

(4) Detailed provisions for identifying the particular currencies, or gold, to be used for obligatory repurchases (Schedule B).

(5) Provisions for voluntary repurchases of the Fund's holdings in excess of the member's quota (Article V, Section 7 (a)).

(6) Provision for the emergency suspension of all the foregoing (Article XVI, Section 1).

The full text of Article V, Section 7, is as follows:

> *Repurchase by a member of its currency held by the Fund.*—(a) A member may repurchase from the Fund and the Fund shall sell for gold any part of the Fund's holdings of its currency in excess of its quota.
>
> (b) At the end of each financial year of the Fund, a member shall repurchase from the Fund with gold or convertible currencies, as determined in accordance

---

[3] E.B. Decision No. 1345-(62/32), May 23, 1962; below, Vol. III, p. 233.

[4] Only the highlights of the Fund's policy on repurchases are described in this section. For a full description of the relevant technicalities the reader is referred to Fund Circular No. 9.

with Schedule B, part of the Fund's holdings of its currency under the following conditions:

(i) Each member shall use in repurchases of its own currency from the Fund an amount of its monetary reserves equal in value to one-half of any increase that has occurred during the year in the Fund's holdings of its currency plus one-half of any increase, or minus one-half of any decrease, that has occurred during the year in the member's monetary reserves. This rule shall not apply when a member's monetary reserves have decreased during the year by more than the Fund's holdings of its currency have increased.

(ii) If after the repurchase described in (i) above (if required) has been made, a member's holdings of another member's currency (or of gold acquired from that member) are found to have increased by reason of transactions in terms of that currency with other members or persons in their territories, the member whose holdings of such currency (or gold) have thus increased shall use the increase to repurchase its own currency from the Fund.

(c) None of the adjustments described in (b) above shall be carried to a point at which

(i) the member's monetary reserves are below its quota, or

(ii) the Fund's holdings of its currency are below seventy-five percent of its quota, or

(iii) the Fund's holdings of any currency required to be used are above seventy-five percent of the quota of the member concerned.

The provisions of Article V, Section 7 (b) (ii), which were intended to deal with the case of a member building up reserves in a reserve currency by operations in that currency in a third country, have proved impracticable and have never been applied by the Fund.

The principal provisions of Schedule B are as follows:

1 (a). If the member's monetary reserves have not increased during the year, the amount payable to the Fund shall be distributed among all types of reserves in proportion to the member's holdings thereof at the end of the year.

1 (b). If the member's monetary reserves have increased during the year, a part of the amount payable to the Fund equal to one-half of the increase shall be distributed among those types of reserves which have increased in proportion to the amount by which each of them has increased. The remainder of the sum payable to the Fund shall be distributed among all types of reserves in proportion to the member's remaining holdings thereof.

1 (c). If after all the repurchases required under Article V, Section 7 (b), had been made, the result would exceed any of the limits specified in Article V, Section 7 (c), the Fund shall require such repurchases to be made by the members proportionately in such manner that the limits will not be exceeded.

3. . . . No account shall be taken . . . of any increase in [a member's] monetary reserves which is due to currency previously inconvertible having become convertible during the year; or to holdings which are the proceeds of a long-term or medium-term loan contracted during the year; or to holdings which have been transferred or set aside for repayment of a loan during the subsequent year.

The principal elements in the definition of monetary reserves, which is of course basic to the calculations needed to assess repurchase obligations, are as follows:

> A member's monetary reserves means its net official holdings of gold, of convertible currencies of other members, and of the currencies of such non-members as the Fund may specify. (Article XIX (a)) [*Note:* The Fund has never "specified" any non-member currency.]

> A member's monetary reserves shall be calculated by deducting from its central holdings the currency liabilities to the Treasuries, central banks, stabilization funds, or similar fiscal agencies of other members . . . together with similar liabilities to other official institutions and other banks in the territories of members. . . . (Article XIX (e))

INTERPRETATIVE DECISIONS

In the early days of the Fund's work the calculation of members' monetary reserves gave rise to a large number of problems, and various decisions were taken which generalized the answers given.[5] For our purposes the following are the most important of these decisions.[6]

Timing of repurchase obligations

Three questions concerning the application of time limits to the calculation of monetary reserves, and hence of repurchase obligations, have been decided by the Board. The first one dealt with the question when the initial calculation of monetary reserves was to be made. The Board decided that

> for the purpose of the repurchase obligations prescribed by Article V, Section 7, increases and decreases in the monetary reserves of a member shall not be considered if they occur on or before the latest date on which the member's subscription must be paid . . . ; and the payment of subscriptions, whether actually made before or after such latest date for payment, shall not be regarded as resulting in a decrease in monetary reserves.[7]

The second decision settled at what point of time the decrease in monetary reserves resulting from a repurchase would be deemed to take effect for the purpose of the next calculation under this provision:

> Whenever a member uses its monetary reserves to repurchase its currency from the Fund in accordance with the provisions of Article V, Section 7 (b) (i) or (ii), the resulting reduction in its monetary reserves and in the Fund's holdings of its currency must be regarded as having occurred, for the purpose of calculating subsequent repurchase obligations under the same provisions of the Fund Agreement, at the end of the financial year of the Fund in respect of which the obligation to make the repurchase arose.[8]

---

[5] See, e.g., in Vol. III below, pp. 220, 243–44, 269–73.

[6] See also E.B. Decision No. 493-3, November 4, 1949; below, Vol. III, p. 272.

[7] E.B. Decision No. 124-2, January 22, 1947; below, Vol. III, p. 244.

[8] E.B. Decision No. 447-5, June 17, 1949; below, Vol. III, p. 244.

The third decision determined the point of time at which the limits set out in Article V, Section 7 (c), were to be regarded as applying:

> In the application of the repurchase obligations of the Fund Agreement the limits specified in Article V, Section 7 (c), apply solely as of the end of the financial year for which the repurchase obligations are calculated.[9]

Abatement of repurchase obligations

The Board considered in 1950 what should be done when a repurchase obligation calculated in accordance with Article V, Section 7, and Schedule B included an amount of a currency which the Fund could not accept because of the terms of Article V, Section 7 (c) (iii), and decided as follows:

> If part of a member's gross repurchase obligation for any financial year is allocated to a currency which the Fund cannot accept because of Article V, Section 7 (c) (iii), that part of the gross obligation is abated for that year under Schedule B, Paragraph 1 (c), and is not required to be discharged in gold or some other currency.[10]

Voluntary repurchases

On several occasions the question has arisen whether the Fund might accept a voluntary repurchase. Provision was made in Article V, Section 7 (a), for a member wishing to repurchase from the Fund the Fund's holdings of its currency in excess of its quota. However, a difficulty arose (as explained below) in connection with other repurchases that were neither (1) required by Article V, Section 7 (b), nor (2) arranged following consultations prescribed by Article V, Section 8 (d), nor (3) made in pursuance of an undertaking given at the time of a drawing (e.g., under a stand-by arrangement or in consideration of the Board's waiving the limits set out in Article V, Section 3 (a)).

The decision eventually reached was as follows:

> (1) Subject to paragraph 3 below, a member may offer in voluntary repurchase, and the Fund has the power to accept, if it so decides, gold or convertible currencies to the extent that (a) the Fund's holdings of the convertible currency of a member which is offered would not be increased above 75% of the quota of that member, and (b) the Fund's holdings of the repurchasing member's currency would not be decreased below 75% of its quota.

> (2) As a matter of legal interpretation it is determined that the consent of the member whose currency is offered in voluntary repurchase is not necessary as a condition precedent to the acceptance by the Fund of such currency.

> (3) Where a member has an accrued and undischarged repurchase obligation under Art. V, Sec. 7 (b), and Schedule B in respect of any financial year of the

---

[9] E.B. Decision No. 419-1, April 11, 1949; below, Vol. III, p. 244.
[10] E.B. Decision No. 521-3, January 16, 1950; below, Vol. III, p. 273.

Fund, the member must discharge the obligation in accordance with those provisions; provided, however, that the payment of currency under those provisions may be combined with the sale of gold to the Fund for the currency under Art. V, Sec. 6 (a).[11]

COLLECTION OF MONETARY RESERVES DATA

The information needed to calculate repurchase obligations under Article V, Section 7, consists of figures for the member's monetary reserves, as defined in the Articles and in the Board's decisions, together with the Fund's holdings of the members' currencies. The latter data are, of course, in the Fund's possession, but for the former it is dependent upon reports from the members. The original Rules and Regulations provided (Rule I-6) that each member should furnish to the Fund the necessary data about its monetary reserves "at the end of each financial year." At first, however, it proved difficult to secure the data, and in July 1950 the Board altered the Rule to require the provision of the information within six months of the end of each financial year. Despite this, the staff had to report in November 1950 that, out of the 49 members of the Fund at that time, 20 had failed to provide information about their monetary reserves as at April 30, 1950, and 14 of these had also failed to provide figures for earlier years.

Thereafter matters improved, and as time went on the staff was able to make the necessary calculations with reasonable promptitude. The provisions of Article V, Section 7 (b) (i), Section 7 (c) (i), and Section 7 (c) (ii), affect only the monetary reserves of the member concerned. As soon, therefore, as data of these reserves is available, the member's repurchase obligation, so far as it is affected by these provisions, can be calculated. Article V, Section 7 (c) (iii), introduces into the calculation a limit related to the Fund's holdings of another member's currency. If there is any doubt whether repurchase obligations in the aggregate exceed the amount of that currency which can be accepted within the limit, none of the calculations can be finalized until this point has been cleared up. Before 1961 this did not much matter, as only a few countries had accepted the obligations of Article VIII, Sections 2, 3, and 4 (thereby making their currencies acceptable in repurchases). Of these few, the only one in whose currency substantial repurchases became due was the United States, and the Fund's holdings of U.S. dollars were well below 75 per cent of the U.S. quota.

In 1961 the calculations became complicated by the acceptability of a number of other currencies, but there was little doubt that the relatively small repurchase obligations accruing in them could be accepted by the Fund. By the end of 1962, however, the position had radically changed. The Fund's holdings of U.S. dollars had risen to 74 per cent of the U.S. quota, and it would not be possible, under the limitation imposed by Article V, Section 7 (c) (iii), to accept

[11] E.B. Decision No. 7-(648), March 8, 1951; below, Vol. III, p. 244.

more than US$34 million in repurchases thereafter. As repurchase obligations arising at April 30, 1963 were bound to include much more than this sum, there would have to be a scaling down of the obligations of all members who were due to repurchase their currencies with U.S. dollars. By how much each obligation would have to be scaled down, however, could not be known until all obligations had been calculated. If the Fund was to wait for six months for members to supply monetary reserves data, then make the requisite calculations, and only then notify all repurchasing members how much they were due to pay, no member would be able to make any repurchase, in respect of the year ended April 30, 1963, until late in that year. This could well have been awkward, as by that time a member's monetary reserves might (as experience in the past had shown) have been depleted to a point at which a repurchase would be embarrassing.

The Board accordingly decided to require members to expedite the provision of monetary reserves data, taking for that purpose the following decision:

> 1. Where on any April 30 the Fund holds a member's currency in an amount exceeding 75 per cent of the member's quota, the member shall make a provisional monetary reserves report to the Fund not later than May 31, preferably by cable.

> 2. The Fund will make a provisional calculation of the amount and distribution of the repurchase obligations of such members and will inform them of the results of the calculation not later than June 15. Members shall discharge within thirty days any repurchase obligations as thus provisionally calculated and agreed with the member.

> 3. All provisional repurchases shall be subject to adjustment by members and the Fund in accordance with Rule I-6 of the Fund's Rules and Regulations.[12]

While each member of whose currency the Fund holds more than 75 per cent of its quota is thus required to supply information annually about its monetary reserves, the Board decided in 1957 that it was not necessary actually to collect repurchases if the amount involved was small. It accordingly decided:

> In cases where a repurchase obligation of less than the equivalent of $500 is calculated the member will be notified, and the obligation collected, on the next occasion thereafter that a repurchase obligation accrues which, together with the first one, will total the equivalent of $500 or more.[13]

LIMITATION OF REPURCHASE OBLIGATIONS

Throughout the Fund's life, repurchase obligations under Article V, Section 7, have been prevented from arising because of Section 7 (c) (ii) and have been substantially reduced by Section 7 (c) (i) and (iii). The effects of these limitations are described in the immediately following paragraphs.

---

[12] E.B. Decision No. 1813-(65/4), January 18, 1965; below, Vol. III, p. 245.

[13] E.B. Decision No. 705-(57/55), November 7, 1957; below, Vol. III, p. 245.

The member most affected by Article V, Section 7 (c) (i), has been the United Kingdom. For instance, between April 1961 and May 1965 the United Kingdom drew over $4 billion from the Fund and repurchased $1.28 billion, but it incurred no repurchase obligation under Article V, Section 7 (b), because of the operation of Article V, Section 7 (c) (i): its monetary reserves were at all times less than its quota. In addition, the limitations contained in the last sentence of Article V, Section 7 (b) (i), and in Article V, Section 7 (c) (ii), applied at April 30, 1963 and April 30, 1964.

As regards Article V, Section 7 (c), it is convenient to consider two periods, the first comprising the twelve financial years 1948/49 through 1959/60, and the second, the six financial years 1960/61 through 1965/66. For the first twelve years it is sufficient to say that actual repurchases, which began in 1949/50, totaled $2,179 million,[14] while repurchase obligations arising at April 30 in each year from 1948 to 1959 (which will normally have become payable in the ensuing fiscal year) totaled less than 60 per cent of this figure, viz., $1,235 million.[15]

For the six years 1960/61 through 1965/66, during which the Fund's operations were on a much larger scale, actual repurchases totaled $4,029 million.[16] But repurchase obligations accruing under Article V, Section 7 (b), totaled only 12 per cent of this sum, viz., $491 million. A total of $1,621 million did not emerge as an obligation or was abated as a result of the impact of Article V, Section 7 (c). This total was made up as follows:

Under Section 7 (c) (i) $198 million, affecting 11 countries
Under Section 7 (c) (ii) $1,106 million, affecting 20 countries
Under Section 7 (c) (iii) $317 million, affecting 26 countries

Of the 67 repurchase obligations, amounting to $2,112 million, which arose during the six years, 16 were affected by Section 7 (c) (i), 35 by Section 7 (c) (ii), and 55 by Section 7 (c) (iii).

The abatements under Section 7 (c) (i), representing the elimination of repurchases which otherwise would have reduced the member's monetary reserves below its quota, largely affected Argentina, Chile, and Spain ($76 million).

Section 7 (c) (ii), which precludes repurchases which would reduce the Fund's holdings of the repurchasing member's currency below 75 per cent of its quota, affected principally France ($253 million). But quite substantial sums were also involved for a number of the other 19 countries concerned. The chief reason was that the members' reserves increased so much that 50 per cent of the increase was greatly in excess of the amount needed to reduce the Fund's holdings of their currencies to 75 per cent of their quotas.

---

[14] *Annual Report, 1966*, Table 55, p. 131.
[15] *Annual Report, 1965*, Table 55, p. 114.
[16] *Annual Report, 1966*, Table 55, p. 131.

Section 7 (c) (iii) precludes the acceptance by the Fund in repurchases of any currency of which its holdings had reached 75 per cent of the issuing member's quota. The effect of this provision was greatly increased during the six years 1960/61 to 1965/66 by two circumstances. The first was the acceptance of the obligations of Article VIII, Sections 2, 3, and 4, by the United Kingdom and 17 other countries. The effect of this was to make their currencies available, in principle, for repurchases. However, as the Fund's holdings were at 75 per cent or more of the British quota except between February and August 1961 and between August 1962 and April 1963, there was little scope for using sterling in repurchases, and most of the other countries' obligations in that currency were abated, to a total equivalent to $45 million. The other factor was that the Fund's holdings of U.S. dollars reached 75 per cent of the U.S. quota during 1963 and subsequently remained above that figure, so that the other countries' obligations in U.S. dollars were also abated, to a total of $268 million.

ALTERNATIVE REPURCHASE PROCEDURES

In addition to the obligatory repurchases called for by Article V, Section 7 (b), and to the voluntary repurchases permitted by Article V, Section 7 (a), four other methods of repurchase have evolved: (1) repurchases called for by the Board's decision of February 1952 (the Rooth Plan), which limits the retention of drawings to "the period reasonably related to the payments problem for which [the currency] was purchased from the Fund" and requires this period to "fall within an outside range of three to five years"; (2) repurchases of drawings under stand-by arrangements, for which the time limit is three years; (3) repurchases in accordance with a schedule agreed with the member, usually after it has been unable to repurchase within three years; and (4) voluntary repurchases.

The effect of repurchases is, of course, also achieved if other members draw from the Fund the currency of a member that has a repurchase obligation. This process has gained in importance in recent years as a result of the widening of the range of currencies drawn from the Fund—see the next section of this chapter.

REPURCHASES IN FLUCTUATING CURRENCIES

In September 1950 Canada abandoned the par value of the Canadian dollar, which thereafter was allowed to fluctuate. The Articles of Agreement make no provision for a fluctuating currency, so that when in 1952 Canada accepted the obligations of Article VIII, Sections 2, 3, and 4, thereby making its currency eligible for use in repurchases, it became necessary to stipulate at what exchange rate the Canadian dollar should be accepted in repurchases.

This was settled by the Board in the course of a comprehensive decision on "Transactions and Computations Involving Fluctuating Currencies" taken on June 15, 1954. The decision provided for the exchange rate for fluctuating

currencies offered in repurchases to be the midpoint between the highest rate and
the lowest rate for the U.S. dollar quoted, for cable transfers for spot delivery, in
the main financial center of the country of the fluctuating currency, on the last
business day before the Fund instructed its depository to receive the fluctuating
currency.[17]

VOLUNTARY REPURCHASES

It will be recalled that the provision in the Articles of Agreement for voluntary
repurchases (Article V, Section 7 (a)) relates only to repurchases of the Fund's
holdings in excess of quota, and provides for such repurchases in gold. It was for
long disputed whether the Fund was entitled to accept voluntary repurchases in
other circumstances. Mr. de Largentaye (France), who was the principal
opponent of such voluntary repurchases, based his argument on Article V, Section 2, which reads:

> *Limitation on the Fund's operations.*—Except as otherwise provided in this
> Agreement, operations on the account of the Fund shall be limited to transactions
> for the purpose of supplying a member, on the initiative of such member, with the
> currency of another member in exchange for gold or for the currency of the
> member desiring to make the purchase.

He also objected that voluntary repurchases other than in gold, such as were in
the main offered, might deprive the Fund of gold which otherwise would have
had to be provided by the member in making repurchases under the terms of
Article V, Section 7 (b), and Schedule B.

The Board, however, believed that it was in principle desirable to encourage
voluntary repurchases, and that the correct view of the limitations set out in
Article V, Section 2, did not debar such repurchases. This view, as expounded
by the General Counsel in February 1950, was that the "operations" referred to
in Section 2 could be simple or complex. They could, for instance, consist of a
combination of a purchase of dollars from the Fund and a repurchase of the
member's currency with dollars. For if "operations" did not mean this, the Fund
would be precluded from accepting any repurchase (other than under the
provisions of Article V, Section 7 (b)) which would reduce the Fund's holdings of
the member's currency below 100 per cent of quota; and this was clearly inconsistent with the emphasis in the Articles of Agreement on the desirability of the
Fund's holdings of members' currencies being equal to 75 per cent of their quotas.

There remained the possibility that a member having an accrued obligation
under Article V, Section 7 (b), might forestall the payment to the Fund of gold
due under that obligation, by making a voluntary repurchase in some currency
which might be of less use to the Fund. To prevent this, the Board decided—as
set out in full earlier in this section—that any accrued and undischarged obliga-

[17] E.B. Decision No. 321-(54/32), June 15, 1954; below, Vol. III, p. 222.

tion under Article V, Section 7 (b), must be fulfilled in accordance with the stipulations of Schedule B, except that it could be paid in gold.

Ten years later the subject recurred. In November 1961 the United Kingdom made a voluntary repurchase of £100 million sterling with U.S. dollars. Mr. de Largentaye argued that the repurchase, being a voluntary one, should have been made in gold. He was answered in a memorandum from the Managing Director which pointed out that the Rooth Plan had imposed on the United Kingdom an obligation to repurchase its drawing within three to five years; that the Fund had made no stipulation at any time as to the medium in which it should be repurchased; and that therefore the United Kingdom was entitled to repurchase with any convertible currency. Article V, Section 7 (a), to which Mr. de Largentaye had referred, offered a privilege, and did not constitute a duty. When the matter came before the Board, Mr. de Largentaye's view was not shared by other Directors, and the Managing Director's answer was approved.

Of the total sum repurchased down to the end of 1965 (including transactions for the purpose of reducing initial currency subscriptions to 75 per cent of quota), about one eighth was voluntarily repurchased as described on page 439. A further 3½ per cent of the total sum was originally repurchased voluntarily, but was subsequently applied to extinguish liabilities arising under Article V, Section 7 (b).

ALLOCATION OF REPURCHASES

The fact that, as mentioned above, the reductions in the Fund's holdings of a member's currency can be effected in a number of different ways, not all of which are related to specific drawings, makes it necessary to allocate such reductions according to fixed principles. (The need for such principles was crystallized by the obligations assumed by the Fund, under the General Arrangements to Borrow (GAB), to repay participants as members repurchased drawings for which the GAB had been activated.) The following are the principles which the Fund has adopted:

Repurchases not accruing under Article V, Section 7 (b). When such a repurchase is made, the member may specify which drawing is being repurchased; if so, its decision is accepted. If it does not specify which drawing is being repurchased, it is invited to do so. If it does not do so, the repurchase is regarded as extinguishing in whole or in part the commitment which matures first.

Repurchases accruing under Article V, Section 7 (b). Where it is practicable to identify which drawing is being repurchased, this is done (e.g., where only one drawing is outstanding in that financial year, or where several drawings are outstanding, but only one was made in the year, and the repurchase obligation arises solely because of the increase in the Fund's holdings of the member's currency). Where it is not possible to identify the drawing, the repurchase is regarded as relating to the drawing which matures first.

Sale by Fund of member's currency. This is regarded as extinguishing, in whole or in part, the drawing by the member concerned that has the earliest maturity.

In effect, the arrangements ensure that the earliest drawings are normally repurchased first, in accordance with the FIFO (first in, first out) principle, in contrast to the LIFO (last in, first out) principle applied to the determination of charges. If the FIFO principle were not used in allocating reductions in holdings, a member making a series of drawings might find itself due to repurchase some of the earliest amounts all at once in order to ensure that none of them remained outstanding for longer than five years.

A related issue was discussed by the Board in 1959, when the staff brought to its notice the question of the extent to which a member could reconstitute a stand-by arrangement by repurchasing a drawing while the arrangement was in force. This feature had been introduced in the stand-by arrangement with Belgium in 1952 [18] and implicitly approved when the Board revised the conditions for stand-by arrangements in 1953.[19] Since then, members had been allowed to reconstitute stand-by arrangements that had been wholly or partially exhausted, by repurchasing not only drawings made under the stand-by arrangement but also drawings made before the arrangement began. The staff suggested that this was probably not the Board's intention, and proposed that in the revision of conditions then in preparation this should be made clear. The Board agreed, and its decision accordingly included the following passage:

> A stand-by arrangement shall provide for a fixed amount that can be purchased under it augmented by amounts equivalent to repurchases in respect of drawings made under the stand-by arrangement or made at the time when the stand-by arrangement is entered into, unless when any such repurchase is made the member informs the Fund that it does not wish the stand-by arrangement to be augmented by the amount of that repurchase.[20]

EFFECTIVENESS OF REPURCHASE ARRANGEMENTS

Since 1952 it has been the declared policy of the Fund that drawings shall be repurchased within three to five years. As with any other drawing, a member wishing to draw further before it has completed the repurchase of an existing drawing is required to justify the further drawing in accordance with the terms of the Board's decision of February 1952. It is not surprising that there has been some increase in the total of drawings outstanding during the later years of the

---

[18] See below, p. 469.

[19] E.B. Decision No. 270-(53/95), December 23, 1953; below, Vol. III, pp. 231–32.

[20] E.B. Decision No. 876-(59/15), April 27, 1959; below, Vol. III, pp. 232–33.

period covered by this volume, but it is of interest to inquire how far the repurchase requirements have succeeded in limiting the period for which members have had continuous use of the Fund's resources. The following analysis results from such an inquiry.

During the twenty years 1946–65 there were twenty-seven members of whose currencies the Fund held more than the equivalent of 75 per cent of their quotas for more than five consecutive years. Fourteen of these, however, were members whose original gold subscriptions were less than 25 per cent of their quotas, and who took more than five years to reduce the Fund's holdings of their currencies to 75 per cent of quota. These members, because of the relative smallness of their monetary reserves, did not incur repurchase obligations for at least a part of the time. For four other members the Fund's holdings, while in excess of 75 per cent of quota for more than five years, did not exceed 100 per cent of quota for that length of time. Since access to drawings in the gold tranche is quasi-automatic, the position of these members scarcely gives cause for concern.

There remain nine members of whose currencies the Fund had held, during the twenty years down to December 31, 1965, more than the equivalent of 100 per cent of their quotas for more than sixty consecutive months. These members are shown in Table 17. For seven of the nine members listed, the Fund's holdings were still in excess of 100 per cent of the member's quota at the end of the period, indicating that, as might have been expected, the members'

Table 17. Continuous Use of the Fund's Resources, 1946–65

Member	Number of Months During Which the Fund's Holdings of the Member's Currency Continuously Exceeded:	
	75 per cent of quota	100 per cent of quota
United Arab Republic [1]	111	106
Argentina	104	104
Turkey	161	101
Brazil [1]	200	98
Yugoslavia	195	95
Bolivia	151	93
Paraguay	160	69
Syrian Arab Republic	67	67
Honduras	68	64

[1] To disregard the special drawings under the arrangements for the compensatory financing of export fluctuations, granted to the United Arab Republic and Brazil, would make no difference to the table.

difficulties were cumulative. The total amount drawn by these seven members in excess of 100 per cent of their quotas was, at December 31, 1965, $388.1 million (equal to 1.9 per cent of the aggregate of Fund quotas).

SELECTION OF CURRENCIES

DRAWINGS IN INCONVERTIBLE CURRENCIES

Before 1952 the only currencies that were convertible in the Fund sense, and therefore acceptable by the Fund in repurchases, were the Cuban peso, Guatemalan quetzal, Honduran lempira, Mexican peso, Panamanian balboa, Salvadoran colón, and U.S. dollar. In 1952 the Canadian dollar was added to the list, and in 1953 the Dominican peso and the Haitian gourde. No further currencies became convertible until 1961. Of those listed, only the U.S. dollar, and to a much more limited extent the Canadian dollar, are used in international trade. In consequence, drawings down to the end of 1960 were concentrated largely on the U.S. dollar, since members did not wish to obtain a currency that was inconvertible, especially since it could not be used in repurchases. Indeed, of the currencies mentioned above, the only ones drawn at all were Canadian and U.S. dollars. This meant that the Fund's holdings of all the other convertible currencies were consistently at or above 75 per cent of their quotas. No repurchases could therefore be made in any currencies except the two dollar currencies.

Of total drawings down to December 31, 1960 amounting to $3,683 million, 87 per cent were drawn in U.S. dollars, 8 per cent in sterling, and 3 per cent in deutsche mark; the remaining 2 per cent were divided between Belgian francs, Canadian dollars, Danish kroner, French francs, and Netherlands guilders (Table 18). Total repurchases amounted to $2,748 million, of which $628 million was repurchased with gold, $2,120 million with U.S. dollars, and $0.1 million with Canadian dollars.

This heavy concentration of drawings and repurchases on one currency had not been intended by the drafters of the Articles of Agreement, who had expected that the majority of countries would accept the obligations of Article VIII, Sections 2, 3, and 4, at a fairly early stage in the Fund's life, thereby making their currencies acceptable in repurchases once they had been drawn. On two occasions before 1961, accordingly, attempts were made to devise means by which members could be encouraged to draw inconvertible currencies.

This subject was among those remitted to the staff Working Party which was set up in November 1951 to draft the proposals for the use of the Fund's resources which were adopted in February 1952.[21] A suggestion was made to the Working Party by Sir George Bolton (United Kingdom) that the disadvantages of drawing an inconvertible currency might be overcome if two members, A and B, mutually agreed that if A drew B's currency, B would (after a specified lapse of time) draw a corresponding amount of A's currency, which it would sell to A for its own (B's) currency. These arrangements would, of course, restore the Fund's

---

[21] See above, p. 402.

holdings of both A's and B's currencies to what they had been before the drawing took place; and provided that the Fund's holdings of neither currency was, at the end of the double transaction, above 75 per cent of quota, neither would finish with a repurchase obligation (although A might have incurred one when it originally drew). Sir George's proposal was commended to the Board by the staff, who added that it would be still more attractive to members if the arrangements, instead of being bilateral, were multilateral—though this would, of course, be much more difficult to arrange.

The staff's recommendation was discussed in the Board on two occasions in 1952, but was not in general favorably received. Some Executive Directors suggested that drawings in inconvertible currencies were to be deprecated

Table 18. Drawings and Repurchases by Currency, 1946–65
(In millions of U.S. dollars or equivalents)

Currency	Drawn 1946–60	Drawn 1961–65	Total Drawn 1946–65	Repurchased 1946–65
Argentine pesos	—	16.0	16.0	—
Australian pounds	—	35.0	35.0	—
Austrian schillings	—	73.0	73.0	11.6
Belgian francs	11.4	360.5	371.9	61.8
Canadian dollars	15.0	474.5	489.5	157.8
Danish kroner	0.8	30.0	30.8	—
Deutsche mark	116.2	1,792.8	1,909.0	709.8
French francs	17.5	1,195.0	1,212.5	267.4
Italian lire	—	753.4	753.4	94.1
Japanese yen	—	241.5	241.5	49.9
Mexican pesos	—	9.5	9.5	—
Netherlands guilders	22.5	469.0	491.5	133.0
Spanish pesetas	—	128.5	128.5	—
Swedish kronor	—	157.0	157.0	22.5
Pounds sterling	297.4	353.6	651.0	96.3
U.S. dollars	3,202.8	1,689.3	4,892.1	3,572.0
Totals in currencies	3,683.5	7,778.9	11,462.4	5,176.0
Repurchases in gold				858.1
Total repurchases				6,034.1

because a country whose currency was inconvertible was *ipso facto* not in a position to extend credit to others. These Directors also thought it unlikely that bilateral balances could be reversed as quickly as would be necessary to enable the drawing to be extinguished within three to five years. Some other Directors, however, welcomed the proposal, believing that some countries with inconvertible currencies could, in fact, afford to assist other members. This point was taken up especially by Mr. de Selliers (Belgium), whose country was then extending credit through the EPU to much of Europe. However, when Mr. de Selliers commended the plan from the point of view of the country with the inconvertible currency, remarking that the drawing of its currency would enable that country to come to the Fund to draw dollars, Mr. Southard objected. He said that a member acquired the right to draw a convertible currency from the Fund by virtue of having contributed gold or convertible assets to its holdings. He also argued that it was implicit in the concept of gold tranche drawings [22] that they should be reversed by repurchases with convertible currencies.

The next occasion for a discussion of the possibility of making more use of inconvertible currencies in drawings arose in 1958. At the Annual Meeting in New Delhi that year the Governors had passed a resolution requesting the Executive Directors to examine the question of enlarging the resources of the Fund.[23] A related issue, which the Board also examined, was whether fuller use could not be made of the resources which the Fund already possessed. To assist in the examination of this question, the staff made two suggestions. One was that the Fund should apply Article XIX (g), which reads as follows:

> The Fund, after consultation with a member which is availing itself of the transitional arrangements under Article XIV, Section 2, may deem holdings of the currency of that member which carry specified rights of conversion into another currency or into gold to be holdings of convertible currency for the purpose of the calculation of monetary reserves.

If the Fund, using this provision, "deemed" members' holdings of specific currencies to be convertible, these holdings could be accepted in repurchases (subject to the limits set out in Article V, Section 7 (c)).

The other suggestion by the staff was an elaboration of that made in 1952 by Sir George Bolton; it set out a series of steps by which the Fund's holdings could be restored, after a drawing and repurchase in inconvertible currency, to exactly the same position as before the drawing.

Simultaneously, however, a further staff memorandum pointed out that in practice the use which could be made of inconvertible currencies in repurchases, even if the legal difficulties could be overcome in this way, was effectually limited by the provisions of Article V, Section 7 (c) (iii). The only inconvertible currency which could be accepted by the Fund without infringing the limits in that Section was the deutsche mark (to the extent of $66 million). The Research Department, which had written this last memorandum, suggested that the practical solution was to encourage a few members with large quotas to be ready to convert other members' holdings of their currencies into dollars to the extent that these other members needed to make repurchases from the Fund.

While the foregoing proposals were before the Board, the major European countries announced, on December 27, 1958, that they had taken steps to

---

[22] See above, pp. 402–406.

[23] Resolution 13-10, *Summary Proceedings, 1958*, p. 178. See above, p. 358.

establish the nonresident convertibility of their currencies. This in effect achieved what the Research Department had in mind, and it became unnecessary for the Board to consider further how to encourage the use of inconvertible currencies. The problem thus minimized vanished altogether when in February 1961 the main European countries accepted the obligations of Article VIII, Sections 2, 3, and 4.

EFFECTS OF CONVERTIBILITY

An analysis of drawings from the Fund during the calendar years 1961 through 1965 shows an entirely different picture from that prevailing in the years 1946–60, as described above. During the years 1961–65 only 22 per cent of drawings were taken in U.S. dollars. As will be seen from Table 18, the currency most used was the deutsche mark (23 per cent of all drawings), and there were also extensive drawings in French francs (15 per cent) and Italian lire (10 per cent). Repurchases were also widely spread.

PRINCIPLES OF SELECTION

The distribution of drawings shown in Table 18 did not come about spontaneously. Because a large proportion of international trade is carried on in the reserve currencies, the currency which a member would normally need in the terms of Article V, Section 3 (*a*) (i), is likely to be either U.S. dollars or sterling. As soon, therefore, as the assumption of convertibility by the major European countries opened up the possibility of using other currencies for repurchases, the Managing Director represented to the Board the need to guide drawings and repurchases toward a range of currencies.

The first step was for the Legal Department to remove any doubts about the meaning of "needed for making in that currency" in Article V, Section 3 (*a*) (i). Its advice was that the phrase, interpreted against the background of Bretton Woods, must be taken to mean that a member was entitled to draw any currency which it could use, directly or indirectly, to support its exchange market. It could therefore draw a currency which was not a reserve currency in order to obtain for it, from the country issuing it, a reserve currency with which to settle its international accounts. This view was tacitly accepted by the Board.

A parallel memorandum prepared by the Research Department proposed a series of principles which should govern the Fund's use of the currencies at its disposal. This concluded that the overriding concept should be that reserves should, through the Fund, flow from countries with strong balances of payments to countries with weak ones. Ideally, therefore, each member's reserve position in the Fund (its quota less the Fund's holdings of its currency) should move in parallel with the movements in its primary reserves. In order to influence the constitution of drawings and repurchases in this direction, the Fund should

(1) ensure that future drawings were preceded by consultation as to the currencies to be drawn; (2) arrange for facilities to be available to convert currencies that were drawn into the currency directly needed by the drawing country; (3) apply the policy not necessarily to individual drawings, but in such a way as to secure the desired result from drawings in general; (4) include more currencies, rather than fewer, in any arrangements set up. At this stage the emphasis was primarily on policy with respect to drawings, and during the ensuing twelve months the members that drew from the Fund were asked to draw individual currencies in such a way as to move toward the goal outlined by the staff.

The Board returned to the subject in April 1962, and attention was then focused also on repurchases, partly as a result of Mr. de Largentaye's protest against a voluntary repurchase by the United Kingdom in U.S. dollars.[24] The staff then suggested that a reasonable starting point for future policy would be to prescribe that currencies to be used in drawings should be selected in proportion to the primary reserves of the countries whose currencies were being used, and that currencies for repurchases should be accepted proportionately to each member's position in the Fund.

Some attention was devoted in the discussion of these proposals to the "reversal" technique, which had been suggested as a solution to the problem of directing drawings toward appropriate currencies. This technique consisted in allowing a member whose currency was drawn, if it considered that this had been done to excess, to draw in turn on the Fund, so as to offset the use of its currency. The staff deprecated this plan because of its limited usefulness. For one thing, the member that sought to draw in order to offset a drawing would itself have to make representations to the Fund within the terms of Article V, Section 3 (a), except to the limited extent that it might be able to have recourse to Article VI, Section 2.[25] Also, any drawing would involve the member concerned in paying a service charge.

In the event, the Board agreed in July 1962 on a lengthy statement which included an explanation of the technique that had been adopted and an elaboration of the criteria used in the selection of currencies.[26] The technique of selection, as it has since been used, may be summarized as follows:

(1) A quarterly budget of currencies to be used in purchases and to be received in repurchases is formulated as described in (5) to (10) below. The basis for this budget is a rough estimate of the requests for drawings that might be made in the coming quarter, and a forecast of the repurchase obligations which are due to be fulfilled during the quarter.

(2) The budget thus evolved is discussed by the Managing Director with the Executive Directors appointed or elected by the countries whose currencies are

---

[24] See above, p. 445.
[25] See above, p. 411.
[26] E.B. Decision No. 1371-(62/36), July 20, 1962; below, Vol. III, p. 235.

included in it. Subject to any modifications made as a result of these discussions, the figures are used to guide members, when drawing or repurchasing, toward the use of the listed currencies in such a manner as to approach the budget targets, taking the transactions for the period as a whole.

(3) Any drawings or repurchases that are too large to be accommodated in the budget are the subject of separate consultations with respect to the currencies to be used. For very large drawings other considerations arise—for example, it may be decided to replenish the Fund's holdings of certain currencies by the sale of gold,[27] or to activate the General Arrangements to Borrow.[28] Even for these transactions, however, the principles in (5) to (10) below guide the decisions taken.

(4) For drawings that are large, but not too large to be met within the budget, a distribution of currencies is worked out individually along the same lines. Very small drawings are arranged in the reserve currency of the member drawing; this is not only operationally convenient, but makes it unnecessary for a small country to handle an unfamiliar currency. For intermediate drawings the procedure is regarded as applying to the transactions of the quarter as a whole rather than to any individual drawing; the currencies used in any one such drawing, therefore, have no great significance.

The principles which guide the selection of currencies, and the decision as to the amounts of each to be used, are as follows:

(5) A relatively short, but growing, list is maintained of countries whose balances of payments and reserves would normally permit them to see a gradual increase in their reserve positions in the Fund, and with which suitable arrangements have been worked out for conversion of amounts of their currencies when drawn. For the most part, these countries have accepted Article VIII and have reserves which exceed $500 million and (except for those of the United Kingdom) are large in relation to their quotas.

(6) On the occasion of any particular budget or large drawing, a few countries may be eliminated from this list on short-term balance of payments grounds, as indicated by the exchange rates and by changes in their reserves. Current and long-term capital accounts are watched as a check. Such countries are eliminated, however, only if they appear likely to have to draw on the Fund.

(7) As between the different currencies thus available, drawings are allocated in proportion to the size of the members' reserves (excluding their reserve positions in the Fund).

(8) Some restraint may be imposed should the Fund's holdings of a particular currency fall very low, but this is disregarded if it is possible to borrow that currency under the GAB.

---

[27] See below, p. 455.
[28] See above, p. 376.

(9) The currencies thus selected will also be available for use in repurchases, if and when the Fund's holdings of them fall below 75 per cent of the quotas of the members issuing them, provided that these members have accepted Article VIII. The budget for repurchases allocates the aggregate commitments expected to arise during the quarter among the acceptable currencies in proportion to each member's reserve position in the Fund.

(10) The long-term aim is to equalize the ratios between each member's reserve position in the Fund on the one hand and its official gold and foreign exchange holdings on the other. The former quantity is defined as the gold tranche drawings which the member could make plus the amount of any indebtedness of the Fund which is readily repayable to the member under a loan agreement (including the GAB and any similar arrangement with one or more members).

U.S. TECHNICAL DRAWINGS

At an early stage, the application of the foregoing procedure to repurchases came up against the difficulty that the Fund's holdings of U.S. dollars had reached 75 per cent of the U.S. quota. When dollars thus became no longer acceptable in repurchases, countries holding dollars and needing to make repurchases could do so only by exchanging them for gold in the United States, or by purchasing with them currencies which the Fund could accept. Since these purchases would usually be those of European creditor countries, the result could be a similar drain on U.S. gold.

In these circumstances the United States offered to draw on the Fund, not for its own needs but in order to obtain a supply of currencies which the Fund could accept; these it would exchange for dollars at the request of members that had repurchases to make and wished to do so. Since currencies thus drawn by the United States would be promptly repaid to the Fund by the member making the repurchases, it was immaterial which currencies were drawn, provided that the Fund's holdings of them were not in excess of 75 per cent of the issuing members' quotas. The United States first drew from the Fund early in 1964, and from then until the end of 1965 it drew and made available for conversion a total equivalent to $660 million in eight different currencies. The arrangement was terminated at the end of 1966.

REPLENISHMENT

Passing reference was made above to the possibility that the Fund might acquire additional supplies of currencies needed to meet requests for drawings by replenishing its holdings of these currencies and by activating the GAB. The Fund's powers for these purposes have been discussed in Chapter 17. Here we shall be concerned with the principles by which the Fund has selected the amounts of currencies to be acquired.

Until 1961 the only currency of which any substantial use was made was, as has been shown, the U.S. dollar. As a result of heavy drawings in 1956, the Fund's holdings of U.S. dollars fell to $1,142 million at the end of that year, while at the same date commitments under stand-by arrangements totaled $1,117 million. The Board decided that it was desirable to replenish the holdings of dollars, and sold $300 million of gold to the United States for this purpose in January 1957. Four months later, when the Fund's holdings of U.S. dollars had been further reduced to $977 million, and commitments under stand-by arrangements totaled $969 million, a second sale of $300 million of gold was authorized. Those were the only occasions on which the Fund has replenished its holdings of a single currency, until it borrowed Italian lire in 1966.

In August 1961 the United Kingdom came to the Fund for a drawing of $1,500 million. The Board then decided that it would replenish the Fund's resources of each of the nine currencies being used to meet the drawing (Belgian francs, Canadian dollars, French francs, deutsche mark, Italian lire, Japanese yen, Netherlands guilders, Swedish kronor, and U.S. dollars) to the extent of one third of the use made of each. This was done by purchasing these currencies for gold.

In July 1964 the United Kingdom renewed a stand-by arrangement for $1 billion from the Fund, and within a few weeks it became apparent to the staff that a substantial drawing under that arrangement was to be expected. The Fund's holdings of the principal continental European currencies were at a low ebb, and there would clearly have to be some reinforcement of them if the drawing was to be met without reducing the holdings to injudiciously low levels. In contrast to the situation in 1961, the GAB had become available in 1963, and during the Annual Meeting, 1964, the Managing Director discussed with the participants in the GAB the possibility of activating these Arrangements when the British request for a drawing should eventuate.

When, therefore, the United Kingdom presented its request to draw the whole amount under the stand-by arrangement late in November, a comprehensive plan was worked out, as shown in Table 19. The principal points to be noted in the table concern the proportions between the constituent columns and the totals.

(a) The proportion of the total obtained from sales of gold was one fourth. At the meeting of the Board on November 20, Mr. Garland (Australia) and Mr. Anjaria (India) questioned whether it was necessary to sell as much as $250 million of gold since, in contrast to 1961, currencies could be obtained by drawing on the GAB. The Managing Director, in reply, said that the proportion obtained by the sale of gold was a matter of judgment; he and the staff believed that one fourth was appropriate. No other Director raised the point. As between the different currencies, the amounts obtained by the sale of gold were related not to the amounts drawn on this occasion but to the cumulative total of net drawings outstanding, including those to be provided for the United Kingdom.

(b) The $750 million needed in addition to the currencies obtained by the sale of gold was apportioned among the countries whose currencies were to be drawn in a rough ratio to their holdings of gold and foreign exchange. As

Table 19. Constitution of Drawing by United Kingdom, December 1964
(In millions of U.S. dollars or equivalents)

Currencies	From Fund Holdings	From GAB	From Sales of Gold	Total
Austrian schillings	20	—	8	28
Belgian francs	10	30	17	57
Canadian dollars	45	15	9	69
Deutsche mark	—	180	93	273
French francs	—	100	63	163
Italian lire	15	5	3	23
Japanese yen	20	20	14	54
Netherlands guilders	—	40	26	66
Spanish pesetas	30	—	10	40
Swedish kronor	5	15	7	27
U.S. dollars	200	—	—	200
Total	345	405	250	1,000

between the Fund's holdings and borrowings under the GAB, the original intention had been to borrow the full amount of the five currencies of which the Fund's holdings were lowest (Belgian francs, deutsche mark, French francs, Netherlands guilders, and Swedish kronor), and to obtain what was required of the other currencies wholly from the Fund's holdings. The signatories of the GAB, however, preferred that the Fund should borrow from each participant except the United Kingdom itself, even if only a token sum were borrowed. The reason for this was partly a wish for solidarity among the participants, and partly a doubt whether the terms of the agreement between the participants which was embodied in Mr. Baumgartner's letters [29] would permit a member of the Group of Ten to vote on the proposal to activate the GAB if its currency was not borrowed.

The Managing Director was prepared to agree to the proposal that the currency of each participant should be borrowed to a greater or lesser degree, except that he demurred at the Fund's borrowing any currency of which its holdings would exceed 75 per cent of the member's quota after the drawing. Until October this would have excluded any borrowing of Canadian dollars, as well as of U.S. dollars, but at the end of that month, prompted by a large increase in its reserves, Canada repurchased its currency from the Fund to an extent that reduced the Fund's holdings to 75 per cent of quota. The final

---

[29] See above, Vol. I, p. 512; below, pp. 520–21 of this volume; and below, Vol. III, p. 252.

allocation of currencies between the Fund's holdings and borrowings under the GAB was made on a sliding scale. For the three currencies of which the Fund's holdings were smallest in relation to quota (ranging from 20 per cent to 42 per cent), the whole sum needed was borrowed; for two currencies, of which the Fund's holdings were 52–55 per cent of quota, the percentage borrowed was 75; for one, of which the Fund's holdings were at 64 per cent of quota, the percentage borrowed was 50; and for the other two, of which the Fund's holdings were at 75 per cent, the percentage borrowed was 25. The appropriate sums were transferred to the United Kingdom's account on December 2.

In February 1965 it became known to the Fund staff that some $3 billion of credits to the United Kingdom, which had been arranged in the previous November concurrently with the drawing, would expire in May. This made it likely that the British authorities would then seek a further drawing to enable them to repay such of the credits as had been used. The staff accordingly gave thought to a possible distribution of currencies to make up a drawing of $1 billion or $1.5 billion.

On April 21 the Managing Director handed to the Executive Directors appointed or elected by the ten countries in the GAB a possible schedule of currencies to be drawn from the Fund's holdings, to be borrowed, and to be obtained from the sale of gold. As it appeared probable that the United Kingdom would wish to draw as much as it could without increasing the Fund's holdings of sterling beyond 200 per cent of the British quota, the draft schedule assumed a drawing of $1,400 million. The main proposal was that the amount of gold sold should be one fourth of the total, as in 1964. This would yield $350 million. It was planned to use $200 million from the Fund's holdings of U.S. dollars, and $25 million each from its holdings of Danish kroner and Spanish pesetas— the substitution of the kroner for Austrian schillings being due to the improvement in the Danish balance of payments, and the deterioration of that of Austria, since the 1964 drawing. The remainder ($800 million) of the drawing would be found in the currencies of the members of the GAB other than the United States and the United Kingdom. The division between drawings on the Fund's holdings and drawings on borrowed funds would depend (as in 1964) on the proportion of the Fund's holdings of each currency to that country's quota.

On April 29 the United Kingdom, which had by then used up $1.1 billion of the $3 billion of inter-central-bank credits, requested a drawing of $1.4 billion. On the same day the Managing Director had a further discussion with the Executive Directors from the countries that were signatories of the GAB, preparatory to issuing a formal proposal for its activation. At this meeting some criticism developed of the plans put forward on April 21. Specifically, it was urged that a larger proportion of the total should be found by the sale of gold, preferably one third, as had been done for the British drawing in August 1961. Directors also wished more use to be made of the Fund's holdings and less of currencies borrowed through the GAB. In consequence, a revised plan was immediately prepared and cleared with the Executive Directors concerned. This provided for a sale of gold amounting to $400 million and for an increase from $187 million (out of $800 million) to $225 million (out of $750 million) in the amount to be taken from the Fund's holdings of the currencies of the GAB countries other than the United States. The proportion of the total needed of each currency that was borrowed under the GAB was again related inversely to the proportion of the Fund's holdings of that currency to the country's quota; it varied from 93 per cent for France and Germany down to 44–45 per cent for Canada, Italy, and Japan. The drawing was approved on May 12; its constitution is shown in Table 20.

Table 20. Constitution of Drawing by United Kingdom, May 1965
(In millions of U.S. dollars or equivalents)

Currencies	From Fund Holdings	From GAB	From Sales of Gold	Total
Belgian francs	17.5	37.5	27.5	82.5
Canadian dollars	45.0	35.0	27.5	107.5
Danish kroner	25.0	—	5.0	30.0
Deutsche mark	12.5	167.5	132.5	312.5
French francs	10.0	140.0	92.5	242.5
Italian lire	85.0	65.0	32.5	182.5
Japanese yen	30.0	25.0	22.5	77.5
Netherlands guilders	17.5	37.5	32.5	87.5
Spanish pesetas	25.0	—	15.0	40.0
Swedish kronor	7.5	17.5	12.5	37.5
U.S. dollars	200.0	—	—	200.0
Total	475.0	525.0	400.00	1,400.0

RESULTS OF POLICY

Despite the difficulty created by the unavailability of U.S. dollars, the policy worked out in 1961 has been successful in reducing the disparities which previously existed between the ratios of the reserve positions in the Fund to official gold and foreign exchange reserves for those members whose currencies have been used for repurchases. Table 21 shows these ratios as they were shortly before the Managing Director made his statement and as they were at the end of the period covered by this volume. It will be seen that, before the policy for the selection of currencies was introduced, the ratios between the members' positions in the Fund and their gold and foreign exchange reserves varied from 2 to 10 per cent. By 1965 the range of ratios had been narrowed, for most of the countries concerned, to 13–17 per cent. The low ratios for the other two countries, Austria and Spain, were due to the imminent exhaustion of the Fund's holdings of their currencies.

Table 21. Ratio of Reserve Position in the Fund to Official Gold and Foreign Exchange Holdings: Selected Countries, as at December 31, 1960 and 1965 [1]

(In per cent)

Country	Ratio, 1960	Ratio, 1965
Austria	3	6
Belgium	6	15
Canada	8	13
France	10	16
Germany	5	17
Italy	2	13
Japan	7	13
Netherlands	7	17
Spain	—	11
Sweden	8	17

[1] The countries selected are those whose currencies have been used regularly, during most of the period, for drawings in accordance with the criteria for the selection of currencies. The United Kingdom and the United States are excluded because of balance of payments weakness. Australia, Denmark, and Mexico are omitted because their currencies were not considered for use until 1965.

STATISTICAL APPENDIX

Table 22 details the amounts drawn by each member of the Fund in each calendar year from 1947 through 1965.

Table 23 shows the amounts of the drawings listed in Table 22 that were repurchased by each member in each year. The final column shows the amount (if any) of the drawings which was still outstanding on December 31, 1965. The following points should be noted:

(*a*) The figure in the last column does not necessarily represent the difference between the amounts drawn and the amounts repurchased by the member. The reason is that if any member A's currency is drawn by another member, the Fund's holdings of A's currency are reduced; if A has itself drawn, the amount that it has to repurchase is correspondingly reduced. (This has affected especially the United States.)

(*b*) The absence of a figure in the last column means only that any drawings have been wholly repurchased. The Fund's holdings of the member's currency may be below, at, or above 75 per cent of the member's quota. They may be below 75 per cent if other members have drawn that currency, or above 75 per cent if the member concerned has not yet paid 25 per cent of its subscription in gold.

Details of stand-by arrangements are appended to Chapter 20.

Table 22. Drawings from the Fund, Calendar Years 1947–65 [1]

(In millions of U.S. dollars)

Member	1947	1948	1949	1950	1951	1952	1953	1954	1955	1956
Afghanistan	•	•	•	•	•	•	•	•	—	—
Algeria	•	•	•	•	•	•	•	•	•	•
Argentina	•	•	•	•	•	•	•	•	•	—
Australia	—	—	20.0	—	—	30.0	—	—	—	—
Austria	•	—	—	—	—	—	—	—	—	—
Belgium	11.0	22.0	—	—	—	—	—	—	—	—
Bolivia	—	—	—	—	—	—	2.5	—	—	3.0
Brazil	—	—	37.5	—	28.0	37.5	65.5	—	—	—
Burma	•	•	•	•	•	—	—	—	—	15.0
Burundi	•	•	•	•	•	•	•	•	•	•
Cameroon	•	•	•	•	•	•	•	•	•	•
Canada	—	—	—	—	—	—	—	—	—	—
Central African Rep.	•	•	•	•	•	•	•	•	•	•
Ceylon	•	•	•	—	—	—	—	—	—	•
Chad	•	•	•	•	•	•	•	•	•	•
Chile	8.8	—	—	—	—	—	12.5	—	—	—
China	—	—	—	—	—	—	—	—	—	—
Colombia	—	—	—	—	—	—	—	25.0	—	—
Congo (Brazzaville)	•	•	•	•	•	•	•	•	•	•
Congo, Dem. Rep.	•	•	•	•	•	•	•	•	•	•
Costa Rica	—	1.2	—	—	—	—	—	—	—	—
Cuba	—	—	—	—	—	—	—	—	—	12.5
Cyprus	•	•	•	•	•	•	•	•	•	•
Czechoslovakia	—	6.0	—	—	—	—	—	—	—	•
Dahomey	•	•	•	•	•	•	•	•	•	•
Denmark	3.4	6.8	—	—	—	—	—	—	—	—
Dominican Rep.	—	—	—	—	—	—	—	—	—	—
Ecuador	—	—	—	—	—	—	—	—	—	—
El Salvador	—	—	—	—	—	—	—	—	—	2.5
Ethiopia	—	0.3	0.3	—	—	—	—	—	—	—
Finland	•	—	—	—	—	4.5	5.0*	—	—	—
France	125.0	—	—	—	—	—	—	—	—	—
Gabon	•	•	•	•	•	•	•	•	•	•
Germany	•	•	•	•	•	—	—	—	—	•
Ghana	•	•	•	•	•	•	•	•	•	•
Greece	—	—	—	—	—	—	—	—	—	—
Guatemala	—	—	—	—	—	—	—	—	—	—
Guinea	•	•	•	•	•	•	•	•	•	•
Haiti	•	•	•	•	•	•	—	—	—	—
Honduras	—	—	—	—	—	—	—	—	—	—
Iceland	—	—	—	—	—	—	—	—	—	—
India	—	68.3	31.7	—	—	—	—	—	—	—
Indonesia	•	•	•	•	•	•	•	15.0	—	55.0
Iran	—	—	—	—	6.6	2.2	—	—	17.5	19.7
Iraq	—	—	—	—	—	—	—	—	—	—
Ireland	•	•	•	•	•	•	•	•	•	•
Israel	•	•	•	•	•	•	•	—	—	—
Italy	—	—	—	—	—	—	—	—	—	—
Ivory Coast	•	•	•	•	•	•	•	•	•	•
Jamaica	•	•	•	•	•	•	•	•	•	•
Japan	•	•	•	•	•	—	124.0	—	—	—
Jordan	•	•	•	•	•	—	—	—	—	—
Kenya	•	•	•	•	•	•	•	•	•	•
Korea	•	•	•	•	•	•	•	•	—	—
Kuwait	•	•	•	•	•	•	•	•	•	•

Footnote on page 462.

Table 22. Drawings from the Fund, Calendar Years 1947–65 [1]

(In millions of U.S. dollars)

1957	1958	1959	1960	1961	1962	1963	1964	1965	Total	Member
—	—	—	—	—	—	5.6	5.6	1.7*	12.9	Afghanistan
—	—	—	—	—	—	—	—	—	—	Algeria
75.0	—	72.5*	70.0*	60.0*	50.0*	50.0*	—	—	377.5	Argentina
—	—	—	—	175.0	—	—	—	—	225.0	Australia
—	—	—	—	—	—	—	—	—	—	Austria
50.0	—	—	—	—	—	—	—	—	83.0	Belgium
1.0*	2.0*	3.4*	1.0*	2.0*	3.5*	4.0*	—	—	22.4	Bolivia
37.5	54.8*	—	47.7	60.0*	—	60.0	—	75.0*	503.4	Brazil
—	—	—	—	—	—	—	—	—	15.0	Burma
•	•	•	•	•	•	—	—	2.0*	2.0	Burundi
•	•	•	•	•	•	—	—	—	—	Cameroon
—	—	—	—	—	300.0	—	—	—	300.0	Canada
•	•	•	•	•	•	—	—	—	—	Central African Rep.
—	—	—	—	11.2	11.2	—	—	23.0*	45.5	Ceylon
•	•	•	•	•	•	—	—	—	—	Chad
31.1*	10.6*	0.7*	—	76.0*	—	40.0*	20.0*	36.0*	235.7	Chile
—	—	—	—	—	—	—	—	—	—	China
5.0*	10.0*	—	—	65.0*	7.5*	48.5*	7.5*	—	168.5	Colombia
•	•	•	•	•	•	—	—	—	—	Congo (Brazzaville)
•	•	•	•	•	•	—	—	—	—	Congo, Dem. Rep.
—	—	—	—	7.5*	2.5*	10.0*	—	10.0*	31.2	Costa Rica
35.0*	25.0	—	—	—	—	—	—	•	72.5	Cuba
•	•	•	•	—	—	—	2.0	—	2.0	Cyprus
•	•	•	•	•	•	•	•	•	6.0	Czechoslovakia
•	•	•	•	•	•	—	—	—	—	Dahomey
34.0	—	—	—	—	—	—	—	—	44.2	Denmark
—	—	—	9.0*	—	—	—	15.0*	5.0*	29.0	Dominican Rep.
5.0	—	—	—	14.0*	4.0*	—	—	11.0*	34.0	Ecuador
—	—	5.5*	13.2*	8.0*	—	—	—	—	29.2	El Salvador
—	—	—	—	—	—	—	—	—	0.6	Ethiopia
—	—	—	—	—	—	—	—	—	9.5	Finland
262.5*	131.2*	—	—	—	—	—	—	—	518.8	France
•	•	•	•	•	•	—	—	—	—	Gabon
—	—	—	—	—	—	—	—	—	—	Germany
—	—	—	—	—	14.2	—	—	—	14.2	Ghana
—	—	—	—	—	—	—	—	—	—	Greece
—	—	—	—	—	5.0*	—	—	5.0	10.0	Guatemala
•	•	•	•	•	•	—	—	—	—	Guinea
1.0	2.5*	1.9*	—	1.5*	3.2*	5.0*	3.0*	2.5*	20.7	Haiti
6.2*	—	3.8*	5.0*	2.4*	5.0*	2.5*	5.0*	—	30.0	Honduras
—	—	—	6.8*	—	—	—	—	—	6.8	Iceland
200.0*	—	—	—	250.0	25.0*	—	—	200.0*	775.0	India
—	—	—	—	61.2*	21.2*	20.0*	—	—	172.5	Indonesia
—	—	5.0	45.0*	7.5*	—	—	17.5	—	121.0	Iran
—	—	—	—	—	—	—	—	—	—	Iraq
—	—	—	—	—	—	—	—	—	—	Ireland
3.8	—	—	—	—	—	—	12.5	—	16.2	Israel
—	—	—	—	—	—	—	225.0	—	225.0	Italy
•	•	•	•	•	•	—	—	—	—	Ivory Coast
•	•	•	•	•	•	—	—	—	—	Jamaica
125.0	—	—	—	—	—	—	—	—	249.0	Japan
—	—	—	—	—	—	—	—	—	—	Jordan
•	•	•	•	•	•	•	—	—	—	Kenya
—	—	—	•	—	—	—	—	—	—	Korea
•	•	•	•	•	—	—	—	—	—	Kuwait

Table 22 *(concluded).* Drawings from the Fund, Calendar Years 1947–65 [1]
(In millions of U.S. dollars)

Member	1947	1948	1949	1950	1951	1952	1953	1954	1955	1956
Laos	•	•	•	•	•	•	•	•	•	•
Lebanon	—	—	—	—	—	—	—	—	—	—
Liberia	•	•	•	•	•	•	•	•	•	•
Libya	•	•	•	•	•	•	•	•	•	•
Luxembourg	—	—	—	—	—	—	—	—	—	—
Malagasy Rep.	•	•	•	•	•	•	•	•	•	•
Malawi	•	•	•	•	•	•	•	•	•	•
Malaysia	•	•	•	•	•	•	•	•	•	•
Mali	•	•	•	•	•	•	•	•	•	•
Mauritania	•	•	•	•	•	•	•	•	•	•
Mexico	22.5	—	—	—	—	—	—	22.5*	—	—
Morocco	•	•	•	•	•	•	•	•	•	•
Nepal	•	•	•	•	•	•	•	•	•	•
Netherlands	52.0	23.3	—	—	—	—	—	—	—	—
New Zealand	•	•	•	•	•	•	•	•	•	•
Nicaragua	—	0.5	—	—	—	—	—	—	—	1.9*
Niger	•	•	•	•	•	•	•	•	•	•
Nigeria	•	•	•	•	•	•	•	•	•	•
Norway	—	9.6	—	—	—	—	—	—	—	—
Pakistan	•	•	•	—	—	—	—	—	—	—
Panama	—	—	—	—	—	—	—	—	—	—
Paraguay	—	—	—	—	—	0.9	—	—	—	1.5
Peru	—	—	—	—	—	—	—	—	—	—
Philippines	—	—	—	—	—	—	—	—	10.0	5.0
Poland	—	—	—	—	•	•	•	•	•	•
Portugal	•	•	•	•	•	•	•	•	•	•
Rwanda	•	•	•	•	•	•	•	•	•	•
Saudi Arabia	•	•	•	•	•	•	•	•	•	•
Senegal	•	•	•	•	•	•	•	•	•	•
Sierra Leone	•	•	•	•	•	•	•	•	•	•
Somalia	•	•	•	•	•	•	•	•	•	•
South Africa	—	10.0	—	—	—	—	—	—	—	—
Spain	•	•	•	•	•	•	•	•	•	•
Sudan	•	•	•	•	•	•	•	•	•	•
Sweden	•	•	•	•	—	—	—	—	—	—
Syrian Arab Rep.	—	—	—	—	—	—	—	—	—	—
Tanzania	•	•	•	•	•	•	•	•	•	•
Thailand	•	•	—	—	—	—	—	—	—	—
Togo	•	•	•	•	•	•	•	•	•	•
Trinidad & Tobago	•	•	•	•	•	•	•	•	•	•
Tunisia	•	•	•	•	•	•	•	•	•	•
Turkey	5.0	—	—	—	—	10.0	20.0	—	—	—
Uganda	•	•	•	•	•	•	•	•	•	•
United Arab Rep.	—	—	3.0	—	—	—	—	—	—	15.0
United Kingdom	240.0	60.0	—	—	—	—	—	—	—	561.5
United States	—	—	—	—	—	—	—	—	—	—
Upper Volta	•	•	•	•	•	•	•	•	•	•
Uruguay	—	—	—	—	—	—	—	—	—	—
Venezuela	—	—	—	—	—	—	—	—	—	—
Viet-Nam	•	•	•	•	•	•	•	•	•	—
Yugoslavia	—	—	9.0	—	—	—	—	—	—	—
Zambia	•	•	•	•	•	•	•	•	•	•
Totals	467.7	208.0	101.5	—	34.6	85.1	229.5	62.5	27.5	692.6

[1] A dot (•) indicates that the country was not a member at the time; a dash (—) indicates that no draw‑ ing was made; an asterisk (*) designates drawings made wholly or partly under stand-by arrangements

Table 22 *(concluded).* Drawings from the Fund, Calendar Years 1947–65 [1]
(In millions of U.S. dollars)

1957	1958	1959	1960	1961	1962	1963	1964	1965	Total	Member
•	•	•	•	—	—	—	—	—	—	Laos
—	—	—	—	—	—	—	—	—	—	Lebanon
•	•	•	•	•	—	3.6*	3.8*	3.0*	10.4	Liberia
•	—	—	—	—	—	—	—	—	—	Libya
—	—	—	—	—	—	—	—	—	—	Luxembourg
•	•	•	•	•	•	—	—	—	—	Malagasy Rep.
•	•	•	•	•	•	•	•	—	—	Malawi
•	—	—	—	—	—	—	—	—	—	Malaysia
•	•	•	•	•	•	—	5.0*	5.0*	9.9	Mali
•	•	•	•	•	•	—	—	—	—	Mauritania
—	—	22.5*	—	45.0*	—	—	—	—	112.5	Mexico
•	—	—	—	—	—	—	13.1	—	13.1	Morocco
•	•	•	•	—	—	—	—	—	—	Nepal
68.8	—	—	—	—	—	—	—	—	144.1	Netherlands
•	•	•	•	—	—	—	—	62.0	62.0	New Zealand
3.8*	1.9*	—	—	6.0*	—	11.5*	12.0*	—	37.5	Nicaragua
•	•	•	•	•	•	—	—	—	—	Niger
•	•	•	•	•	•	—	—	—	—	Nigeria
—	—	—	—	—	—	—	—	—	9.6	Norway
—	—	—	12.5	—	—	—	—	53.5*	66.0	Pakistan
—	—	—	—	—	—	—	—	2.7	2.7	Panama
4.0*	0.8*	—	1.0*	—	—	—	—	—	8.1	Paraguay
—	10.0*	4.5*	—	—	—	—	—	—	14.5	Peru
—	—	8.8	6.2	—	28.3	—	—	—	58.3	Philippines
•	•	•	•	•	•	•	•	•	—	Poland
•	•	•	•	—	—	—	—	—	—	Portugal
•	•	•	•	•	•	—	—	—	—	Rwanda
—	—	—	—	—	—	—	—	—	—	Saudi Arabia
•	•	•	•	•	—	—	—	—	—	Senegal
•	•	•	•	•	—	—	—	—	—	Sierra Leone
•	•	•	•	•	—	—	4.7*	5.6*	10.3	Somalia
—	36.2*	—	12.5	25.0	—	—	—	—	83.7	South Africa
•	—	50.0	—	—	—	—	—	—	50.0	Spain
—	5.0	1.2	—	—	—	—	5.4	18.8	30.4	Sudan
—	—	—	—	—	—	—	—	—	—	Sweden
—	—	—	15.0*	—	5.6*	—	18.5*	—	39.1	Syrian Arab Rep.
•	•	•	•	•	—	—	—	—	—	Tanzania
—	—	—	—	—	—	—	—	—	—	Thailand
•	•	•	•	—	—	—	—	—	—	Togo
•	•	•	•	•	—	—	—	—	—	Trinidad & Tobago
•	—	—	—	—	—	5.2*	11.8*		17.0	Tunisia
13.5	25.0	—	—	16.0*	15.0*	21.5*	19.0*	—	145.0	Turkey
•	•	•	—	—	—	—	—	—	—	Uganda
15.0	—	—	34.8	10.0	67.4*	21.0	25.0*	15.0*	206.2	United Arab Rep.
—	—	—	—	1,500.0	—	—	1,000.0*	1,400.0*	4,761.5	United Kingdom
—	—	—	—	—	—	—	525.0*	435.0*	960.0	United States
•	•	•	•	•	•	—	—	—	—	Upper Volta
—	—	—	—	15.0*	—	—	—	—	15.0	Uruguay
—	—	—	—	—	—	—	—	—	—	Venezuela
—	—	—	—	—	—	—	—	—	—	Viet-Nam
—	22.9	—	—	75.0*	—	30.0	—	50.0*	186.9	Yugoslavia
•	•	•	•	•	•	•	•	—	—	Zambia
977.1	337.9	179.8	279.8	2,478.5	583.8	333.2	1,949.8	2,433.5	11,462.4	Totals

Table 23. Repurchases of Drawings, Calendar Years 1947–65 [1]

(In millions of U.S. dollars)

Member	1947	1948	1949	1950	1951	1952	1953	1954	1955	1956
Afghanistan	•	•	•	•	•	•	•	•	—	—
Algeria	•	•	•	•	•	•	•	•	•	•
Argentina	•	•	•	•	•	•	•	•	•	—
Australia	—	—	—	—	—	—	12.0	24.0	14.0	—
Austria	•	—	—	—	—	—	—	—	—	—
Belgium	—	—	0.9	20.7	—	—	—	—	—	—
Bolivia	—	—	—	—	—	—	—	—	—	—
Brazil	—	—	—	—	—	65.5	37.5	—	—	28.0
Burma	•	•	•	•	•	—	•	—	—	—
Burundi	•	•	•	•	•	•	•	•	•	•
Cameroon	•	•	•	•	•	•	•	•	•	•
Canada	—	—	—	—	—	—	—	—	—	—
Central African Rep.	•	•	•	•	•	•	•	•	•	•
Ceylon	•	•	•	—	—	—	—	—	—	—
Chad	•	•	•	•	•	•	•	•	•	•
Chile	—	—	—	—	3.4	3.7	1.7	—	—	0.2
China	—	—	—	—	—	—	—	—	—	—
Colombia	—	—	—	—	—	—	—	—	—	—
Congo (Brazzaville)	•	•	•	•	•	•	•	•	•	•
Congo, Dem. Rep.	•	•	•	•	•	•	•	•	•	•
Costa Rica	—	—	0.9	0.3	—	—	—	—	—	—
Cuba	—	—	—	—	—	—	—	—	—	—
Cyprus	•	•	•	•	•	•	•	•	•	•
Czechoslovakia	—	—	—	—	—	—	—	—	2.0	0.7
Dahomey	•	•	•	•	•	•	•	•	•	•
Denmark	—	—	—	—	—	—	—	—	10.2	—
Dominican Rep.	—	—	—	—	—	—	—	—	—	—
Ecuador	—	—	—	—	—	—	—	—	—	—
El Salvador	—	—	—	—	—	—	—	—	—	—
Ethiopia	—	—	—	0.3	0.3	—	—	—	—	—
Finland	•	—	—	—	—	—	2.0	4.5	3.0	—
France	—	—	—	—	—	—	—	20.0	60.0	45.0
Gabon	•	•	•	•	•	•	•	•	•	•
Germany	•	•	•	•	•	—	—	—	—	—
Ghana	•	•	•	•	•	•	•	•	•	•
Greece	—	—	—	—	—	—	—	—	—	—
Guatemala	—	—	—	—	—	—	—	—	—	—
Guinea	•	•	•	•	•	•	•	•.	•	•
Haiti	•	•	•	•	•	•	•	•	•	•
Honduras	—	—	—	—	—	—	—	—	—	—
Iceland	—	—	—	—	—	—	—	—	—	—
India	—	—	—	—	—	—	—	46.7	40.7	12.5
Indonesia	•	•	•	•	•	•	•	—	—	15.0
Iran	—	—	—	—	—	—	—	—	8.7	11.9
Iraq	—	—	—	—	—	—	—	—	—	—
Ireland	•	•	•	•	•	•	•	•	•	•
Israel	•	•	•	•	•	•	•	•	—	—
Italy	—	—	—	—	—	—	—	—	—	—
Ivory Coast	•	•	•	•	•	•	•	•	•	•
Jamaica	•	•	•	•	•	•	•	•	•	•
Japan	•	•	•	•	•	—	61.6	—	62.4	—
Jordan	•	•	•	•	•	—	—	—	—	—
Kenya	•	•	•	•	•	•	•	•	•	•
Korea	•	•	•	•	•	•	•	•	—	—
Kuwait	•	•	•	•	•	•	•	•	•	•

Footnotes on page 466.

Table 23. Repurchases of Drawings, Calendar Years 1947–65 [1]

(In millions of U.S. dollars)

1957	1958	1959	1960	1961	1962	1963	1964	1965	Total	Member	Out-standing [2]
—	—	—	—	—	—	—	—	—	—	Afghanistan	12.9
	—	—	—	—	—	—	—	—	—	Algeria	
—	—	—	21.5	13.0	59.0	36.0	42.0	44.0	215.5	Argentina	146.0
—	—	—	—	175.0	—	—	—	—	225.0	Australia	
—	—	—	—	—	—	—	—	—	—	Austria	
—	50.0	—	—	—	—	—	—	—	71.6	Belgium	
—	—	1.0	2.5	4.0	2.3	2.9	4.8	1.0	18.4	Bolivia	4.0
—	17.2	20.2	—	20.0	17.5	55.5	28.0	55.0	344.5	Brazil	159.0
—	3.0	4.0	4.0	4.0	—	—	—	—	15.0	Burma	
•	•	•	•	•	•	—	—	2.0	2.0	Burundi	
•	•	•	•	•	•	—	—	—	—	Cameroon	
—	—	—	—	—	—	79.7	166.0	—	245.7	Canada	
•	•	•	•	•	•	—	—	—	—	Central African Rep.	
—	—	—	—	—	—	—	—	7.5	7.5	Ceylon	38.0
•	•	•	•	•	•	—	—	—	—	Chad	
12.3	—	0.7	12.4	16.7	12.7	—	10.0	37.0	110.7	Chile	125.0
—	—	—	—	—	—	—	—	—	—	China	
5.0	5.0	15.0	15.0	—	—	—	20.0	24.0	84.0	Colombia	84.5
•	•	•	•	•	•	—	—	—	—	Congo (Brazzaville)	
•	•	•	•	•	•	—	—	—	—	Congo, Dem. Rep.	
—	—	—	—	—	6.6	0.4	1.3	1.7	11.3	Costa Rica	20.0
22.5	25.0	—	—	—	—	—	15.0	2.5	65.0	Cuba	7.5
•	•	•	•	—	—	—	—	—	—	Cyprus	2.0
0.7	0.7	0.7	0.7	0.7	•	•	•	•	6.0	Czechoslovakia	
•	•	•	•	•	•	—	—	—	—	Dahomey	
—	25.5	8.5	—	—	—	—	—	—	44.2	Denmark	
—	—	—	—	—	—	9.0	—	—	9.0	Dominican Rep.	20.0
—	5.0	—	—	—	6.2	3.3	6.6	2.0	23.0	Ecuador	11.0
2.5	—	—	7.5	11.2	8.0	—	—	—	29.2	El Salvador	
—	—	—	—	—	—	—	—	—	0.6	Ethiopia	
—	—	—	—	—	—	—	—	—	9.5	Finland	
—	—	200.0	181.1	—	—	—	—	—	506.1	France	
•	•	•	•	•	•	—	—	—	—	Gabon	
—	—	—	—	—	—	—	—	—	—	Germany	
—	—	—	—	—	—	—	—	5.6	5.6	Ghana	8.6
—	—	—	—	—	—	—	—	—	—	Greece	
—	—	—	—	—	—	1.1	3.9	—	5.0	Guatemala	5.0
•	•	•	•	•	•	—	—	—	—	Guinea	
—	—	—	1.3	2.8	1.3	1.5	2.5	2.3	11.7	Haiti	9.0
2.5	3.8	—	3.7	1.2	3.8	2.5	2.5	2.5	22.5	Honduras	7.5
—	—	—	—	—	4.0	2.8	—	—	6.8	Iceland	
—	—	—	72.5	127.5	—	25.0	50.0	75.0	449.9	India	325.1
—	—	9.0	18.5	27.5	—	—	—	39.1	109.0	Indonesia	63.5
—	8.4	16.9	—	19.5	37.9	—	—	3.5	106.9	Iran	14.0
—	—	—	—	—	—	—	—	—	—	Iraq	
—	—	—	—	—	—	—	—	—	—	Ireland	
—	3.8	—	—	—	—	—	12.5	—	16.2	Israel	
—	—	—	—	—	—	—	65.3	—	65.3	Italy	
•	•	•	•	•	•	—	—	—	—	Ivory Coast	
•	•	•	•	•	•	—	—	—	—	Jamaica	
—	125.0	—	—	—	—	—	—	—	249.0	Japan	
—	—	—	—	—	—	—	—	—	—	Jordan	
•	•	•	•	•	•	•	—	—	—	Kenya	
—	—	—	—	—	—	—	—	—	—	Korea	
•	•	•	•	•	—	—	—	—	—	Kuwait	

Table 23 *(concluded)*. Repurchases of Drawings, Calendar Years 1947–65 [1]
(In millions of U.S. dollars)

Member	1947	1948	1949	1950	1951	1952	1953	1954	1955	1956
Laos	•	•	•	•	•	•	•	•	•	•
Lebanon	—	—	—	—	—	—	—	—	—	—
Liberia	•	•	•	•	•	•	•	•	•	•
Libya	•	•	•	•	•	•	•	•	•	•
Luxembourg	—	—	—	—	—	—	—	—	—	—
Malagasy Rep.	•	•	•	•	•	•	•	•	•	•
Malawi	•	•	•	•	•	•	•	•	•	•
Malaysia	•	•	•	•	•	•	•	•	•	•
Mali	•	•	•	•	•	•	•	•	•	•
Mauritania	•	•	•	•	•	•	•	•	•	•
Mexico	—	—	—	—	22.5	—	—	—	22.4	—
Morocco	•	•	•	•	•	•	•	•	•	•
Ncpal	•	•	•	•	•	•	•	•	•	•
Netherlands	—	—	—	—	—	27.3	48.0	—	—	—
New Zealand	•	•	•	•	•	•	•	•	•	•
Nicaragua	—	—	0.5	—	—	—	—	—	—	—
Niger	•	•	•	•	•	•	•	•	•	•
Nigeria	•	•	•	•	•	•	•	•	•	•
Norway	—	—	—	—	9.6	—	—	—	—	—
Pakistan	•	•	•	—	—	—	—	—	—	—
Panama	—	—	—	—	—	—	—	—	—	—
Paraguay	—	—	—	—	—	—	—	0.4	—	—
Peru	—	—	—	—	—	—	—	—	—	—
Philippines	—	—	—	—	—	—	—	—	—	—
Poland	—	—	—	—	•	•	•	•	•	•
Portugal	•	•	•	•	•	•	•	•	•	•
Rwanda	•	•	•	•	•	•	•	•	•	•
Saudi Arabia	•	•	•	•	•	•	•	•	•	•
Senegal	•	•	•	•	•	•	•	•	•	•
Sierra Leone	•	•	•	•	•	•	•	•	•	•
Somalia	•	•	•	•	•	•	•	•	•	•
South Africa	—	—	—	—	10.0	—	—	—	—	—
Spain	•	•	•	•	•	•	•	•	•	•
Sudan	•	•	•	•	•	•	•	•	•	•
Sweden	•	•	•	•	—	—	—	—	—	—
Syrian Arab Rep.	—	—	—	—	—	—	—	—	—	—
Tanzania	•	•	•	•	•	•	•	•	•	•
Thailand	•	•	—	—	—	—	—	—	—	—
Togo	•	•	•	•	•	•	•	•	•	•
Trinidad & Tobago	•	•	•	•	•	•	•	•	•	•
Tunisia	•	•	•	•	•	•	•	•	•	•
Turkey	—	—	—	—	—	5.0	—	6.0	9.0	—
Uganda	•	•	•	•	•	•	•	•	•	•
United Arab Rep.	—	—	—	3.0	—	—	—	—	—	—
United Kingdom	—	—	—	—	—	—	—	108.3	—	—
United States	—	—	—	—	—	—	—	—	—	—
Upper Volta	•	•	•	•	•	•	•	•	•	•
Uruguay	—	—	—	—	—	—	—	—	—	—
Venezuela	—	—	—	—	—	—	—	—	—	—
Viet-Nam	•	•	•	•	•	•	•	•	•	—
Yugoslavia	—	—	—	—	—	•	•	•	—	—
Zambia	•	•	•	•	•	•	•	•	•	•
Totals	—	—	2.3	24.3	45.8	101.5	162.8	210.0	232.4	113.3

[1] A dot (•) indicates that the country was not a member at the time; a dash (—) indicates no repurchase; a blank in the last column means that any drawings made have been wholly repurchased.
[2] At December 31, 1965.

Table 23 *(concluded).* Repurchases of Drawings, Calendar Years 1947–65 [1]
(In millions of U.S. dollars)

1957	1958	1959	1960	1961	1962	1963	1964	1965	Total	Member	Out-standing [2]
•	•	•	•	—	—	—	—	—	—	Laos	
—	—	—	—	—	—	—	—	—	—	Lebanon	
•	•	•	•	•	—	—	—	—	—	Liberia	10.4
•	—	—	—	—	—	—	—	—	—	Libya	
•	—	—	—	—	—	—	—	—	—	Luxembourg	
•	•	•	•	•	•	—	—	—	—	Malagasy Rep.	
•	•	•	•	•	•	•	•	—	—	Malawi	
•	•	—	—	•	•	—	—	—	—	Malaysia	
•	•	•	•	•	•	—	—	—	—	Mali	9.9
•	•	•	•	•	—	—	—	—	—	Mauritania	
—	—	22.5	—	—	45.0	—	—	—	112.5	Mexico	
•	—	—	—	—	—	—	—	5.9	5.9	Morocco	7.2
•	•	•	•	—	—	—	—	—	—	Nepal	
—	63.7	—	—	—	—	—	—	—	139.1	Netherlands	
•	—	•	•	—	—	—	—	—	—	New Zealand	62.0
1.9	3.8	1.9	—	1.5	—	5.5	11.2	—	26.3	Nicaragua	11.2
•	•	•	•	•	•	—	—	—	—	Niger	
•	•	•	•	—	—	—	—	—	—	Nigeria	
—	—	—	—	—	—	—	—	—	9.6	Norway	
—	—	—	—	—	12.5	—	—	—	12.5	Pakistan	53.5
—	—	—	—	—	—	—	—	—	—	Panama	2.7
0.5	—	1.5	0.9	1.6	1.8	0.5	0.5	0.5	8.1	Paraguay	
—	—	14.5	—	—	—	—	—	—	14.5	Peru	
—	—	15.0	2.9	2.9	2.9	—	6.2	14.0	44.0	Philippines	14.3
•	•	•	•	•	•	•	•	•	—	Poland	
•	•	•	•	•	•	—	—	—	—	Portugal	
•	•	•	•	•	•	—	—	—	—	Rwanda	
—	—	—	—	—	—	—	—	—	—	Saudi Arabia	
•	•	•	•	•	—	—	—	—	—	Senegal	
•	•	•	•	•	—	—	—	—	—	Sierra Leone	
•	•	•	•	•	—	—	—	—	—	Somalia	10.3
—	—	36.2	—	—	37.5	—	—	—	83.7	South Africa	
•	—	—	50.0	—	—	—	—	—	50.0	Spain	
•	—	—	0.4	2.9	2.9	—	—	—	6.2	Sudan	24.2
—	—	—	—	—	—	—	—	—	—	Sweden	
—	—	—	—	0.7	2.2	1.2	3.9	7.0	15.0	Syrian Arab Rep.	24.1
•	•	•	•	•	•	—	—	—	—	Tanzania	
—	—	—	—	—	—	—	—	—	—	Thailand	
•	•	•	•	•	—	—	—	—	—	Togo	
•	•	•	•	•	•	—	—	—	—	Trinidad & Tobago	
•	—	—	—	—	—	—	—	—	—	Tunisia	17.1
7.0	8.0	3.0	3.0	5.5	9.5	17.5	16.0	15.0	104.5	Turkey	40.5
•	•	•	•	•	•	—	—	—	—	Uganda	
—	—	2.7	9.6	12.7	10.0	2.5	12.0	28.5	81.0	United Arab Rep.	125.2
—	—	200.0	296.8	420.0	852.2	—	—	—	1,877.4	United Kingdom	2,370.4
—	—	—	—	—	—	—	—	—	—	United States	383.5
•	•	•	•	•	•	—	—	—	—	Upper Volta	
•	•	•	•	•	•	—	—	—	—	Uruguay	15.0
—	—	—	—	—	—	—	—	—	—	Venezuela	
—	—	—	—	—	—	—	—	—	—	Viet-Nam	
9.0	—	—	—	7.5	7.5	7.9	30.0	15.0	76.9	Yugoslavia	110.0
•	•	•	•	•	•	•	—	—	—	Zambia	
63.8	347.7	573.3	654.3	753.6	1,305.8	267.1	510.2	390.5	5,758.6	Totals	4,354.1

CHAPTER

20

Stand-By Arrangements: Purposes and Form

Emil G. Spitzer

Combating inflation by monetary and fiscal policies has been a recognized task of governments, especially since World War I, even though for much of the interwar period the major economic problems which countries had to face derived from the deflationary consequences of the Great Depression rather than from inflationary pressures. The generally expansionary environment which has prevailed in most parts of the world since World War II has intensified the need for anti-inflationary policies, and has encouraged their embodiment in comprehensive stabilization programs. In its work with its members the Fund has devoted much time and thought to fostering such programs.

The link between stabilization programs and the support of them by the Fund has been provided by the Fund's policies on the use of its resources (described in previous chapters), and especially by those governing stand-by arrangements. The importance of these arrangements has grown with time. Nowadays a high proportion of all drawings is made under stand-by arrangements. Table 24 at the end of this chapter lists the arrangements inaugurated or renewed down to the end of 1965.

ORIGINS OF STAND-BY ARRANGEMENTS

The Board's decision of February 13, 1952 establishing the policy for the use of the Fund's resources contained a reference to arrangements by which a member might "ensure that it would be able to draw if, within a period of say 6 or 12 months, the need presented itself." [1] Such an arrangement had, excep-

---

[1] E.B. Decision No. 102-(52/11), February 13, 1952, par. 1; below, Vol. III, p. 228. For the background of this decision see above, p. 402.

tionally, been made with Mexico in May 1949, when the Board decided to inform the member that the Fund would not object to its drawing $22.5 million within the ensuing twelve months. The passage quoted above was also in the Board's mind in April 1952 when Australia came to the Fund for a drawing of $30 million and it was decided to permit this to be made at any time before September 30, 1952. However, in neither of these instances was it thought that the right to draw might be, in itself, sufficient to satisfy the member's requirements without a drawing actually being made. This feature has since been characteristic of stand-by arrangements, even though in many—indeed in most—instances the member has in fact drawn under the arrangement. It was first introduced when Belgium sought the Fund's assistance in June 1952. As explained to the Board by Mr. de Selliers (Belgium), his country

> wished to be able to consider the Fund's resources as a second line of reserves to help meet any sizable dollar deficit without having to resort to measures that would move away from convertibility. . . . The request for the stand-by credit . . . should help give the authorities the confidence they needed to help maintain a liberal economic policy.

The immediate occasion for Belgium's request was that negotiations in Paris to continue the European Payments Union and to settle the Belgian surplus in the Union had included the consolidation of a $50 million debt to be repaid to Belgium at the rate of $10 million a year starting on June 30, 1953. It was this $50 million for which a stand-by arrangement was asked. The Board's decision was:

> 1. The Fund assures Belgium the right for an initial period of six months to purchase the currencies of other members from the Fund in exchange for its own currency so long as such purchases do not bring the Fund's holdings of Belgian francs above their present level increased by the equivalent in Belgian francs of 50 million United States dollars; provided, however, that the amounts Belgium may purchase under this arrangement shall not be increased by reason of any purchases of Belgian francs by other members.

> 2. Belgium will pay a charge of one-quarter of one per cent fifteen days after this arrangement is concluded. This charge will be in addition to any charge that may become due under Article V, Section 8 (a).[2]

> 3. Belgium's right to purchase under this arrangement shall be subject only to the eligibility provisions of the Articles of Agreement.

> 4. Belgium will remain in consultation with the Fund from time to time on its payments situation and its general policies. The arrangement will be renewed for subsequent periods of six months each, unless either Belgium or the Fund determines that conditions have been basically altered so that the arrangement should be terminated. The arrangement will, in any case, be terminated when it has been in effect for five years.

---

[2] See above, p. 429.

In the event, Belgium drew nothing under the stand-by arrangement until almost the end of the five-year period, when it drew the whole $50 million.

At the conclusion of the meeting which approved the Belgian request, the Managing Director undertook that the staff would submit proposals for standard conditions for stand-by arrangements. These were presented in August 1952, and after considerable debate resulted in the Board's first general decision on such arrangements, taken on October 1, 1952.[3] This dealt only with stand-by arrangements for six months, as some Executive Directors had expressed the view that it would not be possible to foresee conditions in a member country for more than six months, and it was therefore inadvisable for the Fund to commit itself for a longer period. The preamble to the decision contained the following general statement concerning drawing rights:

> The Fund is prepared to consider requests by members for stand-by arrangements designed to give assurance that, during a fixed period of time, transactions up to a specified amount will be made whenever a member requests and without further consideration of its position, unless the ineligibility provisions of the Fund Agreement have been invoked.

Other clauses in the decision introduced conditions similar to those in the stand-by arrangement with Belgium, covering charges and the possibility of renewing the arrangement after six months. It was also provided that a stand-by arrangement would be for a sum not larger than the member could draw under the terms of Article V, Section 3, subject to the Fund's powers to waive these limits by the exercise of Article V, Section 4.

In paragraph 5 of the decision the conditions for drawings and for the suspension of drawing rights were elaborated as follows:

> A member having a stand-by arrangement would have the right to engage in the transactions covered by the stand-by arrangement without further review by the Fund. This right of the member could be suspended only with respect to requests received by the Fund after: (a) a formal ineligibility, or (b) a decision of the Executive Board to suspend transactions either generally (under Article XVI, Section 1 (a) (ii)) or in order to consider a proposal, made by an Executive Director or the Managing Director, formally to suppress or to limit the eligibility of the member.

A clause embodying this paragraph has been included in all stand-by arrangements.

In December 1952 the terms of the decision were made applicable for the first time. Finland requested a stand-by arrangement for six months permitting drawings up to $5 million, and undertook to abide by the terms of the decision. It also undertook to repurchase any drawings under the arrangement within three years of the date of drawing.

---

[3] E.B. Decision No. 155-(52/57), October 1, 1952; below, Vol. III, p. 230.

A second policy decision on stand-by arrangements, taken on December 23, 1953,[4] recognized that arrangements might be for periods of more than six months. Although the preamble and paragraph 5 of the first decision (which became paragraph 4 in the second decision) remained unchanged, the following sentence was added to paragraph 1 of the second decision:

> With respect to stand-by arrangements for periods of more than six months, the Fund and the member might find it appropriate to reach understandings additional to those set forth in this decision.

In the course of the discussion in the Board, the need for this sentence was explained by the staff as follows:

> Because of the difficulty of foreseeing a member's situation for a long time in advance, a stand-by beyond 6 months might have to be based on the expectation that the member would maintain certain policies. If the member changed those policies so as to impair the character of the understanding with the Fund, the Fund should have the possibility of cancelling its guarantee. For example, if a stand-by was arranged for the purpose of supporting an attempt at convertibility and the country later called off the attempt, the basis for continuing the stand-by would be gone. Such a situation might be handled by formal ineligibility proceedings as provided in paragraph 5 of the decision, but in most cases such an extreme action would probably not be desirable. Moreover, there might be cases where there would be no basis for a declaration of ineligibility, but nevertheless the stand-by should be terminated.

The provision for stand-by arrangements for more than six months was first utilized in February 1954, when an arrangement for one year was agreed with Peru. The special conditions incorporated in this arrangement are discussed later in this chapter.[5] Here we should note that the arrangement with Peru set a precedent by including as a requirement the offer made by Finland, viz., that drawings under it should be repurchased within three years instead of "within an outside range of three to five years" as prescribed in the decision of February 13, 1952.

It has not been possible to trace a connection between the undertaking offered by Finland and that required of Peru. On the contrary, the immediate reason for stipulating that Peru should complete repurchase within three years appears to have been that Peru had negotiated an arrangement with the U.S. Government parallel to the stand-by arrangement with the Fund, and the U.S. authorities required drawings under that arrangement to be repaid within three years. Mr. de Largentaye (France) suggested, when the Board discussed Peru's request, that it should be possible for Peru to repurchase more quickly than in three years, since it had a fluctuating exchange rate, which should enable it to rectify its balance of payments more quickly. But Mr. Southard (United States) urged

---

[4] E.B. Decision No. 270-(53/95), December 23, 1953; below, Vol. III, p. 231.

[5] Below, p. 478.

that it would be better for the obligations to the Fund and to the United States to be similar, and the Board agreed.

There has been no formal decision by the Board stipulating that repurchases of drawings under stand-by arrangements should be completed within three years, but this has, in fact, been the practice in all subsequent arrangements. It has been rationalized as follows. Drawings under a stand-by arrangement may take place at any time up to a year from the date when the arrangement is agreed, while the Fund's commitment begins as soon as the arrangement comes into force. It is therefore desirable that repurchases should be completed within a shorter time than five years, so that the total time that elapses between the date of the Fund's commitment and the date when repurchase is completed shall not exceed five years. To require drawings to be repurchased within three years ensures, in the circumstances envisaged, that the Fund's position will be fully restored within four years—i.e., by the mid-point of the period of three to five years applicable to drawings not made under a stand-by arrangement.

STABILIZATION PROGRAMS

Before detailing the process by which stand-by arrangements have been adapted to the varying circumstances of members, and especially to the support of stabilization programs, we should consider briefly the value of stabilization programs in encouraging progress toward the Fund's objectives.

It has been the experience of the Fund that in most of its member countries the need for a stable financial base is recognized, and that repeated efforts are made to bring about and maintain this stability. The generic term *stabilization program* is used for such efforts when concerted with the Fund, although this is, in fact, a partial misnomer: the aim both of the country and of the Fund is steady development, not stabilization of the current situation.

PURPOSES

Stabilization programs supported by the Fund have been designed to cope with a great variety of balance of payments difficulties and internal financial problems. The policies incorporated in such programs have naturally differed according to the source and duration of these difficulties and the magnitude of the problems involved. Frequently the foreign exchange reserves held by member countries have been too low to absorb pressures on their payments position arising from temporary or seasonal variations in export earnings. Such variations may follow, for example, a decline in export prices, or a decline in domestic production for export resulting from a drought or some other factors beyond the control of the authorities. In such instances, the stabilization programs adopted have been able to be limited to short-term correctives.

In many countries, however, the problems have been more serious and more complex, especially where the balance of payments difficulties have resulted from persistent inflation. Excessive credit expansion to finance private investment or consumption has sometimes been an important factor in generating inflation; but large fiscal deficits financed by bank credit have been by far the most common cause of inflationary pressure. These deficits have arisen for a variety of reasons. Some have been caused by financing subsidies to producers or consumers through the budget. Others have arisen from increases in the operating losses of public enterprises or from increases in public investment expenditures at a time when consumption expenditures were rising. Frequently the situation has been aggravated by serious deficiencies in the tax structure and the tax collection mechanism. Sometimes, the simultaneous occurrence of droughts or other natural calamities, political disturbances, or adverse movements in the terms of trade have further weakened the fiscal position by reducing revenues and increasing expenditures.

In some countries the process of economic development itself has generated serious pressures on the balance of payments. There has been a tendency for domestic expenditures to outstrip available resources, as countries have attempted to provide desirable public services to their growing populations and to accelerate economic growth. Development plans have frequently called for a considerable increase in public investment expenditures, but the mobilization of additional resources through taxation or other noninflationary means, to finance the rising levels of both current and investment expenditures, has proved difficult. The absence of appropriate institutions for mobilizing private savings has also been a constraining factor. In these circumstances, recourse to inflationary financing has been substantial.

Elsewhere the balance of payments difficulties have been caused by a concentration on investment in industries with a high import content but with little export potential in the near future, while agriculture and the traditional export sectors have received inadequate attention.

The objective of stabilization programs in inflationary situations has been not only to control inflation, to arrest the decline in foreign exchange reserves, and to prevent an increase in debt service, but also to sustain an improvement in the payments position and lay the foundation for sustained economic growth.

The programs have not necessarily aimed at an unchanged price level or the establishment of a balance of payments equilibrium during the period of the program. Some programs have involved a general upward adjustment of prices, resulting from exchange rate depreciation, and other measures aimed at correcting price distortions. Because most domestic prices tend to be inflexible downward, relative price adjustments have usually entailed a general rise in prices. In circumstances of severe and protracted inflation the programs have not attempted to arrest the rise in prices within one year, but to taper it off over several years.

As to the balance of payments, an essential step in formulating a program has been to examine to what extent the exchange rate needs to be adjusted to correct disparities between domestic and foreign prices. Sometimes, if the necessary financing is available, a large increase in imports is planned, in order to reduce inflationary pressures. Much more commonly, however, it has been reasonable to assume that there would be an immediate lessening of pressures on imports and other payments as aggregate demand was controlled, and as inventories built up during the inflationary period were dishoarded. Another general expectation has been that there would be a return of domestic capital that had sought refuge abroad and an increased inflow of public and private foreign capital.

PROBLEMS

A prolonged inflation derives, to a large extent, from a failure to resolve by other means the conflicting claims of different social groups, each aiming at a larger share of the national income. The retrenchment of consumption often proves to be difficult, particularly in developing countries, where public expenditures, for example on welfare, tend to increase with the growth of population and urbanization. In such a situation, not only do the distortions of the price-cost structure deepen with the passage of time, but also the antagonisms become more intransigent, magnifying the difficulty of implementing a stabilization program. The success of a stabilization program in this situation depends largely on the broad acceptance of its objectives (including an appropriate policy for incomes) by the main social, political, and economic forces in the country.

Equally important, in very difficult situations, is the continuity of action over a period of years. A program may be carried through for a year or so, but evolving political and social pressures or unexpected economic difficulties may lead to an eventual slackening of the efforts or even to a reversal of policies. These considerations underscore the obstacles which the authorities face when they feel forced to adopt a gradual attack on inflation—i.e., one which is planned to extend over several years.

The implementation of major policy changes also calls for efficient and stable administrative machinery. The most complex administrative problems have arisen in the fiscal field and have frequently prevented countries from attaining their revenue goals and controlling expenditures. Difficulties have also been experienced in collecting the government's share in the profits of public enterprises or in obtaining repayment of budgetary loans. Furthermore, when budget receipts have not materialized as planned, many governments have not been able to bring about a corresponding reduction in expenditures.

One major problem, with which the Fund is particularly concerned, is the adjustment of the exchange rate. In an acute inflationary situation it is difficult to determine the extent of the necessary change. For one thing, the increase in prices and costs resulting from a devaluation and other measures must be allowed for in determining the extent of the devaluation itself. Some countries do not realize how large an adjustment may for this reason be needed, with the result that the benefits of devaluation are largely offset by consequential price increases. Unless exports receive the stimulus needed to sustain an adequate level of activity, restrictions on imports may have to remain severe, thus perpetuating structural or price distortions. Moreover, expectations about a further change in the rate may adversely affect the movement of capital. Control over suppliers' and other short-term and medium-term foreign credits often proves extremely difficult, in both debtor and creditor countries.

STAND-BY ARRANGEMENTS: GENERAL PRINCIPLES

When introducing or pursuing a stabilization program a country often feels the need to reinforce its reserves, not necessarily for immediate disbursement but as a precaution against pressure on the balance of payments. It was to meet such needs that the Fund's stand-by arrangements were devised. Since the introduction of the technique in 1952, there have been some two hundred stand-by arrangements, most of which have been associated with stabilization programs.

In negotiating a stand-by arrangement, the Fund determines the appropriate degree of conditionality to be applied to drawings under the arrangement in accordance with the particular circumstances, and within the framework of the Fund's tranche policy. This policy, which relates to stand-by arrangements as well as to outright drawings, was described in Chapter 18.[6] In the context of the present discussion it is sufficient to refer to the basic principle of that policy, viz., that "the larger the drawing in relation to a member's quota the stronger is the justification required of the member";[7] and, further, that "requests for such drawings or stand-by arrangements [in the higher credit tranches] are likely to be favorably received where they are intended to support well-balanced and adequate programs. . . ."[8]

The choice of policy instruments for the implementation of these programs has depended not only on the problems facing the country, but also on the stage of its development and the institutional features of its economy. In order for

---

[6] See above, p. 404.

[7] *Annual Report, 1955*, pp. 84–85.

[8] *Annual Report, 1957*, p. 120.

the Fund to be assured of the effective implementation of a program, it has been necessary to formulate the appropriate policies, as far as possible, in quantitative terms. Thus the practice has developed of placing quantitative limits on the expansion of domestic credit by the central bank or the banking system or on the growth of certain types of foreign debt; or of establishing specific goals for the budgetary or balance of payments position or for the level of foreign exchange reserves during the period of the program. These quantitative limits and specific goals have at the same time provided the authorities of the country concerned with a basis for appraisal of monetary, fiscal, and balance of payments developments, which has enabled them, if necessary, to make adjustments in their policies to conform to the objectives. In such arrangements certain protective clauses (detailed below) are used; these clauses call for consultation with the Fund and frequently also for agreement on new terms in the event that the commitments expressed in quantitative terms or the other specific policy intentions of the member are not observed, or that the policies pursued do not appear to be adequate to achieve the objectives of the program. (The problems experienced in defining the factors to be quantitatively expressed are considered in Chapter 21.)

Where there is strong evidence that the problems have arisen from serious weaknesses in policy and that the member has not made reasonable efforts to cope with them, the Fund applies a high degree of conditionality. This is of particular importance if the member chooses a gradual approach to stability and if the expected price and cost increases during the period of the stand-by arrangement are likely to be incompatible with the maintenance of the existing exchange rate. In such instances, drawing rights are generally made contingent upon the observance of binding conditions expressed in quantitative terms, which may call for a flexible exchange rate policy, i.e., periodic exchange rate adjustments when certain balance of payments goals are not reached.

If the member has not yet established a par value, particular attention is given to the efforts that it is making toward the establishment of a realistic exchange rate and the early adoption of an effective par value.[9] In such a situation, it is normally required that the granting of financial assistance be preceded by a reasonably adequate exchange rate adjustment that will enable the country to make progress toward the establishment of an effective par value. In some instances, however, immediate action in the exchange field may not be feasible and a better course of action may be to make the change over time. In either event, if the balance of payments problem of the member indicates a need for continuing policy adjustments, the member has to present a detailed quantitative program and the stand-by arrangement contains an appropriate clause requiring consultation between the Fund and the member.

---

[9] E.B. Decision No. 1687-(64/22), April 22, 1964; below, Vol. III, p. 243.

From the legal point of view a stand-by arrangement embraces two documents: (1) The stand-by arrangement proper, containing certain legal clauses, is designed to fit the operation into the framework of the Articles of Agreement and the Fund's mechanism of financing. (2) The letter of intent, usually signed by the Minister of Finance and the Governor of the central bank, describes in precise terms the policies and measures comprising the stabilization program, especially in the credit, fiscal, balance of payments, and exchange fields. The letter of intent is annexed to the stand-by arrangement proper, and is referred to in the first paragraph of the latter as a "consideration." It frequently contains specific commitments on various aspects of these policies, and whenever these commitments involve legally binding undertakings which are not fulfilled, the member is not entitled to make further drawings under the stand-by arrangement until it consults with the Fund and, where necessary, agrees on new terms. During the period of the stand-by arrangement the Fund maintains close and continuing contact with the country through frequent visits by the staff. Sometimes, at the request of the member, the Fund may station one of its officials in the country as a representative accredited to the central bank or the government, or both.

PROTECTIVE CLAUSES

One of the recurrent problems in the development of the Fund's policy on stand-by arrangements has been to know how to reconcile the assurance to members of their right to draw on the Fund with the duty of the Fund to ensure that proper use will be made of its resources. The general conditions governing all stand-by arrangements, as decided in October 1952 and December 1953, left this matter open; but it will be recalled that the Board's hesitation about entering into arrangements for longer than six months stemmed from a doubt whether a member's economic situation could be foreseen for a longer period. Viewed in historical perspective it was this doubt, and the consequential provision in the December 1953 decision that for stand-by arrangements lasting longer than six months "the Fund and the member might find it appropriate to reach understandings additional to those set forth in this decision," which initiated the Fund's current policies and practices in connection with stand-by arrangements associated with stabilization programs. Such arrangements are usually concluded for periods of one year. But in the first one-year arrangement—with Peru, in 1954—a provision was included permitting the Fund to give notice of the interruption of drawing rights, although certain reservations were expressed about this provision by some Executive Directors. In the course of time, as stand-by arrangements were adopted increasingly for a period of one year and for members with fluctuating rates, uncertain economic conditions, or complex stabilization programs, the feeling persisted that protective clauses were needed to prevent improper use of the Fund's resources and to give reasonable effect to the following standard clause, which appears in all stand-by arrangements:

> In consideration of the policies and intentions set forth in the annexed letter, the International Monetary Fund agrees to this stand-by arrangement to support these policies and intentions.

The need for effective protective clauses was felt all the more strongly because the Executive Board did not wish to resort to procedures associated with ineligibility under paragraph 5 of the first and paragraph 4 of the second policy decisions on stand-by arrangements.

The "prior notice" clause

As a result of these considerations various types of clauses for stand-by arrangements have been developed. One is the "prior notice" clause, which was first used in paragraph 7 of the 1954 stand-by arrangement with Peru and was then worded as follows:

> If the Fund should indicate that developments had occurred that would no longer justify the belief that the Exchange Stabilization Program could be made effective, Peru would not draw further amounts under the stand-by arrangement before consulting the Fund and securing its consent. Under such circumstances Peru would, of course, be free to approach the Fund for financial assistance, but without relying upon the stand-by arrangement.

In presenting the proposed arrangement with Peru to the Executive Board, the management emphasized that "the proposed text of the agreement including paragraph 7 had been adapted to the particular needs of Peru" and that the management "did not want to feel that any fixed pattern had been developed for all countries as a result of the negotiations with Peru. It would not want to regard the Peruvian arrangement as constituting a standard to be followed in other cases." In the ensuing discussions most Executive Directors stressed the point that the arrangement with Peru did not establish a precedent. Mr. Southard, who strongly supported the arrangement, agreed that it would "still be understood that Fund stand-by arrangements generally should involve irrevocable lines of credit as indicated in the December 1953 decision." Nevertheless, several Executive Directors remained unconvinced that the arrangement with Peru could properly be called a stand-by arrangement; they felt that the conditions contained in paragraph 7 of the arrangement could be justified in this particular instance only because the arrangement involved a waiver of the quantitative limits on drawings set out in Article V, Section 4, of the Fund Agreement. (This refers to the provision that the Fund may grant a waiver "on terms which safeguard its interests.")

Under the "prior notice" clause, further drawing rights could be interrupted if, pursuant to a decision of the Board, the Fund gave the member notice to that effect. In most cases, the criteria for giving notice were not made explicit, but were tacitly assumed to be the observance of the policies and intentions in consideration of which the stand-by arrangement was entered into, and the observance of which would ensure that a proper use was made of the Fund's resources. The clause was included in more than thirty arrangements before the end of 1960; and in one instance, that of Bolivia, the Board decided to give notice.[10]

There have been variations in the wording of the "prior notice" clause, as the following examples indicate. A typical formulation (more general than that shown above) has been as follows:

> [The member] will have the right, unless the Fund gives [the member] prior notice to the contrary, to purchase the currencies of other members.

Or, if the clause was to become operative only after the Fund's holdings of the member's currency had reached a certain level:

> If the Fund's holdings of [the member's] currency are increased to the level described in paragraph —, [the member] will have the right, after 30 days from the date when this level is reached, to make further purchases under this arrangement unless the Fund notifies [the member] to the contrary within the period of 30 days. . . .

The details of the decision of September 17, 1958 to give notice to Bolivia under the "prior notice" clause are of some interest as showing the kind of criticism to which it was subjected. The decision was:

> 1. In December 1957 the Fund agreed to a stand-by arrangement with Bolivia to support the stabilization program of the Government of Bolivia as described in the Annex to the stand-by arrangement. During the course of 1958 there were substantial deviations from this program which have created conditions under which it is no longer possible for the Government of Bolivia to use the Fund's resources under the stand-by arrangement for the stabilization purposes indicated in the stand-by.
>
> 2. In these circumstances and in order to establish conditions under which further drawings under the stand-by arrangement will be for the purposes set forth in it, the Fund shall notify Bolivia, pursuant to paragraph 6 of the stand-by arrangement, that no further drawings may be made until the Bolivian Government and the Fund agree on terms for such further drawings.

In the course of the discussion in the Board, Mr. Luzzetti (Argentina), Alternate to Mr. Corominas-Segura, called attention to the fact that when the extension of the stand-by arrangement with Bolivia was discussed by the Board, Mr. Corominas-Segura, as Executive Director of the Fund elected by Bolivia, had objected to the text of the proposed agreement and had pointed out the

---

[10] See above, pp. 389–90.

danger of including, as part of the arrangement with the Fund, government measures which unforeseen circumstances might cause to be modified at any moment. Mr. Luzzetti wished to reiterate Mr. Corominas-Segura's position and express his concern about the way the Fund was handling the Bolivian case. He saw no reason for taking the drastic measure the staff had proposed.

The Deputy Managing Director (Mr. Cochran) commented that

> paragraph 6 of the stand-by arrangement with Bolivia provided that notice for a suspension of further drawings shall be given within 30 days of the date on which Bolivia's drawings under the stand-by reach a level of 140 per cent of quota, increased by the equivalent in Bolivian currency of US$2 million. This level was reached on September 4.

The "prior notice" clause came in for criticism also on various other occasions on the ground that it had not been incorporated in all stand-by arrangements and that when it had been adopted it had not indicated with sufficient clarity the circumstances in which it could be applied. Moreover, the "prior notice" clause gave the Fund the right to stop drawings that had not yet been requested, apparently for any reason that the Fund thought proper. When these controversial features were discussed in 1961, the Executive Board felt that this formulation did not give members an adequate assurance of their ability to draw. The staff accordingly proposed the elimination of the "prior notice" clause and the addition of the following sentence to the provision in the stand-by arrangement dealing with ineligibility (paragraph 5 of the decision of October 1, 1953 and paragraph 4 of that of December 23, 1953):

> When notice of a decision [on ineligibility] is given pursuant to clause (b) of this paragraph, the member will consult the Fund and prior to any further drawings will agree with it the terms on which such further drawings may be made.

This text was not accepted by the Board because some Executive Directors felt that there was no good reason for requiring a member to consult when it had no intention of making further drawings under the stand-by arrangement.

Discussions in the Executive Board led to the conclusion that thenceforth references to the "prior notice" clause in stand-by arrangements should be eliminated in favor of a new official formulation of Fund policy by amendment of the ineligibility provisions; but in formulating the amendment, the Board took into account the objections to the staff proposal mentioned above. The decision agreed on February 20, 1961 included the following:

> 1. There shall be added to the end of paragraph II.4 of Executive Board Decision No. 270-(53/95) the following sentence for use in all future stand-by arrangements:
>
> > When notice of a decision of formal ineligibility or of a decision to consider a proposal is given pursuant to this paragraph, purchases under this stand-by arrangement will be resumed only after consultation has taken place between

the Fund and the member and agreement has been reached on the terms for the resumption of such purchases.

2. "Prior notice" provisions appearing in existing stand-by arrangements, except for the one approved [for Yugoslavia] shall be understood as if the sentence set forth in paragraph 1 above were substituted for such provisions.[11]

By this decision, the "prior notice" clause was replaced by a clause which called for "consultation and agreement" on new terms when a member had become unable to draw, either because it had become ineligible or because the Board had decided to consider a proposal that the member be declared ineligible. At the time when the decision was taken there were seventeen stand-by arrangements in effect which contained "prior notice" clauses in the old form. In all instances but one the new decision involved no disadvantage to the members. An exception had, however, to be made for the stand-by arrangement with Yugoslavia, because in agreement with Yugoslavia the standards for the application of the "prior notice" clause in that arrangement had been spelled out in detail, and an amendment of these precise provisions might have been regarded as an action detrimental to Yugoslavia's interests.

PHASING OF DRAWING RIGHTS

Very soon after one-year stand-by arrangements began to be approved, the practice was developed of relating drawings under the arrangements not only to the implementation of certain policies, but also to the period of time during which the need for using the Fund's resources might be experienced.

This new technique was used for the first time in a stand-by arrangement with Chile, approved by the Executive Board in March 1956, which was the first arrangement granted in support of a comprehensive stabilization program. At that time the Chilean exchange system was being modified to include two free markets with fluctuating rates, viz., (1) a banking free market for permitted imports and exports and associated invisibles and government transactions, and (2) a brokers' free market for transactions not permitted in the banking free market. Paragraph 1 of the stand-by arrangement, containing a general outline of the stabilization program, stated inter alia:

> Chile is undertaking a comprehensive economic stabilization program which includes certain fundamental changes in its exchange system approved by the Fund March 2, 1956. Steps have already been taken toward breaking the wage-price spiral by enactment of legislation providing for the eventual discontinuation of the automatic wage and salary adjustments in relation to changes in the cost of living. Quantitative ceilings have been established on the permissible expansion in bank credit and steps have been taken to limit the use of Central Bank rediscount facilities. The Government of Chile intends to maintain firmly this new restrictive credit policy. As an essential part of the over-all stabilization effort,

---

[11] E.B. Decision No. 1151-(61/6), February 20, 1961; below, Vol. III, p. 234.

the Government intends to take measures to increase revenue and reduce public expenditures. . . . The Government of Chile realizes that the success of the stabilization program requires continued efforts to reduce further the budgetary deficit.

The Fund agreed "in consideration of the stabilization policies and intentions of the Government of Chile" to a stand-by arrangement whereby up to $35 million could be drawn during the period of a year beginning April 1, 1956. Chile's quota in the Fund at that time was $50 million. The right to draw under the stand-by arrangement was, however, subject to certain conditions which were contained in paragraphs 5 and 6 of the arrangement. In essence, these conditions were that after drawings under the stand-by arrangement had reached an amount of $12.5 million further drawings could not exceed, without the consent of the Fund, an amount of $6.25 million within any thirty-day period.

Parallel arrangements made by the U.S. Treasury and various commercial banks provided supplementary credits of $75 million in support of Chile's stabilization program.

In the Board discussion several Executive Directors stressed the point that the arrangement should not be regarded as a precedent. As Mr. Luna-Guerra (Mexico) put it, there was no doubt, to his way of thinking, that the conditions attached to the stand-by arrangement modified the generic and essential features of an irrevocable line of credit intended in the original decision, to convert it into a *sui generis* contract suitable to the specific circumstances in the Chilean case.

Although it cannot be said that the arrangement with Chile was intended to set a pattern for future stand-by arrangements associated with stabilization programs, it did, in fact, initiate the process of adapting the stand-by techniques to the implementation of such programs and of developing the policy instruments used in the supervision of such programs by the Fund.

In the following two years phasing was used infrequently, but since the middle of 1958 phasing clauses have been included in the majority of stand-by arrangements, especially those with Latin American countries: of 141 stand-by arrangements approved between the end of 1957 and the end of 1965, 117 included phasing clauses. In the latter part of this period the use of phasing was even more common: of 101 stand-by arrangements approved between the end of 1960 and the end of 1965, 89 included phasing clauses. The 12 stand-by agreements without phasing which were approved during that period involved only six countries (Iceland, Japan, Pakistan, the Philippines, the United Kingdom, and the United States). In these arrangements the circumstances were such that either the whole amount of the stand-by credit should be available to the members at any time during the period of the arrangement, if needed, or the amount of the drawing was very small or fell within the first credit tranche.

The amounts available for drawings under each phase of a stand-by arrangement have been determined in accordance with the needs of each particular program. In many instances a large proportion of the total amount of the stand-by arrangement has been made available for drawing within a relatively short period. Some typical examples of phasing clauses are shown below to illustrate this point:

(A) Clause limiting amounts of purchases in any thirty-day period (without cumulation):

> For a period of one year from _____ [the member] will have the right . . . to purchase from the Fund the currencies of other members in exchange for its own currency in an amount equivalent to US$__ provided that purchases under the stand-by arrangement shall not, without the consent of the Fund, exceed the equivalent of US$__ within any thirty days.

(B) Clause limiting amounts of purchases in any ninety-day period (without cumulation):

> For a period of one year from _____ [the member] will have the right . . . to purchase the currencies of other members from the Fund in exchange for its own currency in an amount equivalent to US$__ provided that purchases under this stand-by arrangement shall not, without the consent of the Fund, exceed the equivalent of US$__ in any ninety-day period.

(C) Clause limiting amounts of purchases in any three months and permitting cumulation:

> For a period of one year from _____ [the member] will have the right . . . to purchase the currencies of other members from the Fund in exchange for its own currency in an amount of US$__; provided that purchases under this stand-by arrangement shall not, without the consent of the Fund, exceed the equivalent of US$__ in the first three months of the stand-by arrangement and a cumulative total equivalent to US$__ for each subsequent ninety-day period.

(D) Clause limiting amounts of purchases per month and permitting cumulation:

> For a period of one year from _____ [the member] will have the right . . . to purchase the currencies of other members from the Fund in exchange for its own currency in an amount of US$__; provided that purchases under this stand-by arrangement shall not, without the consent of the Fund, exceed at any time a cumulative total equivalent to US$__ plus US$__ per month. . . .

(E) Clause limiting amount of purchases by specified time periods:

> For a period of one year from _____ [the member] will have the right . . . to purchase the currencies of other members from the Fund in exchange for its own currency in an amount equivalent to US$__; provided that purchases under this stand-by arrangement shall not, without the consent of the Fund, exceed the equivalent of US$__ in the first three months, US$__ in the first six months, and US$__ in the first nine months.

An analysis of stand-by arrangements approved between the end of 1960 and the end of 1965 that included phasing shows that in 40 per cent of these arrangements, 50 per cent or more of the amount could be drawn immediately; in 82 per cent of them, 50 per cent or more of the amount could be drawn within three months; and in 83 per cent of them, 75 per cent or more of the amount could be drawn within six months. Moreover, it should be noted that all stand-by arrangements permit acceleration of the use of resources if the member requests it and the Fund agrees.

"BINDING" PERFORMANCE CONDITIONS

By the time the "prior notice" clause was abandoned, another type of technique had come into use which made drawings under stand-by arrangements dependent on the observance of certain specified policies, frequently expressed in quantitative terms. This technique (which is usually combined with the phasing of drawing rights) involves an undertaking by members committed to such "objective" policies as limiting credit to a fixed amount or maintaining specified reserve requirements, that if they should deviate from those policies they would not request drawings under the stand-by arrangement without first consulting the Fund and agreeing on new terms for further drawings. This type of clause, based on the "additional understandings" provision in the second policy decision on stand-by arrangements quoted above, has appeared, according to the member's preference, either in the text of the stand-by arrangement or in the annexed letter of intent. Whichever alternative was adopted, appropriate cross references have been made in the relevant provisions of the arrangement.

The practice of making some of the policy intentions legally binding originated in stand-by arrangements with Latin American countries, and has evolved gradually. The first stand-by arrangement in which binding policy commitments in the credit and fiscal fields (expressed in quantitative terms) were included was that with Paraguay, approved by the Executive Board on July 29, 1957. This arrangement included the following two clauses:

> If, at any time before January 1, 1958, the credit ceiling as described in _____ is exceeded, Paraguay will not draw further amounts under this stand-by arrangement before consulting the Fund and obtaining its consent.

and

> If, at any time before January 1, 1958, the Government of Paraguay exceeds the maximum commitment level for ordinary budget expenditures or the maximum level for the implementation of the four-year public works program as described in the annexed Report, Paraguay will not draw further amounts under this stand-by arrangement before consulting the Fund and obtaining its consent.

A number of Executive Directors expressed misgivings about the inclusion of such specific performance conditions in the proposed arrangement. Mr. Thorold

(United Kingdom) stated that he "would wish the record to show that the decision taken was on the merits of the particular case and was not to be regarded as a precedent for general application," but did not press for the deletion of these provisions. Several other Directors expressed similar views. Mr. Southard, who favored the inclusion of these specific conditions, stated that in the light of its experience the Fund had learned the advisability of adjusting the terms of its stand-by arrangements to the situation of each country and to the circumstances in which the situation had developed. He emphasized the point that the Paraguayan authorities and the Fund had examined the practical situation and concluded that these provisions were essential and that if the authorities were unable to meet them they would consult with the Fund. Following the discussion, the arrangement with Paraguay (which required a waiver under Article V, Section 4, of the Fund Agreement) was approved by the Board.

A subsequent stand-by arrangement with Haiti, approved by the Executive Board about a year later, contained a wider range of specific policy commitments, including the following clause:

> If Haiti, without consultation and agreement with the Fund, departs from the budgetary or credit or other policies and intentions set forth in the annexed letter, Haiti will not draw further amounts under this stand-by arrangement before consulting the Fund and agreeing with it the terms on which further drawings may be made.

Several Executive Directors again expressed misgivings about the conditions attached to the arrangement. Mr. Luzzetti stated that Mr. Corominas-Segura, for whom he spoke, wished to reserve his position with respect to the specific conditions recommended by the staff. Mr. Hockin (Canada) objected to the particularly detailed nature of the specific conditions in the monetary and fiscal fields which, he felt, "went too far, involving as it did judgments of specific detail which the Board had not discussed." After further debate, in which Mr. Southard supported the arrangement, the Chairman (Mr. Jacobsson) expressed his feeling that there was a definite advantage in having the members submit a detailed program. He added that if the member felt that it would not be able to meet a particular commitment, the staff would submit its recommendations to the management, which in turn would bring any proposal for a major change to the Board for its consideration.

The Board discussions mentioned above illustrate the point that binding specific performance conditions for drawings under stand-by arrangements in their early days had to be defended against the charge that they were not in accordance with the concept of an assured line of credit. It was, therefore, considered advisable to make it clear that if there was a deviation from a condition, this did not necessarily mean that there was no possibility of making further drawings during the remaining period of the stand-by arrangement. For this reason, it was made explicit that the member could resume drawings if it consulted and agreed on new terms. The "consult and agree" clause itself did not interrupt drawings because the interruption of drawing rights had already occurred as a result of the deviation from a condition. The main purpose of the clause was, therefore, at that time to draw attention to the possibility of restoring drawing rights.

The use of legally binding specific performance conditions in stand-by arrangements spread quickly. Since 1959 most stand-by arrangements in the higher credit tranches (and even some arrangements confined to the first credit tranche) have included specific policy commitments and an appropriate protective clause which refers to these commitments. This clause, as included in letters of intent, has been most frequently worded as follows:

> During any period in which [the specified limits are exceeded, etc.] [the member] will not request any further drawing under the stand-by arrangement, except after consulting with the Fund and agreeing with it on the terms on which further drawings may be made.

Sometimes, in addition to the above clause, which is designed to interrupt drawings when specific commitments are not observed, another clause is included, in the stand-by arrangement itself, which calls for "consultation and agreement" with the Fund on terms for further drawings when the total drawn reaches a specified amount or increases the Fund's holdings of the member's currency to a certain level, as shown in the following examples:

> . . . when purchases under this stand-by arrangement reach a total equivalent to US$__ million [the member] will consult the Fund and agree with it on the terms for further purchases under this arrangement.

or

> If . . . the Fund's holdings of [the member's currency] are increased to _____ per cent of the present quota, [the member] will consult with the Fund before requesting any further purchases under this arrangement and will agree with it on the terms on which such further purchases may be made.

The specific policies referred to in stand-by arrangements have varied widely in numbers and range of coverage. In addition to a ceiling (or a number of ceilings) on the domestic assets of the central bank, they have frequently included fiscal, exchange rate, and balance of payments policies. There has been a tendency toward the proliferation of specific limitations and targets, especially in stand-by arrangements with certain Latin American countries which have adopted a gradual approach toward stabilization. When a stabilization program is aimed only at a deceleration of the inflationary process, it has been necessary to maintain a flexible exchange rate policy based on certain balance of payments tests and the achievement of certain net foreign exchange reserve targets. In such arrangements, failure to observe the net foreign exchange reserve target generally carries only the standard obligation "not to request any further drawing under the stand-by arrangement, except after consulting with the Fund and agreeing with it on the terms on which further drawings may be made." The link of the balance of payments performance test with exchange rate flexibility is provided by the declared intention of the authorities concerning their exchange rate policy. For example, in a stand-by arrangement with Brazil, approved by the Board on February 2, 1966, the letter of intent included the following statement:

> The Brazilian Government intends to maintain the unification of the exchange rate structure achieved in 1965 and it intends to continue to place major reliance on the exchange rate to achieve a sound improvement in its balance of payments and foreign exchange reserve position. Accordingly the exchange rates quoted by the Central Bank and the Bank of Brazil will follow the fundamental market trends. . . . (b) In carrying out its policy with regard to foreign exchange commitments, the authorities will ensure that their net foreign exchange assets at the end of each month in 1966 will be, in U.S. dollar terms, equal to, or higher than, those existing at the end of October 1965. . . .

In some arrangements, however, an explicit link between the balance of payments performance and the exchange rate policy has not been established. For instance, in the letter of intent provided by Paraguay in connection with a stand-by arrangement approved by the Board on November 20, 1964, it was stated that

> the Paraguayan authorities believe that the policies described in this letter will be sufficient to avoid an over-all balance of payments deficit during the forthcoming year, although seasonal fluctuations are expected in the level of the international reserves. Accordingly, during the period of the requested stand-by arrangement it will be their policy to avoid a reduction of more than $3.5 million in the net international reserves of the Central Bank below the level of October 23, 1964. . . .

The letter of intent attached to a stand-by arrangement with Colombia, approved by the Board on December 15, 1965, unlike others before, included a specific reference to what could appropriately be done after failure of a quarterly balance of payments test:

> Any shortfalls from the balance of payments targets for 1966 described in paragraph 6 above will be corrected as quickly as possible by (i) appropriate adjustments of the exchange rate in the intermediate official market; (ii) shifts of payments from the preferential to the intermediate official selling rate; (iii) increases in tariff duties; or (iv) any combination of these measures. Also, monetary policies could be tightened more than is contemplated in paragraph 9 below.

Circumstances in Colombia and Paraguay, however, were somewhat different from those considered above, in that inflation was less acute and the stabilization program could conceivably be implemented without exchange rate adjustment.

(There was disagreement on this point between the staff and the authorities of the countries concerned.)

THE "MAJOR SHIFT" CLAUSE

Following the rejection of the "prior notice" clause by the Board, another technique was developed to fill the gap resulting from the fact that not all policies can be made the subject of specific "objective" conditions. In contrast to the discarded "prior notice" clause, the "major shift" clause which was then introduced has not been given legal force.

In the letter of intent provided in connection with a stand-by arrangement approved by the Board on April 26, 1961, Australia stated:

> Should any major shift in the direction or emphasis of policy become necessary during the currency of the stand-by arrangement the Australian Government would, at the request of the Managing Director, be ready to consult with the Fund and, if necessary, reach new understandings before any request for a further drawing under the stand-by arrangement is made.

The arrangement with Australia and certain other arrangements in which the "major shift" clause has been used did not contain any "objective" conditions, and originally the clause was undoubtedly intended to be a moral equivalent for those conditions. However, sometimes the clause has been used also in stand-by arrangements which contained numerous "objective" performance conditions. There has even been a tendency to stiffen the clause in some cases. For example, in the letter of intent annexed to the stand-by arrangement with Chile, approved by the Board on February 14, 1964, the clause was worded as follows:

> Should any major shift in the direction or emphasis of any of the policies outlined in this letter become necessary during the period of the requested stand-by arrangement, the Government of Chile will consult with the International Monetary Fund and, if necessary, reach new understandings before any request for a drawing under the stand-by arrangement is made.

In the stand-by arrangement with the United Kingdom approved by the Board on July 27, 1964, the formulation was substantially the one quoted above for Australia. The staff memorandum contained the following explanation:

> The staff's understanding of this formulation is that the member will inform the Fund of any major shift, whatever may be the reason for it. In addition, the staff understands that the member would give the Managing Director such information in sufficient time to enable him to decide whether to request consultation in accordance with the paragraph.

This type of clause calls for consultation if there is a "major shift" of policy, whether or not the member intends to draw again. This is a reasonable requirement in view of the serious implications of a major shift of policy, particularly if there are no "objective" performance conditions that bring about an automatic interruption of drawings. More recently, however, the "major shift" clause has been subject to criticism because of the difficulty of deciding what constitutes a major shift in policy. Although in 1965 the clause was still being used, it was tending to give way to another type of clause which called for consultation when the objectives of the program were not achieved rather than when a shift in policies occurred.

If the amount made available under the stand-by arrangement did not exceed the amount of the first credit tranche, it became the practice to include two clauses, as follows:

(A) If at any time during the period of the stand-by arrangement (*a*) the limits specified in paragraphs _____ of this letter are exceeded, or (*b*) the intentions set forth in paragraphs _____ of this letter are not carried out, the Government of [the member] will consult with the International Monetary Fund regarding measures to be adopted in order to achieve the objectives of the program described above.

(B) If in the opinion of [the member] Government or the Managing Director the policies outlined in this letter turn out to be inadequate to achieve the objectives of the program described above, the Government of [the member] will consult with the International Monetary Fund regarding additional measures to be adopted in order to achieve the objectives of the program of [the member] described above.

Thus , if the amount available under a stand-by arrangement would not raise the Fund's holdings of the member's currency above the first credit tranche, the member's obligation, should the specified limits be exceeded, was to consult the Fund on ways in which to improve its program. In stand-by arrangements above the first credit tranche, on the other hand, the observance of specific policy commitments was normally made binding: if the member deviated from the quantitative limits or targets or other policies specified, it had to consult with the Fund prior to any further drawings and agree with it on the terms on which such further drawings might be made. In addition, the clause shown above in paragraph (B) was used in such arrangements.

Table 24. Stand-By Arrangements Inaugurated or Renewed, Calendar Years 1952–65 [1]

(In millions of U.S. dollars)

Member	1952	1953	1954	1955	1956	1957	1958	1959	1960	1961	1962	1963	1964	1965
Afghanistan	•	•	•	•	—	—	—	—	—	—	—	—	—	6.7
Argentina	•	•	•	•	—	—	75.0	100.0	100.0	100.0	100.0	100.0	—	—
Australia	—	—	50.0*	50.0	50.0	—	—	—	100.0	100.0	—	—	—	—
Belgium	50.0*	50.0*	—	—	—	—	—	—	—	—	10.0	10.0	12.0	—
Bolivia	—	—	—	—	7.5	3.5	3.5*	1.5	1.5*	7.5	—	—	—	14.0
Brazil	•	•	•	•	•	—	37.5	—	—	160.0	—	—	—	125.0
Burundi	—	—	—	—	—	—	—	•	•	•	•	—	—	4.0
Ceylon	—	—	—	—	35.0	35.0	10.0	—	—	75.0	—	40.0	25.0	30.0
Chile	—	—	—	—	—	25.0	—	8.1*	—	—	10.0	52.5	10.0	36.0
Colombia	—	—	—	—	—	—	15.0	41.2	75.0	—	—	—	—	—
Costa Rica	—	—	—	—	12.5*	—	—	—	—	15.0	11.6	—	—	10.0
Cuba	•	•	•	•	—	—	—	—	—	—	—	—	25.0	•
Dominican Rep.	—	—	—	—	—	—	—	11.2	—	—	—	—	13.0	—
Ecuador	—	—	—	—	—	—	—	—	—	10.0	5.0	6.0	—	12.0
El Salvador	—	—	—	—	—	—	7.5*	7.5*	11.2*	11.2	11.2	5.0	—	20.0
Finland	5.0*	—	—	—	—	—	—	—	—	—	—	—	—	—
France	—	—	—	—	262.5	—	131.2	—	—	—	—	—	—	—
Guatemala	—	—	—	—	—	—	—	—	15.0	15.0	6.0	4.0	4.0	—
Haiti	•	—	—	—	—	—	5.0	4.0	6.0	6.0	7.5	7.5	7.5	4.0
Honduras	—	—	—	—	—	3.7*	—	4.5	7.5	7.5	—	—	—	—
Iceland	—	—	—	—	—	—	—	—	5.6	1.6*	1.6	—	—	—
India	—	—	—	—	—	72.5	—	—	—	—	100.0	100.0	—	200.0
Indonesia	•	•	—	—	—	—	—	—	—	41.2	100.0	50.0	—	—
Iran	—	•	—	—	17.5*	—	—	•	35.0	35.0	•	—	—	—
Jamaica	•	•	•	•	•	•	•	•	•	•	•	10.0	—	—

Japan	—	—	—	—	—	—	—	—	—	—	305.0	—	305.0	—
Korea	•	•	•	—	—	—	—	—	—	—	—	—	—	9.3
Liberia	•	•	•	•	•	•	•	•	•	•	—	5.7	4.4	4.0
Mali	•	—	•	•	•	•	•	•	•	•	•	—	9.9	—
Mexico	•	•	50.0*	50.0	•	—	—	90.0*	—	90.0	—	—	—	—
Morocco	•	•	•	•	•	68.7	—	25.0	—	—	—	—	—	45.0
Netherlands	—	—	—	—	—	7.5*	—	—	—	—	—	—	—	—
Nicaragua	—	—	—	—	3.7*	—	7.5*	—	7.5	—	—	11.2	11.2	—
Pakistan	—	—	—	—	—	—	25.0	—	—	—	—	—	—	37.5
Panama	—	—	—	—	—	—	—	—	—	—	—	—	—	7.0
Paraguay	—	—	—	—	—	5.5	1.5	2.7	3.5	5.0	5.0*	—	5.0	—
Peru	—	—	12.5	12.5	12.5	12.5	25.0	13.0	27.5	30.0	30.0	30.0	30.0	30.0
Philippines	—	•	—	—	—	—	—	—	—	40.4	40.4	40.4	40.4	40.4
Somalia	•	•	•	•	•	•	•	•	•	•	—	—	4.7	5.6
South Africa	—	—	—	—	—	—	25.0	—	—	75.0	—	—	—	—
Spain	•	•	•	•	•	•	—	25.0	25.0	—	—	—	—	—
Syrian Arab Rep.	•	•	—	—	•	•	—	—	7.5*	—	6.6*	—	18.5*	—
Tunisia	•	•	•	—	—	—	—	—	—	37.5	—	—	14.2	5.6
Turkey	—	—	—	—	—	—	—	—	—	37.5	31.0*	21.5*	21.5*	21.5*
United Arab Rep.	—	—	—	—	—	—	—	—	—	—	42.5	—	40.0	—
United Kingdom	—	—	—	—	738.5	738.5	738.5	—	—	500.0	1,000.0	1,000.0	1,000.0	—
United States	—	—	—	—	—	738.5	738.5	—	—	1,000.0	1,000.0	—	500.0	—
Uruguay	—	—	—	—	—	—	—	—	—	30.0	30.0	—	—	—
Venezuela	—	—	—	—	—	—	—	—	100.0	—	—	—	—	—
Yugoslavia	—	—	—	—	—	—	—	—	—	30.0	—	—	—	80.0

¹ A dot (•) indicates that the country was not a member at the time; a dash (—) indicates that no stand-by arrangement was in effect; an asterisk (*) indicates that the stand-by arrangement was for less than one year (usually for six months).

CHAPTER

21

Factors in Stabilization Programs

Emil G. Spitzer

T HE PURPOSES OF STABILIZATION PROGRAMS and the evolution of stand-by arrangements as a means by which the Fund is able to assist members undertaking such programs have been described in Chapter 20. It has been shown that in considering members' proposals, the Fund focuses attention on certain critical factors by which the success of a program can be tested.

The main considerations in the selection of the criteria of performance have been (1) that they are capable of being expressed in quantitative or objective terms, (2) that actual performance can be compared with the criteria without delay due to time lags, and (3) that the criteria are significant enough to serve as a basis for an appraisal of the economy as a whole. The present chapter examines typical policy objectives in detail and describes the difficulties experienced in defining them.

CREDIT CONTROLS

DOMESTIC CREDIT CEILINGS

In the majority of financial programs the control of domestic bank credit has been of particular importance. The major instrument used for this purpose is a ceiling on the expansion of the domestic assets of the central bank during the period of the stand-by arrangement. An over-all ceiling is capable of being defined and administered easily; it also has the advantage of providing operational flexibility to the central bank. Frequently, however, separate ceilings have been applied to different categories of central bank credit. For example, in some programs there has been one ceiling on credit to the government and another on credit to the private sector; when budget deficits have been the primary cause of financial instability, this has been useful in indicating the magnitude of the government's share in the total credit expansion. Sometimes there are separate ceilings for central bank credit to the government, to various official agencies or state-owned enterprises, and to the banking system; the use of this technique has been based on the view that separate ceilings on each major category of central bank credit would facilitate the control of over-all credit expansion. Sometimes ceilings on credit to particular official agencies have been not so much an element in the over-all program of credit control as a means of encouraging changes in the financial operations and pricing policies of the agencies concerned or of ensuring that compliance with the over-all ceiling does not involve undue restraint on credit to the private sector.

Credit ceilings have frequently been phased in order to take account of seasonal changes in the demand for bank credit; it has also been necessary to provide some accommodation for the government where revenues or expenditures are subject to significant seasonal variation.

A ceiling on the domestic assets of the central bank has usually been supplemented by provisions regarding the policy to be followed in respect of changes in the legal requirements governing the minimum reserves of the commercial banks. Where, at the beginning of a program, the commercial banks were in a highly liquid position, programs have provided for an increase in reserve requirements in order to reduce excess liquidity and keep the expansion of credit within the desired limit. In some other programs, marginal reserve requirements (i.e., requirements applying only to an expansion of bank deposits after a certain date) have been introduced to increase the control over monetary expansion. On some occasions the amount of rediscounts to the commercial banks has been limited, in order to achieve the desired effect on commercial bank credit. Some programs, however, have aimed at a more comprehensive control of credit by establishing additional ceilings on commercial bank credit to the government or even broader limits on government indebtedness to commercial banks and to the private sector.

Provisions of a more selective nature, regulating the flow of credit to particular purposes or industries, have been part of a number of programs but only rarely have they been quantified. The central bank has exercised such selective controls either by establishing quantitative limits on the amount of the various types of bills which are eligible for rediscounting or by changing the eligibility requirements, or by fixing subceilings for credits to particular industries or purposes under the broader ceiling on credit to the private sector.

In some situations an increase in the central bank's rediscount rate has been used as a supplement to quantitative limits on the supply of credit. However, where the rate of inflation is rapid, it is difficult to use interest rate policy as a credit control device; in such conditions, an adequate interest rate in real terms would necessitate a very considerable increase in the nominal interest rate.

The policy instruments mentioned above are aimed at controlling the total expansion of bank credit indirectly by reducing the liquidity of the commercial banks. Because of particular institutional arrangements, some countries have preferred to regulate the amount of credit extended by the banking system as a whole. This regulation has taken different forms, depending largely upon the degree of flexibility desired by the monetary authorities and the legal powers they possess for controlling commercial bank operations. For example, in some programs a ceiling has been placed on total credit extended by the banking system. In others, a ceiling has been placed on credit extended by the commercial banks, either with or without a ceiling on credit by the central bank. In some circumstances a ceiling has been established for each bank, allowing it to expand its lending by a specified percentage over the level existing as of a base date.

The choice between a ceiling on credit of the banking system as a whole and a ceiling on central bank credit only is influenced largely by institutional factors. Use of the former has usually been confined to countries where commercial banks are relatively few in number and are subject to strong central bank control. Another important consideration in deciding whether a ceiling should cover commercial bank assets has been the promptness with which the relevant data become available. Credit ceilings covering commercial bank credit may prove ineffective as a guide to policy if there are substantial lags in reporting data.

In the formulation of credit ceilings, various problems have arisen with regard to the inclusion or exclusion of certain central bank assets. The practice of covering credit to the central government, to state and local governments where applicable, and to other official entities has been fairly uniform. Further, the inclusion in credit ceilings of loans or discounts to commercial banks and other banking institutions, such as development banks and agricultural banks, has posed no particular problem. In many countries central banks do not lend directly to the private sector, but where they do (i.e., where they engage in commercial banking activities) the ceilings have covered such credit.

In several instances credit for the marketing of major agricultural crops has had to be excluded from domestic credit ceilings because the financial requirements depended on the size of the crops and therefore could not be predicted. For example, in a program for Ceylon the ceiling excluded finance for rice marketing, and in a program for Ghana it excluded financing of cocoa purchases by the Cocoa Marketing Board. In several other programs (e.g., those for the Sudan and the United Arab Republic), such problems have led to the establishment of separate ceilings on the financing of agricultural crops. The advantage of this technique is that it prevents the use of such credit for other purposes. Sometimes the letter of intent has specified the estimated size of the agricultural crop on which the ceiling on marketing finance is based and has provided for an adjustment in the ceiling, if necessary, after consultation and agreement with the Fund.

In the majority of programs, domestic credit ceilings have not covered items which in the balance sheets of the central bank are included in "other assets" (fixed assets, etc.). The smallness of such "other assets" has been sufficient reason for their exclusion. In addition, delays in the availability of data covering "other assets" and their tendency to exhibit random short-term fluctuations would have complicated the task of setting ceilings.

With regard to the coverage of central bank assets, it should be noted that two different approaches have been adopted in defining the assets subject to domestic credit ceilings. The more common method, called the "selected assets" approach, has been to specify for inclusion certain balance sheet items which cover the main domestic assets of the central bank. The alternative method, the "residual" approach, has been to define domestic assets as the difference between the total assets of the central bank and specified assets, primarily foreign assets, which have been excluded from the ceiling. The "residual" approach has been used mainly in programs for countries in the Western Hemisphere. Both the "selected" and the "residual" approach have also been applied to the liability side of the balance sheet. Where the "residual" approach has been adopted on both sides of the balance sheet, the ceiling has sometimes been defined as the difference between the currency issue and the net foreign assets of the central bank.

"Residual" ceilings have tended to be more comprehensive, covering in most cases "other assets" as well as the main credit operations of the central bank. The main argument for adopting the "residual" approach has been that it is likely to reduce the chances of credit being extended outside the coverage of the ceiling; any new type of domestic operation of the central bank, unforeseen at the time of the establishment of the ceiling, is automatically covered. On the other hand, ceilings on "selected assets" have usually been more meaningful to the authorities of the country concerned; when the ceilings are applied to such specific central bank assets as credit to the government and credit to the commercial banks, which are subject to the direct control of the authorities, there is a greater chance of compliance. The "residual" approach, however, does not necessarily preclude the use of additional ceilings on specific components of domestic credit. In some programs, for example, a global ceiling arrived at on a "residual" basis has been supplemented by a ceiling on credit to the government sector, or by a number of separate ceilings each covering an important component of central bank credit.

Some problems in the formulation of credit ceilings have been related to the fact that monetary expansion or contraction may result not only from movements in the domestic assets of the central bank, but also from movements in its domestic liabilities. For instance, the monetary consequences of a reduction in the government's deposits with the central bank are the same as those of an increase in the central bank's advances to the government. Netting of assets and liabilities has therefore been an important aspect of the formulation of credit ceilings.

In establishing most domestic credit ceilings, the government's deposits are netted against its liabilities to the central bank. This is not done, however, when government deposits are low, with little scope for further reduction, or when the government has given other undertakings directly related to its revenue and expenditure.

In the majority of instances, deposits of the commercial banks with the central bank have not been netted, particularly in those programs in which the ceilings have been related to over-all credit operations of the banking system, interbank claims being excluded. However, the freedom of the commercial banks to reduce their deposits with the central bank has been limited by undertakings to maintain specified reserve ratios. This has also been the practice in programs where the ceilings have been applied only to the central bank. Sometimes, commercial banks' deposits with the central bank have been excluded from the ceiling even without a commitment on reserve requirements, either because these deposits were relatively small or because an excessive expansion of commercial bank credit was considered unlikely. In some instances, these deposits have been netted because of the unsatisfactory record of the commercial banks in complying with reserve requirements. In other instances, the authorities of the country concerned have preferred this arrangement because of its greater operational flexibility compared with a commitment to maintain specified reserve requirement ratios.

Other arrangements involve the compulsory holding of deposits with the central bank. The most common practice requires the commercial banks to make advance deposits for imports. Although these deposits are maintained primarily for balance of payments reasons, they also have some monetary effects: an increase in them represents a contractionary factor while a decrease is a source of monetary expansion.

In most programs for countries with compulsory deposit arrangements such deposits have not been netted against liabilities, mainly because the amounts involved were small or were not likely to change substantially. In several programs, however, where compulsory deposits have not been so netted, they have, nevertheless, been taken into account: for example, some items, such as losses on official foreign exchange transactions, have been excluded from the ceilings in the expectation that they would be a source of monetary expansion offsetting the contractionary effects of expected increases in advance deposits for imports.

Foreign transactions

The majority of countries that have stand-by arrangements associated with stabilization programs are recipients of foreign aid as well. As the commodities imported under the various aid arrangements are sold, they generate counterpart funds which in some countries have a significant effect on the monetary situation. While counterpart funds are being accumulated the effect is contractionary, but when the funds are spent they represent a source of monetary expansion. The monetary effects of significant movements in counterpart funds are usually taken into account in the formulation of credit ceilings by netting the counterpart fund accounts. In a few countries where counterpart funds are not deposited with the central bank but with commercial banks, they have not been covered by a ceiling because the amounts involved have not been significant.

In some countries characterized by exchange rate instability, foreign exchange operations have been the source of substantial central bank profits or losses. These may be divided into two groups, those arising from the revaluation of foreign assets and foreign liabilities in connection with exchange rate adjustments, and those arising from a variety of other foreign exchange operations.

As a result of devaluing the exchange rate, the domestic currency value of the central bank's foreign assets and liabilities is increased. If the assets exceed the liabilities, a profit is earned, and if the liabilities are greater, there is a loss; but as revaluation of the assets and liabilities involves only book entries, the profits and losses arising during the period of the stand-by arrangement are not included in credit ceilings. Profits arising from revaluations may, however, pose a problem if they are transferred to the government; in the absence of provisions to the contrary, this increases the margin available for credit expansion under the ceiling. In such cases the stand-by arrangement may specify that the ceiling will be reduced by the amount of any transfer of profits from the exchange revaluation account to the government.

The other category of profits and losses arises from a variety of foreign exchange operations other than revaluations of foreign assets and liabilities. Sometimes, there have been substantial losses on swap arrangements entered into at contractual exchange rates below those prevailing at the time of repayment of the swap. Losses on liquidation of forward exchange contracts have also occurred. In a number of countries, profits or losses (generally the former), have resulted from the existence of multiple currency practices. In some countries, for instance, such practices have yielded substantial profits owing to the application of penalty exchange rates to major export items.

An important characteristic of these profits and losses is that they involve real monetary effects; they have, therefore, usually been covered by the ceiling. In some instances, while the exchange profit accounts as such have not been included, profits yielded by the exchange system have been credited directly to the government's accounts with the central bank and in this way have been covered by the ceiling. In a few instances, where exchange operations have been a source of loss, the accounting system has not permitted an accurate identification of the items involved, but it has been possible to take account of their estimated expansionary effects in constructing the ceiling.

There have usually been excluded from the ceiling domestic loans by a central bank which represent the counterpart of certain foreign loans, such as development loans from the World Bank and the Inter-American Development Bank. In these instances the central bank becomes involved in a credit operation only as an intermediary. Accordingly, the exclusion of such credit from the ceiling has the same result as if the foreign credit had been extended directly to the government or the private sector. However, for the counterpart of the loan to qualify for exclusion from the ceiling, the foreign credit must exceed a specified maturity, generally five years. This minimum maturity limit serves to ensure that exclusion from the ceiling does not extend to the lending of the counterpart of short-term foreign borrowings undertaken by the central bank for balance of payments reasons. The absence of provisions regarding the treatment of loans representing the counterpart of foreign credits channeled through the central bank has generally reflected a judgment that no such credits were likely during the period of the stand-by arrangement, rather than a different view on how they should be treated. However, if the amount of foreign credits to be channeled through the central bank is known when a financial program is drawn up, the ceiling can be set correspondingly higher and the need to provide for the exclusion of counterpart loans will not arise.

Where the government or the private sector has been engaged directly in short-term borrowing abroad, the level of the ceiling has sometimes varied inversely with the amount of foreign borrowing. Thus, the letter of intent has, for example, provided that the ceiling on credit operations of the central bank is to be reduced by the amount of any Treasury bills placed abroad. Some programs have contained provisions setting ceilings on specified forms of short-term and medium-term foreign indebtedness.

The Fund has applied such limitations where a rapid accumulation of foreign debt has threatened to disrupt financial stability and the burden of servicing has become critical, and in the context of multilateral debt renegotiations. In other instances such limitations have been applied in order to reinforce the effectiveness of domestic credit and fiscal policies. The insertion of such provisions has, however, more often been motivated by the desire to avoid external debt problems than by the need to limit domestic credit expansion.

Provisions concerning foreign debt obligations were first included in stand-by arrangements in 1958, when Argentina and Chile decided to curtail authorizations of government imports under deferred payments arrangements. While in early stand-by arrangements no quantitative commitments were undertaken, in later arrangements specific commitments were made with regard to the amount of certain categories of foreign credits that could be contracted, or for which official guarantees could be given during the period of the stand-by arrangement. Access to the Fund's resources was made contingent on the fulfillment of these commitments.

The degree of restrictiveness applied to borrowing abroad has varied considerably. The most restrictive debt limitation used in stabilization programs has been the prohibition of certain categories of foreign credits for a given period. Its effect has been to reduce the level of such foreign indebtedness by the amount of repayments falling due during the period of the stand-by arrangement. Less restrictive have been ceilings permitting new credits, but limiting them to less than net repayments (i.e., repayments less refinancing). In some other programs, ceilings on new credits equal to repayments have been used to ensure that the outstanding level of indebtedness would not increase. In some instances when this method has been used, however, the level of indebtedness has still tended to decline because disbursements have lagged behind the authorization of new credits. The least restrictive limitation on foreign credits has been one which has permitted the total outstanding debt subject to control to increase by a specified amount during the period of the program.

The prohibition of certain types of credit has been used in two situations. First, where an excessive debt servicing burden has emerged, or has threatened to emerge, as a result of a rapid accumulation of debts, a prohibition has been applied to provide a breathing spell in which the magnitude of the debt problem could be assessed and guidelines for the contracting of new debts as well as procedures for the orderly repayment of past debt obligations could be established. The second kind of prohibition has been related to the enforcement of domestic credit ceilings or the strengthening of fiscal measures. This has been necessary when the public or private sector, by borrowing abroad, has tended to circumvent a ceiling imposed on domestic credit expansion.

Sight drafts and letters of credit at the lower end of the time spectrum, and long-term credits at the upper end, have generally been excluded from limitations. The credits most frequently subjected to limitations have been short-term and medium-term suppliers' credits and, to a lesser extent, short-term bank credits not related to commercial transactions. Experience has shown that because of the relatively easier circumstances under which suppliers' credits can be obtained, fairly substantial indebtedness can be incurred in a short time. Moreover, the fact that such credits are frequently handled through private channels on both sides often conceals their magnitude from the authorities unless contingent government liabilities are involved.

Stabilization programs supported by stand-by arrangements have sometimes contained limitations on certain new foreign credits contracted by both the public and private sectors, but in most instances the limitations have been applied only to credits contracted by the government and its agencies. Credits contracted by the private sector have usually been controlled by denying them the benefit of official guarantees. For example, in Chile's 1959 stabilization program the contracting of new suppliers' credits by the public sector was prohibited, while the contracting of such credits by the private sector without official guarantee was permitted. However, in connection with Chile's 1965 multilateral debt rearrangement, the contracting of new suppliers' credits by both sectors was made subject to limitations. The 1965 and 1966 Brazilian stabilization programs prohibited the Bank of Brazil and the commercial banks from guaranteeing short-term and medium-term foreign loans unless these were used to finance foreign trade.

Unguaranteed private sector credits have been subject to reporting in some programs; this has helped the authorities to secure better information on the foreign debt situation of the private sector.

The types of suppliers' credits to be controlled have usually been identified in terms of the number of years to final maturity. The maturity limit has often been placed at eight years on the ground that this period is long enough to account for the bulk of credit transactions which are to be brought under control. The fixing of a maturity limit has, however, created some problems.

The terms traditionally applied to exports of light capital goods and durable consumer goods tend to be of shorter duration than those relating to heavy capital goods. There has been some concern that the exclusion from ceilings of long maturities geared to imports of heavy capital goods may exert pressure on suppliers to extend the terms for other types of goods beyond their typical shorter maturities. It has also been felt that limitations applied to suppliers' credits of less than a certain number of years may discriminate against suppliers who are not able to offer longer terms. The risk of curtailing competition or discriminating against certain suppliers exists in any arrangement prescribing upper time limits on credit.

Limitations on foreign credits applied for the purpose of making domestic credit controls more effective have been placed only on short-term borrowing abroad, defined as credits with maturities up to five years. Longer-term credits not subject to limitations are often extended by foreign governments or government agencies, or by international institutions after scrutiny and evaluation whereby the chances of an unduly large accumulation of such long-term debts are reduced.

Moreover, an important objective of stabilization programs is to create conditions conducive to an orderly growth of the economy, which requires the inflow of long-term capital. Consequently, far from placing limitations on the inflow of long-term capital, stabilization programs are designed to encourage the financing of development by long-term loans. Development loans usually involve relatively small debt servicing obligations in the early years because the terms of such loans usually include grace periods. Hence, there is less immediate danger of a sharp rise in debt servicing obligations resulting from long-term development loans than from short-term and medium-term suppliers' credits.

The complete prohibition of new foreign indebtedness has been regarded as an exceptional debt control procedure to be reserved for extreme situations. Even though short-term commercial credits from abroad (up to one year) are usually exempted, such prohibitions impede the financing of the movements of goods by longer-term credits. Also, domestic enterprises often depend on foreign credits for supplementing their working capital. Some degree of flexibility has been provided in some arrangements by permitting exceptions from the prohibitions through consultation with the Managing Director of the Fund. However, in dealing with such requests, difficult problems are likely to arise. For example, it may be necessary to determine whether the project to be financed will make a direct contribution to the balance of payments and whether the amortization schedule proposed is consistent with the project's earning capacity. It may also be necessary to determine whether financing at lower cost could be obtained from other sources.

Limitations aimed only at some debt reduction are less onerous. Limitations which permit the contracting of new credits up to the amount of repayments during the period of the stand-by arrangement are no more than a standstill device, designed to prevent the level of indebtedness in the restricted category from rising. For administrative and planning purposes, a limitation permitting a specified amount of new credits may be preferable to one which links the contracting of new credits to the irregular flow of repayments. Limitations permitting a certain amount of new credits to be contracted as old credits are repaid have the advantage that they enable the authorities to keep the debt situation under control without disrupting the country's established commercial relations with its creditors.

Some member countries have undertaken, with the support of the Fund, to implement a stabilization program designed to eliminate inflationary conditions at a time when their external debt was large but on the whole sustainable. Limitations on foreign credits have then been applied to strengthen confidence in the creditworthiness of the country by keeping foreign borrowing under careful control. Such limitations have not aimed at reducing foreign indebtedness but rather at restraining its rate of growth, while the main stabilization effort has been directed toward restoring domestic financial stability.

In most stabilization programs containing limitations on foreign credits these limitations have been applied to the public sector as a whole, including public enterprises. As their borrowing capacity is enhanced by the implicit or explicit guarantee of the government, public enterprises have tended to shift to foreign borrowing in order to escape the pressures exerted by domestic financial restraints. A limitation on foreign borrowing by public enterprises is therefore necessary in most instances.

Sometimes domestic credit ceilings have been adjusted for subscriptions to international organizations. This problem has arisen mostly in connection with a prospective increase in a country's quota in the Fund. If the government makes the subscription, the ceiling excludes credit to the government to finance it. If the central bank makes the subscription, there is no need for an adjustment in the ceiling as the subscription to the Fund affects only the foreign assets and liabilities of the central bank and has no effect on the ceiling on domestic assets.

In programs for some Central and South American countries, it has also been necessary to take into account in constructing the ceilings subscriptions to such international organizations as the Central American Bank for Economic Integration (CABEI) and the Inter-American Development Bank (IDB). As far as the gold or foreign exchange component of any subscription has been concerned, the view has been taken that the making of such a subscription should lessen the permissible domestic credit expansion. Accordingly, the usual practice has been to include in the ceiling the credit to the government to finance the subscription where the government rather than the central bank subscribes.

On occasions, the net position on local currency subscriptions to international organizations has been of some importance. The making of a subscription in local currency by the central bank raises both its assets and its liabilities without affecting its net position. However, the net position is affected where the international organization subsequently uses the local currency subscription to finance projects or to lend to other borrowers in the subscribing country. The use by CABEI of the local currency component of subscriptions has been an important source of monetary expansion. Accordingly, in some arrangements with members of that institution (e.g., Costa Rica, Guatemala, and Honduras) the net position on local currency subscriptions has been included in the ceiling. Sometimes the net position on local currency subscriptions to the IDB has also been included in the ceiling, but only when domestic financing from this source has been significant.

Drawings on the Fund or repurchases may have to be taken into account in the formulation of credit ceilings. In the majority of countries, such transactions are carried out by the central bank. Their effect is simply to raise the foreign assets and liabilities of the central bank, and they have no implications for credit ceilings covering domestic assets of the central bank. It makes also no difference whether the central bank records its liability to the Fund in its balance sheet as a noninterest-bearing note or as a deposit. Neither does the meeting of repurchase obligations have any implications for the credit ceiling when effected by the central bank.

In some countries, however, it is the government rather than the central bank which draws on the Fund, and the foreign exchange drawn is usually sold to the central bank for national currency. Some governments leave the proceeds on deposit with the central bank. This may reflect either a voluntary decision on the part of the authorities concerned or the requirements of the national legislation governing transactions with the Fund. In order to cover this aspect, a provision may be included in the letter of intent that the counterpart of Fund drawings will be sterilized. The alternative to leaving the currency on deposit with the central bank is for the government to substitute noninterest-bearing notes, thereby making the national currency counterpart available to the government. Where this has been the practice, one of two measures has been adopted in the relevant programs to take account of this additional source of funds to the government. In some programs where it was considered likely that the amount of drawings available under the stand-by arrangements would be fully utilized, the ceilings have been set at levels lower by this amount than they would have been if the counterpart funds had not been available to the government. Another approach has been to permit the local currency counterpart to be used to meet the needs of the government but to word the letter of intent so that, in effect, the limit on other forms of credit expansion is reduced by the amount of any use of counterpart funds. This has served to ensure that drawings on the Fund do not affect the margin for credit expansion under the ceiling but at the same time has left the government free to use the counterpart funds rather than borrow from the central bank to meet its financial needs. The need to maintain this freedom of choice may exist, for example, because of a statutory limitation on government borrowing from the central bank.

FISCAL CONTROLS

As mentioned before, major inflationary pressures frequently originate in public sector deficits. In such situations it has not been sufficient to place global ceilings on the expansion of bank credit, or separate ceilings on central bank credit to the government or the public sector as a whole. These indirect methods of controlling public finances do not go to the root of the problem; moreover, being subject to strong pressure from the government, the central bank authorities cannot always enforce these credit ceilings. Therefore, more direct fiscal measures have been stipulated in many programs (in addition to limiting access to bank credit).

In order to keep the deficit of the public sector within limits compatible with the monetary objectives, these fiscal measures have been designed to increase budgetary receipts, to reduce the growth of current or capital expenditures, and to strengthen the financial position of public enterprises.

For the most part, measures designed to increase revenue have involved additional taxation, mainly in areas where taxes can be introduced quickly and where they can be easily collected. The most common measure has been the imposition of taxes on foreign trade transactions, especially in connection with exchange rate adjustments. In situations of prolonged inflation, devaluation of the currency (or, where a multiple exchange rate system had existed, unification of the rates at a realistic level) has been a major policy instrument, frequently leading to the removal or the liberalization of restrictions on trade and payments.

Such exchange rate adjustments have often been accompanied by the introduction of new, or the increase of existing, export taxes or import subsidies. For certain primary export commodities the supply is inelastic in the short run, and devaluation may therefore generate excessive profits. An export tax designed to absorb part of these profits has frequently been imposed as a temporary measure. In some instances, the liberalization of quantitative restrictions following the unification of multiple rates has been facilitated by an increase in import duties or, pending an adjustment in the tariff structure, by the imposition of import surcharges. On the other hand, import subsidies for certain items of general consumption have sometimes been granted for a transitional period to minimize the impact of the devaluation on the cost of living; but in view of the distorting effects of import subsidies on the production and consumption of the commodities concerned, and of the burden on the budget, the use of such subsidies has been far less common.

Another frequently used tax measure has been the imposition of indirect taxes on nonessential commodities. Action in the field of direct taxation has been less frequent because it has been difficult to obtain quick and effective results. However, various programs have aimed at improvements in the income tax structure or stricter enforcement of existing income taxes, and the collection of tax arrears.

Measures to restrain the growth of government expenditures have been an important feature of many stabilization programs. For example, limits have been placed on government expenditures by establishing a ceiling on the fiscal deficit, or on current or total government spending. Sometimes also a certain revenue target has been stipulated. These measures have aimed not only at improving the current budgetary situation but also at providing additional resources for the financing of public investment expenditures. This has been done in some programs by establishing minimum targets for the achievement of savings in the public sector, i.e., minimum targets for surpluses of current revenues over current expenditures. In some instances, the program has provided that, in order to comply with the over-all credit policy, the government would refrain from initiating new investment projects unless foreign aid was actually forthcoming, or some other form of noninflationary financing was available. Sometimes new taxes have been imposed to provide the financial resources required to cover the domestic costs of investment projects without undue resort to bank financing.

In several instances an improvement in the over-all budgetary situation has been achieved by bettering the financial position of public enterprises. Some programs, for example, have introduced substantial upward adjustments in the charges for the services of various public utilities, such as electricity, gas, and water, state-owned railroads, or urban transportation, thereby reducing their dependence on budgetary support. Again, some programs have specified measures directed toward raising the efficiency of these enterprises through better management control, more efficient work rules, or the discontinuation of certain uneconomic operations.

EXCHANGE RATE ADJUSTMENT

Sometimes, where a substantial adjustment in the exchange system has been necessary, a gradual approach has been adopted to ease the problems of transition. For example, the devaluation of exchange rates to realistic levels has been carried out in more than one step; in the intervening period subsidies have been given to provide added incentives to some exports, and the demand for imports has been limited by maintaining quantitative restrictions, which have on occasion been reinforced by import surcharges. Similarly, some multiple rate systems have been gradually unified through a succession of simplifying measures.

In a number of instances, the political and administrative difficulties encountered in adjusting a highly complex exchange system have been so great that only a partial or selective adjustment could be made at the initial stage, although the ultimate objective has always been the achievement of a single realistic exchange rate. In these circumstances, the existing rate of exchange has been maintained for certain transactions such as traditional exports, essential imports, and some invisibles, while the rate for other transactions has been devalued either directly or indirectly through exchange taxes and subsidies. Alternatively, a complex multiple rate system has been simplified so as to consist of only a few rates; this has usually involved a devaluation on both the buying and selling sides through the elimination of the more appreciated rates. In general, the provision of a subsidy through the exchange system, i.e., through the maintenance of a more depreciated rate for exports than for imports, has been avoided.

Adjustment of the exchange system to a realistic single rate has not always involved the immediate establishment of a fixed rate. Many programs have provided for a fluctuating exchange rate as a temporary device, because of the difficulty of determining in advance the rate that would be appropriate after the stabilization measures have taken effect. When a combination of restrictions and multiple rates has existed, the effectiveness of the immediate measures to bring inflation under control has frequently been in doubt. A fluctuating rate used in these situations has carried with it a commitment that the rate would be allowed to move in accordance with the market forces, and that the authorities would intervene in the exchange market only to maintain orderly market conditions.

In some programs, the purpose of such a commitment was to ensure that gross foreign exchange reserves would not fall below the level maintained at the beginning of the program. The assumption was that observance of a minimum level for gross reserves would cause the exchange rate to be determined in the market, free from government intervention. This commitment was, however, not sufficiently precise and sometimes proved to be ineffective, because the gross reserve position could be improved by external borrowing. It was also very difficult to distinguish between temporary fluctuations and a long-term trend, especially in countries where export earnings are subject to wide fluctuations.

In recent years, as an alternative to fluctuating rates, exchange rate flexibility through periodic rate adjustment has been introduced in some programs which could not aim at an early restoration of stability. In several countries, inflation has been so acute and prolonged that it has not been feasible to restore financial stability in the immediate future. In such circumstances, the stabilization programs have been aimed at the gradual deceleration of inflation. Continuing domestic inflation, however, is likely to wipe out rapidly the beneficial effects of an exchange rate adjustment, and the exchange rate must therefore be adjusted periodically in order to counteract the adverse effects of domestic price increases on the balance of payments.

Experience has shown that some mutually agreed objective criteria are required to judge the compliance with the commitment on the flexibility of the exchange rate during the period of the stabilization program. Such programs have, in most instances, included certain "balance of payments tests" to ensure that official support does not cause the exchange rate to diverge significantly from the basic market trend. By these tests the minimum level at which the net foreign exchange reserves of the central bank or the banking system are to be maintained during the period of the program has been specified, thus setting limits within which the authorities would intervene in the market to smooth out fluctuations. The minimum limits to the net foreign exchange position of the monetary authorities, as defined in the arrangement, have usually been phased over the period covered by the program. The commitment not to let the net foreign exchange reserves fall below the agreed level (or levels) during the period of the program is binding, and compliance with this commitment is checked periodically.

In some programs the periodic exchange rate adjustments have been linked to movements in the domestic price index rather than to balance of payments performance, i.e., the programs have provided that a specified increase in the price index would be followed by an appropriate adjustment in the exchange rate.

The commitment to follow a flexible exchange rate policy has the advantage of being applicable to countries maintaining a fixed exchange rate. The setting of a minimum level for net reserves aims at preventing the authorities from maintaining an exchange rate which does not yield, in the context of the stabilization program, the desired balance of payments performance. The balance of payments adjustment through exchange rate action becomes necessary when other means of adjustment are judged to be insufficient. Thus, the level of net foreign exchange reserves is used both as a guide for the determination of the exchange rate adjustment and as a test of the effectiveness of this action.

The inclusion of a balance of payments performance test as an additional binding commitment in a stand-by arrangement increases the stringency of the conditions applied to the use of the Fund's resources, and has important policy implications. The main problems involved in the formulation of the test are the definition of net foreign exchange reserves, the choice of the minimum level for reserves, and the linking of the test to the required exchange rate adjustment.

The definition of net foreign exchange reserves has to draw a line between those operations which do not influence the performance under the test, and those which should yield the desired performance. If a foreign credit facility is included in the definition of net reserves as a liability of the monetary authorities, the performance under the test is not affected by the receipts from this source, as the minimum reserves level covers both assets and liabilities of the monetary authorities. If the proceeds from such a foreign loan are redisbursed to meet current obligations, there is a net loss in the reserves as defined. If the proceeds are redisbursed in order to repay an obligation listed as a liability of the monetary authorities, there is no change in the net reserve position. Similarly, any movement in gross reserves may or may not affect the performance under the test depending on whether there is a simultaneous change in the liabilities of the monetary authorities. This does not mean, however, that foreign assistance cannot be used without impairing the results of the test, except to repay a liability of the monetary authorities. To the extent that the amount of foreign assistance was known in advance, it may have been taken into account by lowering the performance target by an equivalent amount when it was fixed. For example, if a balance of payments surplus would have been required in order to meet short-term obligations coming due, a foreign credit (or a drawing on the Fund) may allow the authorities to aim at equilibrium rather than a surplus in the balance of payments. However, once a performance target has been chosen, and unless this target is a deficit, resources from foreign borrowing can be used only to be added to gross reserves or to consolidate the debt of the monetary authorities.

Generally, the performance target has covered the amount of foreign assets and short-term liabilities of the central bank. In one arrangement the liabilities of the central bank were defined as "its liabilities to nonresident banks and other financial institutions, excluding loans with a maturity of over five years granted for development purposes." Sometimes, however, the over-all amount of foreign assets and liabilities of the Treasury and other official agencies has been included when they have formed an important part of foreign indebtedness. In one instance, the performance target covered the net position of the whole banking system, including the commercial banks, because the commercial banks had tended to borrow heavily abroad in order to ease the tightness of domestic credit restrictions. Suppliers' credits have on occasion been taken into account, either by a separate commitment to limit the amount of such credits, or by a clause providing for a reduction or increase in the target in accordance with any decrease or increase in suppliers' credits.

The choice of a level for net reserves involves a projection of the payments and receipts of the monetary authorities as defined; the receipts are estimated as accurately as possible and a certain amount is allowed for payments in order to yield a performance considered as desirable and feasible. If heavy short-term obligations fall due during the program period, the level of gross reserves and of foreign assistance available may indicate that a certain minimum surplus will be necessary in order to meet the payments coming due. Some basic elements in the balance of payments projection, such as the prospective foreign exchange receipts and payments of the government, may be known with some degree of certainty, while some other elements, such as exports, imports, and private capital movements, are difficult to estimate. It is on these elements that certain assumptions have to be made and targets have to be established through negotiation and agreement with the authorities. In general the stabilization program aims at achieving a balance of payments surplus or at least an equilibrium over the whole period, and the rest of the financial program has to be consistent with that target.

After an over-all net reserves target has been chosen, it may be necessary to phase it according to the seasonal pattern of receipts and payments, taking into account any predictable elements that may temporarily affect the level of reserves. The establishment of phased net reserves targets, usually on a quarterly basis, is a difficult task, as foreign exchange reserves may be subject to wide short-term fluctuations, especially in countries where receipts from exports are largely dependent on agricultural crops. The seasonality of such receipts may not be clearly apparent or there may be some leads or lags from one year to the other. In some instances, a fixed margin of deviation from the target for seasonal or accidental factors has been allowed or a more elaborate phasing has been used.

Unexpected circumstances such as strikes, droughts, or fluctuations in world market prices for major export commodities may also temporarily affect the level of receipts. Consequently, some arrangements have included a safeguarding clause for situations where receipts from exports rose above or fell below the estimated level as a result of a change in the export volume or in export prices. The target could then be adjusted downward by the amount of the shortfall, or adjusted upward by an amount equivalent to the excess of receipts over the projected level. These safeguarding clauses, however, change the nature of the test by eliminating certain types of transactions from the balance of payments performance which is tested. If, for instance, compensation is given for some major receipts, the test primarily affects payments, and failure to pass the test may occur only if actual payments differ significantly from estimated payments irrespective of the level of receipts. Therefore, such safeguarding clauses, like the definition of foreign exchange reserves, are closely related to the problem of deciding for which type of transaction a certain performance is desired.

Agreement to submit to a balance of payments performance test implies that appropriate corrective action has to be taken before rather than after the points in time when the performance is checked, since failure to pass the test makes the country ineligible for drawings under the stand-by arrangement. Although the type of appropriate action is not always specified, it is generally understood that the achievement of the target should essentially result from an exchange rate adjustment. Thus, the staff report concerning the stand-by arrangement with Uruguay, of May 25, 1966, contained the following statement:

> Attainment of the balance of payments performance targets will clearly depend on the implementation of the other policies embodied in the program. . . . Any necessary corrections will have to come through movements of the exchange rate, a tightening of monetary policies, or a combination of the two.

Other types of action, such as an increase in quantitative import restrictions or in exchange restrictions, may be specifically barred, but a tightening of monetary policy or of fiscal policy is never specifically ruled out. The timing and magnitude of the corrective action are left to the authorities to the extent that their action is successful in keeping the net foreign exchange reserves above the stipulated minimum limit. In the case of failure to pass the test, their decisions become a subject of the consultations with the Fund in order to agree on "the terms on which further drawings may be made."

If the balance of payments performed better than the net foreign exchange reserve target required, the authorities could, in theory, either accumulate additional reserves or let the exchange rate appreciate. However, sometimes other conditions in the stand-by arrangement prevent any appreciation of the exchange rate, or the further improvement in the net reserves position may be considered preferable in view of the general indebtedness of the country. Thus the flexible exchange rate policies involving a balance of payments performance test have, in practice, resulted in the periodic devaluation of fixed exchange rates.

PRICE AND WAGE CONTROLS

In most programs appropriate monetary and fiscal measures have been sufficient to restore internal financial stability. In some instances, however, direct action in the field of prices and wages has been considered necessary. Thus, some programs have provided for the immediate or gradual removal of price controls where these were hampering production and distorting the allocation of resources. Some other programs have included specific price adjustments, such as the increases in public utility rates mentioned above, within the context of commitments made in the fiscal field.

Wage policies have frequently been of particular concern because the effectiveness of monetary and fiscal measures designed to combat inflation is greatly affected by wage movements. However, the ability of the authorities to influence wage movements differs widely, depending on the institutional framework within which labor unions operate. Consequently, stand-by arrangements have frequently contained general declarations of wage policies, but rarely are these policies made binding commitments. Where the stabilization measures have resulted in a significant upward adjustment of prices, the programs have sometimes provided for an initial increase in wages in the public sector to be followed by a period without change. In the 1959 stand-by arrangement with Bolivia, the adjustment of prices of commissary goods to market levels and certain specific wage increases for workers employed by the Mining Corporation were made binding commitments (and subsequently modified). In the 1965 Brazilian arrangement, the fiscal program included an undertaking not to increase wages and salaries of government employees beyond the budgeted amount, unless further financial resources should be made available through additional taxation. With regard to the private sector, in countries where the government exercises control over wage policy through its role as arbitrator in wage negotiations, some undertakings on wage policy have been included. Where the government has little direct role in connection with wages, some programs have attempted to implement wage policy by moral suasion.

PART V

Constitutional Development and Change

CHAPTER

22

The Institution

Joseph Gold

THE ARTICLES OF THE FUND are one of the great law-making charters of the postwar world. "Something very important happened at Bretton Woods in 1944, and that was that the world consciously took control of the international monetary system."[1] The Articles drafted at Bretton Woods have had the strength and suppleness to permit the institution, by interpretation, rule-making, policy, and practice, to adapt to a world of change.[2] This part of this volume will deal with the Articles as a dynamic instrument of international law. It begins with an account of the career of certain provisions, in the course of which there will be some attempt to compare experience with expectation. The survey must be selective in the choice of both provisions and the episodes in which they have been involved. As is common in the literature on the Fund, the subject is divided into topics dealing with the institution, the resources (Chapter 23), and the code of conduct (Chapter 24). Chapter 25 deals with the techniques that have been employed by the Fund for flexible response to new needs, and Chapter 26 examines some characteristics of the Fund in action. Finally, there is a chapter on the amendments that entered into effect in July 1969. This stresses the uses of the past not only in the transformation of some of the original provisions but also in the fashioning of many of the new provisions.

Two preliminary remarks by way of apologia are in order. In the course of these chapters it is sometimes said that certain influences were responsible for certain developments, but, in the words of Francis Bacon, the causes of causes are infinite and their impulsion one of another. Again, there may be an undue emphasis on the difficulties that have arisen in the application of certain provisions, but no disparagement is intended. If we can see further than the drafters of the original Articles, it is because we are standing on their shoulders.

---

[1] Louis Rasminsky, speech at Guildhall, London, February 3, 1969.

[2] For the text of the Articles, see below, Vol. III, pp. 185–214 and 521–38.

THE ORGANIZATION

The great growth in the membership of the Fund has caused no grave constitutional problems. Membership is not available to countries as of right, but the criteria that the Fund has applied in permitting membership are few. The Fund satisfies itself that an applicant is in full charge of its external affairs and that all of the obligations of the Articles can be observed. The U.S.S.R. participated in the Bretton Woods Conference and influenced the drafting of certain provisions [3] but has not joined the institution. Poland and Cuba have been members but withdrew. Indonesia withdrew and was readmitted. Czechoslovakia withdrew after a decision of the Fund requiring it to withdraw.

The admission of small states has not given rise to the concern that has been felt in some other international organizations. This is largely the result of the system of weighted voting which exists in the Fund.[4] There have been consequences, however, of the membership of small states. One of them has been the necessity to modify the Fund's policies on minimum quotas. Another has been the need to solve legal problems and make special arrangements because of some unusual circumstance in the country's situation, such as its use of the currency of another member as its own legal tender.

The senior organ of the Fund, the Board of Governors, has held only annual sessions. Its meetings have given governors the opportunity to express opinions on the conduct of the Fund and the policies that should guide it, but the actions of the Board are taken normally on the basis of preparatory work or recommendations by the Executive Directors. One consequence of the great increase in the size of the Board of Governors has been a tendency towards the expression of regional views in meetings of the Board.

The powers of the Fund are vested in the Board of Governors, but the Board can delegate all but a small number of reserved powers to the Executive Directors. All the powers that are not reserved were delegated to the Executive Directors by the Board of Governors when it adopted Section 15 of the By-Laws on March 16, 1946. Under the Articles of Agreement as amended, the Board of Governors will have additional reserved powers, some of which are connected with the original powers of the Fund and others with special drawing rights.

The Executive Directors have grown in number from the original twelve to the present twenty. They meet frequently and still retain the camaraderie of an executive committee, although as the number grew with the increase in the membership of the Fund fears were expressed that this spirit might be jeopardized. Under the Articles, five executive directors [5] were appointed by

---

[3] E.g., Article IV, Section 5 (e); Article XIX (c).

[4] Article XII, Section 5.

[5] In this and the following chapters the distinction drawn in the Articles between individual executive directors and the Executive Directors as an organ of the Fund is followed by reserving the use of capital letters for the latter.

the five members with the largest quotas, two were elected by the American Republics not entitled to appoint directors, and five were elected by the rest of the members. The Board of Governors may decide by a four-fifths majority of the total voting power to increase the number of executive directors when new members join the Fund,[6] and the Board has exercised this power in accordance with a policy based on the voting power of new members. By the time of the 1966 election, the number of executive directors elected by the American Republics had been increased to three and the other elected executive directors had been increased from five to twelve. The biennial election of executive directors by members not entitled to appoint executive directors is settled by negotiations among members in which the Managing Director and staff take no part.

The Articles provide for an increase, in certain circumstances, in the number of appointed executive directors.[7] The drafters wanted to be certain that the members which were providing assistance through the Fund because of the net sales of their currencies by the Fund would be able to express their views directly in the Executive Directors and, as a minimum, balance the views of the members making a net use of the Fund's resources. It was provided, therefore, that if the two currencies that had been used in the largest absolute amounts during the two years preceding a biennial election were the currencies of members that were not among those already entitled to appoint executive directors, these two members also were to be entitled to make appointments. Canada was entitled to exercise this right in 1958 and Italy in 1968. In 1950, the question arose whether a member entitled to appoint an additional executive director was bound to exercise the right. The reluctance to exercise it resulted from the fact that the executive director appointed by a member in this position would speak no longer for the other members that had voted for him in earlier elections, and the number of votes that he could cast would be reduced correspondingly. It was concluded that the right was also a duty, and on both occasions the other members, in order to maintain the earlier associations, refrained from participating in the election of executive directors, with the result that no executive director could cast votes corresponding to the votes allotted to these members. Instead, an informal procedure was followed by which these other members have requested the Canadian and Italian executive directors to take care of their interests in the Executive Directors.

The Articles do not define the status of executive directors, but in some ways the silence of the Articles is the most interesting contribution to the definition of their position. For example, the word "representative" is not used in the Articles although it appeared in some earlier drafts. It is not said, as it is in the

---

[6] Article XII, Section 3 (b).

[7] Article XII, Section 3 (c).

case of the Managing Director and the staff, that they owe their duty entirely to
the Fund and to no other authority, but they are officials of the institution and
are paid by it. The absence of definition has enabled executive directors to
work out their own relations with the members that appointed or elected them,
and there is much variety in those relations. Only the United States [8] and a
few other members [9] have provided by law for the way in which an executive
director shall receive instructions on the positions he is to take on issues arising
in the Fund.

It is impossible to understand the Fund without some discussion of voting.
All members have an equal number of basic votes in deference to the classical
principle of the equality of sovereign states, and further votes weighted according
to quota in recognition of the fact that they belong to a financial institution and
have made varying contributions to its resources. For two kinds of financial
decisions, weighted voting power is adjusted on the basis of a member's net
purchases from the Fund or the net sales of a member's currency to other
members. In the drafting of the Articles and in legislative discussions of their
acceptability, relative voting strength, possible blocs, and possible alignments on
particular issues were a major preoccupation. This concern is apparent in the
provisions of the Articles on voting and decisions. Although the basic rule is that
decisions are taken by a majority of votes cast, there is an elaborate network of
special majorities and safeguards.

To understand the Fund it is necessary to know what has happened in connection with voting. In the Board of Governors voting is unavoidable because
most issues are put to the Board by correspondence. It is remarkable, however,
that voting by the Executive Directors, who are in continuous session, has been
almost nonexistent. This has been the result of deliberate policy. As early as
September 25, 1946, a rule was adopted declaring that "the Chairman will
ordinarily ascertain the sense of the meeting in lieu of a formal vote," although
any director is entitled to call for a vote.[10] It did not follow that voting strength
became irrelevant, and it was decided on May 28, 1947 that in ascertaining the
sense of the meeting the Chairman must take account of voting power, but the
avoidance of formal voting has tended to moderate the effect of discrepancies
in voting strength.

Most of the votes that have occurred took place in the early years of the Fund
before satisfactory procedures were developed by which individual executive
directors could record their views. If an executive director was not able to concur
in a decision without qualification, almost the only way in which he could record

---

[8] Bretton Woods Agreements Act, P.L. 171, 79th Congress, 1st Session (59 Stat. 512 (1945)),
Sec. 4 (*Selected Decisions*, pp. 147–50).

[9] For example, Germany, *Bundesgesetzblatt*, Part II, No. 21, July 13, 1956, page 747, Article 5.

[10] Rules and Regulations, Rule C-10; below, Vol. III, p. 290.

his reservations was by voting against the decision. Many of the early votes were on successive motions on the same issue, so that the number of occasions on which there has been resort to voting has been much smaller than the number of votes. There has been no pattern in these votes, and certainly they have not all been on major issues.

For some years the threat of a vote has been regarded as regrettable. The effect of this distaste for voting on the operation of the institution has been profound. It has helped to avoid blocs or at least not to intensify any drive towards routine coalition. On any important question, the Managing Director and executive directors try to reach a decision which all can accept or at least not oppose, and they persist in this effort while there is still reasonable hope that it will succeed. Naturally, there are abstentions or dissents on occasion, but in an atmosphere in which normally more attention is given to the weight of argument than to the weight of voting power the minority does not feel that it has been overborne by force. It would be disingenuous to pretend that the influence of all members is the same, but a policy of not voting has given even members with small voting strength a sense of participation in the process of reaching decisions. In addition, the policy has induced members with great voting power to be restrained in working towards a decision. An incident which involved one of the few votes is revealing. A decision was taken on the morning of March 2, 1951 by 44,510 to 33,155 votes, but the majority consisted only of the U.S., British, and Canadian executive directors, whereas eight executive directors voted against the decision and three abstained. In the afternoon session one of the three executive directors asked that the discussion of the subject be resumed at a later date, and on March 7 there was general agreement on the minority position. The significance of any one incident must not be exaggerated, but it is a defensible proposition that the larger voting power of some members gives them an assurance that enables them to act with moderation. It is the desire for this assurance that has made relative voting power a continuing concern of members, particularly in the negotiation of the amendments to the Articles, even if voting power is exercised only on rare occasions.

One reason why voting has been avoided as a deliberate policy is that, in some of its functions, the Fund, in the international field, closely resembles the regulatory or administrative agency of national law.[11] The exercise of the Fund's functions as an international regulatory agency has an impact on the rights and

---

[11] "Present-day administrative agencies are vested with authority to prescribe generally what shall or shall not be done in a given situation (just as legislatures do); to determine whether the law has been violated in particular cases and to proceed against the violators (just as courts do); to admit people to privileges not otherwise open to members of the public (as the Crown once could do); and even to render what amount to money judgments. Agencies vested with such powers are usually called 'regulatory agencies' in the United States, because their activities impinge upon the personal or property rights of private individuals and regulate the manner in which such rights may be exercised." Bernard Schwartz, *An Introduction to American Administrative Law*, p. 8.

duties of its members. It must have been clear at an early date that members would be more likely to accept the decisions and rules of the Fund if the Fund strove for consensus, at least on important issues. It must have been clear also that the objective of consensus would tend to deter the formation of permanent combinations among members and encourage a more fluid procedure for reaching decisions. The policy of seeking consensus does much to explain the authority of the Executive Directors, because it is largely through them that consensus, or at least widespread agreement, is reached.

THE ORGANIZATION IN THE WORLD

The place of the Fund in international organization at large has helped to shape its role. Two aspects of international organization have had unusual importance. One of them has been the intention to establish an international trade organization, and the other has been the advent of additional institutions or groups with international monetary functions.

At the Bretton Woods Conference it was contemplated that the Fund and the International Bank for Reconstruction and Development (the World Bank) would be joined by a trade organization, and it was resolved that participating governments should reach agreement as soon as possible on the ways in which obstacles to international trade could be reduced, the orderly marketing of staple commodities at fair prices could be ensured, and other related objectives attained. The intention to create an international trade organization and the subsequent history of efforts to carry out this intention affected the Fund in various ways. The effects on the definition of "restrictions on payments and transfers for current international transactions," on which much of the Fund's jurisdiction in bringing about a multilateral system of payments and transfers depends, and on the scope of the Fund's consultations with members, are discussed elsewhere in these chapters.

In the scales of history the emergence of other international entities with authority in monetary matters will probably have greater weight. There is no evidence that at the time of Bretton Woods the world contemplated more than one international monetary entity. A generation later, the Fund is the central but not the sole monetary institution. The Bank for International Settlements is not a newcomer, but its activities are broader now than in the past. Certain committees of the Organization for Economic Cooperation and Development and of the European Economic Community, the Group of Ten, and the members of the Gold Pool are among the entities that have taken an active part or exercised authority in international monetary matters. The Fund is the central institution in the sense that its resources are the most considerable, but, more to the present point, its formal authority is the broadest and its membership the largest of all of the monetary entities. As a result, as was seen in the liquidity debate which led finally to the amendments of the Articles, smaller combinations of members sometimes seem to be exclusionary and for this reason provoke political reactions.

The obligations involved in participation in other organizations or less formal bodies cannot derogate in law from the obligations of membership in the Fund. Inevitably, however, decisions have been taken in other entities that have had major importance for the Fund. The provisions of the Articles are extensive enough to have permitted the adoption of at least some of these decisions within the Fund even if there was no legal necessity that the decisions be taken there. Examples of decisions affecting the international monetary system taken outside the Fund are the establishment of the Gold Pool, the introduction of the two-tier gold system, the Basle Agreements relating to sterling, and the increases in swap arrangements. In some but not in all of the other entities the Managing Director or his representative has participated in the deliberations leading to decisions.

Observers may disagree on the reasons for the proliferation of other entities in international monetary matters. Some of the reasons that may be suggested are related more or less closely to the Fund itself. One of them may be the great growth in the membership of the Fund and the belief that other entities are needed that are based on more homogeneous interests or simply on geography. The original reaction in the Fund that the European Payments Union was an unwelcome discriminatory currency arrangement may have left a residual feeling that the reconciliation between particular interests and universal objectives is not always easy. Inequality of voting power in the Fund, even though voting power is not brandished, may have spurred some members to find an environment in which this disparity would be absent or less marked. The continued deficit in the balance of payments of the United States and its need to find acceptable forms of financing have made it easier to suggest that some other environment would be more convenient. The tranche policies of the Fund may have led the United States to conclude that the Fund was *forum non conveniens*. From time to time, the theory of the special responsibility of certain members for the monetary system has been heard. This is probably not an autonomous influence, but then most of the other reasons that have been suggested are related to each other in one way or another.

In the history of the effect on the Fund of other entities the greatest interest attaches to the Group of Ten. It came into being as part of the search by the United States for financing for its balance of payments deficit and as a result of the fear that the resources of the Fund would be inadequate to enable the United States to make a substantial use of them. As the result of complex negotiations, the Fund adopted the decision which is called the General Arrangements to Borrow.[12] Under it, eight members and the central banks of two other members were invited, and by adherence to the decision have agreed, to lend the currencies

---

[12] E.B. Decision No. 1289-(62/1), January 5, 1962; below, Vol. III, pp. 246–52.

of these members to the Fund to supplement the resources of the Fund for the financing of exchange transactions by any of the ten members with the Fund. The decision, which is also an agreement between the Fund and the participants, became effective on October 24, 1962 for a period of four years, and has been renewed for a further period of four years. The intention of the Fund was to establish a ring of lenders to the Fund and the decision retains evidences of a bilateral nexus between the Fund and individual participants.[13] It became apparent early in the negotiations, however, that a more corporate spirit was intended and that a certain amount of authority would be exercised elsewhere by the incipient collectivity.

The substructure of the Group of Ten consists of the General Arrangements to Borrow and identical letters addressed on December 15, 1961, by Mr. Baumgartner, the then Minister of Finance of France, to the other nine participants.[14] These letters, to which the Fund was not a party, established the procedures for consultation and decision among the Ten. It must be understood that under the General Arrangements participants are not obligated to lend to the Fund but only to consider whether they will accept calls on them by the Fund to lend. The letters establish the procedures by which the participants will reach their conclusions collectively, although each participant responds individually to the call on it made by the Fund. The desideratum stated in the letters is unanimity, but if that is not attainable, decisions are taken by a system of weighted voting that is unrelated to voting power in the Fund. Voting power according to the letters is weighted in relation to the total amount that each participant may be called on to lend under the General Arrangements. Two majorities are needed for a decision: two thirds of the participants voting and three fifths of the weighted votes. The participant requesting a transaction with the Fund, for the purpose of which the Fund seeks to borrow, is not entitled to vote on the question whether the participants asked to lend will agree to lend.

The Baumgartner letters state the understanding that a consultative meeting will be held if proposals for calls are made "or if other matters should arise under the Fund decision requiring consultations among the participants." They also state that to further these consultations participants, to the fullest extent practicable, should use the facilities of the international organizations—the plural is used—to which they belong to keep each other informed of developments in their balances of payments that could give rise to a need to lend under the General Arrangements. The Ministers of Finance and Central Bank Governors of the Group of Ten, however, have given mandates to their deputies to perform other tasks. The work by the Group of Ten in connection with international liquidity is the leading example of an activity that goes beyond the General

---

[13] Paragraph 7 (a); *ibid.*, p. 248.

[14] Below, Vol. III, pp. 252–54.

Arrangements and the Baumgartner letters. The United States has not attempted so far to make a use of the Fund's resources beyond the gold tranche, and the Fund has not found it necessary to invoke the General Arrangements for the purpose of a transaction with the United States, although it has borrowed under them for transactions with the United Kingdom and France.

The General Arrangements caused uneasiness among some members of the Fund. The agreement establishing the General Arrangements seemed to them to be a preferential facility because it was not for the benefit of transactions with the Fund by nonparticipants. One reason why they could not welcome the agreement was that they could discern no convincing principle by which to explain the selection of the Ten as a distinctive group. The reaction of members outside the Ten may have contributed something to the willingness of the Fund community to establish the compensatory financing facility which on its face is available to all members but in practice is likely to be used only by the exporters of primary products.

In time, the disquiet of some members outside the Ten took another form because of the movement towards the deliberate control of more elements in the international monetary system. These members felt that decisions were being reached on problems affecting the international monetary system as a whole by a process in which the rest of the members of the Fund had no direct voice although their views could be communicated to the Ten by the Managing Director or his representative. Even if decisions had to be taken in the Fund on these matters, the outcome might be predetermined by the Ten because of their dominating voting power in the Fund. In the liquidity debate a solution was sought by holding four joint meetings of executive directors and the deputies of the Group of Ten. The problem of a *modus vivendi* remains.

23

Use of the Fund's Resources

Joseph Gold

THE POWER TO CHALLENGE

It is in connection with its financial operations and transactions that the Fund has shown the greatest virtuosity and imagination even though the overture began with discord. "For legal purposes it is normally necessary to try to get rid of ambiguities. . . . In poetry the ambiguities can happily remain." [1] The negotiators of treaties are sometimes more like poets than lawyers in their drafting. It is possible that the dissonant effect of declaring in Article V, Section 3 (*a*) that a member is "entitled" to make purchases from the Fund subject to certain conditions, but that one of the conditions is that the member "represents" that the currency is needed and so on, is not fortuitous. The words permitted two understandings of the right to make purchases from the Fund and each had vigorous supporters. One version, based on the word "entitled," was that, if a member was eligible to use the Fund's resources, it had the right to make purchases without hindrance if they did not require a waiver under Article V, Section 4. "Drawing rights" were often said to be "automatic" according to this view. The other version, based on the word "represents," was that the representation that the currency requested "is presently needed for making in that currency payments which are consistent with the provisions of this Agreement" could be challenged by the Fund if it thought the representation to be incorrect in some respect. The acceptance of this second understanding would reduce the need for the Fund to employ the procedures of ineligibility in order to defend the Fund's resources against an improper use of them. The Fund would be able to challenge the representation made when a member requested a purchase without taking the more disagreeable action of imposing a status on the member which made it ineligible to use the Fund's resources in general or beyond a limited amount prescribed by the Fund.

---

[1] Roy Fuller, "The Lawyer as Poet," *The New Law Journal*, December 19, 1968, p. 1205.

A decision in favor of the second understanding of Article V, Section 3 (*a*) was adopted in May 1947, and, after further examination, this conclusion was confirmed by a decision of March 10, 1948.[2] The later decision states that there is a presumption in favor of the correctness of a representation, but that the Fund may challenge any element in it if the Fund has good reasons to doubt its correctness. If the Fund concludes that a representation is not correct, the Fund may postpone or reject the request or accept it subject to conditions. This decision is one of the major influences in the development of the Fund's law and practice on the use of its resources because in rejecting the theory of "automaticity" the decision opened the way to the tranche policies and "conditionality."

The power to challenge representations was not a substitute for ineligibility if there were grounds for ineligibility, but no member has ever submitted repeated requests that forced the Fund to declare the member ineligible in order to avoid repeated challenges. In fact, there has never been a decision by the Executive Directors to challenge a representation on the occasion of a request. Members seem to feel that even a challenge would convey stigma, and, therefore, once it became clear that the Fund had the power to challenge representations, there developed the tacit understanding that it was wise for a member to consult the Managing Director before it submitted a request to the Fund. Even Rule G-5 of the Rules and Regulations has become a dead letter insofar as it was intended to facilitate small purchases. One purpose of this rule, which was adopted on February 7, 1947, was to allow members an automatic right to make a limited use of the Fund's resources by permitting a member to make a purchase without the need for consideration by the Executive Directors if the purchase would increase the Fund's holdings of the member's currency by no more than 5 per cent of quota during the thirty days ending with the purchase.

The decision establishing the Fund's power to challenge a representation when an eligible member requests an exchange transaction was one of a number taken during March 1948 in order to clarify the Fund's powers to prevent an improper use of its resources,[3] but it is not necessary to say more about the other decisions. The central decision was the one affirming the power to challenge, and the uncertainty which it produced about the circumstances in which the power might be exercised, apart from the notice given in the decisions of April 5 and June 4, 1948 on the use of the Fund's resources by members benefiting under the European Recovery Program, led to an almost complete paralysis in the financial operations of the Fund.

If the decision of March 10, 1948 on the power to challenge representations is a landmark, the decision of February 13, 1952 is the Mount Everest that towers

---

[2] E.B. Decision No. 284-4; below, Vol. III, p. 227.

[3] E.B. Decisions Nos. 287-3, 284-3, 286-1, 292-3; below, Vol. III, pp. 228, 234–35.

over all other decisions on the use of the Fund's resources.[4] The decision of
February 13, 1952 was intended to reinvigorate the Fund by encouraging members to believe that they would be able to use its resources. The decision clarified
what the Fund regarded as an appropriately temporary use of its resources;
initiated the policy of representations of intention as to repurchase; foreshadowed
the stand-by arrangement; and invented the concept of the gold tranche. The
discussion will deal with these elements in the decision and then other developments in the Fund's law and practice on the use of its resources.

TEMPORARY USE AND REPURCHASE

The topics of temporary use and repurchase are related and can be considered
together. The word "temporary" in connection with the use of the Fund's
resources does not appear in the original Articles, although there were clear indications that only temporary use was proper. This was inherent, of course, in the
idea that the Fund provided an addition to a member's monetary reserves during
periods of balance of payments difficulty. In order to pacify those critics in the
United States who feared that the Fund might engage in long-term financing and
undermine the lending practices of the World Bank, the United States provided in
its Bretton Woods legislation that it would seek an interpretation from the Fund
on the proper use of the Fund's resources, and that it would propose an amendment of the Articles if the interpretation was unsatisfactory.[5] This led to the
interpretation of September 26, 1946 on the use of the Fund's resources, on
which more will be said later in this chapter, but which, it is sufficient to note
here, emphasized that the Fund gave no more than "temporary assistance" in
making its resources available.[6]

There could be no quarrel with that conclusion but it was not specific. What
was meant by "temporary"? The Articles did not declare that use must be
temporary and, therefore, they did not define what period could be regarded as
temporary, but nevertheless there was some evidence of the attitude of the
drafters. Article V, Section 8 sets forth a system of charges on the Fund's
holdings of a currency in excess of quota, which increased in relation to both
time and amount, and provided that when the rate of charge on any part of
those holdings reached 4 per cent per annum the Fund and the member must
consider means by which the Fund's holdings could be reduced. The stage of
compulsory consultation might not be reached until seven years had passed after
a purchase on which periodic charges were payable, and therefore it was argued

---

[4] E.B. Decision No. 102-(52/11); below, Vol. III, p. 228.

[5] Sec. 13 (see above, Chapter 22, footnote 8).

[6] E.B. Decision No. 71-2; below, Vol. III, p. 245.

by some that the maximum period of temporary use could not be less than seven years. Their view of the Articles was that the repurchase provisions of Article V, Section 7 (b) were a mechanism under which repurchase obligations were to accrue, and if they did not accrue there would then be consultation on the means to reduce the Fund's holdings under Article V, Section 8 (d), and finally ineligibility could be declared under Article V, Section 5 if a member's use of the Fund's resources was so protracted as to be adjudged "contrary to the purposes of the Fund."

The opponents of this view considered seven years, followed by whatever period was agreed in the consultation for the reduction of the Fund's holdings, to be too lengthy. Moreover, they were troubled by the fact that the provisions of Article V, Section 7 (b) would not produce repurchase obligations for some members. Obligations under that provision depended on monetary reserves and increases in them. A member's monetary reserves were defined substantially as the holdings of gold and convertible currencies of its central institutions minus currency liabilities, i.e., the holdings of the member's currency by the central institutions and other official institutions of other members and by other banks within their territories. A member like the United Kingdom tended to have negative monetary reserves under this formula because its central holdings were less than its currency liabilities. For certain other members, repurchase obligations would not accrue because a large part of their reserves was held in the form of inconvertible currencies which were not included in the calculation of monetary reserves.

Discouraged by the probable ineffectiveness of the repurchase provisions, the U.S. executive director proposed in October 1949 that whenever a member sought to use the Fund's resources it should undertake to make a repurchase equivalent to its purchase not later than five years after the event. The dissenters argued, correctly, that the "conditions" on which a member could make purchases were set forth in Article V, Section 3 (a) and they could not be added to by fiat. The Articles did not establish a fixed term for use of the Fund's resources, and this was one of the ways in which the use of the Fund's resources differed from a loan. The attempt to impose repurchase conditions failed.

A related development was in process at this time. The Fund could not impose repurchase conditions, but could it accept a repurchase that was voluntary because the member was not obligated to make it and the Fund was not obligated to receive it? The question in other words was whether a repurchase could be made by agreement between the Fund and a member. Probably there would have been no dispute about the validity of "voluntary" repurchases in gold, but for a time there was stiff resistance by some to the acceptability of currencies. It was understood that voluntary repurchases would have to be compatible with the concept of repurchase as elaborated in the Articles, and that they could be made, therefore, only in convertible currencies and only to the extent that they did not increase the Fund's holdings of any member's currency above 75 per cent of that member's quota or reduce the Fund's holdings of the repurchasing member's currency below 75 per cent of its quota. Nevertheless, it was argued by a minority that voluntary repurchases in this form were unacceptable. In part, the objection was based on a suspicion of the doctrine of implied powers, on which part of the argument for voluntary repurchases rested. This was not the only occasion on which implied powers have been resisted, but this resistance has not prevented them from making their due contribution to the growth of Fund law. However, the objection to voluntary repurchases in currency was based on more than textual or doctrinal considerations. For example, according to one view, it would be advantageous for the Fund to obtain as much gold as possible, and therefore voluntary repurchases in gold should be encouraged by refusing to recognize that they could be made in currency. Another reason for opposition was that the amount of currency that a member would be able to purchase from the Fund would be reduced by voluntary repurchases made with its currency. This consideration was related more to the future operation of the Fund because when the validity of voluntary repurchases in currency was discussed few currencies were convertible and therefore acceptable in repurchase. It was not then as clear as it became in later years that if the Fund receives a member's currency in repurchase this can be as helpful to the member as an equivalent purchase by it, because it eliminates a claim against the member's resources. Indeed, the repurchase is a less expensive form of assistance because a repurchase, unlike a purchase, involves no service charge. The lengthy debate terminated with a decision of March 8, 1951 which recognized the validity of voluntary repurchases on the ground that, like repurchase obligations, they promoted the revolving character of the Fund's resources, and they were not prohibited by any provision of the Articles.[7] Again, as in the case of repurchase obligations, a voluntary repurchase could be made in a member's currency without the necessity for getting the consent of that member.

When the time arrived for ending the Fund's financial inactivity, it was possible to build on the basis of the decision on voluntary repurchases. The decision of February 13, 1952 relied upon the classic theory of the purpose of the use of the Fund's resources. It is to give a member the time in which to pursue the policies that will correct its balance of payments problem and thereby enable the member to accumulate resources with which to repurchase. Therefore, the appropriate period of use is one that is reasonably related to the problem for which the member makes its purchase. Some term had to be placed on the period of use, and as there were different views on what it should be, the limping phrase of "an outside range of three to five years" was adopted as a compromise

---

[7] E.B. Decision No. 7-(648); below, Vol. III, p. 244.

in the drafting of the decision. Lack of style has not impaired its career. It has become firm practice that if the Fund's holdings of the currency of a purchasing member have not been reduced within three years after a purchase, there must be an understanding under which repurchase will be completed not later than five years after the purchase. Even the paragraph in the decision which was introduced because the new policy was an experiment and which said that the Fund would "consider" some extension beyond five years if "unforeseen circumstances beyond the member's control" made it "unreasonable" to insist that the member repurchase in accordance with the decision [8] has never been applied, although there have been a few attempts to obtain a longer period. There is a strong feeling that there should be no extensions of the period of use beyond five years, either in particular cases or under general policies, even though from time to time those who would like a longer period recall that the determination of what is temporary is a policy decision. Notwithstanding its strict adherence to the limit of five years, the Fund has permitted a small percentage of members to make an effectively longer use of the Fund's resources by allowing these members to make new purchases after they have repurchased. Each stand-by arrangement or purchase in the series has required consultation with the Fund on a new program, and in this way the Fund has been able to stay in close contact with members that have had persistent balance of payments difficulties notwithstanding their efforts to solve their problems.

The technique for putting the understanding on temporary use to work, without stumbling over the objection that the "conditions" in Article V, Section 3 (a) are exhaustive, was as follows. The rates of charge on the Fund's holdings of a member's currency in excess of quota were altered so that the date for consultation under Article V, Section 8 (d) on means to reduce the Fund's holdings of a member's currency would arrive not later than three years after the member's purchase. When making a request for a purchase, a member would be expected, although not required, to declare that in the consultation the member would agree with the Fund on appropriate arrangements to ensure that the Fund's holdings would be reduced by the amount of the purchase as soon as possible and not later than five years after the purchase. The "conditions" of Article V, Section 3 (a) did not preclude a representation of intention as to repurchase, and nothing else in the Articles prevented a member from declaring that it intended to make a voluntary repurchase not later than a date that met the test of temporary use. It was never made clear what would happen if a member refused to make the representation of intention as to repurchase. In practice, this representation has been made in connection with all purchases, and, on the rare occasions when it was omitted as part of the request, this was an oversight that was remedied immediately when it was drawn to the member's attention.

---

[8] E.B. Decision No. 102-(52/11), February 13, 1952, paragraph 2.d; below, Vol. III, p. 229.

A representation as to repurchase became standard practice very quickly, but the original conception of it has been transformed to a very great extent. It has been seen that a representation of intention as to repurchase is not a "condition" of a purchase, and it does not create an obligation of repurchase in any other way. It is a representation of the member's intention to make a repurchase in due time. Members began to make these representations at a time when modest uses of the Fund's resources were foreseen after a period of virtually no use. As the volume of transactions grew under the influence of decisions that gave increasing precision to the Fund's policies on the use of its resources, it became possible for the Fund to employ certain powers which enabled it to insist on binding commitments with respect to repurchase instead of being content with representations of intention. For example, the Fund can grant a waiver under Article V, Section 4 of the conditions in Article V, Section 3 (a) under which members may make purchases, including the condition of use not in excess of 25 per cent of quota during any period of twelve months.[9] It will be seen later that the grant of a waiver permitting use in any period of twelve months beyond this "normal" amount has become common practice. When the Fund grants a waiver, it can impose terms that safeguard its interests, and it invariably makes the repurchase provisions of the decision of February 13, 1952 a term safeguarding its interests. This is not the only way in which repurchase commitments, which differ from representations because they are legally binding, are entered into. For example, when the Fund approves a stand-by arrangement, a term is always included which obligates the member to make a repurchase corresponding to each purchase under the stand-by arrangement, unless the Fund's holdings resulting from the purchase are reduced in some other way, not later than three years after the purchase. The result, therefore, is that in every case in which a purchase is requested the member makes a representation as to repurchase or assumes a commitment to repurchase if there is a legal basis for an obligation. In view of the frequency with which the Fund now grants waivers or approves stand-by arrangements, commitments are far more common than representations.

These developments in Fund practice represent a transformation of certain features of the original theory of the Fund. For example, the practice on repurchase makes the doctrine that the Fund's operations are not for a fixed term somewhat unreal. Repurchase representations and commitments do not replace the provisions of Article V, Section 7 (b), to which they can be regarded as ancillary, but there is now a precise final date for repurchase, which may not be obligatory but usually is. Although this practice was first introduced as a result of the initiative of the United States, it has had widespread support for some years, and not merely from the expanding group of members whose currencies are used in the Fund's operations.

---

[9] For the meaning of 25 per cent of quota in Article V, Section 3 (a) (iii), see E.B. Decision No. 451-(55/52), August 24, 1955; below, Vol. III, p. 228.

The slogan that the Fund's resources should be a "second line of reserves" is another example of the divergence between theory and practice.[10] It was intended that if a member wishes to use the Fund's resources in order to meet a balance of payments problem, it should use its own reserves and the Fund's resources in equal proportions and should not throw the whole burden on the Fund. There is no obligation to make an equal current use, but the object of the repurchase provisions is to bring this about if the member has made a disproportionate use of the Fund's resources. Subject to certain refinements which need not be recalled here, the repurchase provisions are constructed on the principle that if in any year in which a member, in order to meet a deficit, makes a purchase from the Fund in a greater amount than it uses its own reserves, the member will have a repurchase obligation at the end of that year that will put it in the same position as if it had made that equal use. Moreover, if in any year in which a member is making use of the Fund's resources it enjoys an increase in its monetary reserves, it will have to share that increase with the Fund, so as to reduce or eliminate its outstanding use of the Fund's resources. In recent years, for a number of reasons, including the unacceptability in repurchase of both U.S. dollars and sterling because the Fund's holdings of those currencies were at or above the level of 75 per cent of quota, no more than about one fourth by value of repurchases have been the result of obligations that accrued under Article V, Section 7 (b). All other repurchases have been made in accordance with representations or commitments. This phenomenon, coupled with widespread waivers, means that the concept of the second line of reserves as an equal use of a member's own reserves and the Fund's resources has not operated as it would have if the repurchase provisions had been effective on a broad scale. The Fund's resources have been a second line of reserves in a less precise sense because of the condition that a member must "need" the currency that it purchases, which implies in many cases some reduction in its reserves in the recent past, the present, or the immediate future.

Equally little significance remains in the distribution theory of repurchase obligations as written into the Articles. Article V, Section 7 (b), and Schedule B were drafted on the principle that repurchase obligations should be discharged in the types of reserve assets that constitute monetary reserves in proportion to a member's holdings, or increases in its holdings, of each type of reserve asset. The rationale of the distribution rules was that reserve assets might not be of equal quality. For example, a currency would still be "convertible" under the Articles even though the Fund approved many restrictions on its use. This consideration led to the interpretative decision under which if part of an obliga-

[10] See, e.g., *Hearings Before the Committee on Banking and Currency of the U.S. Senate on H.R. 3314* (79th Cong., 1st sess.) (Bretton Woods Agreements Act), p. 575. *Hearings Before the Committee on Banking and Currency, U.S. House of Representatives, on H.R. 2211* (79th Cong., 1st sess.), p. 88.

tion had to be discharged under the distribution rules in a member's currency that could not be accepted by the Fund because its holdings of the currency were already at 75 per cent of quota, that part of the obligation was abated and there was no obligation to discharge it in gold or some other currency that the Fund could accept.[11] The drafters thought that if an obligation allocated to a currency which the Fund could not accept had to be discharged by the automatic reallocation of the obligation to another and more usable currency, the distribution formulas would work too inflexibly and perhaps inequitably. Repurchases under representations and commitments are not based on any formulas for distribution among types of reserve assets, and repurchases of this kind may have to be made on occasion because abatement has operated under the fixed formulas of the Articles. The Fund has developed policies, which are discussed a little later, on the currencies in which repurchases should be made under representations or commitments. It will also be seen in Chapter 27 that the principle of abatement has been abrogated under the amendments, but there will be no automatic redistribution of any repurchase obligation that is distributed to an unacceptable currency. The greater flexibility that developed in practice has been preferred, and the new rule is that the Fund will determine the convertible currencies in which the obligation is to be discharged.[12]

WAIVERS

In the discussion of repurchase there was a reference to the Fund's practice on waivers under Article V, Section 4, and an excursus on that subject will be useful before stand-by arrangements are considered. Under Article V, Section 4, the Fund has the discretion to waive any of the conditions governing use of the Fund's resources, and it may grant a waiver on terms which safeguard the Fund's interests. The provision declares that the Fund may grant a waiver especially in the case of members with a record of avoiding large or continuous use of the Fund's resources. In making a waiver, the Fund is to take into consideration "periodic or exceptional requirements" of the member requesting the waiver. Although the Fund is not required by the provision to confine waivers to members that avoid a large or continuous use of the Fund's resources or to members that have periodic or exceptional requirements, the drafters undoubtedly thought that waivers would be unusual. In particular, they regarded the condition limiting use of the Fund's resources in any period of twelve months to 25 per cent of quota as an indication of the "normal" rate of use of the Fund's resources. The Fund has not developed in accordance with these expectations. The first waiver of the 25 per cent limit was not granted until August 1953, but

[11] E.B. Decision No. 521-3, January 16, 1950; below, Vol. III, p. 273.
[12] Schedule B, paragraph 1 (d); below, Vol. III, p. 534. Cf. E.B. Decision No. 1371-62/36), July 20, 1962; below, Vol. III, pp. 235–36.

it is now granted with great frequency. It is still uncommon for the Fund to waive the limit of 200 per cent on its total holdings of a member's currency, but there is evidence of an attitude towards the waiver of that limit also which is different from that of the drafters. For example, in the decision on the compensatory financing of export fluctuations, the Fund has announced in advance its willingness to waive the latter limit in order to make the decision workable.[13]

The almost routine grant of waivers suggests that it would be possible to realize the expectations of the drafters in connection with waivers only if all quotas were considerably larger. A general increase in quotas of 50 per cent was approved in February 1959 and a further increase of 25 per cent in March 1965. These general increases, together with numerous increases in individual quotas throughout the life of the Fund, have expanded total quotas from under $8 billion to the equivalent of approximately $21 billion, but this has not led to a diminished grant of waivers.[14] The effect of the size of quotas and resources on the development of the Fund is not confined to waivers. The General Arrangements to Borrow and all that has followed on that decision are other consequences. This may be true also, at least to some extent, of other forms of financing balance of payments difficulties that have been negotiated outside the framework of the Fund. Some of these are now recognized by the amendments to the Articles.[15]

The Fund has been modest in its recourse to terms safeguarding its interests when granting waivers. The only terms that it has imposed, apart from the rare exceptions mentioned in the next paragraph, have dealt with repurchase. Whenever a member receives the benefit of a waiver, it is required to undertake a commitment to repurchase either as a term under the waiver provision or as a term in a stand-by arrangement.

Under Article V, Section 4 a further consideration that the Fund is to take into account when deciding whether to grant a waiver is "a member's willingness to pledge as collateral security gold, silver, securities, or other acceptable assets having a value sufficient in the opinion of the Fund to protect its interests" and the Fund may require "the pledge of such collateral security." There has always been resistance to the idea that the Fund should relax the standards of its tranche policies merely because of a member's willingness to give security. In addition, the Fund has drawn back from the prospect that, if a pledgor could not repurchase because of continuing difficulties, the Fund would have to decide either to pursue its remedy against the pledged property or, by foregoing its remedy, admit that the pledge was an illusory security. For these and other reasons, the Fund has shown no more than a glimmer of willingness to accept collateral.

---

[13] E.B. Decision No. 1477-(63/8), February 27, 1963; below, Vol. III, p. 239.

[14] The amendment by which 150 per cent of quota is substituted for quota in Article V, Section 7 (c) should be noted; see below, Vol. III, p. 523.

[15] Schedule B, paragraph 5; below, Vol. III, p. 535.

There have been only three decisions by the Fund to accept gold collateral, and one of them was abortive. It is interesting, however, that one of the cases did not involve a waiver but rested on the proposition that the Fund and a member could agree on the pledge of collateral in any circumstances. As a result of the reaction to some of the features of these three cases, the Fund adopted a general decision on July 1, 1963 which declared that it would be willing to enter into a gold collateral transaction in exceptional circumstances if this would promote the purposes of the Fund and give the member time to work out a program in consultation with the Fund. Certain restrictive conditions were established in order to enforce this objective, including the condition that normally the transaction would not be outstanding for more than six months.[16] There has been no transaction in which this decision has been tested.

The Fund itself, however, has given a negative pledge. When the General Arrangements to Borrow were being negotiated the participants feared that the Fund's liquidity would be enhanced unduly by its receipt of the currency of the participant in an exchange transaction made possible by a loan to the Fund. The Fund might then use that currency in transactions with other members, including nonparticipants. The Fund could not agree that some of its holdings could not be used in its operations, but it was a legitimate use to retain adequate satisfactory resources with which to repay its creditors. It is, therefore, a term of the General Arrangements to Borrow that the Fund shall not reduce its holdings of the currency of a participant below the amount that the Fund has borrowed under the General Arrangements to Borrow in order to finance a transaction with the participant.[17]

STAND-BY ARRANGEMENTS

The stand-by arrangement is the most original instrument of financial policy that the Fund has created. It is wholly an invention because no suggestion of it can be found in the Articles. Among the forces that produced it, as well as the tranche policies, were the affirmation of the Fund's power to challenge representations when members request the use of the Fund's resources, the absence of any clear definition of the circumstances in which there might be a challenge, and the Fund's determination early in 1952 to end its financial inactivity. The possibility of the stand-by arrangement was suggested, therefore, as a technique by which a member could be given an assurance that it would be able to make purchases not going beyond a prescribed limit during a defined period. The essential characteristic of a stand-by arrangement is that a member is given the assurance that it will be able to use the Fund's resources without any further

[16] E.B. Decision No. 1543-(63/39); below, Vol. III, pp. 240–42.
[17] E.B. Decision No. 1289-(62/1); below, Vol. III, p. 250.

review of its position and policies. This assurance means that there will be no challenge of a representation when there is a request to make a purchase under a stand-by arrangement, because it is a review which shows whether there is the basis for a challenge.

The idea imbedded in the decision of February 13, 1952 germinated in the first general decision on stand-by arrangements of October 1, 1952, and it has flourished with ever increasing vigor under the four major decisions of December 23, 1953, April 27, 1959, February 20, 1961,[18] and September 20, 1968. Each decision has been taken after a period in which it had become apparent as the result of experience that the stand-by arrangement could be made to serve the interests of members and the Fund even more effectively than it already had. There has been and continues to be great scope for the adaptation of policy on stand-by arrangements without running athwart the Articles.

There is no need to resume the stages by which the stand-by arrangement has been improved to the point of its present flexibility and variety. A few general reflections on its intricate history are appropriate, however, in a survey of development and change. The first comment must be that the concept of the stand-by arrangement has undergone a complete metamorphosis. Originally, it was considered as something in the nature of a confirmed line of credit that gave a member an absolute right to make purchases subject only to those provisions of the Articles on ineligibility and the general suspension of operations that were *lex cogens* and therefore necessarily applicable. At the present date it has become the main instrument for conditionality, and, in particular, for making the Fund's resources available beyond the first credit tranche only if the member observes certain policies. Annexed to each stand-by arrangement is a letter of intent from the member's authorities in which they set forth the program they will pursue. The stand-by arrangements that permit purchases beyond the first credit tranche include performance clauses establishing criteria on the non-observance of which the member's right to make purchases under the stand-by arrangement will be interrupted without the need for a decision by, or even notice to, the Executive Directors. Performance criteria are invariably objective in character, in the sense that a subjective judgment is not necessary in order to ascertain whether they are being observed, with the result that a member will know at all times whether it is able to make purchases. The movement, therefore, has been from the assurance of use without the review of requests to the definition of the circumstances in which there is assured use without review. It is still proper to speak of assured use because no evaluation is necessary in order to determine whether performance criteria are being observed. No subjective judgment is necessary to determine whether, for example, a limit on

---

[18] E.B. Decisions Nos. 155-(52/57), 270-(53/95), 876-(59/15), 1151-(61/6); below, Vol. III, pp. 230–33, 234.

credit has been transcended or a restriction on payments and transfers for current international transactions has been introduced. Therefore, if a member is unable to make purchases under its stand-by arrangement, it will not be able to complain that its legitimate expectations have been frustrated by a surprise decision of the Fund.

There are a number of reasons why the stand-by arrangement has been transformed into an instrument of conditionality. One reason has been the willingness of the Fund to take into account the fact that quotas are less than they might be and therefore to allow members to make a large outstanding use of the Fund's resources in terms of quota, provided, however, that there are adequate safeguards that the use will be proper. The continuous refinement of protective clauses in stand-by arrangements providing for consultation, review, and performance has made it possible to protect the Fund's resources against improper use. This should not be understood to mean that the provisions of stand-by arrangements have become progressively stricter for members with each development in the Fund's policies on stand-by arrangements. On the contrary, a dominant theme in the history of these arrangements has been an equitable reconciliation of the assurance to members that they will be able to use the Fund's resources with the assurance to the Fund that use by members will be consistent with the Articles and the policies of the Fund. Great care has been taken to ensure that the balance between the two assurances is not disturbed by being tilted unfairly in either direction, with the result that there have been changes in policy that were designed to reduce the severity of certain protective clauses. For example, the Fund does not insist on performance criteria for purchases in the gold tranche or the first credit tranche, and the "prior notice" clause, which was in common use at one time and which enabled the Fund to interrupt the right to make purchases under a stand-by arrangement on the basis of its subjective judgment of performance, has been banished since February 1961. More recently, in September 1968, the Fund has decided that the number of performance criteria affecting purchases beyond the first credit tranche should be confined to those that are truly necessary for determining whether the objectives of the member's program are being achieved.

It must not be assumed that the stand-by arrangement could have become an effective instrument of conditionality without the support of members. It is true that from time to time there have been debates leading to a revision of policy in order to strike a more acceptable balance between the two basic assurances and between the desiderata of flexibility in dealing with the idiosyncrasies of particular cases and the uniform treatment of all members. The stand-by arrangement has had the endorsement of members since its conception, and the Fund's efforts to improve the efficacy of the instrument have had the same response. The Fund's approval of a stand-by arrangement is commonly regarded by other sources of finance as a seal of approval on the member's program as set forth in its letter of intent, although it should be understood that the standards for this judgment depend upon the amount in terms of tranches that is made available by the stand-by arrangement. Other lenders, international, governmental, or private, often await the Fund's decision to approve a stand-by arrangement before entering into their own financial arrangements with the member, sometimes in a total amount exceeding the amount that the member can purchase under the stand-by arrangement. This is one of the reasons why most of the exchange transactions of the Fund now take place under stand-by arrangements and they account for the larger proportion by value as well. Moreover, there are cases in which stand-by arrangements are approved although there is no great likelihood that any purchases will be made under them. Sometimes a member fears that it is not the presence of a stand-by arrangement but its absence that may be interpreted as a criticism of the member's program. This is an unexpected form of testimony by some members to the success of the Fund's erstwhile campaign to encourage a more routine use of the Fund's resources in order to dispel the impression that members resort to the Fund only in a crisis. Now, if one or another member is reluctant to use the Fund's resources the reason is less likely to be the fear that the public will be alarmed than the reluctance of the member to measure its program against the Fund's tranche policies.

The stand-by arrangement has become the main instrument by which the Fund makes a practical contribution to the adjustment process because all stand-by arrangements are approved on the basis of a letter of intent in which the member sets forth its policies after they have been discussed with the representatives of the Fund. The legal character of the stand-by arrangement and letter of intent as clarified by the Fund is itself evidence of the responsiveness of the Fund. In its letter of intent a member states the program that it will pursue during the period of the stand-by arrangement. The stand-by arrangement is the Fund's decision which prescribes the terms on which the member may make purchases consistently with the Articles, including those specific or quantified policies, targets, or ceilings that are to be performance criteria, i.e., the criteria that the member must observe in order that there will be no interruption of its right to make purchases. There are many reasons why a member may not be able to observe a performance criterion, and sometimes the circumstances responsible for non-observance may be beyond the member's control. The Fund has made it clear that a letter of intent does not have contractual effect, and the non-observance of a performance criterion is not the violation of an international agreement. If a member fails to observe a performance criterion, its access to the Fund's resources under a stand-by arrangement will be interrupted not because it is breaking a contractual commitment but because the Fund has decided in the stand-by arrangement that the non-observance may result in an improper use of the Fund's resources and therefore that there should be consultation with the

Fund to determine the circumstances in which further purchases may be made. This analysis is consistent with the disposition of the Fund to avoid actions that may harm the reputation of members. The analysis has made it easier for members to formulate effective programs and accept performance clauses as a basis for access to the Fund's resources. The stand-by arrangement is a wholly original contribution to international finance and international monetary law.

THE GOLD TRANCHE

One of the main purposes of the decision of February 13, 1952 was to give members the maximum assurance that was possible under the Articles that they would be able to make certain purchases without challenge. The purchases for which there was the strongest case were those that would not raise the Fund's holdings of a member's currency above its quota. These purchases would not exceed the net contribution in economic terms that the member had made to the Fund because they would be no more than the member's gold subscription and the net use of the member's currency by the Fund in its operations and transactions. In the first instance, the amount of this contribution was equal to the member's gold subscription, and for this reason it was called the gold tranche. The Fund could not bind itself validly to surrender the right to challenge the representation of a member requesting a transaction, but in order to convey the idea that a challenge was highly unlikely in practice, even though it remained possible in law, the decision informed members that they could count on "receiving the overwhelming benefit of any doubt" if they requested gold tranche purchases. The concept of "adequate safeguards" in Article I (v), under which the Fund makes its resources available, enables it to graduate safeguards according to financial risk. For gold tranche purchases, the Fund could adopt minimum safeguards because its risk would not exceed the member's own net economic contribution to the Fund.

The gold tranche policy thus began as an attempt to encourage a limited use of the Fund's resources, but from this modest origin it has developed into yet another original contribution to international monetary law and financial arrangements. Once the Fund had formulated its full tranche policies and had become an active financial institution, the gold tranche policy ceased to be an experimental first step in the use of the Fund's resources. The Fund and many of its members began to see in the gold tranche a facility that could be treated as a reserve asset under central bank statutes or at least in the public presentation of a member's reserves. One advantage of this treatment of the gold tranche was that it would counteract the decline in reserves that would follow from the payment of a gold subscription to the Fund or from the Fund's sale of a member's currency and the member's conversion of it into a reserve currency. The latter effect would have special importance in connection with the Fund's efforts to bring about the use of a broader range of currencies in its transactions.

The Fund urged its members to regard the gold tranche as an asset, notwithstanding an occasional resistance provoked by the novelty of the idea, and did what it could to emphasize the asset-like character of the gold tranche. In order to facilitate gold tranche purchases, the Fund refrained from making an examination of the member's policies as it did in the case of purchases beyond the gold tranche, and on August 3, 1964 the Fund adopted a further simplification of procedure for dealing with requests for gold tranche purchases. They were not placed on the agenda of the Executive Directors, unless there was a prompt call for discussion, and arrangements were made for an accelerated transfer of currency.[19] There remained, however, certain shortcomings of the gold tranche in the view of some members. Although in practice it had the quality of ready availability, often described as *"de facto* automaticity" or "virtual automaticity," it could not be given this quality *de jure*. It had to remain subject in principle to the possibility of challenge, although it was never necessary for the Fund to clarify in what circumstances it would feel constrained to challenge a representation because even the overwhelming benefit of any doubt would not be an adequate presumption of propriety. The legal possibility of challenge was not the only shortcoming. It was pointed out that, in addition, the gold tranche policy could be abrogated because it was no more than a policy, and again it was not a formal rebuttal of the objection to aver that this was unlikely to occur. These criticisms of the gold tranche became more troublesome as the Fund sought to promote a policy on the use of an increasing number of currencies in its transactions, one result of which would be to produce gold tranches for more members. There was some sympathy for a more solid legal foundation for the gold tranche even before the principle of amendment was accepted at Rio de Janeiro, and it is not surprising, therefore, that a number of the amendments concentrate on the legal status of the gold tranche and its characteristics. Under the amendments, representations by a member when requesting gold tranche purchases will be immune from challenge by legal prescription, and the gold tranche will enter yet another stage in its evolution.

The Fund's success in achieving widespread recognition of the gold tranche as a reserve asset even before the proposals to amend the Articles led it to make a similar effort in connection with the claims of its creditors to repayment under loan agreements negotiated by the Fund in order to replenish its holdings of currencies. The terms of the General Arrangements to Borrow [20] and the bilateral loan agreement with Italy [21] provide that if before the due date for repayment a lender gives notice to the Fund representing that it has a balance of payments

---

[19] E.B. Decision No. 1745-(64/46); below, Vol. III, p. 243.

[20] E.B. Decision No. 1289-(62/1), January 5, 1962, paragraph 11 (f); below, Vol. III, p. 250.

[21] See below, p. 544.

need for repayment, the Fund will give "the overwhelming benefit of any doubt" to the representation and will make prompt repayment. Members lending to the Fund under these agreements have concluded that the characteristics of their claims to repayment warranted recognition of them as reserve assets. It will be seen later that once again the reserve character of these claims will have legal endorsement under the amendments to the Articles.

CREDIT TRANCHE POLICY AND COMPENSATORY FINANCING

The Fund's policies for the use of the "credit" tranches, i.e., for members' purchases beyond the gold tranche, developed after 1952 on the legal basis of the Fund's power to challenge representations and the concept of adequate safeguards. By 1955 the Annual Report could state the policy for the first credit tranche and by 1957 the Annual Report could formulate the policy for the higher tranches.[22] These declarations are the framework within which the Fund supports the policies of members by making its resources available as conditional liquidity. Members have come to recognize the credit tranche policies as applied to both purchases and stand-by arrangements as more than the safeguards by which the Fund attempts to protect its resources against improper use. In a world in which the adjustment process is still largely unregulated by international agreement, the credit tranche policies perform part of the task, although only for members in balance of payments deficit.

The greater part of the financial activity of the Fund is now conducted under its credit tranche policies, but the Fund has been prolific in establishing more specialized operations. Although the Fund still subscribes to the doctrine that its financial operations are entered into for the purpose of assisting members to overcome difficulties in the balance of payments taken as a whole, the Fund has felt that this did not prevent it from identifying the specific character of the difficulty and providing assistance more closely related to the difficulty.

The compensatory financing facility is one of the results of this approach that deserves special notice not only because of the intrinsic interest of the facility but also because it has had an effect on the amendments to the Articles. On February 27, 1963 the Fund adopted a decision under which it declared its willingness to assist all members, but particularly primary producers, by compensating them for temporary shortfalls in their export receipts that were largely attributable to circumstances beyond their control. The Fund had been making its resources available to members suffering from these difficulties under its tranche policies but now it was prepared to give special assistance. Compensation was to be limited normally to 25 per cent of quota and was to be additional to

---

[22] *Annual Report, 1955*, p. 85; *Annual Report, 1957*, p. 119.

the amounts that a member could purchase under the tranche policies. For purchases under the new facility special criteria were prescribed that were less severe than those that applied to the credit tranches or at least the higher credit tranches.[23] On September 20, 1966 the facility was liberalized in amount and in other ways,[24] one of which was the introduction of the "floating" feature. Under the earlier policy, the compensatory financing facility was not separated from the ordinary tranches, with the result that a purchase under the facility might exhaust the gold tranche or the first credit tranche as well and thus deprive the member of the opportunity to make other purchases under the relaxed criteria that apply to those tranches. The revised policy introduced an original development in Fund practice by providing that the facility was to exist alongside the ordinary tranches without overlapping them, so that purchases under the facility would not affect the tranches. The facility has been given statutory recognition in a form that will be mentioned later.

USE OF RESOURCES FOR CAPITAL TRANSFERS

On September 26, 1946 the Executive Directors adopted an interpretation in response to a request made by the Governor for the United States in accordance with the U.S. Bretton Woods Agreements Act.[25] The question was drafted somewhat infelicitously and seemed to ask whether the Fund's authority went beyond the financing of deficits on current account to the length of meeting a large or sustained outflow of capital. The reply to the question was that "authority to use the resources of the Fund is limited to use in accordance with its purposes to give temporary assistance in financing balance of payments deficits on current account for monetary stabilization operations."[26] This appeared to exclude all possibilities for the use of the Fund's resources in respect of an outflow of capital under Article VI ("Capital Transfers"). Section 1 (a) of that Article declares that a member may not make net use of the Fund's resources to meet a large or sustained outflow of capital, and Section 1 (b) provides that this rule does not prevent the use of the Fund's resources for certain capital transactions of reasonable amount. According to these provisions, therefore, it would seem that the Fund's resources could be used to deal with difficulties created by a capital outflow that was not large or sustained or by certain specified capital transactions of reasonable amount.

There was no doubt that the drafters had placed primary emphasis on the financing of deficits on current account but they had left room in Article VI

[23] E.B. Decision No. 1477-(63/8); below, Vol. III, p. 238.
[24] *Compensatory Financing of Export Fluctuations: A Second Report by the International Monetary Fund*; below, Vol. III, pp. 469–96.
[25] Sec. 13; see above, Chapter 22, footnote 8.
[26] E.B. Decision No. 71-2; below, Vol. III, p. 245.

for the financing of difficulties caused by capital transactions in certain circumstances. The interpretation of September 26, 1946 had not been applied so as to preclude this form of financing, and indeed it gave so little difficulty that virtually no reference was made to it in the Fund's conduct of its operations. By 1961 widespread convertibility had been restored for the currencies of members that had major roles in world trade and payments and this movement had been accompanied by a freedom for exchange markets that permitted great mobility for capital movements. This probably involved a greater freedom for capital movements than the drafters had expected. They had assumed that capital transfers would be suppressed by controls if they became troublesome, and this assumption was carried to the point of empowering the Fund to call for capital controls in certain circumstances. The view which developed, however, was that greater freedom was beneficial and would bring about a greater integration among markets, even though there were dangers of disequilibrating movements. As a result, the Fund has never exercised its power to call for capital controls.

Greater permissiveness for capital movements made it more difficult to decide contemporaneously to what extent payments problems were in the current or in the capital account. In these circumstances, it became advisable to ascertain the exact effect of the 1946 interpretation. Studies of the legislative history of the Articles confirmed what seemed apparent from the text of Article VI: use of the Fund's resources for capital outflows was not proscribed if the outflows were not "large or sustained." These terms were not self-executing, and in the application of them the Fund could take a number of factors into account, including the resources, whether subscribed or borrowed, available for its transactions and its continued capacity to help members deal with deficits on current account. Certain special difficulties might have arisen if it had been necessary to rescind or amend the interpretation, but it was decided ultimately that a clarification would suffice because it could not have been intended that the interpretation should reject what seemed so clear on a reading of Article VI. On July 28, 1961 the Executive Directors decided "by way of clarification" that the interpretation of September 26, 1946 "does not preclude the use of the Fund's resources for capital transfers in accordance with the provisions of the Articles, including Article VI." [27]

The clarification did not initiate use of the Fund's resources to meet difficulties occasioned by capital transfers. That kind of use had already occurred. It is probable, however, that it has led to a greater volume of use for this purpose than would have occurred without provoking the anxiety that this could not be defended under Fund law. The reason for this in large part is that the General Arrangements to Borrow became effective on October 24, 1962 "in order to

---

[27] E.B. Decision No. 1238-(61/43); below, Vol. III, p. 245.

enable the . . . Fund to fulfill more effectively its role in the international monetary system in the new conditions of widespread convertibility, including greater
freedom for short-term capital movements." [28] The participants in the General
Arrangements to Borrow stand ready, in accordance with the terms of the
General Arrangements, to make their currencies available to the Fund to supplement its resources for financing the exchange transactions of these members
in order to deal with their balance of payments difficulties, including, but not
limited to, those produced by short-term capital movements.

THE WIDER USE OF CURRENCIES

The last of the leading decisions on the use of the Fund's resources to be
considered here is the decision of July 20, 1962 entitled "Currencies to be drawn
and to be used in repurchases." [29] It is a decision approving a statement that sets
out "what may be regarded as appropriate practices to be followed for the time
being." The tentative note in this language reflects the novelty of the synthesis
that was being attempted. Nevertheless, the statement has not been amended
since it was adopted, although, as in the case of most important declarations of
policy, it has become the nucleus around which conventions and procedures are
constantly forming.

For ten years or more, almost all purchases from the Fund were of U.S. dollars, but in 1958 the Fund began to suggest that other currencies might enter
into its transactions. As the deficit in the balance of payments of the United
States continued, it became less justifiable to concentrate on the dollar in the
Fund's exchange transactions with other members while the United States itself
was reluctant to use the Fund's resources. If the United States had been more
willing to purchase the currencies of other members, it would have been
possible to continue to sell substantial amounts of dollars to other members.
This procedure would have produced fewer problems in applying the provisions
of the Articles. With the reluctance of the United States to resort to the Fund,
it became necessary to sell non-reserve currencies to other members. This
process was encouraged by the *de facto* convertibility of many European currencies and the protracted payments difficulties of both of the main reserve
currency countries. The practices that grew up in the period after 1958 were the
main content of the decision of July 20, 1962.

A policy of a wider use of currencies in Fund transactions had to be considered in relation to Article V, Section 3 (*a*) (i), which speaks of the sale of a
currency that is needed by the purchasing member for making payments "in that
currency." The language could be read to mean that a member is entitled to

---

[28] E.B. Decision No. 1289-(62/1), January 5, 1962; below, Vol. III, p. 246.
[29] E.B. Decision No. 1371-(62/36); below, Vol. III, pp. 235–38.

purchase the currency that the member needs to support its exchange market or that its residents need in order to make international payments. On this view, the member would be able to purchase its intervention currency or the currency demanded by payees, which might be the intervention currency in its role of transactions or "vehicle" currency. This version would preclude the sale by the Fund of currencies that would have to be converted by the currency issuer for the benefit of the purchasing member. In reply to this view, it was argued that in a regime of widespread convertibility a member could be said to need any currency that would be converted in order that the proceeds could be put into the market. There was, however, a different approach to the provision which did not require the elucidation of its language. Whatever the words "for making in that currency payments" meant, the Fund could waive them as one of the conditions that were subject to waiver under Article V, Section 4, and in this way the Fund could eliminate any restrictive effect of the words on the sale of currencies. The choice between these theories was never formally settled. It was sufficient that the sale of currencies that would be converted by the currency issuers into a reserve currency for the benefit of purchasing members could be defended under the Articles. Moreover, the question whether there is an obligation on a member to convert its currency for the benefit of a purchasing member also has been left unresolved. Members have been willing to convert their currencies in the conviction that a policy of collaboration of this kind benefited the whole membership of the Fund. The evolution of procedures satisfactory to members for consulting them on the use of their currencies has encouraged the collaboration on which the wider use of currencies depends.

The decision of July 20, 1962 rests on the principle that the selection of currencies for use in the Fund's transactions should be based on the balance of payments and reserve positions of members as well as on the level of the Fund's holdings of their currencies. The Fund seeks to maintain an equitable proportion among members in the sale of their currencies, but the motive for this now is not so much equality of sacrifice as the fair distribution of a reserve asset resulting from Fund transactions, the gold tranche. It is a desirable asset because it is guaranteed as to gold value and to some extent carries remuneration.

It is now standard practice for a member contemplating a purchase to consult the Fund on the currency or currencies it should select. A similar practice has become established in connection with the choice of currencies to be used in repurchases that do not accrue under Article V, Section 7 (b), and the decision of July 20, 1962 includes criteria for this purpose also. The impact of the decision has extended even beyond the wider use of currencies in purchases and repurchases because the criteria which it established have affected the drafting of the provisions of the General Arrangements to Borrow on the selection of the currencies that should be lent to the Fund to supplement its resources and, more recently, the drafting of the amendments on special drawing rights.

The practices that are described in the decision of July 20, 1962 and that have grown up under it have had a fundamental effect on the operation of the Fund. These practices have made it possible for members to give assistance through the Fund whenever their position warrants this, and to give assistance on a multilateral basis that eliminates any need to link deficits and surpluses bilaterally. Another result is that to a large extent the subscription paid by a member in its currency has become a token of the reserve currency, or even gold, into which the member will convert its currency for use by purchasing members.

The policy has had another interesting effect. The drafters of the Articles were worried that the traditional practice by which trade and payments are conducted largely in a few transactions currencies might lead to the immobilization of the Fund's holdings of many or even most currencies.[30] For example, a member might require that payments to it or to its residents be made in dollars, with the result that the Fund's holdings of the member's currency would not be in demand from the Fund for making payments to it. At the same time, there might be additional pressure on the Fund's holdings of U.S. dollars because other members might have to purchase dollars for making payments to the member or its residents. A member is free to prescribe the currency in which payments must be made to the member or its residents. This is not a restriction on the *making* of payments and transfers. The drafters did not want to interpose any impediment to the traditional use of transactions currencies, and so they adopted a special, although partial, solution for the effect that this practice might have on the Fund's currency holdings. They imposed an additional repurchase obligation on a member that required payments to be made in a "third" currency if it was itself using the Fund's resources. A formula was adopted under which the proceeds of transactions which a member had received in a third currency had to be used for the repurchase of that member's currency from the Fund even beyond the standard repurchase obligation if that obligation did not reduce the Fund's holdings to 75 per cent of the member's quota.[31] But this was a case in which the drafters' reach exceeded the administrators' grasp, because no way was found by which the provision could be made to work. The Fund's policy on the wider use of currencies in its transactions provides a more satisfactory solution. If a member is in an economic position that justifies the use of its currency under the decision, other members can purchase the currency for conversion by the member into its reserve currency and they can use that currency for making international payments. Moreover, these sales by the Fund of the member's currency can be more extensive than the member's repurchases. A member cannot reduce the Fund's holdings of its currency below 75 per cent

---

[30] *Proceedings*, pp. 461–63.

[31] Article V, Section 7 (*b*) (ii); below, Vol. III, pp. 192–93.

of quota by repurchase, but the Fund can sell any of the member's currency which it holds without observing that or any other limit.

It is convenient to refer here to another financial provision that has been dormant most of the time, although it has not become a dead letter. This is Article VIII, Section 4, which created a new form of convertibility. If a member undertakes the obligations of convertibility under the Articles it must convert balances of its currency that are presented to it by the monetary authorities of another member if the balances were recently acquired as the result of current transactions or their conversion is needed for making payments for current transactions. The currency issuer may choose to make the conversion with either gold or the currency of the other member, but the currency issuer will not be obligated to make a conversion unless it is entitled to purchase the currency of the other member from the Fund. This was a new form of convertibility because it is convertibility through the Fund on the theory that if the currency issuer purchases from the Fund the currency of the holder of the balances, the extent to which the latter will be able to make purchases of currencies from the Fund will be increased correspondingly. The provision is based on the assumption of a bilateral balancing of payments that has not occurred among members having convertible currencies.[32] With the restoration of free exchange markets, most conversions take place in the market on an even broader scale than is required by Article VIII, Section 2 (*a*), under which members must refrain from restricting payments and transfers for current international transactions. In the result, there has been only one occasion on which there was an overt reference to Article VIII, Section 4 as the basis of a transaction. This was a sale by the Fund in August 1966 of lire to the United States in an amount equivalent to one quarter of a billion dollars in order to enable it to convert dollars held by Italy. The sale was contemporaneous with an equivalent loan of lire by Italy to the Fund.

The Fund's policy on the selection of the appropriate currencies for its exchange transactions has not departed from the drafters' theory of a "passive" Fund. The main expression of that theory is Article V, Section 2, which places a "limitation on the Fund's operations" by declaring that, except as otherwise provided in the Articles, the Fund's operations are to be confined to transactions for the purpose of supplying a member, "on the initiative of such member," with the currency of another member in return for gold or for the purchasing member's currency. Under this provision, the Fund cannot initiate an exchange transaction, either with a member or in the market. Under the policy on the selection of currencies, the Fund does not initiate exchange transactions, but it is the active party in indicating the currencies that are to be purchased in transactions initiated by members.

---

[32] See *Questions and Answers on the International Monetary Fund*, Question 24; below, Vol. III, pp. 164–65.

Another effect of Article V, Section 2 is that the Fund cannot sell currency A to member A in return for currency B, except under the repurchase provisions, if, for example, the Fund wishes to acquire currency B because member C wishes to purchase it from the Fund. Under the Fund's policy on the selection of currencies, however, the Fund has been able to sell currency A to member C and member A has converted currency A into currency B for the benefit of member C. In this example, it is assumed, of course, that currency B is a reserve currency of A and needed by C. Because the conversion is not carried out in a direct operation with the Fund it need not be made at the par values.[33] Once there is a departure from par values, however, the question of the ultimate value received by the purchasing member C arises, and this consideration has not been absent in the selection of currencies under the policy. The experience with exchange rates in conversions under the policy has been taken into account in the drafting of the provisions dealing with special drawing rights. In transactions between participants in the special drawing rights facility, currency is not provided at the par value, and the exchange rates that are used must be such that the transferor of special drawing rights receives the same value whatever the currencies that are provided.[34]

A BACKWARD GLANCE

In retrospect, there seem to have been two major and related themes in the evolution of the Fund's practice on the use of its resources. The first has been the development of the two forms of liquidity, conditional and unconditional, that the Fund makes available to its members. Once it was accepted that the Articles give the Fund a power to challenge the representation made by a member when requesting the use of the Fund's resources, it became desirable to encourage members to use the Fund's resources by creating the concept of a gold tranche that was to be available as nearly automatically as possible. Because of this and other attributes, the gold tranche became recognized eventually as a new reserve asset. Meanwhile, the tranche policies based on an ascending scale of conditionality were being elaborated, while constant experiment was being devoted to the stand-by arrangement in order to improve it as the main instrument for putting this conditionality to work. A prerequisite of development in this part of the Fund's constitutional history was the solution of the problems of temporary use and repurchase. Both the tranche policies and stand-by arrangements have entered on the scene and played their leading parts without the benefit of express mention in the Articles.

---

[33] Article IV, Section 1 (b). E.B. Decision No. 1371-(62/36), July 20, 1962; below, Vol. III, pp. 237–38.

[34] Article XXV, Section 8; below, Vol. III, p. 530.

The second main theme has been the extension of the Fund's financial operations in both volume and character. The "adequate safeguards" of tranche policies and stand-by arrangements and the liberal approach to waivers have made it possible to permit large individual transactions and large outstanding use of the Fund's resources in terms of quota. Borrowing by the Fund and the employment of a wider range of currencies in its transactions are other techniques that have made this greater use possible. Clarification of the Fund's authority to permit the use of its resources to meet difficulties caused by capital outflows in certain circumstances and the creation of the compensatory financing facility are leading examples of the adaptability of the Fund in helping members to deal with pressing new problems.

The position of the United States in the world and in the Fund has dominated much of the history of this part of the Fund's affairs. For many years it was the member which provided virtually the only currency purchased from the Fund, and it used its influence to insist on adequate safeguards. In a later stage, the United States was in a persistent and troubling deficit in its balance of payments, and the Fund then sought to adjust itself to a situation in which the United States would need to receive assistance in financing its deficit, in greater or less degree through the Fund according to the willingness of the United States itself. It is not surprising that in this stage the members that did not readily accept the caution of the United States in the earlier period are now the most determined advocates of it. This change of opinion has had a decisive effect on the amendments of the Articles that deal with the use of the Fund's resources.

The Code of Conduct

Joseph Gold

PAR VALUES AND EXCHANGE RATES

The basic premise of the provisions dealing with par values and rates of exchange, sometimes referred to as the par value system, was the novel idea that rates of exchange are matters of international concern and therefore should be the subject of international scrutiny and endorsement. It was provided that each member should agree on a par value for its currency with the Fund.[1] Exchange rates should be fixed, and therefore should not fluctuate beyond narrow margins around the par value,[2] and multiple currency practices should be avoided.[3] To ensure stability without rigidity, it was agreed that a par value should be subject to change but only to correct a fundamental disequilibrium. Each member was to have the exclusive privilege of proposing a change in the par value of its currency, but it was required to consult the Fund and in most cases obtain its concurrence before making a change. In deciding whether to concur in or object to a change, the Fund would seek to deter a member from making a change that would be competitive.[4]

The Fund has had to deal with a world for which this model was not completely appropriate, with the result that the model has been adapted in some respects, although without any compromise of the principle that rates of exchange are matters of international concern. The most crucial issue of interpretation in which this principle was involved in the early years of the Fund was the question whether a member could adapt multiple currency practices, or in the case of some members introduce them, without the approval of the Fund because the member was availing itself of the transitional arrangements of Article XIV. Section 2 of that Article enables a member availing itself of the

---

[1] Article XX, Section 4; below, Vol. III, p. 208.
[2] Article IV, Sections 3 and 4 (b).
[3] Article VIII, Section 3.
[4] Article IV, Section 5.

transitional arrangements to adapt restrictions on payments and transfers for current international transactions to changing circumstances, and introduce them where necessary if the member had been occupied by the enemy, and the question that had to be answered was whether this authority applied to multiple currency practices when, as is often true, they are also restrictions. Notwithstanding Article XIV, Section 2, the Fund decided that if a restriction is also a rate of exchange, the rate provisions, and basically Article IV, Section 4 (a), must be observed, and a member is obligated to obtain the approval of the Fund before making the change of rate that would be involved in the adaptation or introduction of a multiple currency practice. The objection that this conclusion put members maintaining multiple currency practices as a form of exchange control at a disadvantage compared with those maintaining other forms of exchange control did not prevail. The decision was communicated to members together with a statement of the Fund's policies on multiple currency practices in a letter of December 19, 1947.[5]

The direct and indirect impact of the decision on the practice of the Fund has been enormous. It is obviously important because so many members maintaining multiple currency practices have availed themselves of the transitional arrangements of Article XIV and also because the postwar transitional period in which those arrangements operate has not been terminated. The ideological importance of the decision has been even more profound. It was animated by the conviction that jurisdiction over rates of exchange is at the heart of the Fund's functions and the constriction of that jurisdiction could maim the Fund's authority. The Fund's letter of December 19, 1947 described the obligations of members in connection with exchange stability, orderly exchange arrangements, and the avoidance of competitive alterations as "fundamental considerations" in the interpretation of the Articles. The decision and the conviction on which it rests have influenced the attitude of the Fund on other questions involving exchange rates. No decision can be recalled in which the Fund has held that it does not have jurisdiction in connection with the adoption of exchange rates for a member's currency. This does not mean that all issues affecting exchange rates have been settled. For example, the Fund has found it necessary to reconcile Article VI, Section 3, which gives members broad powers to control capital transfers, and Article VIII, Section 3, which prevents members from engaging in discriminatory currency arrangements without the approval of the Fund. The Executive Directors held on July 25, 1956 that the members' authority to control capital transfers had to be given primacy and that they could discriminate in the application of their capital controls without the need for the approval of the Fund.[6] The Executive Directors drew back, however, from extending this decision to multiple currency practices that applied to capital transfers, and they

---

[5] E.B. Decision No. 237-2; below, Vol. III, pp. 261-65.
[6] E.B. Decision No. 541-(56/39); below, Vol. III, p. 246.

did this precisely because rates of exchange were involved. The Executive Directors reserved for later decision the question whether under Article VI, Section 3 members may freely introduce or adapt, without the approval of the Fund, multiple currency practices that apply to capital transfers or whether members must obtain the Fund's approval of these actions under Article VIII, Section 3. The Executive Directors have not decided this question so far, but the staff has held the view that the approval of the Fund is required, and in a number of cases in which a multiple currency practice affecting capital transfers was introduced or adapted, and the Fund agreed that the practice was justified, the Fund adopted a formula by which it gave such approval as was necessary. This formula keeps the jurisdictional issue open until such time as it becomes so important in practice that its solution is necessary.

It is clear from the Articles that the drafters assumed that the prevention of competitive devaluation would be a major preoccupation of the Fund, but the overvaluation of currencies has been a greater problem than undervaluation. This phenomenon was reflected in the issue which arose as a result of the unauthorized change of par value by France in January 1948. The question was whether the Fund was required to concur in a change of par value which was in the right direction and not competitive but in the opinion of the Fund inadequate to correct the member's fundamental disequilibrium. The Executive Directors decided on March 1, 1948 that the extent of the change in a par value that is necessary to correct a fundamental disequilibrium cannot be determined with precision, and that in considering a member's proposal to make a change the Fund would give the member the benefit of any reasonable doubt. If, however, the Fund concluded, after giving the member the benefit of any reasonable doubt, that the proposed change was insufficient to correct the fundamental disequilibrium, the Fund had the authority to object to the proposal and was not bound to concur in it.[7] Part of the reasoning on which the decision rested was that the phrases "correct a fundamental disequilibrium" or "necessary to correct a fundamental disequilibrium" mean that the change is sufficient to bring about a correction, with the result that the Fund is not bound to concur in any proposal that would not bring about a full correction.

Another decision that bears on the degree of flexibility in the par value system is the question whether the Fund may approve a fluctuating rate as a transitional device from one par value to another par value. Some experts have had a certain sympathy for a device of this kind because of the difficulty of determining the precise level at which a new par value should be fixed in order to correct a fundamental disequilibrium. A transitional fluctuating rate, it has been argued, would permit a period of experiment in which to determine what the new par value should be. On July 22, 1948 when Mexico ceased to ensure that its par

---

[7] E.B. Decision No. 278-3; below, Vol. III, p. 227.

value would be effective and again on September 19, 1949 when Belgium proposed to adopt such a regime, the Fund's reaction was based on the principle that it had no legal power to approve the regime even as a temporary expedient. If a member ceases to ensure that exchange transactions within its territories take place only within the permitted margins around the par value established under the Articles, the member is failing to fulfill its obligations. The definitive statement affirming this position appeared in the Fund's Annual Report for 1951 [8] after Canada adopted a fluctuating rate in September 1950, and was repeated in the Annual Report for 1962.[9]

The discussion so far illustrates the sensitivity of the Fund to exchange rates as matters of international concern and the pervasiveness of its jurisdiction over them, but indicates that there are certain limits under the Articles on the ability of members to adopt or the Fund to approve certain exchange rate practices or regimes. This brings the discussion to those developments by which the Fund has been able to accommodate itself to something less than the optimal system as foreseen by the drafters. In the three cases in which Mexico, Belgium, and Canada felt that they must cease to support the par value in exchange transactions, the Fund refrained from applying sanctions, and even showed some sympathy, but there is even stronger evidence of the Fund's tolerance. There have been instances in which the Fund has welcomed or encouraged the adoption of a fluctuating rate. In many of these cases the member was eliminating multiple currency practices or simplifying a complex exchange rate regime. In the case of simplification, the Fund is able to approve the remaining rates as multiple currency practices but it has no power to approve if rates are unified. It may seem odd that the Fund can approve multiple currency practices but not a unitary fluctuating rate, but the explanation is the assumption underlying the Articles that if a member is in a position to have a single rate for its currency it should be able to fix a par value and should not allow the rate to fluctuate. On a number of occasions the Fund has approved stand-by arrangements in support of a fluctuating rate as part of a stabilization program. The theory, usually tacit, on which the Fund has welcomed or encouraged a fluctuating rate has been that the member was making progress towards the establishment of an effective par value and the observance of the purposes of the Fund. Nevertheless, in some cases in which the rate has become stabilized no new par value has been established, presumably on the ground that it was not yet certain that the official rate was soundly entrenched.

In some of these cases in which the Fund has put its resources at the disposition of a member, the so-called fluctuating rate has been too rigid to ensure the success of the member's stabilization program. The Fund has developed a num-

---

[8] *Annual Report, 1951*, pp. 36–41.
[9] *Annual Report, 1962*, pp. 58–67.

ber of techniques for incorporation in stand-by arrangements by which to encourage the member to pursue a policy of helpful exchange rate flexibility.

The Fund has exercised its authority over the use of its resources, particularly under stand-by arrangements, in a way that contributes to the adjustment of exchange rates even though they do not purport to be fluctuating rates. It is a member's prerogative to propose what the par value for its currency shall be, but it is the Fund's duty to husband its resources. The Fund has been unwilling, therefore, to make its resources available in support of a par value which it considers untenable. For example, the Fund's criterion for the use of its resources in the higher credit tranches refers to programs aimed at "establishing or maintaining the enduring stability of the currency concerned at a realistic rate of exchange." [10] The Fund's unwillingness to make its resources available to a member that has an inappropriate par value for its currency does not entitle the Fund to make a proposal that the par value be changed. The initial discussion of a transaction with the Fund takes place with the Managing Director or staff so that the member need not be embarrassed by further debate of the appropriateness of the exchange rate for its currency.

The Fund has been patient if new members have felt that their adherence to the full exchange rate regime of the Articles might be premature. The standard form of membership resolution under which a new member joins the Fund contains a paragraph empowering the Fund to call on the member to proceed with the establishment of a par value. In recent years many new members have been new countries as well and for this or other reasons the establishment of a viable par value by some of them has been difficult. The Fund has refrained from initiating the procedure that would require these members to establish par values. This policy gives greater weight to the provision in membership resolutions under which a member may change exchange rates before the establishment of a par value only after consulting the Fund and reaching agreement with it on the change.

The Fund's understanding of the special problems of these new members is apparent in more than its restraint in calling for the establishment of par values for their currencies. It has been forthcoming in its disposition to assist them with its resources. The general theory of the drafters was that after a member established a par value, it would be able to use the Fund's resources for the purpose of defending the par value if it were tenable and if support for a temporary period became necessary.[11] The Articles also provide that the Fund may determine the amounts of, and conditions for, purchases by a member belonging to a defined and limited class before it establishes a par value for its currency.[12]

---

[10] *Annual Report, 1958*, p. 24.

[11] Article III, Section 3; Article XX, Section 4 (*c*) and (*i*).

[12] Article XX, Section 4 (*d*).

In June 1953 the Executive Directors examined the question whether there was general authority to prescribe the amounts of and conditions for pre-par-value transactions, but there was no decision at that time largely because there was no authority in the Articles to do this for the benefit of one original member (Uruguay) that had not yet established a par value. After that member had established an initial par value and become eligible to use the Fund's resources, the Executive Directors decided on April 22, 1964 that the Fund had authority under the Articles to provide in all membership resolutions that it might permit pre-par-value transactions in such amounts and on such conditions as it saw fit.[13] The Fund would encourage members to follow policies leading to the establishment of realistic exchange rates and the adoption of effective par values at the earliest possible date, and, in deciding whether to give access to its resources, would take into account the efforts that the member was making to reach this objective. The Fund also decided that it would permit a member that had not yet established a par value to make gold tranche purchases and enjoy the benefits of the compensatory financing facility on the same basis as other members. The decision eliminated the anomaly that, whereas a member that has established an initial par value is able to use the Fund's resources even after it is forced by events to cease to ensure its effectiveness in exchange transactions, with a few exceptions a member that had not yet established an initial par value did not enjoy access to the Fund's resources even though its exchange rate regime might be an orderly one. The theory of the drafters was not offended because members in this latter condition were not entitled to use the Fund's resources but could make use of them only in the amounts and on the conditions permitted by the Fund.

This survey of actions by the Fund in favor of greater exchange rate flexibility will be concluded with one that relates to the margins for spot exchange transactions. These are fixed by the Articles at 1 per cent from par, and members must adopt appropriate measures consistent with the Articles to ensure that these margins are not transcended in exchange transactions within their territories. This meant, in effect, that each member could establish a margin of $\frac{1}{2}$ of 1 per cent for gold transactions in its currency. There is evidence that these were regarded as generous margins,[14] although there is also evidence that the drafters thought that the margins might become inadequate.[15] In December 1958, certain European members that were contemplating the adoption of "external" convertibility concluded that it would help them to restore convertibility and free exchange markets, but with a certain economy in the use of reserves, if they were to adopt margins up to $\frac{3}{4}$ of 1 per cent on the U.S.

[13] E.B. Decision No. 1687-(64/22); below, Vol. III, p. 243.

[14] *Questions and Answers on the International Monetary Fund*, Question 19; below, Vol. III, pp. 158–60.

[15] Article XVI, Section 1.

dollar for their currencies. This meant that the margins for exchange transactions between any two of these currencies might be as much as 1½ per cent from par. Moreover, if a currency pegged on a currency that was itself pegged on a convertible currency, the margin in an exchange transaction involving the first currency and a third currency might be more than 1½ per cent from par. Basing itself on some early decisions,[16] the Fund decided that if a member takes official action to confine exchange transactions involving its own and another member's currency within 1 per cent of par and permits transactions involving its own and other currencies to go beyond those margins, this constitutes a multiple currency practice. In order, therefore, to assist members to move towards convertibility, the Fund decided on July 24, 1959 that it would not object to the cumulation of margins in such a system provided that the resulting margin from par for transactions between any two member currencies was no more than 2 per cent.[17]

RESTRICTIONS

The establishment of a multilateral system of payments in respect of current transactions between members is one of the purposes of the Fund and it is to be attained by the avoidance of restrictions on the making of payments and transfers for current international transactions as defined by the Articles. Article VIII, Section 2 requires members to refrain from imposing these restrictions without the approval of the Fund unless they are authorized by the transitional arrangements of Article XIV. The question of the definition of restrictions for the purposes of Article VIII, Section 2 was raised as a problem of interpretation in 1951. There were forces pulling in opposite directions: some wished to arrive at a definition that would make it clear that the Fund's jurisdiction did not embrace restrictions on trade, even if they were imposed for balance of payments reasons, because these were within the competence of the CONTRACTING PARTIES to the GATT, whereas others were troubled by the fact that this might limit the competence of the Fund in connection with members' balances of payments. There was a division of opinion on the primary question of definition and therefore no agreement on the secondary question whether the same measure might be a restriction on both payments under the Fund's Articles and on trade under the GATT. The differences of opinion could not be reconciled and discussion petered out.

The problem did not come to the surface again until 1960 when it seemed that a solution should be found because of the likelihood that a number of

---

[16] See E.B. Decision No. 237-2, December 18, 1947, and the accompanying statement on multiple currency practices; below, Vol. III, p. 265.

[17] E.B. Decision No. 904-(59/32); below, Vol. III, p. 226.

European members would accept the obligations of Article VIII. By that time, attitudes had become less uncompromising, partly because the scope of consultations under Article XIV, and the manner of conducting them, had become established. It had become clear also that certain measures were of a mixed character and came under the jurisdiction of both the Fund and the CONTRACTING PARTIES.

A 1959 staff study said that there were three possible approaches to the definition of what constitutes a restriction on payments and transfers for current international transactions under the Articles. One approach would deem a measure to be a restriction if the effect on the balance of payments was the motive with which the measure was adopted. The second approach was not concerned with motive but took account of the effect of a measure and would regard it as a restriction if the direct or indirect effect was to hinder payments or transfers for current international transactions. It was concluded that neither approach was acceptable and that the third of the possible approaches was correct. This looked simply at the way in which the measure was formulated and made to operate. The main elements responsible for this conclusion were the language of the Articles, which emphasized the financial or settlement aspect of a transaction, and the intention of the Bretton Woods Conference that there should be an international trade organization with a jurisdiction that would complement and in principle not overlap the jurisdiction of the Fund. Either of the other approaches would have resulted unavoidably in a very considerable coincidence of jurisdiction for the two organizations.

The conclusion that the test must be a technical one was accepted by the Executive Directors although with some regret by those who continued to feel a strong attachment to the balance of payments motive as the appropriate criterion. In their view, the fact that the Fund acted as the advisor of the CONTRACTING PARTIES on balance of payments and reserve questions and that the CONTRACTING PARTIES had bound themselves to accept the Fund's advice was not an adequate substitute for the direct jurisdiction of the Fund because not all members of the Fund were contracting parties. Nevertheless, agreement was reached, and the Fund's decision of June 1, 1960 records it in the sentence which reads: "The guiding principle in ascertaining whether a measure is a restriction on payments and transfers for current transactions under Article VIII, Section 2, is whether it involves a direct governmental limitation on the availability or use of exchange as such." [18] In order to help reconcile those who had held a different view, although they would insist on it no longer, the formula is expressed as a "guiding principle" and not as a definition or interpretation.

---

[18] E.B. Decision No. 1034-(60/27); below, Vol. III, pp. 260–61. See also James G. Evans, Jr., "Current and Capital Transactions: How the Fund Defines Them," *Finance and Development*, Vol. 5 (1968), No. 3, pp. 30–35; Stephen A. Silard, "The Impact of the International Monetary Fund on International Trade," *Journal of World Trade Law*, Vol. 2 (1968), No. 2, pp. 121–61.

Some executive directors, however, said that they would regard the guiding principle as an interpretation, and in practice it has operated in that way.

The settlement of this fundamental question of jurisdiction is interesting for a number of reasons. It illustrates the caution with which questions of jurisdiction under the code of conduct have been approached. It is an example of self-imposed discipline, and one that is all the more noteworthy because it was inspired by a design for international economic organization even though that design had not been realized. The presumed intention of the drafters prevailed even though some thought that it had lost its cogency because it had been based on an expectation that had been frustrated.

TRANSITIONAL ARRANGEMENTS

Article XIV deals with a "post-war transitional period" and permits members to avail themselves of "transitional arrangements" under which, notwithstanding the provisions of any other articles, they may maintain, and adapt to changing circumstances, restrictions on payments and transfers for current international transactions. There was also a limited authority for some members to introduce restrictions of this kind. A member exercising its privileges under the transitional arrangements is not required to seek the approval of the Fund under Article VIII for the maintenance, adaptation, or introduction of restrictions in accordance with Article XIV, Section 2. One of the conditions on which these privileges can be enjoyed by a member is that it is satisfied that it needs the restrictions for balance of payments reasons. Once it concludes that it has no balance of payments justification for restrictions, they can be maintained, adapted, or introduced only with the approval of the Fund under Article VIII.

From time to time it has been assumed by some commentators that the transitional period was of defined duration. Sometimes, this misapprehension was induced by the references in Article XIV, Section 4 to a period of three years after which the Fund began to report on restrictions and a period of five years after which members began to consult the Fund on the further retention of restrictions. In fact, there is no transitional period of defined length, and there is evidence that this was deliberate because of the fear of some countries that they might be pressed to adopt a premature convertibility for their currencies. There is, however, a procedure by which the Fund can make representations to a member that conditions are favorable for the withdrawal of particular restrictions or the abandonment of all of them. The caution of the drafters is illustrated by the fact that these representations may be made "in exceptional circumstances," but on January 6, 1947, the Fund's concern that a too extensive use might be made of the privileges of Article XIV led to a decision emphasizing that the Fund is the judge of what is meant by "exceptional circumstances."[19] If the Fund makes a representation to a member and finds that it persists in maintaining restrictions, the member becomes ineligible to use the Fund's resources. The Fund has made general policy declarations recommending or urging all members to withdraw certain kinds of restrictions,[20] and has adopted numerous decisions concluding consultations with individual members under Article XIV in which the Fund expressed the opinion in one way or another that the use of restrictions could be reduced or eliminated, but the Fund has never addressed a formal representation to a member under Article XIV, Section 4.

On a few occasions, but not since 1960, the question has been asked whether the Fund could terminate the transitional period by interpretation or in some other way. Another question that has been asked is whether the Fund could find that a member was no longer availing itself of the transitional arrangements and was in the same position as if it had given notice under Article XIV, Section 3 that it was prepared to accept the obligations of convertibility of Article VIII, Sections 2, 3, and 4. Neither of these questions has been resolved by the Fund.

The main reason why at least the first of these questions has not been answered is the transformation in the Fund's attitude to Article XIV which can be traced to 1960. On June 1 of that year the Executive Directors adopted a decision in the expectation that in the near future there would be a concerted acceptance of the obligations of Article VIII by a number of European members.[21] There was a widespread feeling that the legal convertibility of a currency under Article VIII should correspond with a real convertibility. It was clear that a member is entitled to decide for itself whether to give notice that it is prepared to accept the obligations of Article VIII, and the Fund cannot reject the notice, although it can refuse to approve any remaining restrictions. Once a member gives the notice, its currency is "convertible" under the Articles. Moreover, acceptance of the obligations of Article VIII is a one-way street, and a member cannot retreat to Article XIV after it has given the notice. There was no way to ensure that the convertibility of a currency would never be impaired, but it was at least possible to prevent convertibility from being turned into a legal fiction by discouraging a member from accepting the obligations of Article VIII if there was a risk that soon after acceptance it would have to request the Fund's approval for the introduction of restrictions.

The Fund's position can be discerned in paragraph 2 of the decision of June 1, 1960. The paragraph recognizes the right of members to give notice but states

---

[19] E.B. Decision No. 117-1; below, Vol. III, p. 269.

[20] E.B. Decisions Nos. 433-(55/42), June 22, 1955, 201-(53/29), May 4, 1953, 955-(59/45), October 23, 1959; below, Vol. III, pp. 258–60.

[21] E.B. Decision No. 1034-(60/27); below, Vol. III, pp. 260–61.

that before taking that step "it would be desirable that, as far as possible, they eliminate measures which would require the approval of the Fund, and that they satisfy themselves that they are not likely to need recourse to such measures in the foreseeable future." The Fund warned that it would not readily approve the maintenance or introduction of restrictions by a member once it had accepted the obligations of Article VIII. If a member proposed to maintain or introduce restrictions for balance of payments reasons, the Fund would grant approval "only where it is satisfied that the measures are necessary and that their use will be temporary while the member is seeking to eliminate the need for them." If the justification is not related to the balance of payments, "the Fund believes that the use of exchange systems for nonbalance of payments reasons should be avoided to the greatest possible extent."

The implication of this declaration of policy is that the Fund will not be complaisant about the maintenance or introduction of restrictions by a member that accepts the obligations of Article VIII but might be more tolerant about the use of restrictions by a member that has not yet accepted those obligations. This attitude reflects a willingness to see members continue to opt for the transitional arrangements if there is still doubt about the strength of their position, with the result that the postwar transitional period has become literally a period, of undefined duration, after the war. Even new members joining the Fund in these days are allowed a choice between the regimes of Article VIII and Article XIV. Moreover, there are members that are still technically under Article XIV even though they maintain no restrictions and therefore can take no action under Article XIV. If these members were to wish to introduce restrictions, they would have to request approval under Article VIII. Presumably, they retain their status under Article XIV because they believe their position to be such that they cannot say with confidence that "they are not likely to need recourse to" measures requiring approval "in the foreseeable future."

CONSULTATION

According to the first purpose of Article I, the Fund is to provide the machinery for consultation on international monetary problems, and the functioning of the Fund would be impossible without consultation with members. Under Article XIV, Section 4, members are required to consult the Fund each year on the further retention of any restrictions that are inconsistent with the Articles. This is a narrow jurisdictional basis for consultation and in earlier years there were difficulties in convincing some members that even the limited objective of this form of consultation required consideration of the economic context in which exchange restrictions were retained. Part of the problem was the suspicion that the Fund was extending its authority into the field of trade in which it had no jurisdiction to approve or disapprove trade practices. This problem persisted for a time even though it is a purpose of the Fund to facilitate the expansion and balanced growth of international trade and even though Article XIV, Section 2 requires members, as soon as conditions permit, to develop such commercial and financial arrangements with other members as will facilitate international payments and the maintenance of exchange stability.

One of the great advances in the Fund's activities has been the progressive acceptance of the idea that consultation under Article XIV should encompass all aspects of a member's economy that have a direct or indirect effect on the member's balance of payments. The scope of these consultations has not been limited even though there has been a steady withdrawal of restrictions to the point where some members still availing themselves formally of the transitional arrangements have few or even no restrictions still in force. The scope of consultation under Article XIV has become more extensive as confidence has grown between members and the Fund and as members have realized that the review is useful to the member with which the consultation is conducted and to other members as well. It is useful to other members because the consultation report is often the most comprehensive international report of its kind. One evidence of the value of these reports has been the increasing requests for the descriptive part of them by other international organizations. Discussion of the reports has made it possible for the Executive Directors to maintain multilateral surveillance over members, propose the adjustment of their policies, and gather knowledge on the basis of which to formulate the general policies of the Fund.

The acceptance of broad consultations on the narrow jurisdictional basis of Article XIV has been accompanied by increased consultation in connection with the use of the Fund's resources. Consultation clauses in stand-by arrangements have been refined over the years so as to make them more effective, and it is now established policy for a member to consult with the Fund whenever this seems advisable for as long as the member is using the Fund's resources beyond the first credit tranche. It would be reasonable to conclude that the greater use of the Fund's resources and the confidence that this has instilled in members have been influences in the progress towards searching but amicable consultations under Article XIV and even under Article VIII.

It is in relation to consultation under Article VIII that one of the most striking advances in the field of consultation was made by the decision of June 1, 1960. It had been understood that if a member had undertaken the obligations of Article VIII, Sections 2, 3, and 4, it could not be required to consult unless it maintained practices that were inconsistent with these provisions, and the decision states the principle with great firmness that consultation is not obligatory except in these latter circumstances. The decision goes on to acknowledge, however, that because the Fund is able to provide technical

facilities and advice, or because of the opportunity to exchange views on monetary and financial developments, "there is great merit in periodic discussions
between the Fund and its members even though no questions arise involving
action under Article VIII." [22] These modest words are a considerable achievement because they record the readiness of some members that had been free of
any duty to consult under Article VIII and had been unenthusiastic about consultation to make the experiment, with an awareness, of course, of the advantages that would follow from similar consultations by other members that were
about to undertake the obligations of Article VIII. The decision went on to
state, therefore, that agreement would be reached on the place and timing of
consultations, and that ordinarily they would occur at intervals of about a year.
There was to be one difference, however, between consultations under
Article VIII and Article XIV although it is not mentioned in the decision. Consultations under Article XIV are concluded with a decision of the Executive
Directors, but, although the report on a consultation under Article VIII is
discussed by the Executive Directors, they take no decision unless there are
exchange measures that require approval. There is testimony in this to the
seriousness with which members regard the formal decisions of an international
organization even though the organization may take no action on the basis of
the decisions. Notwithstanding the absence of a decision in an Article VIII
consultation, the practice of consultation with all members has enabled the
Fund to increase its contribution to the problems of adjustment by exercising
some influence on members in surplus as well as those in deficit.

The distance traveled by the Fund and its members in the field of consultation
is evident in the last paragraph of the decision also. This called on members which
are contracting parties to the GATT and which impose import restrictions for
balance of payments reasons to continue to send information concerning those
restrictions to the Fund so as to facilitate the work of the Fund in advising the
CONTRACTING PARTIES. The decision concluded by envisaging agreements between
the Fund and members that are not contracting parties under which the Fund
would seek to obtain similar information.

THE AMBIGUITIES OF GOLD

It is possible to understand the international monetary system as embodied
in the Articles as one in which convertible currencies are convertible into U.S.
dollars and U.S. dollars held by the monetary authorities of other members are
convertible into gold. This may be one meaning of the frequent but delphic
reference to gold as the "final" or "ultimate" asset. If this was indeed the theory
of the drafters, they probably assumed the continued invulnerability of the

---

[22] E.B. Decision No. 1034-(60/27); below, Vol. III, p. 261.

U.S. dollar and the readiness of other members to hold dollars in the quantities that were likely to become available to them. This view of the world and the assumptions on which it rested were not made explicit in the Articles. For example, there is no obligation under the Articles for the United States or any other member to buy and sell gold for its own currency. The Articles recognize the possibility that the monetary authorities of a member may freely buy and sell gold in fact, within the margins of par established by the Fund for gold transactions, for the settlement of international transactions.[23] If a member engages in this practice, it will be maintaining the value of its own currency in direct relation to gold, and therefore the Articles provide that the member is deemed to be fulfilling its obligation to ensure that exchange transactions in its territories involving its own and another member currency are within the permitted margins for exchange transactions. In short, the Articles hold that the member is discharging the duty that is laid on each member to maintain the value of its own currency. The United States is the only member which has informed the Fund that it freely buys and sells gold within the meaning of the provision that recognizes that practice. In addition, France has informed the Fund that the monetary authorities of French Somaliland freely buy and sell gold by freely buying and selling U.S. dollars for Djibouti francs so that the exchange rate obligations of the Articles could be deemed to be fulfilled in respect of the Djibouti franc.

It may seem extraordinary that the Fund has not adopted a final view of the meaning of the provision dealing with the free purchase and sale of gold. The view held by the staff in January 1948 was that a member is freely buying and selling gold within the meaning of the provision if it satisfies two conditions, of which one is that the member in fact buys and sells gold for its own currency whenever requested to engage in these transactions by the monetary authorities of other members whether or not the practice is required by the member's law. The other condition is that the member has no exchange restrictions on either current or capital transactions. The staff concluded that, if these two conditions are satisfied, the member is doing all that can be reasonably expected of it to maintain the value of its own currency, and it is not expected, in addition, to hold other currencies and intervene in the market with them, much less apply exchange controls, in order to maintain appropriate exchange rates. If exchange transactions involving the member's currency and another member currency should take place at rates outside the permitted margins, the responsibility for them could not be attributed to the member that was freely buying and selling gold for its currency. When the question was considered in 1948, the Executive Directors did not endorse this as the sole or necessary meaning of the provision, but, in effect, left the full or final meaning for some future debate if there should

---

[23] Article IV, Section 4 (b).

ever be a challenge of the declaration of a member that it was freely buying and selling gold.

The reluctance to arrive at a full or final view of the provision was based less on the unwillingness of the United States to be held to so strict a standard than on the preference of some members for another standard that might be helpful to them. The staff opinion and the Executive Directors' debate on the provision in February 1948 were the result of a contention by a member that had numerous exchange restrictions that it was freely selling gold for its currency to the extent that the monetary authorities of other members were able to acquire its currency. The incompatibility of that contention with the principle that the member must maintain the value of its currency in terms of gold by means of gold transactions induced the staff to dissent from the member's contention that it was freely buying and selling gold within the intent of the provision. The member then withdrew its contention but without prejudice to the question of interpretation.

In March 1949 the Executive Directors held that a member that does meet the two conditions as explained by the staff will be freely buying and selling gold within the meaning of the provision, even if the provision can be satisfied by less rigorous conditions as well. It was on this basis that the Executive Directors were able to agree that the Djibouti franc was covered by the provision. The reasoning was that because the United States at the time clearly met the two conditions, monetary authorities that permitted the full convertibility of their currency into dollars also met the conditions, provided that the cost of converting their currency into dollars and then into gold was no greater than the cost of transactions involving the currency and gold directly. In these circumstances, monetary authorities could be said to be freely buying and selling gold indirectly. The Fund has adopted no other decisions on the meaning of the free purchase and sale of gold.

Another fundamental question involving gold on which the "last verse is not yet sufficiently explicated" is the role of the Fund itself in gold transactions. Gold enters and leaves the Fund in a variety of operations and transactions. The inflow results mainly from subscriptions, repurchases, and charges, the outflow largely from sales to replenish the Fund's holdings of particular currencies. The Fund has been conscious of the effects of the flow of gold into and out of the Fund, and its policies have been affected by this awareness. An understanding of those policies would have to be derived from the study of such transactions and operations as sales of gold contemporaneously with borrowing under the General Arrangements to Borrow, sales of gold for investment of the proceeds in U.S. Government securities in order to create a special reserve to deal with possible administrative deficits, and the placing of gold on general deposit in order to counteract the effect of the provision of gold by the reserve currency countries to other members paying gold subscriptions to the Fund when increasing their quotas. These are only a few examples of issues relating to gold, sometimes legal and sometimes economic, that have been resolved by the Fund, but although some of them have been debated with great intensity and over long periods, probably none of them has so profound a legal and philosophical importance as a category of transactions that has occurred hardly at all.

Article V, Section 6 provides that a member desiring to obtain the currency of another member for gold shall "acquire it by the sale of gold to the Fund," "provided that it can do so with equal advantage." This provision is deemed not to preclude any member from selling in any market gold newly produced from mines within its territories. Article V, Section 6 resulted from a diversity of views among the negotiators of the Articles on the extent to which gold should be directed to the Fund so as to harden its resources. Clearly, not all gold had to be sold to the Fund and room was left for the restoration of a private market in gold once the Articles took effect.

Some have seen Article V, Section 6, coupled with Article VII, Section 2, as establishing the legal foundation for gold as a reserve asset. For them, it is possible to understand why the monetary authorities of members have no obligation under the Articles to engage in gold transactions between themselves because the historic acceptability of gold has been reinforced by agreement on a buyer that is required to buy. They believe that the Fund has this role. They believe that a member can be assured that if it wishes to acquire currency for gold, it will be able to sell its gold to the Fund because the member's obligation to acquire the currency from the Fund in accordance with Article V, Section 6 connotes a reciprocal obligation on the Fund to purchase the gold and supply the currency. In its turn, the Fund can compel a member to supply its currency to the Fund for gold under Article VII, Section 2 whenever the Fund deems it appropriate to replenish its holdings of the member's currency. Here then is the market assured to members by international monetary law for the disposition of gold.

Another view of Article V, Section 6 has become apparent since the institution of the two-tier gold system on March 17, 1968. This is the view that the only obligation under the provision is the obligation of a member to offer gold to the Fund if a member is seeking the currency of another member for gold, but the Fund itself has no obligation to purchase the gold. The Fund has a discretion to accept or refuse the offer, and in deciding whether to purchase any gold that is offered, the Fund must be guided by its purposes, including the maintenance of exchange stability.

Once again it may be surprising that so fundamental an issue was not settled by the Fund many years ago. In part, this is because there was little financial or other inducement for members to sell gold to the Fund under the provision, and there have been very few purchases by the Fund other than purchases of small amounts held by the Fund under earmark for members as the result of their transactions and operations with the Fund, or purchases of small amounts accepted in discharge of repurchase obligations that had accrued in currency. As part of its decision on voluntary repurchases adopted on March 8, 1951, the Fund held that if a repurchase obligation accrues in a currency under Article V, Section 7 (b), the member may combine the payment of that currency with a sale of gold to the Fund for the currency under Article V, Section 6.[24] In effect, therefore, the member may substitute gold for the currency. The decision seems to have been based on the assumption that the Fund has no discretion to refuse the gold, but the issue was not raised, and the decision does not preclude the interpretation that the Fund was exercising a discretion. Apart from cases of this kind and purchases by the Fund of small amounts held under earmark for members, the last purchase of gold by the Fund under Article V, Section 6 took place in November 1948. One reason why the traffic has been negligible is that the Fund has not attempted to deflect gold sales to itself by reducing or forgoing charges so as to offer terms that would be competitive with those offered by the monetary authorities of members.

Other aspects of the role of gold under the Articles have been given greater precision as the Fund's practice developed. It was apparent to the drafters that certain gold transactions by members at non-parity prices could have an adverse effect on par values. Article IV, Section 2 prevents purchases of gold at a premium or sales at a discount by members, whoever the other party may be. This provision permits members to sell gold at a premium or buy it at a discount, except in transactions with other members, because a sale by one member at a premium would be a purchase by the other party at a premium and a purchase by one member at a discount would be a sale by the other at a discount. Therefore, transactions in gold outside the margins from par established by the Fund are inconsistent with the Articles if both parties are members of the Fund.

The leading problems connected with this provision have involved the payment of subsidies to gold producers and external sales of gold by members at premium prices. On gold subsidies the Fund's position basically was that the prohibition of the payment of a premium price by a member applied to purchases from domestic producers also, but other forms of subsidy were not precluded.[25] More complex issues were involved in the controversy with respect to external sales at a premium. These were not sales to another member and therefore they did not fall within the prohibitions of the Articles. In June 1947, however, the Fund reached the conclusion that the volume of external sales of gold at premium prices tended to undermine exchange stability and that the

[24] E.B. Decision No. 7-(648); below, Vol. III, p. 244.
[25] E.B. Decision No. 233-2, December 11, 1947; below, Vol. III, pp. 225–26.

interests of members would be served if as much gold as possible could be held in official reserves instead of private hoards. The Fund issued a recommendation to members that they take effective action to prevent external sales of gold at premium prices.[26] The legal basis for this recommendation was Article IV, Section 4 (*a*), which obligates members to collaborate with the Fund for certain specific purposes. The part played by this obligation in the history of the Fund is considered in greater detail in the next chapter.

The difficulties in supervising and ensuring observance of its recommendation led to the Fund's abandonment of the effort in its statement of September 28, 1951, although it did not resile from its judgment that gold should be channeled to official reserves.[27] In March 1954, the London gold market was re-established, an action that could be taken consistently with the provision that permits members to sell gold at a premium except to other members and did not require them to sell it to the Fund if the gold was newly produced from domestic mines. The creation of the Gold Pool in the fall of 1961 and its operation through the London market solved the problem of premium prices because prices were kept within the margins established by the Fund for gold transactions. The solution of the problem was found in supplying the market instead of starving it as the Fund had recommended. In time, however, supplying the market became too costly for the active partners in the Gold Pool, and this led them to institute the two-tier system.

A SECOND BACKWARD GLANCE

The development of the code of conduct in the Articles has called for delicacy because essentially it has been a process of clarifying the division of authority between the Fund and members in matters that were exclusively within the domestic jurisdiction before the Articles took effect. Exchange rates are at the heart of the code. The Articles subject rates of exchange to international scrutiny and, in most instances, agreement. The Fund has not been disposed to hold that an issue relating to exchange rates is beyond its jurisdiction. The system envisaged by the drafters was one in which par values would be established under the procedures of the Articles, and changed only in order to correct a fundamental disequilibrium. The Fund has held that members are not entitled to correct a fundamental disequilibrium by changes of par values in installments, and if a par value is to be changed a period of fluctuation as the prelude to a new par value is not permissible. Nevertheless, the Fund has been willing to support a fluctuating rate with sympathy and resources, even when the practice could not be validated by Fund approval, if the practice was an improvement in a member's

---

[26] See below, Vol. III, p. 310.

[27] E.B. Decision No. 75-(705); below, Vol. III, p. 225.

exchange system and represented progress towards the establishment of an effective par value.

The Fund cannot propose a change of par value but has been able to exercise influence in favor of realistic rates of exchange by withholding the use of its resources to support untenable rates. Although the support of par values is a basic objective of the availability of the Fund's resources, the Fund has found it possible to engage in exchange transactions with a member on terms that the Fund prescribes even though the member has not yet established an initial par value.

A member must ensure that spot exchange transactions within its territories involving its own and another member currency take place within margins of 1 per cent from par. The Fund has been able to introduce additional flexibility by approving certain multiple exchange practices under which, in effect, the 1 per cent margin need apply only to transactions involving a member's intervention currency and wider margins up to 2 per cent are possible for transactions involving other member currencies. The Fund has the authority to prescribe reasonable margins in excess of 1 per cent for other exchange transactions. The Fund has not prescribed margins for forward exchange transactions, and the effect has been to permit some additional flexibility in the management of exchange rates.

The Fund has not adopted the most extensive conceivable theory of what constitutes restrictions on payments and transfers for current international transactions. It has chosen the test of the technical formulation and operation of an exchange measure and not the tests of balance of payments motive or the effect on payments and transfers. Adoption of the more modest decision was influenced by the intention to establish a parallel international trade organization with authority over trade practices. That intention and the limited jurisdiction conferred on the Fund as a result made it difficult at one time to gain general acceptance of the idea that annual consultations under Article XIV should have a wide range. That difficulty has been overcome, and regular consultations are held now even with members that have accepted the obligations of Article VIII.

Members are still able to avail themselves of the transitional arrangements of Article XIV, which in many instances means only that they have not given notice of the acceptance of the obligations of Article VIII. The Fund has not discouraged this continued but largely or even wholly formal retention of the privileges of Article XIV. It has acquiesced in the protraction of the transitional arrangements in order to give greater reality to the concept of the convertibility of currencies under Article VIII.

The Fund has had to deal with the problems of gold at all stages of its history. Nevertheless, certain fundamental questions relating to the place of gold in the international monetary system as embodied in the Articles remain unresolved even at this date. In the earlier years of the Fund when the international monetary system was not being tested by some of the problems that have demanded attention in more recent years, there was little practical reason for trying to settle these questions. Now that the questions have a practical immediacy, the problems that have brought them to the fore impede easy agreement on the answers.

CHAPTER

25

The Techniques of Response

Joseph Gold

INTERPRETATION

The Fund is one of a growing number of international organizations, mostly financial or economic in character, that have the authority to adopt final interpretations of their own charters. Under Article XVIII of the Fund's charter, any question of interpretation of the provisions of the Articles arising between any member and the Fund or between any members must be settled by the Executive Directors. In any case in which the Executive Directors have given a decision, any member may require that the question be referred to the Board of Governors, whose decision is final. Pending the result of the reference to the Board, the Fund may decide to act on the basis of the decision of the Executive Directors. The drafters attached importance to keeping disputes concerning the interpretation of the Articles within the framework of the Fund, while at the same time establishing safeguards for members and providing for external arbitration for disputes with a country in the liquidation of the Fund or after withdrawal from the Fund.[1]

The Fund has adopted no more than ten interpretations under Article XVIII, and there has been a special reason for resort to the formality of proceeding under that provision in each of these cases. The first interpretation was adopted on May 8, 1946, in response to a request by India, and in order to clarify what happens to an executive director who was appointed by a member which, between elections, ceases to be one of the members with the five largest quotas and entitled, therefore, to appoint executive directors.[2] Two interpretations were adopted by the Executive Directors on September 26, 1946 in response to requests by the United Kingdom and the United States respectively, which wanted assurances on certain matters that were of particular interest to them,

---

[1] Joseph Gold, *Interpretation by the Fund*, IMF Pamphlet Series, No. 11.
[2] E.B. Decision No. 2-1; below, Vol. III, pp. 267–68.

in part because these matters had raised political issues. The United Kingdom, committed to a policy of maintaining full employment, sought and received an interpretation that steps necessary to protect a member from unemployment of a chronic or persistent character, arising from pressure on its balance of payments, are among the measures necessary to correct a fundamental disequilibrium.[3] The United States, fearing that the Fund might engage in long-term lending that could undermine the policies of the World Bank, requested an interpretation with respect to the use of the Fund's resources, and was given the answer that use was limited in accordance with the Fund's purposes to give temporary assistance in financing balance of payments deficits on current account for monetary stabilization purposes.[4]

The next interpretation was adopted on June 10, 1949. It took the form of a letter addressed to members and was intended to make it clear that Article VIII, Section 2 (b) had modified private international law in many countries in connection with the recognition of the exchange control regulations of other members. The interpretation dealt with the prime example of "lawyer's law" in the whole Articles. The provision declares that exchange contracts involving the currency of a member which are contrary to the exchange control regulations of that member maintained or imposed consistently with the Articles shall be unenforceable in the territories of any member. The interpretation explained that a court in a member country in which a litigant seeks to enforce such a contract should not refuse to recognize the exchange control regulations on the ground that exchange control regulations are against the public policy of the forum or because the regulations are not part of the law governing the contract or its performance under the traditional private international law of the forum.[5] The novelty and compressed language of the provision have raised many legal issues, and both the provision and the interpretation have been relied on in numerous cases throughout the world.[6] There is also a growing legal literature on the effect of the Articles on the recognition of foreign exchange control, but the Fund has not ventured into further interpretation of the provision.

In response to a question put by the executive director appointed by the United States, the Fund, on February 20, 1950, adopted an interpretation of the provision which requires a member to give the Fund the same treatment for its official communications as the member accords to the official communications of

---

[3] E.B. Decision No. 71-2; below, Vol. III, p. 227.

[4] Ibid., p. 245; cf above, pp. 524, 539.

[5] E.B. Decision No. 446-4; below, Vol. III, pp. 256–57.

[6] See Joseph Gold, The Fund Agreement in the Courts; "The Fund Agreement in the Courts—VIII," Staff Papers, Vol. XI (1964), pp. 457–89; "The Fund Agreement in the Courts—IX," ibid., Vol. XIV (1967), pp. 369–402; The Cuban Insurance Cases and the Articles of the Fund, IMF Pamphlet Series, No. 8; "The International Monetary Fund and the International Recognition of Exchange Control Regulations: The Cuban Insurance Cases," Revue de la Banque (Brussels), Vol. 31 (1967), pp. 523–38.

other members.[7] The U.S. Federal Communications Commission recognized this interpretation as binding on the United States in a proceeding brought by the Fund and the World Bank against U.S. cable companies.[8]

The sixth interpretation was adopted by the Executive Directors on August 11, 1954, in reply to a question put by Czechoslovakia, against which proceedings had been instituted that led to a decision requiring it to withdraw from the Fund. Czechoslovakia argued that the failure to fulfill obligations for which a member could be compelled to withdraw meant a failure for which there was no legal justification, and that reasons of national security were recognized as a justification of that character in international law. In their interpretation, the Executive Directors did not accept this argument in connection with the provisions under which it was alleged that Czechoslovakia had failed to fulfill its obligations.[9] This was the only case in which an interpretation under Article XVIII was appealed to the Board of Governors. The Board, on September 28, 1954, confirmed the interpretation of the Executive Directors.

The seventh interpretation was adopted on August 24, 1955 and dealt with the troublesome question of the amount of exchange that a member is entitled to purchase from the Fund without a waiver. One of the conditions on which a member is entitled to make a purchase is that the proposed purchase will not cause the Fund's holdings of the member's currency to increase by more than 25 per cent of quota during the period of twelve months ending on the date of the purchase. The Fund recoiled from reading the provision to mean that the 25 per cent referred to is measured simply by the difference between its holdings of the member's currency at the beginning of the period and the level to which they would be increased by the proposed purchase. This could permit a member to purchase huge amounts in terms of its quota and could enable it to make long-term use of the Fund's resources. This would follow because any reduction in the Fund's holdings of a member's currency by repurchase, by a sale of its currency, or as the result of other operations, during the preceding twelve months, would enable the member to purchase an amount equivalent to the reduction and a further 25 per cent of quota without the need for a waiver. The Executive Directors decided that such a view would be repugnant to the basic ideas of the temporary use and revolving character of Fund resources and adopted a view under which during any twelve months a member may make purchases amounting to 25 per cent of quota augmented only by the amount of any reductions in the Fund's holdings of the member's currency, not in excess of those purchases, which take place after the purchases have occurred.[10]

---

[7] E.B. Decision No. 534-3; below, Vol. III, pp. 266–67.

[8] On the binding effect of interpretations, see Gold, *Interpretation by the Fund*, pp. 31–42.

[9] E.B. Decision No. 343-(54/47); below Vol. III, p. 269.

[10] E.B. Decision No. 451-(55/52); below, Vol. III, p. 228.

On January 25, 1956, the Executive Directors adopted their eighth interpretation under Article XVIII by deciding, after years of debate, that the Fund has the legal authority to sell part of its gold for investment of the proceeds in U.S. Government securities in order to prevent the impairment of its capital as a result of the excess of its administrative expenses over income. The interpretation laid down the conditions on which this could be done, including the condition that the Fund must be able to reacquire the gold.[11] On the disappearance of its accumulated deficit, the Fund, on November 27, 1957, decided under Article XVIII that the investment could be continued in order to provide a reserve against any similar deficits that might occur in the future.[12] A third interpretation dealing with investment was adopted on July 24, 1959 and dealt with the length of the maturity of the securities in which the Fund might invest.[13] That has been the last interpretation under Article XVIII so far.[14]

Nobody could claim that these ten decisions constitute an impressive body of legal principles, or even that all of them have made outstanding contributions to the constitutional development of the Fund. It is unlikely that anyone would deny the constitutional importance of the interpretations dealing with fundamental disequilibrium, use of the Fund's resources, and the meaning of the 25 per cent limit, but opinions might differ about the impact of some of the others. It would be difficult to insist that certain of the interpretations have had more than a minor effect on the work of the Fund.

The modest number of interpretations under Article XVIII gives no impression of the considerable volume of interpretative decisions that have been taken without recourse to that provision. Many of these decisions have been drafted in general terms and quite obviously as interpretations. Others have been rendered in particular cases and have dealt with the facts of the individual case. All in all, these decisions do amount to a very substantial body of law. The progressive development of its interpretative decisions has been one of the outstanding techniques of the Fund in dealing with the problems under the Articles with which it has been confronted by a far from quiescent international monetary order.

It has not been the attitude of members of the Fund, the Executive Directors, the Managing Director, or the staff that interpretative decisions can be held in lower esteem if they are not taken under Article XVIII. The procedures for arriving at decisions and the techniques of interpretation have been the same for both categories of decision. Clearly, any distinction between the two cate-

---

[11] E.B. Decision No. 488-(56/5); below, Vol. III, pp. 275–76.

[12] E.B. Decision No. 708-(57/57); below, Vol. III, p. 276.

[13] E.B. Decision No. 905-(59/32); below, Vol. III, p. 277.

[14] But see E.B. Decision No. 1107-(60/50), November 30, 1960; below, Vol. III, p. 277.

gories on the basis of their importance in the working of the Fund would be in favor of the decisions taken without recourse to Article XVIII.

The preference for interpreting the Articles without raising questions under Article XVIII is not the result of any conscious decision and it is not easy to explain the practice. The feeling of greater formality that necessarily accompanies the invocation of Article XVIII may be one explanation. Members regard interpretative decisions with respect and there is no need, therefore, to give these decisions maximum solemnity in order to ensure observance of them. Perhaps this informality may seem more compatible with the cooperation, consultation, and collaboration that are referred to in the first purpose of Article I. Another explanation may be the subconscious conviction that if an interpretative decision will have to be modified for good cause, this will be easier if it has not been adopted under Article XVIII. The debate on the clarification of the Executive Directors' interpretation of September 26, 1946 on the use of the Fund's resources shows that there may be great reluctance to re-examine a decision taken under Article XVIII.[15] A similar desire to minimize rigidity can be detected in some of the legal systems in which the volume of appeals to higher tribunals is closely controlled. Finally, it is possible that the assurance which members enjoy that they can raise any questions of interpretation under Article XVIII if they wish makes it unnecessary for them to overindulge in the privilege.

There are many approaches to the interpretation of treaties and the last word on this subject is always being written. The Fund has adopted an eclectic approach to problems of interpretation and has never decided that its technique would be based exclusively on the grammatical elucidation of the text, the determination of the intent of the drafters, the object of the provision, or the wider purposes of the Fund. A study of the interpretative work of the first two decades would show that a number or all of these techniques have been applied to most problems of interpretation. There is probably nothing unique in the experience of the Fund in this respect.

In the process of interpretation, what is sometimes called a "constitutional" or a "teleological" approach, or an approach that seeks to make the purposes of the institution effective, has found a place, although again the approach may have been no more pronounced in the Fund than in other international organizations. Perhaps the best public expression of the Fund's consciousness of this technique occurred in a speech by Mr. Jacobsson, who included the law among his many interests:

> In this and in other matters under the Fund's charter, I am reminded of what an English Lord Chancellor, Lord Sankey, said of the Canadian Constitution. It was, he said, "a living tree capable of growth and expansion within its natural limits." [16]

---

[15] See above, pp. 539–40.

[16] Per Jacobsson, *International Monetary Problems, 1957–1963*, p. 284. The quotation is from *Edwards v. Att.-Gen. for Canada* (1930) A.C. 124, 136.

His quotation from Lord Sankey was taken from an opinion in which the following passage also is relevant to Mr. Jacobsson's attitude of mind:

> Their Lordships do not conceive it to be the duty of this Board—it is certainly not their desire—to cut down the provisions of the Act by a narrow and technical construction, but rather to give it a large and liberal interpretation so that the Dominion to a great extent, but within certain fixed limits, may be mistress in her own house, as the Provinces to a great extent, but within certain fixed limits, are mistresses in theirs. "The Privy Council, indeed, has laid down that Courts of law must treat the provisions of the British North America Act by the same methods of construction and exposition which apply to other statutes. But there are statutes and statutes; and the strict construction deemed proper in the case, for example, of a penal or taxing statute or one passed to regulate the affairs of an English parish, would be often subversive of Parliament's real intent if applied to an Act passed to ensure the peace, order and good government of a British Colony" (see Clement's *Canadian Constitution*, 3rd ed., p. 347).[17]

In presenting his plan to the Executive Directors on February 10, 1961 for the development of the Fund's activities in an era of widespread convertibility, Mr. Jacobsson explained his position even more clearly:

> It is frequently suggested that one or another of the activities of the Fund indicated above might require amendment of the Articles of Agreement. I have an open mind on this; but I do know that the Articles provide considerable flexibility in many respects. The Articles are a constitutional charter, and constitutional interpretation recognizes that such a document must meet needs when this can be done without offending its spirit, purposes, or provisions.

In this approach he was supported, of course, by the last sentence of Article I, which declares that "the Fund shall be guided in all its decisions by the purposes set forth in this Article."

As in any body of men who are called on to exercise the art of interpretation, there have been differences of opinion on technique among executive directors. Some have seen interpretation as a more mechanical and less creative task than have those others who have held that, if there is a choice among readings, the best answer must be considered the right answer, and what is the best answer calls for knowledge, experience, and an understanding of the purposes of the Fund. Whatever differences of opinion may have existed about technique, and the frequency of this kind of disputation should not be exaggerated, it has been the unanimous view in the Fund that its power to interpret its charter was not a *laissez-passer* that authorized it to move beyond the law in order to achieve some end that was not attainable within the law. Strict adherence to this view has sometimes provoked lengthy and meticulous scrutiny of propositions that in retrospect seem obvious. The legality of voluntary repurchases and the decision of February 13, 1952 are examples of issues that were debated with

---

[17] *Edwards v. Att.-Gen. for Canada, ibid.*, pp. 136–37.

ardor over long periods. But this behavior has encouraged the law-abidingness of which it is itself a product. Furthermore, it has produced a body of interpretative decisions that are harmonious and therefore stable.[18] Indeed, some critics have thought that there was too much rigidity in the jurisprudence of the Fund, although the critics who have said the reverse must not be neglected.

It is interesting to speculate whether there have been special reasons in the Fund for the legalism, in the non-pejorative sense, which it has observed. Once again it is possible that its special character as an international regulatory institution may be an explanation. It would have been unreasonable to expect members to observe their obligations, and particularly the code of conduct, if the Fund had acted in the spirit of the old maxim that it is the function of a good judge to extend his jurisdiction (*boni judicis est ampliare jurisdictionem*).

THE UNDERTAKING TO COLLABORATE

One of the purposes of the Fund is to promote exchange stability, to maintain orderly exchange arrangements among members, and to avoid competitive exchange depreciation.[19] This purpose is matched by Article IV, Section 4 (*a*), under which members undertake "to collaborate with the Fund to promote exchange stability, to maintain orderly exchange arrangements with other members, and to avoid competitive exchange alterations." The provision is a source of authority on which the Fund has drawn in order to promote the purposes of exchange stability and orderly exchange arrangements. Sometimes the Fund has done this expressly, but at other times the spirit of the undertaking has affected relations between the Fund and its members even though the undertaking was not openly invoked.

Three examples drawn from the early years of the Fund illustrate the protean quality of the provision. In deciding that members are not entitled to adapt or introduce multiple currency practices, without the approval of the Fund, as restrictions on payments and transfers under Article XIV, Section 2, the Fund held as a matter of interpretation that because multiple currency practices are also rates of exchange the Fund must judge whether the adaptation is justified by "changing circumstances" or the introduction is "necessary."[20] The Fund relied largely on Article IV, Section 4 (*a*) as the source of this interpretation.

---

[18] ". . . the Executive Board has habitually shown a close regard for the legal arguments on both sides of a controversial question before it, and is probably more careful for the rule of law than many boards of directors, which have only municipal law to contend with, and it is slow to come to a decision until it can be legally well based. In the result the Fund's decisions since it commenced operations in March 1947 show a high degree of coherence and consistency." J. E. S. Fawcett, "The Place of Law in an International Organization," in *The British Year Book of International Law, 1960*, p. 327.

[19] Article I (iii); below, Vol. III, p. 188.

[20] See above, p. 548.

In its letter of December 19, 1947 to members, the Fund referred to the purposes of the Fund and the undertaking of members under the provision as "fundamental considerations in an interpretation of the rights and obligations of members" in connection with multiple currency practices. The widespread importance of this decision and its influence on the Fund's attitude to its jurisdiction in connection with exchange rate practices have been referred to in Chapter 24.

When in January 1948 France made an unauthorized change of par value and introduced discriminatory multiple currency practices of which the Fund disapproved, the Fund's action under Article IV, Section 4 (a) was of a different character. The Fund advised other members that neither the former par value nor the new rates of exchange adopted by France were binding on them and members were not bound to take appropriate measures to ensure that these rates were observed in exchange transactions in their territories. Nevertheless, members were bound to avoid exchange disorder. Therefore, the Fund was willing to agree in advance if by a bilateral arrangement between France and another member an exchange rate between their currencies was established on the basis of the unauthorized par value. If these arrangements contemplated other rates of exchange, the Fund did not give advance approval even if they corresponded with another rate in the French exchange system. The parties negotiating the agreement on a rate had to request the approval of the Fund because in the context of the French exchange system the rate inevitably would constitute a discriminatory currency arrangement. In this case, the Fund drew from Article IV, Section 4 (a) an obligation of members to seek prior approval for the introduction or adaptation of discriminatory currency arrangements involving rates of exchange.

In the third case, the Fund made yet a third kind of use of Article IV, Section 4 (a). In 1947, the Fund came to the conclusion that external sales of gold by members at premium prices tended to undermine exchange stability. It has been seen that whereas Article IV, Section 2 prevents members from buying gold at a price above par plus the Fund's margin for gold transactions or selling it at a price below par minus the margin, sales by a member or its residents at a premium to a purchaser that is not another member are not proscribed. Whether these latter sales continue to be permitted if the Fund finds that they undermine, and not merely tend to undermine, exchange stability was not decided. For a number of reasons, including perhaps the desire to avoid the settlement of that question, the Fund decided not to go beyond a recommendation to members. In its letter to members of June 18, 1947 the Fund deprecated premium sales in external markets and recommended that its members take effective action to prevent them.[21] The legal authority on which this policy pronouncement was based was Article I (iii) and Article IV, Section 4 (a).

---

[21] See above, pp. 563–64.

In these three episodes, the Fund made the undertaking of members in Article IV, Section 4 (*a*) more specific when dangers threatened exchange stability and orderly exchange arrangements. The Fund acted by formulating the obligations of members, by employing the provision in the interpretation of other provisions, or by addressing recommendations to members, when problems arose that imperiled the purposes of the Fund and the provisions of the Articles were not sufficiently clear or detailed in their relation to the problems. A study of the three episodes shows that there may be legal problems in reconciling an obligation or recommendation drawn from Article IV, Section 4 (*a*) with other provisions or with the silence of other provisions. Therefore, the acceptability to members at large of the Fund's reliance on the provision has been an element in the success of the Fund's action. The obligations of members to seek prior approval for the adaptation or introduction of multiple currency practices or discriminatory currency arrangements involving rates of exchange are firmly established. The history of the Fund's policy on premium transactions in gold shows that an application of Article IV, Section 4 (*a*) may be unsuccessful if it is not supported by the cooperation of those members from which cooperation is thought to be necessary.[22]

The recognized usefulness of Article IV, Section 4 (*a*) induced the drafters of the amendments dealing with special drawing rights to formulate a similar provision. This progeny of Article IV, Section 4 (*a*) is entitled "General Obligations of Participants," and it provides that:

> In addition to the obligations assumed with respect to special drawing rights under other Articles of this Agreement, each participant undertakes to collaborate with the Fund and with other participants in order to facilitate the effective functioning of the Special Drawing Account and the proper use of special drawing rights in accordance with this Agreement.[23]

VARIATION WITHOUT AMENDMENT

One of the techniques for adaptation at the disposal of the Fund is a power to vary certain provisions in the Articles without the need for amendment, and the exercise of this power has made at least one vital contribution to the operation of the Fund. The provisions in the original Articles under which variation is possible have been the precedents for a broader use of the technique in the amendments. Agreement on a power to vary without amendment enabled the negotiators of the amendments to arrive at a compromise on a basic feature of special drawing rights that was the subject of a particularly stubborn difference of opinion. The power to vary is one of the more obvious responses to Keynes,

---

[22] See Joseph Gold, "The Duty to Collaborate with the International Monetary Fund and the Development of Monetary Law," in *Law, Justice and Equity*, edited by R.H. Code Holland and G. Schwarzenberger, pp. 137–51.

[23] Article XXVIII; below, Vol. III, p. 531.

who said at Bretton Woods of the lawyer that: "I want him to tell me how to do what I think sensible, and, above all, to devise means by which it will be lawful for me to go on being sensible in unforeseen conditions some years hence." Full disclosure makes it necessary to report that the second use of the word "I" appears in italics.[24]

There were four examples of the technique in the original Articles. It is provided that when countries not listed in Schedule A become members of the Fund, the Board of Governors has authority, by a four-fifths majority of the total voting power, to increase the number of elected executive directors from the original seven.[25] The exercise of this power has enabled the Fund to increase the number of executive directors over time from twelve to twenty by increasing the number elected by the American Republics from two to three and the number elected by other members not appointing executive directors from five to twelve. The Fund has followed a policy of providing for further elected executive directors on the basis of the voting power exercised by newcomers, and one of the results of this policy has been to permit emerging countries to participate directly in the affairs of the Fund through executive directors of their choice.

The Articles also provide that whenever the Board of Governors increases the number of elected executive directors, it shall issue regulations making appropriate changes in the proportions of votes required to elect executive directors as laid down in the Articles.[26] The Board of Governors has made a flexible use of this power. For each election once countries not listed in Schedule A had joined the Fund, the Board of Governors has established the minimum number of votes required for the election of an executive director and the maximum number that he may retain. In determining these limits the Board of Governors has been guided by the objective of maintaining an approximate equality in the number of votes that elected executive directors can cast and by the further objective of making it possible, up to a point, for members to combine as they wish in electing an executive director.

The original Articles provide for a service charge of ¾ of 1 per cent on exchange transactions with the Fund but allow the Fund to alter this charge within a range of ½ of 1 per cent to 1 per cent.[27] On November 19, 1951 the Fund reduced the charge to the minimum in order to encourage short-term transactions as one means of reviving the use of the Fund's resources.[28]

The Articles also include a system of periodic charges on the Fund's holdings of currency in excess of quota under which the rates ascend in relation to both

---

[24] *Proceedings*, p. 1241.

[25] Article XII, Section 3 (*b*); below, Vol. III, p. 200.

[26] Article XII, Section 3 (*d*).

[27] Article V, Section 8 (*a*); below, Vol. III, p. 193.

[28] Rules and Regulations, Rule I-2; below, Vol. III, p. 294.

holdings and time.[29] It is provided that when the charge applicable to any bracket of the Fund's holdings of a member's currency reaches the rate of 4 per cent per annum, the Fund and the member have to consider means by which the Fund's holdings can be reduced.[30] That rate could be reached as late as seven years after a transaction with the Fund. The Fund is empowered to change the rates in the Articles, including the rate at which consultation occurs on the reduction of the Fund's holdings, by a three-fourths majority of the total voting power.[31]

In the discussions leading to the decision of February 13, 1952 the view was advanced that seven years was not an ideal period for the use of the Fund's resources, although obviously it had been considered tolerable by the drafters, and that a shorter period not exceeding five years was preferable. There was a more basic difference of opinion, however, on whether any fixed period was compatible with the notion of the Fund and whether it could be made effective in any way that was acceptable legally. The solution to the latter question was found in the variation of the charges in the Articles so that the date for consultation on the reduction of the Fund's holdings would occur not later than three years after a transaction. With that revision of the charges, members were willing to assure the Fund, in advance of the consultation that they would be obligated to enter into, that in the consultation they would agree upon appropriate arrangements for reducing the Fund's holdings of their currency as soon as possible but in any event not later than five years after a transaction.[32] On the basis of that settlement it became possible also to agree on a modified form of repurchase representation for gold tranche purchases on which periodic charges are not payable and to which, therefore, the requirement of consultation does not apply if only those purchases are outstanding. It is not an exaggeration to say that the Fund's power to vary the charges included in the Articles provided the legal basis on which it became possible to establish the policy that the temporary use of the Fund's resources meant use not in excess of three to five years.

The further powers of the Fund under the amended Articles to vary provisions without amendment relate to both the General Account and the Special Drawing Account. In the former category is the power of the Executive Directors to vary a basic rate of remuneration of 1½ per cent per annum payable on the amount by which the Fund's holdings of a member's currency are below 75 per cent of quota; a three-fourths majority of the total voting power is required for a decision to vary the rate beyond a band of 1 to 2 per

---

[29] Article V, Section 8 (c); below, Vol. III, p. 193.

[30] Article V, Section 8 (d).

[31] Article V, Section 8 (e).

[32] E.B. Decision No. 102-(52/11); below, Vol. III, p. 229. Rules and Regulations, Rule I-4; below, Vol. III, pp. 294–95.

cent per annum.[33] In addition, the Board of Governors has received the power to vary, by a majority of 85 per cent of the total voting power, a number of amendments that have been made in the provisions relating to repurchase.[34] This power was created because of the uncertainty about the way in which the amendments of the repurchase provisions might work not only from the point of view of equity but also in relation to the complexities of the original repurchase mechanism.

In the field of special drawing rights, there are powers to vary within a defined band the prescribed rate of 1½ per cent payable as interest on participants' holdings and as charges on net cumulative allocations of special drawing rights,[35] and to vary the rules for the designation of participants as recipients of special drawing rights that are intended to promote over time a balanced distribution of holdings of special drawing rights among participants.[36] Both powers may be exercised by the Executive Directors by a majority of votes cast.

The most striking power to vary a provision without amendment relates to "reconstitution." Those who favored the view that the new instrument of unconditional liquidity should take the form demonstrably of a reserve asset and not credit, or that it should be a "unit" and not a "drawing right," argued that a participant should have no legal obligation to restore its holdings of the new instrument after they had been used. Those who preferred the concept of "credit" or a "drawing right" insisted that there should be a duty of restoration. The compromise between the two schools was an agreement that there would be an obligation on each participant, in accordance with the rules in Schedule G, to maintain over time an average balance of 30 per cent of its net cumulative allocation of special drawing rights beginning five years after the first allocation. The rules for reconstitution, however, are to be reviewed before the end of the first and each subsequent basic period and new rules may be adopted if they are considered necessary but they may be abrogated altogether. Any decision to adopt, modify, or abrogate reconstitution rules will be taken by the Board of Governors and will require a majority of 85 per cent of the total voting power.[37]

RULE-MAKING

The Board of Governors, and the Executive Directors to the extent that they have been authorized, may adopt "such rules and regulations as may be necessary or appropriate to conduct the business of the Fund."[38] In accordance with

---

[33] Article V, Section 9; below, Vol. III, p. 523.

[34] Article V, Section 7 (d); Article XII, Section 2 (b) (ix).

[35] Article XXVI, Sections 1–3.

[36] Article XXV, Section 5 (b) and (c), and Schedule F.

[37] Article XXV, Section 6.

[38] Article XII, Section 2 (g); below, Vol. III, p. 199.

this provision in the Articles, the Board of Governors adopted By-Laws on March 16, 1946 and the Executive Directors adopted Rules and Regulations on September 25, 1946.[39]

Most of the By-Laws and Rules and Regulations now in force were adopted on those occasions, although there have been amendments and additions over the years. The words "necessary or appropriate," which are the criterion for rule-making, are broad and flexible, but the Fund has not made conspicuous use of either the By-Laws or the Rules and Regulations as a medium of adaptation to changing circumstances. Nevertheless, some rule-making actions have had more than a routine character. The changes already noted in the service charge on members' exchange transactions with the Fund and in the periodic charges on the Fund's holdings of currencies were incorporated in the Rules and Regulations. Another noteworthy example is the amendment of Rule F-4 of the Rules and Regulations on October 15, 1954 by which the Executive Directors adopted an alternative to the original margin for gold transactions which they had established on June 10, 1947. The new margin of 1 per cent facilitated the reopening of the London gold market, through which, in due course, the operations of the Gold Pool were conducted. Yet another interesting example of rule-making is Rule M-6, adopted on June 7, 1950, in which the Fund deemed it prejudicial to the interests of members and contrary to the purposes of the Fund for a member to impose restrictions on non-members that have entered into special exchange agreements under the GATT, or with persons in their territories, which the member would not be authorized in similar circumstances to impose on transactions with members or with persons in their territories.[40]

The last rule to be mentioned here as worthy of particular notice is Rule K-2, which was adopted on September 25, 1946. It declares that whenever the Fund is authorized to declare a member ineligible to use the resources of the Fund, it may refrain from taking that action and instead indicate the circumstances in which, or the extent to which, the member may make use of the Fund's resources. The rule expresses the Fund's philosophy that its powers should be exercised not to obstruct access to its resources but to clarify the circumstances in which members can rely on the availability of those resources.

DEFINING THE UNDEFINED

The restraint which the drafters observed in defining basic concepts has given the Fund a degree of flexibility by enabling it to decide how those con-

---

[39] See below, Vol. III, pp. 278–303.

[40] Joseph Gold, *The Fund and Non-Member States*, IMF Pamphlet Series, No. 7.

cepts are to be applied. It is true that Article XIX explains a number of terms, but they deal with little more than payments for current transactions and the calculation of net official holdings and monetary reserves. Net official holdings were relevant to the determination of members' gold subscriptions, and monetary reserves are important mainly in connection with repurchase obligations under Article V, Section 7 (b) and the payment of charges. Notwithstanding the explanation of terms in Article XIX, further elucidation of them was necessary before they could be put to work. The Net Official Holdings Committee of the Executive Directors met during the period March 1947 to April 1948 to unravel the complications of the concept by means of a number of case studies. This detailed work had a permanent usefulness because of the intersection of the concepts of "net official holdings" and "monetary reserves." One of the most fundamental of the determinations common to both concepts was the decision that the "holding" of a reserve asset involves the ownership of the asset and not merely a claim to acquire it against another member that has the ownership of it. No committee was established in connection with monetary reserves, but the intricacies of both that concept and the repurchase formulas based on it were clarified as issues arose over the years in the practice of the Fund.

The other main topic on which Article XIX gives guidance is "payments for current transactions." This concept sets the bounds within which the Fund exercises jurisdiction over restrictions on payments and transfers under Article VIII, Section 2. Problems of definition have arisen in connection with "payments for current transactions" but problems of application, such as the mode of operation of particular exchange control regulations, have been more frequent. One reason for the predominance of problems of application over problems of definition is the breadth of the first category in Article XIX (i): "All payments due in connection with foreign trade, other current business, including services, and normal short-term banking and credit facilities."

In a discussion of the techniques of adaptation, it must be recalled that certain discretions were given to the Fund to extend particular definitions. Article XIX (d) defines "currency" for the purposes of that provision and declares that the term shall include "without limitation" the items that are specified. The definition has been applied, as was to be expected, to other references to "currency" in the Articles. Similarly, Article XIX (i) declares that payments for current transactions means payments that are not for the purpose of transferring capital and include "without limitation" the categories that then follow. The "without limitation" clause empowers the Fund to add items or categories to those enumerated, but no addition has been made to either list.

Obviously, the concepts that are wholly undefined have given the Fund no less opportunity for evolving a realistic and consistent body of practice than the concepts on which the drafters provided guidance by an explanation of terms. The Articles contain no definitions of such terms as "multiple currency practices," "discriminatory currency arrangements," "fundamental disequilibrium," or even "rates for exchange transactions." Sometimes, the Fund has made a specific project of the clarification of a particular concept. The Executive Directors' Committee on Spreads and Multiple Currency Practices which sat in May to July 1947 mapped a large part of the terrain in this area of the Articles, and its work led to the letter to members of December 19, 1947 which still explains much of the Fund's policy and interpretation in connection with multiple currency practices.[41] With other concepts the Fund has refrained from making so systematic an effort and has allowed a body of practice to develop more slowly as problems arose. The concept of the rate of exchange has been formed in this way, and it has central importance in the work of the Fund. It is established that the rate of exchange with which the Fund is concerned is the "effective" rate, which means that it includes not only the formal *quid pro quo* for the exchange but also other payments, such as exchange taxes or charges, that are directly exigible in connection with the exchange transaction.

Reliance on the future administrators of the Fund to give substance to basic concepts of its operation is not an accident of hurried negotiation. There is the evidence of Mr. White himself who wrote in August 1946 that:

> In the drafting of the Articles of Agreement no attempt was made to define fundamental disequilibrium. This, as we know, was not an oversight. It was generally agreed that a satisfactory definition would be difficult to formulate. A too rigid or narrow interpretation would be dangerous; one too loose or general would be useless in providing a criterion for changes in currency parities. It was felt too that the subject matter was so important, and the necessity for a crystallization of a harmonious view so essential that it were best left for discussion and formulation by the Fund.

There can be few negotiators of a major international treaty who have been so enlightened as to hold that because of the basic importance of a concept, its definition had best be left to those who later would administer the treaty. It need only be said that those who have followed the drafters and administered the Fund have been equally enlightened, at least in connection with "fundamental disequilibrium." They have not yet ventured a formal definition of it. There are other cases in which the administrators, like angels, have not rushed in, and by their reluctance to adopt definitions, or on occasion even interpretations, have preserved a valuable flexibility for the Fund.

---

[41] See above, pp. 548, 574.

CHAPTER

26

Some Characteristics of Operation

Joseph Gold

THE AVOIDANCE OF SANCTIONS

A student of the development of the Fund must note how little use the Fund has made of sanctions. This characteristic of the way in which the Fund has operated has had a formative influence on Fund law and practice. The Articles authorize the Fund to take certain actions of which some are clearly sanctions and others have been regarded as comparable to sanctions if only because there is a tacit view that they involve an adverse judgment on the member against which the action is taken. One of the most obvious sanctions is a declaration of ineligibility to use the Fund's resources either because a member "is using the resources of the Fund in a manner contrary to the purposes of the Fund"[1] or because a member "fails to fulfill any of its obligations" under the Articles.[2] If a member makes an unauthorized change of par value despite the objection of the Fund in circumstances in which the Fund is entitled to object, this is technically not a failure by the member to fulfill any of its obligations, but it becomes automatically unable to make purchases unless the Fund decides to forestall ineligibility.[3]

The most radical of all obvious sanctions is the compulsory withdrawal of a member from the Fund. This can be required if after a reasonable period a member persists in its failure to fulfill any of its obligations under the Articles or if a difference between the Fund and a member persists on its unauthorized change of par value.[4]

A member must consult with the Fund on means to reduce the Fund's holdings of the member's currency once the rate of charge on any part of them reaches 4 per cent per annum. If the member fails to reach an agreement on repurchase

---

[1] Article V, Section 5; below, Vol. III, p. 192.

[2] Article XV, Section 2 (*a*).

[3] Article IV, Section 6.

[4] Article XV, Section 2 (*b*).

within three to five years after a purchase, or fails to observe the terms of an agreement, the Fund may levy penalty rates of charge after the charge has reached 5 per cent per annum.[5]

Under Article XII, Section 8, the Fund may communicate its views informally to any member on any matter arising under the Articles, and may publish a report regarding a member's monetary or economic conditions and developments which directly tend to produce a serious disequilibrium in the international balance of payments of members. In exceptional circumstances, the Fund may make representations to a member that is availing itself of the transitional arrangements of Article XIV that conditions are favorable for the withdrawal of any particular restriction, or for the general abandonment of restrictions, that are inconsistent with any other provision of the Articles.[6] There are other actions that the Fund may take that might be regarded by some observers as sanctions, but it is not necessary to complete the list, although one of them will be singled out later because of its special relationship to the international monetary system.

In the elaborate congressional hearings on the proposed U.S. Bretton Woods legislation in 1945, there was much discussion of the sanctions and safeguards in the Articles in order to rally public opinion in the United States to support of the Fund by showing that abuse of the proposed institution by its members could be prevented or deterred. The Fund has found it necessary to make a negligible use of this armory of sanctions and quasi-sanctions. The most dramatic employment of a sanction in the history of the Fund was the declaration of Czechoslovakia's ineligibility in November 1953 and the decision in September 1954 to compel it to withdraw because of its failure to provide information under Article VIII and consult under Article XIV. There have been no other declarations of ineligibility or decisions to compel withdrawal, although ineligibility proceedings were initiated against Cuba in February 1964 for failure to repurchase after it had requested and been refused a postponement beyond five years from its purchase, and in these circumstances Cuba withdrew voluntarily. France became ineligible in January 1948 when it adopted an unauthorized par value, but ineligibility was automatic under Article IV, Section 6 and called for no declaration by the Fund.[7] Under Article XV, Section 2, if a difference between a member and the Fund on an unauthorized change of par value continues, the member may be required to withdraw. The Fund took no further action in the case of France, and eligibility was restored by the Fund in October 1954, even though a new par value was not established until December 1958. Only two members have had to pay rates of charge in excess of 5 per cent per

---

[5] Article V, Section 8 (*d*); Rules and Regulations, Rule I-4 (g); below, Vol. III, pp. 193, 296.

[6] Article XIV, Section 4.

[7] See above, pp. 549, 574.

annum, and then for no more than brief periods. The Fund has made no formal representations under Article XIV, Section 4, and has not published any report under Article XII, Section 8.

The sparing use of sanctions can be evaluated only if it is known to what extent sanctions could have been applied, but it is not easy to arrive at a judgment on that question. One reason for the difficulty is that the practices and procedures that have been developed to avoid sanctions, particularly in connection with the use of the Fund's resources, make it unnecessary to determine whether members are making an improper use. There have been numerous failures by members to observe their obligations to seek the prior approval of the Fund for the introduction of multiple currency practices or restrictions on payments and transfers for current international transactions, but in most cases these failures were the subject of consultation with the Fund after the adoption of the measures and the Fund then took decisions to approve them. Many of the failures to observe obligations in the code of conduct were the result of oversight, but there have been a few cases in which the violation has been a conscious choice under what was thought to be the pressure of events. There have been no more than a handful of cases in which members have failed to honor their financial obligations meticulously. Only in rare instances have charges been paid or repurchases made after the due date, and there has never been a protracted or permanent default. Although there is no legal or logical distinction between financial and other obligations, financial institutions and their members have a special sensitivity about the prompt and full performance of financial obligations.

One must conclude that there has been a high degree of law observance by members, but not complete impeccability, and sanctions could have been applied more frequently than they have been. It should be added that the Rules and Regulations require the Managing Director to report to the Executive Directors any case in which it appears to him that a member is not fulfilling its obligations.[8] There has been no formal decision to minimize the use of sanctions, and it is not easy, therefore, to explain fully why they have been avoided. Sanctions involve an adverse judgment by the international community, and it is painful not only to the member against which the judgment is delivered but also to its fellow members that adopt the judgment. Another reason is the conviction that persuasion based on consultation and collaboration are more likely to encourage the widespread observance of obligations than punitive methods. This conviction rests not only on the prescription of the Articles but also on the experience of the Fund. In any event, it seems to have been concluded that usually there is no advantage in reacting to the violation of one obligation by imposing sanctions that may lead to withdrawal from the Fund and the release from all obligations.

---

[8] Rules and Regulations, Rule K-1; below, Vol. III, p. 299.

The Fund's attitude to sanctions has affected its practice most profoundly in connection with the use of its resources. The power to challenge a member's representation when it requests a purchase is not a complete safeguard for the Fund because a challenge is not a proper substitute for a declaration of ineligibility if there are grounds for ineligibility. In the early years of the Fund, informal procedures were employed, such as warning some members that Article XX, Section 4 (*i*) might be invoked to postpone exchange transactions with them if they submitted requests. Under this provision the Fund has the power to postpone transactions with a member if, in the opinion of the Fund, they would lead to use of its resources in a manner contrary to the purposes of the Articles or prejudicial to the Fund or its members. However, this provision also could provide only a partial defense against improper use because the Fund decided on March 10, 1948 that the power could be exercised only in the case of a member that had not already had an exchange transaction with the Fund.[9]

The major contribution to the protection of the Fund's resources without the need to rely on the sanction of ineligibility has been made, of course, by the technique of the stand-by arrangement. Here again, however, the desire to avoid ineligibility has affected the development of that instrument. In early stand-by arrangements a paragraph was employed, as a result of the decision of October 1, 1952,[10] which provided that the Fund would not permit a member to make purchases under a stand-by arrangement that were requested after the member became ineligible or after the Executive Directors adopted a decision to consider a proposal made by the Managing Director or an executive director to suppress or limit the member's eligibility. The reluctance to employ procedures related to ineligibility in order to interrupt the right to make purchases under a stand-by arrangement was responsible for the introduction of two features of stand-by arrangements that were meant to be substitutes for these procedures. The first was the evolution of performance clauses containing performance criteria as described in Chapter 23.[11]

The second of the two features of the Fund's practice that were designed to avoid ineligibility procedures under stand-by arrangements was the use of the "prior notice" clause. This was a clause in stand-by arrangements by which the Fund reserved to itself the privilege of giving notice and thereby interrupting a member's right to request purchases after the date of the notice. Nothing was said about the criteria for giving notice. The clause became standard practice because a member's program might be jeopardized by the non-observance of certain policies in its letter of intent even though, by their nature, they could not be given the objective formulation that is required for performance criteria.

---

[9] E.B. Decision No. 284-2; below, Vol. III, p. 272.

[10] E.B. Decision No. 155-(52/57); below, Vol. III, pp. 230–31.

[11] See above, pp. 533–35.

Notwithstanding the widespread use of the prior notice clause before it was repudiated, it was invoked on only one occasion, on September 17, 1958.[12] All of the inhibitions that attended the ineligibility procedures for which the prior notice clause was to be a substitute obstructed action under the clause as well. The embarrassment that was felt by the Executive Directors on the one occasion on which they decided to give notice helped to bring about the demise of the clause. That event occurred not because of the profligate use of the clause, but because of the conviction that it did not produce the most desirable balance between assurance to a member that it could use the Fund's resources and assurance to the Fund that use would be consistent with the Articles. The Fund decided in February 1961 to proscribe prior notice clauses and even deleted them from stand-by arrangements then in operation.[13]

When the decision to abandon prior notice clauses was taken, the staff and some executive directors urged that ineligibility procedures should not be regarded as an impeachment, and that, with this change in attitude, more use could be made of them. These recommendations have not been followed. Instead, the consequences of the decision have been, first, a greater vigilance than ever in ensuring that performance criteria are truly objective, because, if they are not, they will suffer from the same vice of subjectivity as the prior notice clause. Second, the decision led to a greater sophistication in the formulation of performance criteria as determinants of the effectiveness of a member's program. Third, performance criteria tended to proliferate until this tendency was curbed by a decision of September 20, 1968 which declares that they must be confined to those that are truly necessary for evaluating the progress of a program.

Earlier in this discussion of sanctions it was said that one further sanction would be singled out. That was a reference to Article VII, which is entitled "Scarce Currencies." Under Section 1, if the Fund finds that a general scarcity of a particular currency is developing, the Fund may inform members and issue a report setting forth the causes of the scarcity and containing recommendations for bringing it to an end. Section 2 empowers the Fund to borrow a member's currency or to acquire it for gold if the Fund deems it appropriate to replenish its holdings of that currency. Section 3 provides that if it becomes evident to the Fund that the demand for a member's currency seriously threatens the Fund's ability to supply the currency, the Fund, whether or not it has issued a report under Section 1, must make a formal declaration of the scarcity of the currency, apportion its existing and future supply of the currency, and issue a report. The formal declaration operates as an authorization to any member, after consulting the Fund, to impose temporary limitations on the freedom of exchange operations in the scarce currency. There are certain qualifications on the exercise of the

---

[12] See above, Vol. I, p. 433.
[13] E.B. Decision No. 1151-(61/6), February 20, 1961; below, Vol. III, p. 234.

authority, but, subject to them, members "have complete jurisdiction in determining the nature of [the] limitations"[14] on exchange operations, and therefore members would be able to discriminate against transactions in the scarce currency.

Action by the Fund under Section 1 or Section 3 was considered by the drafters to be the way in which the Fund could put pressure on a member that enjoys a substantial and persistent surplus in its balance of payments while a considerable number of other members suffer from deficits in their balance of payments. It is possible to detect a difference in tone in the explanations of these provisions before the Articles took effect, with Keynes describing the forerunner of Section 3 as "a sanction" and U.S. representatives generally avoiding quite so harsh a description.[15]

The provisions of Sections 1 and 3 and their relevance to conditions at the time were discussed by the Executive Directors in August 1947. The staff prepared a memorandum in which it was explained that the provisions were intended to prevent a general contraction of world trade as a result of inadequate imports and foreign investments by a great trading country. The insufficient monetary reserves of members at that time were not the result of any decline in demand in the United States or inadequate loans and grants by it; the abnormal demand for dollars was caused by an imbalance between the needs and the productive resources of many members. The implication of the staff's approach was that an adverse judgment would be implied by action under Section 1 and more particularly Section 3. In fact, the judgment would have been more disturbing than its legal consequences because many members were able to discriminate against transactions involving the U.S. dollar even in the absence of a declaration of the scarcity of the dollar. These were the members availing themselves of the transitional arrangements of Article XIV which permitted discrimination for balance of payments reasons. The Executive Directors decided on August 14, 1947 that there was no justification for action under Article VII, Sections 1 or 3. The possibility of invoking these provisions has not been discussed by the Executive Directors since August 1947, although the effectiveness of the provisions was the subject of debate in the CONTRACTING PARTIES to the GATT in 1955.

It seems to have become a received idea that a report under Section 1 or a declaration under Section 3 is an adverse judgment; certainly the consequences of the declaration, and perhaps also the report, could be grave. It was not to be expected that the Fund's customary caution in applying sanctions would be relaxed in the case of sanctions as serious as those that are available under

---

[14] Article VII, Section 3 (*b*); below, Vol. III, p. 195.

[15] See, for example, *Hearings Before the Committee on Banking and Currency of the U.S. Senate on H.R. 3314* (79th Cong., 1st sess.), pp. 168–72. See also *Questions and Answers on the International Monetary Fund*, Questions 30–32; below, Vol. III, pp. 171–75.

Article VII. This has led some observers to conclude that the only provision under which effective pressure could be applied against a member that has a substantial and persistent surplus in its balance of payments is sterile, and that the international adjustment process is all the weaker for that loss.

This discussion of the scarce currency provisions can be completed by a brief mention of the practice that has developed under Article VII, Section 2. Under that provision, the Fund can replenish its holdings of a currency by borrowing or by the sale of gold, and the Fund has now done this on a number of occasions. The provision would have had a more appropriate place in Article V among those dealing with the operations of the Fund, and it did appear in the forerunner of that article at one stage in its legislative history. Not only was the provision moved but the somewhat maladroit word "scarce" was introduced in its title. It has been necessary for the Fund to emphasize that the replenishment of a member's currency under Section 2 does not require action under either Section 1 or Section 3 and is not an animadversion on the member. On the contrary, the replenishment makes action under Section 3 less justifiable, because, if the replenishment takes the form of lending to the Fund, the member is making a contribution to the operation of the international monetary system by increasing the Fund's capacity to assist members in deficit. A member is required to provide its own currency to the Fund for gold but no member is obligated to lend to the Fund.

STRICT OBLIGATIONS AND PRACTICAL SOLUTIONS

The Fund's reluctance to employ sanctions is not associated with a relaxed understanding of the obligations of members. The Fund has tended to the view that obligations are not to be construed more narrowly than the terms in which they are written, and therefore it has not been responsive to alleged legal justifications for failures to observe obligations. An example of this strict construction has been cited in connection with par values: if a member wishes to change the par value of its currency it may do this only by the immediate adoption of a new par value in accordance with the Articles and without any intervening period of fluctuation in the exchange rate for its currency or an intervening unauthorized par value. Another example is the Fund's position on the scope of the obligation of members to refrain from imposing restrictions on payments and transfers for current international transactions without the approval of the Fund. The question arose whether the obligation applies to restrictions that are imposed for such political reasons as the preservation of national or international security and not for economic reasons. The Fund has made strenuous efforts at all times to exclude political considerations from its discussions and decisions. The desire to operate as a technical organization is reflected in the

Fund's agreement with the United Nations which was entered into pursuant to Article X of the Fund's Articles and Article 63 of the Charter of the United Nations and came into force on November 15, 1947. The agreement recognizes that

> by reason of the nature of its international responsibilities and the terms of its Articles of Agreement, the Fund is, and is required to function as, an independent international organization.[16]

It is an accepted convention of the Fund that political issues are not allowed to intrude into operating decisions, and thus there have been occasions on which the executive director appointed or elected by one disputant in a political controversy outside the Fund has not opposed an exchange transaction involving another disputant. It will be realized that the dilemma involving restrictions for security reasons was acute. In their decision of August 14, 1952, the Executive Directors expressed their conviction that the Fund does not provide a suitable forum for the discussion of the political and military considerations that are responsible for the adoption of these restrictions. The Executive Directors were aware, however, that it is not possible to distinguish sharply between cases involving only these considerations and other cases involving economic motivations and effects as well, that the Fund must protect the legitimate interests of its members, and that the language of the Articles makes no exception for any category of restrictions. They concluded, therefore, that the Fund's jurisdiction over restrictions applies whatever the motivation with which, or the circumstances in which, they are imposed.[17]

The Fund's skeptical attitude to alleged legal justifications for the nonperformance of obligations that are written in absolute form can be illustrated by two cases. The first of these arose in June 1948 and related to the responsibility of the United Kingdom for a subsidy paid by Southern Rhodesia to its domestic gold producers which appeared to be inconsistent with the Articles and the Fund's policy. A member accepts the Articles not only on its own behalf but also in respect of all colonies, overseas territories, territories under its protection, suzerainty, or authority and all territories in respect of which it exercises a mandate.[18] The United Kingdom felt that it could not require Southern Rhodesia to modify the subsidy because the colony was wholly self-governing in domestic matters. The Fund relied, however, on the traditional principle that a state cannot invoke its constitutional or domestic law as a legal excuse for noncompliance with a treaty obligation, and the United Kingdom withdrew its objection.

The second case relates to the compulsory withdrawal of Czechoslovakia. It was contended by Czechoslovakia that the complaint that it had failed to fulfill

---

[16] Below, Vol. III, p. 215.

[17] E.B. Decision No. 144-(52/51); below, Vol. III, p. 257.

[18] Article XX, Section 2 (g); below, Vol. III, p. 207.

its obligations under Article VIII, Section 5 and Article XIV, Section 2 was unfounded because the failure referred to in Article XV, Section 2 meant noncompliance for which there was no legal justification. Reasons of national security were a legal justification and Czechoslovakia had reasons of this kind for noncompliance. The reply was that the conditions on which the Fund may compel a member to withdraw are set forth in the Articles; failure to perform an obligation was one of these conditions; and no exception was made for reasons of national security in connection with the obligations on which the complaint was based. In the Board of Governors, the Governor for Czechoslovakia proposed an interpretative resolution which would have held that:

> 1. "Failure to fulfill the members' obligations under the Agreement" in Article XV, Section 2, means legally not justified nonfulfillment of the provisions of the Articles of Agreement.

> 2. Reasons of national security are under the general concept of international law legal justification for "failure to fulfill the members' obligations under the Agreement."

> 3. Members of the Fund are entitled not to comply with the provisions of the Articles of Agreement if to comply would endanger their national security, and, in particular, are entitled to withhold information under Article VIII, Section 5, the disclosure of which would endanger their national security.

The Board of Governors refused to adopt this proposed resolution and confirmed the interpretation of the Executive Directors.[19]

It must not be inferred from what has been said that the attitude of the Fund has been "let justice be done though the Fund perish" (*fiat justitia pereat Argentaria*). Faced by the problems that a strict view of obligations may provoke, the Fund has been prepared to find practical solutions within its constitutional framework. The decision on restrictions imposed for security reasons on payments and transfers for current international transactions can be reverted to as an example. In order to give effect to all interests, including the Fund's interest in avoiding political controversy, the decision established a special procedure by which a member can perform its obligation to obtain the approval of restrictions imposed for security reasons. Any member contemplating the adoption of restrictions that in its view are related solely to the preservation of national or international security may give notice under the decision and apply for prior approval, and the Fund will act promptly on the request. If the member finds that circumstances preclude advance notice to the Fund, it should give notice as promptly as possible but ordinarily not later than thirty days after imposition of the restrictions. Each notice is circulated immediately to the Executive Directors, and unless the Fund informs the member within thirty days after receiving the notice that the Fund is not satisfied that the restrictions are imposed

---

[19] *Summary Proceedings, 1954*, pp. 97–102, 112–14, 121–22, 135–80.

solely to preserve security, the member may assume that the Fund has no objection to the imposition of the restrictions. Notices have been given under the decision in connection with a number of international incidents of a political character. In no instance has there been any request to place a notice on the agenda of the Executive Directors, and the Fund has not objected to the imposition of any of the restrictions to which notices have related.

The decision dealing with restrictions established a procedure to enable members to stay within the law. A further illustration will be cited but of a different kind because it deals with the consequences of a situation that is contrary to the law. After Canada decided that it would not observe the obligations of Article IV, Sections 3 and 4 (b) and would allow the exchange rate for its currency to be determined by market forces, the Fund was faced with the problem of conducting transactions or making calculations in such a currency. It must be emphasized that a par value agreed with the Fund continues to be the par value for the purposes of the Articles until a new par value is established even though the member fails to perform its obligations to make the par value effective in exchange transactions taking place in its territories. If the Fund continued to stand ready to sell the currency at the par value, the practical effect would be to deprive other members of the opportunity to purchase the currency if it depreciated in the market, while there might be too great a readiness to purchase it from the Fund if the currency appreciated. The solution was an elaborate decision under which the Fund deals at market rates in a fluctuating currency to which the decision is applied, and makes all of its computations on the same basis.[20] The Fund employs the maintenance of gold value provisions in the Articles [21] to adjust all of its holdings in accordance with market rates prevailing on or about the dates as of which computations are made or transactions are carried out because it would produce a chaotic situation if the Fund were to value its currency holdings at one rate and at the same time use another rate in any of its operations or calculations.[22]

RECIPROCITY AND LEGAL ORDER

It has been suggested by some commentators that the Articles establish a legal system of reciprocity. For example, when the issue before a court in one member has been whether it must declare an exchange contract unenforceable under Article VIII, Section 2 (b) because it is contrary to the exchange control regulations of another member, the court has felt on occasion that it was relevant

---

[20] E.B. Decisions Nos. 321-(54/32), June 15, 1954, 1245-(61/45), August 4, 1961, 1283-(61/56), December 20, 1961; below, Vol. III, pp. 222–24.

[21] Article IV, Section 8.

[22] Joseph Gold, *Maintenance of the Gold Value of the Fund's Assets,* IMF Pamphlet Series, No. 6.

to inquire whether the other member was applying Article VIII, Section 2 (*b*) or other provisions in the Articles.[23] It is true that the Articles envisage benefits for all members because all have assumed obligations by subscribing to the Articles. It does not follow from this, however, that there is a legal principle of reciprocity by which the failure of one member to observe an obligation releases another member or members from their obligations to the delinquent member. The purpose of the Articles is to preserve legal order notwithstanding failures by a member from time to time to fulfill any of its obligations under the Articles. It is the function of the Fund to decide whether there has been a failure and what the legal consequences shall be. Even if the Fund is satisfied that there has been a failure, it does not follow that the legal consequence will be the release of other members from any of their obligations in relation to the defaulter or other members.

There is an eloquent statement of this principle by a Netherlands court that was asked to refrain from applying Article VIII, Section 2 (*b*) to an exchange contract that was said to be contrary to the exchange control regulations of Indonesia because of alleged violations of treaty obligations owed by Indonesia to the Netherlands:

> The Dutch forum must refrain from evaluating the Indonesian foreign exchange provisions and must also refrain from judging the question whether in view of its behavior Indonesia can be considered as a treaty partner. Apart from the fact that a partner to a treaty which has had to protest against violations of international agreements must itself fulfill its obligations, the paramount interest is that the international order to which the Netherlands and Indonesia have both adhered be respected.[24]

The principle on which the Articles are based and which guides the operation of the Fund is the one expressed by the Netherlands court. If, therefore, a member introduces restrictions on payments and transfers for current international transactions, this gives no license to other members to retaliate at will. They must observe this restraint even if the restrictions are discriminatory. Indeed, although one of the objectives of the Fund is the elimination of discrimination, and although the Fund has pursued this objective with vigor,[25] it must be recalled that the Fund does have the legal authority to approve discriminatory currency arrangements.[26] But even if a member introduces discriminatory or other restrictions without the approval of the Fund, other members are not entitled to adopt countermeasures without the Fund's approval if they are measures that require the Fund's approval. The Fund's Rules and Regulations

[23] *Pan American Insurance Co. v. Blanco*, 311 F. 2d 424, 427 fn. 8 (1962).

[24] *Frantzmann v. Ponijen*, Nederlandse Jurisprudentie (1960), No. 290. Gold, *The Fund Agreement in the Courts* (1962), pp. 113–18.

[25] E.B. Decisions Nos. 433-(55/42), June 22, 1955, 201-(53/29), May 4, 1953, 955-(59/45), October 23, 1959; below, Vol. III, pp. 258–60.

[26] Article VIII, Section 3.

establish procedures under which members can lodge complaints against a member that is alleged to be neglecting its obligations,[27] but, in accordance with the tendency to avoid formal procedures, most discussions of a member's practices take place informally and usually during regular consultations. By common consent, these consultations are a convenient and effective procedure for expressing an international opinion on a member's practices. In fact, the opportunities offered by consultations are considered so useful that occasionally members air informal complaints about an economic or financial policy of a member even though the complainants are aware that it is not within the jurisdiction of the Fund to approve or disapprove the policy. Some of these complaints are made in the forum of the Executive Directors because the present state of international economic organization does not provide another international forum with direct jurisdiction.

A leading example of the fact that the Articles establish a legal order which does not entitle members to take the law into their own hands in matters within the Fund's jurisdiction is the episode in which France adopted an unauthorized change of par value and discriminatory multiple rates of exchange on January 26, 1948.[28] The principle of the exchange rate obligations of the Articles is that each member is responsible for maintaining the value of its own currency. If it fails in this obligation, the obligation is not shifted to other members. Accordingly, the Fund held that other members were not bound to regard the former par value for the franc or the new rates of exchange for the franc as binding on them and as rates that they would have to enforce by appropriate measures in exchange transactions in their territories. However, both they and France remained bound by their obligations under Article IV, Section 4 (a), and the Fund called on them to maintain close contact with the Fund on the negotiation of new exchange arrangements. As a practical solution, the Fund agreed that any bilateral arrangements establishing rates of exchange based on the unauthorized change of par value, or the evolution of such rates in exchange transactions in the absence of bilateral arrangements, were not inconsistent with the objectives of the Articles. The Fund declared that specific approval had to be sought for bilateral arrangements for the adoption, or for the adoption without bilateral agreement, of rates not compatible with the unauthorized change of par value even if they were based on other rates introduced by France as part of its exchange reform. The Fund received a number of requests from France and other members for the approval of rates of exchange between the franc and other currencies that were justified because of special economic or other stated reasons. Some of these rates were not acceptable to the Fund and were modified. The general approach of the Fund was to resist the proliferation of rates beyond those already in existence.

---

[27] Rules and Regulations, Rules H-2, H-3, K-4, M-4, M-5; below, Vol. III, pp. 293–94, 299, 301.

[28] See above, pp. 549, 574, 583.

The adoption by France of its new exchange system did not release other members from their obligations although the new system involved a par value to which the Fund objected and multiple rates which it did not approve. The Fund insisted that other members were not entitled to retaliate by establishing rates of exchange between their currencies and the franc as they saw fit or even to establish rates by agreement with France in view of the interests of members that were not parties to the agreements. The relationships between the currencies of members are not simply bilateral but fit into an orderly design involving all currencies which is supervised by the Fund. If the design is disturbed at one place, the disturbance must be contained and order restored. One of the economic features of the French exchange system that the Fund found most undesirable was the introduction of broken cross rates. Rates of exchange ceased to be uniform among members in terms of gold as a common measure. This is a condition that can produce the most damaging distortions in trade and payments, and the Fund has opposed it relentlessly.

CHAPTER

27

The Amendments

Joseph Gold

SPECIAL DRAWING RIGHTS

In the 1960's the conviction grew that some more rational method of controlling international liquidity was needed in order to strengthen the international monetary system. The volume of reserves available to the community of Fund members was determined by the balance of payments deficits of the reserve currency countries, by the amount of gold production and the pattern of its absorption and use, by the conversion of reserve currencies into gold, and by fluctuations in the total of the newly recognized assets, gold tranches and readily repayable loan claims against the Fund, that arise as the result of the operations of the Fund. The determination of the reserve currency countries to reduce or eliminate their balance of payments deficits supported the credibility of the argument that unconditional liquidity might not increase sufficiently to prevent global stagnation and deflation. The long debate and negotiations on measures to deal with this threat led to the resolution of the Board of Governors at their Annual Meeting at Rio de Janeiro requesting the Executive Directors to prepare the text of an amendment of the Articles on the basis of an Outline attached to the resolution. The main tenet of the Outline was that the Fund should be empowered to allocate "special drawing rights" to its members as a supplement to existing reserve assets. The text of the amendments was prepared,[1] approved by the Board of Governors on May 31, 1968, and submitted to members for their acceptance in accordance with Article XVII. The amendments became effective on July 28, 1969. They are the first that have been adopted in the

---

[1] *Establishment of a Facility Based on Special Drawing Rights in the International Monetary Fund and Modifications in the Rules and Practices of the Fund: A Report by the Executive Directors to the Board of Governors Proposing Amendment of the Articles of Agreement* (Washington, April 1968); below, Vol. III, pp. 497–541. And see Joseph Gold, *Special Drawing Rights*, IMF Pamphlet Series, No. 13; "The Next Stage in the Development of International Monetary Law: The Deliberate Control of Liquidity," *American Journal of International Law*, Vol. 62 (1968), pp. 365–402.

history of the Fund. Although from time to time the idea of an amendment has been suggested, the general attitude has been that amendment was too complicated a process to undertake unless there was an overwhelming case for it. That case existed for the amendments that have been adopted. They represent the most important development in the Fund and in the legal regulation of the international monetary system since the original Articles became effective.

The facility through which special drawing rights will come into being is the Special Drawing Account, which became operative on August 6, 1969 in accordance with the provisions of the amendments.[2] This facility within the Fund will coexist with the General Account. The Fund will conduct its original operations and transactions, as well as a few new operations and transactions involving special drawing rights, through the General Account. The two Accounts will be separate in the manner indicated in the amendments, but neither will be a legal entity in itself.[3] The Special Drawing Account is not an affiliate, although that technique was considered possible at one time during the negotiations.[4] The Fund will remain a single legal entity and will be the same international person as before the amendments.

All members of the Fund have the privilege of participating in the Special Drawing Account but are not bound to participate. Decisions to allocate or cancel special drawing rights will be taken by the Board of Governors by a majority of 85 per cent of the total voting power of participants on the basis of a proposal by the Managing Director concurred in by the Executive Directors.[5] In decisions on matters pertaining exclusively to special drawing rights, only governors appointed by participants or executive directors appointed or elected by participants will be entitled to vote.[6]

Special drawing rights may be allocated to participants on the basis of their quotas for basic periods of five years. A participant may opt out of allocations.[7] The central right of a participant is to use its special drawing rights to meet its balance of payments needs, or in the light of developments in its official holdings of gold, foreign exchange, and special drawing rights, and its reserve position in the Fund, by transferring its special drawing rights in return for currency convertible in fact to another participant designated by the Fund. Although a participant is expected to use its special drawing rights only in the circumstances described and not for the sole purpose of changing the composition of its official holdings as between the total of its gold, foreign exchange, and reserve position

---

[2] Article XXIII, Section 1; below, Vol. III, pp. 525–26.

[3] Article XXII, Sections 1 and 2.

[4] Joseph Gold, "Legal Technique in the Creation of a New International Reserve Asset," *Case Western Reserve Journal of International Law*, Vol. I, No. 2 (1969), pp. 105–23.

[5] Article XXIV, Section 4.

[6] Article XXVII (*a*).

[7] Article XXIV, Section 2 (*e*).

in the Fund on the one hand and its special drawing rights on the other hand, the use of special drawing rights cannot be challenged on the basis of this expectation, although the Fund may take certain actions after the event.[8] A participant may use its special drawing rights up to the hilt but it must maintain an average balance of them over time, according to a prescribed formula, and must do this by an appropriate "reconstitution" of its balance of special drawing rights if they fall below the average for a time.[9]

There are three ways in which the provisions dealing with special drawing rights have been affected by the Fund's past experience. First, some provisions have been based on the Fund's practices and policies in the evolution of its original operations and transactions. Second, some provisions have been based on the original provisions. Third, some provisions deliberately depart from the original provisions.

(1) Some of the central characteristics of special drawing rights have been influenced profoundly by the experience of the Fund in the conduct of its original operations and transactions. For example, it was intended that special drawing rights should be a form of unconditional liquidity, and therefore the closest analogue in the General Account, the gold tranche, was the model for the unchallengeable right of a participant to use special drawing rights when it considers that it has a need to use them. The ability of a member to make gold tranche purchases without challenge rested on policy and practice before the amendments, but special drawing rights will begin life with a participant's unchallengeable right to use them as a legal characteristic of special drawing rights.

A participant is entitled to use its special drawing rights in accordance with the expectation of need by transferring them to another participant designated by the Fund. Alternatives to the concept of designation were considered, notably use by agreement between participants or use as determined solely by the participant using its special drawing rights. The choice in favor of use in accordance with designation by the Fund [10] was made because of the success of the Fund's policy on the selection of currencies purchased by members in exchange transactions with the Fund. The balance of payments and reserve criteria on which designation will be based have been adapted from that policy. Similarly, the provisions on the balanced distribution of special drawing rights among participants as a principle of designation derive from the attempt to achieve an equitable distribution of gold tranche positions under the policy.

There are other examples of a similar influence of policy on the new facility, but they need not be pursued here, except to note that the term "special drawing

---

[8] Article XXV, Section 3 (b).

[9] Article XXV, Section 6; Schedule G.

[10] Article XXV, Section 5.

rights" itself is a link, although an odd one, with the terminology of the Fund's original transactions. The importance of the point, however, goes beyond terminology. The original Articles speak of the purchase and sale of currencies and never of "drawings," but this word has become the popular way of referring to the Fund's exchange transactions. In the negotiations leading to the agreement on special drawing rights there was much dispute about whether the outcome should be a new monetary "unit" or "reserve asset" or a new form of "credit." This was not decided at the international level, but each participant is enabled to decide for itself whether it will regard special drawing rights as a reserve asset and include them in its reserves for domestic legal or policy purposes, and special drawing rights have been given the qualities which will permit participants to come to that conclusion. At the international level, a number of compromises were made, one of which was that the new instrument of liquidity would be called special drawing rights. The words "drawing rights" were used as an echo of the exchange transactions of the Fund, because these words connoted to some a credit element, although the Articles avoid all language that suggests the indebtedness of members to the Fund or the extension of credit by it. The adjective "special" was added to the popular term "drawing rights" to indicate that new drawing rights differing from the old were being established, and the result was the creation of a new term of art.

(2) The provisions dealing with special drawing rights that have been adapted, with more or less fidelity, from the original provisions are too numerous to mention here in full. In Chapter 25 the inspiration for the provision setting forth "general obligations of participants" in Article XXVIII was identified as Article IV, Section 4 (a), which establishes general obligations regarding exchange stability. In addition, the association between the new provisions that give the Fund authority to adopt variations in the operation of certain Articles without the need to amend and similar provisions in the original Articles has been noted. Provisions closely parallel to the original provisions have been adopted on such matters as administration of the Special Drawing Account,[11] emergency,[12] settlement on the termination of participation,[13] and interpretation.[14]

(3) In some ways, the decisions not to adopt parallel provisions are even more interesting. One of the most important divergences is the normal absence of any resources of gold or currency in the Special Drawing Account.[15] A participant receiving special drawing rights from another participant will provide currency to the latter on the occasion of the transaction.[16] The balance of payments need

[11] Article XXVII.
[12] Article XXIX, Section 1.
[13] Article XXX; Schedule H.
[14] Article XXVII (c).
[15] Article XXII, Section 2.
[16] Article XXV, Section 4.

for which a participant may make a use of its special drawing rights does not distinguish between difficulties in the current and capital accounts of the balance of payments, whereas a distinction of this kind is made in connection with a member's use of the Fund's resources through the General Account.[17] Special drawing rights have an absolute gold value guarantee,[18] whereas it is possible, theoretically at least, for the gold value of gold tranches to be decreased. This would occur if the Fund were to waive the maintenance of the gold value of its assets on a uniform proportionate reduction in the par values of all currencies.[19] The Fund sells currencies from the General Account at the par value,[20] but currency will be provided by participants in return for special drawing rights on the basis of market rates of exchange.[21] The liquidity of the Special Drawing Account is superior to that of the General Account because the net obligation of a participant to receive special drawing rights in transactions is equal to twice its net cumulative allocation of special drawing rights,[22] whereas the member's corresponding obligation in the General Account is limited to its subscription. The system of liquidation of the Special Drawing Account differs somewhat from that of the General Account [23] in order to establish a more desirable apportionment among participants of the burden of a default by a participant in the liquidation settlement and in order to ensure that a participant's exposure to risk will not be increased because it increases its holdings of special drawing rights.[24]

REFORM OF THE FUND

The resolution of the Board of Governors at Rio de Janeiro requested the Executive Directors to perform a second task: to proceed with their work relating to "improvements in the present rules and practices of the Fund based on developments in world economic conditions and the experience of the Fund since the adoption of the Articles of Agreement of the Fund" and to report on their proposals for amending the Articles and By-Laws for this purpose. The members of the European Economic Community had insisted that the establishment of the new facility and the improvement of the Fund had to be regarded as contemporaneous projects. One of the major developments in world economic conditions since the creation of the Fund which these members thought should be recognized by appropriate amendments was their economic and financial strength

[17] Article VI, Sections 1 and 2.
[18] Article XXI, Section 2.
[19] Article IV, Section 8 (d).
[20] Article IV, Section 1 (b).
[21] Article XXV, Section 8.
[22] Article XXV, Section 4.
[23] Article XVI, Section 2; Schedule E.
[24] Article XXXI; Schedule I.

in the world and their role in the Fund. This had been reflected in the volume of the Fund's sales of their currencies. Their voting strength in the Fund, however, was 16.45 per cent of the total in comparison with the 21.76 per cent of the United States.

All the basic reforms that have been incorporated in the amendments were proposed by the EEC members, although there are certain associated or consequential amendments that are the result of proposals by other members during the negotiations. The basic reforms proposed by the EEC members were few in number and only a small proportion of those originally considered by the EEC. They can be assembled into a few categories.[25] Foremost among them in their dramatic effect are those amendments that introduce the need for a special majority of 85 per cent of voting strength by analogy to the majority that is required for decisions to allocate or cancel special drawing rights. The argument for these amendments was the logical link that was alleged to exist between these latter decisions and certain other decisions of the Fund. The link was the effect on global liquidity. It was argued that decisions approving adjustments in quotas as the result of a general review of quotas and decisions on uniform proportionate changes in the par values of all currencies affect the volume of global liquidity, and these decisions, therefore, should command the same general support as decisions on the allocation or cancellation of special drawing rights. It was agreed that the same majority should be required for quota adjustments resulting from a general review [26] and for uniform proportionate changes in par values as well as for a number of associated decisions.[27]

A second group of amendments relate to the original provisions governing repurchase and the calculation of monetary reserves by which repurchase obligations are determined. The negotiation of these amendments began with the thesis that two aspects of these provisions involving reserve currencies were unsatisfactory. One of these was the deduction of "currency liabilities" in the calculation of monetary reserves. The currency liabilities of a member, it will be recalled, are the holdings of its currency by the central or other official institutions of other members or by banks in their territories. The view was advanced that this was a preference for the reserve currency members because it was mainly their currencies that were held by others, and the deductions that were made in respect of these holdings had resulted in negative monetary reserves or monetary reserves below the quota level for both the United Kingdom and the United States. The other objection was to the abatement of repurchase obligations, i.e., the principle by which a calculated repurchase obligation was

---

[25] Joseph Gold, *The Reform of the Fund,* IMF Pamphlet Series, No. 12. For the revisions to the Articles see below, Vol. III, pp. 521–38.

[26] Article III, Sections 2 and 4 (*c*); below, Vol. III, p. 521.

[27] Article IV, Sections 7 and 8 (*d*).

canceled if it accrued in the currency of a member which the Fund could not accept because the Fund's holdings of that currency cannot be increased above 75 per cent of the member's quota by repurchases. The member for which the obligation was calculated was not required to use another convertible currency or gold, which it might have had to obtain from a reserve center, in discharge of the obligation that was abated. It was contended that there was no economic justification for abatement because the repurchase obligation resulted from an improvement in the member's monetary reserves. The effects of abatement had been enhanced in recent years because the Fund had been unable to accept either U.S. dollars or sterling. Indeed, in order to enable members to make a temporary use of the Fund's resources in accordance with repurchase representations or commitments, the United States had made purchases of currencies from the Fund and had sold them, in return for dollars, to members which then returned them to the Fund immediately by way of repurchase. In view of the nature of these operations, the terms "turnstile" or "technical" purchases were in popular use for a time.

It was agreed that there should be amendments under which currency liabilities would not be deductible in the calculation of monetary reserves [28] and repurchase obligations that had been abated because the Fund could not accept the currency in which they had accrued would be discharged in another convertible currency which the Fund could accept.[29] These two basic amendments were accompanied by a large number of other amendments in relation to repurchase,[30] some of which were intended to soften the impact of the increase in repurchase obligations that might have followed from the two basic reforms. The possibility of eliminating the whole mechanism of repurchase and replacing it with a more discretionary system was raised but rejected, although the amendments introduce further qualifications of the principles of sharing or the concept of the Fund's resources as a second line of reserves for members, on which the original provisions had been based.

Amendments have been made in relation to the use of the Fund's resources. The gold tranche enters the third stage in its history and now receives constitutional recognition.[31] The former policy by which representations made in connection with requests for gold tranche purchases were not challenged in practice although they remained challengeable in principle has been converted into a legal guarantee of immunity from challenge.[32] This amendment has been accompanied by another which prevents the future creation of new forms of

---

[28] Article XIX (e).

[29] Schedule B, paragraph 1.

[30] See Report (cited above in footnote 1), Section 35; below, Vol. III, p. 515.

[31] Article XIX (j). See above, pp. 536–37.

[32] Article V, Section 3 (d).

unconditional or virtually unconditional facilities in the General Account.[33] Some of the members that had been vigorous supporters in the early days of the Fund of the thesis that access to the Fund's resources should be unconditional, and that had opposed the Fund's power to challenge requests or call for repurchase commitments, were among those that pressed for the prohibition of new forms of unconditional liquidity through the General Account. Their position was that the creation of this kind of liquidity in the future was a function of the Fund acting through the Special Drawing Account. In addition, they pointed out that it would not be logical to permit the creation of unconditional liquidity through one Account by a majority of votes cast while requiring a high majority for the same purpose through the other Account. Finally, Article VI, Section 2, which gave members that were not making a net use of the Fund's resources a special privilege to make purchases of certain currencies without encountering the objection that the purchases were to meet a large or sustained outflow of capital, has been eliminated in that form.[34] The original provision contained some fundamental obscurities, and in any event, it had not been useful because of the limitation on the currencies that could be purchased.

This brings the discussion to the next group of amendments, which can be described as improvements in the qualities of the gold tranche or in that part of it which is below the level of 75 per cent of quota and is sometimes referred to in practice as the "super gold tranche." For example, requests may be made for any gold tranche purchases without challenge on the ground that they are to meet a large or sustained outflow of capital. Under the original provision this rule had been confined to purchases that did not increase the Fund's holdings of the purchasing member's currency above 75 per cent of quota. The limitation on the currencies that may be purchased in this way has been removed. Other improvements include the assured remuneration that is payable on "super gold tranches"[35] and the possible reduction or elimination of service charges on gold tranche purchases.[36]

Finally, an amendment has been made in Article XVIII, the provision on interpretation. It may seem extraordinary in view of the conclusions of this history that the question was raised whether the principle of final and authoritative interpretation of its Articles by the Fund itself should be replaced by the procedure of settlement by three arbitrators which applies to disagreements between the Fund and a member which has withdrawn or which arises in the course of liquidation. The legal, political, and other reasons why the issue was raised are complex and can be left to some future historian. Here it can be said that the arbitration tribunal as the final authority was not acceptable. Instead,

---

[33] Article V, Section 3 (c).

[34] Article VI, Section 2; below, Vol. III, pp. 194, 523.

[35] Article V, Section 9.

[36] Article V, Section 8 (a).

a new organ with certain novel attributes was established within the framework of the Fund itself in order to provide a new mode of appeal. The Executive Directors will continue to take decisions on questions of interpretation in accordance with the original Articles. Within three months of any decision, any member may appeal to the Board of Governors, whose decision will continue to be final. However, any question referred to the Board of Governors in this way will be considered by a Committee on Interpretation of the Board of Governors. The Board of Governors is to establish the membership, procedures, and voting majorities of the committee, but each member of the committee is to have one vote. The decisions of the committee will be the only decisions within the structure of the Fund that are taken without weighted voting. This is particularly important because a decision of the committee will be deemed to be the decision of the Board of Governors unless the Board repudiates the decision by a majority of 85 per cent of the total voting power.

THE "CODIFICATION" OF POLICIES AND INTERPRETATIONS

In a chapter dealing with constitutional development it is appropriate to emphasize a further characteristic of the amendments. This is the incorporation of a number of policies and interpretative decisions into the amendments, a process that was frequently referred to in the discussions of the draft amendments as "codification." The Executive Directors were aware that the transformation of policies in this way could be a dangerous process because it could inhibit the evolution of future policy. Similarly, there was a risk that it might be thought to be the view of the Fund that from time to time interpretations should be transformed into amendments. The Executive Directors recommended, therefore, that only a modest number of policies and interpretative decisions should be treated in this way.

Among the policies that are given a legal foundation, it has been noted already that the *de facto* unchallengeability of representations connected with requests for gold tranche purchases is now a *de jure* unchallengeability. The compensatory financing facility and its "floating" character are now recognized, although there is no compulsion on the Fund to perpetuate either the facility or its floating character.[37] The Fund's investment in U.S. Government securities of the proceeds of the sale of gold in order to establish a Special Reserve against future administrative deficits has been recognized indirectly by broadening the use of the Special Reserve to cover operational deficits as well.[38] The policy by

---

[37] Article XIX (j).
[38] Article XII, Section 6 (c).

which various techniques have been adopted in order to soften the impact on members of the gold subscriptions payable on quota increases has been given a statutory basis by requiring an 85 per cent majority for decisions, taken as part of a general review of quotas, for the sole purpose of mitigating the effect of these subscriptions.[39]

Various important interpretative decisions are given statutory expression. The first of these is that the use of the Fund's resources must be temporary.[40] That word was not used in the Articles, although it was implicit in a number of provisions. Another relates to "conditionality" in the provision of Fund resources to members. Conditionality was inherent in the concept of "adequate safeguards," but it is now made express in a provision which requires the Fund to have policies on the use of its resources and to examine the representation made in connection with a request to make a purchase, other than a gold tranche purchase, in order to determine the consistency of the request with the Articles and the Fund's policies.[41] A third example is the express reference to the voluntary and other repurchases that are not made as the result of obligations accruing under the repurchase mechanism in the Articles and that account for the bulk of actual repurchases.[42]

Finally, three concepts that have emerged in past practice have been recognized and given operative effect. One of these is "reserve position in the Fund," which is now defined as the sum of the gold tranche purchases that a participant in the Special Drawing Account could make and the amount of any indebtedness of the Fund which is "readily repayable" to the participant under a loan agreement.[43] Developments in a member's reserve position in the Fund are among those that a member may take into account in deciding whether to use its special drawing rights.[44] The concept also appears in the amendments in connection with the desideratum of the harmonized use by a member of its resources, including its special drawing rights.[45] A readily repayable loan is one under which the lender may obtain early repayment at its request by representing that there is a balance of payments need for repayment. The concept, although not the term, was first used in the General Arrangements to Borrow [46] and again in the 1966 loan agreement with Italy. It was adapted from the gold tranche by giving the lender's representation the overwhelming benefit of any doubt. Lastly, "currency convertible in fact" also emerged from the General Arrangements to Borrow,

---

[39] Article III, Sections 2 and 4 (c).

[40] Article I (v); Article V, Section 3 (c).

[41] Article V, Section 3 (c) and (d).

[42] Article XXV, Section 7 (c).

[43] Article XXXII (c).

[44] Article XXV, Section 3 (a).

[45] Schedule G, paragraph 1 (b).

[46] E.B. Decision No. 1289-(62/1), January 5, 1962, paragraph 11 (f); below, Vol. III, p. 250.

where it was not defined.[47] It is now elaborately defined, and is of course a vital concept in connection with special drawing rights.[48] In particular, it is the currency that a participant designated to receive special drawing rights from another participant must supply in return for them.

"Each phrase and each sentence is an end
and a beginning."—T. S. Eliot, *Four Quartets*

---

[47] *Ibid.*, paragraph 11 (a); below, Vol. III, p. 249.
[48] Article XXXII (*b*); below, Vol. III, p. 534.

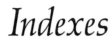

Indexes

Index A. Subjects

References in this index are arranged in alphabetical order of subject within each main heading. References are to pages; page numbers marked with an asterisk (*) refer to tables, and those including the letter n refer to footnotes.

A

ALTERNATE EXECUTIVE DIRECTORS *see* EXECUTIVE DIRECTORS, ALTERNATE.

ANGLO-AMERICAN FINANCIAL AGREEMENT: 29, 219, 252.

ANNUAL MEETINGS: 6; **4th (1949)**, 98, 189; **5th (1950)**, 194; **13th (1958)**, 450; **20th (1965)**, 423-24; *and see* INDEX E, *s.v.* International Monetary Fund, *Summary Proceedings of the Board of Governors.*

ANNUAL MEETINGS, COMMITTEES: 189, 194, 255, 261.

ANNUAL MEETINGS, SYMPOSIA: 272.

ANNUAL REPORT OF THE EXECUTIVE DIRECTORS *see* INDEX E, *s.v.* International Monetary Fund.

ANNUAL REPORT ON EXCHANGE RESTRICTIONS: 256; *and see* INDEX E, *s.v.* International Monetary Fund.

ARTICLES OF AGREEMENT: 514-16; ambiguities in, 393-94; amendment of, 575, 595-605; interpreted, 236, 368-69, 384-89, 438-40, 567-73; provisions for interpretation, 9, 567, 602-603; revision deprecated, 416, 596; variations without amendment, 575-78; *and see* INDEX C.

B

BANK FOR INTERNATIONAL SETTLEMENTS: 322, 323, 518.

BASLE AGREEMENTS: 519.

BILATERALISM: defined, 228, 297-98; Fund action, 228, 276, 308-309, 315-16; Fund policy, 276, 302-307, 314-16; prevalence of, 281-82, 297-300, 308, 310-14; 312*, 318; reasons for, 297-98, 303, 305-306, 312-16; relation to convertibility, 303-304, 310; relation to discrimination, 281, 299, 303, 306-307, 315; relaxed, 273, 301-302, 306, 310; with nonmembers, 305-307, 312*, 313-16; *and see* EXCHANGE RESTRICTIONS.

BRETTON WOODS CONFERENCE: 124, 203, 205, 513, 514, 518, 554.

BY-LAWS OF FUND: 514, 578-79.

C

CAPITAL MOVEMENTS *see* INTERNATIONAL CAPITAL MOVEMENTS.

COMPENSATORY FINANCING OF EXPORT FLUCTUATIONS *see* FUND'S RESOURCES, USE OF, POLICY

CONSULTATIONS, FUND: 27, 33, 229-48, 557-59; content and form of conclusions, 231-32, 234-38, 241, 246-48; Fund's representations, 231-32, 234-35, 308, 555-56, 583-84; initiated, 231; locale, 243-45; numbers of, 248*; procedure, 12-13, 231, 233, 241-48; required by scale of charges, 383, 401, 431, 524-25, 577, 582; required by stand-by arrangements, 476, 489, 535-36, 558; role of, 27, 557-58; scope of, 137, 235-41, 558, 593; use of reports on, 242-43, 558; with Article VIII countries, 27, 246-48, 287, 558-59.

CONVERTIBILITY: achieved (Article VIII), 29, 289-90; by buying and selling gold freely, 560-61; currency convertible in fact, 604-605; external, 81, 226, 250, 277-79, 451, 541; foreseen, 266-70; hinges on sterling, 219, 266-67, 274; list of countries, 225, 250, 285, 292*, 448; need for par value, 75-76, 287; of sums drawn from Fund, 452, 542; **pre-1961**, 28-29, 225, 250; significance of Article VIII, 76, 270, 278, 283-88, 290, 544, 556; through Fund, 544; use of Article XIX(g), 450; *and see* EXCHANGE RESTRICTIONS.

D

DEPUTY MANAGING DIRECTOR: functions, 9, 14-17.

DEVALUATION *see* EXCHANGE RATES, CHANGES IN.

DEVELOPMENT INSURANCE FUND: 420.

DISCRIMINATION *see* EXCHANGE RESTRICTIONS.

DOLLAR SHORTAGE: 28, 45, 47, 138, 141, 251, 256.

DRAWINGS *see* FUND'S RESOURCES, USE OF, POLICY, *and* FUND TRANSACTIONS.

E

ECONOMIC COOPERATION ADMINISTRATION: 320-22, 328-29.

EUROPEAN ECONOMIC COMMUNITY: 599-600.

EUROPEAN FUND: 374.

EUROPEAN MONETARY AGREEMENT: 269, 323.

EUROPEAN PAYMENTS UNION: 223, 318, 322; effects of, 223, 275-76, 300-301; Fund relations with, 32, 317-31, 469; Fund views on, 224, 276, 323-29, 340, 519; Managing Board, 322, 327-30; precursors, 319-21; problem of sterling area, 321; role of BIS, 322, 323.

EUROPEAN RECOVERY PROGRAM: 320, 324, 328, 394-98, 523.

EXCHANGE CONTROLS: capital movements, 29-31, 224, 291-92, 295-96, 540, 548-49; defined, 217n; obligations of other members to recognize, 220, 568, 591-92; prevalence of, 218-19, 250; *and see* EXCHANGE RESTRICTIONS.

EXCHANGE RATES: 39-173; and international transactions, 63-65; defined, 581; fixed rates as objective, 21, 40, 170-73, 547; Fund's role, 21, 53-60, 114-16, 547-53, 564-66, 591-94; rigidity of, 44-45, 96; *and see following headings.*

EXCHANGE RATES, CHANGES IN: 90-116; adequacy questioned, 93-95, 134, 549; Ad Hoc Committee of Directors, 97; competitive depreciation, 91, 94, 100-10, 130, 549; effected, 44-45, 54, 61, 74, 90, 96-107, 116*-18*, 217; effects of, 46, 109-10, 115-16, 189; fundamental disequilibrium, 21-22, 62, 91-92, 547, 549, 568, 581; Fund's procedures, 46, 549; Fund's role, 22, 92-105, 111, 114-16, 551; magnitudes of, 111-14, 112*, 119*-21*; members' reluctance to introduce, 44-45, 96; nonmetropolitan currencies, 99-103; obligation to fix new par value, 74, 549-51, 588; profits or losses from, 497; revaluation, 110-11; stabilization programs, 475, 505-10; uniform change, 192-94, 600; ways of effecting, 90; *and see* INDEX B.

EXCHANGE RATES, CROSS RATES: 32, 43-44, 48, 76-82, 129-30, 133, 141, 180, 594.

J

JOINT STATEMENT: 124.

K

KEYNES PLAN: 124.

L

LOCAL CURRENCY COUNTERPART FUNDS: 497-98, 503.

LONDON: gold market, 185, 202, 564, 579.

M

MANAGING DIRECTOR: functions, 9, 11-17, 515-16.

MEMBERSHIP OF FUND: 4-5, 87*-89*, 514.

MEMBERSHIP RESOLUTIONS: 54, 66-71, 408-10, 552.

MEMBERS' OBLIGATIONS: 19-23, 25, 547-66, 573-75, 591-94, and *passim*.

MONETARY RESERVES: adequacy examined, 356; calculation for repurchases, 438, 440-43, 525, 580, 600; collection of data, 440-41; increase in, 271; *International Reserves and Liquidity*, 358; Net Official Holdings Committee, 580; stabilization programs, 506-10.

MULTIPLE CURRENCY PRACTICES *see* EXCHANGE RATES, MULTIPLE RATES.

N

NET OFFICIAL HOLDINGS *see* MONETARY RESERVES.

NONMETROPOLITAN AREAS: devaluations, 99-103; members' responsibilities, 207, 589.

O

ORGANIZATION OF AMERICAN STATES: 420, 423.

ORGANIZATION FOR ECONOMIC COOPERATION AND DEVELOPMENT: 518.

ORGANIZATION FOR EUROPEAN ECONOMIC CO-OPERATION: 223-24; liberalization policy, 30, 223-24, 250, 261-62, 273, 275; Ministerial Examination Group on Convertibility, 269, 302; receives Fund documents, 330; *and see* EUROPEAN MONETARY AGREEMENT *and* EUROPEAN PAYMENTS UNION.

P

PAR VALUES *see* EXCHANGE RATES, PAR VALUES.

PARIS CLUB: 273, 305, 310.

PRICE CONTROLS: stabilization programs, 510.

Q

QUOTAS: 349-63, 378*-80*; adequacy questioned, 355-63, 373; Articles, 349-51; Committee of the Whole on Review of Quotas, 355, 356-57, 359; compensatory financing revisions, 421-23; *Enlargement of Fund Resources Through Increases in Quotas*, 358; formula, 5, 351, 354, 360; *International Reserves and Liquidity*, 358; mitigation of gold subscriptions, 358-59, 361-63, 604; revised, 5-6, 354-55, 357, 359, 361-63, 378*-80*, 423, 531; significance, 5, 351-52, 354, 531; small quotas, 356-61, 514; voting on general increases, 600.

R

REFORM OF THE FUND: 599-605.

REPURCHASES *see* FUND'S RESOURCES, USE OF, REPURCHASES, *and* FUND TRANSACTIONS.

RESERVE POSITION IN FUND: defined, 451, 454, 604.

RESOURCES OF FUND *see* FUND'S RESOURCES.

RETENTION QUOTAS *see* EXCHANGE RESTRICTIONS.

RULES AND REGULATIONS OF FUND: 82, 195, 355, 388, 428, 440-41, 516, 523, 576n, 577n, 578-79, 584, 592-93.

S

SCARCE CURRENCY CLAUSE: 373, 586-88.

SELECTION OF CURRENCIES *see* FUND'S RESOURCES, USE OF, POLICY.

SPECIAL DRAWING RIGHTS: 35, 545, 578, 595-99, 604-605.

STABILIZATION PROGRAMS: balance of payments policies, 486-87, 506-10; content and purposes, 25-27, 472-74; definition, 472; domestic credit controls, 476, 486, 492-96, 502; exchange rate adjustment, 476, 504-10; fiscal controls, 476, 503-505; fluctuating exchange rates, 170, 505-506, 550-51; foreign transactions, 497-503; gradualism, 473-74, 476, 505-506; letter of intent, 477, 535; policy instruments, 475-76, 492-510; price and wage controls, 510; problems, 474-75, 492-510.

STAFF: functions, 11-17, 515-16; numbers and organization, 10, 13, 293.

STAND-BY ARRANGEMENTS *see* FUND'S RESOURCES, USE OF, STAND-BY ARRANGEMENTS.

STERLING *see* INDEX B, *s.v.* UNITED KINGDOM.

STERLING AREA: constitution, 217-18; devaluations, 99; discrimination, 226-27; dollar expenditure reduced, 338; Fund's views, 339-40; GATT consultations, 230, 261, 337-40; in EPU, 321; par values, 53; *raison d'être*, 218, 339-40; reserves, 252, 274, 391, 399-400; *and see* INDEX B, *s.v.* UNITED KINGDOM.

SUBSCRIPTIONS: 349-50.

SUBSCRIPTIONS, GOLD: 350-51, 358-59, 361-63, 371, 604.

T

TECHNICAL ASSISTANCE: 26, 34.

TRANSIT TRADE: 47, 264.

TRANSITIONAL PERIOD: 22-23, 224-25, 270, 284, 288, 384, 555-57, 583.

U

UNITED NATIONS: CICT, 360-61, 418-23; ECOSOC experts' reports, 355, 417-18; Fund agreement with, 589; UNCTAD, 109, 345, 423-26.

V

VOTING PROVISIONS IN FUND: 7-9, 352-53*, 514, 516-17, 596, 600, 604.

W

WAGE POLICIES: stabilization programs, 510.

WHITE PLAN: 124.

Index B. Countries

In this index the word "exchange" should be understood before the word "rate" in the expressions "fluctuating rate," "forward rate," and "multiple rate." References are to pages. Page numbers marked with an asterisk (*) refer to tables; however, no references are given to the following comprehensive tables:

Table 1. Initial Par Values Established, 1946–65 (pp. 84-86)

Table 2. Dates of Membership and of Initial Par Values, December 27, 1945–December 31, 1965 (pp. 87-89)

Table 3. Magnitudes of Exchange Depreciation, End 1948 to End 1965: Distribution of 105 Countries by Degree of Depreciation (p. 112)

Table 4. Changes in Par Values, 1948–65 (pp. 116-18)

Table 5. Exchange Rates Used in Table 3 (pp. 119-21)

Table 6. Principal Developments in Multiple Exchange Rates, 1946–65 (pp. 147-51)

Table 14. Quotas of Members at Selected Dates (pp. 378-80)

Table 22. Drawings from the Fund, Calendar Years 1947–65 (pp. 460-63)

Table 23. Repurchases of Drawings, Calendar Years 1947–65 (pp. 464-67)

Table 24. Stand-By Arrangements Inaugurated or Renewed, Calendar Years 1952–65 (pp. 490-91)

A

AFGHANISTAN: bilateral agreements, 311-12; multiple rates, 137, 146; par value, 70, 408.

ALGERIA: devaluation, 102; membership resolution, 71; par value, 53.

ARGENTINA: bilateral agreements, 299-300, 310; currency drawn, 449*; devaluation, 57; drawings, 447*; exchange restrictions, 218; fluctuating rate, 167, 168; multiple rates, 125, 126, 143; "Paris Club," 273, 305, 310; par value, 57-58; repurchase obligations, 442; stand-by arrangement, 498.

AUSTRALIA: consultations, GATT, 230, 261, 338-40, 345; convertibility, 292; currency drawn, 449*; devaluation, 99; drawings, 469; gold producers, subsidies to, 206-208, 210, 211-12, 214; par value, 54; quota, 354, 359; stand-by arrangement, 488; views on Fund's jurisdiction, 236, 240, 284, 337-40.

AUSTRIA: bilateral agreements, 300, 309, 312; consultation, GATT, 345; convertibility, 277, 292; currency drawn, 449*, 456*; currency holdings by Fund replenished, 456*; currency used in repurchases, 449*; devaluation, 54, 105, 111; exchange controls, 218; membership resolution, 66; multiple rates, 55, 105, 123; par value, 54-55, 59, 105.

B

BELGIAN CONGO: gold production, 182; par value, 53; *and see* CONGO, DEMOCRATIC REPUBLIC OF.

BELGIUM: bilateral agreements, 298, 300, 309, 310; consultation, Fund, 83, 234; convertibility, 277, 289, 292*, 309; creditor in Europe, 319, 330, 469; currency drawn, 448, 449*, 456*, 458*; currency holdings by Fund replenished, 455, 456*, 458*; currency used in repurchases, 449*; devaluation, 99-100; drawing, 470; EPU, 80; fluctuating rate, 99, 155-56, 550; forward rate, 83; GAB, 17, 374-77, 456*, 458*; gold sales at premium prices, 181-82; multilateral compensation agreement, 319; multiple rate, 137-38; par value, 53, 84; stand-by arrangement, 330, 446, 469.

BOLIVIA: devaluation, 74, 105-106; drawings, 447*; exchange restrictions, 218; fluctuating rate, 47, 167, 168; ineligible to draw, 389-90, 479-80; multiple rate, 43, 74, 106, 125, 141; par value, 53, 74; stand-by arrangements, 389-90, 479-80, 510.

BRAZIL: bilateral agreements, 299, 300, 310, 311, 313; consultation, GATT, 345; drawings, 399, 423, 447*; exchange restrictions, 218; fluctuating rate, 167; "Hague Club," 273, 305, 310; multiple rates, 47, 107, 125, 146; par value, 54; stabilization program, 500, 510; stand-by arrangement, 487, 510; trade with Germany, 123.

BRITISH GUIANA *see* GUYANA

BRITISH HONDURAS: par value, 53.

BURMA: drawings, 386, 403, 406; membership resolution, 66; par value, 46, 53, 54, 69, 408.

BURUNDI: bilateral agreements, 309; membership resolution, 71.

C

CAMEROON: devaluation, 102; membership resolution, 70, 71; par value, 53.

CANADA: appoints Executive Director, 7, 515; convertibility, 75, 225, 292*, 443; currency drawn, 448, 449*, 456*, 458*; currency holdings by Fund replenished, 455, 456*, 458*; currency used in repurchases, 449*; devaluation, 90, 100, 111, 165; exchange controls abolished, 262; fluctuating rate, 44, 47, 48, 59, 75, 90, 111, 159-67, 171, 443, 550, 591; GAB, 17, 374-77, 456*, 458*; gold output, 208, 214; gold producers, subsidies to, 204-10, 214; par value, 49, 53, 164; quota, 358; repurchases, 456.

CENTRAL AFRICAN REPUBLIC: membership resolution, 70, 71.

CEYLON: bilateral agreements, 311, 313, 314-15; consultations, GATT, 230, 261, 338-40, 345; par value, 46, 53, 54; stabilization program, 494.

CHAD: membership resolution, 70, 71.

CHILE: bilateral agreements, 310, 314; consultations, GATT, 230, 261, 338-40; drawing, 403; exchange restrictions, 218; fluctuating rate, 47, 167, 168, 182; gold sales at premium prices, 182-83; multiple rates, 43, 125, 126, 141, 146, 182, 481; par value, 53; quota, 359; repurchase obligations, 442; stabilization program, 481-82, 500; stand-by arrangements, 403, 481-82, 488, 498.

CHINA: appoints Executive Director, 353*; bilateral agreements, 300; multiple rates, 132, 137; not qualified to draw, 68n; quota, 354.

COLOMBIA: bilateral agreements, 313; consultation, Fund, 237; devaluation, 44; fluctuating rate, 167, 170; gold producers, subsidies to, 210-11; gold sales at premium prices, 175-77, 203; multiple rates, 43, 47, 125, 146, 170; par value, 53; quota, 359; stand-by arrangement, 487.

CONGO (BRAZZAVILLE): membership resolution, 70, 71.

CONGO, DEMOCRATIC REPUBLIC OF: bilateral agreements, 309; membership resolution, 71; and see BELGIAN CONGO.

COSTA RICA: convertibility, 292; devaluation, 143; fluctuating rate, 143; multiple rates, 43, 47, 125, 126, 143; par value, 49, 53; stand-by arrangement, 502.

CUBA: convertibility, 225, 292; drawings, 412; exchange tax, 43, 47, 125, 126-27, 237-38, 286; fails to repurchase drawings, 389, 435; ineligibility to draw considered, 389, 583; par value, 53; restrictions for security reasons, 259; stand-by arrangement, 412; withdraws from Fund, 5, 292, 389, 514.

CYPRUS: bilateral agreements, 312; par value, 53, 59.

CZECHOSLOVAKIA: adduces national security reasons, 569, 589-90; bilateral agreements, 298; devaluation, 123; exchange controls, 218; fails to supply information, 65, 389, 583, 589-90; ineligible to draw, 65, 389, 583; interpretation of Articles obtained, 569, 590; par value, 53, 63-65; unauthorized change in par value, 63-65, 389; withdraws from Fund, 5, 389, 514, 569, 583.

D

DAHOMEY: membership resolution, 70, 71.

DENMARK: bilateral agreements, 298, 300, 310; consultation, Fund, 234; consultation, GATT, 345; convertibility, 277; currency drawn, 448, 449*, 458*; currency holdings by Fund replenished, 458*; devaluation, 99, 217; EPU, 80; multiple rates, 47; par value, 53.

DOMINICAN REPUBLIC: convertibility, 225, 292*; par value, 54.

E

ECUADOR: devaluation, 74; multiple rates, 43, 47, 74, 125, 126; par value, 53.

EGYPT: bilateral agreements, 300; devaluation, 99; multiple rates, 47, 137; par value, 53; quota, 354; and see UNITED ARAB REPUBLIC.

EL SALVADOR: convertibility, 225, 250, 292*; par value, 53, 74; quota, 359, 361.

ETHIOPIA: drawing, 386; par value, 53; quota, 356.

F

FIJI: gold producer, subsidy to, 213; par value, 53.

FINLAND: bilateral agreements, 300, 310, 312; consultation, GATT, 345; convertibility, 277; devaluation, 100, 112, 143, 217; membership resolution, 66; multiple rates, 47, 137, 143; par value, 49, 54; stand-by arrangement, 470.

FRANCE: appoints Executive Director, 7, 353*; bilateral agreements, 298, 300, 309, 310; broken cross rates, 129-30; consultation, GATT, 345; convertibility, 277, 289, 292*; currency drawn, 448, 449*, 451, 456*, 458*; currency holdings by Fund replenished, 455, 456*, 458*; currency used in repurchases, 449*; devaluation, 44, 93, 100, 111, 129-30, 389, 549, 574, 583, 593-94; EPU, 80; exchange restrictions, 262; GAB, 17, 374-77, 456*, 458*; import restrictions, 262; ineligible to draw, 130, 389, 583; multilateral compensation agreement, 319; multiple rates, 44, 100, 129-30, 389, 574, 593-94; par value, 44, 53, 354; quota, 350-51, 354; repurchase obligations, 442; subscription, 350-51.

FRENCH COLONIES: devaluations, 102; par values, 53.

FRENCH SOMALILAND: convertibility of Djibouti franc, 560-61; devaluation, 44.

G

GABON: membership resolution, 70, 71.

GAMBIA, THE: par value, 53.

GERMANY: appoints Executive Director, 7, 353*; bilateral agreements, 122-23, 297-98, 300, 305, 310; consultations, Fund, 237, 248*; consultation, GATT, 345; convertibility, 277-78, 289, 292*; currency drawn, 448, 449*, 451, 456*, 458*; currency holdings by Fund replenished, 455, 456*, 458*; currency used in repurchases, 449*; EPU, 80; exchange arrangements, pre-1939, 122-23, 218, 297; GAB, 17, 374-77, 456*, 458*; multiple rates, 122-23, 138; par value, 46, 54; quota, 358; revaluation of currency, 110-11.

GHANA: bilateral agreements, 311, 313; gold producers, subsidies to, 214; par value, 59; stabilization program, 494; and see GOLD COAST.

GOLD COAST: par value, 53; and see GHANA.

GREECE: bilateral agreements, 300, 312; consultation, GATT, 345; convertibility, 277; devaluation, 100, 105; exchange controls, 218; multiple rates, 105, 137; par value, 48, 49, 56.

GUATEMALA: convertibility, 225, 250, 292*; par value, 53; stand-by arrangements, 502.

GUINEA: bilateral agreements, 311-12; membership resolution, 70, 71.

GUYANA: par value (as British Guiana), 53.

H

HAITI: convertibility, 225, 250, 292*; par value, 46, 54; stand-by arrangement, 485.

HONDURAS: convertibility, 225, 250, 292*; drawings, 447*; exchange tax, 125, 127; multiple rates, 43, 125; par value, 53; quota, 354-55, 357, 361; stand-by arrangement, 502.

HONG KONG: broken cross rates, 79-80; par value, 53.

HUNGARY: exchange controls, 218; multiple rates, 123.

I

ICELAND: bilateral agreements, 300, 312; devaluation, 99, 102-103, 112; multiple rates, 47, 103, 137; par value, 49, 53; stand-by arrangement, 482.

INDIA: appoints Executive Director, 7, 353*; bilateral agreements, 311, 313; consultations, GATT, 230, 261, 338-40, 345; devaluation, 60, 99; import restrictions relaxed, 262; interpretation of Articles obtained, 567; par value, 53, 60; quota, 354.

INDONESIA: bilateral agreements, 299, 300, 309; membership resolution, 66-70, 408; multiple rates, 107, 137, 146.

IRAN: bilateral agreements, 300; multiple rates, 43, 47, 125, 143; offers gold collateral, 407; par value, 49, 53; quota, 354.

IRAQ: devaluation, 99; par value, 53.

IRELAND: convertibility, 277, 289, 292*; par value, 59.

ISRAEL: bilateral agreements, 299-300; devaluation, 143; multiple rates, 107, 137, 143; par value, 49, 53; quota, 361.

ITALY: appoints Executive Director, 515; bilateral agreements, 300, 309, 310; broken cross rates, 77; consultation, GATT, 345; convertibility, 277, 289, 292*; currency drawn, 449*, 451, 456*, 458*, 544; currency holdings by Fund replenished, 455, 456*, 458*, 537-38, 544, 604; currency used in repurchases, 449*; devaluation, 44, 123; exchange controls, 218; fluctuating rate, 55-56, 77; GAB, 17, 374-77, 456*, 458*; loan to Fund, 455, 537-38, 544, 604; membership resolution, 66, 408; multilateral compensation agreement, 319; multiple rates, 55; par value, 49, 55-56; quota, 361; right to draw, 66.

IVORY COAST: membership resolution, 70, 71.

J

JAMAICA: convertibility, 60, 292; membership resolution, 70; par value, 53, 59.

JAPAN: bilateral agreements, 298, 300, 310; consultation, GATT, 345; convertibility, 292; currency drawn, 449*, 456*, 458*; currency holdings by Fund replenished, 455, 456*, 458*; currency used in repurchases, 449*; GAB, 17, 374-77, 456*, 458*; par value, 46, 54; quota, 358; stand-by arrangement, 482.

JORDAN: bilateral agreements, 311, 314; fluctuating rate, 143; multiple rates, 47; par value, 46, 49, 54.

K

KENYA: membership resolution, 71; par value, 53.

KOREA: bilateral agreements, 300, 312; fluctuating rate, 143, 146; membership resolution, 70, 71; multiple rates, 137, 146.

KUWAIT: convertibility, 60, 292; membership resolution, 70; par value, 59.

L

LAOS: membership resolution, 70, 71; quota, 361.

LEBANON: broken cross rates, 79-80; fluctuating rate, 47, 165; par value, 54.

LIBERIA: membership resolution, 70; par value, 59.

LIBYA: par value, 59.

LUXEMBOURG: bilateral agreements, 300, 309, 310; consultation, Fund, 234; convertibility, 277, 289, 292*; devaluation, 99; multilateral compensation agreement, 319; par value, 53.

M

MALAGASY REPUBLIC: devaluation, 102; membership resolution, 71; par value, 53.

MALAYSIA: par value, 53, 60; quota, 361.

MALI: bilateral agreements, 311-12; membership resolution, 71.

MALTA: par value, 53.

MAURITANIA: membership resolution, 71.

MAURITIUS: par value, 53.

MEXICO: bilateral agreements, 310; convertibility, 225, 250, 292*; currency drawn, 449*; devaluation, 44, 90, 106-107, 154, 412; eligibility to draw, 154: fluctuating rate, 44, 153-54, 164, 549-50; gold sales at premium prices, 179-80; par value, 53, 549-50; stand-by arrangements, 412, 469.

MOROCCO: bilateral agreements, 311; par value, 53.

N

NEPAL: membership resolution, 70, 71; quota, 361.

NETHERLANDS: bilateral agreements, 298, 300, 309, 310; consultation, GATT, 345; convertibility, 277, 289, 292*, 309; currency drawn, 448, 449*, 456*, 458*; currency holdings by Fund replenished, 455, 456*, 458*; currency used in repurchases, 449*; devaluation, 99; drawings, 397-98; EPU, 80; GAB, 17-18, 374-77, 456*, 458*; multilateral compensation agreement, 319; multiple rates, 47; par value, 53; revaluation of currency, 111.

NETHERLANDS COLONIES: par value, 53.

NEW ZEALAND: consultations, GATT, 230, 261, 338-40, 345; par value, 59; special exchange agreement, 332.

NICARAGUA: convertibility, 292; drawing, 398; fluctuating rate, 143; multiple rates, 43, 47, 125; par value, 49, 53.

NIGER: membership resolution, 70, 71.

NIGERIA: membership resolution, 70; par value, 53, 59, 60.

NORWAY: bilateral agreements, 298, 300, 310; consultation, GATT, 345; convertibility, 277; devaluation, 99, 217; par value, 53.

P

PAKISTAN: consultations, GATT, 230, 261, 338-40, 345; devaluation, 61, 90; multiple rates, 146; par value, 46, 54, 60-61; stand-by arrangement, 482.

PANAMA: convertibility, 225, 250, 292*; par value, 53; quota, 361.

PARAGUAY: bilateral agreements, 299, 310; devaluation, 74, 241; drawings, 447*; fluctuating rate, 47, 74, 167, 168; multiple rates, 43, 74, 126, 141; par value, 53, 74; quota, 354; stand-by arrangements, 484-85, 487.

PERU: broken cross rates, 79-80; convertibility, 76, 159, 289, 292*; eligibility to draw, 156, 159; fluctuating rate, 44, 47, 76, 156-59, 165-67, 171; gold mining problems, 180, 203-204; gold sales at premium prices, 175; multiple rates, 43, 79, 125, 156-57, 166; par value, 53, 158-59, 211; stand-by arrangements, 73, 471, 477-78; trade with Germany, 123.

PHILIPPINES: devaluation, 90; fluctuating rate, 90, 143, 146, 168-69; gold producers, subsidies to, 210-11, 214; gold sales at premium prices, 180; multiple rates, 137, 141, 146; par value, 49, 53; stand-by arrangement, 482.

POLAND: exchange controls, 218; withdraws from Fund, 5, 514.

PORTUGAL: bilateral agreements, 298, 311; convertibility, 277; devaluation, 217; par value, 59.

R

RHODESIA AND NYASALAND: consultation, GATT, 345; *and see* SOUTHERN RHODESIA.

RUANDA URUNDI: access to Belgian gold market, 182; *and see* BURUNDI *and* RWANDA.

RUMANIA: exchange controls, 218; multiple rates, 123.

RWANDA: bilateral agreements, 309; membership resolution, 71.

S

SAUDI ARABIA: convertibility, 289, 292*; fluctuating rate, 143; par value, 59.

SENEGAL: membership resolution, 71.

SIERRA LEONE: membership resolution, 70, 71; par value, 53, 59.

SOMALIA: membership resolution, 70; par value, 59.

SOUTH AFRICA: consultations, GATT, 261n, 337-40, 345; devaluation, 99, 189; drawings, 398, 413, 414-15; gold price, 188, 191-94; gold producers, subsidies to, 213, 214; gold production, 214; gold sales at premium prices, 183-99; import restrictions, 337; par value, 53; repurchase, 414; stand-by arrangement, 413.

SOUTHERN RHODESIA: consultation, Fund, 248*; consultations, GATT, 230, 261, 338-40; gold producers, subsidies to, 206-208, 213, 214, 589; par value, 53.

SPAIN: bilateral agreements, 300, 310, 311, 312; currency drawn, 449*, 456*, 458*; currency holdings by Fund replenished, 456*, 458*; devaluation, 143; multiple rates, 143; par value, 59; repurchase obligation, 442.

STERLING AREA *see* INDEX A.

SUDAN: drawing, 423; par value, 59; stabilization program, 494.

SWEDEN: bilateral agreements, 298, 309, 310; consultation, GATT, 345; convertibility, 277, 292*; currency drawn, 449*, 456*, 458*; currency holdings by Fund replenished, 455, 456*, 458*; currency used in repurchases, 449*; devaluation, 46, 217; EPU, 80; GAB, 17-18, 374-77, 456*, 458*; multiple rates, 47; par value, 46, 54.

SWITZERLAND: bilateral agreements, 298; EPU, 80; GAB, 376.

SYRIAN ARAB REPUBLIC: bilateral agreements, 311-12; broken cross rates, 80; drawings, 447*; fluctuating rate, 47, 165; multiple rates, 47, 141; par value, 54; quota, 359, 361.

T

TANZANIA: membership resolution, 70, 71; par value, 53.

THAILAND: broken cross rates, 79-80; devaluation, 90; fluctuating rate, 47, 74, 79, 90, 143, 158, 165; membership resolution, 66-70, 408; multiple rates, 74, 79, 141, 158; par value, 56, 74; right to draw, 66-70, 408.

TOGO: devaluation, 102; membership resolution, 70, 71; par value, 53.

TRINIDAD AND TOBAGO: membership resolution, 71; par value, 53.

TUNISIA: bilateral agreements, 314; membership resolution, 70, 71; par value, 53.

TURKEY: bilateral agreements, 300, 310, 312; consultation, GATT, 345; devaluation, 112, 143; drawings, 403, 447*; multiple rates, 47, 137, 143; par value, 54.

U

UGANDA: membership resolution, 71; par value, 53.

UNION OF SOUTH AFRICA *see* SOUTH AFRICA.

U.S.S.R.: at Bretton Woods, 5, 514.

UNITED ARAB REPUBLIC: bilateral agreements, 311-12; drawings, 403, 407, 423, 447*; offers gold collateral, 407; quota, 359; stabilization programs, 407, 494; stand-by arrangement, 407; *and see* EGYPT.

UNITED KINGDOM: Anglo-American Financial Agreement, 29, 219, 252; appoints Executive Director, 7, 353*; Basle Agreements, 519; bilateral payments agreements, 298, 300, 305; bullion market, 185, 202, 564, 579; Commonwealth conferences, 267; concern about broken cross rates, 77-80; consultations, GATT, 230, 261, 338-40, 345; convertibility, 29, 219, 226, 252-53, 266-68, 274, 277, 289, 292*, 300, 368; currency drawn, 448, 449*; currency used in repurchases, 449*; devaluation, 45, 97-99, 217; drawings, 376, 403, 412, 442, 455-58; EPU, 80, 321; exchange controls and restrictions, 31, 218, 252, 260, 262, 296; fluctuating rate suggested, 47; GAB, 17-18, 374-77; import restrictions, 262; interpretation of Articles obtained, 92, 567-68; investment currency, 146; par value, 53; repurchases, 442, 445, 452; reserves, impact of quota increases on, 362; reserves, monetary, 391, 442, 525, 600; responsibility for Southern Rhodesia, 207, 589; restrictions for security reasons, 260; stand-by arrangements, 376, 412, 455, 482, 488; sterling, strains on, 30-31, 252, 412-13; sterling balances, 252, 388; *and see* INDEX A, *s.v.* STERLING AREA.

UNITED KINGDOM COLONIES: par values, 53.

UNITED STATES: Anglo-American Financial Agreement, 29, 219, 252; appoints Executive Director, 6-7, 353*; Bretton Woods Agreements Act, 386, 516, 524, 539; capital controls, 31, 296; convertibility, 225, 250, 292*; currency drawn, 448, 449*, 456*, 458*, 546; currency holdings by Fund replenished, 455-58, 456*; currency used in repurchases, 440, 448, 449*; drawings, 454, 520, 544, 546, 601; ECA and ERP, 320-22, 324, 328-29, 394-98; Federal Communications Commission, 569; Federal Reserve Bank of New York, 369-70; GAB, 17-18, 374-77, 456*, 519; gold policy, 180, 187, 191, 560; interpretation of Articles obtained, 385, 411, 414-16, 524, 539, 567-69; National Advisory Council, 97, 206; obligations *re* Fund investment, 366, 369, 372; par value, 53; Randall Commission, 138, 268; recession, international effects of, 154; reserves, impact of quota increase on, 362, 371; reserves, monetary, 600; restrictions for security reasons, 259; stand-by arrangement, 482; unwillingness to draw, 541.

UPPER VOLTA: bilateral agreements, 311-12; membership resolution, 70, 71.

URUGUAY: bilateral agreements, 299, 300, 310; fluctuating rate, 58; multiple rates, 107, 125; par value, 56, 58, 68, 552; right to draw, 68, 552; stand-by arrangement, 509.

V

VENEZUELA: Article XIV, 248*; multiple rates, 43, 47, 74, 125, 126, 146; par value, 43, 54; stand-by arrangement, 413.

VIET-NAM: membership resolution, 70, 71; multiple rates, 146.

Y

YUGOSLAVIA: bilateral agreements, 300, 311-12; devaluation, 63, 112; drawings, 447*; exchange controls, 218; multiple rates, 47, 63, 123, 137, 143; par value, 49, 54, 62-63; quota, 359; stand-by arrangement, 481.

Index C. Articles of Agreement

The page numbers given for an Article may also refer to individual Sections of that Article. References given for Sections of an Article are not necessarily repeated against the Article itself. The Article is usually cited in a footnote.

The text of the Articles will be found in Volume III of this history; those adopted at Bretton Woods are on pages 185-214, and those embodied in the Amendment that came into force in July 1969 are on pages 521-38.

Index D. Executive Board Decisions

Decisions Referred to by Number

The citation is usually in a footnote. The text of these decisions is given in full in Volume III of this history, pp. 219-77.

Index E. Publications Cited

Numbers refer to pages. The publication is usually cited in a footnote.

Germany, Ministry of Justice. *Bundesgesetzblatt*, Part II, July 13, 1956: 516.

Germany, Sachverstandigenrat zur Begutachtung der gesamtwirtschaftlichen Entwicklung, *Jahresgutachten 1964-65* [Annual Report of the Council of Experts on Economic Development]: 50.

Gold, Joseph. *The Cuban Insurance Cases and the Articles of Agreement of the Fund*, IMF Pamphlet Series, No. 8 (Washington, 1966): 568.

——. "The Duty to Collaborate with the International Monetary Fund and the Development of Monetary Law," in *Law, Justice and Equity*, R. H. Code Holland and G. Schwarzenberger, eds. (London, 1967), pp. 137-51: 575.

——. *The Fund Agreement in the Courts*, IMF Monograph Series, No. 2 (Washington, 1962): 220, 568, 592.

——. "The Fund Agreement in the Courts—VIII," *Staff Papers*, Vol. XI (1964), pp. 457-89: 220, 568.

——. "The Fund Agreement in the Courts—IX," *Staff Papers*, Vol. XIV (1967), pp. 369-402: 220, 568.

——. *The Fund and Non-Member States: Some Legal Effects*, IMF Pamphlet Series, No. 7 (Washington, 1966): 579.

——. "The International Monetary Fund and the International Recognition of Exchange Control Regulations: The Cuban Insurance Cases," *Revue de la Banque* (Brussels), Vol. 31 (1967), No. 6, pp. 523-38: 568.

——. *Interpretation by the Fund*, IMF Pamphlet Series, No. 11 (Washington, 1968): 9, 567, 569.

——. "Legal Technique in the Creation of a New International Reserve Asset: Special Drawing Rights and the Amendment of the Articles of Agreement of the International Monetary Fund," *Case Western Reserve Journal of International Law* (Cleveland, 1969), Vol. I, No. 2, pp. 105-23: 596.

——. *Maintenance of the Gold Value of the Fund's Assets*, IMF Pamphlet Series, No. 6 (Washington, 1965): 591.

——. "The Next Stage in the Development of International Monetary Law: The Deliberate Control of Liquidity," *The American Journal of International Law* (Washington), Vol. 62 (1968), pp. 365-402: 595.

——. *The Reform of the Fund*, IMF Pamphlet Series, No. 12 (Washington, 1969): 600.

——. *Special Drawing Rights*, IMF Pamphlet Series, No. 13 (Washington, 1969): 595.

Gordon, Margaret S. *Barriers to World Trade: A Study of Recent Commercial Policy* (New York, 1941): 123, 219, 297.

Group of Ten. *Ministerial Statement of the Group of Ten and Annex Prepared by Deputies* (Paris, August 1964): 50.

Gutt, Camille. *The Practical Problem of Exchange Rates: An Address Before the Littauer School of Public Administration, Harvard University, Cambridge, Mass., February 13, 1948* [Washington, 1948]: 54.

H

Hexner, Ervin P. "Interpretation by Public International Organizations of Their Basic Instruments," *The American Journal of International Law* (Washington), Vol. 53 (1959), No. 2, pp. 341-70: 9.

——. "The Executive Board of the International Monetary Fund: A Decision-Making Instrument," *International Organization* (Boston), Vol. XVIII (1964), pp. 74-96: 15.

——. "The General Agreement on Tariffs and Trade and the Monetary Fund," *Staff Papers*, Vol. I (1950-51), pp. 432-64: 335, 336.

Hicks, Earl, Graeme S. Dorrance, and Gerard R.

Aubanel, "Monetary Analyses," *Staff Papers*, Vol. V (1956-57), pp. 342-433: 272.

Holtrop, M. W. "Method of Monetary Analysis Used by De Nederlandsche Bank," *Staff Papers*, Vol. V (1956-57), pp. 303-15: 272.

I

[International Monetary Fund]. "The Adequacy of Monetary Reserves," *Staff Papers*, Vol. III (1953-54), pp. 181-227: 356.

——. *Annual Report of the Executive Directors:* **1946**, 221, 252, 392; **1947**, 43, 54, 58, 249, 254, 392; **1948**, 25, 44, 58, 78, 96, 135, 249, 252, 254, 396-97; **1949**, 44, 207, 255, 399; **1950**, 194, 208, 258; **1951**, 80, 171, 550; **1952**, 63; **1953**, 105, 202; **1954**, 138, 202, 268-69; **1955**, 139, 202, 209, 211, 250, 271, 276, 305, 404, 475, 538; **1956**, 202, 274; **1957**, 202, 209, 271, 475, 538; **1958**, 48, 80, 171, 211, 212, 551; **1959**, 209, 213, 279, 404; **1960**, 212; **1961**, 145, 202, 209, 374; **1962**, 35, 171, 211, 212, 550; **1963**, 110, 211, 212, 295, 316, 404; **1964**, 209, 211, 213, 295, 362; **1965**, 211, 212, 213, 362, 442; **1966**, 110, 202, 211, 213, 442; **1967**, 111.

——. *Annual Report on Exchange Restrictions:* 121, 131; **1st** (1950), 134, 257; **2nd** (1951), 230, 262, 263; **3rd** (1952), 267; **4th** (1953), 137, 263; **5th** (1954), 301; **6th** (1955), 138; **7th** (1956), 141; **9th** (1958), 58; **10th** (1959), 58; **12th** (1961), 58, 291; **17th** (1966), 146, 260.

——. *Compensatory Financing of Export Fluctuations: A Report by the International Monetary Fund on Compensatory Financing of the Fluctuations in Exports of Primary Producing Countries* (Washington, 1963): 361, 421.

——. *Compensatory Financing of Export Fluctuations; Developments in the Fund's Facility: A Second Report by the International Monetary Fund on Compensatory Financing of the Fluctuations in Exports of Primary Producing Countries* (Washington, 1966): 425, 539.

——. *Enlargement of Fund Resources Through Increases in Quotas: A Report by the Executive Directors to the Board of Governors of the International Monetary Fund* (Washington, 1958): 358.

——. *Establishment of a Facility Based on Special Drawing Rights in the International Monetary Fund and Modifications in the Rules and Practices of the Fund: A Report by the Executive Directors to the Board of Governors Proposing Amendment of the Articles of Agreement* (Washington, 1968): 595, 600.

[——]. "Fund Policies and Procedures in Relation to the Compensatory Financing of Commodity Fluctuations," *Staff Papers*, Vol. VIII (1960-61), pp. 1-76: 418.

——. *International Financial News Survey* (Washington), Vol. XVI (1964), pp. 115-16: 172.

——. *International Financial Statistics* (Washington), various dates: 113, 121, 131, 406.

——. *International Reserves and Liquidity: A Study by the Staff of the International Monetary Fund* [Washington, 1958]: 358.

——. *Schedule of Par Values*, 41st issue (Washington, February 15, 1966): 167.

——. *Selected Decisions of the Executive Directors and Selected Documents*, 3rd issue (Washington, January 1965): 385, 516.

——. *Selected Documents, Board of Governors Inaugural Meeting* (Washington, 1946): 92, 385.

——. *Summary Proceedings of the Board of Governors:* **1946**, 55, 354; **1947**, 253, 354; **1948**, 355; **1949**, 188, 255; **1950**, 194, 261; **1952**, 67, 265, 408; **1953**, 69, 70, 408; **1954**, 270, 590; **1955**, 274; **1956**, 272; **1957**, 357; **1958**, 358, 450; **1959**, 279, 282-83, 331, 359; **1960**, 290, 359; **1961**, 374; **1962**, 359; **1963**, 70, 361, 409; **1964**, 71, 361, 362, 410; **1965**, 361, 363, 406; **1966**, 363.